UNDERSTANDING CRIMINAL LAW

FOURTH EDITION

JOSHUA DRESSLER

Frank R. Strong Chair in Law
Michael E. Moritz College of Law
The Ohio State University

LexisNexis™

Library of Congress Cataloging-in-Publication Data

Dressler, Joshua.

Understanding criminal law / Joshua Dressler. — 4th ed.

   p. cm.

Includes index.

ISBN 0-8205-7001-X (soft cover)

1. Criminal law — United States. I. Title.

KF9219.D74 2006

345.73 — dc22

2006009852

Editorial Offices
744 Broad Street, Newark, NJ 07102 (973) 820-2000
201 Mission St., San Francisco, CA 94105-1831 (415) 908-3200
701 East Water Street, Charlottesville, VA 22902-7587 (434) 972-7600
www.lexis.com

(Pub.0789)

DEDICATION

Thank you, Casey Irene, Lucy Belle, and Maya Shoshana

PREFACE TO THE FOURTH EDITION

This text is primarily designed for use by law students enrolled in a course in Criminal Law. However, it will also serve nicely in undergraduate courses covering substantive criminal law. As well, based on comments I have received from practicing attorneys, judges, and scholars (and citations to this text in judicial opinions and scholarly works), this text should be helpful to *anyone* looking for a survey of criminal law substance and theory. The text considers common law doctrine, statutory reform (with particular emphasis on the Model Penal Code), and constitutional law affecting the substantive criminal law.

I am gratified by the extremely favorable response UNDERSTANDING CRIMINAL LAW has received from users. Therefore, I have avoided the temptation to tinker. Each chapter has been updated from the third edition, to ensure that the criminal law described here is up-to-date. As before, I have included citations to new scholarship in the field, in the hope that users will look to some of these sources for additional insights into the various subjects.

Gender policy of the text. For most of Anglo-American legal history men monopolized the critical roles in the system of criminal justice. With only a few exceptions, lawyers, judges, legislators, jurors, and criminals were men. The only place for a woman in the system was as a crime victim. Such sexual inequality, of course, is changing, slowly but presumably surely. As an author of a book that will be read and used by readers of both sexes, I wanted to make sure that the text recognized the increasing importance of women in the law. Therefore, when discussing hypothetical defendants and victims, and when writing in general terms about other parties in the legal system — e.g., lawyers, judges, and legislators — I balance the account between male and female parties. In odd-numbered chapters the parties are female; in the even-numbered chapters males get equal time. I diverge from this approach when the gender policy would distort history (e.g., there were no female property-holders in sixteenth century England), prove inaccurate as a principle of law, or confuse the reader.

Acknowledgements. A book of this length cannot be written without help from many people. I wrote the first edition while I was on the faculty at Wayne State University. My colleague there, Leroy Lamborn, read the first, and often the second, draft of every chapter of the book. He provided remarkably helpful editorial and substantive suggestions. I will be grateful forever.

Many readers assisted me in improving the text. I have been blessed over the years with letters, e-mail messages, and telephone calls from professors (here and in Europe, Australia, and New Zealand), judges, practitioners, and law students, all providing advice. Although I know I have missed some names, for which I apologize, I thank the following people for their input: Marcia Baron; Robert Batey; Charles Bobis; William Bridge; Anthony Dillof; Madame Justice Claire L'Heureux-Dubé; Antony Duff; Susan Beth Farmer; Jeffry Finer; Stanley Fisher; Norman Garland; Stephen Garvey; Abner Greene; Peter Henning; Christopher Johnson; Cynthia Lee; Alan Michaels; David Moran; Stephen

Morse; Frederick Moss; Mary Rose; Richard Rosen; William Schabas; Kenneth Simons; Richard Singer; James Alexander Tanford; George Thomas; and Welsh White. I also thank the many scholars whose writings have influenced my thinking and, I hope, improved this text.

I received wonderful research assistance on the fourth edition from Leigh Anne Williams (Moritz '07).

Finally, and importantly, I thank my family. My wife and life partner, Dottie, has been my support and counsel for more than three decades. My son, David, not yet even in high school when I began working on the first edition of this book, has moved on to college, graduate school, theater work, rabbinical studies, marriage to a wonderful woman, Debra, and life bringing up their daughters, Casey Irene, Lucy Belle, and Maya Shoshana. Although my son is an American League fan and tolerates the DH rule, I love him dearly. And, Debra, Casey, Lucy Belle and Maya have made my life immeasurably happier and fuller. I thank them with all of my heart.

Joshua Dressler
November, 2005
Columbus, Ohio

FREQUENTLY CITED SOURCE

This Text frequently cites to the MODEL PENAL CODE COMMENTARIES, found in two volumes:

American Law Institute, MODEL PENAL CODE AND COMMENTARIES (OFFICIAL DRAFT AND REVISED COMMENTS) (PART I: GENERAL PROVISIONS) (1985); and

American Law Institute, MODEL PENAL CODE AND COMMENTARIES (OFFICIAL DRAFT AND REVISED COMMENT) (PART II: DEFINITION OF SPECIFIC CRIMES) (1980)

* * *

These sources are cited in footnotes of this Text by use of the shorthand "American Law Institute."

* * *

TABLE OF CONTENTS

CHAPTER 1
CRIMINAL LAW: AN OVERVIEW

CHAPTER 2
PRINCIPLES OF CRIMINAL PUNISHMENT

CHAPTER 3
SOURCES OF THE CRIMINAL LAW

CHAPTER 4
CONSTITUTIONAL LIMITS ON THE CRIMINAL LAW

CHAPTER 5
LEGALITY

CHAPTER 6
PROPORTIONALITY

CHAPTER 7
BURDENS OF PROOF

CHAPTER 8
PRESUMPTIONS

CHAPTER 9
ACTUS REUS

CHAPTER 10
MENS REA

CHAPTER 11
STRICT LIABILITY

CHAPTER 12
MISTAKES OF FACT

CHAPTER 13
MISTAKES OF LAW

CHAPTER 14
CAUSATION

CHAPTER 15
CONCURRENCE OF ELEMENTS

CHAPTER 16
DEFENSES: AN OVERVIEW

CHAPTER 17
JUSTIFICATIONS AND EXCUSES

CHAPTER 18
SELF-DEFENSE

CHAPTER 19
DEFENSE OF OTHERS

CHAPTER 20
DEFENSE OF PROPERTY AND HABITATION

CHAPTER 21
LAW ENFORCEMENT

CHAPTER 22
NECESSITY

CHAPTER 23
DURESS

CHAPTER 24
INTOXICATION

CHAPTER 25
INSANITY

**CHAPTER 26
DIMINISHED CAPACITY**

**CHAPTER 27
ATTEMPT**

CHAPTER 28
SOLICITATION

CHAPTER 29
CONSPIRACY

CHAPTER 30
LIABILITY FOR THE ACTS OF OTHERS: COMPLICITY

CHAPTER 31
CRIMINAL HOMICIDE

CHAPTER 32
THEFT

CHAPTER 33
RAPE

Chapter 1

CRIMINAL LAW: AN OVERVIEW

§ 1.01 NATURE OF "CRIMINAL LAW"[1]

The study of the criminal law is the study of crimes and the moral principles of criminal responsibility.

[A] Crimes

[1] Comparison to Civil Wrongs

What is a crime? If we are to believe many judicial opinions and treatises, the answer is simple, circular, and largely useless: A "crime" is anything that lawmakers say is a crime. We need to look deeper for an answer to this question and, thus, to understand how a crime differs from a civil wrong, such as a tort or breach of contract.

First, unlike torts and contracts, the criminal law involves *public* law. That is, although the direct and immediate victim of a crime typically is a private party (e.g., the person who is robbed, assaulted, or kidnapped), and other individuals may indirectly be injured (e.g., the spouse of the direct victim), a crime involves more than a private injury. A crime causes "social harm,"[2] in that the injury suffered involves "a breach and violation of the public rights and duties, due to the whole community, considered as a community, in its social aggregate capacity."[3] For this reason, crimes in the United States are prosecuted by public attorneys representing the community at large, and not by privately retained counsel.

---

[1] See generally John C. Coffee, Jr., *Paradigms Lost: The Blurring of the Criminal and Civil Law Models—And What Can Be Done About It*, 101 Yale L.J. 1875 (1992); Claire Finkelstein, *Positivism and the Notion of an Offense*, 88 Cal. L. Rev. 335 (2000); Henry M. Hart, Jr., *The Aims of the Criminal Law*, 23 Law & Contemp. Probs. 401 (1958); Sanford H. Kadish, *Why Substantive Criminal Law—A Dialogue*, 29 Clev. St. L. Rev. 1 (1980); Susan R. Klein, *Redrawing the Criminal-Civil Boundary*, 2 Buff. Crim. L. Rev. 679 (1999); Stephen J. Morse, *Fear of Danger, Flight from Culpability*, 4 Psych. Pub. Pol'y and L. 250 (1998); Stephen J. Schulhofer, *Two Systems of Social Protection: Comments on the Civil-Criminal Distinction, With Particular Reference to Sexually Violent Predator Laws*, 7 J. Contemp. Legal Issues 69 (1996); Carol S. Steiker, *Punishment and Procedure: Punishment Theory and the Criminal-Civil Procedural Divide*, 85 Geo. L.J. 775 (1997); William J. Stuntz, *Substance, Process, and the Civil-Criminal Line*. 7 J. Contemp. Legal Issues 1 (1996).

[2] For a definition of this term, see § 9.10[B], *infra*.

[3] 4 William Blackstone, Commentaries on the Laws of England *5 (1769).

There is more, however, that *should* distinguish a criminal wrong from its civil counterpart. A person convicted of a crime is punished. The technical definition of "punishment" awaits consideration in the next chapter,[4] but what is significant here is that the "the essence of punishment . . . lies in the criminal conviction itself,"[5] rather than in the specific hardship imposed as a result of the conviction. The hardship suffered as a result of the criminal conviction may be no greater (or even less) than that which results from a civil judgment. For example, a person who lacks substantial financial resources might prefer to spend a few days in jail than to pay a civil judgment of $10,000. And, it is *not* the case that a civil proceeding can *never* result in loss of liberty: A mentally ill person may involuntarily be committed to a mental institution,[6] and so-called "sexual predators" may be confined, supposedly "civilly," due to their perceived dangerousness to the community.[7] What, then, distinguishes the criminal law from its civil counterpart is, or at least should be, the societal condemnation and stigma that accompanies the conviction.[8]

When the factfinder (ordinarily, a jury) determines that a person is guilty of an offense, the resulting conviction is an expression of the community's moral outrage, directed at the criminal actor, for her act. It follows, therefore, that a crime might properly be defined as "an act or omission and its accompanying state of mind which, if duly shown to have taken place, will incur a formal and solemn pronouncement of the moral condemnation of the community."[9] To the extent that conduct that does *not* justify condemnation is treated as criminal, as is sometimes the case,[10] the line between the civil and the criminal processes is unfortunately blurred.[11]

---

[4] See § 2.02, *infra.*

[5] George K. Gardner, *Bailey v. Richardson and the Constitution of the United States*, 33 B.U. L. Rev. 176, 193 (1953).

[6] See § 25.05[A], *infra.*

[7] E.g., Kan. Stat. Ann. § 59-29a01-05 (Supp. 2004) (defining a "sexually violent predator" as "any person who has been convicted of or charged with a sexually violent offense and who suffers from a mental abnormality or personality disorder which makes the person likely to engage in repeat acts of sexual violence"; and making such a person eligible for indefinite, even life-long, civil commitment). These laws are controversial because they blur the line, perhaps to the point of extinction, between civil and criminal commitment.

[8] Hart, Note 1, *supra*, at 404; see also Leo Katz, Bad Acts and Guilty Minds: Conundrums of the Criminal Law 28 (1987) ("[P]unishment condemns, the [civil] penalty does not").

[9] Hart, Note 1, *supra*, at 405.

[10] See Chapter 11, *infra.*

[11] Even if all criminal conduct arguably should involve morally wrongful behavior — a controversial assumption — it does not follow that all morally wrongful conduct is, or should be, criminal. In a society that values individual liberty, the criminal law serves a *minimalist* role — it only seeks to identify and regulate wrongful conduct that results in significant social harm. The criminal law does not seek "to purify thoughts and perfect character," United States v. Hollingsworth, 27 F.3d 1196, 1203 (7th Cir. 1994), which is the responsibility of family, and religious and other private institutions. For example, telling lies may be a character flaw and, in many contexts, morally wrongful, but the criminal law only punishes the most harmful lies, e.g., material misstatements made under oath in judicial proceedings (perjury).

[2] Classification of Crimes

The English common law[12] divided crimes into two general categories: felonies and misdemeanors.[13] A felony "comprise[d] every species of crime which occasioned at common law the forfeiture of lands and goods."[14] All common law felonies were punishable by death. The list of felonies was short: felonious homicide (later divided by statute into murder and manslaughter), arson, mayhem, rape, robbery, larceny, burglary, prison escape, and (perhaps) sodomy.[15] All other criminal offenses were misdemeanors.

In modern penal codes, the line distinguishing felonies from misdemeanors is drawn differently than in the past. Very generally speaking, an offense punishable by death or imprisonment in a state prison is a felony; an offense for which the maximum punishment is a monetary fine, incarceration in a local jail, or both, is a misdemeanor. For sentencing purposes, the Model Penal Code,[16] and the statutory schemes of various jurisdictions,[17] divide felonies into degrees.[18] Some states, as well, have added an additional classification of crime, e.g., "violations"[19] or "infractions." These offenses encompass misconduct so minor that incarceration is prohibited.

[B] Principles of Criminal Responsibility

As one scholar has observed, "[i]t is deeply rooted in our moral sense of fitness that punishment entails blame and that, therefore, punishment may not justly be imposed where the person is not blameworthy."[20]

The study of the criminal law is, therefore, much more than the study of crimes. It is also the investigation of the doctrines that have developed over the centuries for determining when a person may justly be held criminally responsible for harm that she has caused. Put another way, the principles of criminal responsibility, which are at the core of the criminal law, identify the point at which it is believed fair to go from the factual premise, "*D* caused or assisted in

---

[12] The "common law" is judge-made law. See § 3.01[A], *infra*.

[13] Because of its special heinousness, treason was categorized separately, but strictly speaking it was a felony. 4 Blackstone, Note 3, *supra*, at *95.

[14] *Id.* at *94.

[15] Rollin M. Perkins & Ronald N. Boyce, Criminal Law 14 (3d ed. 1982). The authors state that sodomy originally was punished as an ecclesiastical offense, and later made a felony by statute, but it is "old enough to be recognized as common law in this country." *Id.* at 15.

[16] For an explanation of the Model Penal Code, see § 3.03, *infra*.

[17] E.g., N.Y. Penal Law § 55.05 (Consol. 2004).

[18] E.g., Model Penal Code § 6.01(1) (dividing felonies into three degrees); §§ 6.03 and 6.06 (setting out the fines and terms of imprisonment, by degree of felony).

[19] Model Penal Code § 1.04(5).

[20] Kadish, Note 1, *supra*, at 10.

causing X (a social harm) to occur," to the normative judgment, "*D should* be punished for having caused or assisted in causing X to occur." The rules of criminal responsibility are considered in Chapters 9-30, *infra*.

§ 1.02 PROVING GUILT AT THE TRIAL

[A] Right to Trial by Jury

[1] In General

The Sixth Amendment to the United States Constitution provides that "in all criminal prosecutions, the accused shall enjoy the right to a speedy and public trial, by an impartial jury." The right to trial by jury is "fundamental to the American scheme of justice," and therefore applies in all criminal proceedings, both state and federal.[21] The Supreme Court has stated that the constitutional guarantee reflects a "profound judgment about the way in which law should be enforced and justice administered." The right is granted "in order to prevent oppression by the Government. . . . If the defendant prefer[s] the common-sense judgment of a jury to the more tutored but perhaps less sympathetic reaction of the single judge, he [is] to have it."[22]

Despite the Sixth Amendment phrase, "in all criminal prosecutions," the jury-trial right only applies to "non-petty" offenses. According to the Supreme Court, "no offense can be deemed 'petty' for purposes of the right to trial by jury where imprisonment for more than six months is authorized."[23] An offense is also non-petty, even if the maximum authorized period of confinement is six months or less, if any additional statutory penalties (including fines) "are so severe that they clearly reflect a legislative determination that the offense in question is a 'serious' one."[24] As a practical matter, this means that a criminal defendant has a constitutional right to trial by jury in all felony and many misdemeanor prosecutions.

[2] Scope of the Right

In the federal courts[25] and in most states, a jury in a criminal trial is composed of twelve persons who must reach a unanimous verdict to convict or acquit. Juries as small as six, however, are constitutional.[26] State laws per-

---

[21] Duncan v. Louisiana, 391 U.S. 145, 149 (1968).

[22] *Id.* at 155-56.

[23] Baldwin v. New York, 399 U.S. 66, 69 (1970).

[24] Blanton v. City of North Las Vegas, 489 U.S. 538, 543 (1989).

[25] Fed. R. Crim. P. 23(b)(1) (setting the size of the jury at 12); 31(a) (unanimity requirement).

[26] Williams v. Florida, 399 U.S. 78 (1970) (a jury of six is permissible); Ballew v. Georgia, 435 U.S. 223 (1978) (a jury of five is too small).

mitting non-unanimous verdicts are also allowed, as long as the vote to convict represents a "substantial majority" of the jurors.[27]

Because the jury system is meant to protect an accused from governmental oppression and to provide her with the common-sense judgment of the community, a defendant is entitled to a jury drawn from a pool of persons constituting a fair cross-section of the community.[28] This Sixth Amendment right is violated if large, distinctive groups of persons, such as women, racial minorities, or adherents of a specific major religion, are systematically and unjustifiably excluded from the jury pool.

[B] Burden of Proof

The Due Process Clauses of the United States Constitution[29] require the prosecutor in a criminal trial to persuade the factfinder "beyond a reasonable doubt of every fact necessary to constitute the crime . . . charged."[30] The meaning of this language, and the effect of failing to meet this burden of proof, are matters considered in detail in Chapter 7.

[C] Jury Nullification[31]

[1] The Issue

Are there circumstances in which a jury should acquit an individual, even if the prosecutor proves beyond a reasonable doubt that the accused committed the offense charged? For example, should jurors acquit a defendant if they believe that the criminal law she violated is immoral or unwise, or because they feel that she has been "punished enough" already (perhaps because the defendant has lost her job or feels guilty about her conduct), or because they believe that the police or prosecutors misbehaved in some manner in bringing her to trial? Should jurors, in short, "nullify" the law if they feel there are justifications for doing so?

Jurors have the raw power to do so. Two factors make this possible. First, a jury ordinarily returns a general verdict — "guilty" or "not guilty" — in crimi-

---

[27] Johnson v. Louisiana, 406 U.S. 356 (1972) (a 9-3 guilty verdict is constitutional).

[28] Taylor v. Louisiana, 419 U.S. 522 (1975).

[29] The Fifth and Fourteenth Amendments each contain a Due Process Clause. The Fifth Amendment applies in the federal system, whereas the Fourteenth Amendment pertains to the states.

[30] In re Winship, 397 U.S. 358, 364 (1970).

[31] See generally Thomas Andrew Green, Verdict According to Conscience (1985); Erick J. Haynie, Comment, *Populism, Free Speech, and the Rule of Law: The "Fully Informed" Jury Movement and Its Implications*, 88 J. Crim. L. & Criminology 343 (1997); Alan Scheflin & Jon Van Dyke, *Jury Nullification: The Contours of a Controversy*, 43 Law & Contemp. Probs. 51 (1980); Phillip B. Scott, *Jury Nullification: An Historical Perspective on a Modern Debate*, 91 W. Va. L. Rev. 389 (1989).

nal proceedings.[32] A jury is not required to explain its verdict. Second, the Fifth Amendment of the United States Constitution provides that "[n]o person shall . . . be subject for the same offense to be twice put in jeopardy." Therefore, the government may not reprosecute a defendant for the same crime after a "not guilty" verdict. Consequently, a jury *can* acquit a defendant they are convinced committed an offense, fail to state their reason for acquittal, and leave the government powerless to reprosecute. But, is such jury *power* of nullification a good thing? Should we conclude that jurors not only have the *power* to nullify, but also the *right*? We turn to the debate.

[2] The Debate

"Jury nullification" has been the subject of rich and sometimes eloquent debate over the centuries. Advocates of jury nullification point out that the trial-by-jury right is recognized in order to protect against governmental oppression, and to provide the accused with the common sense judgment of lay people.[33] As Judge Learned Hand put it, the institution of the jury "introduces a slack into the enforcement of the law, tempering its rigor by the mollifying influence of current ethical conventions."[34] This "slack" makes sense, advocates of nullification claim: A finding of guilt is not simply a determination that the accused did the acts charged; it also represents a judgment by the jury — the "conscience of the community"[35] and "the oracle of the citizenry"[36] — that the defendant *should* be subjected to the condemnation and formal punishment that results from a conviction.

The jury-nullification power, therefore, serves as the community's safeguard against morally unjust or socially undesirable (albeit legally proper) criminal convictions that inflexible judges might impose.[37] For example, a colonial jury in 1735 acquitted Peter Zenger, the confessed printer of a journal that published articles critical of British authorities, of seditious libel. And, in the nineteenth century, Northern juries acquitted individuals who assisted slaves to escape their "owners," who were prosecuted under then-existing federal fugitive slave laws.

---

[32] One common exception exists: In many states a jury that acquits a defendant on the basis of insanity may return a verdict of "not guilty by reason of insanity." See § 25.02[C], *infra*.

[33] See § 1.02[A][1], *supra*.

[34] United States *ex rel.* McCann v. Adams, 126 F.2d 774, 776 (2d Cir.), reversed on other grounds, 317 U.S. 269 (1942).

[35] Witherspoon v. Illinois, 391 U.S. 510, 519, 519 n.15 (1968).

[36] United States v. Gilliam, 994 F.2d 97, 101 (2d Cir. 1993).

[37] There is very little discussion in the literature of *judicial* nullification, although it doubtlessly occurs on occasion. The Model Penal Code provides for judicial authority to dismiss a prosecution in specified circumstances, notwithstanding the defendant's possible factual guilt. The Code does not characterize this as judicial nullification, but rather as the implementation of a "de minimis" defense. Model Penal Code § 2.12.

Critics of jury nullification respond that juries should not exercise their raw power to nullify the law. For every benevolent example of jury nullification to which its advocates point, there are "numerous and notorious examples" of malignant nullification, such as when Southern juries in the 1950s refused to convict white men for lynchings and other murders of civil rights workers, despite overwhelming evidence of guilt.[38] Moreover, to the extent that a jury acts on the basis of its conclusion that a particular law is unjust, the jury-nullification power "[c]ast[s] aside . . . our basic belief that only our elected representatives may determine what is a crime and what is not, and only they may revise that law if it is found to be unfair."[39] Critics also point out that jurors take an oath before they are empaneled to obey the judge's instructions on the law. If jurors understand and yet ignore the law out of sympathy for the defendant, lack of compassion for the victim, or dislike for the governing law, the jurors have violated their oath. To require jurors to take such an oath and yet recognize jury nullification "would confuse any conscientious citizen serving on a jury."[40]

[3] The Law

The issue of jury nullification may arise in various legal contexts. First, the judge might instruct the jury that, if it finds beyond a reasonable doubt that the defendant committed the crime charged, it "must" find her guilty. Or, the judge might expressly inform the jury that it has a duty to follow her instructions, even if it disagrees with them. The general rule is that such instructions are permissible because, while the *power* to nullify exists, there is no concomitant *right* to nullify.[41]

Second, the defense may be bold enough to request the judge to instruct the jury that it is entitled to act upon its conscientious feelings to acquit the defendant, or the issue may arise in the context of a defense counsel's call to the jury during closing arguments to exercise its power to nullify the law and acquit. Although a very few courts have allowed jury-nullification arguments to the jury,[42] the overwhelming rule is that such arguments and pro-nullification jury instructions are impermissible.[43]

---

[38] See United States v. Thomas, 116 F.3d 606, 616 (2d Cir. 1997).

[39] State v. Ragland, 519 A.2d 1361, 1369 (N.J. 1986).

[40] *Id.* at 1371.

[41] E.g., Watts v. United States, 362 A.2d 706 (D.C. 1976) (*en banc*) (approving use of "must" in an instruction); State v. Ragland, 519 A.2d 1361 (N.J. 1986) (same).

[42] E.g., United States v. Datcher, 830 F. Supp. 411 (M.D. Tenn. 1993) (permitting the defense to argue to the jury that it should acquit because of a "draconian sentence" hanging over the defendant; but stating in dictum that it would not have permitted an instruction on jury nullification if it had been requested).

[43] E.g., United States v. Dougherty, 473 F.2d 1113 (D.C. Cir. 1972); State v. Hatori, 990 P.2d 115 (Haw. Ct. App. 1999); Holden v. State, 788 N.E.2d 1253 (Ind. 2003); State v. Ragland, 519 A.2d 1361 (N.J. 1986); State v. Bjerkaas, 472 N.W.2d 615 (Wis. Ct. App. 1991).

Third, a prosecutor may seek to have a juror discharged before or during deliberations if there is evidence that she intends to nullify the law and vote to acquit. Trial courts are exceedingly hesitant to grant such motions. Jury deliberations occur in secret, so that jurors may talk freely amongst themselves; a discharge motion cannot realistically be granted without intruding into the deliberative process. Moreover, it is often difficult to distinguish between a juror who plans to ignore the judge's legal instructions and one who simply believes that the government has failed to satisfy its burden of proof. Although there is little case law on point, the better rule seems to be that judges "may not delve too deeply into a juror's motivations," and that "if the record evidence discloses any possibility that the request to discharge stems from the juror's view of the sufficiency of the government's evidence, the court must deny the request."[44] Nonetheless, if a trial judge determines that a juror *is* "unable or unwilling" to discharge her legal duty "to determine the facts and render a verdict in accordance with the court's instruction on the law," the juror may be discharged.[45]

[4] Race-Based Nullification[46]

Professor Paul Butler, a former prosecutor, recently wrote: "[F]or pragmatic and political reasons, the black community is better off when some nonviolent lawbreakers remain in the community rather than go to prison."[47] Therefore, he has called on African-American jurors to acquit African-American defendants charged with victimless and nonviolent offenses, even if they are guilty, except in unusual circumstances. For example, Butler suggests, a jury should acquit a black thief who steals goods from an expensive department store, but perhaps should not acquit if the victim is a neighbor.

Butler states that his "goal is the subversion of American criminal justice, at least as it now exists."[48] He advocates "black self-help" outside the courtroom (through community-building activities, such as mentoring, tutoring, providing medical and legal care for the poor) and inside the courtroom (through jury nullification).[49] He defends his proposal on the ground that African-Americans are imprisoned disproportionately as a result of malignant factors (e.g., racial

---

[44] United States v. Brown, 823 F.2d 591, 596 (D.C. Cir. 1987).

[45] People v. Williams, 21 P.3d 1209, 1223 (Cal. 2001).

[46] See generally Paul D. Butler, *Race-Based Jury Nullification: Case-In-Chief*, 30 J. Marshall L. Rev. 911 (1997); Paul Butler, *Racially Based Jury Nullification: Black Power in the Criminal Justice System*, 105 Yale L.J. 677 (1995); Andrew D. Leipold, *Race-Based Jury Nullification: Rebuttal (Part A)*, 30 J. Marshall L. Rev. 923 (1997); Andrew D. Leipold, *The Dangers of Race-Based Jury Nullification: A Response to Professor Butler*, 44 UCLA L. Rev. 109 (1996).

[47] Butler, Yale Law Journal, Note 46, *supra*, at 679.

[48] *Id.* at 680.

[49] Butler, John Marshall Law Review, Note 46, *supra*, at 912-13.

discrimination in the criminal justice system and society as a whole), and on the ground that imprisonment of nonviolent offenders causes more harm than good in the African-American community. Butler states that black jurors should send a message of their disapproval of, and lack of faith in, the justice system by acquitting nonviolent and victimless offenders.

Professor Andrew Leipold, while sympathetic to many of Butler's criticisms of the justice system, has argued forcefully against race-based jury nullification. First, he provides a narrow, technical argument: Given ordinary rules of evidence, the typical jury will not have the information it needs (for example, information relating to the defendant's degree of dangerousness) to make an informed decision whether to nullify the law. Second, he fears that "[o]nce we have agreed that jurors can legitimately decide the outcome of cases by a cost-benefit analysis rather than by applying the law as written to the evidence presented, we have started down a dangerous road."[50] If blacks begin nullifying the law, other groups will do the same, and the result could be legal anarchy. For example, a jury might acquit a guilty wife beater because the victim nagged him: "We might be repelled by this reasoning, but we [would] not have any standing to complain about the process by which the outcome was reached."[51] Finally, Leipold rejects the Butler proposal because "whether you go to jail or get set free should not depend on the color of your skin."[52] He argues that race-based judgments are bad on principle, and bad because they encourage precisely the type of stereotyping that has unfairly led to the evils that inspired Butler's plan.

---

[50] Leipold, John Marshall Law Review, Note 46, *supra*, at 925.

[51] *Id.* at 926.

[52] *Id.*

Chapter 2

PRINCIPLES OF CRIMINAL PUNISHMENT

§ 2.01 "PUNISHMENT" AND CRIMINAL LAW THEORY

The subject of this chapter is punishment, and more specifically the moral theories used to justify it.[1] Why should we care about these theories? First, the criminal law is a blunt instrument, used in our name. The criminal justice system, which enforces our criminal laws, inflicts pain on persons convicted of criminal conduct, typically by taking their life, liberty, or property. Any system that intentionally causes such suffering requires a justification. The principles discussed in this chapter provide potential bases for legitimizing our criminal justice system.

Second, lawmakers must ascertain not only what conduct is wrongful, but must determine which persons may properly be held accountable for wrongful conduct; and when punishment is deemed appropriate, legislators must decide *what* and *how much* punishment fits the offense and the offender. The principles discussed here provide different means for making these determinations.

Third, criminal laws ought to be fair and, to the extent possible, deal coherently with persons charged with crime. The penal theories considered below provide intellectual foundations for evaluating the fairness and coherence of our criminal laws.

---

[1] Professor Guyora Binder has asked whether "the justification of punishment [is] a moral question." Guyora Binder, *Punishment Theory: Moral or Political?*, 5 Buff. Crim. L. Rev. 321, 321 (2002). As he observes, most modern writers on the subject of punishment — philosophers and legal scholars alike, not to mention courts and practicing lawyers — answer his question in the affirmative. In his useful article, however, Professor Binder contends that debate regarding the various justifications for punishment "will become more productive once [the debate] is redefined as a political debate about institutions" — a discussion, if you will, of political theory — "rather than a moral debate about the conduct of criminals and officials." *Id.* at 371.

Binder contends that the competing moral theories of punishment — those discussed in this chapter — are *all* implausible unless they are bound up with questions regarding the legitimacy "of the institutions promulgating the norm[s]." *Id.* at 322. As stated in the text above, this chapter focuses on the moral justifications of punishment, but it is certainly true that these questions should be considered within the context of political theory. The ultimate issue is how we should justify punishment — and principles of criminal responsibility predicated on penal theory — in a democratic legal system. Professor Binder's discussion of punishment theory from a political-theory context is worthwhile reading.

§ 2.02 "PUNISHMENT": DEFINED[2]

[A] In General

What does it mean to "punish" someone? The issue is a critical one. For example, the Constitution provides that a person may not be *punished* twice for the same criminal offense, may not be *punished* retroactively, and may not be subjected to cruel and unusual *punishment*; state laws, as well, typically provide greater procedural protections to persons subject to punishment than to those who may suffer "mere" civil penalties.

Clearly, sending a convicted criminal to prison for his offense is punishment. Suppose, however, that a wealthy person is required by a court to pay a small fine for violating a criminal statute. Is this punishment? Is a physician "punished" when he is compelled by a criminal court to perform public service in a hospital? What if a convicted criminal must undergo outpatient psychiatric care in lieu of a prison sentence? Is an alleged or convicted wrongdoer "punished" if a mob lynches him? May we say that a lawyer has been punished if he is disbarred for embezzlement of a client's funds?

Unfortunately, there is no universally accepted non-arbitrary definition of the term "punishment." Criminal law scholars have generally concluded, however, that *D* may be said to suffer "punishment" when, but only when, an agent of the government, pursuant to authority granted to the agent by virtue of *D*'s criminal conviction, intentionally inflicts pain on *D* or otherwise causes *D* to suffer some consequence that is ordinarily considered to be unpleasant.[3] Pursuant to this definition, payment of a fine by a wealthy individual for a criminal violation constitutes punishment, albeit perhaps inadequate punishment, because the fine is a consequence that ordinarily is considered unpleasant. For the same reason, post-conviction court-compelled public service[4] and outpatient psychiatric care of a convicted actor both constitute punishment. On the other hand,

---

[2] See generally Steven Sverdlik, *Punishment*, 7 Law & Phil. 179 (1988); Kent Greenawalt, *Punishment, in* 4 Encyclopedia of Crime and Justice 1282 (Joshua Dressler ed., 2d ed. 2002). For reflections on, and accounts of, the punitive process, see Michel Foucault, Discipline and Punish (Alan Sheridan trans., 1977); Robert Blecker, *Haven or Hell? Inside Lorton Central Prison: Experiences of Punishment Justified*, 42 Stan. L. Rev. 1149 (1990); Dan M. Kahan, *What Do Alternative Sanctions Mean?*, 63 U. Chi. L. Rev. 591 (1996); Stephen D. Sowle, *A Regime of Social Death: Criminal Punishment in the Age of Prisons*, 21 N.Y.U. Rev. L. & Soc. Change 497 (1994).

[3] E.g., H.L.A. Hart, Punishment and Responsibility 4-5 (1968); Greenawalt, Note 2, *supra*, at 1282-83.

[4] In *United States v. Bergman*, 416 F. Supp. 496 (S.D.N.Y. 1976), *B*, a rabbi and nursing home operator, pleaded guilty to two counts of Medicaid and tax fraud, relating to operation of his nursing homes. *B* proposed to the trial judge that he be required to create and run a program of Jewish vocational and religious high school training or a "Committee on Holocaust Studies." The judge expressed doubt that this would constitute punishment, because the proposed work was "honorific" in nature and "not unlike that done [by *B*] in other projects" prior to his legal difficulties. *Id*. at 500-01. According to the definition in the text, however, the proposed community service *is* punishment.

penalties imposed outside the criminal justice system, such as the disbarment of a lawyer by the licensing authority or the actions of a lynch mob, although painful and unpleasant, do not constitute "punishment."

[B] Constitutional Law Analysis

The constitutional line between "punishment" and civil remedies is exceptionally difficult to draw and may, in fact, be illusory. For example, various states have enacted "sexual predator" laws that authorize a "civil" process that can result in the confinement of a person who, as a result of a sexual disorder, is determined to be dangerous to the community. The proceeding may be initiated if the person has been convicted of (or, often, simply charged with) a specified sexual offense. And, a person declared to be a sexual predator may remain "civilly" confined until he no longer is dangerous, which may never occur. During the period of confinement, the sexual predator may be, but is not always, offered treatment for his mental condition.

Is such confinement of a person, who has already been punished for the original sexual offense, a violation of the individual's right not to be punished twice for the same offense? Or, does it constitute cruel and unusual punishment to restrict an individual's liberty, perhaps for the duration of his life, simply on the speculative ground that he may cause harm in the future, rather than on the basis of proof of prior criminal wrongdoing? The answer to these constitutional questions depends on whether the confinement is characterized as "punishment."

The United States Supreme Court has held that the categorization of a proceeding as "civil" — and, therefore, that the restriction on a person's liberty imposed at such a proceeding is not "punishment" — "is first of all a question of statutory construction."[5] That is, if the legislature apparently intended to treat a proceeding as civil — for example, by placing the questioned law in the civil code, rather than in the jurisdiction's penal code[6] — it presumptively will be treated as such.

The "civil" label the legislature attaches to a law, however, is not dispositive: The presumption that a restriction is non-punitive is not conclusive. If there is clear proof that the statutory scheme is "so punitive in either purpose or effect as to negate [the legislature's presumed] intention"[7] to treat it as "civil," then a court may characterize the law as "criminal" in nature, and thus treat the consequences arising from the proceeding as "punishment." But, there is no bright-

---

[5] Smith v. Doe, 538 U.S. 84, 92 (2003) (quoting Kansas v. Hendricks, 521 U.S. 346, 361 (1997)).

[6] But see Smith v. Doe, 538 U.S. 84, 94 (2003) (in which placement of a sexual predator provision in the state's criminal procedure code was not considered dispositive of its "criminal" nature: "The location and labels of a statutory provision do not by themselves transform a civil remedy into a criminal one.").

[7] United States v. Ward, 448 U.S. 242, 249 (1980).

line basis for determining "punitiveness": Courts generally characterize commitment as penal in nature if there is clear evidence (which there rarely is) that the primary legislative purpose is to further the traditional goals of punishment, namely, retribution and deterrence of wrongdoing.[8] The chapter sections that follow explain the essence of these theories of punishment.

§ 2.03 THEORIES OF PUNISHMENT[9]

[A] Utilitarianism[10]

[1] Basic Principles

According to classical utilitarianism, formulated by Jeremy Bentham,[11] the purpose of all laws is to maximize the net happiness of society. Laws should be used to exclude, as far as possible, all painful or unpleasant events. To a utilitarian, both crime and punishment are unpleasant and, therefore, normally undesirable occurrences. In a perfect world, neither would exist.

As we do not live in a perfect world — some persons are disposed to commit crimes — utilitarians believe that the pain inflicted by punishment is justifiable if, but only if, it is expected to result in a reduction in the pain of crime that would otherwise occur. For example, the imposition of five units of pain (however the "units" are measured) on D is justifiable if it will prevent more than five units of pain (in the form of crime) that would have occurred but for D's punishment.

---

[8] Although each statute must be considered individually, sexual predator laws have typically been characterized by courts as civil in nature. However, in the minds of many scholars, such laws seriously undermine the traditional distinction between civil commitment and criminal punishment. See generally John Q. LaFond, *Can Therapeutic Jurisprudence Be Normatively Neutral? Sexual Predator Laws: Their Impact on Participants and Policy*, 41 Ariz. L. Rev. 375 (1999); Stephen J. Morse, *Fear of Danger, Flight from Culpability*, 4 Psychol. Pub. Pol'y & L. 250 (1998).

[9] For broad overview of the competing theories of punishment, see generally Hart, Note 3, *supra*, at 1-27; Herbert L. Packer, The Limits of the Criminal Sanction 9-70 (1968); Nigel Walker, Why Punish? (1991); Albert W. Alschuler, *The Changing Purposes of Criminal Punishment: A Retrospective on the Past Century and Some Thoughts about the Next*, 70 U. Chi. L. Rev. 1 (2003); Greenawalt, Note 2, *supra*; Mark A. Michael, *Utilitarianism and Retributivism: What's the Difference?*, 29 Am. Phil. Q. 173 (1992).

[10] See generally Johannes Andenaes, Punishment and Deterrence (1974); Contemporary Utilitarianism (Michael D. Bayles ed., 1968); Jeremy Bentham, An Introduction to the Principles of Morals and Legislation (J. Bowring ed., 1843); John Stuart Mill, Utilitarianism (1863); Franklin E. Zimring & Gordon J. Hawkins, Deterrence (1973); Louis Michael Seidman, *Soldiers, Martyrs, and Criminals: Utilitarian Theory and the Problem of Crime Control*, 94 Yale L.J. 315 (1984); J.J.C. Smart, *Utilitarianism and Punishment*, 25 Isr. L. Rev. 361 (1991); Michael Vitiello, *Reconsidering Rehabilitation*, 65 Tulane L. Rev. 1011 (1991); Andrew von Hirsch & Lisa Maher, *Can Penal Rehabilitationism be Revived?*, Crim. Just. Ethics, Winter/Spring 1992, at 25.

[11] Bentham, Note 10, *supra*.

Classical utilitarians reason that the threat or imposition of punishment can reduce crime because, in Bentham's words, "[p]ain and pleasure are the great springs of human action," and "[i]n matters of importance every one calculates."[12] Put slightly differently, utilitarians believe that human beings generally act hedonistically and rationally. That is, a person will act according to his immediate desires to the extent that he believes that his conduct will augment his overall happiness. As a calculator, however, a person contemplating criminal activity (to augment his happiness) will balance the expected benefits of the proposed conduct against its risks, taking into account such factors as the risk of detection and conviction, and the severity of the likely punishment. He will avoid criminal activity if the perceived potential pain (punishment) outweighs the expected potential pleasure (criminal rewards).[13]

[2] Forms of Utilitarianism

Utilitarianism as applied to the criminal law takes different forms. Most commonly, utilitarians stress *general deterrence*. That is, *D* is punished in order to convince the *general* community to forego criminal conduct in the future. In this model, *D*'s punishment serves as an object lesson to the rest of the community; *D* is used as a means to a desired end, namely, a net reduction in crime. *D*'s punishment teaches us what conduct is impermissible; it instills fear of punishment in would-be violators of the law; and, at least to a limited extent, it habituates us to act lawfully, even in the absence of fear of punishment.

Specific (or *individual*) *deterrence* is an alternative utilitarian goal. Here, *D*'s punishment is meant to deter future misconduct by *D*. Specific deterrence may occur in two ways. First, there is deterrence by *incapacitation*: *D*'s imprisonment prevents him from committing crimes in the outside society during the period of segregation.[14] Second, upon release, there is deterrence by *intimida-*

---

[12] Jeremy Bentham, Principles of Penal Law, *in* J. Bentham's Works 396, 402 (J. Bowring ed., 1843).

[13] E.g., at least theoretically, if *D* believes that there is a 50 percent chance of being caught, prosecuted, convicted, and subjected to 10 units of punishment, he will commit the crime if his expected gain from the offense is more than 5 units of pleasure (10 units of pain-by-punishment x .50 chance of its infliction = 5 units of expected pain). On the other hand, if *D* thinks that the risk of detection, conviction, and punishment is 90 percent, he will not commit the crime unless he believes that the likely benefits are much greater (more than 9 units of pleasure). Notice that if an actor believes that there is virtually no chance of detection and punishment, virtually no threat of punishment will deter him. In general, therefore, an increase in the *likelihood* of punishment will deter more effectively than an increase in the *severity* of punishment. See Steven Klepper and Daniel Nagin, *The Deterrent Effect of Perceived Certainty and Severity of Punishment Revisited*, 27 Criminology 721 (1989).

[14] This theory does not justify the simplistic notion that society should put all convicts in prison and "throw away the key." To a utilitarian, punishment is unjustifiable on incapacitative grounds unless *D*'s likely future anti-social behavior is expected to result in more pain to society than the pain inflicted on *D* and society (e.g., costs of incarceration and the loss of the offender's potential productivity in the community) by his lifetime imprisonment. See generally Linda S. Beres & Thomas

tion: *D*'s punishment reminds him that if he returns to a life of crime, he will experience more pain.

A non-classical variety of utilitarianism is *rehabilitation* (or *reform*). Although the goal is the same — to reduce future crime — advocates of this model prefer to use the correctional system to reform the wrongdoer rather than to secure compliance through the fear or "bad taste" of punishment. The methods of reformation will vary from case to case, but could consist of, for example, psychiatric care, therapy for drug addiction, or academic or vocational training.[15]

[B] Retributivism[16]

[1] Basic Principles ·

Retributivists believe that punishment is justified when it is deserved. It is deserved when the wrongdoer freely chooses to violate society's rules. To an uncompromising retributivist,[17] the wrongdoer should be punished, whether or not it will result in a reduction in crime. As Immanuel Kant made the latter point, "[e]ven if a civil society resolved to dissolve itself . . . the last murderer lying in the prison ought to be executed. . . ." This act of punishment, which can provide no utilitarian benefit, is required because of the "desert of [the murderer's] deeds."[18] According to a retributivist, "[i]t is morally fitting that an offender should suffer in proportion to [his] desert or culpable wrongdoing."[19]

Notice two basic differences between retributivism and utilitarianism. First, retributivism looks backward and justifies punishment solely on the basis of the

---

D. Griffith, *Do Three Strikes Laws Make Sense? Habitual Offender Statutes and Criminal Incapacitation*, 87 Geo. L.J. 103 (1998); Michael Vitiello, *Three Strikes: Can We Return to Rationality?*, 87 J. Crim. L. & Criminology 395 (1997).

[15] Adherents of rehabilitation prefer to call the reformative process "treatment" or "healing," rather than "punishment." However, because the process does not require the criminal's consent and is the result of a criminal conviction, reformative procedures constitute "punishment." See § 2.02[A], *supra*.

[16] See generally Immanuel Kant, The Metaphysical Elements of Justice (J. Ladd trans., 1965); Immanuel Kant, The Philosophy of Law (W. Hastie translation 1887); Michael S. Moore, Placing Blame (1997); Jeffrie G. Murphy & Jean Hampton, Forgiveness and Mercy (1988); Joshua Dressler, *Hating Criminals: How Can Something That Feels So Good Be Wrong?*, 88 Mich. L. Rev. 1448 (1990); Jean Hampton, *Correcting Harms versus Righting Wrongs: The Goal of Retribution*, 39 UCLA L. Rev. 1659 (1992); Herbert Morris, *Persons and Punishment*, 52 Monist 475 (1968); Benjamin B. Sendor, *Restorative Retributivism*, 5 J. Contemp. Legal Issues 323 (1994); Roger Wertheimer, *Understanding Retribution*, Crim. Just. Ethics, Summer/Fall 1983, at 19.

[17] Some people support a mixture of retributivism and utilitarianism; others favor a weaker version of retributivism than is set out here. See § 2.05, *infra*.

[18] Kant, The Philosophy of Law, Note 16, *supra*, at 197-98. Many retributivists disagree with proposition that the death penalty must inevitably be imposed for the offense of murder.

[19] Russell L. Christopher, *Deterring Retributivism: The Injustice of "Just" Punishment*, 96 Nw. U. L. Rev. 843, 860 (2002).

voluntary commission of a crime. In contrast, utilitarians look forward. They care about the past only to the extent that it helps them predict the future: No matter how egregious the wrongdoing, utilitarians do not advocate punishment unless they believe it will provide an overall social benefit. Second, whereas the premise of utilitarianism is that people are generally hedonistic and rational calculators, retributivists focus on their view that humans generally possess free will or free choice[20] and, therefore, may justly be blamed when they choose to violate society's mores.[21]

[2] Forms of Retributivism

Although retribution is based on the dual premises that humans possess free will and that punishment is justified when it is deserved, retributivists differ among themselves regarding the best way to defend their "just deserts" philosophy. According to one form of retribution, variously described as *assaultive retribution*,[22] *public vengeance*, or *societal retaliation*, "it is morally right to hate criminals."[23] Because the criminal has harmed society, it is right for society to "hurt him back." This version of retribution is apt to "regard[] criminals rather like noxious insects to be ground under the heel of society."[24]

---

[20] This is not to say that retributivists reject the idea that humans generally are capable of rational calculation, but they emphasize that the actor ordinarily has the capacity to choose whether to act in conformity with the calculation.

[21] Some philosophers, termed "hard determinists," deny the existence of free will. The thesis of determinism is that every event has a cause. According to hard determinists, humans are little more than marionettes whose strings are pulled by genetic and environmental forces beyond their control. Because free will is a fiction, there is no basis for praising good samaritans or blaming wrongdoers. The hero acts selflessly because he is programmed to act in this manner; the criminal acts selfishly for the same reason. According to this view, a criminal is "more a victim of misfortune than a villain on the cosmic stage." Greenawalt, Note 2, *supra*, at 1284. Hard determinism, therefore, is incompatible with retributivism.

By contrast, "soft determinists" or "compatibilists" reason that although human actions are caused, they are not necessarily compelled. A person is free, and therefore properly the recipient of praise or blame, if he is able to act according to the determinations of his own will, i.e., if his actions spring from his own rationally-based motives. A person is unfree when he must do something against his own will — the result of external constraints — or when he lacks the capacity to reason. Soft determinism, therefore, is said to be compatible with retributivism.

For a provocative article that suggests that the determinism/free-will debate is a "false problem" and, as such, that the "proper response . . . is not to wrestle with it but to escape it," and to "recognize that nothing can possibly come of [the debate] and, hence, that nothing can possibly turn on it," see Peter Westen, *Getting the Fly out of the Bottle: The False Problem of Free Will and Determinism*, 8 Buff. Crim. L. Rev. 599, 652 (2005).

[22] Margaret Jane Radin, *Cruel Punishment and Respect for Persons: Super Due Process for Death*, 53 S. Cal. L. Rev. 1143, 1168 (1980). Professor Radin also coined the term "protective retribution" discussed in the text, *infra*.

[23] 2 James Fitzjames Stephen, A History of the Criminal Law of England 81 (1883).

[24] Murphy & Hampton, Note 16, *supra*, at 3 (describing the attitude of James Fitzjames Stephen).

Some advocates of this view argue that retributive punishment gratifies the passion for revenge that would otherwise be satisfied through private vengeance. However, this justification is a disguised form of utilitarianism, since it defends punishment in order to deter private revenge. On the other hand, Professor Jeffrie Murphy has defended what he characterizes as "retributive hatred" this way: When a person is the victim of a crime, he justifiably resents the criminal for violating his rights; such resentment takes the form of righteous anger or hatred, in which the resenter wants to see the wrongdoer suffer; these passions are morally desirable because they demonstrate that the crime victim respects himself, i.e., that he believes that he should be treated with dignity.[25]

A second, quite different, version of retribution may be called *protective retribution*. For adherents of this form of retribution, punishment is not inflicted because society wants to hurt wrongdoers, as with assaultive retribution, but because punishment is a means of securing a moral balance in the society. As Professor Herbert Morris has explained, society is composed of rules that forbid various form of harmful conduct; compliance with these rules burdens each member of the community that exercises self-restraint.[26] These same rules provide a benefit in the form of "noninterference by others with what each person values, such . . . as continuance of life and bodily security."[27] As long as everyone follows the rules, an equilibrium exists — everyone is similarly benefitted and burdened. If a person fails to exercise self-restraint when he could have — when he renounces a burden that others have assumed — he destroys the balance. He becomes a free rider: He has the benefits of the system of rules, without accepting the same burdens. Thus, a criminal owes a debt to society. It is fair, therefore, to require payment of the debt, i.e., punishment equal or proportional to the debt owed (i.e., the crime committed).

Advocates of this form of retribution emphasize that by punishing the wrongdoer, society demonstrates its respect for him: By stating that the criminal deserves punishment and is morally blameworthy, society treats him as a responsible moral agent. Indeed, according to this school of thought, the wrongdoer has a *right* to be punished. Punishment permits the offender to pay his debt to society, and to return to it free of moral guilt and stigma.

A third form of retribution might be termed *victim vindication*.[28] According to Jean Hampton, punishment is a way to "right a wrong." By committing an offense, a criminal implicitly sends a message to the victim and society that his (the criminal's) rights and desires are more valuable than those of the victim. Thus, by committing a crime, the offender elevates himself with respect to oth-

---

[25] *Id.* at 88-110.

[26] Morris, Note 16, *supra*.

[27] *Id.* at 477.

[28] Hampton, Note 16, *supra*, at 1686 ("retribution is a response to a wrong that is intended to vindicate the value of the victim"); and Murphy & Hampton, Note 16, *supra*, at 111-61.

ers. By doing so, the criminal makes a false moral claim as to his relative worth: In reality the criminal and the victim have equal moral worth as human beings. Retributive punishment corrects this false claim. It reaffirms the victim's worth as a human being in the face of the criminal's challenge. Retributive punishment, therefore, represents a "defeat of the wrongdoer"; he is mastered in much the way that he mastered the victim. Once the criminal receives punishment proportional to the offense, the "score" is made even.

[C] Denunciation (Expressive Theory)[29]

Most efforts to justify punishment are based on utilitarianism or retributivism. *Denunciation* or, alternatively, the *expressive* view of punishment, is probably the most frequently suggested alternative basis of punishment. According to this view, punishment is justified as a means of expressing society's condemnation, and the relative seriousness, of a crime. Upon a closer look, denunciation turns out to be a hybrid of sophisticated aspects of utilitarianism and the victim vindication form of retribution. According to one commentator, however, "[i]t might be the case that any plausible conception of the expressive view can be fit into the framework of deterrence or retributivism, but it would be fallacious to conclude that the expressive theory can therefore be ignored. . . ."[30] The view here is that any sensible version of utilitarianism or retribution must include the ideas found in the denunciatory theory.

Why is denunciation desirable? First, it is educative. We inform individuals that the community considers specific conduct improper and that we value the victim's worth. Second, public denunciation through the criminal justice system channels community anger away from personal vengeance. The collective expression of condemnation also serves to maintain social cohesion.[31] In all of these ways denunciation is utilitarian in nature, in that it affects future conduct.

Denunciation is also retributive, in that it is a form of moral condemnation: Denunciation serves to stigmatize the offender for his offense. It vindicates the victim. By denunciation, society announces that the wrongdoer deserves punishment, precisely because he has "engage[d] in behavior that conveys disrespect for important values."[32] As Professor Samuel Pillsbury has explained, "[t]hose persons who rationally resolve to hurt others in certain fundamental respects should be punished in order that they, and others, can see the moral significance of their actions."[33] These expressive feelings are consistent with retributivism.

---

[29] See generally Kahan, Note 2, *supra*, at 594-605.

[30] Kahan, Note 2, *supra*, at 601.

[31] Emile Durkheim, The Division of Labor in Society 108-09 (G. Simpson trans., 1933).

[32] Kahan, Note 2, *supra*, at 602.

[33] Samuel H. Pillsbury, Judging Evil: Rethinking the Law of Murder and Manslaughter 35 (1998).

§ 2.04 THE DEBATE BETWEEN THE COMPETING THEORIES[34]

Debate between utilitarians and retributivists has raged for centuries, and it won't end soon. Nonetheless, it is important to get a sense of the nature of the disagreement. What follows is a brief summary of some of the criticisms of the theories, and common responses to the objections.

[A] Criticisms of Utilitarianism

[1] Deterrence

Retributivists criticize deterrence theory on the ground that it justifies using persons solely as a means to an end. To the utilitarian, the punished individual is an instrument for the improvement of society. This system ignores the dignity and human rights of the wrongdoer. Utilitarians respond that humans possess no immutable rights for utilitarians to ignore.[35] The right each member of society possesses is the right to have the law used to benefit the whole community. Furthermore, since the wrongdoer is a member of society, he benefits from his own punishment. Therefore, he is not used *solely* as a means to an end.

A second criticism of utilitarianism, closely allied to the first charge, is that utilitarianism can justify the punishment of a person known to be innocent of wrongdoing.[36] The following hypothetical illustrates the issue:[37] A white woman, living in a racially divided community, is brutally raped by an unidentified black male. A mob of white racists respond by surging into an area of town with a predominantly African-American population, intending to indiscrimi-

---

[34] See generally Contemporary Utilitarianism, Note 10, *supra*; Christopher, Note 19, *supra*; David Dolinko, *Three Mistakes of Retributivism*, 39 UCLA L. Rev. 1623 (1992); David Dolinko, *Some Thoughts About Retributivism*, 101 Ethics 537 (1991); Morris B. Hoffman & Timothy H. Goldsmith, *The Biological Roots of Punishment*, 1 Ohio St. J. Crim. L. 627 (2004); Dan M. Kahan, *The Theory of Value Dilemma: A Critique of the Economic Analysis of Criminal Law*, 1 Ohio St. J. Crim. L. 643 (2004); Paul H. Robinson & John M. Darley, *The Role of Deterrence in the Formulation of Criminal Law Rules: At Its Worst When Doing Its Best*, 91 Geo. L.J. 949 (2003).

[35] Bentham wrote that "*[n]atural rights* is simple nonsense; natural and imprescriptible rights, rhetorical nonsense, — nonsense upon stilts." Jeremy Bentham, Anarchical Fallacies, *in* 2 The Works of Jeremy Bentham 501 (J. Bowring ed., 1843).

[36] This accusation has been the subject of a great deal of literature. See generally Guyora Binder & Nicholas J. Smith, *Framed: Utilitarianism and Punishment of the Innocent*, 32 Rutgers L.J. 115 (2000); H.J. McCloskey, *A Non-Utilitarian Approach to Punishment*, *in* Contemporary Utilitarianism, Note 10, *supra*, at 239; James McCloskey, *Convicting the Innocent*, Crim. Just. Ethics, Winter/Spring 1989, at 2; Jeffrey Reiman & Ernest van den Haag, *On the Common Saying that It Is Better that Ten Guilty Persons Escape than that One Innocent Suffer: Pro and Con*, Soc. Phil. & Pol'y, Spring 1990, at 226; T.L.S. Sprigge, *A Utilitarian Reply to Dr. McCloskey*, *in* Contemporary Utilitarianism, Note 10, *supra*, at 261.

[37] The hypothetical is based on H.J. McCloskey, Note 36, *supra*, at 248.

nately lynch many innocent persons and burn their houses. The town's sheriff lacks the personnel to stop the mob. According to retributivist critics, a utilitarian sheriff could justify immediately arresting and framing an innocent African-American for the crime in order to placate the mob. Retributivism flatly rejects this outcome: An innocent person never deserves punishment because he has no debt to repay society; therefore, punishment of an innocent person is unalterably wrong.

Some utilitarians do not deny the *theoretical* possibility that punishment of an innocent person could be justified, but they insist that the real-world circumstances supporting such a result would never come into play. In the hypothetical above, for example, the sheriff could have arrested the innocent man, and then released him after the mob dispersed. Furthermore, utilitarians argue, the sheriff ignored the wider consequences of his actions. By framing an innocent person, a guilty individual remained free to kill and rape again. Moreover, it is said, a sensible utilitarian would consider the possibility that the public would eventually learn that the sheriff had framed an innocent person. The loss of the public's respect for the criminal justice system, anger at the sheriff, and fear of similar treatment of other innocents, would cause more harm than the mob would have committed.

Indeed, the latter defense raises a more fundamental claim of some utilitarians: The accusation that framing the innocent could be justifiable "rests on a misunderstanding of utilitarian penology as an application of an 'act-utilitarian' ethic governing individual behavior."[38] That is, the sheriff hypothetical only makes sense if one applies (improperly, the argument is made) *act-utilitarianism* — a calculation of whether a particular act, on this immediate occasion, is justified on utilitarian grounds. In contrast is *rule-utilitarianism* — the determination of whether a particular act, publicly announced as a rule of law that applies to an entire community, would be justified. A *rule* that an innocent person should be framed whenever it would do more good than harm would conflict with a theory of law and legal process that intends to create not only happiness in general, but which favors the formulation and publication of rules, legal decisionmaking, and a sense of security among the public.

[2] Rehabilitation

Critics doubt that criminals can be reformed. They ask, in essence: "If family, school, and religion have failed, why should we think that prisons, psychiatric care, or any other treatment will succeed?" Opponents of rehabilitation point to studies that suggest that reform efforts have failed.[39]

---

[38] Binder & Smith, Note 36, *supra*, at 118-19.

[39] E.g., Robert Martinson, *What Works? Questions and Answers about Prison Reform*, 35 Pub. Int. 22 (1974).

Proponents contend that empirical studies demonstrate "that opponents . . . [have] grossly overstated the case against rehabilitation."[40] Although reformation may not be possible in all circumstances, advocates argue that it will often work if society is prepared to commit the necessary resources to the process. And, in the long run, the costs of rehabilitation may result in long-term cost savings.[41]

Retributivists criticize rehabilitation on the ground that, in the name of humanitarianism, the "theory removes from Punishment the concept of Desert. . . . [W]hen we cease to consider what the criminal deserves and consider only what will cure him . . . , we have tacitly removed him from the sphere of justice altogether."[42] Critics state that proponents of rehabilitation demean offenders by treating them as sick, childlike, or otherwise unable to act as moral agents. Moreover, a system based on rehabilitation can justify "cures" (e.g., a lobotomy) that violate the offender's personhood.

Advocates of rehabilitation believe that reformation is preferable to punishment based on fear (classical utilitarian theory) or the "hurt the criminal, he deserves it" attitude of assaultive retribution. They point out that the rehabilitative model preserves the concept of redemption evident in Judeo-Christian values. When such a transformation occurs, "it is difficult to find a continued justification for imposing suffering on that offender."[43]

[B] Criticisms of Retributivism

Utilitarians state that punishment — the intentional infliction of pain — is senseless and even cruel if it does no good, and yet retributivists favor precisely that, i.e., the infliction of pain that need not result in future benefit. Society's goal should be to reduce overall human suffering, not purposely cause more of it. This criticism focuses on the consequentialist nature of utilitarianism — that the propriety of an act depends on the consequences. In contrast, retributivists believe that there are moral imperatives, i.e., acts that are unalterably right or wrong, regardless of their consequences. To a retributivist, once it is determined that a crime has been committed and that the wrongdoer is morally responsible for committing it, a measured response in the form of punishment proportional to the crime is unalterably right.

---

[40] Vitiello, Note 10, *supra*, at 1032. One early critic of rehabilitation (see Note 39, *supra*) has since pointed to successes in the field. Robert Martinson, *New Findings, New Views: A Note of Caution Regarding Sentencing Reform*, 7 Hofstra L. Rev. 243 (1979).

[41] E.g., Christopher S. Wren, *Arizona Finds Cost Savings in Treating Drug Offenders*, N.Y. Times, Apr. 21, 1999, at A16 (reporting on an Arizona Supreme Court finding that the state's new policy of treating, rather than jailing, addicts, had saved an estimated $2.5 million in its first year and would reap greater long-term savings; and reporting the view that such early intervention may be more beneficial to the addict than incarceration).

[42] C.S. Lewis, *The Humanitarian Theory of Punishment, in* Contemporary Punishment: Views, Explanations, and Justifications 194 (R. Gerber & P. McAnany eds., 1972).

[43] Vitiello, Note 10, *supra*, at 1051.

Second, some utilitarians criticize retributivism because, they say, it glorifies anger and legitimizes hatred.[44] The reality of retribution, therefore, conflicts with its purported respect for the rights of all persons, including criminals. A retributivist response is that this observation, if valid at all, applies only to the assaultive form of retribution.[45]

Third, and closely related to the preceding argument, is the claim that retributivism is irrational, because it is founded on emotions, such as anger, rather than on reason. Retributivists believe, however, that emotion can have a moral content.[46] Just as most people believe that an emotion such as compassion is morally good — it says something good about the character of the person — anger, when directed at a wrongdoer for his wrongdoing, is also a morally proper emotion. Our anger demonstrates our awareness that the criminal has violated our rights, has acted unjustly and, therefore, deserves punishment. That anger — including the retributive urge to punish — is morally good when it demonstrates that we value ourselves and the rights of other crime victims.

§ 2.05 MIXED THEORIES OF PUNISHMENT[47]

Utilitarianism and retributivism conflict with each other. Although adherents of both theories may agree on results in particular cases, a criminal justice system that seeks, exclusively, to prevent future crime will look very different from one that seeks, exclusively, to impose punishment based on a just-deserts philosophy. The difficulty is that, although some people are thoroughgoing utilitarians or uncompromising retributivists, most people find aspects of each theory attractive.

The criminal law that has, in fact, developed in the United States is not philosophically consistent. Some rules of criminal responsibility are primarily retributive in nature, whereas others are utilitarian in character. In part this is because each theory has dominated intellectual thought at separate times, but neither has won the ultimate debate; in part, this is because courts and legislatures find both theories attractive; in part, this is because of a failure on the part of lawmakers to attend to the conflicting theories of punishment.

Although some of the mixture of theories that has developed is a function of happenstance or incoherence, many scholars have sought to justify a mixed theoretical system. For example, as Professor H.L.A. Hart has shown,[48] we

---

[44] Dolinko, *Three Mistakes of Retributivism*, Note 34, *supra*, at 1650.

[45] See § 2.03[B][2], *supra*.

[46] See generally Samuel H. Pillsbury, *Emotional Justice: Moralizing the Passions of Criminal Punishment*, 74 Cornell L. Rev. 655 (1989).

[47] See generally Stephen P. Garvey, *Lifting the Veil of Punishment*, 7 Buff. Crim. L. Rev. 443 (2004); Paul H. Robinson, *Hybrid Principles for the Distribution of Criminal Sanctions*, 82 Nw. U. L. Rev. 19 (1987); Andrew von Hirsch, *Hybrid Principles in Allocating Sanctions: A Response to Professor Robinson*, 82 Nw. U. L. Rev. 64 (1987).

[48] Hart, Note 3, *supra*, at 8-13.

may want to ask two different questions in the criminal law. The first question is: Why have we set up a criminal justice system, i.e., devised criminal laws prohibiting certain conduct, created a police force to arrest law violators, set up courts to adjudicate guilt and innocence, and imposed penalties for violations of those laws? In short, what is the general justifying aim of the criminal law: Is our primary purpose to punish murderers, rapists, and robbers (retribution), or is to prevent those crimes in the first place (utilitarianism)? A separate question is: Given our justice system, *who* should be held responsible for their actions, and *how much* punishment is appropriate for those who are held responsible?

According to Hart, a person may coherently argue that the general aim of the criminal law is to deter unwanted behavior, but that retributive concepts of just deserts should be applied in determining *whether* and *how much* to punish a particular person. For example, suppose that *D*, suffering from a severe mental illness, kills *V*. An advocate of this hybrid penal system might say that the criminal homicide statutes were enacted to deter unjustified killings, but that *D* should only be punished if he is morally blameworthy, which he might not be in light of his mental illness. And, even if he *is* blameworthy, his punishment should be in proportion to his moral desert (retribution) and not his future dangerousness (utilitarianism).

Especially when one shifts from the general justifying aim of the criminal law, and even from the question of *who* deserves punishment, to the question of *how much* punishment should be imposed, there are mixed theories of punishment. For example, some theorists favor a concept of "limiting retributivism."[49] The idea here is that, pursuant to retributivist thought, punishment should be proportional to the crime and the criminal's blameworthiness. Retributivists, however, cannot realistically identify the precise amount of punishment deserved in any particular case. They can only provide a "range of severity" of proportional punishment: Punishment below a certain amount would be too little, and punishment above a certain amount would be too much. Within that range, advocates of "limited retributism" suggest, utilitarian factors should predominate. Others would go further and say that, although punishment should never exceed that which is retributively justifiable (even if there are utilitarian reasons for exceeding it), it is permissible to inflict *less* punishment than is deserved, if there is no good utilitarian justification for the punishment.[50]

---

[49] American Law Institute, Model Penal Code Sentencing, Preliminary Draft No. 3 (May 28, 2004), at 8.

[50] Garvey, Note 47, *supra*, at 450.

§ 2.06 SENTENCING[51]

Criminal codes generally provide that a defendant convicted of a noncapital felony offense may receive a sentence consisting of a term of years of imprisonment in a state prison, a monetary fine, or a combination thereof.[52] Alternative non-incarcerative sanctions — for example, compelled community service or shaming[53] — are far less common, but permitted in some circumstances. In most cases a trial judge also has the option of sentencing a defendant to a term of years in prison, for example, five years, but then suspending the sentence and placing the individual on probation for that term.[54] In the latter case, the offender remains free subject to conditions set by the judge (e.g., that he undergo random drug testing, avoid contact with known ex-felons, not possess a firearm, and/or report to a probation officer on regularly scheduled dates). If the probationer violates any of the conditions of release, the judge may order the offender to serve the suspended sentence or part thereof.

A state's sentencing structure should be consistent with the theories of punishment that are at the foundation of that particular jurisdiction's criminal justice system. Modern penal codes often set out those penal theories expressly. For example, Model Penal Code § 1.02, subsections (2)(a) and (b), provide that the Code's sentencing provisions are intended "to prevent the commission of crimes" (deterrence), and "to promote the correction and rehabilitation of offenders." Consistent with the latter rehabilitative goal, subsection (e) states that sentences should "differentiate among offenders with a view to a just individualization of treatment."

---

[51] See generally 2 Joshua Dressler & Alan C. Michaels, Understanding Criminal Procedure ch. 15 (4th ed. 2006); Samuel H. Pillsbury, *Understanding Penal Reform: The Dynamic of Change*, 80 J. Crim. L. & Criminology 726 (1989); William J. Powell & Michael T. Cimino, *Prosecutorial Discretion Under the Federal Sentencing Guidelines: Is the Fox Guarding the Hen House?*, 97 W. Va. L. Rev. 373 (1995).

[52] E.g., Model Penal Code §§ 6.03, 6.06.

[53] A highly controversial and uncommon form of punishment is shaming. For example, one defendant convicted of driving under the influence of alcohol was required by a judge to attach a sign to his car identifying himself as a convicted drunk driver. People v. Letterlough, 655 N.E.2d 146 (N.Y. 1995). In another case, a husband was ordered to stand on the City Hall steps at lunchtime, face lunchtime workers and battered-woman advocates, and apologize for striking his wife. Jan Hoffman, *Crime and Punishment: Shame Gains Popularity*, N.Y. Times, Jan. 16, 1997, at A1. Many shaming sentences have been struck down by appellate courts on the ground that the judges lacked statutory authority to impose the sentences. See generally Stephen P. Garvey, *Can Shaming Practices Educate?* 65 U. Chi. L. Rev. 733 (1998); Kahan, Note 2, *supra*; Toni M. Massaro, *Shame, Culture, and American Criminal Law*, 89 Mich. L. Rev. 1880 (1991).

[54] Increasingly, legislatures are enacting laws providing for mandatory minimum sentences for specific crimes. In such circumstances, a judge lacks the authority to place a defendant on probation. Many trial judges dislike mandatory-minimum-sentence laws because they believe these provisions compel them to impose a more severe sentence than is justified in individual cases. E.g., United States v. Patillo, 817 F. Supp. 839 (C.D. Cal. 1993) (in which the trial judge expressed his conscientious opposition to imposing a mandatory minimum prison sentence of ten years on a 27-year-old, college educated, first-time drug offender).

The sentencing features of the Model Penal Code, which were published by the American Law Institute in 1962,[55] are consistent with the rehabilitative goals dominant in legal thought in the 1960s.[56] Indeed, consistent with rehabilitation, most states by 1960 utilized some form of "indeterminate sentencing."[57] During this period, judges had considerable sentencing discretion. They were encouraged to individualize a defendant's maximum sentence based on information obtained in a post-conviction sentencing hearing, regarding the defendant's character and the circumstances of the offense. However, what made a sentencing system "indeterminate" was that the judge only defined the outer reaches of the sentence. Correctional officers (primarily parole boards) had the authority to release the prisoner *before* completion of the sentence imposed by the judge, if the prisoner satisfied rehabilitative goals.

Most states have abandoned indeterminate sentencing systems for a determinate one. This trend is the result of many factors and social forces, including disillusionment with the rehabilitative model, pressure from the public during high-crime periods for longer prison sentences, increased interest in retributive goals, and a widespread desire to cut back on judicial sentencing discretion because of perceived unjustifiable disparity in sentences meted out by different judges for similar offenses.[58]

Determinate sentencing systems vary, but have one feature in common: The offender's sentence is determined at the time of sentencing. In such a system, corrections officers lack authority to reduce the sentence based on evidence of rehabilitation in prison. In most states, judges retain limited discretion in imposing a sentence. For example, a state code may set a range of incarcerative penalties for a crime, and the judge may select a fixed sentence within that range (e.g., robbery may be punishable by imprisonment, ranging from two to five years; the judge determines the precise sentence within that range).

In the federal courts, sentences are imposed in conformity with complicated and controversial Federal Sentencing Guidelines.[59] The guidelines require a

---

[55] See § 3.03, *infra*.

[56] Because rehabilitative goals no longer are dominant in American legal thought, a committee of the American Law Institute is considering revisions of the Code's sentencing provisions. Professor Kevin Reitz is serving as the Reporter on the revisions.

[57] Powell & Cimino, Note 51, *supra*, at 378.

[58] Sanford H. Kadish, *Fifty Years of Criminal Law: An Opinionated Review*, 87 Cal. L. Rev. 943, 979-80 (1999) (characterizing the change in sentiment as the result of the "unlikely coincidence of views between two historically antagonistic schools of thoughts": law-and-order advocates who have long rejected rehabilitative measures because they "coddled" offenders; and traditional supporters of such sentencing who were disturbed by "indefensible inequities," often racially based, in sentencing and release procedures).

[59] See generally Stephen Breyer, *The Federal Sentencing Guidelines and the Key Compromises Upon Which They Rest*, 17 Hofstra L. Rev. 1 (1988). For a critique of the guidelines, especially from a judge's perspective, see Kate Stith & Jose Cabranes, Fear of Judging: Sentencing Guidelines in the Federal Courts (1998).

court to proceed through various regulated steps to determine an offender's actual sentence within a range of incarcerative penalties set by the legislature. Although a judge may impose a sentence above or below the guidelines (although, of course, the sentence must be within the legislatively set range), the judge is expected to provide reasons for the departure, those reasons should meet certain guideline requirements, and the judge's departure is subject to appellate review.

Chapter 3

SOURCES OF THE CRIMINAL LAW

§ 3.01 ORIGINS OF THE CRIMINAL LAW[1]

[A] Common Law

American criminal law is primarily English in its heritage and judicial in its origin. In large measure, the original thirteen American states and most later states adopted English law as their own.[2]

Originally, English criminal law was "common law" in nature. That is, it was judge-made law: The definitions of crimes and the rules of criminal responsibility were promulgated by courts rather than by the Parliament. When American courts and criminal lawyers use the term "common law," therefore, they are describing the law developed over the centuries by English judges and imported to this country. However, the common law of England was reworked by American courts to meet local needs and mores, so that by the turn of the twentieth century this country's common law diverged in significant respects from its British progenitor.

[B] Criminal Statutes

Inspired by the Enlightenment, a movement in eighteenth and nineteenth century Europe and United States shifted the locus of lawmaking from the courts to legislative bodies. In part, the effort to enhance legislative authority was based on the belief that crimes should be defined by an institution more representative of those being governed than the judiciary.[3] The "romance with reason" also inspired reformers of different philosophical stripes (both utilitarians and believers in natural law) to try to codify the criminal law in order to produce "a legislated body of reordered, reformed, and reconceived law" in accordance with their respective principles.[4]

---

[1] See generally Markus Dirk Dubber, *Reforming American Penal Law*, 90 J. Crim. L. & Criminology 49 (1999); Ford W. Hall, *The Common Law: An Account of its Reception in the United States*, 4 Vand. L. Rev. 791 (1951); Sanford H. Kadish, *The Model Penal Code's Historical Antecedents*, 19 Rutgers L.J. 521 (1988); Sanford H. Kadish, *Codifiers of the Criminal Law: Wechsler's Predecessors*, 78 Colum. L. Rev. 1098 (1978).

[2] See Hall, Note 1, *supra*, at 798-805.

[3] See John Calvin Jeffries, Jr., *Legality, Vagueness, and the Construction of Penal Statutes*, 71 Va. L. Rev. 189, 190 (1985).

[4] Kadish, *The Model Penal Code's Historical Antecedents*, Note 1, *supra*, at 521-22.

In general, early codification efforts failed. Over time, however, legislatures asserted themselves and enacted penal statutes, initially to supplement, but ultimately to replace, the common law. Today, the change-over is virtually complete. The legislature is the pre-eminent lawmaking body in the realm of criminal law.

§ 3.02 MODERN ROLE OF THE COMMON LAW

Although the legislative branch of government now has primary lawmaking authority, the common law of crimes remains important to modern lawyers.

[A] "Reception" Statutes

Most states, often by statute, have abolished common law crimes.[5] In these jurisdictions, a person may only be convicted and punished for conduct defined as criminal by statute or other legislative enactment.

A few states, however, expressly recognize common law offenses. These states have enacted "reception" statutes, which essentially provide that "[a]ny person who shall commit any . . . offense at the common law, for the punishment of which no provision is expressly made by any statute . . . [is] guilty of a felony"[6] or misdemeanor. In effect, such a statute "receives" the common law offenses in place at the time of the statute's enactment; these crimes become an unwritten part of the state's criminal law, and are defined as they existed at the time of their reception.[7]

As a practical matter, prosecutions of common law offenses in jurisdictions that retain the common law are rare. Common law crimes, although not abolished in such states, are superseded by statutes prohibiting similar conduct.[8] A common law prosecution is not possible, therefore, unless there is a true gap in the statutory system, and today there are few lacunae. Nearly all legislatures have enacted statutes encompassing the common law felonies and most of the misdemeanors.

---

[5] E.g., Cal. Penal Code § 6 (Deering 2005) ("No act or omission . . . is criminal or punishable, except as prescribed or authorized by this code. . . ."); Model Penal Code § 1.05(1) ("No conduct constitutes an offense unless it is a crime or violation under this Code or another statute of this State").

[6] Mich. Comp. Laws § 750.505 (2005); see also R.I. Gen Laws § 11-1-1 (2004).

[7] Where the criminal code is silent on the matter — it has neither expressly abolished common law offenses nor does it contain a reception statute — it may be, as one court has claimed, that "so much of the common law as has not been abrogated or repealed by statute [remains] in full force and effect." *Gervin v. State*, 371 S.W.2d 449, 454 (Tenn. 1963).

[8] E.g., State v. Palendrano, 293 A.2d 747 (N.J. Super. Ct. Law Div. 1972) (holding that the common law offense of "being a common scold" — a woman who habitually acts in a quarrelsome manner — was no longer a crime, in part because the non-gender-biased elements of the offense were encompassed by New Jersey's Disorderly Persons Act).

A lingering issue in the few states recognizing common law offenses is whether a court may assert its traditional authority to devise *new* crimes. The authors of early twentieth century treatises assumed that this judicial power remained intact, and a few courts have exercised such authority,[9] but it is now commonly accepted that "[j]udicial crime creation [in the United States] is a thing of the past."[10] In contrast, at least a few modern courts believe that they are empowered by reception statutes to *abolish* common law offenses that they consider no longer "compatible with . . . local circumstances and situation."[11]

[B] Statutory Interpretation

Even in states without reception statutes, the common law retains significance. Almost without exception, these jurisdictions have codified the common law felonies and most common law misdemeanors. These statutory offenses are usually defined, at least in part, in common law terms.[12] A familiar maxim of statutory interpretation is that when a statute contains a common law term, the presumption is that such a term retains its common law meaning, absent a statutory definition to the contrary.[13] Therefore, lawyers should be familiar with, and courts must often apply, the common law.

For example, in *Keeler v. Superior Court*,[14] *K* learned that his ex-wife was pregnant by another man. He intentionally struck her in the abdomen in order to kill the fetus. The fetus was delivered stillborn. *K* was prosecuted for murder,

---

[9] E.g., Commonwealth v. Donoghue, 63 S.W.2d 3 (Ky. 1933) (upholding an indictment for participation in "a nefarious plan for the habitual exaction of gross usury," although no such offense had previously existed). An example of judicial crime-creation in England is *Shaw v. Director of Public Prosecutions*, [1962] A.C. 220, in which the House of Lords affirmed a conviction for conspiracy to corrupt public morals, for the publication of a telephone directory of prostitutes. Viscount Simonds stated that he "entertain[ed] no doubt that there remains in the courts of law a residual power to enforce the supreme and fundamental purpose of the law, to conserve . . . the moral welfare of the State" against "novel and unprepared for" attacks. *Id.* at 268.

[10] Jeffries, Note 3, *supra*, at 195. However, some courts have maintained that they have authority to expand the definition of *existing* crimes, including statutory offenses. See Note 15, *infra*.

[11] Pope v. State, 396 A.2d 1054, 1078 (Md. 1979) (concluding that the common law offense of "misprision of felony" should be abolished because "its origin, the impractical and indiscriminate width of its scope, its other obvious deficiencies, and its long non-use" rendered it incompatible with that state's "general code of laws and jurisprudence"); see also State v. Palendrano, 293 A.2d 747 (N.J. Super. Ct. Law. Div. 1972) (holding that the common law offense of "being a common scold" was no longer an offense, in part because the crime had been ignored by the state legislature and had been mentioned only twice in the reports of judicial proceedings during almost two centuries of statehood).

[12] At times, a state will enact a common law offense but not define it, in which case the common law definition applies. E.g., Mich. Comp. Laws § 750.321 (1991) (prohibiting, but not defining, manslaughter).

[13] Taylor v. United States, 495 U.S. 575, 592 (1990); State v. Coria, 48 P.3d 980, 987 (Wash. 2002) (dissenting opinion) (citing this Text).

[14] 470 P.2d 617 (Cal. 1970).

which was defined by statute, as at common law, as the "unlawful killing of a human being, with malice aforethought."

K sought to bar his prosecution. He claimed that a fetus born dead was not a "human being" within the meaning of the state's murder statute. Because the statute did not define this critical term, the court sought to identify legislative intent by looking to the common law of 1850, the year the murder statute was enacted and the same year the state legislature abolished common law offenses. In short, absent evidence to the contrary, the court assumed that the 1850 legislature defined "human being" in common law terms. The court ruled that a fetus born dead was not a "human being" for purposes of homicide law under the common law and, therefore, could not be the basis for a modern-day prosecution, in the absence of legislative action.[15]

The common law may also be used to fill in gaps in a penal code. For example, a common law principle is that a person may not be charged with murder if the victim did not die within a year and a day of the assault.[16] Federal law defines murder in common law terms,[17] but is silent regarding the year-and-a-day rule. In the absence of legislative history suggesting that Congress intended to eliminate the rule's requirements, a court may interpret this silence as evidence that the common law rule still applies.[18]

§ 3.03 MODEL PENAL CODE[19]

Although criminal code drafting by legislatures was a major project in the United States through the first half of the nineteenth century, subsequent codification and reform efforts stalled. One result of this long neglect of penal reform was "a substantive criminal law that was often archaic, inconsistent,

---

[15] Accord Vo v. Superior Court, 836 P.2d 408 (Ariz. Ct. App. 1992); Meadows v. State, 722 S.W.2d 584 (Ark. 1987); Passley v. State, 21 S.E.2d 230 (Ga. 1942); People v. Greer, 402 N.E.2d 203 (Ill. 1980); State v. Gyles, 313 So. 2d 799 (La. 1975); State v. Beale, 376 S.E.2d 1 (N.C. 1989); State *ex rel.* Atkinson v. Wilson, 332 S.E.2d 807 (W. Va. 1984).

In jurisdictions in which the judiciary retains residual common law authority, a few courts have expanded the definition of "human being" to include viable fetuses born dead. Commonwealth v. Cass, 467 N.E.2d 1324 (Mass. 1984); Hughes v. State, 868 P.2d 730 (Okla. Crim. App. 1994); State v. Horne, 319 S.E.2d 703 (S.C. 1984). Such changes, however, should only apply prospectively. See § 5.01, *infra*.

[16] See § 31.01[C], *infra*.

[17] 18 U.S.C. § 1111(a) (2004).

[18] E.g., United States v. Chase, 18 F.3d 1166 (4th Cir. 1994); Ex Parte Key, 890 So. 2d 1056 (Ala. 2003) (in the absence of express evidence, the state legislature's enactment of a new criminal code did not abolish the common law year-and-a-day rule); *but see* State v. Rogers, 992 S.W.2d 393 (Tenn. 1999), *affirmed*, Rogers v. Tennessee, 532 U.S. 451 (2002) (finding that the common law year-and-a-day rule was inconsistent with modern public policy, and judicially abolishing it).

[19] See generally Commentary Symposium, *Model Penal Code Second: Good or Bad Idea?*, 1 Ohio St. J. Crim. L. 157-244 (2003); Symposium, *The 25th Anniversary of the Model Penal Code*, 19 Rutgers L.J. 519-954 (1988).

unfair, and unprincipled."[20] Therefore, in 1952 the American Law Institute, an organization composed of judges, lawyers, and law professors, began to draft a penal code intended to inspire a new reformative spirit among state legislatures.

In 1962, after completion of thirteen tentative drafts and accompanying explanatory commentaries, the American Law Institute approved and published its Proposed Official Draft of the Model Penal Code, a carefully drafted code containing general principles of criminal responsibility, definitions of specific offenses, and sentencing provisions.

The impact of the Model Penal Code on American criminal law has been "stunning."[21] Although the Code, as such, is not the law in any jurisdiction — it is, after all, a *model* penal code — it stimulated adoption of revised penal codes in at least thirty-seven states.[22] As Professor Sanford Kadish has put it, the Model Penal Code "has become a standard part of the furniture of the criminal law."[23] Although some state legislatures have adopted only small portions of the Model Code as their own, other jurisdictions (including New Jersey, New York, Pennsylvania, and Oregon) have enacted many of its provisions; and courts, on their own, sometimes turn to the Model Code and its supporting commentaries for guidance in interpreting non-Code criminal statutes.

Many criminal law professors treat the Model Penal Code as "the principal text in criminal law teaching,"[24] because its influence on the law has been so dramatic. As a consequence, this Text considers in detail both the common law and Model Penal Code, the primary sources of modern statutory law.

---

[20] Sanford H. Kadish, *Fifty Years of Criminal Law: An Opinionated Review*, 87 Cal. L. Rev. 943, 947 (1999).

[21] Kadish, *The Model Penal Code's Historical Antecedents*, Note 1, *supra*, at 538.

[22] Peter W. Low, *The Model Penal Code, the Common Law, and Mistakes of Fact: Recklessness, Negligence, or Strict Liability?*, 19 Rutgers L.J. 539, 539 (1988).

[23] Kadish, *The Model Penal Code's Historical Antecedents*, Note 1, *supra*, at 521.

[24] *Id.*

Chapter 4

CONSTITUTIONAL LIMITS
ON THE CRIMINAL LAW

§ 4.01 THE CONSTITUTION: OVERVIEW

Are there limits to a legislature's lawmaking authority? For example, may a state legislature or Congress make it an offense to desecrate an American flag, or prohibit consensual sexual conduct among adults in their home? May it make it a crime to be a drug addict, to suffer from cancer, or to be infected with the HIV virus? May a state legislature abolish common law defenses, such as self-defense and insanity, and thereby punish persons who kill in self-defense or who act due to an insane delusion?

As explained in Chapter 3, modern legislatures, rather than judges, ordinarily determine what conduct is criminal and the circumstances under which a person may be held accountable for his actions. Their considerable authority, however, is not unlimited: Various provisions of the United States Constitution, as interpreted by the judiciary, limit legislative action. A state legislature is also limited by its own state constitution, which may place greater restrictions on it than does the federal Constitution.

This chapter provides a brief overview of some of the federal constitutional provisions that limit legislative authority in the realm of criminal law, and which are considered throughout this Text. These provisions, however, are not interpreted by judges in a policy vacuum. Various overarching policy considerations, which may motivate a court to interpret the Constitution either narrowly or broadly, are also considered here.

§ 4.02 RELEVANT CONSTITUTIONAL PROVISIONS[1]

[A] Bill of Rights

The first ten amendments to the United States Constitution, the so-called "Bill of Rights," restrict the power of the federal government in its relationship to individuals. Various provisions of the Bill of Rights are relevant in the study and practice of the substantive criminal law. The First Amendment provides, in part, that "Congress shall make no law . . . abridging the freedom of speech." Criminal laws that prohibit speech or chill expression, such as some laws pro-

---

[1] See also § 5.01[C][1], *infra* (Bill of Attainder and *Ex Post Facto* Clauses considered).

hibiting the defacing or burning of the American flag, are subject to constitutional attack under this amendment.[2]

The Fourth Amendment provides in pertinent part that "[t]he right of the people to be secure in their persons, houses, papers, and effects against unreasonable searches and seizures, shall not be violated. . . ." Evidence obtained by the police in violation of this amendment may be excluded at a defendant's criminal trial.[3] This amendment also limits the degree of force that a police officer may use in arresting a suspect or preventing an arrestee from escaping. This limitation can affect the scope of criminal law defenses that would otherwise apply to law enforcement officers.[4]

The Eighth Amendment states that "cruel and unusual punishment [shall not be] inflicted." This amendment restricts legislative action in two ways: (1) it imposes limitations on what legislators may define as criminal;[5] and (2) it prohibits punishment that is barbarous in its infliction[6] or grossly disproportional to the offense committed.[7]

[B] Fourteenth Amendment

Whereas the Bill of Rights limits the *federal* government in its relations with individuals, the Fourteenth Amendment to the United States Constitution imposes limits on *state* government. The amendment reads in full:

> No State shall make or enforce any law which shall abridge the privileges or immunities of citizens of the United States; nor shall any State deprive any person of life, liberty, or property, without due process of law; nor deny to any person within its jurisdiction the equal protection of the laws.

The most significant portion of the Fourteenth Amendment as it pertains to the criminal law is the Due Process Clause.[8] Although the meaning of this clause has been the source of great controversy, it is now settled that it requires states not only to guarantee procedural fairness to criminal defendants, but also to respect substantive principles of justice "so rooted in the traditions and con-

---

[2] See § 9.11, *infra*.

[3] Mapp v. Ohio, 367 U.S. 643 (1961); see generally 1 Joshua Dressler & Alan C. Michaels, Understanding Criminal Procedure Ch. 4-20 (4th ed. 2006).

[4] See § 21.04, *infra*.

[5] See § 9.04, *infra*.

[6] Weems v. United States, 217 U.S. 349, 368 (1910).

[7] See § 6.05, *infra*.

[8] The Fifth Amendment, which applies to the federal government, includes a Due Process Clause. In most respects, the scope of the two Due Process Clauses are the same. See West Coast Hotel Co. v. Parrish, 300 U.S. 379, 391 (1937).

science of our people as to be ranked as fundamental."[9] The "fundamental rights" that states must respect are virtually the same as those that the federal government must honor, i.e., nearly all of the provisions of the Bill of Rights have been "incorporated" to the states through the Fourteenth Amendment Due Process Clause.

Citizens also possess certain unenumerated fundamental rights (rights not expressly specified in the Constitution) that are protected within the constitutional term "liberty" found in the Fourteenth Amendment. The Supreme Court has held that among the implicit constitutional rights of Americans is a right of privacy.[10] However, the precise contours of this right remain highly controversial.[11]

The Fourteenth Amendment also prohibits states from denying citizens "the equal protection of the laws."[12] A criminal law that distinguishes on its face between two classes of persons (e.g., females and males, felons and misdemeanants, wealthy and poor people),[13] or which is discriminatory in the manner in which it is applied, may be subject to constitutional attack.[14]

§ 4.03 POLICY FACTORS IN ENFORCING THE CONSTITUTION[15]

[A] In General

Courts are often called upon to determine whether a criminal statute, or the punishment of an offender pursuant to statute, violates one or more of the constitutional principles summarized in Section 4.02. In determining whether a violation has occurred, various competing principles come into play.

---

[9] Snyder v. Massachusetts, 291 U.S. 97, 105 (1934).

[10] Griswold v. Connecticut, 381 U.S. 479 (1965).

[11] See § 9.11, *infra*.

[12] By judicial interpretation this provision applies to the federal government through the Fifth Amendment Due Process Clause. Bolling v. Sharpe, 347 U.S. 497, 499 (1954).

[13] E.g., the common law offense of "being a common scold" expressly applies to women, but not to men. See § 3.02, Note 8, *supra*. As there is no valid justification for this sex-based distinction, the offense violates the Equal Protection Clause. State v. Palendrano, 293 A.2d 747, 752 (N.J. Super. Ct. Law Div. 1972).

[14] This equality right is not absolute. The legislature may lawfully distinguish between groups if there is rational basis for the distinction. Classifications such as race and religion, however, are inherently suspect and subject to much closer judicial scrutiny. See In re Griffiths, 413 U.S. 717 (1973).

[15] See generally Louis D. Bilionis, *Process, the Constitution, and Substantive Criminal Law*, 96 Mich. L. Rev. 1269 (1998); Joshua Dressler, *Kent Greenawalt, Criminal Responsibility, and the Supreme Court: How a Moderate Scholar Can Appear Immoderate Thirty Years Later*, 74 Notre Dame L. Rev. 1507 (1999); Kent Greenawalt, *"Uncontrollable" Actions and the Eighth Amendment: Implications of Powell v. Texas*, 69 Colum. L. Rev. 927 (1969).

In some sense, the Constitution is divided against itself.[16] On the one hand, the document embodies the principles of separation-of-powers and federalism, which are doctrines that suggest that courts should hesitate to intervene in constitutional disputes; on the other hand, the Constitution guarantees persons certain fundamental rights from governmental encroachment, which means that the judiciary may need to act forthrightly to ensure those rights. These competing policies are briefly explained below.

[B] Separation of Powers

Many judges are reluctant to intrude on the lawmaking domain of the legislature, because members of the latter branch of government are elected, whereas federal judges are appointed and hold office for life. Although judges in many states are elected, legislators are viewed as more immediately subject to the will of the public.

Because criminal laws intimately affect the lives of citizens and are intended to represent the moral values of the community, judges believe that, whenever possible, they should defer to the wishes of the public as represented by legislative action. As a consequence, courts presume the constitutionality of criminal statutes, i.e., the party attacking a statute must demonstrate its constitutional invalidity.[17]

[C] Federalism

State governments have primary authority for defining and enforcing the criminal laws of their respective jurisdictions. The Constitution does not give the federal government the right to compel statutory uniformity among the states. In fact, legislative experimentation and interstate diversity is welcomed in our federal system.

Left to their own devices, state legislatures are apt to generate criminal codes that differ from each other in key respects. For example, State X might consider polygamy a serious moral offense and prohibit and punish it as a felony, whereas the people of State Y might consider polygamy morally tolerable conduct or too trivial a matter to prohibit. At the same time, State Y, with an agriculturally-based economy, might believe that it needs to punish theft of crops more severely than urban neighbor State X does. And each of the fifty states might choose to deal with the burgeoning problem of crime on the Internet, but they might do so in a myriad of ways, as each jurisdiction experiments in search of a viable solution.

---

[16] See Akhil Reed Amar, *Of Sovereignty and Federalism*, 96 Yale L.J. 1425, 1426 (1987).

[17] United States v. Watson, 423 U.S. 411, 416 (1976).

[D] Protecting Individual Rights

Although the principles discussed above support caution by the judiciary, especially the federal judiciary, in dealing with statutes, the Constitution "explicitly compels the States [and federal government] to follow . . . constitutional commands."[18] Among the most important constitutional commands are those found within the Bill of Rights and Fourteenth Amendment. These provisions guarantee that the fundamental rights of individuals will *not* be trampled upon by the majority. In short, these provisions serve as a "minority rights' charter," in the sense that the constitutional framers intended to place some limits on the extent to which majority will may prevail over the interests of the less powerful.

The legislative branch of government represents the public, as a whole. Some branch of government must protect the constitutional rights of individuals. That branch is the judiciary.[19] Therefore, a court that defers to legislative judgment out of respect for the doctrines of separation-of-powers and federalism may be guilty of abdicating its institutional duty to enforce constitutional edicts. Judges concerned about potential governmental overreaching are apt to de-emphasize the doctrines of separation-of-powers and federalism. Judges concerned about the vitality of the latter principles are likely to de-emphasize the principle that the judiciary should serve as a watchdog against governmental overreaching.

---

[18] Rummel v. Estelle, 445 U.S. 263, 303 (1980) (Powell, J., dissenting).

[19] See Marbury v. Madison, 5 U.S. (1 Cranch) 137 (1803).

Chapter 5

LEGALITY

§ 5.01 PRINCIPLE OF LEGALITY[1]

[A] "Legality": Definition

Some conduct is immoral, harmful, or both. Some conduct is criminal and punishable. The fact that conduct is immoral or harmful does not mean, however, that it is criminal and punishable. The American legal system espouses the principle, *nullum crimen sine lege, nulla poena sine lege*, or "no crime without law, no punishment without law." That is, a person may not be punished unless her conduct was defined as criminal — today, in the United States, by statute, rather than the result of judicial crime-creation[2] — before she acted.[3] This prohibition on retroactive criminal lawmaking constitutes the essence of the principle of legality.

The doctrine of legality, which has been characterized as reflective of the "central values of liberal societies,"[4] is considered the first principle of American criminal law jurisprudence.[5] That is, the legality principle should override all other criminal law doctrines. It applies even though its exercise may result in dangerous and morally culpable persons escaping punishment.[6] As one court stated when it reversed the conviction of a defendant on the basis of the principle of legality:

> That [the defendant] will go largely unpunished . . . is frustrating. There are, however, basic principles upon which this country is founded

---

[1] See generally Herbert L. Packer, The Limits of the Criminal Sanction 79-102 (1968); Francis A. Allen, The Habits of Legality: Criminal Justice and the Rule of Law (1996); Timothy Endicott, *Law Is Necessarily Vague*, 7 Legal Theory 379 (2001); Douglas N. Husak & Craig A. Callender, *Wilful Ignorance, Knowledge, and the "Equal Culpability" Thesis: A Study of the Deeper Significance of the Principle of Legality*, 1994 Wis. L. Rev. 29; John Calvin Jeffries, Jr., *Legality, Vagueness, and the Construction of Penal Statutes*, 71 Va. L. Rev. 189 (1985); Dan M. Kahan, *Some Realism About Retroactive Criminal Lawmaking*, 3 Roger Williams U. L. Rev. 95 (1997); Paul H. Robinson, *Legality and Discretion in the Distribution of Criminal Sanctions*, 25 Harv. J. on Legis. 393 (1988).

[2] See § 3.02[A], *supra*.

[3] E.g., Model Penal Code § 1.01(2).

[4] Allen, Note 1, *supra*, at 15.

[5] Packer, Note 1, *supra*, at 79-80.

[6] Donald A. Dripps, *The Constitutional Status of the Reasonable Doubt Rule*, 75 Cal. L. Rev. 1665, 1685 (1987) ("[T]he legality principle enjoys nearly complete priority over the public interest in punishing wrongdoers. . . ."); see Kahan, Note 1, *supra*, at 97-103 (agreeing that this is the effect of the principle, but deploring this outcome).

which compel the result we reach. . . . [Legality] is one of them. The retroactive application of criminal law . . . is so abhorrent that we must occasionally endure some frustration in order to preserve and protect the foundation of our system of law.[7]

There are three interrelated corollaries to the legality principle: (1) criminal statutes should be understandable to reasonable law-abiding persons; (2) criminal statutes should be crafted so as not to "delegate[] basic policy matters to policemen, judges, and juries for resolution on an *ad hoc* and subjective basis";[8] and (3) judicial interpretation of ambiguous statutes should "be biased in favor of the accused" (the lenity doctrine).[9]

The legality principle is explained in this chapter section. Its corollaries are considered in the following sections of this chapter. As will be seen, the corollaries (especially the first and third ones) are often not enforced rigorously.

[B] Rationale

Advocates of the legality doctrine defend it on various grounds. First, enforcement of the principle is designed to serve fundamental justice by preventing the "arbitrary and vindictive use of the laws."[10] Second, the legality principle enhances individual autonomy, and "maximizes the opportunity of individuals to pursue their own purposes and ends,"[11] by reducing the risk that a person's lawful conduct will be punished retroactively.

Third, the legality principle is justified on fair notice grounds. Specifically, the existence of "legislative enactments 'give fair warning of their effect and permit individuals to rely on their meaning until explicitly changed.' "[12] Without fair notice — if a person can be punished for conduct that was lawful at the time that she acted — a citizen lacks adequate opportunity to conform her conduct to the law. And, some argue, in the absence of such an opportunity, the retributive basis for moral condemnation of the actor is lacking. Also, the requirement of fair notice is said by some to enhance general deterrence principles: A person cannot be deterred from committing what is subsequently determined to be a socially unacceptable act unless she has fair notice at the time of her conduct of the line separating proper from improper behavior.

---

[7] Hughes v. State, 868 P.2d 730, 736 (Okla. Crim. App. 1994); see also Dripps, Note 6, *supra*, at 1685 ("punishment unauthorized by law is, in civilized communities, simply beyond the pale").

[8] Grayned v. City of Rockford, 408 U.S. 104, 108-09 (1972).

[9] Jeffries, Note 1, *supra*, at 189.

[10] Rogers v. Tennessee, 532 U.S. 451, 460 (2001).

[11] Kahan, Note 1, *supra*, at 100 (but rejecting this rationale).

[12] Miller v. Florida, 482 U.S. 423, 430 (1987) (quoting Weaver v. Graham, 450 U.S. 24, 28-29 (1981)); see also Model Penal Code § 1.02(1)(d) (stating that one purpose of the Code is to "give fair warning of the nature of the conduct declared to constitute an offense").

As some commentators have demonstrated,[13] however, the fair notice argument is not entirely persuasive. It assumes that individuals always, or even commonly, consult criminal codes before acting and, thus, can legitimately claim surprise if the legislature acts retroactively to criminalize their conduct. Moreover, in some cases, those who investigate the law in advance, do so for the purpose of looking for loopholes in the law, rather than to enhance obedience to the law. In short, "rule-of-law benefits . . . always come at a price."[14]

Although courts often reject claims that a particular criminal statute is unduly vague,[15] the rule of legality — the basic principle that, in order to properly prosecute and punish a person, there must be a criminal law in existence at the time of the defendant's conduct — is rather strictly enforced, and retroactive lawmaking is barred.

[C] Constitutional Law

The legality principle has constitutional foundations.

[1] Bill of Attainder and *Ex Post Facto* Clauses

According to the Supreme Court, the "presumption against the retroactive application of new laws is an essential thread in the mantle of protection that the law affords the individual citizen."[16] This presumption, "deeply rooted in our jurisprudence" and "centuries older than our Republic,"[17] is meant to place "limits on the sovereign's ability to use its law making power to modify bargains it has made with its subjects."[18]

Specifically, Article I, Sections 9 and 10 of the United States Constitution prohibit federal and state legislatures from enacting bills of attainder and *ex post facto* (after the fact) legislation.[19] A bill of attainder is special legislation that declares a specific person to be guilty of a crime and subject to punishment without either a trial or conviction.[20] The *Ex Post Facto* Clause prohibits:

> 1st. Every law that makes an action done before the passing of the law, and which was innocent when done, criminal; and punishes such action.

---

[13] E.g., Kahan, Note 1, *supra*, at 99-101.

[14] Endicott, Note 1, *supra*, at 380.

[15] See § 5.02, *infra*.

[16] Lynce v. Mathis, 519 U.S. 433, 439 (1997).

[17] Landgraf v. USI Film Prod., 511 U.S. 244, 265 (1994).

[18] Lynce v. Mathis, 519 U.S. at 440.

[19] "No Bill of Attainder or ex post facto Law shall be passed." U.S. Const. art. I, § 9, cl. 3. "No State shall . . . pass any Bill of Attainder [or] ex post facto Law." U.S. Const. Art. I, § 10, cl. 1.

[20] Cummings v. Missouri, 71 U.S. (4 Wall) 277, 325 (1867).

2d. Every law that aggravates a crime, or makes it greater than it was, when committed. 3d. Every law that changes the punishment, and inflicts a greater punishment, than the law annexed to the crime, when committed. 4th. Every law that alters the legal rules of evidence, and receives less, or different testimony, than the law required at the time of the commission of the offense, in order to convict the offender.[21]

Under the first category of protection noted in the above quotation, if *D* performs lawful act X on December 31, 2004, she cannot be convicted of a criminal offense prohibiting X, enacted by the legislature on January 1, 2005. Similarly, if *D* kills *V* in self-defense on December 31, 2004, *D* may not be convicted of murder if the legislature subsequently abolishes the statutory defense of self-defense. Although murder was an offense on December 31, the legislature may not retroactively criminalize what was an innocent act (a killing in self-defense) at the time of the conduct. Under the third category above, it is impermissible to disadvantage a defendant by applying stricter sentencing guidelines, adopted after the crime was committed;[22] and, pursuant to the fourth category, a legislature may not enact a new criminal statute of limitations permitting prosecutions of offenses for which the prior limitations-period has expired.[23]

[2] Due Process Clause

The *Ex Post Facto* and Bill of Attainder Clauses discussed in subsection [1] apply to state and federal *legislatures*, but not to the judiciary.[24] Nonetheless, the legality principle — or, more specifically, the requirement of fair notice that specific conduct constitutes an offense — applies as well to the judicial branch of government through the Fifth and Fourteenth Amendment Due Process Clauses. However, the Supreme Court warned in *Rogers v. Tennessee*[25] that the Due Process Clause does *not* "incorporate jot-for-jot" the specific categories of *Ex Post Facto* Clause protections set out in subsection [1] above, in regard to the retroactive application of *judicial* decisions. That is, in the legality context, the *Ex Post Facto* Clause provides somewhat broader constitutional protections to citizens than does the Due Process Clause.

According to *Rogers*, a court (as distinguished from a legislative body) *may* give its interpretation of a common law doctrine or statute retroactive effect unless such a reading of the doctrine or statute is "unexpected and indefensible," when interpreted in light of judicial opinions expressed before the conduct in question.

---

[21] Calder v. Bull, 3 U.S. (3 Dall.) 386, 390 (1798) (emphasis omitted).

[22] Miller v. Florida, 482 U.S. 423 (1987).

[23] Stogner v. California, 539 U.S. 607 (2003).

[24] Rogers v. Tennessee, 532 U.S. 451, 456 (2001).

[25] *Id.* at 459.

Notwithstanding this limitation, the Due Process Clause provides significant protection. For example, "it is clear the courts cannot go so far as to create an offense by enlarging a statute, by inserting or deleting words, or by giving the terms used false or unusual meanings."[26] Thus, a criminal trespass statute that prohibits "*entry* upon the lands of another . . . after notice from the owner . . . prohibiting such entry" cannot be expanded unforeseeably by judicial interpretation and then applied retroactively to prohibit the act of *remaining* on land *lawfully* entered after being told to leave.[27] However, such an interpretation of the statute may be applied *prospectively*, because future actors are put on constructive notice by the court's decision of the broader reading of the statute.

§ 5.02 STATUTORY CLARITY[28]

A corollary of the legality principle is that a criminal statute must not be "so vague that men of common intelligence must necessarily guess at its meaning and differ as to its application."[29] A statute must give "sufficient warning that men may conduct themselves so as to avoid that which is forbidden."[30] A person is denied due process of law if she is convicted and punished for violation of a statute that lacks such clarity. Vague statutes are unacceptable because they deny a law-abiding person fair notice, and they provide police and prosecutors the opportunity (and may even encourage them) to act in an arbitrary and discriminatory manner.[31]

The requirement of reasonable statutory clarity is easy to state but difficult to apply. Supreme Court Justice Felix Frankfurter has conceded that the doctrine "is itself an indefinite concept. There is no such thing as 'indefiniteness' in the abstract. . . . The requirement is fair notice that conduct may entail punishment. But whether notice is or is not 'fair' depends on the subject matter to which it relates."[32] As a practical matter, in an effort to determine how much clarity is required, courts look at the purpose of the statute (the societal interest at stake by the legislation), the extent to which the statutory ambiguity was necessary to further the legislative goal, and the impact of the statute on the protected rights of the individual.[33]

---

[26] Keeler v. Superior Court, 470 P.2d 617, 625 (Cal. 1970).

[27] Bouie v. City of Columbia, 378 U.S. 347 (1964).

[28] See generally Robert Batey, *Vagueness and the Construction of Criminal Statutes — Balancing Acts*, 5 Va. J. Soc. Pol'y & L. 1 (1997); Endicott, Note 1, *supra*; Jeffries, Note 1, *supra*.

[29] Connally v. Gen. Constr. Co., 269 U.S. 385, 391 (1926).

[30] Rose v. Locke, 423 U.S. 48, 50 (1975) (footnote omitted).

[31] City of Chicago v. Morales, 527 U.S. 41, 56 (1999). The issue of arbitrariness is considered in § 5.03, *infra*.

[32] Winters v. New York, 333 U.S. 507, 524 (1948) (dissenting opinion).

[33] Batey, Note 28, *supra*, at 4-39.

In one particular set of circumstances, courts apply a particularly strict standard: "Statutes governing potential First Amendment and similarly sensitive constitutional rights [are] strictly tested for certainty by interpreting their meaning from the face of the statutes."[34] For example, in *Lewis v. City of New Orleans*,[35] *L* was prosecuted for breach of the peace. The statute provided that it was an offense "wantonly to curse or revile or to use obscene or opprobrious language toward . . . any member of the city police in the actual performance of his duties." The Supreme Court ruled that the statute could not withstand constitutional attack if it were "susceptible of application to speech, although vulgar or offensive, that is protected by the First . . . Amendment[]." That is, even if a person's conduct *in fact* is not constitutionally protected, her conviction must be overturned if the statute could reasonably be construed to prohibit constitutionally protected speech or other conduct.

Courts are much slower to hold that an ordinary criminal statute — one that does not touch on fundamental constitutional rights — is unconstitutionally vague. Judges do not want to reward ignorance or misunderstandings of law; and they are cognizant of the "practical difficulties in drawing criminal statutes both general enough to take into account a variety of human conduct and sufficiently specific to provide fair warning that certain kinds of conduct are prohibited."[36]

The "root of the vagueness doctrine is a rough idea of fairness,"[37] and fairness requires only "that there is sufficient warning to one bent on obedience that he comes *near* the proscribed area."[38] As a consequence, a statute is *not* invalid "simply because it requires conformity to an imprecise normative standard,"[39] such as the requirement that a person not act "negligently,"[40] or that she not harm others by "cruel or inhumane treatment."[41] As Justice Holmes observed, "the law is full of instances where a man's fate depends on his estimating rightly, that is, as the jury subsequently estimates it, some matter of degree."[42]

Furthermore, "[e]ven trained lawyers may find it necessary to consult legal dictionaries, treatises, and judicial opinions before they may say with any certainty what some statutes may compel or forbid."[43] Therefore, the Due Process

---

[34] State v. Flinn, 208 S.E.2d 538, 543 (W. Va. 1974).

[35] 415 U.S. 130 (1974).

[36] Colten v. Kentucky, 407 U.S. 104, 110 (1972); see also Endicott, Note 1, *supra*, at 382 ("Laws can be precise, but a legal system with no vague laws is impossible. The reason is that any legal system needs to regulate a *variety* of human activity in a *general* way.").

[37] Colten v. Kentucky, 407 U.S. at 110.

[38] Winters v. New York, 333 U.S. 507, 539 (1948) (Frankfurter, J., dissenting) (emphasis added).

[39] Eanes v. State, 569 A.2d 604, 615 (Md. 1990).

[40] See Nash v. United States, 229 U.S. 373 (1913).

[41] Bowers v. State, 389 A.2d 341 (Md. 1978).

[42] Nash v. United States, 229 U.S. at 377.

[43] Rose v. Locke, 423 U.S. 48, 50 (1975).

Clause is not violated unless a law-abiding person would still have to guess as to the meaning of a statute after she or her attorney conducts research into the meaning of the law. For example, consider a statute that provides that "[w]hoever commits the abominable and detestable crime against nature, either with mankind or beast, shall be guilty of a felony. . . ." On it face, the statute is vague. Ordinary persons would probably have to guess as to the meaning of the critical phrase "crime against nature."[44] Nonetheless, the statute is not unconstitutional if its meaning can be ascertained by reading prior state court opinions construing the law.[45] And, if these prior opinions indicate that judicial interpretations of a statute in *another* state are relevant in ascertaining the first statute's meaning, a person may be held responsible for learning the applicable law of the other jurisdiction![46] And, if a statute uses, but does not define, a common law term, a law-abiding person may be assumed to have read the treatises of Blackstone, Coke, or other common law sources in order to learn the term's common law meaning.[47]

In view of these prior interpretations of the vagueness doctrine, it is fair to state that the vagueness doctrine is largely fictive in nature because "it focuses on a sort of 'lawyer's notice' that seems far removed from ordinary life."[48] The doctrine is all the more removed from real life when one remembers that the ordinary individual does not, and often lacks the financial resources to, seek legal advice prior to acting.

§ 5.03 AVOIDING UNDUE DISCRETION IN LAW ENFORCEMENT

A statute that lacks clarity not only provides insufficient notice to law-abiding persons, but is susceptible to enforcement in an arbitrary or discriminatory manner. The Supreme Court observed in *Kolender v. Lawson*[49] that a statute or ordinance must "establish minimal guidelines to govern law enforcement." In the absence of such guidelines, the *Kolender* Court warned, "a criminal statute may permit a standardless sweep [that] allows policemen, prosecutors, and juries to pursue their personal predilections." The Due Process Clause forbids the enforcement of any statute that, due to vagueness in language, "vests vir-

---

[44] In its broadest meaning, the crime consists of consensual or nonconsensual oral or anal sexual relations between persons of the same or opposite sex, or sexual relations between a human being and a "brute beast."

[45] Wainwright v. Stone, 414 U.S. 21 (1973) (*per curiam*); see also In re Banks, 244 S.E.2d 386 (N.C. 1978) (holding that a statute prohibiting "peep[ing] secretly into any room occupied by a female" was not vague in light of prior judicial interpretative clarifications of the statute).

[46] See Rose v. Locke, 423 U.S. at 52-53.

[47] See Keeler v. Superior Court, 470 P.2d 617, 620, 633 (Cal. 1970).

[48] Batey, Note 28, *supra*, at 5 (quoting Jeffries, Note 1, *supra*, at 211).

[49] 461 U.S. 352, 358 (1983) (internal quotation marks omitted).

tually complete discretion in the hands of the police to determine whether the suspect has satisfied [its requirements]."[50]

So-called vagrancy statutes are prime examples of such impermissible legislation. For example, in *Papachristou v. City of Jacksonville*,[51] a city ordinance prohibited a person from being a "vagrant." Under the ordinance, "[r]ogues and vagabonds," "common drunkards," "persons wandering or strolling around from place to place without any lawful purpose," "habitual loafers," and others, were "vagrants."

On its face, of course, this language is vague. What is a "common" drunkard? What makes a person an "habitual loafer"? Worse than its imprecision, however, is that the ordinance gives the police virtually unfettered discretion to determine who is a vagrant. According to *Papachristou*, such laws, "though long common in Russia, are not compatible with our constitutional system." A primary concern is that a prosecution "may be merely the cloak for a conviction which could not be obtained on the real but undisclosed grounds for the arrest,"[52] for example, that the "vagrant" was an African-American person "strolling" in a white community,[53] a poorly dressed person found in a wealthy business district, or a person whose lawful conduct, e.g., males holding hands or kissing, offended the sensibilities of the arresting officer.

The Supreme Court invalidated another ordinance on similar grounds in *City of Chicago v. Morales*.[54] In an effort to reduce criminal street gang activity, the Chicago City Council enacted a criminal ordinance that provided that "[w]henever a police officer observes a person whom he reasonably believes to be a criminal street gang member loitering in any public place with one or more other persons, he shall order all such persons to disperse and remove themselves from the area."[55] The ordinance defined "loitering" as "remain[ing] in any one place with no apparent purpose." Any person who did not "promptly" obey the dispersal order was subject to a fine or jail sentence.

Three members of the Supreme Court stated that the ordinance was unconstitutionally vague. For example, these justices pointed out, it is unclear how far loiterers, once ordered to disperse, must move apart from each other, and how long they must remain separate before they can meet again. But, the more sig-

---

[50] *Id.*

[51] 405 U.S. 156 (1972).

[52] *Id.* at 169.

[53] In fact, in *Papachristou* two black males and two white females driving to a nightclub were arrested for "prowling by auto."

[54] 571 U.S. 41 (1999).

[55] For the background to this ordinance, see Tracey L. Meares & Dan M. Kahan, *The Wages of Antiquated Procedural Thinking: A Critique of Chicago v. Morales*, 1998 U. Chi. Legal F. 197 (defending the ordinance); Albert W. Alschuler & Stephen J. Schulhofer, *Antiquated Procedures or Bedrock Rights?: A Response to Professors Meares and Kahan*, 1998 U. Chi. Legal F. 215 (criticizing the ordinance).

nificant problem, according to six members of the Court, was that the ordinance provided absolute discretion to police officers to determine what activities constituted loitering. Based on the language of the ordinance, "[i]t matters not whether the reason that a gang member and his father, for example, might loiter near Wrigley Field is to rob an unsuspecting fan or just to get a glimpse of Sammy Sosa leaving the ballpark." The Court worried that "in either event, if their purpose is not apparent to a nearby police officer, she may . . . order them to disperse." Thus, the ordinance could be applied by the police to attack entirely innocent activity.

The ordinance's triggering mechanism — making the decision that the street gang member and another are in one place "with no apparent purpose" — "is inherently subjective because its application depends on whether some purpose is 'apparent' to the officer on the scene." The ordinance permits an officer to treat some purposes, "perhaps a purpose to engage in idle conversation or simply to enjoy a cool breeze on a warm evening . . . as too frivolous to be apparent if he suspected a different ulterior [criminal] motive."

In contrast, an ordinance that is drafted more narrowly to attack incipient street gang activity would be constitutional. For example, the *Morales* Court stated it had "no doubt that a law that directly prohibited . . . intimidating conduct" by street gang members would be constitutional. Likewise, two justices (with the apparent approval of three dissenting justices) stated that the ordinance might have been constitutional if "loitering" had been defined to mean "to remain in any one place with no apparent purpose other than to establish control over identifiable areas, to intimidate others from entering those areas, or to conceal illegal activities." Such language, it seems, would meet the *Kolender* requirement that a criminal law "establish minimal guidelines to govern law enforcement."

Model Penal Code Section 250.6 ("Loitering or Prowling"), drafted prior to *Papachristou* and *Morales*, provides in part that a person commits a violation if she "loiters or prowls in a place, at a time, or in a manner not usual for law-abiding individuals, under circumstances that warrant alarm for the safety of persons or property in the vicinity." Except when it is impracticable (e.g., the suspect flees), the Code requires a police officer, prior to arrest, to "afford the actor an opportunity to dispel any alarm which would otherwise be warranted"; the Code provision further provides that a person may not be convicted if the officer failed to comply with this requirement or if the explanation given by the actor was true and, if believed, would have dispelled the alarm. Courts that have considered statutes patterned on Section 250.6 have reached conflicting conclusions as to their constitutionality under the Due Process Clause.[56]

---

[56] Compare Fields v. City of Omaha, 810 F.2d 830 (8th Cir. 1987) (invalidating the law), with State v. Ecker, 311 So. 2d 104 (Fla. 1975) (upholding the law).

§ 5.04 STRICT CONSTRUCTION OF STATUTES (RULE OF LENITY)[57]

When the language of a statute is clear and unambiguous, "there is no room for judicial construction and the courts must give the statute its plain and definite meaning."[58] When a statute in unclear or ambiguous, however, a court's primary function is to ascertain the intent of the legislature that enacted the law.[59] To do this, a court may seek assistance by all "appropriate means and *indicia*, such as the purposes appearing from the statute taken as a whole, the phraseology, the words ordinary or technical, the law as it prevailed before the statute, the mischief to be remedied, . . . statutes *in pari materia*, the preamble, the title, and other like means."[60] In the effort to divine the legislative intent, courts will often turn to dictionaries, to legislative debates, and to careful parsing of the language and punctuation used in the statute.

But, what does a court do if, after careful analysis, the meaning of a statute remains uncertain? In response to a "vast and irrational" expansion in the number of capital offenses in eighteenth century England, British courts developed the rule that when a criminal statute is subject to two, conflicting reasonable interpretations, the statute (including sentencing provisions thereto) should be interpreted in the manner favorable to the criminal defendant.[61] This so-called rule of lenity (the "junior version of the vagueness doctrine"[62]) is not constitutionally compelled, but is said to support the principle of legality by preventing a court from inadvertently enlarging the scope of a criminal statute through its interpretive powers.

If the lenity doctrine requires strict construction of statutes, it should be observed that some courts, including the United States Supreme Court in its interpretation of federal statutes, strictly construe *the lenity doctrine itself*. The lenity doctrine only comes into play if a statute is ambiguous, and it is *not* ambiguous unless, "after seizing everything from which aid can be derived, we can make no more than a guess as to what Congress intended."[63] In essence, the lenity doctrine serves as a tie breaker; but it only comes into play if there *truly* is a "tie" — two or more *equally* reasonable interpretations of a statute.

---

[57] See generally Batey, Note 28, *supra*; Jeffries, Note 1, *supra*; Dan M. Kahan, *Lenity and Federal Common Law Crimes*, 1994 Sup. Ct. Rev. 345; Lawrence M. Solan, *Law, Language, and Lenity*, 40 Wm. & Mary L. Rev. 57 (1998).

[58] In re Banks, 244 S.E.2d 386, 388 (N.C. 1978).

[59] Whitner v. State, 492 S.E.2d 777, 779 (S.C. 1997).

[60] In re Banks, 244 S.E.2d at 389 (quoting State v. Partlow, 91 N.C. 550 (1884)).

[61] Jeffries, Note 1, *supra*, at 198.

[62] Packer, Note 1, *supra*, at 95.

[63] Reno v. Koray, 515 U.S. 50, 65 (1995) (internal quotation marks omitted).

Even the most well-drafted criminal statutes are often susceptible to multiple, reasonable interpretations. Overuse of the lenity doctrine, therefore, may result in an application of a statute contrary to legislative intent. As a result, many American states have abolished the rule of lenity outright.[64]

The Model Penal Code does not recognize the lenity principle. It requires instead that criminal statutes be construed according to their "fair import," and that ambiguities be resolved in a manner that furthers "the general purposes [of the Code] and the special purposes of the particular provision involved."[65] That is, although one general purpose of the Code is to provide fair warning regarding the nature of the conduct that is deemed to be criminal,[66] a statute should be interpreted to further, not frustrate, the legislative policies behind the specific law in question.

---

[64] Jeffries, Note 1, *supra*, at 198.

[65] Model Penal Code § 1.02(3).

[66] Model Penal Code § 1.02(1)(d).

Chapter 6

PROPORTIONALITY

§ 6.01 "PROPORTIONALITY" IN THE CRIMINAL LAW: OVERVIEW[1]

"Proportionality" is an important and recurring concept in the criminal law. For example, all justification defenses, e.g., self-defense, defense-of-others, defense-of-property, contain a proportionality requirement: A person is not justified in using force against another unless it is "proportional or reasonable in relation to the harm threatened or the interest to be furthered."[2] Thus, a person may not justifiably kill another in order to prevent a minor battery to himself or another, or to prevent a theft of personal property.

The doctrine of proportionality is also asserted in the context of sentencing, to ensure that an offender receives punishment appropriate to the crime he has committed. Both utilitarians and retributivists recognize proportionality in their theoretical structures, although the doctrine is more closely linked to retribution.[3] Modern penal codes, as well, acknowledge that one purpose of a criminal code is "to safeguard offenders against excessive, disproportionate or arbitrary punishment."[4] And, according to Supreme Court case law, the Constitution, through the Eighth Amendment, prohibits grossly disproportional punishment.

This chapter considers two questions relating to proportionality of punishment. First, how much (or what) punishment is excessive or disproportionate to a particular crime? Utilitarians and retributivists go about answering this question differently. Punishment that is proportional according to utilitarian principles might be retributively disproportional, or vice-versa. Second, under what circumstances is disproportional punishment not only unwise or unfair,

---

[1] For an understanding of the philosophical underpinnings of the subject, see generally John Kleinig, Punishment and Desert ch. VII (1973); Herbert L. Packer, The Limits of the Criminal Sanction 139-45 (1968); Paul H. Robinson & John M. Darley, Justice, Liability and Blame: Community Views and the Criminal Law 157-99 (1995); Andrew von Hirsch, Censure and Sanctions (1993); Andrew von Hirsch, *Proportionality in the Philosophy of Punishment: From "Why Punish?" to "How Much?"*, 1 Crim. L.F. 259 (1990); Andrew von Hirsch & Nils Jareborg, *Gauging Criminal Harm: A Living-Standard Analysis*, 11 Oxford J. Legal Stud. 1 (1991); Jeremy Waldron, *Lex Talionis*, 34 Ariz. L. Rev. 25 (1992). See also § 2.03, *supra*.

[2] 1 Paul H. Robinson, Criminal Law Defenses 87 (1984).

[3] Harmelin v. Michigan, 501 U.S. 957, 989 (1991) (opinion of Scalia, J., & Rehnquist, C.J.) ("Proportionality is inherently a retributive concept . . .").

[4] Model Penal Code § 1.02(2)(c).

but also unconstitutional? Few criminal law issues have more sharply divided the United States Supreme Court than this one.

§ 6.02 UTILITARIANISM AND PROPORTIONALITY

[A] General Principles

Utilitarian philosophy directs that punishment be neither too little nor too much, but rather that it be proportional, i.e., that punishment be inflicted in the amount required — but no more than is required — to satisfy utilitarian crime prevention goals. In his classic account on utilitarianism, Jeremy Bentham announced five rules intended to ensure proportional punishment.[5]

In order to deter crime, the first rule is that punishment must not be less than is required to outweigh the potential profit to the criminal of committing the offense. If too little punishment is imposed, criminal conduct will remain profitable and, as a consequence, the threat of punishment will be ineffective. It follows from this, according to the second rule, that "[t]he greater the mischief of the offense, the greater is the expense, which it may be worth while to be at, in the way of punishment."

Utilitarian analysis also directs lawmakers (Rule 3) to grade offenses in a manner that will induce a person "to choose always the least mischievous of two offences," by making sure that "[w]here two offenses come into competition, the punishment for the greater offense must be sufficient to induce a man to prefer the less." For example, a battery should be punished less severely than a murder, in order to induce a wrongdoer to commit the less harmful act. Punishment should also be set in a manner to induce the criminal "to do no more mischief than what is necessary for his purpose" (Rule 4).

The final rule of proportionality is that "punishment ought in no case to be more than what is necessary to bring it into conformity with the [previous] rules." In other words, because punishment is itself a mischief that should be avoided to the extent possible, punishment is disproportional if more pain is inflicted than is required to satisfy the previous goals.

[B] Application of the Principles

[1] General Deterrence

Very dangerous crimes should be punished more severely than less dangerous ones. To a utilitarian legislator concerned with general deterrence, however, the degree of dangerousness of an offense is not measured by calculating the

---

[5] See generally Jeremy Bentham, An Introduction to the Principles of Morals and Legislation ch. 14 (1789).

injury likely to be caused in a single incident by a particular offender, but rather by predicting the overall mischief that is likely to result from commission of the offense in the future by this and other offenders. This means that the appropriate punishment for a crime may differ over time and among jurisdictions. For example, in a rural community in which theft of cattle occurs frequently and is apt to cause serious economic hardship to its inhabitants, it would be appropriate to punish this conduct more severely than in an urban community where the crime rarely occurs and does not threaten the economic well-being of its people.

In setting the punishment for an offense, a utilitarian lawmaker will also consider the degree to which the conduct in question can be deterred. Consider, for example, how a utilitarian might treat the offense of driving an automobile under the influence of alcohol. Little or no injury may occur in a specific case of intoxicated driving. In terms of future mischief, however, the offense is relatively serious, because drunk driving frequently results in loss of life or injury to persons and property. Moreover, some criminologists claim that drunk driving is especially difficult to deter by threat of punishment.[6] If this is the case, it may be appropriate to impose penalties greater than would be set for equally dangerous, but more easily deterred, behavior. Conversely, if drunk driving can only be deterred by directing substantial law enforcement efforts away from violent crimes, thereby increasing the frequency of the latter offenses, or only by application of such draconian punitive measures that the community would lose respect for the justice system, a utilitarian might favor attacking the problem in a non-penal manner.

[2] Specific Deterrence

When deterrence of a specific offender is desired, punishment is proportional to the extent, *but only to the extent*, that it is necessary to prevent the individual offender from committing future criminal acts more painful to society than the punishment that will be inflicted on the wrongdoer.

Evidence may exist that a specific criminal is less susceptible to deterrence than the ordinary offender. As a result, he may be more likely than the usual wrongdoer to commit future crimes. Consistent with concepts of specific deterrence, a more dangerous offender may be punished more severely than an ordinary offender who commits the same crime. For example, the offense of battery may merit "x" units of punishment pursuant to general deterrence principles.

---

6 Dale E. Berger et al., *Deterrence and Prevention of Alcohol-Impaired Driving in Australia, the United States, and Norway*, 7 Just. Q. 453 (1990) (finding general deterrence relatively weak in the United States); Rodney F. Kingsnorth et al., *Specific Deterrence and the DUI Offender: The Impact of a Decade of Reform*, 10 Just. Q. 265 (1993) (showing no decrease in recidivism associated with an increase in the severity of penalties); Lonn Lanza-Kaduce, *Perceptual Deterrence and Drinking and Driving Among College Students*, 26 Criminology 321 (1988) (finding that perceptions of risk of arrest and severity of punishment were not related to later drinking and driving).

D, however, may be more dangerous and less easily deterred than the usual battterer, as evidenced by his previous convictions for violent offenses. Enhanced punishment of *D*, e.g., "x + 5" units of punishment, might be appropriate. Under these hypothesized circumstances, *D*'s punishment would be significantly greater than that imposed for battery under general deterrence principles, and his punishment would cause more pain than the harm suffered by the victim of the specific battery.

[3] Rehabilitation

Proportionality of punishment has little meaning in a rehabilitative system of treatment. C.S. Lewis has written that it is possible to speak of "just punishment," but not of "just cure," where "just" means "proportional."[7] Although compelled rehabilitation constitutes "punishment" for purposes of the criminal law,[8] Lewis's observation is still pertinent, because the duration of such treatment and the potential harshness of some rehabilitative techniques are logically unrelated to the severity of the offense committed and to the degree to which the treatment/punishment will deter others from committing the offense. Unless limited by other doctrines, rehabilitative procedures may be exercised until they have succeeded (if ever).

§ 6.03 RETRIBUTIVISM AND PROPORTIONALITY

[A] General Principles

The concept of proportional punishment is closely allied with retributivism.[9] Retributivists justify punishment on the ground that a crime has been committed. The offender owes a debt to society; punishment is the mode of repayment. The payment due varies with the crime committed: Punishment must be proportional to the offense committed, taking into consideration both the harm caused and the wrongdoer's degree of moral desert for having caused it.

Most modern retributivists reject the concept of *lex talionis* — the infliction upon the wrongdoer of the same injury he has caused the victim — except, perhaps, in the case of murder. For example, to punish a rapist by raping him, whatever that would mean in practice, would violate most modern schools of retributive thought, which require that the offender be treated with dignity and as a person possessing moral worth.[10] Moreover, with the exception of the death

---

[7] C.S. Lewis, *The Humanitarian Theory of Punishment*, 6 Res Judicatae 224, 225 (1953).

[8] See § 2.02, *supra*.

[9] Margaret Jane Radin, *Cruel Punishment and Respect for Persons: Super Due Process for Death*, 53 S. Cal. L. Rev. 1143, 1167 n.83 (1980)

[10] See § 2.03[B][2], *supra* (the protective retribution and victim vindication models).

penalty for murder, punishment equivalent in kind to the offense committed is impractical. Therefore, retributivists only require that the wrongdoer symbolically repay the debt he owes, by undergoing punishment proportional in severity to the offense committed.

[B] Application of the Principles

[1] In General

As discussed more fully in subsequent chapters of this Text, a crime has two basic components: the external part, involving the harm inflicted by the actor; and an internal portion, involving the actor's moral blameworthiness, as represented by the offender's mental state in causing the harm inflicted. Both components must be considered in calculating the actor's retributive just deserts.

Regarding the harm component, a legislature seeking to impose retributively fair punishment looks backward at the crime committed and determines what harm — physical, psychological, moral, economic, etc. — ordinarily results from the commission of the offense in question. To the extent that a trial judge has sentencing discretion, the judge may consider, as well, the actual harm inflicted (which might be more or less than ordinary) in the case before him.

Regarding the blameworthiness component, retributivists consider a person more deserving of punishment if he intentionally, rather than, for example, negligently, causes the particular harm. Thus, a retributivist would punish an automobile driver who negligently kills a pedestrian less severely than an assassin who purposely takes a human life. The retributivist would take into consideration other factors as well, relating to an offender's moral blameworthiness. For example, if A intentionally kills $V1$ as the result of a delusion, he is less blameworthy (if he is blameworthy at all) than B, a contract killer who intentionally, but rationally, kills $V2$.

[2] Devising a Proportional Retributive System

Developing a retributively fair sentencing system is not easy. In the absence of *lex talionis* punishment, penalties can only roughly approximate the seriousness of the crimes committed. One real-world way to scale deserts in a sentencing system based on retribution is to proportion punishment *between* offenses, rather than *to* offenses.

Consider for a moment a society in which there are only three statutory offenses: criminal homicide, rape, and theft. The first step for the legislator is to rank these crimes in the order of their seriousness. The lawmaker must determine the harmfulness of each offense, taking into consideration the immediate victim, family members, and society as a whole. People generally consider crimes of violence more serious than non-violent offenses; and, among violent crimes, the unjustifiable taking of human life (criminal homicide) is ordinarily viewed as the most heinous offense.[11] Therefore, the legislature would probably rank an intentional killing as the most serious offense, rape as less serious, and theft as the least severe.

The next step would be to impose punishment commensurate to the relative gravity of the offenses. One way to do this is to begin with the least serious offense — here, theft — and to set its punishment at the low end of the continuum of acceptable forms and degrees of punishment. For example, theft would receive "x" units of punishment, such as two years' imprisonment. Then, each successively more serious crime would be compared to the last one in terms of increased degree of seriousness, with penalties set in rough proportion to the last crime. If rape is considered approximately ten times more serious than the ordinary theft (based on the comparative harm of the two offenses), then rape would receive "10x" units of punishment (20 years' imprisonment). If an intentional homicide is two times as serious as rape, then the homicide would merit "20x" units of punishment (40 years', or perhaps life, imprisonment). Alternatively, the grading system could start at the top (setting the maximum punishment for murder at death or life imprisonment) and the legislature could work its way down through the lesser offenses.[12]

The preceding analysis considered only the harm component of criminal offenses. As previously indicated, however, the personal blameworthiness of an actor in causing the harm is also a critical factor. Therefore, a legislature would subdivide criminal homicide and other serious offenses into sub-offenses based on the actor's degree of culpability. For example, an intentional killing would be graded as a more serious offense than a negligent homicide.[13]

§ 6.04 COMPARING THE TWO THEORIES
OF PROPORTIONALITY

For purposes of determining the appropriate punishment for an offense, retribution and utilitarianism differ in two key respects. First, utilitarian punishment is linked to predictions of future harm and the extent to which the undesired conduct is deterrable. In contrast, retributivists seek to proportion punishment to the offense already committed, without consideration of future

---

[11] Peter H. Rossi et al., *The Seriousness of Crimes: Normative Structure and Individual Differences*, 39 Am. Soc. Rev. 224 (1974).

[12] Of course, in a real system, involving many more offenses, the differences in seriousness between crimes will be relatively small. Once the ranking is done, and the upper and lower limits of punishment are set, penalties can be graduated in a relatively simple manner.

[13] What is especially difficult to determine is whether, for example, *intentional* nonconsensual sexual intercourse is more, equally, or less serious than the *negligent* taking of a human life.

harm. Second, retributivists believe that punishment for wrongdoing is morally right, perhaps obligatory. Utilitarians contend that punishment is undesirable unless it will result in a net benefit to society. Because of these differences in outlook, utilitarian and retributive versions of proportionality may differ substantially in specific cases.

For example, for some retributivists the death penalty for the most serious forms of murder is justifiable,[14] but death is disproportional for offenses in which no life is taken. In contrast, utilitarians favor capital punishment for murder and/or other offenses if, but only if, its deterrent benefits outweigh its human and economic costs.

The two theories may also lead in very different directions if the offense in question involves dangerous conduct that does not result in significant harm on a specific occasion. For example, as discussed earlier,[15] under one scenario, general deterrence theorists might justify substantial punishment of persons who drive under the influence of intoxicants because such conduct is a major social problem, resulting in great harm on many occasions, and is especially difficult to deter. The retributivist, however, would not consider the difficulty-of-deterrence or likely-future-harm factors in calibrating the proper punishment. Instead, the penalty would be based on the harm of drunk driving *per se*, which is apt to be fairly minor,[16] and on the actor's culpability in causing the minor harm. Under such circumstances, the penalty is likely to be relatively slight.[17]

Retributivists and specific-deterrence utilitarians may also differ, for example, in their approach to recidivists. As noted before,[18] utilitarians can justify enhanced punishment of repeat offenders, assuming there is reliable evidence of such actors' future dangerousness. For a retributivist, however, heightened punishment cannot be approved on the basis of the offender's predicted future conduct. Also, assuming that the repeat offender has been punished for his prior crimes — he has paid his debt to society — a retributivist cannot justify

---

[14] Other retributivists reject capital punishment on the ground that humans lack the knowledge required to determine with sufficient reliability a wrongdoer's degree of depravity, a necessary component of retributive analysis. See Jeffrie G. Murphy, *Moral Epistemology, The Retributive Emotions, and the "Clumsy Moral Philosophy" of Jesus Christ, in* The Passions of Law 149 (Susan Bandes ed., 1999). Other retributivists, while not opposed philosophically to capital punishment, oppose it because of increasing evidence (particularly in light of the DNA revolution) that innocent persons are finding their way to the nation's death rows. Lawrence C. Marshall, *The Innocence Revolution and the Death Penalty*, 1 Ohio St. J. Crim. L. 573 (2004).

[15] See § 6.02[B][1], *supra*.

[16] If a drunk driver kills another, he may be prosecuted for criminal homicide.

[17] See Douglas N. Husak, *Is Drunk Driving a Serious Offense?*, 23 Phil. & Pub. Aff. 52 (1994) (concluding that the offense is not a serious one, and that drunk drivers should not be imprisoned).

[18] See § 6.02[B][2], *supra*.

punishing the offender more for the present offense merely because of the prior wrongs.[19]

§ 6.05 CONSTITUTIONAL REQUIREMENT OF PROPORTIONALITY

[A] General Principles

The Eighth Amendment to the United States Constitution prohibits the infliction of "cruel and unusual punishment" by agents of the federal government on persons convicted of criminal conduct. Freedom from such punishment is a fundamental right that state governments must also respect.[20]

The Supreme Court ruled in 1910 that an implicit requirement of the Eighth Amendment is that "punishment for crime . . . be graduated and proportioned to [the] offense."[21] This interpretation of the Eighth Amendment is controversial. Although the Supreme Court has stated that the proportionality doctrine is "deeply rooted" in common law jurisprudence,[22] two members of the Court have stated that, based on their historical study, "the Eighth Amendment contains no proportionality guarantee."[23] Nonetheless, the Supreme Court is presently wedded to the principle in some form. Accordingly, courts are sometimes called upon to determine whether punishment imposed for violation of a criminal statute was grossly disproportional to the offense.

Proportionality can be calculated by use of either utilitarian or retributive tools of analysis, and results may differ depending upon the approach followed.[24] As seen below, the Supreme Court has sometimes applied retributive proportionality doctrine to invalidate a statute or the sentence in a specific case. On other occasions, however, it has deferred to legislative will, allowing the state to justify punishment on retributive or (more commonly) utilitarian grounds.

---

[19] Although many retributivists reject laws that authorize enhanced punishment of repeat offenders, see, e.g., George Fletcher, Rethinking Criminal Law 459-66 (1972), some retributivists have sought to justify some habitual offender laws. E.g., Andrew von Hirsch, *Desert and Previous Convictions in Sentencing*, 65 Minn. L. Rev. 591 (1981).

[20] See Robinson v. California, 370 U.S. 660 (1962).

[21] Weems v. United States, 217 U.S. 349, 367 (1910).

[22] Solem v. Helm, 463 U.S. 277, 284-85 (1983); see also Roper v. Simmons, 543 U.S. 551 (2005) ("the Eighth Amendment reaffirms the duty of the government to respect the dignity of all persons").

[23] Harmelin v. Michigan, 501 U.S. 957, 965 (1991) (opinion of Scalia, J., & Rehnquist, C.J.).

[24] See § 6.04, *supra*.

[B] Death Penalty[25]

In 1971, Ehrlich Coker raped a woman and stabbed her to death. Still free eight months later, he kidnapped and twice raped a second woman. Finally caught, Coker was sentenced to three life terms in prison for his offenses. A year and a half later, however, he escaped from prison and robbed and raped a 16-year-old married female in front of her husband, threatening to kill her. Ultimately caught and convicted for the latest rape and robbery, Coker was sentenced to death by a Georgia jury.

Based on these facts, a compelling utilitarian argument for Coker's execution is possible. He was an exceedingly dangerous man for whom incapacitation had proven to be an insufficient remedy. The community, as represented by the jury that sentenced him to death, had reason to fear that, if he were not executed, Coker would escape prison again and commit additional rapes and murders. On specific deterrence principles, therefore, death was quite arguably proportional punishment for Coker's deed. Nonetheless, in *Coker v. Georgia*,[26] the United States Supreme Court ruled that death is grossly disproportional punishment for the crime of rape of an adult woman.[27]

Writing for the Court, Justice Byron White utilized two methods of constitutional analysis in reaching the conclusion that Coker could not properly be executed. First, pursuant to an approach followed in prior death penalty opinions, he considered objective indicia of the public's attitude regarding the death penalty for rape. At the time, only a few states authorized capital punishment for rape and, even in Georgia, juries rarely sentenced rapists to death. Justice White determined, therefore, that death was now a societally unacceptable punishment for rape.[28]

---

[25] See generally Annaliese Flynn Fleming, Comment, *Louisiana's Newest Capital Crime: The Death Penalty for Child Rape*, 89 J. Crim. L. & Criminology 717 (1999); Scott W. Howe, *Resolving the Conflict in the Capital Sentencing Cases: A Desert-Oriented Theory of Regulation*, 26 Ga. L. Rev. 323 (1992); Michael Mello, *Executing Rapists: A Reluctant Essay on the Ethics of Legal Scholarship*, 4 Wm. & Mary J. Women & L. 129 (1997).

[26] 433 U.S. 584 (1977).

[27] The Court's reasoning, as developed in the text below, would extend the death penalty bar to *all* rapes and, indeed, to all offenses where human life is not taken. However, the Court stated the issue to be whether the rape of an "adult woman" (apparently because the teenage victim was married) constituted cruel and unusual punishment. As a result of the Court's apparent narrow ruling, one state, Louisiana, has enacted legislation authorizing capital punishment for the rape of victims under the age of twelve. La. Rev. Stat. 14:42(D)(2)(a) (2005). The Supreme Court has not yet considered the statute's constitutionality.

[28] Unstated by the Court, but perhaps determinative, was the fact that capital punishment historically was "reserved overwhelmingly for black defendants, especially those convicted of raping white women." James R. Acker, *Social Science in Supreme Court Death Penalty Cases: Citation Practices and Their Implications*, 8 Just. Q. 421, 431 (1991).

The jury statistics, however, only proved that juries did not want to sentence *all* rapists to death. They did not demonstrate that Georgians viewed the penalty as excessive in all "adult woman" cases, as the Court ultimately concluded. Also, if concepts of federalism are to be respected,[29] the fact that Georgia was among a small minority of states permitting death as a sentence for rape should not, by itself, have served as a basis for overturning the legislature's judgment.

Perhaps because of these difficulties with his analysis, Justice White stated that the foregoing evidence did not resolve the issue, "for the Constitution contemplates that in the end our own judgment will be brought to bear on the question of the acceptability of the death penalty under the Eighth Amendment." As a consequence, the Court conducted a second, potentially more subjective, analysis, and again concluded that death was an excessive penalty for Coker's crime.

In effect, Justice White applied a strictly retributive conception of proportionality to the Georgia law. Coker's dangerousness was ignored. As well, the Court did not seriously consider whether death was a suitable penalty according to principles of general deterrence.[30] Instead, as a retributivist would do, Justice White compared the harm caused by rape with the penalty of death. He described rape as "highly reprehensible" and "[s]hort of homicide . . . the 'ultimate violation of self.'" Nonetheless, applying what the dissenters described as the "primitive simplicity" of *lex talionis*, Justice White concluded that rape "does not compare with murder, which . . . involve[s] the unjustified taking of human life. . . . The murderer kills; the rapist, if no more than that, does not." Therefore, the Court overturned Coker's sentence of death on constitutional proportionality grounds.

In essence, *Coker* implicitly suggests that punishment that is excessive on retributive grounds violates the Eighth Amendment bar on grossly disproportional punishment. However, as will be seen in the next subsection, whatever *Coker*'s continued vitality may prove to be in the realm of capital punishment, Justice White's mode of analysis does not apply in non-capital circumstances.

[C] Terms of Imprisonment

The Supreme Court's Eighth Amendment proportionality jurisprudence relating to non-death penalty sentences has not been a model of clarity or consistency. It is helpful, therefore, to follow the Court's struggle in this area case-by-case.

---

[29] See § 4.03[C], *supra*.

[30] The issue received one sentence of attention in a footnote. *Coker*, 433 U.S. at 592-93 n.4.

[1] *Rummel v. Estelle*[31]

William Rummel was convicted in 1973 in Texas of the felony of obtaining a check for $120.75 by false pretenses, and then cashing it. The offense carried a two-to-ten year prison term. However, Rummel had twice previously been convicted of theft (in which he fraudulently amassed property or cash valued at $108.36), so he was sentenced under the state's habitual offender law to life imprisonment. Rummel was eligible for parole consideration after approximately twelve years in prison.

Rummel argued that his life sentence constituted grossly disproportional punishment. If the Supreme Court had applied its *Coker*[32] analysis, Rummel's argument almost certainly would have been persuasive. Texas did not, nor could it seriously, claim that pursuant to retributive theory, life imprisonment fit the offense of obtaining $120.75 by false pretenses. Nonetheless, by a 5-4 vote, the Supreme Court upheld Rummel's sentence.

Rummel and the dissenting justices asserted that the disproportionality of his life sentence could be established by weighing three objective factors: (1) the gravity of the offense compared to the severity of the penalty; (2) penalties imposed within Texas for similar offenses ("*intra*-jurisdictional" analysis); and (3) penalties imposed in other jurisdictions for the same offense ("*inter*-jurisdictional" analysis). Speaking for the majority, however, Justice William Rehnquist rejected the proposition that the excessiveness of Rummel's sentence could be determined by use of this three-pronged test.

Regarding the first factor, Rummel reasoned that his offense (indeed all three offenses) were petty, nonviolent crimes, which did not justify the severe sentence he received. The Court rejected his characterization of the offenses as petty. It stated that the state legislature was entitled to draw the line between felony theft and petty larceny as it wished, "subject only to those strictures of the Eighth Amendment that can be informed by objective factors." As for the fact that Rummel's offenses were nonviolent in nature, Justice Rehnquist made the utilitarian observation that the label of violence "does not always affect the strength of society's interest in deterring a particular crime or in punishing a particular criminal."

As for the intra-jurisdictional factor, persons convicted of far more serious offenses in Texas, e.g., first-time rapists, were not subject to the mandatory sentence of life imprisonment. The Court disapproved of this test, however,

---

[31] 445 U.S. 263 (1980); see generally Joshua Dressler, *Substantive Criminal Law Through the Looking Glass of Rummel v. Estelle: Proportionality and Justice as Endangered Doctrines*, 34 Sw. L.J. 1063 (1981); Charles Walter Schwartz, *Eighth Amendment Proportionality Analysis and the Compelling Case of William Rummel*, 71 J. Crim. L. & Criminology 378 (1980).

[32] Coker v. Georgia, 433 U.S. 584 (1977). See § 6.05[B], *supra*.

because identification of some offenses as more serious than others was "inherently speculative."

As for inter-jurisdictional analysis, the Texas recidivist statute was among the three most severe in the country in Rummel's circumstances. Again, the five-justice majority was unimpressed. First, the Court observed that Rummel was eligible for parole consideration after twelve years, which meant that it could not know with certainty how long Rummel would actually be imprisoned. Furthermore, even if it could be shown that Texas' recidivist law was the harshest in the nation, this would not render Rummel's sentence excessive: "Absent a constitutionally imposed uniformity inimical to traditional notions of federalism, some State will always bear the distinction of treating particular offenders more severely than any other State." Justice Rehnquist also made the following utilitarian observation about recidivist laws:

> [T]he interest of the State of Texas here is not simply that of making criminal the unlawful acquisition of another person's property; it is in addition the interest . . . in dealing in a harsher manner with those who by repeated criminal acts have shown that they are simply incapable of conforming to the norms of the society. . . . [T]he State of Texas, or any other State, has a valid interest in so dealing with that class of persons.

The implicit message of *Rummel* appeared to be that, although states are prohibited from inflicting grossly disproportional punishment, the Supreme Court will almost always defer to a state legislature's judgment in a non-capital case. On a more theoretical level, *Rummel* stands for the proposition that legislatures may constitutionally apply utilitarian factors in setting non-capital criminal penalties, even if this process results in *retributively* disproportional sentencing.

[2] *Solem v. Helm*[33]

Jerry Helm was sentenced to life imprisonment without possibility of parole pursuant to South Dakota's habitual offender law, upon conviction of fraudulently passing a "no account" check for $100.00. This was Helm's seventh conviction. Although the Court described Helm's prior felonies as nonviolent in nature, his crimes included three burglaries, and driving an automobile while intoxicated.

Helm asserted that his sentence constituted grossly disproportional punishment. Based on *Rummel*, his legal claim seemed exceptionally weak. Nonetheless, by a 5-4 vote, the Court invalidated Helm's sentence. In an opinion written by Justice Lewis Powell, author of the dissent in *Rummel*, the Court stated that

---

[33] 463 U.S. 277 (1983); see generally Thomas E. Baker & Fletcher N. Baldwin, Jr., *Eighth Amendment Challenges to the Length of a Criminal Sentence: Following the Supreme Court "From Precedent to Precedent"*, 27 Ariz. L. Rev. 25 (1985).

although reviewing courts should grant substantial deference to legislatures in setting punishments for crimes, "no penalty is *per se* constitutional."

The Court applied the same three-pronged test the dissent used in *Rummel*, and concluded that the sentence was excessive on the basis of each prong: Helm received a severe sentence for "relatively minor" conduct; he was treated more harshly than other criminals in South Dakota who committed more serious crimes; and the recidivist statute was one of the two toughest in the country. The Court distinguished *Rummel* on the ground that Texas had a relatively liberal parole policy, whereas Helm's life sentence was without possibility of parole — absent executive pardon or commutation, life imprisonment definitely meant life imprisonment.

[3] *Harmelin v. Michigan*[34]

By 1991, when the Supreme Court again tackled the proportionality issue in *Harmelin v. Michigan*, Justice Powell, the author of *Solem v. Helm* and a dissenter in *Rummel v. Estelle*, had retired from the Court, as had two other members of the *Solem* Court. These personnel changes resulted in a very different constitutional picture.

In *Harmelin*, the defendant was convicted of possessing 672 grams of cocaine. Although this was his first offense, he received the statutory mandatory term of life imprisonment without possibility of parole. Because there was no death penalty in Michigan, this was the harshest penalty available for any offense in the state, and was reserved for only two other crimes: first-degree murder; and manufacture, distribution, or possession with intent to manufacture or distribute 650 grams or more of narcotics. Moreover, the Michigan drug possession statute was by far the harshest in the nation. Based on the three-pronged test of *Solem*, therefore, a strong case of unconstitutionality could be made.

Justice Antonin Scalia announced the judgment of the Court, which was that Harmelin's sentence did *not* violate the Eighth Amendment.[35] However, only Chief Justice Rehnquist joined his opinion. Based on an examination of the background of the Eighth Amendment, Justices Scalia and Rehnquist concluded that the framers of the Constitution did not include within the Eighth Amendment a guarantee against disproportionate sentences. Therefore, they would have overruled *Solem*.[36]

---

[34] 501 U.S. 957 (1991); see generally Steven Grossman, *Proportionality in Non-Capital Sentencing: The Supreme Court's Tortured Approach to Cruel and Unusual Punishment*, 84 Ky. L.J. 107 (1995); Peter Mathis Spett, *Confounding the Gradations of Iniquity: An Analysis of Eighth Amendment Jurisprudence Set Forth in Harmelin v. Michigan*, 24 Colum. Hum. Rts. L. Rev. 203 (1993).

[35] Subsequently, the Michigan Supreme Court invalidated the statute pursuant to that state's own constitutional bar on excessive punishment. People v. Bullock, 485 N.W.2d 866 (Mich. 1992).

[36] However, they would not have overruled *Coker v. Georgia*, considered in subsection [B], *supra*, because the holding in that case was "an aspect of our death penalty jurisprudence, rather than a generalizable aspect of Eighth Amendment law."

As the *Rummel* Court did a decade earlier, the two justices rejected as unduly subjective the first two prongs of the test applied in *Solem*. As for the first prong (seriousness of the offense), Justice Scalia said that although violent crimes are serious, "that is only half the equation. The issue is *what else* should be regarded to be *as serious* as these offenses." On this matter, the justices deferred to the state legislature: "The members of the Michigan Legislature, and not we, know the situation on the streets of Detroit."[37] Nor were Justices Scalia and Rehnquist willing to compare penalties for offenses *within* Michigan: "[S]ince deterrent effect depends not only upon the amount of the penalty but upon its certainty, crimes that are less grave but significantly more difficult to detect may warrant substantially higher penalties."

Justice Scalia conceded that the inter-jurisdictional test "can be applied with clarity and ease. The only difficulty is that it has no conceivable relevance to the Eighth Amendment." Just as one state may punish conduct that another state permits, it follows, he said, that one state may "treat with stern disapproval an act that other States punish with the mildest of sanctions."

Justices Anthony Kennedy, Sandra Day O'Connor, and David Souter concurred in the judgment against Harmelin, but refused to overrule *Solem*. Justice Kennedy conceded that the Court's "proportionality decisions have not been clear or consistent in all respects, [but] they can be reconciled. . . ." According to the concurring justices, the previous cases yielded the following four principles: (1) the fixing of prison terms "involves a substantive penological judgment that, as a general matter, is 'properly within the province of legislatures, not courts'"; (2) "the Eighth Amendment does not mandate adoption of any one penological theory"; (3) substantial divergences in penological theories and in prison sentences are the "inevitable, often beneficial" result of living in a federal system; and (4) proportionality analysis should be informed by objective factors whenever possible.

In light of these principles, Justice Kennedy announced a new way to apply the three-pronged test in imprisonment cases: "[I]ntrajurisdictional and inter-jurisdictional analyses are appropriate only in the rare case in which a threshold comparison of the crime committed and the sentence imposed leads to an inference of gross disproportionality." That is, a court should apply the first prong of *Solem*, and if it determines that the offense was a serious one, any penalty short of death is proportional. The other prongs of the test only come into play if a court determines that the offense at issue is petty and the sentence imposed was severe. In the present case, the three-justice plurality determined

---

[37] In response to the dissent's argument that by this reasoning a legislature could properly make overtime parking a felony punishable by life imprisonment, Justice Scalia responded that it was unlikely "that the horrible example imagined would ever in fact occur, unless, of course, overtime parking should one day become an arguably major threat to the common good, and the need to deter it arguably critical."

that the offense for which Harmelin was convicted was a serious one. Further analysis was unnecessary.

The four dissenters in *Harmelin* would have applied the standards announced in *Solem* without variation. Although Justice White, the author of the primary dissent, agreed that "[d]rugs are . . . a serious societal problem," he did not believe that mere possession of drugs justified a mandatory life sentence. In view of the severity of the penalty in comparison to other laws within the state, and in comparison to similar laws elsewhere, the dissenters would have held that the Michigan law "fail[ed] constitutional muster."

[4] *Ewing v. California*[38]

Twelve years after the Supreme Court ruled in *Harmelin v. Michigan*, the justices again confronted the proportionality issue in *Ewing v. California*. In 2000, Gary Ewing stole three golf clubs, each worth $399. He was convicted of one count of felony grand theft. Because Ewing had previously been convicted of robbery and three counts of burglary, Ewing was sentenced to a term of imprisonment of 25-years-to-life, pursuant to California's "three strikes" recidivist law.

By 2003, three of the four dissenters in *Harmelin* (Justices White, Blackmun, and Marshall) had retired from the Supreme Court. Nonetheless, the Court's division in *Harmelin* repeated itself in *Ewing*: two justices again held that the Eighth Amendment contains no proportionality guarantee; three justices defended a limited proportionality doctrine; four justices would have upheld a broad, *Solem v. Helm*, approach to the Eighth Amendment; and, as in each earlier case discussed in this chapter section, the Court overall split 5-4 — as in *Rummel* and *Harmelin* finding no Eighth Amendment violation.

Justice O'Connor, now writing for Chief Justice Rehnquist and Justice Kennedy, asserted that the Eighth Amendment contains a "narrow proportionality principle" in non-capital cases. Rather than re-define this narrow principle, the plurality adopted Justice Kennedy's four principles from *Harmelin*. And, in view of the additional factor raised in *Ewing* — the defendant's recidivism — Justice O'Connor observed:

> Throughout the States, legislatures enacting three strikes laws [have] made a deliberate policy choice that individuals who have repeatedly engaged in serious or violent criminal behavior, and whose conduct has not been deterred by more conventional approaches to punishment,

---

[38] 538 U.S. 11 (2003); see also Lockyer v. Andrade, 538 U.S. 63 (2003) (companion case); see generally James J. Brennan, *The Supreme Court's Excessive Deference to Legislative Bodies Under Eighth Amendment Sentencing Review*, 97 J. Crim. L. & Criminology 551 (2004); Erwin Chemerinsky, *The Constitution and Punishment*, 56 Stan. L. Rev. 1049 (2004); Erwin Chemerinsky, *Cruel and Unusual: The Story of Leandro Andrade*, 52 Drake L. Rev. 1 (2003).

must be isolated from society in order to protect the public safety. Though three strikes laws may be relatively new, our tradition of deferring to state legislatures in making and implementing such important policy decisions is longstanding.

Echoing Justice Kennedy's observation in *Harmelin*, the plurality stated that the Constitution does not require the adoption of any particular penological theory, and that incapacitation, as here, "may play a role in a State's sentencing scheme."

The plurality then turned to the specifics of Ewing's punishment. It first "address[ed] the gravity of the offense compared to the harshness of the penalty." But Justice O'Connor stated that the case did not involve "merely 'shoplifting three golf clubs.' Rather, Ewing was convicted of felony grand theft for stealing nearly $1,200 worth of merchandise after previously having been convicted of at least two 'violent' or 'serious' felonies." According to the plurality, "[i]n weighing the gravity of Ewing's offense, we must place on the scales not only his current felony, but also his long history of felony recidivism."

In short, these justices controversially were not determining that the punishment (25-years-to-life) fit the crime (grand theft), but whether the punishment fit the crime *plus* "his long history of felony recidivism." To avoid the impression that this meant that California improperly was punishing Ewing *again* for his *prior* crimes, Justice O'Connor stated that "Ewing's sentence is justified by the State's public-safety interest in incapacitating and deterring recidivist felons" from committing *future* crimes, which was "amply supported by [Ewing's] own long, serious criminal record."

Justice Scalia (now joined by Justice Thomas) concurred in the judgment. He reasserted his *Harmelin* claim that there is no proportionality principle, narrow or otherwise, contained in the Eighth Amendment. He also criticized the plurality for its proportionality analysis set out above. He pointed out that proportionality, "inherently a concept tied to the penological goal of retribution," has always meant that punishment must fit a crime, but that the plurality had "not convincingly establish[ed] that 25-years-to-life is a 'proportionate' punishment for stealing three golf clubs." The plurality had to "*add* an analysis" — the utilitarian consideration of protecting society from future crime. Scalia stated that legislatures have every right to consider public safety, "though why that has anything to do with the principle of proportionality is a mystery."

Justice Breyer, joined by Justices Stevens, Souter, and Ginsburg, dissented. They believed that *Solem v. Helm*, and its three-pronged test, controlled the present case, and that the facts of that case and the present one were similar enough to suggest that Ewing's sentence violated the Eighth Amendment. The dissenters also believed that, even applying Justice Kennedy's *Harmelin* approach, the 25-years-to-life sentence here was grossly disproportional.

[5] Summary

After *Ewing*, the Court remained deeply divided on Eighth Amendment, non-death penalty, proportionality analysis. Seven justices believed that the Eighth Amendment prohibits grossly disproportional punishment, but they were divided as to whether the relatively broad *Solem v. Helm* three-pronged test, or Justice Kennedy's narrow formulation from *Harmelin v. Michigan*, should be applied. Although the broader approach had four votes, compared to three votes for the narrow formulation, the latter test will remain the more influential as long as there are two votes for the view that the Eighth Amendment contains no proportionality principle at all. But, since *Ewing* was decided, two justices have left the Court (Chief Justice Rehnquist and Justice O'Connor). Therefore, this 4-3-2 breakdown may change.

Chapter 7

BURDENS OF PROOF

§ 7.01 PUTTING THE ISSUES IN PROCEDURAL CONTEXT

During a criminal trial, the prosecutor, representing the state, will introduce evidence pertaining to the crime or crimes charged. Usually, although not always, the defendant will dispute many of the relevant facts. She may assert an alibi defense ("I wasn't there"), or she may attack the prosecutor's version of the facts more narrowly, e.g., by claiming that she did not intend to cause the harm charged, or by pleading a defense, such as self-defense. At the conclusion of the trial, the factfinder, usually a jury, determines whose version of the evidence was more persuasive.

The jury is not wholly free in its deliberative process. Rules exist to ensure that the jury considers only those legal issues about which sufficient factual evidence was presented at trial that it can reach a rational, rather than speculative, verdict. Moreover, assuming that an issue is properly before it, the jury will be instructed as to "how to decide close cases, and when to regard a case as close."[1]

Among the rules that guide the factfinding process are those establishing two types of burdens of proof: (1) the burden of production (sometimes called the "burden of going forward (with evidence)"; and (2) the burden of persuasion. As to any particular issue raised at a criminal trial, both burdens of proof may fall on a single party, or one party may have the burden of production while the other has the burden of persuasion. Although states have wide discretion in determining on whom the burdens should be allocated, and how substantial the burdens should be, the Due Process Clause of the United States Constitution circumscribes legislative authority.

§ 7.02 BURDEN OF PRODUCTION

[A] Nature of the Burden

Prior to trial the prosecution must file a document with the court that indicates the crime or crimes it believes that the defendant has committed. This document provides the accused with notice of the essential elements of the

---

[1] Barbara D. Underwood, *The Thumb on the Scales of Justice: Burdens of Persuasion in Criminal Cases*, 86 Yale L.J. 1299, 1299 (1977).

offense(s) charged, and the basic facts that the prosecutor intends to prove at trial to support her allegation that the defendant committed the crime(s).[2] In turn, the defendant is sometimes required to provide advance notice to the prosecution of defenses she intends to assert at trial.

At trial, the parties may be expected to introduce evidence supporting their pre-trial claims. The rule establishing the "burden of production" identifies the party on whom the initial obligation is placed to introduce evidence at trial to support the particular legal claim in question.

[B] Who Has the Burden?

In general, the prosecutor has the burden of production regarding each element of the crime charged.[3] Almost always, the defendant has the burden of producing evidence pertaining to any affirmative defense she wishes to raise. For example, assume that murder is defined by statute as "the killing of a human being by another human being with malice aforethought." For current purposes, this definition may be divided into four elements: (1) a killing; (2) of a human being; (3) by another human being; (4) with malice aforethought. The prosecutor has the burden of producing evidence at trial regarding each of these elements. That is, she must introduce evidence that a life was taken, that the victim was a human being,[4] that the killer was the defendant, and that the killing occurred with the mental state described by the law as "malice aforethought." If the prosecutor fails to introduce sufficient evidence (as discussed below) regarding each of these elements, she has not met her burden of production.

In the preceding example, if the defendant intends to have the jury consider a defense to the murder charge, for example, that she killed in self-defense or that she was insane at the time of the crime, she — not the prosecutor — is usually obligated to introduce evidence at trial supporting the claim.

[C] How Great Is the Burden?

The prosecutor must produce enough evidence that a rational trier of fact — typically, a jury — may fairly determine that the elements of the crime have

---

[2] "In all criminal prosecutions, the accused shall enjoy the right . . . to be informed of the nature and cause of the accusation. . . ." U.S. Const. amend. VI. The document that charges the defendant with a crime (called an "indictment" if prepared by a grand jury, or called an "information" if a grand jury is not involved) must "be a plain, concise and definite written statement of the essential facts constituting the offense charged." Fed. R. Crim. P. 7(c)(1).

[3] See Jackson v. Virginia, 443 U.S. 307, 314-20 (1979); 1 Paul H. Robinson, Criminal Law Defenses § 4 (1984).

[4] This would be a serious issue if the victim were a fetus that arguably was born dead. See § 31.01[B][1], *infra*.

been proved beyond a reasonable doubt.[5] Thus, in the hypothetical murder prosecution discussed immediately above, the prosecutor has not met her burden of production unless she puts on enough evidence that a rational juror could believe beyond a reasonable doubt that the defendant killed another human being with malice aforethought.

Regarding affirmative defenses to crimes, for which the defendant has the burden of production, jurisdictions differ in the way they characterize the amount of evidence required. In some jurisdictions the defendant does not meet her burden of production if she produces a "mere scintilla" of evidence supporting an affirmative defense;[6] in other jurisdictions it is stated that the defendant must introduce enough evidence to raise a reasonable doubt on the issue of the defense claimed.[7]

[D] Effect of Failing to Meet the Burden

The trial judge — and not the jury — decides whether the parties have met their respective burdens of production. If the judge concludes that the prosecutor failed to satisfy her burden of production regarding *any* element of the offense charged, the defendant is entitled to a directed verdict of acquittal at the conclusion of the prosecutor's case-in-chief or at the end of the trial. This result follows from the fact that, as discussed in the next section, the prosecutor must *persuade* a jury beyond a reasonable doubt that the defendant committed the crime. If the prosecutor failed to introduce enough evidence for a jury to so find, there is no reason for it to deliberate on the matter.

If the defendant fails to meet her burden of production regarding an affirmative defense, the judge will not instruct the jury on the law pertaining to the defense, and the defendant is not entitled to have the issue considered by the jury in its deliberations.

§ 7.03 BURDEN OF PERSUASION[8]

[A] Nature of the Burden

Once a party satisfies her burden of production pertaining to an issue, that matter is properly before the jury as factfinder, i.e., it will decide whose factual claims are more persuasive. But, how is the jury supposed to make this deter-

---

[5] See Jackson v. Virginia, 443 U.S. at 319. For a definition of the phrase "beyond a reasonable doubt," see § 7.03[C][1], *infra*.

[6] E.g., United States v. Buchmeier, 255 F.3d 415, 427 (7th Cir. 2001).

[7] E.g., State v. Schumaier, 603 N.W.2d 882 (N.D. 1999) (also stating that the defendant is entitled to a jury instruction even if the evidentiary basis for the defense is weak, inconsistent, or of doubtful credibility).

[8] See generally Larry Alexander, *The Supreme Court, Dr. Jekyll, and the Due Process of Proof,* 1996 Sup. Ct. Rev. 191; Ronald J. Allen, *Montana v. Egelhoff — Reflections on the Limits of Leg-*

mination? Rules are needed to instruct it on how to weigh the conflicting evidence.

The rules establishing the "burden of persuasion" determine who is obligated to convince the jury of the accuracy of the particular factual claim in question. Put slightly differently, the party who has the burden of persuasion bears the risk of failing to convince the jury that her factual claim is true.

[B] Who Has the Burden?

[1] The Presumption of Innocence: The *Winship* Doctrine (In General)

The Fifth and Fourteenth Amendments to the United States Constitution provide that a person may not be deprived of her life, liberty, or property without due process of law. Pursuant to the Due Process Clause, a person charged with a crime is presumed innocent and, to enforce this presumption, the Supreme Court held in *In re Winship*[9] that the prosecution must persuade the factfinder beyond a reasonable doubt of "every fact necessary to constitute the crime charged." This rule has come to be known as "the *Winship* doctrine."

According to *Winship*, the presumption of innocence "lies at the foundation of the administration of our criminal law." Although this presumption increases the risk that a guilty person will go free, the Supreme Court has determined that "a society that values the good name and freedom of every individual" does "not view the social disutility of convicting an innocent man as equivalent to the disutility of acquitting someone who is guilty." Our commitment to protecting the innocent is so great that, according to Blackstone, "the law holds that it is better that ten guilty persons escape, than that one innocent suffer."[10]

---

islative Imagination and Judicial Authority, 87 J. Crim. L. & Criminology 633 (1997); Ronald J. Allen, *The Restoration of In re Winship: A Comment on Burdens of Persuasion in Criminal Cases After Patterson v. New York*, 76 Mich. L. Rev. 30 (1977); Donald A. Dripps, *The Constitutional Status of the Reasonable Doubt Rule*, 75 Cal. L. Rev. 1665 (1987); John Calvin Jeffries, Jr. & Paul B. Stephan III, *Defenses, Presumptions, and Burden of Proof in the Criminal Law*, 88 Yale L.J. 1325 (1979); Rinat Kitai, *Protecting the Guilty*, 6 Buff. Crim. L. Rev. 1163 (2003); Rinat Kitai, *Presuming Innocence*, 55 Okla. L. Rev. 257 (2002); Irene Merker Rosenberg, *Winship Redux: 1970 to 1990*, 69 Tex. L. Rev. 109 (1990); Louis B. Schwartz, *"Innocence" — A Dialogue with Professor Sundby*, 41 Hastings L.J. 153 (1989); Scott E. Sundby, *The Reasonable Doubt Rule and the Meaning of Innocence*, 40 Hastings L.J. 457 (1989); Peter Westen, *Egelhoff Again*, 36 Am. Crim. L. Rev. 1203 (1999).

[9] 397 U.S. 358 (1970).

[10] 4 Blackstone, Commentaries on the Laws of England *352 (1769). Not everyone agrees with Blackstone. For a thoughtful dialogue on this matter, see Jeffrey Reiman & Ernest van den Haag, *On the Common Saying that It Is Better that Ten Guilty Persons Escape than that One Innocent Suffer: Pro and Con*, 7 Soc. Phil. & Pol'y, Spring 1990, at 226; see also Vidar Halvorsen, *Is it Better that Ten Guilty Persons Go Free Than that One Innocent Person be Convicted?*, 23 Crim. Justice Ethics, Summer/Fall 2004, at 3 (discussing the Reiman-van den Haag debate, and answering the question in the title in the affirmative).

Winship teaches that the prosecutor must prove (beyond a reasonable doubt) every fact necessary to constitute the crime charged, but what precisely *are* the "facts" for which the government must constitutionally carry the burden of persuasion? Unfortunately, the Supreme Court has had enormous difficulty answering this question.

[2] *Mullaney v. Wilbur*[11]

W was charged with murder by a Maine prosecutor. Evidence presented at his trial tended to show that W intentionally killed the victim, but that he may have done so "in the heat of passion on sudden provocation." The trial court instructed the jury that Maine recognized two forms of criminal homicide, murder and manslaughter, and that the common elements of both offenses were that the homicide be: (1) "unlawful — *i.e.*, neither justifiable nor excusable"; and (2) that it be committed intentionally. The jury was instructed that the prosecution was required to prove both of these elements (beyond a reasonable doubt), and only if it met this burden was the jury to consider the distinction between murder and manslaughter.

On the distinction between murder and manslaughter, the trial court further informed the jury that if the prosecution proved that W killed the victim unlawfully and intentionally, then the killing was murder, unless W persuaded the jury by a preponderance of the evidence that the killing was "in the heat of passion on sudden provocation," in which case it constituted the lesser offense of manslaughter. That is, the prosecution had the burden of persuading the jury beyond a reasonable doubt that W unlawfully and intentionally killed the victim; if it did, the burden of persuasion shifted to W to prove that he was provoked into killing the victim. If W failed in this proof, he was guilty of murder; if he succeeded, he was guilty of manslaughter.

W appealed his conviction on the ground that the preceding jury instructions, which placed on him the burden of persuasion that the killing occurred "in the heat of passion on sudden provocation," violated the *Winship* doctrine. The State of Maine responded, however, that the instructions were constitutional — the prosecution only had the responsibility to prove (beyond a reasonable doubt) that W was guilty of some form of criminal homicide. Under the instructions given, the State did not require W to prove his innocence; he only had the burden of persuasion regarding his level of guilt (murder versus manslaughter). In such circumstances, the State argued, "the defendant's critical interests in liberty and reputation are no longer of paramount concern since, irrespective of . . . the heat of passion on sudden provocation, he is likely to lose his liberty and certain to be stigmatized."

The Supreme Court disagreed. In an opinion written by Justice Lewis Powell, the Court summarized the historical roots of homicide law, and concluded

---

[11] 421 U.S. 684 (1975).

that the presence or absence of heat of passion was "the single most important factor in determining the degree of culpability attaching to an unlawful homicide." It observed that "the clear trend has been toward requiring the prosecution to bear the ultimate burden of proving this fact."

The Court criticized Maine's argument as unduly formalistic. It pointed out:

> [If the *Winship* doctrine] were limited to those facts that constitute a crime as defined by state law, a State could undermine many of the interests that [the Due Process Clause] sought to protect without effecting any substantive change in its law. It would only be necessary to redefine the elements that constitute different crimes, characterizing them as factors that bear solely on the extent of punishment.

In contrast to such formalism, the Supreme Court held that the Due Process Clause required the prosecution not only to prove that W was guilty of criminal homicide, but also to persuade the jury regarding the facts relating to W's "degree of criminal culpability."

Although the precise contours of the *Mullaney* decision were disputed by scholars, one highly plausible interpretation of the opinion was that, once a defendant satisfies her burden of *production* regarding an affirmative defense, the prosecution is constitutionally required to disprove the defense.[12] This potential reading of *Mullaney* proved short-lived.

[3] *Patterson v. New York*[13]

Patterson narrowed the import of *Mullaney*. Indeed, without saying so expressly, *Patterson* "signal[ed] that it [believed it] had erred in *Mullaney*."[14]

In *Patterson*, P was charged with murder. He believed that he was guilty of the lesser offense of manslaughter because he suffered from what New York law described as an "extreme emotional disturbance." This provision, based on the Model Penal Code,[15] was a broader version of the "heat of passion on sudden provocation" doctrine considered in *Mullaney*.

Under New York law, murder required proof of three facts: (1) a human death; (2) that the accused caused it; and (3) that the accused intended the result. The homicide statute expressly provided that "extreme emotional disturbance" was an affirmative defense to murder which, *if proved by the defendant*, reduced the criminal homicide to manslaughter. The jury was instructed consistently with these statutory provisions.

---

12 See Ronald J. Allen, *Mullaney v. Wilbur, the Supreme Court, and the Substantive Criminal Law — An Examination of the Limits of Legislative Intervention*, 55 Tex. L. Rev. 269 (1977).

13 432 U.S. 197 (1977).

14 Allen, *Montana v. Egelhoff*, Note 8, *supra*, at 645.

15 Model Penal Code § 210.3(1)(b). See § 31.10[C][3], *infra*.

P argued that *Mullaney* invalidated the statute because the homicide law permitted the State of New York to shift to him the burden of proving his lesser level of culpability due to extreme emotional disturbance. Nonetheless, in an opinion written by Justice Byron White, the Supreme Court upheld the statute. The Court conceded that there was "language in *Mullaney* that has been understood as perhaps construing the Due Process Clause to require the prosecution to prove . . . any fact affecting 'the [defendant's] degree of criminal culpability.'" It rejected this reading of *Mullaney* as unduly restrictive of legislative authority to allocate burdens of proof. The *Patterson* Court reasoned that if such a broad reading of *Mullaney* were correct, legislatures might be inclined to repeal defenses altogether or, at least, not to broaden them as New York had done here. Justice White suggested that such a response would serve only to prejudice defendants' interests and undermine legislative reform. The Court stated that it did not intend *Mullaney* to have such a far-reaching effect.

According to *Patterson*, the prosecution is constitutionally required to prove "every *ingredient* of an offense." As used in this opinion, however, *Winship*'s "facts" and *Patterson*'s "ingredients" are essentially synonyms for the word "elements." That is, a state is required by the Due Process Clause to prove every element in the definition of an offense, but the legislature may, if it chooses to do so, ordinarily allocate to the defendant the burden of persuasion regarding defenses to crimes.

The Court claimed that this interpretation of *Winship* was consistent with *Mullaney*. It pointed out that one element of the crime of murder in Maine was that the killing be "unlawful." In turn, "unlawful" meant "neither justifiable nor excusable." "Heat of passion," however, is an excuse defense. Therefore, to be guilty of murder, there had to be an *absence* of heat of passion (or any other justification or excuse). This *absence* of a defense, then, was an element of murder, as defined by Maine law. To require the prosecutor to prove the *absence* of heat of passion was consistent, therefore, with the proposition that the government should prove every element of the crime charged.

In contrast, absence of "extreme emotional disturbance" was not an element of the New York murder statute. Instead, existence of such a disturbance was, expressly, an affirmative defense to murder that mitigated the crime to manslaughter. As a non-element of murder, *Patterson* stated, New York could properly place the burden of proving its existence on the defendant.

Justice Powell, author of *Mullaney*, sharply dissented in *Patterson*. He understandably complained that the majority's explanation of the *Mullaney* holding bore "little resemblance to the basic rationale of that decision." In Justice Powell's mind, and in the view of many scholarly critics of *Patterson*,[16] the holding elevated form over substance: It permitted legislatures to "shift, virtually at will, the burden of persuasion with respect to any factor in a criminal case, so long

---

[16] See Alexander, Note 8, *supra*, at 193.

as it is careful not to mention the nonexistence of that factor in the statutory language that defines the crime." Indeed, Powell worried, a legislature could now constitutionally redefine murder as, for example, "mere physical contact causing death," and then set up an affirmative defense requiring the defendant to prove that she acted blamelessly.[17] This was exactly the formalism rejected in *Mullaney*.

[4] Post-*Patterson* Case Law

[a] In General

A prosecutor must prove every element of an offense beyond a reasonable doubt, and, except "in certain limited circumstances," a legislature may allocate to the defendant the burden of persuasion regarding "facts not formally identified as elements of the offense charged."[18] Thus, generally speaking, a legislature may allocate to the defendant the burden of persuasion regarding facts that relate to an affirmative defense. The challenge — one that the Court has struggled mightily to meet in a number of sharply divided opinions — is to determine, as a matter of legislative intent, whether a particular "fact" relates to an "element" of an offense or to a "defense."

[b] Element of an Offense versus a Defense

In *Martin v. Ohio*,[19] *M* was prosecuted for aggravated murder, defined in Ohio as "purposely, and with prior calculation and design, caus[ing] the death of another." *M* claimed he acted in self-defense, the elements of which defense were that he: (1) was not at fault in creating the situation giving rise to the argument; (2) had an honest belief that he was in imminent danger of death or great bodily harm; and (3) did not violate any duty to retreat. The jury was instructed that to convict *M*, it had to find, in light of all of the evidence, that each of the elements of aggravated murder had been proved by the State of Ohio beyond a reasonable doubt. However, the jury was told that *M* had the burden of proving self-defense by a preponderance of the evidence.

---

[17] Some scholars have argued that the Eighth Amendment bar on cruel and unusual punishment might limit legislative authority to redefine criminal offenses in the manner feared by Justice Powell. E.g., Jeffries & Stephan, Note 8, *supra*, at 1365-97. However, in view of the Supreme Court's restrictive reading of the proportionality doctrine outside the death penalty context, see § 6.05[C], *supra*, this avenue now seems foreclosed.

[18] McMillan v. Pennsylvania, 477 U.S. 79, 86 (1986). One exception to this rule is that any fact relating to the offense charged (other than the defendant's criminal history) that will have the effect of increasing the penalty for a crime beyond the prescribed statutory maximum — even if the fact is identified by the legislature as a "sentencing" factor, rather than an "element" of the crime — must be proved beyond a reasonable doubt. Apprendi v. New Jersey, 530 U.S. 466 (2000).

[19] 480 U.S. 228 (1987).

M argued that these instructions violated the *Winship* doctrine, as interpreted by *Patterson*. He reasoned that one element of self-defense — the presence of an "imminent" deadly threat — negates one element of the crime of aggravated murder, "prior calculation and design." (If a person experiences an imminent threat, she does not have time to premeditate.) In effect, *M* argued that the *absence* of the right to kill in self-defense was an implicit ingredient of the offense charged; therefore, it was wrong to allocate to *M* the burden of persuasion on self-defense.

By a 5-4 vote, the Supreme Court rejected *M*'s plausible argument. It emphasized the fact that the trial court did *not* instruct the jury "that self-defense evidence could not be considered in determining whether there was a reasonable doubt about the State's case. . . . Such an instruction would . . . plainly run afoul of *Winship*'s mandate." That is, the jury *was* permitted to consider self-defense evidence, along with all other evidence introduced by either side, in order to determine whether Ohio proved the elements of the offense beyond a reasonable doubt. The Court warned that it "would be quite different if the jury had been instructed that . . . self-defense evidence must be put aside for all purposes unless it satisfied the preponderance standard."

The Court agreed with *M* "that the elements of aggravated murder and self-defense overlap in the sense that evidence to prove the latter will often tend to negate the former." However, a jurisdiction may allocate to a defendant the burden of persuasion regarding an affirmative defense, as long as the jury may *also* consider the evidence relating to the defense as a basis for negating an element of a crime. The dissenters, with good reason, feared that the confusing instructions approved by the Supreme Court could cause a jury to wrongly believe "that by raising the defense, the accused has assumed the ultimate burden of proving that particular element."

Martin was a controversial opinion, but nowhere near as much (or as confusing) as the Court's ruling in *Montana v. Egelhoff*.[20] The State of Montana defined the offense of "Deliberate Homicide" (murder) as "purposely" or "knowingly" causing the death of another human being. This murder statute was supplemented, however, by another statute that provided that a voluntarily-induced "intoxicated condition is not a defense to any offense and may not be taken into consideration in determining the existence of a mental state which is an element of the offense. . . ."[21]

The Court, again 5-4, approved the Montana statutory system. *Egelhoff*'s long-term meaning is unclear, however, because the Court badly split. Justice Antonin Scalia announced the judgment of the Court, but delivered an opinion for only four justices; a fifth justice (Ruth Bader Ginsburg) only concurred in the judgment. The four dissenters wrote three opinions amongst themselves.

---

[20] 518 U.S. 37 (1996).

[21] Mont. Code Ann. § 45-2-203 (1995).

There are two ways to read the Montana statutory system.[22] One reading of Montana law is that the murder definition supplemented by the intoxication statute stands for the proposition that a person is guilty of Deliberate Homicide if she kills purposely or knowingly or, *in the case of a voluntarily intoxicated person, if she simply kills another person, even if the killing was not purposeful or knowing.* According to this reading, which approximates concurring Justice Ginsburg's understanding of Montana law, *Winship* and *Patterson* are not violated because, in essence, the legislature has defined murder two ways, one way to deal with sober killers (they are not guilty of murder unless they purposely or knowingly — intentionally — took a human life), and another way to deal with intoxicated killers (they are guilty of murder if they took a human life, even accidentally). Therefore, according to this reading of Montana law, in regard to voluntarily intoxicated defendants, there is no mental state element in the murder statute for the State to prove beyond a reasonable doubt. This is arguably a highly objectionable way to define murder, but it would not offend the *Winship* doctrine (all elements of the crime are proven beyond a reasonable doubt).

But, there is another way to read the Montana homicide law, which seems to conform with the understanding of the Scalia plurality. According to *this* version, the Montana legislature intended to retain the ordinary culpability requirement for murder (proof that the homicide was purposeful or knowing) *in all cases*, but then with "a certain Alice-in-Wonderland quality,"[23] it bars a voluntarily intoxicated defendant from introducing evidence relating to her intoxication that might cause a jury to possess a reasonable doubt that she acted with the statutorily required purpose or knowledge (for example, that she was so intoxicated that she did not know what she was doing). According to Justice Scalia, as long as an evidentiary rule such as the present one does not offend fundamental principles of justice, it does not violate the Due Process Clause for a state to make "changes in their criminal law that have the effect of making it easier for the prosecution to obtain convictions."[24]

---

[22] See Allen, *Montana v. Egelhoff*, Note 8, *supra*, at 636.

[23] Sanford H. Kadish, *Fifty Years of Criminal Law: An Opinionated Review*, 87 Calif. L. Rev. 943, 955 (1999).

[24] *Egelhoff*, 518 U.S. at 55 (quoting McMillan v. Pennsylvania, 477 U.S. 79, 89 (1986)).

[C] How Great Is the Burden?

[1] Elements of Crimes: Proof Beyond a Reasonable Doubt[25]

The Due Process Clause requires the prosecutor to prove every element of a crime "beyond a reasonable doubt."[26] This burden of proof "defies easy explication."[27] In terms of probability, it is the highest burden recognized in the law. Guilt is not proven on the basis of the traditional civil standard of "preponderance of the evidence" (i.e., 50.1%), or even on the heightened basis of "clear and convincing evidence." Instead, a "very high level of probability [is] required."[28] Jurors must "reach a subjective state of near certitude of . . . guilt."[29] However, courts hesitate to quantify the "inherently qualitative" reasonable-doubt standard.[30]

Chief Justice Shaw of the Massachusetts Supreme Judicial Court crafted the traditional definition of "beyond a reasonable doubt," which served for more than a century as the basis for many reasonable-doubt jury instructions. In *Commonwealth v. Webster*,[31] he explained that "reasonable doubt" is "not merely possible doubt; because every thing relating to human affairs, and depending on moral evidence, is open to some possible or imaginary doubt." Instead, reasonable doubt exists when the "state of the case . . . leaves the minds of jurors in that condition that they cannot say they feel an abiding conviction, to a moral certainty, of the truth of the charge."

In *Victor v. Nebraska*,[32] the Supreme Court warned trial courts that the term "moral certainty" may have "lost its historical meaning, and that a modern jury [might] understand it to allow conviction on proof that does not meet the

---

[25] See generally Barbara J. Shapiro, "Beyond a Reasonable Doubt" and "Probable Cause": Historical Perspectives on the Anglo-American Law of Evidence (1991); Ronald J. Allen, *On the Significance of Batting Averages and Strikeout Totals: A Clarification of the "Naked Statistical Evidence" Debate, the Meaning of "Evidence," and the Requirement of Proof Beyond a Reasonable Doubt*, 65 Tulane L. Rev. 1093 (1991); Henry L. Chambers, Jr., *Reasonable Certainty and Reasonable Doubt*, 81 Marq. L. Rev. 655 (1998); Irwin A. Horowitz & Laird C. Kirkpatrick, *A Concept in Search of a Definition: The Effects of Reasonable Doubt Instructions on Certainty of Guilt Standards and Jury Verdicts*, 20 Law & Hum. Behav. 655 (1996); William S. Laufer, *The Rhetoric of Innocence*, 70 Wash. L. Rev. 329 (1995); Lawrence M. Solan, *Refocusing the Burden of Proof in Criminal Cases: Some Doubt About Reasonable Doubt*, 78 Tex. L. Rev. 105 (1999).

[26] See § 7.03[B], *supra*.

[27] Victor v. Nebraska, 511 U.S. 1, 5 (1994).

[28] *Id*. at 14.

[29] Jackson v. Virginia, 443 U.S. 307, 315 (1979).

[30] McCullough v. State, 657 P.2d 1157, 1159 (Nev. 1983).

[31] 59 Mass. (5 Cush.) 295, 320 (1850).

[32] 511 U.S. 1 (1994).

beyond a reasonable doubt standard." The critical language in *Webster*, the Court said, is that the jurors must have "an abiding conviction" — a "settled and fixed" conviction — of the defendant's guilt.

[2] Defenses[33]

Jurisdictions differ in their allocation of the burden of persuasion regarding affirmative defenses. Some states require the government to disprove beyond a reasonable doubt some or all defenses, once the defendant has met her burden of production. In states that allocate to the defendant the burden of persuasion regarding defenses, it is typical to require her to prove the validity of the claim by the less strict preponderance-of-the-evidence standard.

[D] Effect of Failing to Meet Burden

[1] Elements of Crimes

If the prosecutor fails to prove each element of the crime charged beyond a reasonable doubt, the defendant must be acquitted of the offense charged. Procedurally, the acquittal may occur in either of two ways. First, after the prosecution completes its presentation of evidence or immediately before the case is due to be submitted to the jury, upon motion of the defendant, the trial court must direct a verdict of acquittal if the evidence, viewed in the manner most favorable to the prosecution,[34] can support no reasonable verdict other than acquittal.[35] Alternatively, if the judge believes that reasonable minds can differ and, therefore, permits the case to go to the jury, the jury must acquit if *it* possesses a reasonable doubt regarding one or more elements of the offense charged.

[2] Defenses

If a defendant presents sufficient evidence to meet her burden of *production* regarding a defense to the crime charged, the jury must be permitted to evaluate the defense claimed. When the defendant also has the burden of *persuasion*

---

[33] See generally 1 Robinson, Note 3, *supra*, at § 5.

[34] Because the factfinder may rationally decide to believe the prosecutor's version of disputed facts, the judge must consider the evidence in the manner most favorable to the government on a motion to direct a verdict in favor of the defendant. The same test is applied in any appeal of a conviction. See Jackson v. Virginia, 443 U.S. 307, 319 (1979).

[35] Curley v. United States, 160 F.2d 229, 232-33 (D.C. Cir. 1947). No matter how overwhelming the evidence of guilt, the prosecution is never entitled to a directed verdict of conviction. Sullivan v. Louisiana, 508 U.S. 275, 277 (1993). The grant of such a motion would deny the accused her constitutional right to trial by jury. See § 1.02[A], *supra*.

regarding the defense, a jury should reject the claimed defense if she fails to satisfy the stated burden. Assuming that the state has proven the elements of the crime beyond a reasonable doubt, and that no other defenses have been proven, the defendant may be convicted.

If the prosecution has the burden of disproving a defense, the jury must acquit the defendant if the prosecution fails to persuade the jury beyond a reasonable doubt of the defense's non-existence.

§ 7.04 MODEL PENAL CODE

The Model Penal Code provides that the prosecutor has the burden of *production* regarding each element of an offense. Regarding affirmative defenses, the prosecutor is not required to disprove an affirmative defense "unless there is evidence supporting such defense."[36] The Code does not specify the strength of the evidence required to satisfy the defendant's burden of production, choosing instead to leave the matter to the courts.[37]

Regarding the burden of *persuasion*, the general rule is that the prosecution must prove every "element" of an offense beyond a reasonable doubt.[38] The term "element" as used in the Code, however, includes conduct that "negatives an excuse or justification" for the action.[39] That is, the Model Penal Code allocates to the prosecution the duty to disprove defenses, assuming that the defendant has satisfied her burden of production. However, this rule does not apply to defenses that the Code expressly requires the defendant to prove by a preponderance of the evidence.[40]

---

[36] Model Penal Code § 1.12(2)(a).

[37] American Law Institute, Comment to § 1.12, at 193.

[38] Model Penal Code § 1.12(1).

[39] Model Penal Code § 1.13(9)(c).

[40] E.g., Model Penal Code § 2.13 (the defense of entrapment).

Chapter 8

PRESUMPTIONS

§ 8.01 THE NATURE OF A PRESUMPTION[1]

Assume that murder is defined by statute as the "unlawful and intentional killing of a human being by another human being." The prosecutor must prove beyond a reasonable doubt that: (1) a human being was killed; (2) the defendant was the killer; (3) the defendant intended to take a human life; and (4) the killing was unlawful.

Sometimes, a prosecutor will find it difficult to prove an element of an offense. For example, it might be hard to prove the third element — the defendant's subjective intent to kill — in a prosecution based on the hypothetical murder statute. Assume, therefore, that in order to prove that D intended to kill V, the prosecutor introduces evidence that D picked up a loaded gun, pointed it in V's direction, and fired it. Has the prosecutor proved the requisite intent beyond a reasonable doubt? Perhaps so, but perhaps not: depending on the context it may appear, for example, that D intended only to frighten or wound V.

Suppose, however, that a legislature or court establishes the following rule: "Whenever it is proved in a criminal trial that a person fired a loaded gun at another person, the factfinder must [or may] presume that the actor intended to kill the other person."

This rule establishes a presumption. Presumptions operate in the following manner: Upon proof of Fact (or set of Facts) A, a factfinder must (or "may," depending on the language of the instruction) presume Fact B. In the nomenclature of presumptions, Fact A is the *basic* fact, and Fact B is the *presumed* fact. Usually, although not always, the presumed fact in a criminal prosecution is an element of the crime charged. In our hypothetical, the presumption requires (or permits) the jury to presume intent to kill (Fact B) upon proof that D fired a loaded gun at V (Fact A).[2]

If a jury is instructed that it *must* presume Fact B upon proof of basic Fact A, the presumption is a "mandatory presumption." If the jury is told that it *may*, but need not, presume Fact B, the instruction is called a "permissive presumption."

---

[1] See generally Ronald J. Allen, *Structuring Jury Decisionmaking in Criminal Cases: A Unified Constitutional Approach to Evidentiary Devices*, 94 Harv. L. Rev. 321 (1980); Charles R. Nesson, *Reasonable Doubt and Permissive Inferences: The Value of Complexity*, 92 Harv. L. Rev. 1187 (1979).

[2] Of course, the basic fact here is actually a set of facts: (1) that the weapon used was a gun (rather than some other weapon); (2) that it was loaded; (3) that D aimed it at V; and (4) that D fired it. If one of these facts is not proved, the presumption does not apply.

The practical effect of presumptions, especially those of a mandatory nature, is to make it easier for the party with the burden of proof — typically, the prosecutor — to persuade the factfinder regarding the issue in question. It is not necessarily improper for the legislature or a court to make the prosecutor's job easier in this manner. At times, however, a presumption runs counter to constitutional protections of the defendant.

§ 8.02 MANDATORY PRESUMPTIONS

[A] Rebuttable Presumptions

A mandatory rebuttable presumption requires a finding of the presumed fact upon proof of the basic fact, unless that finding is rebutted by the opposing party. Essentially, in a criminal trial, the jury is instructed regarding a presumption that "if the State proves Fact A, then you must find Fact B, unless the defendant disproves Fact B by a preponderance [or some other quantum] of the evidence."

The procedural effect of a mandatory rebuttable presumption is to shift to the defendant the burden of persuasion regarding the presumed fact, upon proof by the prosecution of the basic fact. Applying this presumption to the example described in Section 8.01, the jury would be required to find that D intended to kill V [Fact B] if the prosecution proved that D fired a loaded gun at V [Fact A], unless D disproved his intent to kill by a preponderance of the evidence.

Rebuttable mandatory presumptions are unconstitutional when the presumed fact is an element of the crime charged. For example, in *Sandstrom v. Montana*,[3] S was charged with "deliberate homicide," that is, that S "purposely or knowingly caused the death" of V. At trial, S admitted that he killed V, but he denied that he did so purposely or knowingly. At the conclusion of the trial, the judge instructed the jury that "the law presumes that a person intends the natural and probable consequences of his voluntary acts." As the Supreme Court explained the effect of this presumption, "upon proof by the State of the slaying, and of additional facts not themselves establishing the element of intent, the burden was shifted to the defendant to prove that he lacked the requisite mental state." The Court held that the presumption was unconstitutional. By shifting to S the burden of proof regarding his mental state, the presumption "conflict[ed] with the overriding presumption of innocence with which the law endows the accused and which extends to every element of the crime."

Similarly, in a prosecution for theft of a rented car, it is unconstitutional to charge the jury that "intent to commit theft by fraud is presumed if one who has leased or rented the personal property of another pursuant to a written contract

---

[3] 442 U.S. 510 (1979).

fails to return the . . . property . . . within 20 days." By shifting the burden of proof regarding intent, this instruction "subvert[s] the presumption of innocence accorded to accused persons."**4**

A mandatory rebuttable presumption is not saved by the requirement that the prosecution prove the basic fact beyond a reasonable doubt. In the hypothetical case described in Section 8.01, even if *D* undoubtedly fired a loaded gun at *V*, this does not necessarily prove beyond a reasonable doubt that he intended to kill *V*. *D* may have believed that the gun was unloaded, or he may have intended to fire in the direction of, but purposely miss, *V*, in order to frighten him. Yet, pursuant to the presumption, the jury would be required to find the element of the offense, unless *D* disproved his intent to kill. The Constitution does not permit this, because the presumption "invade[s] the truth-finding task assigned solely to juries in criminal cases."**5**

[B] Irrebuttable ("Conclusive") Presumptions

An irrebuttable or conclusive presumption requires the jury to find the presumed fact upon proof of the basic fact, even if the opposing party introduces rebutting evidence. For example, a jury might be charged that "upon proof that *D* fired a loaded gun at *V*, you *must* find that *D* intended to kill *V*."

True irrebuttable presumptions are hard to find in the criminal law. However, occasionally a judge will instruct the jury regarding a *rebuttable* presumption in language that could cause a reasonable juror to believe that it is irrebuttable, in which case an appellate court will treat it as such. A mandatory irrebuttable presumption pertaining to an element of an offense is unconstitutional for the same reasons that mandatory rebuttable ones are impermissible.**6**

§ 8.03 PERMISSIVE PRESUMPTIONS ("INFERENCES")

A permissive presumption is one in which the factfinder may, but need not, find the existence of the presumed fact upon proof of the basic fact.

A permissive presumption is not a true presumption. It is more accurately described as an "inference." An inference is not a rule that formally shifts the burden of proof from one party to another, as a true presumption does. Rather, an inference is a (hopefully) logical bridge between one fact believed to be true and a second fact, the truth of which is at issue. Thus, in the hypothetical posed in Section 8.01, if the jury were informed that it "may" — not "must" — presume Fact B from proof of Fact A, the jury would not be required to find that

---

4 Carella v. California, 491 U.S. 263, 265 (1989) (per curiam).

5 *Id.*

6 Sandstrom v. Montana, 442 U.S. at 521-24.

D intended to kill V on the basis of evidence that he fired a loaded gun at V, even if D introduced no evidence to disprove his intent to kill. However, if it wished, the jury could cross the inferential bridge and find the intent based on the aiming and firing of the loaded gun.

Because permissive presumptions, or inferences, do not formally affect the prosecution's constitutional obligation to prove every element of an offense beyond a reasonable doubt, they are not unconstitutional *per se*.[7] Nonetheless, an inference is constitutionally impermissible if there is no rational connection between the basic fact and the presumed (inferred) fact. As the Court explained in *Tot v. United States*,[8] "where the inference [created] is so strained as not to have a reasonable relation to the circumstances of life as we know them," the factfinding process is rendered unreliable, and the defendant is denied due process of law.

An inference is rational if, but only if, the presumed fact more likely than not flows from the basic fact.[9] For example, an appellate court held that a trial judge should not have instructed the jury that it could infer criminal recklessness upon proof that the defendant drove slightly in excess of the maximum lawful speed limit.[10] In such circumstances, the inferred fact did not more likely than not flow from the basic fact. On the other hand, it is rational, and therefore permissible, for a jury to infer that "any person who enters or remains unlawfully in a building . . . [has the] intent to commit a crime . . . therein."[11]

The constitutionality of a permissive presumption often depends on the particular facts of the case. For example, in *County Court of Ulster County v. Allen*,[12] the Supreme Court upheld an instruction to the jury that permitted it to infer from the presence of two firearms in an automobile that all four car occupants were in illegal possession of the weapons. In the case, two very heavy, large-caliber handguns were positioned crosswise in the open handbag belonging to a sixteen-year-old female occupant. The bag was either on the front seat or front floor of the car that contained her and three adult males.

The Supreme Court held that, as applied to the facts of this case, the inference of constructive possession by the four defendants was rationally based. As the weapons were heavy, large, and in full view, the Court reasoned that it was more likely than not true that the youth was not solely responsible for their presence in her purse. More likely that not, the Court said, each of the adult male occupants could exercise control over the weapons, and therefore were also in constructive possession of them. If the evidence at trial had been different — for

---

[7] County Court of Ulster County v. Allen, 442 U.S. 140, 157 (1979).

[8] 319 U.S. 463 (1943).

[9] Ulster County, 442 U.S. at 165.

[10] Hanna v. Riveland, 87 F.3d 1034 (9th Cir. 1996).

[11] State v. Brunson, 905 P.2d 346 (Wash. 1995).

[12] 442 U.S. 140 (1979).

example, if one of the occupants had been a hitchhiker — the inference of possession by this casual occupant might not have withstood analysis. Or, if the weapons in this case had been small and concealed in the girl's purse, the inference of possession by the adult males might not have satisfied the more-likely-than-not test.

§ 8.04 MODEL PENAL CODE

The Model Penal Code does not recognize mandatory presumptions. The drafters of the Code took the position that when a legislature wishes to allocate to the defendant the burden of persuasion regarding a particular issue, it should do so directly by recognizing an affirmative defense, and expressly requiring the defendant to establish the facts pertaining to the defense by the preponderance of the evidence.[13]

The Code permits *permissive* presumptions (inferences) regarding elements of criminal offenses. Such presumptions, when established by the legislature, affect a criminal trial in two procedural ways. First, if any evidence of the basic fact is presented at trial, the issue of the existence of the presumed fact — i.e., the element of the crime — must be submitted to the jury unless, in the language of the Code, the trial judge is "satisfied that the evidence as a whole clearly negatives the presumed fact."[14] In essence, the permissive presumption is triggered unless the presumption is so lacking in foundation that the defendant is entitled to a directed verdict on the matter.

Second, assuming that the permissive presumption is not irrational, the Model Code requires the judge to instruct the jury that the element at issue must still be proved by the prosecutor beyond a reasonable doubt, but that the law permits it to regard the basic facts as sufficient evidence of the presumed fact.[15] Thus, with the ongoing hypothetical considered in this chapter, if the prosecutor introduced evidence that D fired a loaded gun at V, the jury would be instructed (assuming that the inference has a rational foundation) that the prosecutor must prove beyond a reasonable doubt that D intended to kill V, but that the law allows the jury, if it chooses, to treat proof of the fact that D fired the loaded gun at V as adequate evidence to meet the prosecutor's burden of persuasion on the matter of D's mental state.

---

[13] American Law Institute, Comment to § 1.12 at 203. See § 7.04, *supra*.

[14] Model Penal Code § 1.12(5)(a).

[15] Model Penal Code § 1.12(5)(b).

Chapter 9

ACTUS REUS

§ 9.01 *ACTUS REUS*: GENERAL PRINCIPLES[1]

[A] Definition

Generally speaking, crimes have two components: the "*actus reus*," the physical or external portion of the crime; and the "*mens rea*," the mental or internal feature. The concept of "*actus reus*" is the focus of this chapter.

The term "*actus reus*" reportedly was not generally used by scholars in criminal law treatises prior to the twentieth century,[2] but it has found currency in modern Anglo-American jurisprudence. Unfortunately, there is no single accepted definition.

As used in this Text, the term "*actus reus*" generally includes three ingredients of a crime, which can be encapsulated in a single sentence: The *actus reus* of an offense consists of (1) a voluntary act;[3] (2) that causes; (3) social harm.[4] For example, if *A* picks up a knife and stabs *B*, killing *B*, the *actus reus* of a criminal homicide has occurred: *A* has performed a *voluntary act* (stabbing *B*) that *caused B*'s death (the *social harm*). As is developed in this chapter, "voluntary act" and "social harm" are legal terms of art that require special attention. The element of causation, which links the defendant's voluntary act (or omission) to the social harm, is discussed in Chapter 14.[5]

---

[1] See generally Michael Moore, Act and Crime (1993); Paul H. Robinson, *Should the Criminal Law Abandon the Actus Reus-Mens Rea Distinction? in* Action and Value in Criminal Law 187 (Stephen Shute, John Gardner & Jeremy Horder eds., 1993); Albin Eser, *The Principle of "Harm" in the Concept of Crime: A Comparative Analysis of the Criminally Protected Legal Interests*, 4 Duq. L. Rev. 345 (1965); Exchange, *The Actus Reus Requirement*, Crim. Just. Ethics, Winter/Spring 1991, at 11-26; A.P. Simester, *On the So-Called Requirement for Voluntary Action*, 1 Buff. Crim. L. Rev. 403 (1998).

[2] Jerome Hall, General Principles of Criminal Law 222 (2d ed. 1960).

[3] In exceptional circumstances, failure to perform an act — an omission — may serve as the basis for criminal responsibility. See §§ 9.06-.08, *infra*.

[4] Eser, Note 1, *supra*, at 386.

[5] Warning: Because "*actus reus*" has no universally accepted meaning, some courts and commentators use the term more narrowly than is suggested in the text, simply to describe the defendant's conduct (in the example given, the voluntary acts of picking up the knife and stabbing *B*) or the result of that conduct (the social harm of *B*'s death), rather than a combination thereof.

[B] Punishing Thoughts: Why Not?

Suppose that three people separately want the President dead: *A* idly wishes that the President were dead; *B* intends to kill the President and devises a mental plan to commit the offense; and *C* actually kills the President. A society might plausibly punish all three persons. *A* would be punished for her morally wrongful thoughts; *B* would be punished for devising her plan; and *C* would be punished for acting our her intentions. In Anglo-American criminal law, however, only *C* is punishable, as "[t]he reach of the criminal law has long been limited by the principle that no one is punishable for his thoughts."[6] Put differently, the legal requirement of conduct resulting in harm — the *actus reus* component of a crime — insures that *A* and *B,* although morally censurable, are not criminally responsible for their thoughts.

Reasons of pragmatism and principle justify the non-criminalization of mere thoughts. On a pragmatic level, the requirement of conduct is "[r]ooted in skepticism about the ability . . . to know what passes through the minds of men."[7] We often have difficulty accurately reconstructing our own thoughts, much less "reading" another person's mind.

But, suppose that we *could* read another's mind? Suppose that the government implanted an electrode in every infant's brain, and that this device allowed law enforcement officers to read our thoughts with clarity. Even if this were possible, punishment for thoughts alone would be objectionable. First, virtually all people, most of whom are entirely law-abiding, occasionally hope (like *A*) that some harm will befall another. A society that would punish for such idle thoughts would be an intolerable place to live (not to speak of a society whose government would invade mental privacy in this manner).[8]

But, what about *B*? Many people have momentary antisocial thoughts, but few actually devise a plan of criminal action. On its face, a rule that allows *B* to escape punishment is counter-utilitarian. For various reasons, however, *B*'s punishment would be unacceptable. First, practically speaking, there is no way to distinguish "between desires of the day-dream variety and fixed intentions that may pose a real threat to society."[9]

---

[6] United States v. Muzii, 676 F.2d 919, 920 (2d Cir. 1982); see Proctor v. State, 176 P. 771, 772 (Okla. Crim. Ct. App. 1918) ("Guilty intention, unconnected with an overt act . . . [is not] the subject of punishment") (quoting Ex Parte Smith, 36 S.W. 628 (Mo. 1896)). The English Statute of 1351 punished "compassing [devising] the death of the King," but even this statute was interpreted to require an overt act. George Fletcher, Rethinking Criminal Law 207-13 (1978).

[7] Abraham S. Goldstein, *Conspiracy to Defraud the United States*, 68 Yale L.J. 405, 405 (1959).

[8] 2 James Fitzjames Stephen, A History of the Criminal Law in England 78 (1883) ("If [the law] were not so restricted it would be utterly intolerable; all mankind would be criminals, and most of their lives would be passed in trying and punishing each other. . . .").

[9] Powell v. Texas, 392 U.S. 514, 543 (1968) (Black & Harlan, JJ., concurring).

Second, in a society that values individual freedom, use of the criminal law should be limited to situations in which harm is seriously threatened, and not simply "to purify thoughts and perfect character."[10] Respect for individual liberties, therefore, requires that the criminal law be exercised only in response to conduct.[11]

Finally, and perhaps most basically, the *actus reus* requirement — the refusal to punish for thoughts alone — is premised on the retributive belief that it is morally wrong to punish people for their unacted-upon intentions. Retributive theory justifies punishment of those who freely choose to harm others; the corollary of this is that society must give each person some breathing space, i.e., the opportunity to choose to desist from wrongful activity. To a retributivist, voluntary conduct serves as a minimum precondition for the infliction of punishment.

§ 9.02 VOLUNTARY ACT: GENERAL PRINCIPLES[12]

[A] General Rule

Subject to a few limited and controversial exceptions,[13] a person is not guilty of a crime unless her conduct includes a voluntary act. Few statutes defining criminal offenses expressly provide for this requirement. Nonetheless, the voluntary act requirement has common law support, modern courts usually treat it as an implicit element of criminal statutes,[14] and an increasing number of states now include a general statutory provision, cast in terms similar to the Model Penal Code, that sets out this rule.[15]

For analytical purposes the voluntary act rule may be separated into two components, the "act" and its "voluntary" nature.

---

[10] United States v. Hollingsworth, 27 F.3d 1196, 1203 (7th Cir. 1994) (en banc).

[11] See Herbert L. Packer, The Limits of the Criminal Sanction 74 (1968).

[12] See generally Larry Alexander, *Reconsidering the Relationship Among Voluntary Acts, Strict Liability, and Negligence in Criminal Law*, Soc. Phil. & Pol'y, Spring 1990, at 84; Deborah W. Denno, *Crime and Consciousness: Science and Involuntary Acts*, 87 Minn. L. Rev. 269 (2002); Douglas Husak & Brian P. McLaughlin, *Time-Frames, Voluntary Acts, and Strict Liability*, 12 Law & Phil. 95 (1993); Michael S. Moore, *Responsibility and the Unconscious*, 53 S. Cal. L. Rev. 1563 (1980); Kevin W. Saunders, *Voluntary Acts and the Criminal Law: Justifying Culpability Based on the Existence of Volition*, 49 U. Pitt. L. Rev. 443 (1988); William Wilson, *Impaired Voluntariness: The Variable Standards*, 6 Buff. Crim. L. Rev. 1001 (2003); and the sources in Note 1, *supra*.

[13] See §§ 9.06.-.07, *infra*.

[14] E.g., Martin v. State, 17 So. 2d 427 (Ala. Ct. App. 1944) (*M* was charged with violation of an offense that provided that "[a]ny person who, while intoxicated or drunk, appears in any public place . . . and manifests a drunken condition [shall be convicted of an offense]"; the court interpreted the word "appears" to presuppose a voluntary appearance in public, which was not proven at *M*'s trial).

[15] Model Penal Code § 2.01. See § 9.05, infra.

[B] The "Act"

For purposes of the *actus reus* requirement, an "act" is, simply, a bodily movement, a muscular contraction.[16] A person "acts" when she pulls the trigger of a gun, raises her arm, blinks her eyes, turns the ignition key in an automobile, or simply puts one leg in the front of the other to walk. Understood this way, an act involves *physical*, although not necessarily *visible*, behavior. For example, the muscular contractions involved in talking — the movements of the vocal chords and tongue — constitute "acts" for present purposes. However, the term "act" *excludes* the internal mental processes of thinking about, or of developing an intention to do, a physical act (e.g., "mental acts").

Three aspects of the term "act" should be noted here. First, sometimes there can be bodily movement, but really no "act" at all by the person whose body has moved. For example, if *A* grabs *B*'s arm and swings it into *C*'s body, *B* has not acted (voluntarily or involuntarily), although her arm has moved. In this case, *B*'s arm was simply propelled, like a leaf blown by the wind, as the result of *A*'s act of grabbing her arm.

Second, the term "act" does *not* apply to the *results* of a person's bodily movements. For example, suppose that *D*, intending to kill *V*, places dynamite around *V*'s house, where *V* is asleep, and then activates a detonator that causes an explosion, killing *V*. In a criminal homicide prosecution, the pertinent acts by *D* are the positioning of the dynamite around *V*'s house and her activation of the detonator. The term "act," however, does *not* include the result of *D*'s conduct, i.e., *V*'s death. The latter constitutes the "social harm" element of the *actus reus*.[17]

Third, some courts and many scholars contend that, to be an "act" — or, more specifically, a human act — the muscular contraction must itself be voluntarily performed (as defined below). As one court put it, "[a]n [involuntary] 'act' . . . is in reality no act at all. It is merely a physical event. . . ."[18] Most modern lawyers and the Model Penal Code,[19] however, use the term "act" as it is defined in this subsection, as a bodily movement that can be voluntarily or involuntarily performed, as these terms are discussed immediately below.

[C] "Voluntary"

Unfortunately, the word "voluntary" is used by criminal lawyers in two different senses. The two usages of the term are often confused.

---

[16] Oliver Wendell Holmes, The Common Law 54 (1881).

[17] See § 9.10, *infra*.

[18] State v. Utter, 479 P.2d 946, 950 (Wash. Ct. App. 1971).

[19] See § 9.05, *infra*.

[1] Broad Meaning: In the Context of Defenses

The terms "voluntary" and "involuntary" are often used in discussing criminal law defenses to express the general conclusion that the defendant possessed or lacked sufficient free will to be blamed for her conduct.[20] Thus, it is sometimes said that a person who acted under duress or as the result of a mental disorder acted "involuntarily." This simply means that because the actor faced an extremely hard choice or was irrational, she does not deserve to be punished for her actions. This is *not* how the term is used in the context of the *actus reus* requirement.

[2] Narrow Meaning: In the Context of the *Actus Reus*

The term "voluntary" has a much narrower meaning when used to determine whether the *actus reus* of an offense has occurred. Nineteenth century scholar John Austin defined a "voluntary act" in this sense as a "movement of the body which follows our volition."[21] Similarly, Holmes described it as a "willed" contraction of a muscle.[22]

What did Austin mean by "volition," or Holmes by a "willed" act? Austin posited a view of human behavior, in which a person consciously decides to move a part of the body, and then that part of the body "invariably and immediately [follows] our wishes or desires for those same movements."[23] Applying this definition, nearly all human acts are voluntary,[24] and thus it may be more useful to give examples of *involuntary* acts. Examples of these include reflexive actions, spasms, epileptic seizures, and bodily movements while the actor is unconscious[25] or asleep.[26]

Austin's explanation of volition is too simplistic. Today, we realize that bodily movements occur as the result of complicated physiological and psychological mechanisms, many of which are not fully understood even now. However, no human act occurs simply as the result of wishing it to take place.[27] A person

---

[20] Fletcher, Note 6, *supra*, at 803.

[21] 1 John Austin, Lectures on Jurisprudence 426 (3d ed. 1869).

[22] Holmes, Note 16, *supra*, at 54.

[23] Austin, Note 21, *supra*, at 426 (emphasis omitted).

[24] Notice that if X points a gun at D and threatens to kill her unless she shoots V, D's coerced act of pulling the trigger of a gun to shoot V is "voluntary" in the Austinian sense, although it is arguably "involuntary" in the broader sense described in subsection [1], *supra*.

[25] The claim of unconsciousness is sometimes described as "automatism."

[26] See generally Rogers v. State, 105 S.W.3d 630, 636-38 (Tex. Crim. App. 2003); see also Fain v. Commonwealth, 78 Ky. 183 (1879) (sleepwalking); People v. Newton, 8 Cal. App. 3d 359 (Ct. App. 1970) (actions while unconscious); Fulcher v. State, 633 P.2d 142 (Wyo. 1981) (same).

[27] Denno, Note 12, *supra*, at 326 ("Some of the most powerful research in neuroscience suggests that the unconscious may be in charge of how human beings make decisions about willed movements, such as choosing when to flex a wrist, bend a figure, or . . . even to fire a gun.").

receives stimuli from outside and from within herself, which themselves act as further stimuli, some of which ultimately produce electrical impulses from the brain that result in bodily movements.[28]

So, what does it *really* mean to say that a person may not be punished unless her conduct includes a voluntary — "willed" — act? The concept of volition is tied to the notion that criminal law responsibility should only attach to those who are accountable for their actions in a very personal way. As Professor Sanford Kadish has explained, the criminal law distinguishes

> between genuine human actions, which are susceptible of praise and blame, and mere events brought about by physical causes which happen to involve a human body. . . . When a person claims the involuntary-act defense he is conceding that his own body made the motion but denies responsibility for it.[29]

Professor Kadish's point can be seen if one considers the difference in meaning of the following two sentences: (1) "I raised my arm"; and (2) "My arm came up."[30] Both statements suggest that a bodily movement has occurred. Yet, the difference in language expresses our understanding of the difference between a voluntary act (as described in the first sentence) and an involuntary one (the second sentence). In both cases, the arm movement was the result of impulses from the actor's brain. But, in the first sentence, the implication is that the act was the result of something more than mere physiological brain activity. That extra "something" was the more sophisticated thought process that goes into the "decision" to raise one's arm. Put slightly differently, a voluntary act involves the use of the human *mind*; an involuntary act involves the use of the human *brain*, without the aid of the mind.[31] With a voluntary act, a human being — a person — and not simply an organ of a human being, causes the bodily action.

Thus, when *D*'s arm strikes *V* as the result of an epileptic seizure, we sense that *D*'s *body*, but not *D* the person, has caused the impact. The movement of *D*'s arm is similar to a tree branch bending in the wind and striking *V*. When *D* "wills" her arm to move, however, we feel that *D*, and not simply her body, is responsible for *V*'s injury. Her "acting self" is implicated. A personal, human agency is involved in causing the bodily contact.[32] Another way of making this point is to say that involuntary acts are "inappropriate" actions, i.e., they are

---

[28] D. O'Connor, *The Voluntary Act*, 15 Med. Sci. L. 31, 32 (1975).

[29] Sanford H. Kadish, *Excusing Crime*, 75 Cal. L. Rev. 257, 259 (1987).

[30] Ludwig Wittgenstein, Philosophical Investigations 161 (G. Anscombe trans., 3d ed. 1958) ("[W]hat is left over if I subtract the fact that my arm goes up from the fact that I raise my arm?").

[31] See Bratty v. Attorney-General, [1963] A.C. 386, 409 (House of Lords) (an involuntary act is one "which is done by the muscles without any control by the mind").

[32] Moore, Note 12, *supra*, at 1576.

bodily movements not "required for any action . . . which the agent believed himself to be doing." They are "wild" acts, "not 'governed by the will' in the sense that they are not subordinated to the agent's conscious plans of action."[33]

One should be careful not to assume that an act is legally-speaking involuntary simply because the actor is unaware of what she is doing as she is doing it. For example, people act habitually: A chain-smoker may light up a cigarette "without thinking"; a driver coming home from work may change lanes on the freeway at precisely the same place each day, without even noticing that she is doing this. Although, at our best, we are aware of both our external and internal (mental) surroundings, sometimes we "don't notice that [we] notice. . . . [We are] aware of everything except [ourselves]."[34] In this sense, consciousness is a matter of degree,[35] and the law treats habitual acts as falling on the voluntary side of the continuum.

[3] "Voluntariness": At the Edges

[a] Hypnotism[36]

Suppose that X hypnotizes D to immediately shoot and kill V, or suppose that X uses post-hypnotic suggestion to get D to kill V. When D shoots V, is she acting "voluntarily," in the narrow (*actus reus*) sense of the term?

Depending on our ultimate understanding of how hypnotism works upon the human mind, D's acts might be classified as involuntary. The idea to kill V was planted in D's mind by X. If D lacked the ability to disregard X's "suggestions" — a matter of considerable dispute[37] — one may view D as little more than a marionette whose strings were pulled by X. The hypnotized subject might be equated to a sleepwalker, whose acts are considered legally involuntary.

A very plausible case, however, can be developed for the proposition that acts under hypnosis or as the result of hypnotic suggestion are voluntary. After all, in the hypnosis example, D *did* "will" her finger to pull the trigger of the gun. Although this "willed" act was in response to hypnotist X's suggestion, it is dif-

---

[33] H.L.A. Hart, Punishment and Responsibility 105 (1968).

[34] Leo Katz, Bad Acts and Guilty Minds: Conundrums of the Criminal Law 120 (1987).

[35] Denno, Note 12, *supra* (controversially arguing for the law to recognize voluntary, involuntary and "semi-voluntary" acts).

[36] See generally William P. Swain, Note, *Hypnotism and the Law*, 14 Vand. L. Rev. 1509 (1961); for discussion of the related issue of brainwashing, see Richard Delgado, *Ascription of Criminal States of Mind: Toward a Defense Theory for the Coercively Persuaded ("Brainwashed") Defendant*, 63 Minn. L. Rev. 1 (1978); Joshua Dressler, *Professor Delgado's "Brainwashing" Defense: Courting a Determinist Legal System*, 63 Minn. L. Rev. 335 (1979).

[37] Early scientific evidence in this regard is summarized in Ernest R. Hilgard, *Hypnosis*, 26 Ann. Rev. Psych. 19 (1975).

ficult to draw a principled line between this situation and that of a "weak-willed" person *not* under hypnosis who submits "blindly" to the suggestions of a far more dominant personality. It may be better — and more consistent with our assumptions about human free will[38] — to recognize the acts of the hypnotized subject as voluntary (in the narrow sense under discussion), and deal with her culpability, if any, as a potential excusing defense.

[b] Multiple Personality (or Dissociative Identity) Disorder[39]

As suggested in subsection [2], a voluntary act involves the use of the mind, and not simply of the brain. But, is it possible for more than one mind to inhabit a single brain?[40] William James reported[41] that in 1811 a melancholy Pennsylvania woman fell into a profound sleep from which she could not be awakened, and woke up eighteen hours later as a "different person," with an exuberant personality and no memory of her past. Five weeks later, after another deep sleep, her old personality returned. This woman may have suffered from what has been described as "multiple personality disorder" (MPD), and is now called "dissociative identity disorder" (DID), a recognized mental disease.[42]

A person suffering from MPD/DID may be insane, but the condition, in a strange way, arguably implicates the voluntary act requirement. For example, in *State v. Grimsley*,[43] G (Robin Grimsley), who suffered from MPD, drove an automobile under the influence of alcohol while she was dissociated from her primary personality. G introduced psychiatric evidence that she had a secondary personality, Jennifer, who had a drinking problem, which was in control when she was in the automobile. As a consequence, she argued that she, Robin, was unconscious while Jennifer was acting. The court rejected G's reasoning. It stated:

> There was only one person driving the car and only one person accused of drunken driving. It is immaterial whether she was in one state of consciousness or another, so long as in the personality then controlling her behavior, she was conscious and her actions were a product of her own volition.

---

[38] See § 9.02[D], *infra*.

[39] See generally Elyn R. Saks, Jekyll on Trial: Multiple Personality Disorder and Criminal Law (1997).

[40] See Katz, Note 34, *supra*, at 104.

[41] William James, The Principles of Psychology 359-63 (1981).

[42] American Psychiatric Association, Diagnostic and Statistical Manual of Mental Disorders 257 (4th ed. 1994).

[43] 444 N.E.2d 1071 (Ohio Ct. App. 1982).

But, who is the "her" in the phrase "product of her own volition"? Robin and Jennifer had separate identities; Jennifer did not think of herself as Robin, or vice-versa. With separate memories, separate feelings, and separate characters, can we genuinely treat *G* as a single volitional agent? Although few courts have confronted this question, *Grimsley*'s approach is typical. As another court that has confronted the issue has put the matter, "we will not begin to parcel criminal accountability out among the various inhabitants of the mind."[44]

[D] Voluntary Act Requirement: Rationale

Why should an involuntary actor who causes harm escape punishment? One frequent explanation is that the law cannot deter involuntary movement.[45]

This utilitarian explanation is insufficient. Although the threat of punishment cannot deter a person while she is acting involuntarily, e.g., during a seizure, it can motivate her to adjust her behavior, e.g., to take medication or not use a dangerous instrumentality, so as to reduce the risk to others from her involuntary conduct. Moreover, even if the *threat* of the criminal sanction cannot deter, its *use* is one rational way to segregate (or in some other manner render less dangerous) involuntary actors. To a utilitarian lawmaker, whose overall goal is to protect society from dangerous people, the criminal justice system is "simply another method of social control."[46] That is, the line between civil commitment and criminal punishment is blurry, at best, in a purely utilitarian system of laws,[47] so there is no reason categorically to exclude liability for involuntary actions.

The voluntary act requirement is far more closely linked to the retributivist's respect for human autonomy. Retributive theory is premised on the view that "the critical distinction between criminal law and other systems of confinement . . . is that the criminal sanction carries with it something more — the stigmatization of moral blameworthiness."[48] Criminal punishment, with its attendant pain, stigma and formal condemnation of the offender, should only be imposed on those who deserve it, i.e., on those who act as the result of free choice. In the absence of a voluntary act, there is no basis for social censure.

---

[44] Kirkland v. State, 304 S.E.2d 561, 564 (Ga. Ct. App. 1983).

[45] American Law Institute, Comment to § 2.01, at 214-15.

[46] Richard Singer, *The Resurgence of Mens Rea: II — Honest But Unreasonable Mistake of Fact in Self Defense*, 28 B.C. L. Rev. 459, 512 n.285 (1987).

[47] Packer, Note 11, *supra*, at 77-78.

[48] Singer, Note 46, *supra*, at 512 n.285.

[E] Burden of Proof

Courts frequently describe "involuntariness" as a "defense."[49] To the extent that the word "involuntariness" is used in the broad sense of the term,[50] this characterization is appropriate. However, omissions aside,[51] a "voluntary act" (in the narrow, *actus reus*, sense of the term) is a prerequisite to criminal responsibility, i.e., it is an element of every criminal offense.[52]

This distinction — that a voluntary act is an element of a criminal offense and not simply a defense to it — is of procedural significance. Under the Due Process Clause, the government must prove beyond a reasonable doubt every element of an offense, but it is not constitutionally required to carry the burden of persuasion regarding affirmative defenses.[53] Despite the appellation "defense," therefore, the prosecution should be required to prove beyond a reasonable doubt that a defendant's conduct included a voluntary act.[54] Thus, for example, one who is unconscious at the time of the alleged act, but whose unconsciousness was not the result of a mental disease or defect, should not need to plead insanity, an affirmative defense; and, if acquitted on the basis of unconsciousness, such a person, unlike an insanity acquittee, is not subject thereby to automatic commitment to a mental hospital.[55]

[F] The Issue of "Time-Framing"[56]

As explained in this chapter section, a person is not ordinarily guilty of an offense in the absence of a voluntary act. The prosecution does not need to show, however, that *every* act, or even that the defendant's *last* act, was voluntary in order to establish criminal liability.[57] It is sufficient that the defendant's conduct *included* a voluntary act.

But, what does it mean to say that the defendant's "conduct" must "include" a voluntary act? If one identifies the defendant's conduct broadly enough, it will always include a voluntary act. After all, even if *D*, a killer, was unconscious at the time of the homicide, she was surely conscious and acting voluntarily some

---

[49] E.g., People v. Newton, 8 Cal. App. 3d 376-77 (Ct. App. 1970); People v. Grant, 377 N.E.2d 4, 7 (Ill. 1978); Fulcher v. State, 633 P.2d 142, 145 (Wyo. 1981).

[50] See § 9.02[C][1], *supra*.

[51] See § 9.07, *infra*.

[52] 2 Paul H. Robinson, Criminal Law Defenses 263 (1984).

[53] See § 7.03[B], *supra*.

[54] E.g., Baird v. State, 604 N.E.2d 1170, 1176 (Ind. 1992).

[55] McClain v. State, 678 N.E.2d 104 (Ind. 1997); Fulcher v. State, 633 P.2d 142 (Wyo. 1981).

[56] See generally Moore, Note 1, *supra* at 35-37; Alexander, Note 12, *supra*; Husak & McLaughlin, Note 12, *supra*; Mark Kelman, *Interpretive Construction in the Substantive Criminal Law*, 33 Stan. L. Rev. 591 (1981).

[57] State v. Burrell, 609 A.2d 751, 753 (N.H. 1992).

time prior to the moment of the victim's death, if only when she woke up in the morning, dressed, and drove to the scene of the crime.

Professor Mark Kelman has suggested that courts can choose between narrow and broad "time-frames" in identifying the conduct that must include a voluntary act.[58] He contends that the time-framing choice is "arational"; the decision to frame the actor's conduct broadly — or narrowly — is based (if only subconsciously) on a court's desired outcome. If a court wants to convict a defendant who acted involuntarily at some point during the commission of an offense, it will construct a time-frame broad enough to include some remote, but voluntary, act; if it wants the defendant to escape responsibility, it will construct a narrower time-frame, which excludes the prior voluntary movements. If Kelman is right in this regard, of course, the voluntary act requirement is "vacuous."[59]

Manipulation of the voluntary act requirement can be avoided if a court applies the fully stated rule of criminal responsibility: *A person is not guilty of an offense unless her conduct, which must include a voluntary act, and which must be accompanied[60] by a culpable state of mind (the mens rea of the offense), is the actual and proximate cause of the social harm, as proscribed by the offense.* That is, in time-framing, a court may not properly choose *any* conduct it wishes; it must focus on the *relevant* conduct, i.e., the conduct (performed with the requisite *mens rea*) that actually and proximately caused the social harm of the offense charged. Once it identifies *this* conduct, the court can fairly determine whether it includes a voluntary act.

To see how a court should construct the proper time-frame, consider, first, a simple example. *D* decides to kill *V*. She builds a bomb and mails it to *V* in a package. The bomb reaches its destination three days later. Coincidentally, at precisely the moment *V* opens the package and is killed in the ensuing explosion, *D* is asleep 3000 miles away. *D* is prosecuted for murder, which for current purposes is defined as the "intentional killing of another human being." At the murder trial, it will do no good for *D* to point out that she was asleep at the time of *V*'s death. The relevant conduct — the acts that were the actual and proximate cause of *V*'s death, and which were accompanied by the requisite intent to kill — occurred three days earlier, when *D* acted voluntarily.

Now, consider a more difficult case. In *People v. Decina*,[61] *D* was an epileptic who killed four children when the car he was driving went out of control during a seizure. The prosecutor alleged that *D* knew that he was highly susceptible to seizures and failed to take proper precautions. As a result, *D* was

---

[58] Kelman, Note 56, *supra*, at 593-94, 603-05.

[59] Alexander, Note 12, *supra*, at 91.

[60] See Chapter 15 (Concurrence of Elements), *infra*.

[61] 138 N.E.2d 799 (N.Y. 1956).

prosecuted for "criminal negligence in the operation of a vehicle, resulting in death."

Notice that if a court constructed an extremely narrow time-frame — specifically, the conduct at the instant the car struck the victims — *D*'s conduct did not include a voluntary act. A broader time-frame, however, would include the voluntary acts of entering the car, turning the ignition key, and driving.

The appellate court properly affirmed *D*'s conviction. This is because *D* was charged with "the *operation of a vehicle* resulting in death." It was perfectly appropriate, therefore, for the prosecution to include in its focus the voluntary acts immediately preceding the epileptic seizure that constituted the arguably negligent operation of the car.[62]

In contrast is *Martin v. State*:[63] *M*, while intoxicated, was taken from his home by the police and placed by them on a public highway, where he used loud and profane language. *M* was charged with an offense that provided in relevant part that "[a]ny person who, while intoxicated . . . , appears in any public place . . . and manifests a drunken condition by boisterous or indecent conduct" is guilty of a misdemeanor. A broad time-frame might suggest that *M* was guilty because he presumably became drunk voluntarily, before the police arrived at his home. However, the court applied a narrower time-frame, one that discounted these prior voluntary acts; it held that *M*'s conviction had to be overturned because the statute required a voluntary appearance on the highway, which did not occur here.

A careful inspection of the statute shows that the *Martin* court was correct in its analysis. To be guilty of this offense, *M* had to: (1) appear in public; and (2) act there in a boisterous or indecent manner; (3) while intoxicated. The conduct stated in (1) had to include a voluntary act. The same was true for the conduct specified in (2). By the express wording of the statute, this conduct had to occur "while" *M* was intoxicated; it did not matter, therefore, how *M* became intoxicated, only that *while* he was in that condition he voluntarily appeared in public and voluntarily acted boisterously. Thus, the court was right to focus on how *M* ended up on the highway, rather than on how he became intoxicated.

---

[62] See State v. Burrell, 609 A.2d 751, 753 (N.H. 2003); Rogers v. State, 105 S.W.3d 630, 638 (Tex. Crim. App. 2003) (both cases stating that the last act of the defendant, pulling the trigger of a gun, need not be voluntary, as long as the homicidal conduct, as a whole, includes a voluntary act).

[63] 17 So. 2d 427 (Ala. Ct. App. 1944).

§ 9.03 VOLUNTARY ACT: SUPPOSED (BUT NOT REAL) EXCEPTIONS TO THE REQUIREMENT

[A] Poorly Drafted Statutes

Some statutes appear to dispense with the requirement of a voluntary act. For example, a Vermont statute prohibited persons not married to one another "to be *found* in bed together."[64] Read literally, this statute would unfairly and implausibly allow the conviction of a person who, while unconscious, was placed in a bed with someone to whom she was not married. Although a court could conceivably apply such a statute literally,[65] it is likely (and to be hoped) that it would interpret the law to require a voluntary act.

[B] Status Offenses

In the past, many legislatures enacted so-called status offenses. For example, vagrancy laws made it an offense to "be a vagrant." Likewise, a California statute prohibited one "to be addicted to the use of narcotics." These offenses required proof of a status (vagrancy or addiction), rather than conduct.

The Supreme Court has not looked kindly upon status offenses. It invalidated a typical vagrancy law on the ground that it was unduly vague and could result in arbitrary police enforcement;[66] and it held that a California addiction statute violated the Eighth Amendment bar on cruel and unusual punishment.[67] Very likely any statute that punishes a person for a mere propensity to act will run afoul of constitutional principles.[68]

[C] Crimes of Possession

Virtually all states prohibit possession of contraband (e.g., cocaine) or criminal instrumentalities (e.g., "burglars' tools"[69]). On their face, these penal pro-

---

[64] See State v. Woods, 179 A. 1 (Vt. 1935) (applying Vt. Pub. L. § 8602 (1933), repealed in 1979) (emphasis added).

[65] E.g., Regina v. Larsonneur, (1933) 24 Cr. App. R. 74 (upholding the conviction of *L*, a French citizen, for being an alien "found" in the United Kingdom without permission, based on the following facts: She entered England with permission; when English authorities learned she was committing acts of prostitution there, she left for Ireland; Irish officials arrested her and handed her back to English police, whereupon *L* was charged with the offense).

[66] Papachristou v. City of Jacksonville, 405 U.S. 156 (1972). See generally § 5.03, *supra*.

[67] Robinson v. California, 370 U.S. 660 (1962).

[68] See § 9.04, *infra*.

[69] E.g., Cal. Penal Code § 466 (Deering 2005) ("Every person having upon him or her in his or her possession a picklock, crow, keybit, . . . or other instrument or tool with intent feloniously to break or enter into any building . . . is guilty of misdemeanor.").

visions do not require the defendant to act, only that she passively possess the prohibited objects.

Crimes of possession are "inchoate," or incomplete, offenses. That is, their real purpose is to provide the police with a basis for arresting those whom they suspect will later commit a socially injurious act (e.g., sell narcotics, or use the tools to commit a burglary).

Possession crimes do not necessarily dispense with the voluntary act requirement. Courts interpret possession statutes to require proof that the defendant knowingly procured or received the property possessed (thus, a voluntary act must be proven), or that she failed to dispossess herself of the object after she became aware of its presence.[70] In the latter case, "possession" is equivalent to an omission, in which the defendant has a statutory duty to dispossess herself of the property.[71] She is not guilty if the contraband was "planted" on her, and she did not have sufficient time to terminate her possession after she learned of its presence.

§ 9.04 VOLUNTARY ACT: CONSTITUTIONAL LAW[72]

The United States Supreme Court has twice considered the question of whether voluntary conduct is a constitutional prerequisite to criminal punishment.

[A] *Robinson v. California*[73]

The California legislature enacted a law making it an offense, punishable by incarceration of from ninety days to one year, for a person to "be addicted to the use of narcotics." No act by the defendant — just his present addiction — was required for conviction. The Supreme Court ruled that the statute violated the Eighth and Fourteenth Amendments to the United States Constitution.

The Court focused on the fact that the statute made the illness of drug addiction (a status that it pointed out could be contracted innocently or involuntarily) a criminal offense. The justices analogized drug addiction to other illnesses

---

[70] See, e.g., People v. Ackerman, 274 N.E.2d 125, 126 (Ill. App. Ct. 1971); State v. Flaherty, 400 A.2d 363, 366 (Me. 1979).

[71] See § 9.07, *infra*.

[72] See generally Joshua Dressler, *Kent Greenawalt, Criminal Responsibility, and the Supreme Court: How a Moderate Scholar Can Appear Immoderate Thirty Years Later*, 74 Notre Dame L. Rev. 1507 (1999); Kent Greenawalt, *"Uncontrollable" Actions and the Eighth Amendment: Implications of Powell v. Texas*, 69 Colum. L. Rev. 927 (1969); David Robinson, Jr., *Powell v. Texas: The Case of the Intoxicated Shoeshine Man; Some Reflections a Generation Later by a Participant*, 26 Am. J. Crim. L. 401 (1999).

[73] 370 U.S. 660 (1962).

— mental illness, leprosy, venereal disease, and the common cold: If a state were to punish persons for suffering from *these* ailments, it would "doubtless be universally thought to be an infliction of cruel and unusual punishment." The Court believed that the same discernment should be shown the status of drug addiction.

The constitutional infirmity in this case was not that a drug addict might receive a ninety-day or longer jail sentence, but rather that he could be punished at all. "Even one day in prison," the justices said, would have rendered Robinson's fate impermissible. Essentially, the Court held that, although a legislature may use criminal sanctions against the unauthorized manufacture, sale, purchase, or possession of narcotics, and may attack the social problems arising from drug addiction through health education, civil commitment, and other non-penal programs, California lacked constitutional authority to treat Robinson as a criminal solely because of his addiction.

The Court's approach to the Eighth Amendment is intriguing. Perhaps unwittingly, it invoked retributive, rather than utilitarian, values of punishment. That is, retributivism is based on the principle that punishment should not be inflicted unless a person voluntarily chooses to commit a socially harmful act; the condemnatory feature of criminal punishment should not be used against one whose only "crime" is her illness. In contrast, a utilitarian would not categorically rule out the use of the criminal justice system, among other methods, to deal with drug addiction. To utilitarians, there is no wall absolutely separating civil from criminal commitment; the law should be permitted to use every weapon available to it to reduce net social pain.

Essentially, the retributive message of *Robinson* seemed to be the following: Although drug addicts constitute a danger to society and, therefore, it may be *rational* to incarcerate some of them, it is *indecent* to punish them simply because they are sick.

[B] *Powell v. Texas*[74]

Leroy Powell was charged with violation of a Texas statute that prohibited "get[ting] drunk or be[ing] found in a state of intoxication in any public place." Powell attempted to prove at trial that he suffered from the disease of chronic alcoholism and that, therefore, he was unable to avoid appearing in public in a drunken condition. His punishment, he argued, violated the underlying principles enunciated in *Robinson*. After all, Powell was a sick person. To the extent that he represented a social problem, Texas should be required to deal with him in a non-criminal manner.

Speaking for only four justices, Justice Thurgood Marshall upheld Powell's conviction and $20 fine. He distinguished *Robinson* on the ground that Powell

---

[74] 392 U.S. 514 (1968).

"was convicted, not for being a chronic alcoholic, but for being in public while drunk on a particular occasion." As such, Texas was punishing conduct, not an illness. The plurality explained the import of *Robinson* as follows:

> The entire thrust of *Robinson*'s interpretation of the Cruel and Unusual Punishment Clause is that criminal penalties may be inflicted only if the accused has committed some act, has engaged in some behavior, which society has an interest in preventing, or perhaps in historical common law terms, has committed some *actus reus*.

Although this statement of *Robinson* is correct in terms of its holding, *Powell*'s underlying reasoning runs counter to *Robinson*'s retributivist thrust. In *Powell*, Justice Marshall said that the Court was "unable to assert that the use of the criminal process as a means of dealing with the public aspects of problem drinking can never be defined as rational." He said it would be "tragic to return large numbers of helpless, sometimes dangerous and frequently unsanitary inebriates to the streets of our cities without even the opportunity to sober up adequately which a brief jail term provides." Thus, the plurality blurred the rather bright line drawn in *Robinson* between the civil and criminal processes.

If Justice Marshall's test of rationality had been applied in *Robinson* to drug addicts, the Court might have determined that the use of the criminal sanction was one rational way to deal with the addiction problem. To the *Robinson* Court, however, it was wrong to punish an addict for her disease, even if housing her in a prison until she could "get clean" was one sensible approach to her rehabilitation.

Why did the Court back off from the possible implications of *Robinson*? The answer lies in Justice Marshall's observation that a broad reading of *Robinson* would have made the Supreme Court, "under the aegis of the Cruel and Unusual Punishment Clause, the ultimate arbiter of the [states'] standards of criminal responsibility."[75] That is, if the Eighth Amendment prevents a state from punishing an alcoholic for the act of becoming drunk in public, it might also bar punishing a drug addict for possessing drugs[76] or even for committing a robbery in order to secure the money necessary to feed her habit. It would then be just a small step to the proposition that the Eighth Amendment requires states to draft specific criminal law defenses (e.g., insanity and duress) that would exculpate persons whose conduct was "involuntary" in some sense of that term.[77] The Court was unwilling to intrude that far into the state penal systems.

---

[75] In concurrence, too, Justices Black and Harlan observed that a broad reading of *Robinson* "would have [had] a revolutionary impact on the criminal law."

[76] See United States v. Moore, 486 F.2d 1139 (D.C. Cir. 1973) (rejecting the petitioner's claim that he could not be convicted of possession of heroin because of his overpowering addiction to drugs).

[77] Sanford H. Kadish, *Fifty Years of Criminal Law: An Opinionated Review*, 87 Cal. L. Rev. 943, 965 (1999) ("The *Robinson* decision could plausibly have been seen as a vital opening toward establishing lack of self-control as a constitutional bar to punishment.").

[C] Current Law: *Powell* in Light of *Robinson*

The Court was splintered in *Powell*: there was a four-justice plurality, a concurrence in the result by a fifth justice, and a four-justice dissent. Nonetheless, this much is clear: (1) *Powell* did not overrule *Robinson*; and (2) these two cases stand for the proposition that a state may not dispense with the criminal law requirement of an *actus reus*. That is, the government may not punish a person for her thoughts alone, or for her mere propensity to commit crimes: The special rule of omissions aside, *some* conduct by the defendant is constitutionally required.

Powell might stand for more than this, however. The four-vote dissent would have held that a person may not constitutionally be punished for exhibiting "a characteristic part of the pattern of [a] disease . . . which . . . [is] not the consequence of [her] volition." Following this reading, an addict could be punished if she robbed a bank to support her habit, but she could *not* be punished for possession or use of narcotics, a "characteristic part of the pattern" of drug addiction. Because this broad reading of the Constitution "cancels out" the four-justice plurality opinion, the views of the remaining member of the Court, Byron White, are critical. He observed:

> If it cannot be a crime to have an irresistible compulsion to use narcotics, *Robinson v. California*, . . . I do not see how it can constitutionally be a crime to yield to such a compulsion. Punishing an addict for using drugs convicts for addiction under a different name. Distinguishing between the two crimes is like forbidding criminal conviction for being sick with flu or epilepsy but permitting punishment for running a fever or having a convulsion.

In *Powell*, the defendant was not prosecuted for use or possession of alcohol, but for the "voluntary" act (in the willed-muscular-contraction sense of the term) of going from a private place into a public area in an intoxicated condition.[78] Therefore, Justice White did not dissent, but instead concurred in the result. The thrust of his opinion is that as long as *Robinson* is the law, he was prepared to recognize a constitutional defense to involuntary conduct that is an inevitable symptom of the disease syndrome from which the person suffers. In light of the dissent, therefore, there were five votes — a majority — for *this* proposition.

None of the justices involved in *Powell* still sit on the bench. In light of the more conservative nature of the present-day Supreme Court, it is foolhardy to assume that today's high court would constitutionalize a voluntariness requirement (in *any* sense of the term "voluntary"), if the proper case came along.

---

[78] Justice White suggested that some homeless alcoholics might be entitled to a defense under the Texas statute: "I would think a showing [by them] could be made that resisting drunkenness is impossible and that avoiding public places when intoxicated is also impossible."

Therefore, the only safe propositions are those set out in the first paragraph of this subsection.

§ 9.05 VOLUNTARY ACT: MODEL PENAL CODE

[A] General Principles

The Model Penal Code provides that no person may be convicted of a crime in the absence of conduct that "includes a voluntary act or the omission to perform an act of which he is physically capable."[79] The Code allocates to the prosecution the responsibility to persuade the factfinder beyond a reasonable doubt of the existence of a voluntary act.[80]

The Code defines the term "act" as a "bodily movement whether voluntary or involuntary."[81] It does not define the term "voluntary," except "partially and indirectly,"[82] by listing bodily movements that are involuntary: reflexes; convulsions; conduct during unconsciousness, sleep, or due to hypnosis;[83] and, generally, any conduct that "is not a product of the effort or determination of the actor, either conscious or habitual."[84] The Model Code also provides that, for purposes of the voluntary act rule, "possession" is an "act" if the possessor either knowingly obtained the object possessed or knew she was in control of it "for a sufficient period to have been able to terminate . . . possession."[85]

[B] Exception to the Rule

The "voluntary act" rule stated in Section 2.01 of the Model Penal Code applies to liability for "crimes," i.e., felonies, misdemeanors, and petty misdemeanors.[86] However, Section 2.05(1) of the Code provides that the requirements set out in Section 2.01 do not apply to offenses that constitute "violations," unless a court determines that application of Section 2.01 is "consistent with

---

[79] Model Penal Code § 2.01(1).

[80] Model Penal Code § 1.12(1).

[81] Model Penal Code § 1.13(2).

[82] American Law Institute, Comment to § 2.01, at 219.

[83] The drafters of the Code justified this controversial inclusion on the ground that conduct during hypnosis or resulting from hypnotic suggestion is "characterized by the subject's dependence on the hypnotist, [so] it does not seem politic to treat conduct [in such circumstances] as voluntary, despite the state of consciousness involved." *Id*. at 221 (footnote deleted). The Commentary acknowledged, however, that the general view is that a hypnotized subject will not follow suggestions contrary to her moral views. For more on hypnosis, including arguments against the Code's position, see § 9.02[C][3][a], *supra*.

[84] Model Penal Code § 2.01(2)(d).

[85] Model Penal Code § 2.01(4).

[86] Model Penal Code § 1.04(1) (classifying crimes).

effective enforcement of the law defining the offense." A "violation" is an offense for which the maximum penalty is a fine or civil penalty.[87]

Accordingly, under Section 2.05, a driver who suffers an unforeseeable blackout and, as a consequence, fails to halt at a stop sign, may be convicted of a motor vehicle violation in the absence of proof of any voluntary act. The Commentary to Section 2.05 concedes that the fairness of this outcome is "debatable";[88] but with extremely minor offenses, the drafters of the Code determined that litigation of involuntary-act claims should not be permitted to undermine effective law enforcement.

§ 9.06 OMISSIONS: GENERAL PRINCIPLES[89]

[A] General Rule

Consider the following two incidents. First, in *People v. Beardsley*,[90] a married man failed to come to the aid of the woman with whom he was having an affair after she took a lethal dose of poison in his presence. She died. Second, in an infamous after-midnight 1964 assault in Queens, New York, a young woman, Kitty Genovese, cried out for help for approximately thirty minutes as she was attacked and ultimately killed outside her apartment building. It was later determined that thirty-eight of her neighbors heard her cries and saw the attack in progress from their apartment windows, but did nothing.[91]

In both situations, a human being died. In both situations, one or more persons knew that a life was in jeopardy. In both situations, the harm that occurred might have been prevented or mitigated at no apparent physical risk of harm to those aware of the victim's plight. Nonetheless, adulterer Beardsley was not held criminally responsible for his omission; and none of Genovese's neighbors were prosecuted in relation to her death.

---

[87] Model Penal Code § 1.04(5).

[88] American Law Institute, Comment to § 2.05, at 292.

[89] See generally Hall, Note 2, *supra*, at 190-211; Katz, Note 34, *supra*, at 135-53; Moore, Note 1, *supra*, at 22-34, 46-59; Larry Alexander, *Criminal Liability for Omissions: An Inventory of Issues in Criminal Law Theory*, in Criminal Law Theory: Doctrines of the General Part 121 (2002); Joshua Dressler, *Some Brief Thoughts (Mostly Negative) About "Bad Samaritan" Laws*, 40 Santa Clara L. Rev. 971 (2000); George P. Fletcher, *On the Moral Irrelevance of Bodily Movements*, 142 U. Pa. L. Rev. 1443 (1994); Graham Hughes, *Criminal Omissions*, 67 Yale L.J. 590 (1958); F.M. Kamm, *Action, Omission, and the Stringency of Duties*, 142 U. Pa. L. Rev. 1493 (1994); Arthur Leavens, *A Causation Approach to Criminal Omissions*, 76 Cal. L. Rev. 547 (1988); A.P. Simester, *Why Omissions Are Special*, 1 Legal Theory 311 (1995); Patricia Smith, *Omission and Responsibility in Legal Theory*, 9 Legal Theory 221 (2003); A.D. Woozley, *A Duty to Rescue: Some Thoughts on Criminal Liability*, 69 Va. L. Rev. 1273 (1983).

[90] 113 N.W. 1128 (Mich. 1907).

[91] See generally Abraham M. Rosenthal, Thirty Eight Witnesses (1964).

The lesson to be learned from these two incidents is that not every moral obligation to act creates a concomitant legal duty. *Subject to a few limited exceptions, a person has no criminal law duty to act to prevent harm to another, even if the person imperiled may lose her life in the absence of assistance.* In essence, the criminal law distinguishes between an act that affirmatively *causes* harm, on the one hand, and the failure of a bystander to take measures to *prevent* harm, on the other hand. As Professor Woozley has described the principle: "[T]he law should see to it that we do not do harm, but not see to it that, in the absence of a specific statutory duty, we do things to prevent harm."[92] As a matter of criminal law doctrine, we are not our brothers' and sisters' keepers.

[B] Criticisms of the General Rule

Many critics of the omission rule consider it morally repugnant. As one scholar stated in relation to *Beardsley*, "[i]n a civilized society, a man who finds himself with a helplessly ill person who has no other source of aid should be under a duty to summon help, whether the person is his wife, his mistress, a prostitute or a Chief Justice."[93] The implication is that there is no meaningful moral difference between an act and an omission: There is no moral difference between walking into the Pacific Ocean and drowning oneself, and sitting on the beach until one is submerged by the incoming tide;[94] there is no meaningful difference between slamming shut one's open door to bar entry of a child trying to escape a wild animal, and failing to open a closed door for the same child.[95]

The effect of the omission rule is to exonerate people who are guilty of moral indifference, such as Kitty Genovese's neighbors in Queens. The rule may even absolve one who is guilty of a more culpable state of mind. For example, consider *S*, an Olympic-level swimmer, who stands by and watches an infant (not her own) drown in a wading pool. According to the general no-liability rule, *S* is not criminally responsible for the death, although she could have saved the child at no risk to herself, even if she failed to act because she experiences sadistic pleasure watching others suffer.

From a utilitarian perspective, the callousness of the omission rule may breed contempt for society's system of criminal justice. In contrast, a rule that requires people to assist others in peril might promote social cohesion; and some wrongdoers might desist from planned criminal activity if they knew that others were likely to intervene.

---

[92] Woozley, Note 89, *supra*, at 1273.

[93] Hughes, Note 89, *supra*, at 624.

[94] Cruzan v. Dir., Mo. Dep't. of Health, 497 U.S. 261, 296 (1990) (Scalia, J., concurring).

[95] Katz, Note 34, *supra*, at 140.

[C] Defense of the General Rule

Arguments vary in defense of the general no-liability-for-omissions rule. There are pragmatic arguments. First, if people were as legally responsible for their "not-doings"[96] as they are for their harmful "doings," criminal prosecutions would burgeon, adding to the expense of litigation and creating huge backlogs of cases.

A second practical problem is one of line-drawing. For example, in the Genovese case, should all thirty-eight persons who heard her cries for help be held responsible, or only those who heard her in the early moments and, therefore, had the maximum time to help? Either the police and prosecutors would have nearly unbridled discretion in determining whom to prosecute, thereby raising legality concerns,[97] or a legislature would need to devise difficult-to-apply standards, which might result in similar vagueness problems for juries.

Third, liability for non-actions would create serious problems of proof of *mens rea*. For example, if Beardsley had poisoned his mistress, a jury could easily have inferred that he intended to kill her. Or, if a person puts a loaded gun to another's head and pulls the trigger, it is sensible to infer an intent to kill. Omissions, however, are more ambiguous. In the Genovese tragedy, it is possible that some of the apartment residents assumed that someone else had called the police;[98] and one who stands by as a murder occurs may quite plausibly do so out of fear or shock, rather than malice.

How, too, does one go about proving causation in omission cases? As developed in Chapter 14, a person is not responsible for an offense unless she caused the harm in question. Some philosophers argue that a non-act is *never* the cause of a consequence — how can nothing be the cause of something? — but even if this claim is false,[99] more line-drawing problems arise. It is easy to determine that the victim in *Beardsley* "caused" her own death by ingesting poison; it is far more difficult to say that Beardsley's failure to secure medical care for his paramour caused her death. She might have died from the poison despite his best efforts. Similarly, even if one of Genovese's neighbors had called the police, how can we

---

[96] Simester, Note 89, *supra*, at 320.

[97] See § 5.03, *supra*.

[98] See Bibb Latané & John Darley, *Group Inhibition of Bystander Intervention in Emergencies*, 10 J. Personality & Soc. Psych. 215, 215 (1968) ("We have found that the mere perception that other people are also witnessing the event will markedly decrease the likelihood that an individual will intervene in an emergency."); Katz, Note 34, *supra*, at 150 ("For Kitty Genovese, then, there was no safety in numbers.").

[99] There is rich debate on the subject of causation-for-omissions. For example, see John Harris, *The Marxist Conception of Violence*, 4 Phil. & Pub. Aff. 192 (1975); Eric Mack, *Bad Samaritanism and the Causation of Harm*, 9 Phil. & Pub. Aff. 230 (1980); see also H.L.A. Hart & Tony Honoré, Causation in the Law 48 (2d ed. 1985) (concluding that some non-actions are causes because they represent an unexpected "deviation from a system or routine").

know whether help would have come in time? For that matter, if they *were* a cause of her death, isn't *everyone* in the world a cause, since *nobody* helped her?

The line-drawing problems raise more than purely pragmatic concerns. If it is difficult to determine a non-actor's mental state or degree of contribution to resulting harm, there is an enhanced risk that a jury will *incorrectly* resolve these issues. That is, they might find an intent to cause harm when none was present, or they may attach causal responsibility where none exists. Thus, the risk of punishing a legally innocent person is substantially enhanced.

A general rule that persons are criminally responsible for their omissions could also have an unintended counter-utilitarian effect. Although bystanders sometimes prevent harm, they often cause injury to themselves and others by their intervention. An intervenor, helping out of fear of criminal responsibility if she stands by, may provide poor medical assistance, or fire a weapon unsafely, or misconstrue what she observes (e.g., she may believe that an undercover police officer in performance of her duties is a criminal wrongdoer).

Defenders of the general rule also reject the moral claim that omissions and acts are morally symmetrical. Causing harm and allowing it to occur are not morally similar. "[A] doctrine of general liability for not-doings would result in a system that is largely insensitive to ideas of individual responsibility and authorship."[100] The man who stabbed Kitty Genovese is the person who harmed her. Those who figuratively stood by and did nothing did not hurt her. "[W]ithout an act/omissions doctrine like the one our legal system presently recognizes, this truth would be valueless."[101]

Or, consider the drowning child hypothetical involving S, the Olympic swimmer. Suppose that we learned that X pushed the child into the pool. Even assuming that S obtained sadistic pleasure from watching the child die, would we say that X's act and S's omission are morally equivalent? X *caused* the child to die; S merely *permitted* it. X changed the state of affairs by putting the child in jeopardy; S merely failed to put things right. X killed the child; S withheld a benefit. Advocates of the no-liability-for-omissions rule contend that the positive duty not to make the world worse is, morally speaking, more stringent than the duty to make it better.[102]

The latter point leads to a final justification for the general no-liability rule, which is that the omission doctrine is consistent with the principle of autonomy. In a society such as ours, which values individual freedom and limited governmental power, the criminal justice system should be used discriminately. Even if a person is *morally* obligated to come to the aid of others, not every violation of a moral duty should result in criminal punishment. It is the role of religion

---

[100] Simester, Note 89, *supra*, at 329.

[101] *Id.*

[102] Kamm, Note 89, *supra*, at 1493.

and other moral institutions to perfect human character; the purpose of the criminal law is limited to deterring or punishing persons for causing harm. If it were otherwise, the criminal justice system would intrude too deeply into peoples' lives.

§ 9.07 OMISSIONS: EXCEPTIONS TO THE NO-LIABILITY RULE

[A] Common Law Duty to Act: "Commission by Omission"

[1] Overview

In the limited circumstances set out below in subsection [2], liability for a criminal offense may be predicated on an omission, rather than on a voluntary act. Such cases involve what may be termed "commission by omission"[103] liability. Put more fully, a defendant's omission of a common law duty to act, *assuming that she was physically capable of performing the act*, serves as a legal substitute for a voluntary act. If the remaining elements of the charged offense are proven (that is, the omitter caused[104] the social harm of the offense with the requisite *mens rea*), the defendant may be convicted of the crime. Thus, for example, courts have upheld criminal homicide convictions based on omissions. A person with a legal duty to act who negligently fails to provide needed care to someone in great medical distress may be guilty of manslaughter if the person dies as a result of the omission.[105] A person who has a legal duty to report a fire may be convicted of some form of criminal homicide if her failure to report the fire recklessly or negligently results in death.[106] A parent who has a duty to act may be convicted of child or sexual abuse if she fails to prevent such harm from being committed by another person.[107]

Punishment for "commission by omission," even if otherwise defensible, has been criticized by a few scholars[108] as violative of the legality principle. That is, the definitions of most criminal offenses contain verbs such as "kill," "burn," or "break and enter." It is questionable whether, for example, a person who stands by passively while another dies, even if she has a duty to intervene, can be said to have "killed" the other person, as distinguished from "permitting" such a

---

[103] Fletcher, Note 89, *supra*, at 1447.

[104] But see the text to Note 99, *supra*.

[105] E.g., People v. Oliver, 210 Cal. App. 3d 138 (Ct. App. 1989).

[106] Commonwealth v. Levesque, 766 N.E.2d 50 (Mass. 2002).

[107] Degren v. State, 722 A.2d 887 (Md. 1999) (sexual abuse); Pope v. State, 396 A.2d 1054 (Md. Ct. App. 1975) (child abuse).

[108] E.g., Fletcher, Note 89, *supra*, at 1448-49.

death to occur. Nonetheless, courts rarely bar convictions on legality or statutory construction grounds.

We turn now to those uncommon circumstances in which a person *does* have a common law duty to act.

[2] When There Is a Duty to Act

[a] Status Relationship

A person may have a common law duty to act to prevent harm to another if she stands in a special status relationship to the person in peril. Such a relationship is usually founded on the dependence of one party on the other, or on their interdependence. Such status relationships include: parents to their minor children;[109] married couples to one another;[110] and masters to their servants.[111] For example, a mother who allows her children to remain with their father, whom she knows is abusing them, is herself guilty of child abuse by her omission;[112] and, a parent's failure to seek medical attention for her seriously ill child, which omission results in the child's death, will support a conviction for criminal homicide, assuming that the parent acted with the requisite *mens rea*.[113]

[b] Contractual Obligation

A duty to act may be created by implied or express contract. For example, one who breaches an agreement to house, feed, and provide medical care to an infirm stranger,[114] or to care for one's mentally and physically disabled parent,[115] may be held criminally responsible for an ensuing death. Similarly, a babysitter owes an implied contractual duty to protect her ward, and a doctor has a duty to provide ordinary medical care for her patient.

---

[109] Jones v. United States, 308 F.2d 307 (D.C. Cir. 1962).

[110] State v. Smith, 65 Me. 257 (1876); see also State ex rel. Kuntz v. Thirteenth Judicial District, 995 P.2d 951 (Mont. 2000) (unmarried couple who lived together for approximately six years owed each other the same protective duty as exists between spouses).

[111] Rex v. Smith, 2 Car. & P. 449, 172 Eng. Rep. 203 (1826).

[112] State v. Williquette, 385 N.W.2d 145 (Wis. 1986).

[113] State v. Williams, 484 P.2d 1167 (Wash. Ct. App. 1971).

[114] Commonwealth v. Pestinikas, 617 A.2d 1339 (Pa. Super. Ct. 1992).

[115] Davis v. Commonwealth, 335 S.E.2d 375 (Va. 1985).

[c] Omissions Following an Act

In some circumstances an act, followed by an omission, will result in criminal responsibility for the omission, even when there is no liability for the original act.

[i] Creation of a Risk

A person who wrongfully, or perhaps even innocently, harms another or another's property, or who places a person or her property in jeopardy of harm, has a common law duty to aid the injured or endangered party. If she breaches her duty in this regard, she may be held criminally responsible for the harm arising from the omission. For example, if D negligently injures V, D has a common law duty to render aid to V. If D fails to do so, and V dies as the result of the omission, D may be held criminally responsible for V's death, even if she is not guilty of any offense regarding the initial injuries.[116]

Although there is considerably less case law in this regard, a duty to act could arise from non-culpable risk-creation. For example, a few courts have held that one who *accidentally* starts a house fire, and who, therefore, is free of liability for the initial blaze, may be convicted of arson if (with the requisite wrongful state of mind) she fails to act to extinguish the fire or prevent damage to property therein.[117] There is a split of authority regarding whether one who *justifiably* shoots an aggressor in self-defense, seriously wounding the latter, has any subsequent duty to obtain medical aid for the wounded aggressor.[118]

[ii] Voluntary Assistance

One who voluntarily commences assistance to another in jeopardy has a duty to continue to provide aid, at least if a subsequent omission would put the victim in a worse position than if the actor had not initiated help. This rule applies even if the omitter had no initial responsibility to rescue the victim.

For example, a well-meaning individual who takes a sick person into her home, but then fails to provide critical care, may be held responsible for a death arising from this failure. By letting the victim rely on her for care, and by secluding the victim so that others are unaware of her deteriorating condition,

---

[116] See also Jones v. State, 43 N.E.2d 1017 (Ind. 1942) (J raped V; emotionally distraught, V jumped or fell into a creek; J did not attempt to rescue V, although he was aware of her peril; J was convicted of murder for V's death resulting from his omission).

[117] Regina v. Miller, [1983] 1 All ER 978 (House of Lords); see Commonwealth v. Cali, 141 N.E. 510 (Mass. 1923).

[118] State ex rel. Kuntz v. Thirteenth Judicial District, 995 P.2d 951 (Mont. 2000) (duty owed); King v. Commonwealth, 148 S.W.2d 1044 (Ky. 1941) (no duty owed).

the defendant has made matters worse than if she had never become involved.[119]

[B] Statutory Duty (Including "Bad Samaritan" Laws)[120]

Independent of any existing common law duty to act, a duty to act may statutorily be imposed. Examples of such statutes are those that require: a person to pay taxes on earned income;[121] a driver of a motor vehicle involved in an accident to stop her car at the scene;[122] and parents to provide food and shelter to their minor children.[123] Failure to satisfy a statutory duty (assuming, again, that the actor had the capacity to perform the duty and failed to do so with the requisite *mens rea*) constitutes a violation of a statutory "duty to act" offense.

Especially controversial in this regard are "Bad Samaritan" laws, which have been adopted in a few states. These statutes make it an offense, usually a misdemeanor, for a person not to come to the aid of a stranger in peril under specified circumstances. For example, a Vermont statute provides that it is an offense for a bystander to fail to give "reasonable assistance" to another person whom she "knows . . . is exposed to grave physical harm," if such aid "can be rendered without danger or peril" to the bystander, "unless that assistance or care is being provided by others."[124]

Even if such offenses are otherwise desirable, they are difficult to enforce fairly. It is unclear, for example, who (if anyone) would have been guilty of such an offense in the Kitty Genovese tragedy.[125] How many of the persons awakened by the cries for help "knew" the nature of her plight? What would have constituted "reasonable assistance"? Suppose a young woman, awakened by the cries, lacked a telephone to call the police: Would she have been obligated

---

[119] E.g., People v. Oliver, 210 Cal. App. 3d 138 (Ct. App. 1989) (*O* permitted *V*, who was extremely intoxicated, to come to her home, and then allowed *V* to use her bathroom, where *V* injected himself with narcotics; when *V* collapsed, *O* did not summon aid; held: *O* was guilty of manslaughter because "she took [*V*] from a public place where others might have taken care to prevent him from injuring himself, to a private place — her home — where she alone could provide such care"); Regina v. Instan, 17 Cox Crim. Cas. 602 (1893) (*I*, who lived alone with *V*, her elderly and sick aunt, in *V*'s house, failed to obtain needed food and medical care for *V*, who died as a result; held: *I* was properly convicted of manslaughter).

[120] See generally Dressler, Note 89, *supra*; Alison McIntyre, *Guilty Bystanders? On the Legitimacy of Duty to Rescue Statutes*, 23 Phil. & Pub. Aff. 157 (1994); Sandra Guerra Thompson, *The White-Collar Police Force: "Duty to Report" Statutes in Criminal Law Theory*, 11 Wm. & Mary Bill Rts. J. 3 (2002); Woozley, Note 89, *supra*; Daniel B. Yeager, *A Radical Community of Aid: A Rejoinder to Opponents of Affirmative Duties to Help Strangers*, 71 Wash. U. L.Q. 1 (1993).

[121] 26 U.S.C. § 7203 (2005).

[122] E.g., Cal. Vehicle Code § 20001 (Deering 2005).

[123] E.g., Cal. Penal Code § 270 (Deering 2005).

[124] Vt. Stat. Ann. tit. 12, § 519(a) (2004).

[125] See § 9.06[A], *supra*.

to do anything, such as scream out the window for the assaulter to stop? Is there a risk in this action, i.e., that the attacker might come to her premises and attack *her*? And, would any of the thirty-eight neighbors have known, as statutorily required, that assistance (e.g., a phone call to the police) had *not* already been provided?

Critics of Bad Samaritan laws assert that either nobody can fairly be prosecuted under them (thus rendering them of no practical benefit) or a prosecutor might single out one person for prosecution, even though that individual was no more culpable than the other bystanders not prosecuted. There is also the risk that juries, inflamed by the facts, will convict a bystander even though her guilt is legally doubtful.

§ 9.08 OMISSIONS: MODEL PENAL CODE

The Model Penal Code does not differ significantly from the common law regarding omissions. A person is not guilty of any offense unless his conduct "includes a voluntary act or the omission to perform an act of which he is physically capable."[126]

Liability based on an omission is permitted in two circumstances: (1) if the law defining the offense provides for it;[127] or (2) if the duty to act is "otherwise imposed by law."[128] The latter category incorporates duties arising under civil law, such as torts or contract law.[129]

§ 9.09 MEDICAL "OMISSIONS": A SPECIAL PROBLEM[130]

Consider this problem. Patient, *P*, is in an irreversible coma, kept alive by use of a respirator. *D*, *P*'s doctor, concludes that future medical treatment would be useless, so she turns off the respirator, aware that the effect will be to cause *P*'s imminent death, which occurs.

[A] Act or Omission?

One way to analyze the scenario set out above is as follows: *D* committed a voluntary act by turning off the respirator; this conduct caused *P*'s death, the

---

[126] Model Penal Code § 2.01(1).

[127] E.g., Model Penal Code § 220.1(3) (failure to control or report a dangerous fire).

[128] Model Penal Code § 2.01(3)(b).

[129] American Law Institute, Comment to § 2.01, at 222-23.

[130] See generally George P. Fletcher, *Prolonging Life*, 42 Wash. L. Rev. 999 (1967); Sanford H. Kadish, *Letting Patients Die: Legal and Moral Reflections*, 80 Cal. L. Rev. 857 (1992); Arthur Leavens, Note 89, *supra*; H.M. Malm, *Killing, Letting Die, and Simple Conflicts*, 18 Phil. & Pub. Aff. 238 (1989); Judith Jarvis Thomson, *Physician-Assisted Suicide: Two Moral Arguments*, 109 Ethics 497 (1999).

social harm of murder; *D* caused *P*'s death knowingly, the *mens rea* of murder; therefore, the elements of common law murder have been proven. As there is no recognized legal defense of euthanasia, *D* is guilty of murder.

Is it self-evident, however, that *D* is performing an act, rather than omitting conduct, when she turns off a respirator on a comatose patient? Literally, of course, *D*'s conduct *does* include the voluntary act of pulling the plug or turning off the switch on the respirator. But, does this scenario differ significantly from one in which *D fails* to turn the respirator *on* in the first place, a clear-cut omission? From a semantic point of view, the act/omission distinction seems to fail us here. One can as reasonably describe what occurred by saying "*D* failed to provide medical treatment to *P*" as by saying, "*D* voluntarily turned off the machine."

To some it seems morally obtuse for the line in such cases to be drawn on the basis of the fortuity of whether a doctor initially turned on a respirator (and, thus, must turn it off, a voluntary act) or simply refused to initiate medical treatment in the first place. What troubles us about *D*'s behavior (if anything does) is that a doctor, trained to heal others, has chosen — initially or later — to deny future treatment to her patient. The voluntary act of turning off the machine is merely the means of omitting future medical care. Arguably, therefore, we ought to analyze *D*'s behavior as an omission.

[B] Analysis as an Omission

Even if the act of turning off a respirator or discontinuing other medical treatment is analyzed as an omission, this does not necessarily save a doctor from a criminal prosecution. A physician ordinarily has a duty to provide medical treatment for her patients; therefore, she may be held criminally responsible for an omission of this duty.

But, what is the scope of a doctor's duty to her patient? Modern technology has required courts to consider this question, and it is often stated that a physician owes a duty to provide "ordinary," but not "extraordinary," care.[131] If the process of keeping a comatose person artificially alive is considered "extraordinary," a doctor does not violate her duty of care when she omits further medical treatment.

The "ordinary" versus "extraordinary" care distinction, however, arguably raises more questions than it answers. What is "extraordinary" care? Human heart transplants once seemed extraordinary; today they are commonplace. Would the physician who fails to perform a needed transplant operation be violating a duty of ordinary care to her patient? Some new approach to the problem may be needed.

---

[131] See Superintendent of Belchertown State Sch. v. Saikewicz, 370 N.E.2d 417, 424 (Mass. 1977); In re Quinlan, 355 A.2d 647, 667-68 (N.J. 1976).

[C] The *Barber* Approach

In *Barber*,[132] the defendants were physicians charged with murder and conspiracy to commit murder of Clarence Herbert, their patient. Herbert had been in a deep coma from which he was unlikely to recover. After they received permission from the patient's family, the doctors caused life-sustaining equipment to be turned off and, when Herbert continued to live, they removed intravenous tubes that provided needed hydration and nourishment to their patient. Herbert eventually died from the loss of fluids and nourishment.

The court stated that the physicians' conduct amounted to a withdrawal, or omission, of further treatment, rather than an affirmative act. It reasoned that although the life-support devices were "self-propelled," each drop of fluid introduced into the patient's body by intravenous feeding was "comparable to a manually administered injection or item of medication." Therefore, it concluded, the disconnection of the mechanical devices that fed and hydrated the patient was tantamount to withholding medical treatment.

The court framed the resulting omission issue in terms of what "duties [are] owed by a physician to a patient who has been reliably diagnosed as in a comatose state from which any meaningful recovery of cognitive brain function is exceedingly unlikely." In resolving this issue, the court expressed the view that the ordinary/extraordinary care distinction begged the real question. In its place, the court asked "whether the proposed treatment [was] proportionate . . . in terms of the benefits to be gained versus the burdens caused." The court reasoned that medical treatment that is even minimally painful or intrusive is apt to constitute disproportionate treatment when the patient has no meaningful chance of medical improvement. In such circumstances, a physician owes no duty to provide further medical treatment to her patient.

Who determines whether the proposed medical treatment is disproportionate? The court's answer was that "the patient's interests and desires are the key ingredients of the decision making process." When the patient is unable to indicate her wishes, the immediate family is the proper "surrogate" for the patient. In the absence of legislation to the contrary, the court held that medical personnel, along with the family, may decide whether to withdraw treatment without prior judicial authorization.

[D] Reflections Regarding *Barber*

The act/omission distinction is based, at least in part, on the premise that the law should prevent people from actively causing harm, but that it should not compel persons to benefit others.[133] Based on this reasoning, did the doctors

---

[132] Barber v. Superior Court, 147 Cal. App. 3d 1006 (Ct. App. 1983).

[133] See § 9.06[C], *supra*.

here withhold a benefit from their patient, or did they cause his death (i.e., kill him)?

Before the respirator was turned off, Herbert was medically and legally alive. Even after the physicians shut off the machinery, he was not in imminent danger of death. Only after the doctors stopped providing nourishment and fluids to Herbert did he finally die. Therefore, "it is difficult to avoid concluding that the doctors caused [Herbert's] death."[134] From this perspective, the situation was no different than if Herbert's wife had starved her comatose husband to death at home, in order to speed his death. Whether family members or health professionals should be allowed to cut off food and fluids to a chronically comatose person in order to hasten death is a matter of considerable moral controversy. Arguably, however, the matter ought to be resolved directly — through debate regarding whether euthanasia (and, with competent patients, suicide assistance) should be permitted — rather than indirectly through the act/omission, duty/no-duty analysis.[135] But, given that euthanasia is not a recognized defense, "such intentional conduct seems unavoidably to constitute criminal homicide."[136]

§ 9.10 SOCIAL HARM: GENERAL PRINCIPLES

[A] Overview

Holmes has written that the "aim of the law is not to punish sins, but is to prevent certain external results."[137] Joel Feinberg has stated that "[a]cts of *harming* . . . are the direct objects of the criminal law."[138] These statements remind us that, to be guilty of an offense, a person must do more than think bad thoughts; she must be guilty of wrongdoing. The voluntary act is the "doing"; the

---

[134] Leavens, Note 89, *supra*, at 586; see also Thomson, Note 130, *supra*, at 501 (in such a circumstance, the act "seems to be most plausibly seen as not merely letting nature take its course but rather causing it to").

[135] Constitutional issues are raised in some medical omission cases. A competent patient has a "liberty" interest encompassed by the Due Process Clause of the Constitution to refuse medical treatment. This interest must be weighed against the state's legitimate interest in preserving life. In the case of an incompetent patient, as in *Barber*, a state has the right to refuse to accept the substituted judgment of a close family member, and it may refuse to permit the cessation of medical care in the absence of clear and convincing evidence of the person's pre-incompetency expressed desire for withdrawal of medical care in such circumstances. Cruzan v. Dir., Mo. Dep't. of Health, 497 U.S. 261 (1990). However, even though a person has a liberty interest in refusing medical treatment, she has no constitutional right to medical assistance in causing her own death by way of suicide. Washington v. Glucksberg, 521 U.S. 702 (1997).

[136] Leavens, Note 89, *supra*, at 586-87.

[137] Commonwealth v. Kennedy, 48 N.E. 770, 770 (Mass. 1897).

[138] Joel Feinberg, Harm to Others 31 (1984).

harm caused by the voluntary act is the "wrong."[139] The harm is the body — the linchpin — of the crime. Because crimes are public wrongs, however, we may describe the harm caused in a criminal case as "social harm."

Some scholars state that "social harm" is an essential element of every crime.[140] This is only true, however, if the term "social harm" is broadly defined. Some conduct that is criminal may cause no injury at all, in the usual sense of the term. What is the "social harm," for example, in driving while intoxicated, if nobody is hurt and no property is damaged? Or, if D, intending to kill V, who is asleep, pulls the trigger of what turns out to be an unloaded gun, D may be charged with attempted murder, but where is the harm in D's conduct? If all crimes require "social harm," must such conduct go unpunished?

To a utilitarian, there is no reason why resulting harm should be considered a prerequisite to criminal liability, as long as the actor's conduct demonstrates her propensity to cause *future* harm, or if punishment of the person will deter future harm by others. In contrast, many retributivists believe that punishment of an actor is unjustified in the absence of social injury. Only then has the actor taken something from society. Only then is a debt owed. Only then is it right for society to take something from the actor, by means of punishment.

In most circumstances the views of both schools of thought converge. Murder needs to be deterred and, in any case, causes harm that justifies punishment as repayment; so both utilitarians and retributivists typically can justify punishing murderers. Moreover, even in the case of an intoxicated driver who causes no immediate tangible harm, but who threatens future harm, a retributivist may be able to justify punishment: A drunk driver weaving on the highway, for example, endangers others by her conduct, which endangerment frequently causes apprehension of harm in other drivers. Disturbing the public repose is a form of intangible, albeit real, injury that may justify penal sanction.

Frequently, however, it is hard to conclude that dangerous conduct has hurt anyone, even intangibly. If nobody is on the highway to see the intoxicated driver weaving, there is no public alarm. If V, asleep, is alone when D pulls the trigger of an unloaded gun, nobody is put in fear by D's conduct. In these situations, however, the intoxicated driver and attempted murderer *are* subject to criminal punishment. For us to say, therefore, that "social harm" is an essential element of all offenses, the term "social harm" must be carefully — and broadly — defined.

---

[139] In the unusual case in which a person may be punished for an omission, "wrong*non*doing" would be a more apt characterization of the situation.

[140] E.g., Eser, Note 1, *supra*, at 346.

[B] Definition of "Social Harm"

Society values and has an interest in protecting people and things. The "things" that society values and has an interest in protecting may be tangible (e.g., an automobile) or intangible (e.g., emotional security, reputation, personal autonomy). Society is wronged when an actor invades *any* socially recognized interest and diminishes its value.[141] Specifically, "social harm" may be defined as the "negation, endangering, or destruction of an individual, group or state interest which was deemed socially valuable."[142] Thus, the drunk driver and the attempted murderer of the sleeping party have endangered the interests of others, and have caused "social harm" under this definition.

[C] Finding the "Social Harm" Element in a Criminal Statute

Every crime contains an *actus reus* and, as discussed in the next chapter, nearly all crimes require proof of a culpable state of mind (*mens rea*). The definition of an offense will set out the *actus reus* component of the crime. More specifically, the definition of the offense will identify the proscribed social harm.

For example, the common law definition of murder is "**the killing of a human being by another human being** *with malice aforethought.*" The italicized words constitute the *mens rea* of the offense, i.e., the culpable state of mind required to be guilty of the crime. The words in bold state the *actus reus*. More specifically, these words tell us what society does not want to occur (the social harm) — the taking of a human life by another human being. The voluntary act/omission component of the *actus reus* is implicit in this definition — the "killing" of a human being must be the result of conduct that includes a voluntary act or an omission (when there is a duty to act).

Of course, the social harm of murder is not simply the loss of one human life. This is the *definitional* social harm. The *underlying* social harm — the *full* reason why society prohibits murder — is broader and deeper: When a human life is taken by another person, there are deep psychological injuries to loved ones and friends; there are apt to be financial losses suffered by family members and by those with whom the victim worked; there is harm to strangers who, upon learning of the homicide, become fearful for their own safety and, consequently, restrict their public activities; and, of course, there is the tear in the fabric of society that results when one of its members unjustifiably takes the life of another.

---

[141] See Hall, Note 2, *supra*, at 217.

[142] Eser, Note 1, *supra*, at 413.

[D] Dividing "Social Harm" Into Sub-Elements

The social harm of an offense, as defined by statute or at common law, may consist of wrongful conduct, wrongful results, or both. Moreover, the offense will contain "attendant circumstance" (or, simply, "circumstance") elements. Frequently, it is necessary for a lawyer or court to distinguish between "conduct," "result," and "attendant circumstance" elements of the *actus reus* of the crime.

[1] "Conduct" Elements (or "Conduct" Crimes)

Some crimes are defined, at least in part, in terms of harmful conduct. Harmful *results* are not required. An example of a "conduct" crime would be the offense of "intentionally **driving under the influence of alcohol**." The words in bold state the *actus reus* of the offense. More specifically, they state the social harm of the crime — the wrongful conduct of driving a car in an intoxicated condition (which conduct implicitly must include a voluntary act). This is a "conduct" crime because no harmful result is required. That is, the offense is complete whether or not anyone or any property is tangibly injured because of the intoxicated driving. It is enough that socially valuable interests have been endangered by the actor's conduct.

[2] "Result" Elements (or "Result" Crimes)

An offense may be defined in terms of a prohibited result. Common law murder is a "result" crime, because the social harm of the offense, as defined, involves "the death of another human being." Although the killing of another — the result — obviously occurs because of some conduct, the *nature* of the actor's conduct *definitionally* is irrelevant. That is, it does not matter *how* the result occurs (e.g., whether the actor kills by gun or knife or poison), just that it does.

On the other hand, some offenses contain both "conduct" and "result" elements. For example, a statute may define first-degree murder as the "killing of another human being, by means of a destructive device, explosive, poison, or torture."[143] The *actus reus* of this hypothetical statute includes a result (another person's death) brought about by a certain type of conduct (use of a destructive device, explosives, poison, or torture).

[3] Attendant Circumstances

In order for *any* offense to occur, certain facts or conditions — "attendant circumstances" — must be present when the actor performs the prohibited conduct

---

[143] See, e.g., Cal. Penal Code § 189 (Deering 2005).

and/or causes the prohibited result that constitutes the social harm of the offense.

These "attendant circumstance" are found in the definition of the crime. *The "social harm" of the offense, definitionally speaking, has not occurred unless the specified attendant circumstances are present.* For example, the social harm of common law burglary is the "breaking and entering of the dwelling house of another at nighttime." This means that for the defendant's conduct to constitute the criminal offense of burglary, the breaking and entering by the actor *must* be of a "dwelling house" (not, for example, of a commercial structure or chicken coop); the dwelling *must* belong to someone other than the actor; and the events *must* occur at night. These elements of the offense — "dwelling house," "of another," and "at night" — are the "attendant circumstance" elements of burglary, as defined above. In the absence of these facts or conditions, the *social harm* of burglary has not occurred (although the social harm of another offense, e.g., trespass, may have occurred), and thus the *crime* of burglary cannot be proven.

§ 9.11 SOCIAL HARM: CONSTITUTIONAL LIMITS

Various constitutional provisions limit the extent to which a legislature may properly prohibit socially harmful conduct. For example, the Supreme Court has held that the First Amendment bars a legislature from making it a crime to place on property a Nazi swastika, burning cross, or other symbol that the actor should know "arouses anger, alarm or resentment in others on the basis of race, color, creed, religion, or gender."[144] The Court is *not* suggesting by this that there is no social harm in such circumstances, but rather is asserting that constitutional rights — here, freedom of speech — outweigh the society's interest in preventing this social harm in the manner chosen by the legislature.

The Supreme Court has also stated that constitutionally protected liberty "presumes an autonomy of self that includes . . . certain intimate conduct."[145] As a consequence, the high court has invalidated laws that prohibit women from obtaining abortions before fetal viability,[146] physicians from dispensing contraceptive information to married and unmarried persons,[147] and adults from possessing obscene literature in their homes[148] or engaging in intimate consensual sexual conduct.[149]

---

[144] R.A.V. v. City of St. Paul, 505 U.S. 377 (1992).

[145] Lawrence v. Texas, 539 U.S. 558, 562 (2003).

[146] Roe v. Wade, 410 U.S. 113 (1973); Planned Parenthood v. Casey, 505 U.S. 833, 836 (1992) (reaffirming, as the "essential holding" of *Roe*, the "right of [a] woman to choose to have an abortion before viability and to obtain it without undue [governmental] interference.").

[147] Griswold v. Connecticut, 381 U.S. 479 (1965); Eisenstadt v. Baird, 405 U.S. 438 (1972).

[148] Stanley v. Georgia, 394 U.S. 557 (1969).

[149] Lawrence v. Texas, 539 U.S. 558 (2003) (constitutionally protecting same-sex sexual conduct).

Chapter 10

MENS REA

§ 10.01 GENERAL PRINCIPLE[1]

Actus non facit reum nisi mens sit rea, or "an act does not make [a person] guilty, unless the mind be guilty," expresses the principle that, except in relatively rare circumstances,[2] a person is not guilty of a criminal offense unless the government not only proves the *actus reus* of the crime (discussed in the last chapter), but also the defendant's *mens rea* (literally, a "guilty mind"). As the Supreme Court has nicely put it, criminal liability requires proof of "an evil-meaning mind with an evil-doing hand."[3]

This has not always been the case. In ancient English law, criminal responsibility was based solely on proof of commission of an *actus reus*. The actor's state of mind was irrelevant. By as early as the thirteenth century, however, English courts had begun to require proof that the person charged with a criminal offense had a culpable state of mind.[4]

By the twentieth century, the concept of *mens rea* had become so deeply entrenched in American law that the Supreme Court could state that "[t]he contention that an injury can amount to a crime only when inflicted by [*mens rea*] is no provincial or transient notion. It is . . . universal and persistent in mature systems of law. . . ."[5] As one scholar has put it, "the requirement of mens rea contributes to the meaning and value of our lives as moral beings."[6] Today, *mens rea* is "the criminal law's mantra."[7]

---

[1] See generally Jerome Hall, General Principles of the Criminal Law 70-104 (2d ed. 1960); H.L.A. Hart, Punishment and Responsibility 105-45 (1968); Rollin M. Perkins, *A Rationale of Mens Rea*, 52 Harv. L. Rev. 905 (1939); Stephen J. Morse, *Inevitable Mens Rea*, 27 Harv. J.L. & Pub. Pol'y 51 (2003); Paul H. Robinson, *A Brief History of Distinctions in Criminal Culpability*, 31 Hastings L.J. 815 (1980); Francis Bowes Sayre, *Mens Rea*, 45 Harv. L. Rev. 974 (1932).

[2] See Chapter 11 (Strict Liability), *infra.*

[3] Morissette v. United States, 342 U.S. 246, 251 (1952).

[4] Robinson, Note 1, *supra*, at 821-46; Sayre, Note 1, *supra*, at 975-94.

[5] Morissette v. United States, 342 U.S. at 250.

[6] Morse, Note 1 *supra*, at 61.

[7] United States v. Cordoba-Hincapie, 825 F. Supp. 485, 490 (E.D.N.Y. 1993).

§ 10.02 DEFINITION OF *"MENS REA"*

[A] Ambiguity of the Term

Professor George Fletcher has observed that "there is no term fraught with greater ambiguity than that venerable Latin phrase that haunts the Anglo-American criminal law: *mens rea*."[8] Holmes, too, has noted "that most of the difficulty as to the *mens rea* was due to having no precise understanding what the *mens rea* is."[9] "*Mens rea*" has been described as "chameleon-like, [because it] takes on different colors in different surroundings."[10] Professor Sanford Kadish has ruefully observed that "the term '*mens rea*' is rivaled [by few legal terms] for the varieties of senses in which it has been used and for the quantity of obfuscation it has created."[11]

Generally speaking, "*mens rea*" has two meanings. Particularly during the early development of the doctrine, the term had a broad meaning, described below in subsection [B]. Over time, however, "the law [has] embarked upon the long journey of refinement and development"[12] of the doctrine, resulting in a narrower, more precise meaning, considered in subsection [C]. Although the latter meaning has gained prominence, both usages of the term "*mens rea*" persist today.

[B] Broad Meaning: The "Culpability" Meaning of *"Mens Rea"*

Broadly speaking, "*mens rea*" is defined as "a general immorality of motive,"[13] "vicious will,"[14] or an "evil-meaning mind."[15] Although each of these phrases has a slightly different connotation, "*mens rea*" as used here suggests a general notion of moral blameworthiness, i.e., that the defendant committed the *actus reus* of an offense with a morally blameworthy state of mind. For current purposes, this may be termed the "culpability" meaning of "*mens rea*."

According to this definition of "*mens rea*," guilt for an offense is not dependent on proof that the actor caused the proscribed harm with any specific men-

---

[8] George Fletcher, Rethinking Criminal Law 398 (1978).

[9] Letter from Oliver Wendell Holmes to Harold J. Laski (Jul. 14, 1916), *in* Holmes-Laski Letters 4 (Mark DeWolfe Howe ed., 1953).

[10] Francis Bowes Sayre, *The Present Signification of Mens Rea in the Criminal Law*, *in* Harvard Legal Essays 399, 402 (1934) (italics omitted).

[11] Sanford H. Kadish, *The Decline of Innocence*, 26 Cambridge L.J. 273, 273 (1968).

[12] United States v. Cordoba-Hincapie, 825 F. Supp. 485, 491 (E.D.N.Y. 1993).

[13] Sayre, Note 10, *supra*, at 411-12.

[14] 4 William Blackstone, Commentaries on the Laws of England *21 (1769).

[15] Morissette v. United States, 342 U.S. 246, 251 (1952).

tal state, i.e., it is not necessary to show that he committed the offense "intentionally," "knowingly," or with any other particular frame of mind. Indeed, common law definitions of many offenses failed to specify any *mens rea*.[16] It was sufficient that the defendant committed the proscribed acts in a manner that demonstrated his bad character, malevolence, or immorality.

For example, in *Regina v. Cunningham*,[17] C entered the cellar of a building, where he tore the gas meter from the gas pipes and stole the coins deposited in the meter. As a consequence, gas escaped from the pipes, seeped through the cellar wall, and nearly asphyxiated V. Although C had not intended to endanger anyone's life by his actions, he was charged with an offense that provided, in part, that "[w]hosoever shall . . . maliciously . . . cause to be administered to or taken by any other person any poison . . . or noxious thing, so as thereby to endanger the life of such person, . . . shall be guilty of a felony. . . ."

The evidence presented at trial demonstrated that C committed the *actus reus* of the offense: As a result of his voluntary conduct, C "caused to be administered" to V a "noxious thing" that endangered V's life. The primary issue was whether C had the requisite *mens rea*. The trial judge instructed the jury that the statutory term "maliciously" meant only that the prosecution had to show that the defendant acted "wickedly." Thus, the court invited the jury to convict C if it found that he caused the social harm with a morally culpable state of mind. Since C caused the harm, albeit unintentionally, while attempting to steal money from the meter, the jury found the requisite wickedness.[18]

[C] Narrow Meaning: The "Elemental" Meaning of *"Mens Rea"*

"Mens rea" may also be defined, simply, as "the particular mental state provided for in the definition of an offense." This is the "elemental" meaning of *"mens rea."* A person may possess *"mens rea"* in the *culpability* sense of the term, and yet lack the requisite *elemental "mens rea."*

For example, assume that murder is defined by statute as "the intentional killing of a human being by another human being." The *actus reus* of the offense is "the killing of a human being by another human being." The *"mens rea"* — the particular mental state provided for in the definition of the offense — is "intentional." Applying the elemental meaning of *"mens rea,"* D is guilty of murder if he intentionally kills another human being. However, if he kills *un*intentionally, albeit with a morally blameworthy state of mind (for example, if he *recklessly*

---

[16] Early on, some offenses did specify a particular mental state in their definition. These offenses came to be known as "specific intent" crimes. See § 10.06, *infra*.

[17] 41 Crim. App. 155, 2 Q.B. 396, 2 All. E.R. 412 (1957) (Court of Criminal Appeal).

[18] However, the Court of Criminal Appeal in *Cunningham* allowed C's appeal on the ground that the trial judge's *mens rea* instruction was erroneous. See § 10.04[E], *infra*.

takes another's life), he would *not* be guilty of murder as defined, because he lacked the particular mental state required in the definition of the offense.

§ 10.03 RATIONALE OF THE *MENS REA* REQUIREMENT[19]

[A] Utilitarian Arguments

Some persons justify the *mens rea* requirement on grounds of deterrence. A person cannot be deterred from criminal activity, it is argued, unless he "appreciate[s] that punishment lies in store" if he persists in his actions.[20] Therefore, punishment of one who lacks a culpable state of mind will be ineffective and, as a consequence, wasteful. It may also be reasoned that one who causes harm accidentally, rather than intentionally or with an "evil-meaning mind," is harmless and not in need of reformation.

These claims are only partly persuasive. Even if one acting without a culpable state of mind cannot be deterred on the present occasion, his punishment may serve as a useful warning to others to be more careful in their activities, thereby reducing the number of accidentally inflicted injuries.[21] Furthermore, although it may be agreed that one who acts with a *mens rea* is apt to be dangerous and in need of reformation, the accidental harmdoer may also need incapacitation or some other corrective influence. Some people are accident-prone; the criminal sanction may be a rational way to protect society from them. At a minimum, their punishment may influence them to change their lifestyle and to avoid activities that may result in injury to others.

The *mens rea* requirement may be counter-productive for another reason. The prosecution is constitutionally required to prove beyond a reasonable doubt every element of a criminal offense, including the defendant's *mens rea*.[22] This is sometimes a difficult burden to satisfy; consequently, some persons who *do* act with a *mens rea* are able to avoid conviction. Their acquittals send the potential counter-utilitarian message to would-be wrongdoers — those who are looking for a legal loophole — that they might also be able to escape the criminal sanction.

[B] Retributive Arguments

The Supreme Court once observed that "[a] relation between some mental element and punishment for a harmful act is almost as instinctive as the child's

---

[19] See generally the sources in Note 1, *supra*.

[20] Glanville Williams, Criminal Law: The General Part 30 (2d ed. 1961).

[21] Richard A. Wasserstrom, *Strict Liability in the Criminal Law*, 12 Stan. L. Rev. 731, 736-37 (1960).

[22] See § 7.03[B], *supra*.

familiar exculpatory [statement], 'But I didn't mean to.'"**23** Oliver Wendell Holmes has made the same point with animals rather than children when he suggested that "even a dog distinguishes between being stumbled over and being kicked."**24**

Whether Holmes' observation about dogs is right or wrong, the preceding observations assist in making the vital point that the principle of *mens rea* has its roots far deeper in retributive than in utilitarian soil. Although a society presumably wants to deter harmful conduct, the *mens rea* requirement "flows from our society's commitment to individual choice";**25** the principle is founded on the belief that it is morally unjust to punish those who accidentally, rather than by choice, cause social injury.

Crimes are public wrongs. The implication of a guilty verdict is that the convicted party wronged the community as a whole. By convicting a criminal defendant, society denounces the actor; it condemns and stigmatizes him as a wrongdoer.**26** Respect for human dignity suggests, if it does not dictate, that such stigma should not attach, and liberty should not be denied, to one who has acted without a culpable state of mind.

§ 10.04 FREQUENTLY USED *MENS REA* TERMS[27]

[A] "Intentionally"

[1] Definition

Many common law and statutory offenses are defined in terms of "intent," that is, the prosecution must prove that the defendant intentionally committed the social harm that constitutes the *actus reus* of the offense. On occasion, the "intent" to cause a particular result (e.g., to kill another) or to engage in specified conduct (e.g., drive an automobile) is defined narrowly in a statute to mean that it was the actor's purpose, desire, or conscious objective to cause the result or to engage in the specified conduct.**28**

---

23 Morissette v. United States, 342 U.S. 246, 250-51 (1952).

24 Oliver Wendell Holmes, The Common Law 3 (1881).

25 United States v. Cordoba-Hincapie, 825 F. Supp. 485, 495 (E.D.N.Y. 1993).

26 See § 1.01[A][1], *supra*.

27 See generally Larry Alexander, *Insufficient Concern: A Unified Conception of Criminal Culpability*, 88 Cal. L. Rev. 1 (2000); Joshua Dressler, *Does One Mens Rea Fit All?: Thoughts on Alexander's Unified Conception of Criminal Culpability*, 88 Cal. L. Rev. 25 (2000); Douglas N. Husak, *The Sequential Principle of Relative Culpability*, 1 Legal Theory 493 (1995); Kenneth W. Simons, *Rethinking Mental States*, 72 B.U. L. Rev. 463 (1992).

28 People v. Conley, 543 N.E.2d 138 (Ill. App. Ct. 1989) (applying an Illinois statute defining "intent").

The ordinary common law definition of "intent," however, is broader. At common law, a person "intentionally" causes the social harm of an offense if: (1) it is his desire (i.e., his conscious object) to cause the social harm; or (2) he acts with knowledge that the social harm is virtually certain to occur as a result of his conduct.[29] For example,[30] suppose that bomb expert D wants to kill V, his wife, in order to obtain the proceeds from her life insurance policy. D constructs a bomb and places it on an airplane on which V is a passenger. He sets the bomb to explode while the plane is in air. Although D does not want anyone on the plane other than V to die — indeed, he prays that the others will survive — he knows that the bomb will destroy the airplane. The bomb goes off as planned, killing V and the other 100 persons on board.

According to the common law definition, how many people did D "intentionally" kill? Clearly, D "intentionally" killed V. This follows from the simple fact that D wanted V to die; it was his conscious object to take her life. Under the first prong of the definition of "intent" set out above, it does not matter how likely it is that the result will occur; it is enough that D desires his wife's death.

D's mental state as to the other victims must be analyzed differently. He did not desire their deaths; in fact, he prayed that they would live. Nonetheless, assuming that D was not mentally incapacitated in some manner, a jury could determine that he "intended" their deaths as well.[31] According to the second meaning of "intent" set out above, he *knew* that the social harm of their deaths was *virtually certain* to occur when his bomb exploded. This second prong may be termed the "known certainties" prong, for it is not satisfied if the outcome was merely highly probable; the actor must realize that, short of a divine intervention or a secular "miracle," the undesired event will occur "for sure."[32]

Both versions of "intent" involve subjective fault. An actor's fault is "subjective" if he possesses a wrongful state of mind — in this case, the conscious desire to cause the social harm, or the awareness that the harm will almost certainly result from his conduct. If the defendant lacks either of these states of mind, he has not "intentionally" caused the harm.

---

[29] Mill v. State, 585 P.2d 546, 549 (Alaska 1978).

[30] As explained in § 9.10, *supra*, the prohibited "social harm" may be an unwanted result or wrongful conduct. The "intent" definition encompasses both types of offenses. However, because most "intent" issues arise in the context of results, rather than conduct, the examples here focus on "result" offenses, such as murder or manslaughter.

[31] Arguably, a person who *desires* a certain outcome (the first prong of the "intent" definition) is more culpable than one who does not want it to occur but who proceeds with *knowledge* that it will result (the alternative second prong). The common law definition, however, merges these two types of culpability. In contrast, the Model Penal Code distinguishes between these two states of mind. See § 10.07[B], *infra*. For a different view of the subject, see Alexander, Note 27, *supra* (arguing for a single conception of culpability), and Simons, Note 27, *supra* (dividing mental states into two categories, those that are based on states of desire and others based on states of belief, and arguing that one cannot create a hierarchy of culpability between the two categories).

[32] Glanville Williams, *Oblique Intention*, 46 Cambridge L.J. 417, 418 (1987).

The significance of the subjective nature of "intent" is seen by a minor change in the bombing hypothetical. Suppose that *D* belonged to a religious sect that espoused the belief that members of the faith always have their wishes fulfilled by God. Therefore, as a member of the sect, *D* genuinely believed that his fervent prayers would save everyone on the airplane except his wife, for whom he did not pray for divine protection. Based on these revised facts, *D* (as before) intentionally killed his wife, because he desired her death. However, assuming that a jury believes his testimony about his religious beliefs, *D* did not "intentionally" kill the other passengers — he was not subjectively aware that their deaths were a near certainty. "Intent" requires such awareness; it is insufficient that he *should have been aware*, as a reasonable person, that they would be killed.

[2] "Motive" Distinguished[33]

Some legal scholars state that motive is irrelevant in the substantive criminal law.[34] This statement is only correct if they mean that the "intention" to cause social harm is no less "intentional" simply because the actor's motive was not evil in character. For example, a doctor who kills his terminally ill patient to "put him out of his misery" arguably has a good motive, but the killing is still "intentional."[35]

A defendant's motive *is* often relevant in the criminal law. First, some offenses (called "specific intent" crimes[36]) *by definition* require proof of a specific motive. For example, common law larceny is the trespassory taking and carrying away of the personal property of another *with the intent to steal, i.e., with the intent to permanently deprive the other of the property*. Although this definition includes the term "intent" — English scholars sometimes call it an "ulterior intention" — the italicized language denotes the actor's motive for committing the *actus reus* of the offense. In the absence of this motive — for example, if *D* intentionally takes and carries away an automobile in order to "joyride" and return the vehicle — no larceny has occurred.

Second, motive is relevant to claims of defense. That is, if the defendant's motive for his intentional actions is legally justifiable (e.g., he intentionally kills an aggressor in order to protect his own life), he will be acquitted. As this

---

[33] See generally Martin R. Gardner, *The Mens Rea Enigma: Observations on the Role of Motive in the Criminal Law Past and Present*, 1993 Utah L. Rev. 635; Douglas N. Husak, *Motive and Criminal Liability*, Crim. Just. Ethics, Winter/Spring 1989, at 3; Paul H. Robinson, *Hate Crimes: Crimes of Motive, Character, or Group Terror?*, 1992/1993 Ann. Surv. Am. L. 605.

[34] E.g., Hall, Note 1, *supra*, at 88 ("[H]ardly any part of penal law is more definitely settled than that motive is irrelevant.").

[35] Even here, however, the doctor's motive is relevant to the criminal law, in the sense that proof of his motive *reinforces* the prosecution's claim that the doctor acted with the requisite intent.

[36] See § 10.06, *infra*.

example demonstrates, the existence of a justifiable motive does not render the defendant's conduct or the consequences of it any less intentional.

Third, motive is relevant at the sentencing phase of a criminal proceeding. For example, if it wishes to do so, a state may impose enhanced punishment for an offense if the actor selected his victim on account of an unlawful factor, such as race, religion, disability, or sexual orientation.[37] Likewise, in jurisdictions permitting sentencing discretion, a defendant's good motive for wrongful conduct may be considered in mitigation.

[3] "Transferred Intent"[38]

[a] General Doctrine

Suppose A wrongfully fires a gun at B, intending to kill him, but the bullet instead strikes and kills unintended victim C, a bystander. Is A guilty of intent-to-kill murder of C? Or, suppose A attempts to hit B, B ducks, and A's fist strikes C. May A be convicted of battery of C (for current purposes, hypothetically defined as "intentional touching or striking of another").

In both hypotheticals, the answer is "yes." Courts typically reach this outcome by applying the legal fiction of "transferred intent."[39] According to this doctrine, which originated in the sixteenth century,[40] we attribute liability to a defendant who, intending to kill (or injure) one person, accidentally kills (or injures) another person instead.[41] The law "transfers" the actor's state of mind regarding the intended victim to the unintended one. Some judges unwisely[42] instruct juries in these "bad aim" cases that "the intent follows the bullet."[43]

The transferred intent doctrine is justified on grounds of necessity and proportionality. The necessity argument is that the bad aimer should not avoid conviction for intent-to-kill homicide simply because he killed the "wrong person," i.e., someone he did not intend to kill. The proportionality argument is that the

---

[37] E.g., Wis. Stat. § 939.645(1)(b) (2004) (originally upheld against constitutional attack in Wisconsin v. Mitchell, 508 U.S. 476 (1993)).

[38] See generally Anthony M. Dillof, *Transferred Intent: An Inquiry into the Nature of Criminal Culpability*, 1 Buff. Crim. L. Rev. 501 (1998); Douglas N. Husak, *Transferred Intent*, 10 Notre Dame J.L., Ethics & Pub. Pol'y 65 (1996); Mitchell Keiter, *With Malice Toward All: The Increased Lethality of Violence Reshapes Transferred Intent and Attempted Murder Law*, 38 U.S.F. L. Rev. 261 (2004).

[39] People v. Bland, 48 P.3d 1107, 1110 (Cal. 2004) (characterizing the result in such cases as "universally accepted").

[40] Regina v. Saunders, 2 Plowd. 473, 75 Eng. Rep. 706 (1576).

[41] Poe v. State, 652 A.2d 1164, 1169 (Md. App. 1995), aff'd, 671 A.2d 501 (Md. 1996).

[42] See Note 49 and text, *infra*.

[43] *Poe*, 652 A.2d at 1168.

doctrine is meant "to ensure that prosecution and punishment accord with culpability."[44] That is, one who intends to cause a particular harm to one individual, and instead causes precisely the same harm to another person, is "as culpable, and society is harmed as much, as if the defendant had accomplished what he had initially intended."[45]

Unfortunately, as uncontroversial and simple as transferred intent seems on quick inspection, it is neither. Some scholars have argued against the moral soundness of the transferred intent doctrine,[46] which has been characterized as a "name attached to an unexplained mystery."[47] This "mystery" is not only a legal fiction — states of mind hardly follow bullets to unintended victims[48] — but it is a potentially misleading and, therefore, mischievous doctrine.[49] Moreover, as suggested immediately below, the doctrine is unnecessary to ensure a proper outcome.

[b] An Unnecessary and Potentially Misleading Doctrine

It is submitted here that the transferred intent doctrine is unnecessary and, if invoked without great care, misleading. Consider the typical "bad aim" case: A intends to kill B, but instead kills C, and is prosecuted for intent-to-kill murder. In this case, there is no need to transfer A's intention to kill B to unintended victim C; A has the requisite intent *without* the doctrine. There is no need to think in terms of A's *mens rea* following a bullet to its eventual victim. One need only look at the definition of criminal homicide to see this: The social harm of murder is the "killing of a human being by another human being." The requisite intent, therefore, is the intent to kill a, not a specific, human being. In the present case, A intended to kill a human being (B), so the *mens rea* is satisfied; and he did in fact kill a human being (C), so the *actus reus* is proven. Thus, the elements of murder are proved without invoking the legal fiction of transferred intent.[50]

The correctness of this assertion — and the danger of applying the transferred intent doctrine mindlessly — is demonstrated if one looks at offenses that

---

[44] People v. Czahara, 203 Cal. App. 3d 1468, 1474 (Ct. App. 1988).

[45] People v. Scott, 927 P.2d 288, 291 (Cal. 1996).

[46] E.g., Dillof, Note 38, *supra*.

[47] Husak, Note 38, *supra*, at 67.

[48] "By thinking of the *mens rea* in such finite terms — as some discrete unit that must be either here or there — we have created a linguistic problem for ourselves where no real-life problem existed. . . . It neither follows nor fails to follow the bullet. . . . It remains in the brain of the criminal actor and never moves." Harvey v. State, 681 A.2d 628, 637 (Md. App. 1996).

[49] People v. Scott, 927 P.2d at 295 (Mosk, J., concurring) ("a peculiarly mischievous legal fiction").

[50] Ramsey v. State, 56 P.3d 675, 681 (Alaska Ct. App. 2002); People v. Scott, 927 P.2d at 295-96 (Mosk, J., concurring) (citing Dressler, Understanding Criminal Law (2d ed.)); Millen v. State, 988 S.W.2d 164, 165 (Tenn. 1999).

do require proof of a specific victim. For example, in *Ford v. State*,[51] *F* threw rocks at a moving vehicle, with the intention of disabling the driver. He was charged according to an assault statute that made it an offense to "assault or beat any person, with intent to maim, disfigure, or disable *such person*." The trial judge instructed the jury that *F*'s intent could be transferred to an injured passenger. Essentially, the judge believed that the intent to disable followed the rock, but it does not. The appellate court correctly ruled that the transferred intent doctrine does not apply to "statutory offenses which require that the defendant's criminal intent be directed towards the actual victim."

Another subtle error can occur if courts thoughtlessly apply the transferred intent doctrine. By its terms, the doctrine serves to transfer the intent from the intended victim to the unintended one, but it does *not* transfer the intent to cause one type of social harm to another. For example, if *A* intends to kill a dog, but the bullet strikes and unintentionally kills a human, it would be impermissible to charge *A* with intent-to-kill murder and transfer the intent from the dog to the human, because the social harm of murder involves the death of humans and not canines. Similarly, if *A* throws a rock at *B*, intending to injure him, but the rock instead breaks a window in a building behind *B*, *A*'s intent to batter — one type of social harm — may not be used to prove that *A* intended to cause property damage, the social harm of the offense charged.[52]

Overall, confusion could be avoided if courts rejected the transferred intent doctrine, and simply sought to determine whether an actor had the intent to cause the particular social harm required in the definition of the charged offense.

[c] Looking Past the Easy Cases

The paradigmatic transferred intent case has these characteristics: (1) *A* intends to cause a specific harm to one, specific, individual, *B*;[53] (2) *B* escapes unscathed; and (3) an unintended victim, *C*, suffers the harm meant for *B*.[54]

---

[51] 625 A.2d 984 (Md. 1993).

[52] Regina v. Pembliton, 12 Cox C.C. 607 (1874) (Court of Criminal Appeal); see also Mordica v. State, 618 So. 2d 301 (Fla. Dist. Ct. App. 1993) (*M*, a prison inmate, attempted to kick fellow inmate *X*; *M*'s foot hit *V*, a prison guard; held: the transferred intent doctrine does not apply in a prosecution for "battery upon a law enforcement officer"; *M* intended to commit a battery, but not battery of a police officer, a different and more serious type of social harm).

[53] This is an important, and sometimes forgotten characteristic. There is no need to "transfer" intent to a second victim if the actor intended the harm to both victims. For example, so-called "kill zone" cases do not really involve "transferred intent" issues. Assume that *A*, intending to kill *B*, who is holding her baby *C* in her arms, shoots at *B*, knowing that the bullet will have to go through *C* to kill *B*. In short, although *A* only desires to kill *B*, he knows that he will concurrently kill *C*, who is in the line of fire. Therefore, on these facts, *A* has the "intent" — purpose or knowledge, either one of which constitutes common law "intent" — to kill *two* people (*B* purposely, *C* knowingly).

[54] See State v. Hough, 585 N.W.2d 393, 395 (Minn. 1998).

Many supposed transferred intent cases are not so simple.[55] Reconsider the classic case, where A fires at B, misses him entirely, and hits C instead. Or, suppose that the bullet meant for B wounds him and then strikes and kills C. The transferred intent doctrine would obviously permit a prosecutor to charge A with intentional murder of C (the intent "transfers" from B to C). But may the prosecutor *also* charge A with *attempted* murder — an offense also requiring an intent to kill — of B? Or, suppose that the bullet meant for B *does kill B*, but also kills bystander C. Can *two* counts of intent-to-kill murder be permitted here?

It is submitted that the answer in such circumstances normally ought to be "no," yet courts frequently, although not always, invoke the transferred intent doctrine in these and similar circumstances.[56]

It is important to remember that the purpose of the transferred intent doctrine is to put the "bad aim" wrongdoer in the same position he would have found himself if his aim had been good. The doctrine is meant to result in punishment proportional to the wrongdoer's culpability. Often, however, invocation of the transferred intent doctrine will result in disproportional punishment.

This can be seen by the following hypothetical, with two scenarios: Assume A observes B hugging A's wife, C. A, therefore, intends to kill B. A is confident that he can shoot and kill B from a distance without harming C. In Scenario 1, A does exactly what he intended: He kills B and does not kill or wound C. A is guilty of intent-to-kill murder of B. And, in many modern penal codes, A would also be guilty of misdemeanor reckless endangerment of C.[57] In short, the single act of firing one bullet may justifiably result in conviction of A for two offenses, one for each victim, *because A had two culpable states of mind, the intent to kill A, and recklessness as to B.*

In Scenario 2, assume that A's aim is bad, and not good, and the bullet kills C, his wife, and not his intended victim, B. Although the identities of the homicide victim and the person endangered have been switched, A's moral culpabil-

---

[55] Harvey v. State, 681 A.2d 628, 634 (Md. Ct. Spec. App. 1996) (there is "a matrix of no less than nine combinations of criminal harms" that arguably fall under the "transferred intent" umbrella).

[56] E.g., People v. Scott, 927 P.2d 288 (Cal. 1996) (*A* may be convicted of attempted murder of intended victim *B*, who was not hit, and intentional murder of unintended victim *C*); Poe v. State, 671 A.2d 501 (Md. 1996) (under the transferred intent doctrine, *A* may be convicted of attempted murder of intended victim *B*, who was wounded, and intentional murder of unintended victim *C*); Lloyd v. United States, 806 A.2d 1243 (D.C. 2002) (answering affirmatively the question of "whether the transferred intent doctrine, firmly embedded in our jurisprudence, permits a first-degree murder conviction for the shooting death of an unintended victim when the intended victim has also been shot dead"); but see People v. Czahara, 203 Cal. App. 3d 1468 (Ct. App. 1988) (if *A* shoots to kill *B*, wounding *B* and *C*, *A* may be charged with attempted murder of *B*, but not of *C*); Bell v. State, 768 So. 2d 22 (Fla. Dist. Ct. App. 2000) (same); Ford v. State, 625 A.2d 984 (Md. 1993) (if *A* intends to kill *B*, misses him, and wounds but does not kill *C*, *A* may be charged with attempted murder of *B*, but the transferred intent doctrine does not apply to *C*).

[57] E.g., Model Penal Code § 211.2 ("recklessly engages in conduct which places or may place another person in danger of death or serious bodily injury").

ity for the incident remains the same — he intended to kill one person, and he recklessly endangered another. Therefore, it would seem that *A* should still be guilty of one count of intentional murder and one count of reckless endangerment. But, if courts apply the transferred intent doctrine in this case as they often do, *A* will be convicted in Scenario 2, the bad aim case, more severely — he will be guilty of two intent-based offenses, murder (of *C*) and attempted murder (of *B*) — than if his aim had been good.

[B] "Knowingly" or "With Knowledge"[58]

As explained in subsection [A][1], a person who knowingly causes a particular result or knowingly engages in specified conduct is commonly said to have "intended" the harmful result or conduct. Sometimes, however, knowledge of a material fact — an attendant circumstance[59] — is a required element of an offense. For example, it is a federal crime for a person knowingly to import any controlled substance into the country.[60] Under this statute, a person, *D*, who drives an automobile containing marijuana into the United States, is not guilty unless he "knows" of the presence of the contraband — the attendant circumstance — when he crosses the border.

A person has "knowledge" of a material fact if he: (1) is aware of the fact; or (2) correctly believes that the fact exists. Thus, in the marijuana importation hypothetical, *D* "knows" of the presence of the marijuana if he concealed it in the vehicle himself or personally observed its presence ("actual knowledge"); alternatively, he "knows" of the marijuana's existence if he smells it and, as a consequence, believes that it is present ("correct belief" form of "knowledge").

Most jurisdictions also permit a finding of knowledge of an attendant circumstance in a third, more controversial, circumstance, namely, when the actor is guilty of so-called "wilful blindness" or "deliberate ignorance."[61] Although courts and scholars do not agree entirely on the definition of this term, it generally exists if the actor: (a) is aware of a high probability of the existence of the

---

[58] See generally Robin Charlow, *Wilful Ignorance and Criminal Culpability*, 70 Tex. L. Rev. 1351 (1992); Douglas N. Husak & Craig A. Callender, *Wilful Ignorance, Knowledge, and the "Equal Culpability" Thesis: A Study of the Deeper Significance of the Principle of Legality*, 1994 Wis. L. Rev. 29; David Luban, *Contrived Ignorance*, 87 Geo. L.J. 957 (1999); Alan C. Michaels, *Acceptance: The Missing Mental State*, 71 S. Cal. L. Rev. 953 (1998); Ira P. Robbins, *The Ostrich Instruction: Deliberate Ignorance as a Criminal Mens Rea*, 81 J. Crim. L. & Criminology 191 (1990); Kenneth W. Simons, *Does Punishment for "Culpable Indifference" Simply Punish for "Bad Character"? Examining the Requisite Connection Between Mens Rea and Actus Reus*, 6 Buff. Crim. L. Rev. 219 (2002).

[59] See § 9.10[D][3], *supra*.

[60] 21 U.S.C. § 952(a) (2005).

[61] E.g., United States v. Lara-Velasquez, 919 F.2d 946 (5th Cir. 1990); United States v. Jewell, 532 F.2d 697 (9th Cir. 1976); State v. LaFreniere, 481 N.W.2d 412 (Neb. 1992); contra, State v. Nations, 676 S.W.2d 282 (Mo. App. 1984) (interpreting a statute, rejecting the "wilful blindness" concept, and requiring proof of actual knowledge).

fact in question; and (b) deliberately fails to investigate, in order to avoid confirmation of the fact. An instruction to the jury in this regard is sometimes called an "ostrich instruction." One federal judge has explained the ostrich analogy this way:

> [Supposedly, real ostriches] do not just fail to follow through on their suspicions of bad things. They are not merely *careless* birds. They bury their heads in the sand so that they will not see or hear bad things. They *deliberately* avoid acquiring unpleasant knowledge. The ostrich instruction is designed for cases in which there is evidence that the defendant, knowing or strongly suspecting that he is involved in shady dealings, takes steps to make sure that he does not acquire full or exact knowledge. . . .[62]

Thus, in the importation hypothetical, *D* would be guilty of "wilful blindness" or "deliberate ignorance" if, for example, he agreed to drive *X*'s car into the country, although he was highly suspicious that drugs had been concealed in it, and he purposely avoided looking in the trunk or elsewhere because he was afraid that it would confirm his suspicions.[63]

This "wilful blindness" form of "knowledge" is controversial. First, notwithstanding the ostrich analogy, the actor need not take steps of an active nature, equivalent to putting his head in the sand, to be found guilty of wilful blindness; as a practical matter, his culpability can be based on his *failure* to take obvious and simple steps to confirm or dispel his suspicions. The risk in giving an ostrich instruction is that a jury might convict a defendant for merely being a careless bird, i.e., for being negligent, which is a far less culpable state of mind than knowledge. At most, one who suspects the existence of a fact and fails to investigate is *reckless* in acting on the basis of a known suspicion, but recklessness is not the equivalent of knowledge.[64]

Advocates of the wilful blindness doctrine contend that in the real world, absolute knowledge is hard to come by. Therefore, a narrow definition of "knowledge" would reward persons who seek to avoid criminal responsibility by purposeful ignorance. And, it is said, such a person is as culpable as one who is actually aware of a fact or correctly believes that it exists. Critics of the doctrine respond, however, that even if "wilful blindness" is *morally equivalent* to "knowledge," that is not the same as saying that "wilful blindness" *is* "knowledge." As long as an offense is defined in terms of "knowledge," the principle of legality

---

[62] United States v. Giovannetti, 919 F.2d 1223, 1228 (7th Cir. 1990).

[63] See United States v. Jewell, 532 F.2d 697 (9th Cir. 1976).

[64] Robbins, Note 58, *supra*, at 220-27. "Recklessness" is defined in subsection [D][3], *infra*.

Professor Alan Michaels would abandon the wilful blindness doctrine in favor of a *mens rea* concept that he terms "acceptance": "The accepting actor is someone who, aware of a substantial risk that a particular circumstance is present . . . , is so determined to act that he would do so even if he *knew* the circumstance was present." Michaels, Note 58, *supra*, at 957. Michaels reasons that "accepting actors" should be treated the same as those who act knowingly.

teaches that an equivalent — but different — state of mind should be insufficient for conviction.[65]

[C] "Wilfully"[66]

"Wilful" (or, alternatively, "willful") is a "word of many meanings."[67] It is sometimes used as a synonym for "intentional."[68] Sometimes, however, the term means "an act done with a bad purpose"[69] or with "an evil motive."[70] "Wilful" may also connote an "intentional violation of a known legal duty,"[71] or "a purpose to disobey the law."[72] The meaning of the term often cannot be determined except in the context of the legislative history of the offense being charged.

In most circumstances, an intentional wrongdoer acts with a bad purpose or evil motive, and with knowledge that he is violating the law, so it does not matter which meaning of "wilful" is applied. Sometimes, however, the difference is significant. For example, in one federal case, D asserted what he believed to be his constitutional privilege not to incriminate himself, by refusing to answer questions propounded to him by a government agency. As it turned out, the constitutional provision did not apply in his circumstances. Therefore, he was charged with "wilfully" refusing to answer the questions.[73]

If "wilful" means "intentional," D was guilty because he intentionally refused to answer the questions. D's conviction was overturned, however, because his refusal, although intentional, was based on an erroneous belief that he had a lawful right to refuse to answer. Therefore, he lacked an evil motive for the violation, and did not act with the purpose of disobeying the law. It should be noted that when the latter meaning of "wilful" is applied, the presence of this term in the definition of an offense results in an exception to the usual rule that a mistake of law is not a basis for exculpation of an actor.[74]

---

[65] See generally Husak & Callender, Note 58, *supra*.

[66] See generally Michael E. Tigar, *"Willfulness" and "Ignorance" in Federal Criminal Law*, 37 Cleve. St. L. Rev. 525 (1989).

[67] Ratzlaf v. United States, 510 U.S. 135, 141 (1994) (quoting Spies v. United States, 317 U.S. 492, 497 (1943)).

[68] E.g., Commonwealth v. Welansky, 55 N.E.2d 902, 910 (Mass. 1944).

[69] See Townsend v. United States, 95 F.2d 352, 358 (D.C. Cir. 1938).

[70] United States v. Murdock, 290 U.S. 389, 395 (1933), overruled on other grounds by Murphy v. Waterfront Comm'n, 378 U.S. 52 (1964).

[71] Cheek v. United States, 498 U.S. 192, 200 (1991); see also State v. Azneer, 526 N.W.2d 298, 300 (Iowa 1995) ("a voluntary and intentional violation of a known legal duty").

[72] Ratzlaf v. United States, 510 U.S. at 141; see also United States v. Hayden, 64 F.3d 126, 128 (3d Cir. 1995) ("an intent to violate the law itself")

[73] United States v. Murdock, 284 U.S. 141 (1931), overruled in Murphy v. Waterfront Commission, 378 U.S. 52 (1964).

[74] See generally § 13.02[D][2], *infra*.

[D] "Negligence" and "Recklessness"[75]

[1] Overview

Risk-taking is an ever-present aspect of life. Virtually every human act can cause harm to the actor, other persons, property, or non-human life. Nonetheless, society rewards some risk-taking, even as it requires some risk-takers to compensate those who are injured by their conduct, and punishes still others for their risk-taking.

Basically risk-taking falls into four categories: (1) desirable or, at least, neutral risk-taking; (2) risk-taking that justifies civil liability ("civil negligence"); (3) criminally negligent risk-taking ("criminal negligence"); and (4) reckless conduct ("recklessness"). The lines between these categories are not bright and, at times, in dispute. And, unfortunately, courts have often used terms such as "negligence" and "recklessness" interchangeably, so it is even more difficult to distinguish between these types of risk-taking.

[2] "Negligence"

[a] In General

A person's conduct is "negligent" if it constitutes a deviation from the standard of care that a reasonable person would have observed in the actor's situation. Conduct constitutes such a deviation if the actor takes an *unjustifiable* risk of causing harm to another. Thus, "negligence" constitutes *objective* fault, i.e., an actor is not blamed for a wrongful state of mind, but instead is punished for his failure to live up to the standards of the fictional "reasonable person."[76]

Three factors come into play when determining whether a reasonable person would have acted as the defendant did: (1) the gravity of harm that foreseeably would result from the defendant's conduct; (2) the probability of such harm occurring; and (3) the burden — or loss — to the defendant of desisting from the risky conduct, which is simply another way of evaluating the reason for taking the risk. Judge Learned Hand described the relationship of these factors "in

---

[75] See generally Hall, Note 1, supra, at 105-45; Larry Alexander, *Reconsidering the Relationship Among Voluntary Acts, Strict Liability, and Negligence in Criminal Law*, Social Phil. & Pol'y, Spring 1990, at 84; Alexander, Note 27, *supra*; Dressler, Note 27, *supra*; Kimberly Kessler Ferzan, *Opaque Recklessness*, 91 J. Crim. L. & Criminology 597 (2001); George P. Fletcher, *The Theory of Criminal Negligence: A Comparative Analysis*, 119 U. Pa. L. Rev. 401 (1971); Jerome Hall, *Negligent Behavior Should be Excused from Penal Liability*, 63 Colum. L. Rev. 632 (1963); Kyron Huigens, *Virtue and Criminal Negligence*, 1 Buff. Crim. L. Rev. 431 (1998); Heidi M. Hurd, *The Deontology of Negligence*, 76 B.U. L. Rev. 249 (1996); Michaels, Note 58, *supra*; Samuel H. Pillsbury, *Crimes of Indifference*, 49 Rutgers L. Rev. 105 (1996); Kenneth W. Simons, *Culpability and Retributive Theory: The Problem of Criminal Negligence*, 5 J. Contemp. Issues 365 (1994).

[76] The nature of the "reasonable person" is considered in § 10.04[D][2][d], *infra*.

algebraic terms: if the probability [of harm] be called P; the [gravity of] injury, L; and the burden, B; liability depends upon whether B is less than L multiplied by P: i.e., whether B [is less than] PL."[77] Although this formula cannot be applied with scientific precision, its expression emphasizes the point that, as the gravity and/or probability of harm increases, the more substantial the actor's reason for taking the risk must be.

For example, suppose that driver *D* thoughtlessly darts between lanes in his car at a very fast rate of speed on a busy public road, in order to get to a friend's birthday party. As a result, *D* causes an accident and kills *V*. If *D* were sued or prosecuted for negligence in *V*'s death, a jury might find that *D*'s conduct was negligent: The gravity of harm was substantial (loss of life); the probability of such harm occurring was not insubstantial; and the burden to defendant of driving in a safer manner was small (he would have reached his party a bit late). On the other hand, if *D* drives in precisely the same manner in order to get his gravely ill child to the hospital, a jury might determine that *D* took a justifiable — non-negligent — risk, in light of the child's condition.

[b] Distinguishing Civil from Criminal Negligence

A person who breaches his duty of care to another has acted negligently, as defined in subsection [a]. However, not every breach constitutes a crime. As Jerome Hall has observed, " '[b]lame' is a very wide notion and, like praise, it permeates almost all of daily life. Important differences exist between raising an eyebrow and putting a man in jail. . . ."[78] More specifically, the blame expressed in a civil finding of negligence is not the same as the blame communicated by a jury when it returns a verdict of guilty of criminal negligence in a criminal prosecution.

Although rare exceptions exist, "civil negligence ordinarily is [considered] an inappropriate predicate by which to define . . . criminal conduct."[79] To establish *criminal* responsibility for negligence, the prosecution must ordinarily show more than mere deviation from the standard of care that would constitute *civil* negligence.[80]

"Criminal negligence" is conduct that represents a *gross* deviation from the standard of reasonable care.[81] Put more precisely, a person is criminally negligent if he takes a *substantial*, unjustifiable risk of causing the social harm that constitutes the offense charged. Applying the Learned Hand formula, crim-

---

[77] United States v. Carroll Towing Co., 159 F.2d 169, 173 (2d Cir. 1947).

[78] Hall, Note 75, *supra*, at 641.

[79] Santillanes v. State, 849 P.2d 358, 365 (N.M. 1993).

[80] State v. Jones, 126 A.2d 273, 275 (Me. 1956).

[81] State v. Hazelwood, 946 P.2d 875, 878 (Alaska 1997).

inal negligence exists when "PL" *far* outweighs "B";[82] the level of negligence should be so great "that it would be shocking to allow the actor's lack of awareness to excuse his actions in the circumstances."[83]

Frequently courts describe criminal negligence as "gross negligence," "culpable negligence," or "recklessness." However, as explained in subsection [3], *infra*, the term "recklessness" should not be equated with criminal negligence.[84]

[c] Should Negligence Be Punished?

Punishment for negligence is controversial. It should be remembered that "*mens rea*" means "guilty mind," and yet the negligent actor is blamed and punished for what *isn't* in (or on) his mind, namely, attention to risk that a reasonable person would display.

Some opponents of punishment for negligence contend that, by definition, a negligent actor fails to perceive the risks of his conduct and, therefore, cannot be deterred. Since utilitarians believe that punishment should be avoided if it will not result in a net reduction in societal pain, negligent harmdoers should not be punished.

The utilitarian defense of punishment for negligence primarily focuses on general deterrence. Holmes has bluntly observed that "public policy sacrifices the individual to the general good."[85] In this context, punishment of an individual negligent actor, even if he was undeterrable on this occasion, may send a useful message to others: "Conduct yourself more safely, or else you will be punished." Punishment of the negligent harmdoer may also have an incidental specific deterrence benefit: The negligent actor who is punished may act more carefully in the future.

Turning away from utilitarianism, retributivists disagree amongst themselves on the moral propriety of punishment for negligence.[86] Some retributivist opponents of such punishment reason that the basis for just punishment is voluntary wrongdoing.[87] People who intentionally cause harm choose to act

---

[82] The common law generally requires proof that the actor took a substantial *and* unjustifiable risk. But, it might be better to say that the actor must take a *substantially* unjustifiable risk. That is, "substantial" should not be an adjective modifying "risk," but an adverb modifying the unjustifiability of the risk. Even a non-substantial risk, if taken for *no* good reason at all, should constitute criminal negligence. Dressler, Note 27, *supra*, at 27-28. Thus, one who, "just for the hell of it," takes a tiny risk of causing death to another should be deemed criminally negligent, on the ground that the small risk is substantially outweighed by the virtually non-existent justification for the risk-taking.

[83] Commonwealth v. Heck, 491 A.2d 212, 225 (Pa. Super. Ct. 1985).

[84] State v. Hazelwood, 946 P.2d at 878 (criminal negligence "does not spill over into recklessness").

[85] Holmes, Note 24, *supra*, at 48.

[86] For a useful discussion of the competing arguments, see Simons, Note 75, *supra*.

[87] Hall, Note 75, *supra*, at 635.

wrongly and, consequently, may properly be punished. Similarly, one who is consciously aware that his planned conduct is unjustifiably risky, but proceeds anyway,[88] exercises a choice for which he may fairly be held responsible. The negligent actor's risk-taking, however, is inadvertent: He does not appreciate that his conduct is dangerous, although a jury may believe that he *should have been aware*. As a consequence, we cannot blame him for bad choice-making. We can only blame him in the civil tort sense for failing to live up to the "reasonable person" standard, and even here blame may be unjustifiable, if the actor was incapable of living up to such a standard.

Retributive defenders of punishment contend that, at least in some circumstances, criminal blame *is* justified for negligence, on the ground that the negligent actor's failure to perceive the riskiness of his conduct constitutes "culpable indifference" to the rights and interests of those around him.[89] On occasion, it may be fair to argue that a negligent actor, by his lack of awareness of the risk, manifests an insensitivity to the rights of others to be free from unnecessary risk. If *"mens rea"* implies that the actor is morally blameworthy, or that his conduct demonstrates a character flaw, then the ethically insensitive wrongdoer may possess sufficient *"mens rea"* to deserve punishment for the harm he causes.[90] The negligent actor's explanation for the injury is frequently something like: "But, I just didn't think." Defenders of punishment for negligence argue that if a person can be blamed because he failed to act, there is no reason why he should not be blamed because he failed to think.[91]

[d] Who Really Is the "Reasonable Person"?: Initial Observations[92]

Jurists have struggled for centuries to identify the "reasonable person," or what used to be called the "reasonable prudent *man*." He was once described as "an ideal, . . . the embodiment of all those qualities which we demand of the good citizen."[93] A leading torts treatise has stated that "[h]e is not to be identified with any ordinary individual, who might occasionally do unreasonable things; he is a prudent and careful person, *who is always up to standard*."[94] According

---

[88] Such a person is acting recklessly. See subsection [3], *infra*.

[89] Simons, Note 75, *supra*, at 388-90.

[90] Fletcher, Note 75, *supra*, at 416-18.

[91] Hart, Note 1, *supra*, at 151-52.

[92] See generally Mayo Moran, Rethinking the Reasonable Person (2003); Ronald K.L. Collins, *Language, History and the Legal Process: A Profile of the "Reasonable Man"*, 8 Rutgers-Cam. L.J. 311 (1977); Caroline Forell, *Essentialism, Empathy, and the Reasonable Woman*, 1994 U. Ill. L. Rev. 769; Robert Unikel, Note, *"Reasonable" Doubts: A Critique of the Reasonable Woman Standard in American Jurisprudence*, 87 Nw. U. L. Rev. 326 (1992). See also the discussion and cites at §§ 18.05[A] and 31.07[B][2][b][ii], *infra*.

[93] A.P. Herbert, Misleading Cases in the Common Law 12 (1930).

[94] Dan B. Dobbs et al., Prosser and Keeton on Torts 175 (5th ed. 1984).

to this description, nobody is *always* a reasonable person; every one of us, at least occasionally, acts negligently, even if most of us are fortunate enough not to injure others in the process.

Although the stated standard is objective — the defendant's conduct is compared to this external ideal — there are constant pressures on courts to "subjectivize" the "reasonable person," that is, to incorporate into the "reasonable person" some of the mental and/or physical characteristics of the defendant, or by incorporating the defendant's personal life experiences. For example, if the defendant, a man of low education or low mental acuity, is prosecuted for negligently causing the death of his child, the defendant may seek to have his conduct judged by the standard of a reasonable person with a similar level of education and/or mental acuity. Or, suppose that the father failed to obtain traditional medical care for his child because he is a Christian Scientist who believes that medicine is unnecessary or wrong. He may ask to be judged by the standards of a reasonable Christian Scientist. Or, a prior mugging victim suddenly confronted by "threatening youths" may seek to have his self-defensive actions, which must be reasonable, measured against the standard of the reasonable prior mugging victim.

The traditional rule, which is under considerable attack and undergoing significant modern change, is that, although a defendant's unusual physical characteristics (e.g., blindness), if relevant to the case, are incorporated into the "reasonable person" standard, a defendant's unusual mental characteristics are not. Holmes expressed the traditional view that the law does not take "account of the infinite varieties of temperament, intellect and education which make the internal character of a given act so different," and that it "does not attempt to see men as God sees them."[95]

There are few easy or uncontroversial lines drawn in this realm. Just as there is great debate about whether negligence should be punished at all, there is considerable disagreement today on whether the law should "swat the subjectivist bug"[96] or, instead, encourage more subjectivism. This issue is considered in various places in this Text, and is more profitably considered in the context of specific legal doctrines. However, it may be noted here that one's views of whether the criminal law should primarily be concerned with deterrence or, instead, retributive just deserts will inevitably color one's approach to the issue of whether (and to what extent) the characteristics and experiences of the person being evaluated should be included in the "reasonable person."

---

[95] Holmes, Note 24, *supra*, at 108.

[96] Celia Wells, *Swatting the Subjectivist Bug*, 1982 Crim. L. Rev. 209.

[3] "Recklessness"

In the past, "recklessness" was a synonym for "criminal negligence." Today, however, a line is drawn between these two concepts, with "recklessness" falling on the more culpable side of the line.

As an independent concept, two definitions of "recklessness" have developed. According to the tort law definition, which also has some support in the criminal law, a person acts "recklessly" if he takes a *very* substantial and unjustifiable risk. So understood, "civil negligence," "criminal negligence," and "recklessness" lie on a continuum: Each involves unjustifiable risk-taking; they differ only in respect to the degree of the actor's deviation from the standard of due care.

Today, however, most jurisdictions reject this definition of "recklessness." Instead, a finding of recklessness requires proof that the actor disregarded a substantial and unjustifiable risk *of which he was aware*.[97] According to this prevailing view, the line between "criminal negligence" and "recklessness" is *not* drawn on the basis of the extent of the actor's deviation from the standard of reasonable care — the deviation is gross in both cases — but rather is founded on the actor's state of mind. Criminal negligence involves inadvertent risk-taking (we are saying that the defendant, as a reasonable person, *should have been aware* of the substantial and unjustifiable risk he was taking); in contrast, recklessness implicates *subjective* fault, in that the actor was aware of the substantial and unjustifiable risk he was taking, and yet he consciously disregarded it and proceeded with his dangerous conduct.[98]

[E] "Malice"

"Malice" is a critical common law and statutory *mens rea* term. Although the term has a more complicated meaning in the context of murder,[99] in most circumstances a person acts with "malice" if he intentionally or recklessly causes the social harm prohibited by the offense.[100] Although language to the contrary can be found in common law treatises,[101] the term "malice" is rarely employed today in its popular, nonlegal sense, as meaning, simply, "ill-will," "spite," or "wickedness."

---

[97] Farmer v. Brennan, 511 U.S. 825, 837-38 (1994).

[98] Mata-Medina v. People, 71 P.3d 973, 978 (Colo. 2003).

[99] See § 31.02[B][2], *infra*.

[100] Regina v. Cunningham, 41 Crim. App. 155, 2 Q.B. 396, 2 All. E.R. 412 (1957) (Court of Criminal Appeal).

[101] 4 Blackstone, Note 14, *supra*, at *198-99 (in the context of common law murder, defining "malice aforethought" as "any evil design in general; the dictate of a wicked, depraved, and malignant heart").

For example, in *Regina v. Cunningham*,[102] *C*, a thief, wrenched a gas meter from gas pipes in the cellar of a building in which *V* resided, in order to steal coins inside the meter. Gases escaped into *V*'s living quarters, unintentionally harming *V*. *C* was prosecuted for "maliciously" causing the injury to *V*.

The trial judge defined "malice" in terms of wickedness. In that sense, *C* could be convicted because the harm was the consequence of his immoral efforts to steal money. However, according to the more modern definition of "malice" set out above, which the appellate court said was appropriate, the issue is more complicated. *C* did not intentionally cause the social harm to *V*, but he may have recklessly caused it. By tearing the meter from the gas pipes, *C* arguably disregarded a substantial and unjustifiable risk to *V*'s safety. If so, and if *C* was aware of this risk and consciously disregarded it, then it is correct to state that *C* recklessly caused the social harm and, therefore, acted with "malice." If he did *not* have such foresight — if he *should* have been aware of the risk, but was not — then he acted in a criminally negligent manner, which would fall outside the definition of "malice."

§ 10.05 STATUTORY INTERPRETATION: WHAT ELEMENTS DOES A *MENS REA* TERM MODIFY?[103]

In *United States v. X-Citement Video, Inc.*,[104] the Supreme Court was required to interpret a federal statute that made it a felony to knowingly transport, receive, or distribute in interstate or foreign commerce any visual depiction "involv[ing] the use of a minor engaging in sexually explicit conduct."[105] The defendant did not deny that he knowingly transported and distributed non-obscene sexually explicit materials in interstate commerce. He claimed, however, that he did not know that the person depicted in the videos was a minor. The issue for the Court was whether such knowledge was required under the statute. A fairly straightforward reading of the statute suggests that the term "knowingly" modifies the conduct or result elements ("transport, receive, or distribute") of the offense. But, does "knowingly" *also* modify the statutory attendant circumstance that the person depicted in the videos is underage?

There is no foolproof method for interpreting criminal statutes. The general rule is that if a statute is not clear on its face, the court will seek to interpret the statute in the manner that best gives effect to legislative intent. In determining legislative will, judges often consider the "legislative history of an act

---

[102] Regina v. Cunningham, 41 Crim. App. 155, 2 Q.B. 396, 2 All. E.R. 412 (1957) (Court of Criminal Appeal). The case is more fully discussed in § 10.02[B], *supra*.

[103] See generally Peter J. Henning, *Statutory Interpretation and the Federalization of Criminal Law*, 86 J. Crim. L. & Criminology 1167 (1996); John Shepard Wiley, Jr., *Not Guilty by Reason of Blamelessness: Culpability in Federal Criminal Interpretation*, 85 Va. L. Rev. 1021 (1999).

[104] 513 U.S. 64 (1994).

[105] 18 U.S.C. § 2252 (2005).

and the circumstances surrounding its adoption; earlier statutes on the same subject; the common law as it was understood at the time of the enactment of the statute; and previous interpretations of the same or similar statutes."[106]

Courts also consider the structure of a statute, taking into consideration rules of grammar. For example, if there is only one statutory *mens rea* term, and it is set out at the beginning of the statute, a court *may* interpret this to mean that the word modifies every *actus reus* element that follows it. A different result would probably apply, however, if the culpability term *follows* various *actus reus* elements, but *precedes* others, in which case the court may conclude that the *mens rea* element applies in a "forward," but not "backward" direction. For example, assume that a statute is drafted in this form: "A person is guilty of a felony if he [does X] with the *intent* of [causing Y and Z]." Here, the term "intent" probably modifies Y and Z, but not X.[107]

Sometimes courts are reluctant to follow the most grammatical reading of a statute if such an interpretation would conflict with "background assumption[s] of our criminal law,"[108] one of the most important of which is that a "presumption in favor of a scienter [*mens rea*] requirement should apply to each of the statutory elements that criminalize otherwise innocent conduct."[109] For example, in *X-Citement Video*, the Supreme Court held that, to be convicted, the defendant must know that the person depicted in the video was underage. Although a grammatical reading of the statute might have worked just as well, the Court instead reasoned that distribution of sexually explicit, but non-obscene, videos of adults was lawful; therefore, it was essential that the government prove that the defendant knew of the underage status of those involved in the sexually explicit activities, since this was what converted otherwise legally innocent conduct into criminality.

§ 10.06 "SPECIFIC INTENT" AND "GENERAL INTENT"

The terms "specific intent" and "general intent" are the bane of criminal law students and lawyers. This is because the terms are critical to understanding various common law rules of criminal responsibility,[110] yet the concepts are so

---

[106] In re Banks, 244 S.E.2d 386, 389 (N.C. 1978).

[107] E.g., United States v. Yermian, 468 U.S. 63 (1984) (a federal offense provided that "whoever, in any matter within the jurisdiction of any department or agency of the United States knowingly . . . makes any false . . . statements . . . shall be fined"; Y admitted that he knowingly made false statements in a questionnaire sent by his employer to the Department of Defense, but he denied that he knew that the false statements pertained to any "matter within the jurisdiction of any department or agency of the United States"; held: "knowingly" did not modify the introductory phrase).

[108] Liparota v. United States, 471 U.S. 419, 426 (1985).

[109] United States v. X-Citement Video, Inc., 513 U.S. at 72. For further discussion of the general presumption in favor of a culpability requirement, see Chapter 11, *infra*.

[110] E.g., see §§ 12.03 (mistake of fact); 13.02[D] (mistake of law); 24.03 (voluntary intoxication); 26.02 (diminished capacity), *infra*.

"notoriously difficult . . . to define and apply . . . [that] a number of text writers recommend that they be abandoned altogether."[111]

Historically, "general intent" referred to any offense for which the only *mens rea* required was a blameworthy state of mind; "specific intent" was meant to emphasize that the definition of the offense expressly required proof of a particular mental state.[112] In other words, an offense that only required proof of "*mens rea*" in the "culpability" sense of the term was a "general intent" crime; offenses that required "*mens rea*" in the "elemental" sense were "specific intent" in nature.[113] This dichotomy was understandable: The definitions of most common law and early statutory offenses were silent in regard to *mens rea*; those offenses that expressly required a particular state of mind — e.g., murder ("malice aforethought"), larceny ("intent to steal"), and burglary ("intent to commit a felony [inside a dwelling]") — stood out, and were thus denominated as "specific intent."

Today, however, most criminal statutes expressly include a *mens rea* term, or a particular state of mind is judicially implied, so the line between "general" and "specific" intent is much more difficult to draw. Making matters worse, there is no universally accepted meaning of the terms. Sometimes, courts draw the following distinction: An offense is "specific intent" if the crime requires proof that the actor's conscious object, or purpose, is to cause the social harm set out in the definition of the offense.[114] In contrast, a crime is "general intent" in nature if the actor can be convicted upon proof of any lesser state of mind, such as when he causes the harm knowingly, recklessly, or negligently.

But, this is not the only way the term is explained. Generally speaking, a "specific intent" offense is one in which the definition of the crime expressly: (1) includes an intent or purpose to do some future act, or to achieve some further consequence (i.e., a special motive for the conduct), beyond the conduct or result that constitutes the actus reus of the offense;[115] or (2) provides that the actor must be aware of a statutory attendant circumstance. An offense that does not contain one of these features is termed "general intent."

For example, common law burglary is defined as "breaking and entering of the dwelling of another in the nighttime with intent to commit a felony."[116] The *actus reus* of this offense is complete when the offender breaks and enters

---

[111] People v. Hood, 462 P.2d 370, 377 (Cal. 1969).

[112] Commonwealth v. Sibinich, 598 N.E.2d 673, 675 n.2, 676 n.3 (Mass. App. Ct. 1992).

[113] For discussion of the "culpability" and "elemental" meanings of "*mens rea*," see § 10.02, *supra*.

[114] United States v. Bailey, 444 U.S. 394, 405 (1980); United States v. Blair, 54 F.3d 639, 642 (10th Cir. 1995); Harris v. State, 728 A.2d 180, 183 (Md. 1999).

[115] People v. Hood, 462 P.2d at 378; Dorador v. State, 573 P.2d 839, 843 (Wyo. 1978).

[116] Mondie v. Commonwealth, 158 S.W.3d 203, 207 (Ky. 2005).

another person's dwelling at night; he need not commit a felony inside to be convicted of burglary. The requisite *mens rea*, therefore, pertains to a planned future act (commission of a felony) that is not part of the *actus reus*. Consequently, common law burglary is a specific-intent offense.

Similarly, larceny is the trespassory taking and carrying away of the personal property of another *with the intent to permanently deprive the other person of his property* ("intent to steal"). That is, a person not guilty of the offense if he, merely, intentionally takes and carries away another person's property. Instead, he must have a particular motive for his actions, namely, to deprive the owner of the property permanently (and not, simply, temporarily). Therefore, larceny is a specific-intent offense, as defined above.

Another example of a specific-intent crime would be "receiving stolen property with knowledge that it is stolen." According to this definition, the actor who receives the stolen property (the *actus reus* of the offense) must have knowledge — awareness — of the attendant circumstance that the property was "stolen" in nature.

In contrast to these offenses, consider battery, sometimes defined statutorily as "intentional application of unlawful force upon another." This is a general-intent crime, for the simple reason that the definition does not contain any specific intent. The only mental state required in its definition is the intent to "apply unlawful force upon another," the *actus reus* of the crime.

§ 10.07 MODEL PENAL CODE[117]

No aspect of the Model Penal Code has had greater influence on the direction of American criminal law than Section 2.02 of the Code, which sets out the "General Requirements of Culpability." As one commentator has observed, the purpose of Section 2.02 was to "obliterate[ ] ill-defined, confusing common law language and concepts and replace[ ] them with four specifically defined hierarchical levels of culpability in relation to the three objective element types [conduct elements; result elements; and attendant circumstances][118] used to define crimes."[119]

---

[117] See generally Kimberly Kessler Ferzan, *Don't Abandon the Model Penal Code Yet! Thinking Through Simons's Rethinking*, 6 Buff. Crim. L. Rev. 185 (2002); Ronald L. Gainer, *The Culpability Provisions of the Model Penal Code*, 19 Rutgers L.J. 575 (1988); Paul H. Robinson & Jane A. Grall, *Element Analysis in Defining Criminal Liability: The Model Penal Code and Beyond*, 35 Stan. L. Rev. 681 (1983); Kenneth W. Simons, *Should the Model Penal Code's Mens Rea Provisions Be Amended?*, 1 Ohio St. Crim. L.J. 179 (2003).

[118] See § 9.10[D], *supra*.

[119] Dannye Holley, *The Influence of the Model Penal Code's Culpability Provisions on State Legislatures: A Study of Lost Opportunities, Including Abolishing the Mistake of Fact Doctrine*, 27 Sw. U. L. Rev. 229, 230 (1997).

[A] Section 2.02: In General

Section 2.02 takes an exclusively "elemental"[120] approach to the concept of *mens rea*. Subsection (1) provides that, except in the case of offenses characterized as "violations,"[121] a person may not be convicted of an offense unless "he acted purposely, knowingly, recklessly or negligently, as the law may require, with respect to *each* material element of the offense." In other words, the Code requires the prosecution to prove that the defendant committed the *actus reus* of the offense — *indeed, each material ingredient of the offense* — with a culpable state of mind, as set out in the specific statute. Furthermore, the legislature may choose to require different levels of culpability for each material element. For example, a statute could be drafted with the following structure: "It is a felony to *purposely* do X and *knowingly* do Y, so as to *recklessly* cause Z."

This provision is noteworthy in various regards. First, a person may not be convicted solely on the ground that he acted with a morally blameworthy state of mind, i.e., the Code eschews the "culpability" meaning of *"mens rea."* Second, the common law distinction between "general intent" and "specific intent"[122] is discarded.

Third, the Model Penal Code removes the clutter of common law and statutory *mens rea* terms, and replaces them with just four carefully defined terms: "purposely"; "knowingly"; "recklessly"; and "negligently."[123]

Fourth, the phrase "material element of the offense," as used in Section 2.02 and throughout the Code, includes "elements" relating to the existence of a justification or excuse for the actor's conduct,[124] i.e., to defenses to crimes. As a consequence, since Section 2.02 states that one of the four culpability terms applies to *every* material element of a crime, this Section is also relevant in determining whether a person is entitled to acquittal on the grounds of an affirmative defense.

---

[120] See § 10.02[C], *supra*.

[121] A "violation" is an offense (but not a "crime"), for which no sentence other than a fine or civil penalty is authorized. Model Penal Code § 1.04(5). Section 2.05, rather than § 2.02, pertains to violations.

[122] See § 10.06, *supra*.

[123] Because "wilful" is a commonly used non-MPC statutory term, see § 10.04[C], *supra*, the drafters of the Code deal with it expressly: A person who acts "knowingly" satisfies the requirement of wilfulness. Model Penal Code § 2.02(8).

[124] Model Penal Code § 1.13(10)(ii).

[B] Culpability Terms

[1] "Purposely"

The term "purposely" has two definitions, depending upon whether the material element of the offense under consideration pertains to a result or conduct, on the one hand, or to an attendant circumstance, on the other. In the context of a result or conduct, a person acts "purposely" if it his "conscious object to engage in conduct of that nature or to cause such a result."[125] So defined, "purposely" is a mental state comparable to the first of the two alternative common law definitions of the word "intentional."[126] For example, in the airplane bombing hypothetical discussed earlier,[127] the death of V, D's wife, was "purposeful" because it was D's conscious object to take V's life, but the deaths of the remaining passengers were not purposeful.[128]

A person acts "purposely" with respect to attendant circumstances if he "is aware of the existence of such circumstances or he believes or hopes that they exist."[129] For example, if D enters an occupied structure in order to commit a felony inside, he has acted "purposely" regarding the attendant circumstance that the structure was occupied, if he was aware it was occupied or hoped that it would be, but not otherwise.

---

[125] Model Penal Code § 2.02(2)(a)(i). The Code effectively applies the common law "transferred intent" doctrine. See § 10.04[A][3], *supra*. Section 2.03(2)(a) provides that when purposely causing a particular result is an element of an offense, that element is established if "the actual result differs from that designed or contemplated . . . , only in respect that a different person or different property" is harmed. For example, if A's purpose is to kill B, but he accidentally kills C instead, the requisite element of "purpose" is established. Or, if D, intending to set E's house on fire, causes F's home to burn down instead, D may be convicted of an offense prohibiting the purposeful destruction of another's property.

The Code also provides that a defendant is not relieved of liability for an offense if *less* harm occurs than it was the actor's conscious object to cause. For example, if D's conscious object is to kill two persons, but he only succeeds in killing one, the element of "purpose" is established. Model Penal Code § 2.03(2)(a). But, if D intends to kill X and instead kills X and Y, D's purpose to kill X would not apply as to Y, since here he has caused more, not less, harm than was designed. D's liability, if any, for Y's death would have to be based on a different state of mind, perhaps on the ground that firing a gun at X in Y's proximity constitutes recklessness as to Y's safety.

[126] See § 10.04[A], *supra*.

[127] See the example in the text at Note 30, *supra*.

[128] What if an actor's purpose to cause a certain result is conditional? For example, suppose that D threatens to kill V, the driver of an automobile, unless V relinquishes the car to D. Is D guilty of taking a motor vehicle with the "purpose to cause death or serious bodily harm"? See Holloway v. United States, 526 U.S. 1 (1999) (applying the Model Penal Code to a non-MPC statute). The Code provides that "[w]hen a particular purpose is an element of an offense, the element is established although the purpose is conditional, *unless* the condition negatives the harm or evil sought to be prevented by the law defining the offense." Model Penal Code § 2.02(6). In this case, the condition of handing over the car to avoid an assault does not negative the harm sought to be prevented by the carjacking law, which is that an automobile not be taken by the use of force or threat of force. See generally Gideon Yaffe, *Conditional Intent and Mens Rea*, 10 Legal Theory 273 (2004).

[129] Model Penal Code § 2.02(2)(a)(ii).

[2] "Knowingly"

The Code provides two definitions of the term "knowingly," one that applies to results, and the second that pertains to conduct and attendant circumstances. A *result* is "knowingly" caused if the actor "is aware that it is practically certain that his conduct will cause such a result."[130] Thus, in the airplane bombing hypothetical, *D knowingly* killed *V*'s fellow passengers, assuming *D* was aware that his bomb would almost certainly kill those on board.[131] If *D* lacked normal mental faculties, or for any other reason had a distorted sense of reality, so that he was not subjectively aware that their deaths were practically certain to result, then a finding of "knowledge" would not be appropriate.

With "attendant circumstances" and "conduct" elements, one acts "knowingly" if he is "aware that his conduct is of that nature or that such [attendant] circumstances exist."[132] For example, suppose *D* fired a loaded gun in *V*'s direction, and was prosecuted for "knowingly endangering the life of another." *D* is guilty if he was aware that his conduct endangered the life of another person. If he was not aware (perhaps because he did not see anyone in the vicinity), then *D* did not act knowingly, no matter how obvious *V*'s presence may have been.

The same approach is used with attendant circumstances. If *D* purchased stolen property and was prosecuted for "knowingly receiving stolen property," *D* would be guilty of the offense if, when he received the property, he was aware that it had been stolen. In order to deal with the problem of "wilful blindness"[133] the Code includes a special and controversial provision that states that knowledge is established, if "a person is aware of a high probability of . . . [the attendant circumstance's] existence, unless he actually believes that it does not exist."[134] The latter definition is subject to criticisms similar to those generally directed at the wilful blindness doctrine.

[3] "Recklessly" and "Negligently"

[a] In General

The Code provides that a person acts "recklessly" if he "consciously disregards a substantial and unjustified risk that the material element exists or will result from his conduct." A risk is "substantial and unjustifiable" if "considering the

---

[130] Model Penal Code § 2.02(2)(b)(ii).

[131] Observe, therefore, that the common law term "intent" is separated into two Model Code terms, "purposely" and "knowingly." This separation permits the legislature, if it chooses to do so, to make finer culpability distinctions than the common law permits.

[132] Model Penal Code § 2.02(2)(b)(i).

[133] See § 10.04[B], *supra*.

[134] Model Penal Code § 2.02(7).

nature and purpose of the actor's conduct and the circumstances known to him, its disregard involves a gross deviation from the standard of conduct that a law-abiding person would observe in the actor's situation."[135]

A person's conduct is "negligent" if the actor "should be aware of a substantial and unjustifiable risk that the material element exists or will result from his conduct."[136] The definition of "substantial and unjustifiable"[137] is the same as that provided for in the definition of "recklessness," except that the term "reasonable person" is substituted for "law-abiding person."

"Negligence" and "recklessness," therefore, require the same degree of risk-taking: "substantial and unjustifiable." The difference between them lies in the fact that the reckless actor "consciously disregards" the risk, whereas the negligent actor's risk-taking is inadvertent.[138] This tracks the modern common law approach to these doctrines; indeed, the Model Penal Code influenced modern courts, and not vice-versa, in this regard.

[b] Nature of the "Reasonable Person"

The conduct of the "reasonable person" (and "law-abiding person" in the context of "recklessness") is evaluated from the perspective of a person "in the actor's situation." This phrase is ambiguous, but the Commentary opines that physical characteristics, such as an actor's blindness, or the fact that he has just suffered a heart attack, "would certainly be facts to be considered in judgment involving criminal liability," but hereditary factors and matters of intelligence and temperament "would not be held material . . . and could not be without depriving the criterion of all its objectivity." The drafters of the Code did not intend "to displace discriminations of this kind, but rather to leave the issue to the courts."[139] Thus, more than four decades after the American Law Institute adopted the Code, courts continue to struggle to find the proper balance between the opposing poles of pure subjectivism and objectivism.

[C] Principles of Statutory Interpretation

The Model Code provides solutions to some of the difficult problems of statutory interpretation that have confounded courts dealing with pre-Code statutes.[140] First, according to Section 2.02(4), if a statute defining an offense "prescribes the kind of culpability that is sufficient for the commission of the offense, without distinguishing among the material elements thereof," a court

---

[135] Model Penal Code § 2.02(2)(c).

[136] Model Penal Code § 2.02(2)(d).

[137] For potential criticism of this terminology, see Note 82, *supra*.

[138] State v. Brooks, 658 A.2d 22, 26-27 (Vt. 1995).

[139] American Law Institute, Comment to § 2.02, at 242.

[140] See § 10.05, *supra*.

will interpret such culpability provision as applying to *every* material element of the offense, "unless a contrary purpose plainly appears." In other words, a single *mens rea* term — whatever it is — modifies *each actus reus* element of the offense, absent a plainly contrary purpose of the legislature.

For example, Section 212.3 (False Imprisonment) provides, in part, that it is an offense to "knowingly restrain another unlawfully." Applying Section 2.02(4), this means that the prosecution must prove that the defendant knowingly restrained the victim, *and* that he knew that the restraint was unlawful.[141] In contrast, if a single culpability term is placed by the drafters in the middle of the statute, i.e., some material elements of the offense precede the culpability term and some come after, this should suggest a contrary purpose. For example, Section 221.1 (Burglary) provides in part that it is an offense to "enter an occupied structure with purpose to commit a crime therein." The placement of "purpose" after the phrase "enter an occupied structure" plainly demonstrates the drafters' intention not to require "purpose" as to the preceding phrase, or else it would have placed the word "purposely" at the start.[142]

In the burglary example, does this mean that *no* culpability is required as to the "entry of the occupied structure"? No. It must be remembered that Section 2.02(1) provides that *some* form of culpability — purpose, knowledge, recklessness, or negligence — is required for *each* material element of an offense. Therefore, when the definition of a criminal offense is silent regarding the matter of culpability as to a material element of the offense, as in the burglary statute, Section 2.02(3) provides an interpretive solution: The material element "is established if a person acts purposely, knowingly, or recklessly."

In the current case, the phrase "entry of an occupied structure" actually consists of two material elements: (1) the conduct element of "entry"; and (2) the attendant circumstance that the entry be of an "occupied structure." Therefore, in accordance with Section 2.02(3), a person may not be convicted of burglary under the Code unless he purposely, knowingly, or recklessly entered an occupied structure, with the purpose to commit a crime inside. For example, if *D*, with the purpose to commit a crime therein, purposely entered an occupied structure *believing it was unoccupied*, he could *not* be convicted of burglary if he was negligent in his belief that the structure was unoccupied. He could be convicted, however, if he was reckless in this regard.

---

[141] American Law Institute, Comment to § 2.02, at 245-46.

[142] See *id.* at 246.

Chapter 11
STRICT LIABILITY

§ 11.01 GENERAL PRINCIPLES[1]

[A] "Strict Liability": Definition

The term "strict liability" is used in various contexts.[2] Generally speaking, however, it is important to distinguish between strict liability *doctrines* and strict liability *crimes*. A strict liability doctrine is a rule of criminal responsibility that authorizes the conviction of a morally innocent person for violation of an offense, even though the crime, by definition, requires proof of a *mens rea*. An example is the rule that a person who is ignorant of, or who misunderstands the meaning of, a criminal law may be punished for violating it, even if her ignorance or mistake of law was reasonable. Strict liability doctrines of this sort are discussed elsewhere in the Text.[3]

The focus of this chapter is on strict liability offenses, or crimes that, by definition, do not contain a *mens rea* requirement regarding one or more elements of the *actus reus*. This chapter considers the nature, wisdom, and constitutionality of such offenses.

---

[1] See generally Appraising Strict Liability (A.P. Simester, ed. 2005); Stuart P. Green, *Why It's a Crime to Tear the Tag off a Mattress: Overcriminalization and the Moral Content of Regulatory Offenses*, 46 Emory L.J. 1533 (1997); Douglas N. Husak, *Varieties of Strict Liability*, 8 Canadian J. L. & Jurisprudence 189 (1995); Stephen J. Morse, *Inevitable Mens Rea*, 27 Harv. J. L. & Pub. Pol'y, 51 (2003); Gerhard O.W. Mueller, *Mens Rea and the Law Without It*, 58 W. Va. L. Rev. 34 (1955); Steven S. Nemerson, Note, *Criminal Liability Without Fault: A Philosophical Perspective*, 75 Colum. L. Rev. 1517 (1975); Herbert L. Packer, *Mens Rea and the Supreme Court*, 1962 Sup. Ct. Rev. 107; Francis Bowes Sayre, *Public Welfare Offenses*, 33 Colum. L. Rev. 55 (1933); Kenneth W. Simons, *When Is Strict Liability Just?*, 87 J. Crim. L. & Criminology 1075 (1997); Richard Singer & Douglas Husak, *Of Innocence and Innocents: The Supreme Court and Mens Rea Since Herbert Packer*, 2 Buff. Crim. L. Rev. 859 (1999); Richard G. Singer, *The Resurgence of Mens Rea: III — The Rise and Fall of Strict Criminal Liability*, 30 B.C. L. Rev. 337 (1989); Richard A. Wasserstrom, *Strict Liability in the Criminal Law*, 12 Stan. L. Rev. 731 (1960); John Shepard Wiley, Jr., *Not Guilty By Reason of Blamelessness: Culpability in Federal Criminal Interpretation*, 85 Va. L. Rev. 1021 (1999).

[2] Husak, Note 1, *supra* (discussing seven different ways the term is used).

[3] See, e.g., §§ 13.01 (mistake-of-law) and 19.01 (defense-of-others rule), *infra*.

[B] Presumption Against Strict Liability

As discussed more generally in Chapter 10, "[t]he contention that an injury can amount to a crime only when inflicted by [*mens rea*] is no provincial or transient notion. It is . . . universal and persistent in mature systems of law. . . ."[4] As a consequence, the Supreme Court warned in *United States v. United States Gypsum Co.*[5] that offenses that do not contain a *mens rea* element have a "generally disfavored status," and "at least with regard to crimes having their origin in the common law, an interpretative presumption [exists] that *mens rea* is required" in federal statutes. Indeed, although the Supreme Court has typically shied away from holding that there is a constitutional requirement of *mens rea*,[6] it frequently will interpret a federal statute, otherwise silent in regard to *mens rea*, as containing an implicit requirement of some level of moral culpability. Although the case law is not entirely consistent in this regard, two scholars recently declared that the high court has "reinvigorated its concern with protecting innocent persons as a bedrock of federal criminal law."[7] Generally speaking, state courts apply the same presumption against strict liability.[8]

When will a court interpret a statute to be one of strict liability? Judge (later Justice) Harry Blackmun set out in *Holdridge v. United States*[9] various factors that may overcome the presumption against strict liability: (1) that the statutory crime is not derived from the common law; (2) that there is an evident legislative policy that would be undermined by a *mens rea* requirement; (3) that the standard imposed by the statute is "reasonable and adherence thereto properly expected of a person"; (4) that the penalty is small; and (5) that the "conviction does not gravely besmirch."

Unfortunately, "[f]ederal judges have toyed casually and unsystematically with the concept of strict criminal liability. . . ."[10] Therefore, one cannot rely on a court applying the five factors set out above in a consistent or systematic

---

[4] Morissette v. United States, 342 U.S. 246, 250 (1952).

[5] 438 U.S. 422 (1978).

[6] See § 11.03, *infra*.

[7] Singer & Husak, Note 1, *supra*, at 861.

[8] E.g., In re Jorge M., 4 P.3d 297, 300, 305 (Cal. 2000) ("The requirement that, for a criminal conviction, the prosecution must prove some form of guilty intent, knowledge, or criminal negligence is of such long standing and so fundamental to our criminal law that penal statutes will often be construed to contain such an element despite their failure expressly to state it"; "at least where the penalties imposed are substantial, [California penal law] can fairly be said to establish a presumption against criminal liability without mental fault . . . , rebuttable only by compelling evidence of legislative intent to dispense with mens rea entirely").

[9] 282 F.2d 302, 310 (8th Cir. 1960).

[10] Wiley, Note 1, *supra*, at 1161.

manner; it is often difficult to predict when a court will accept a statute on its own terms and permit it to be strictly enforced.[11]

[C] Public Welfare Offenses

Until the middle of the nineteenth century, Anglo-American crimes almost exclusively involved conduct *malum in se* (inherently wrongful), such as murder, arson, rape, and robbery. Conviction for such offenses, which required proof of *mens rea*, was gravely stigmatizing, and the penalties for their violation were severe.

With the advent of the Industrial Revolution, legislatures found it necessary to deal with a new problem: Conduct by a single actor that, although not morally wrongful, could gravely affect the health, safety, or welfare of a significant portion of the public. Consequently, Congress and state legislatures enacted laws, most of which contained no express *mens rea* requirement, that came to be characterized as "public welfare offenses." Such offenses, in contrast to traditional crimes, involve conduct *malum prohibitum* (wrong because it is prohibited). Examples include statutes that prohibit the manufacture or sale of impure food or drugs to the public, anti-pollution environmental laws, as well as traffic and motor-vehicle regulations.

Notwithstanding the presumption against strict criminal liability, courts frequently authorize it in the case of public welfare offenses. The factors set out in subsection [B] often support such an outcome: (1) public welfare offenses are not derived from the common law; (2) a single violation of such an offense can simultaneously injure a great number of people, which may explain the legislature's desire to disregard questions of personal moral guilt, in favor of a "sense of the importance of collective interests";[12] (3) the standard imposed by the statute (e.g., "do not sell alcohol to minors," or "be in possession of an unexpired license when driving a motor vehicle") is reasonable; (4) the penalty for violation is relatively minor, sometimes involving only a fine;[13] and (5) conviction rarely damages the reputation of the violator.

---

[11] For one effort to explain most, although not all, of the Supreme Court's interpretive efforts in this area, see *id.* at 1053 (describing the unstated rule to be that "[t]he Court will interpret a statute to require the government to prove moral blameworthiness if the Court can imagine an extreme hypothetical in which the government's interpretation would reach action that is not culpable according to an unwritten moral code").

[12] Sayre, Note 1, *supra*, at 67.

[13] However, in recent decades, courts have become more willing to justify strict liability, even though incarceration is implicated. For example, in *United States v. Flum*, 518 F.2d 39 (8th Cir. 1975), the court characterized as "relatively small" a potential penalty of incarceration for one year.

[D] Non-Public-Welfare Offenses

A few non-public-welfare offenses can be characterized as "strict liability" because they do not require proof that the defendant possessed a *mens rea* regarding a material element of the offense. Perhaps the most common example is statutory rape, i.e., consensual intercourse with an underage female. This offense is characterized in most states as strict liability because the statute does not require, and most courts have refused to imply, any *mens rea* element regarding the defendant's knowledge of the female's underage status.[14] That is, a male may be convicted of statutory rape, even if he innocently believed that the female was old enough to consent to intercourse.[15]

Non-public-welfare strict liability offenses differ from their public welfare counterparts in at least two significant regards. First, whereas public welfare crimes usually carry only minor penalties, non-public-welfare strict liability offenses often result in severe punishment.[16] Second, non-public-welfare offenses typically involve conduct *malum in se*. Violators of such laws, therefore, are stigmatized, although proof of moral fault is not required. Therefore, strict liability non-public-welfare offenses are aberrant and especially controversial.

§ 11.02 POLICY DEBATE REGARDING STRICT LIABILITY OFFENSES[17]

[A] Searching for a Justification for Strict Liability

Most modern criminal law scholars look unkindly upon the abandonment of the *mens rea* requirement. As developed elsewhere,[18] the *mens rea* requirement is consistent with the retributive principle that one who does not choose

---

[14] E.g., Garnett v. State, 632 A.2d 797 (Md. 1993) (authorizing conviction of a 20-year-old male with an I.Q. of 52, who had consensual intercourse with an underage female; holding that the male's mistake regarding the girl's age was immaterial); see Catherine L. Carpenter, *On Statutory Rape, Strict Liability, and the Public Welfare Offense Model*, 53 Am. U. L. Rev. 313, 385-91 (2003) (listing thirty states that impose strict liability for sexual activity with an underage female).

Of course, in statutory rape cases, the sexual intercourse will be intentional, but what makes the conduct criminal is the attendant circumstance that the female is under a specified age. The absence of any *mens rea* element in this regard makes the offense "strict liability."

[15] Felony-murder, see § 31.06, *infra*, is also "strict liability" in the sense that a felon, although culpable for committing a felony, may be punished for murder as well, even though the *result* of his felonious conduct — the death of another person — was unintentional and even unforeseeable. Simons, Note 1, *supra*, at 1080.

[16] E.g., Garnett v. State, 632 A.2d 797 (Md. 1993) (statutory rape; maximum punishment is imprisonment for twenty years); State v. Yanez, 716 A.2d 759 (R.I. 1998) (denominating first-degree child molestation as a strict liability offense because a defendant's mistaken belief as to the victim's age is irrelevant; *minimum* sentence is twenty years' imprisonment).

[17] See generally the Note 1 cites to Morse, Nemerson, Simons, Singer, and Wasserstrom.

[18] See § 10.03[B], *supra*.

to cause social harm, and who is not otherwise morally to blame for its commission, does not deserve to be punished. In most circumstances, society places the interest of the blameless harmdoer above its concern for deterring social harm, by requiring proof of the actor's *mens rea*.

Such support for strict liability as exists is largely limited to its use in the enforcement of public welfare offenses, and is premised on utilitarian grounds. In these circumstances, punishing innocent actors is still retributively unfair, but the penalties attached to such offenses usually are slight. Society is willing, therefore, to permit this "mitigated unfairness"[19] to the individual, in order more effectively to deter socially dangerous conduct.

Among the utilitarian arguments for strict liability are: (1) the absence of a *mens rea* requirement may have the desirable effect of keeping a relatively large class of people, namely those who doubt their capacity to act safely, from participating in dangerous activities, such as manufacturing pharmaceutical drugs or using dangerous instrumentalities; (2) those who do choose to engage in the risky activity will act with greater caution in light of the strict liability nature of the law; and (3) an inquiry into the actor's *mens rea* "would exhaust courts, which have to deal with thousands of 'minor' infractions every day."[20]

[B] Alternatives to Strict Liability

Even if public welfare offenses should be treated differently than traditional crimes, mechanisms other than abandonment of the *mens rea* requirement are available to legislatures seeking to protect the public. First, a legislature might require proof of recklessness, but set higher penalties, including significant prison sentences, for violation of public welfare offenses. This approach might be a more effective means of deterring dangerous conduct than strict liability coupled with small fines or very short jail sentences.

Second, a legislature might retain the minor penalties that apply to public welfare offenses, but require proof of an extremely low level of *mens rea*, such as *civil* negligence. Third, a legislature might continue to define public welfare offenses in strict liability terms, but permit a "lack of *mens rea*" affirmative defense.[21] For example, if a person sold liquor to a minor, she would be convicted unless she persuaded the factfinder by a preponderance of the evidence that she took all reasonable care to determine the customer's age.

---

[19] The unfairness is not really mitigated. If a person has a moral right not to be punished in the absence of moral blameworthiness, as retributivist principles would suggest, that right is no less violated simply because the punishment imposed is slight.

[20] Singer, Note 1, *supra*, at 389.

[21] E.g., Regina v. City of Sault Ste. Marie, 85 D.L.R.3d 161 (1978) (Canada).

§ 11.03 CONSTITUTIONALITY OF STRICT LIABILITY OFFENSES[22]

The late professor Herbert Packer once summarized the constitutional law regarding strict liability offenses this way: "*Mens rea* is an important requirement, but it is not a constitutional requirement, except sometimes."[23] Packer only partially had his tongue in his cheek.

As Packer's remarks suggest, generally speaking the Supreme Court has rejected the claim that strict liability crimes are unconstitutional. In *United States v. Balint*,[24] B and others were indicted for sale of narcotics without a required order form supplied by the Commissioner of Internal Revenue. The maximum penalty for the strict liability public welfare offense was five years' imprisonment. In a single sentence that cited dictum from an earlier opinion, the Supreme Court held that strict liability offenses do not violate the Fifth Amendment Due Process Clause. The Court provided no principled explanation for this assertion, however, nor did they mention the offense's potentially substantial prison sentence.

In contrast, in *Morissette v. United States*,[25] the Supreme Court spoke of the common law *mens rea* requirement in glowing terms, stating that it "is no provincial or transient notion. It is . . . universal and persistent in mature systems of law. . . ." Nonetheless, the Court observed that, "wisely or not," legislatures usually do not require proof of *mens rea* with public welfare offenses, and that courts, "not . . . without expressions of misgiving," have approved such statutes. With offenses that have evolved from the common law, however, the Court stated that "mere omission . . . of any mention of intent will not be construed as eliminating that element from the [crime]." For example, at trial, M was convicted of conversion of government property that he believed had been abandoned. The statute did not expressly require proof of an intent to steal property. However, because the statute evolved from the common law offense of larceny, which contains such a requirement, the Supreme Court construed the conversion statute as requiring this specific intent.

Morissette's finding of a *mens rea* requirement was not constitutionally based. It left *Balint*'s constitutional holding intact in the context of public welfare offenses. Moreover, the Court did not suggest that a legislature could not abandon the *mens rea* requirement with *traditional* criminal offenses; it held only that a requirement of *mens rea* would be presumed in the absence of a contrary legislative purpose.

---

[22] See generally Alan C. Michaels, *Constitutional Innocence*, 112 Harv. L. Rev. 829 (1999).

[23] Packer, Note 1, *supra*, at 107; see also Singer & Husak, Note 1, *supra*, at 859 (stating that "Packer's assessment still seems valid . . .").

[24] 258 U.S. 250 (1922).

[25] 342 U.S. 246 (1952).

On a few occasions, the Supreme Court has invalidated strict liability laws on constitutional grounds. For example, in *Lambert v. California*,[26] the Court overturned *L*'s conviction for failing to register with the city of Los Angeles as a prior convicted felon, as required pursuant to a strict liability ordinance of which *L* was unaware. Notwithstanding the usual rule that ignorance of the law is no excuse, the Court reversed on "lack of fair notice" due process grounds.[27] The Court has also on occasion applied the First Amendment to strike down strict liability legislation in the obscenity field.[28]

Despite the Court's occasional use of the Due Process Clause and the First Amendment to invalidate strict liability legislation,[29] the justices have never expressly developed a constitutional theory that ties together their decisions, although a few scholars have attempted to do so.[30]

§ 11.04 MODEL PENAL CODE

The Code "attempted a bold assault upon strict liability."[31] Section 2.02, subsection (1), provides that, subject to one exception, no conviction may be obtained

---

[26] 355 U.S. 225 (1957).

[27] See § 13.02[C], *infra*, for more discussion of *Lambert*.

[28] Smith v. California, 361 U.S. 147 (1959) (reversing a conviction of a bookstore owner for possessing an obscene book in a place where books were sold, based on a statute that did not require proof of knowledge that the material was obscene).

[29] The Supreme Court has not ruled on the applicability of the proportionality requirement of the Eighth Amendment in the context of strict liability legislation. The argument would be that substantial punishment of a morally blameless person constitutes grossly disproportional punishment. Based on current case law, such an argument would fail. See § 6.05[C], *supra*.

[30] Perhaps the most impressive effort in this regard comes from Professor Alan Michaels, Note 22, *supra*. He claims that the Court's rulings can be explained by an unstated "constitutional innocence" doctrine, which provides that a legislature may employ strict liability regarding an element of the offense if, but only if, the legislature has the constitutional power to criminalize the elements of the offense that require *mens rea*, with the strict liability element excluded.

For example, bigamy typically has two elements: (1) knowingly marrying another person while (2) still being married. The second element is often strict liability: A person is guilty even if she reasonably believes, for example, that her husband is dead or has obtained a valid divorce. The constitutionality of this statute should be determined by asking, according to Michaels, "Could the state constitutionally punish her simply for knowingly getting married?," the first element of the offense. *Id.* at 835. If yes, then strict liability with regard to the second element could be constitutional; if not, the statute is unconstitutional as a strict liability offense. Based on this reasoning, Professor Michaels argues that strict liability bigamy statutes should be declared unconstitutional.

For an analysis of Michaels' approach regarding statutory rape, see Arnold H. Loewy, *Statutory Rape in a Post Lawrence v. Texas World*, 58 SMU L. Rev. 77 (2005) (concluding that, at least in some cases, there should be a constitutional defense for a person who engages in sexual intercourse with an underage female whom he non-negligently believes is an adult).

[31] Sanford H. Kadish, *Fifty Years of Criminal Law: An Opinionated Review*, 87 Cal. L. Rev. 943, 954 (1999); see also American Law Institute, Comment to § 2.05, at 282 (the Code "makes a frontal attack on . . . strict liability in the penal law").

unless the prosecution proves some form of culpability regarding each material element of an offense. The sole exception is found in Section 2.05, which provides that the voluntary act and *mens rea* requirements need not apply to offenses graded as "violations," rather than "crimes." "Violations" are offenses that cannot result in imprisonment or probation, but may result in fines.[32]

---

[32] Model Penal Code § 1.04(5).

Chapter 12

MISTAKES OF FACT

§ 12.01 PUTTING MISTAKE-OF-FACT IN CONTEXT[1]

D1, a hunter, shoots and kills *V1*, believing he is killing a wild animal. *D2* has nonconsensual sexual intercourse with *V2*, mistakenly believing that *V2* consented. *D3* carries away property belonging to *V3*, incorrectly thinking that he has permission to take it. *D4* drives above the speed limit because his speedometer is inaccurate.

In each of these cases the actor has caused the proscribed social harm. Looking only at their external behavior, one might also initially infer that the defendants intended to cause the harms inflicted. In fact, however, each actor was either unaware of, or mistaken about, a fact pertaining to an element of the offense for which he might be prosecuted. *D1* did not know that he was shooting a human being, yet the death of a human being is an element of murder; *D2* erroneously believed that *V2* was willing to have sexual intercourse with him, which, if true, would have negated the "lack of consent" element of rape; *D3* believed that he had the right to take *V3*'s property, which, if true, would mean that he did not intend to steal the property; and *D4* did not know that he was driving above the speed limit, the *actus reus* of the traffic offense.

This chapter considers why and when a mistake (or ignorance[2]) of a fact relating to an element of an offense[3] exculpates an actor for the social harm he

---

[1] See generally George Fletcher, Rethinking Criminal Law §§ 9.1-9.3.3 (1978); Rollin M. Perkins, *Ignorance and Mistake in Criminal Law*, 88 U. Pa. L. Rev. 35 (1939); Benjamin B. Sendor, *Mistakes of Fact: A Study in the Structure of Criminal Conduct*, 25 Wake Forest L. Rev. 707 (1990); Kenneth W. Simons, *Mistake and Impossibility, Law and Fact, and Culpability: A Speculative Essay*, 81 J. Crim. L. & Criminology 447 (1990); Richard Singer, *The Resurgence of Mens Rea: II — Honest But Unreasonable Mistake of Fact in Self Defense*, 28 B.C. L. Rev. 459 (1987).

[2] "Ignorance" and "mistake" are not synonyms. "Ignorance" implies a total want of knowledge — a blank mind — regarding the matter under consideration, whereas "mistake" suggests a wrong belief about the matter. Because this distinction typically is not drawn in mistake-of-fact cases, no effort will be made in this chapter to distinguish between the terms.

[3] The focus of this chapter, it should be reiterated, is on mistakes pertaining to *elements* in the definitions of crimes. Frequently, however, a defendant will allege that he was mistaken as to the existence of facts that would provide an affirmative defense to his conduct (e.g., *D* kills in "self-defense" because he mistakenly believes *V* is about to kill him). The latter type of mistake is discussed at § 17.04, *infra*.

A person may also be mistaken about some fact unrelated to the *actus reus* of an offense or to an affirmative defense. For example, *D* may be unaware of the fact that the person he has intentionally killed was standing on the Ohio side of the Michigan-Ohio border, and, therefore, *D* does not know that his murder falls within Ohio's jurisdiction. Such jurisdictional mistakes are never exculpatory.

causes. As will become evident, the common law's resolution of this issue is complicated. The Model Penal Code's solution is straightforward.

§ 12.02 WHY DOES A FACTUAL MISTAKE SOMETIMES EXCULPATE?

Aristotle believed that a person is not morally responsible for his actions unless he acts voluntarily, and that "[b]y the voluntary I mean . . . any of the things in a man's own power which he does with knowledge, *i.e. not in ignorance.* . . ."[4]

Use of the word "voluntary" in this context is potentially misleading because the term has multiple meanings in the criminal law.[5] Nonetheless, it points us in the proper direction. An actor who is mistaken about some fact "does not have the same kind of opportunity to avoid doing evil that he would have if he knew what he was doing."[6] Consequently, the mistaken actor's freedom of choice — and ultimately the moral basis for punishing him — is undermined.

Perhaps a better way to understand why a mistake of fact may exculpate an actor is to observe that what makes a person's mistaken action "involuntary" has more to do with his cognition (i.e., what he is aware of) than with his volition (i.e., his capacity to control his conduct). From this realization, "the trail leads plainly to *mens rea.*"[7]

Unfortunately, if the trail leads to "*mens rea,*" then the common law leads us down two paths. This is so because courts use the term "*mens rea*" in two ways: in a general sense to describe the actor's "vicious will," or his moral culpability for causing the social harm; and, in the narrower sense, to describe the particular mental state that is an express element of the offense.[8] A mistake of fact may negate the actor's "*mens rea*" in one or both senses of the term.

In some cases, proof that a person was factually mistaken demonstrates that, despite appearances, he acted in a morally blameless manner and that, therefore, he is not deserving of punishment for causing the social harm. In this sense a mistake of fact negates "*mens rea*" in the "culpability" meaning of the term.

A mistake of fact may also negate "*mens rea*" in the "elemental" sense. That is, because of a mistake, a defendant may not possess the specific state of mind required in the definition of the crime. In such circumstances, the defendant

---

[4] Aristotle, *Nicomachean Ethics* 1135a (W.D. Ross trans.), *in* 2 The Complete Works of Aristotle 1791 (Jonathan Barnes ed., 1984) (emphasis added).

[5] See § 9.02[C], *supra.*

[6] Michael S. Moore, *Causation and the Excuses*, 73 Cal. L. Rev. 1091, 1149 (1985).

[7] Jerome Hall, General Principles of Criminal Law 360 (2d ed. 1960).

[8] See § 10.02, *supra.*

must be acquitted because the prosecutor has failed to prove an express element of the offense.

Once one sees the relationship between mistake and *mens rea* it is easy to see that the rule that a mistake of fact is exculpatory is not a special rule — either the actor had the *mens rea* required to be guilty of the crime, or he did not.

Courts frequently characterize mistake-of-fact as a "defense." However, since an exculpatory mistake negates the *mens rea* of an offense — an element of the crime — a mistake-of-fact claim is only a "defense" in the sense that the defendant may be initially required to produce evidence that he was mistaken.[9] Once the "mistake" issue is raised, the defendant "is entitled to have the jury understand that the State must still prove each element of the crime [including *mens rea*] beyond a reasonable doubt and that the burden never shifts to the defendant."[10] Put differently, once the defendant produces some evidence he was mistaken, the prosecutor must prove (beyond a reasonable doubt) that the defendant was *not* mistaken, or that the defendant's mistake did *not* negate the *mens rea*.

§ 12.03 COMMON LAW RULES

[A] General Approach

The common law rules pertaining to mistakes of fact, although complicated, are understandable if the reader reconsiders the historical context in which the rules developed.[11] Originally, the definitions of most common law crimes omitted any mention of a mental-state requirement: A person was guilty if he committed the *actus reus* under circumstances manifesting his moral culpability. A few crimes, however, included a specific mental-state element in their definitions (typically, "intent" or "knowledge"). The latter offenses came to be known as "specific intent" crimes.

From these two types of crimes and two types of "*mens rea*" came a dual approach to mistakes of fact. With specific-intent crimes,[12] common law jurists developed the rule that a mistake of fact is exculpatory if it negates the particular element of *mens rea* — the "specific intent" — in the definition of the offense. In other words, the common law adopted an *elemental* approach to mistakes. However, with general-intent offenses — crimes that did not include a specific-intent element — the jurists sought to determine if the actor's mistake

---

[9] "Mistake-of-fact" is properly denominated as a "failure-of-proof" defense. See § 16.02, *infra*.

[10] General v. State, 789 A.2d 102, 108 (Md. 2002). Regarding burdens of proof generally, see Chapter 7, *supra*.

[11] See § 10.02, *supra*.

[12] The concepts of "specific intent" and "general intent" are defined at § 10.06, *supra*, and should be reviewed here.

negated his moral culpability for the crime. This is the *culpability* approach to mistakes.

This dual system, as sensible as it might have been centuries ago, is more difficult to justify today in light of the fact that, strict-liability offenses aside, modern penal codes typically include a *mens rea* element in the definition of each felony and serious misdemeanor. Logically, therefore, the elemental approach should be followed with *all* non-strict-liability crimes today. Although the trend is in this direction, largely as the result of the promulgation of the Model Penal Code,[13] the common law's two approaches to mistakes — depending on whether the offense charged is characterized as general-intent or specific-intent — has endured.

As a consequence, the first step in analyzing a mistake-of-fact claim in a jurisdiction that follows common law doctrine is *to identify the nature of the crime for which the defendant is being prosecuted*: Is it a strict-liability, specific-intent, or general-intent, crime? The separate rules for each type of offense are described below.

[B] Strict-Liability Offenses

The mistake-of-fact rule for strict-liability crimes is straightforward: Under no circumstances does a person's mistake of fact negate his criminal responsibility for violating a strict-liability offense.

This rule is sensible. By definition, a strict-liability offense is one that does not require proof of any *mens rea*. Inasmuch as the basis for exculpation on the ground of mistake is that it negates the actor's *"mens rea,"* the absence of any *mens rea* to negate necessarily precludes the use of this defense. For example, if *D* drives above the lawful speed limit because his speedometer is inaccurate, he will be convicted of a strict-liability driving offense, even if the speedometer's faulty calibration was unknown and unforeseeable to him.

Similarly, statutory rape is a strict-liability offense in most states, at least regarding the attendant circumstance of the female's age. Thus, *D*'s erroneous belief, *no matter how reasonable*, that the female with whom he is having intercourse is old enough to consent, will not exculpate him.[14] Any unfairness in this outcome is a function of the strict-liability nature of the offense, and not of the mistake-of-fact rule pertaining to such offenses.

---

[13] See § 12.04, *infra*.

[14] See § 11.01[D], *supra*. A few jurisdictions treat statutory rape as a general-intent offense, subject to the principles relating thereto. See subsection [D], *infra*.

[C] Specific-Intent Offenses

Consider the following two examples of mistake-of-fact claims in the prosecution of specific-intent offenses. First, *D1* takes *V1*'s property, incorrectly believing that the property has been abandoned and, therefore, does not belong to anyone.[15] *D1* is charged with larceny, a specific-intent offense defined at common law as the "trespassory taking and carrying away of the personal property of another with intent to permanently deprive the other of the property (or, in shorthand, the intent to steal)."

In the second case, *D2* attempts to have sexual intercourse with *V2*. Because of a language barrier, *D2* incorrectly believes that *V2* was a consenting prostitute.[16] *D2* is arrested before the intercourse occurs, so he is charged with the specific-intent crime of assault with the intent to commit rape.

In each case, the defendant's mistake relates to the specific-intent portion of the applicable offense. *D1*'s mistaken belief that the property does not belong to anyone is relevant in determining whether he had the specific intent to steal from *V1*. *D2*'s mistaken belief that *V2* consented to intercourse is pertinent in determining whether he "intended to rape" *V2*, the specific intent in the prosecuted offense.

The rule of law here is simple: A defendant is not guilty of an offense if his mistake of fact negates the specific-intent portion of the crime, i.e., if he lacks the intent required in the definition of the offense. Thus, if *D1* genuinely believed that the property he took had been abandoned, then *D1* did not intend to permanently deprive *V1* of the property; if *D2* truly believed that *V2* was consenting to intercourse, then *D2* did not intend to rape *V2*.[17] It does not matter that the defendants' mistakes in these cases may have been entirely unreasonable — reckless or negligent — under the circumstances. Acquittal follows inextricably from the fact that a person may not be convicted of an offense unless every element thereof, including the mental-state element (the *intent* to steal and rape, respectively), is proved, which did not occur here.

On the other hand, suppose that *D3* obtains *heroin* from *X*, believing that the substance is *cocaine*, and is prosecuted for "knowingly receiving a controlled substance," a specific-intent offense.[18] In this case, *D3* may properly be convicted, notwithstanding his mistake, because his error, whether reasonable or unrea-

---

[15] E.g., People v. Navarro, 99 Cal. App. 3d 1 (Ct. App. 1979); see also United States v. Brinegar, 55 M.J. 1 (2001) (in larceny prosecution, soldier *B* incorrectly believed that he had authority to take the property in question).

[16] See United States v. Short, 4 C.M.A. 437 (1954).

[17] United States v. Langley, 33 M.J. 278 (1991).

[18] This is a specific-intent offense because it requires proof of the actor's awareness of the attendant circumstance of the offense, i.e., that he has received a "controlled substance."

sonable, does not negate the requisite specific intent. *D3* knew that he was receiving a controlled substance; he was only mistaken regarding its nature (heroin versus cocaine).

[D] General-Intent Offenses

[1] Ordinary Approach: Was the Mistake Reasonable?

The ordinary rule is that a person is not guilty of a general-intent crime if his mistake of fact was reasonable, but he is guilty if his mistake was unreasonable.[19] For example, suppose that *D* has nonconsensual sexual intercourse with *V*, whom he incorrectly believes is consenting. *D* is charged with rape, defined for current purposes as "sexual intercourse by a male with a female not his wife, without her consent." Inasmuch as rape is a general-intent offense, courts utilize the *culpability* approach to analyze *D*'s mistake of fact. If his mistake regarding *V*'s "consent" was reasonable, then he is not guilty of the offense.[20] This follows because, although the *actus reus* of the offense has occurred, *D*'s state of mind in regard to the prohibited conduct was *nonculpable*, i.e., his belief that she was consenting was one that a reasonable person might have harbored. If *D*'s belief as to *V*'s "consent" was unreasonable, however, then he acted with a culpable state of mind that justifies his conviction of the offense.[21]

The mistake-of-fact rule is not without its critics.[22] The practical effect of denying the defense to those who act on the basis of an unreasonable mistake of fact is to permit punishment on the basis of negligence. Punishment for negligence is controversial in its own right,[23] but in the mistake context its potential unfairness is aggravated in two ways. First, when a crime is defined in terms of negligence, a person is not ordinarily liable unless his negligence is gross. With mistakes of fact, however, "unreasonableness" is not always defined in a manner that requires this heightened degree of fault. Therefore, the unreasonably mistaken actor, although perhaps responsible for conduct that would

---

[19] People v. Mayberry, 542 P.2d 1337 (Cal. 1975); see Ind. Code § 35-41-3-7 (2004) ("It is a defense that the person who engaged in the prohibited conduct was reasonably mistaken about a matter of fact, if the mistake negates the culpability required for commission of the offense.").

[20] United States v. Parker, 54 M.J. 700 (A. Ct. Crim. App. 2001).

[21] Notice the anomaly in the common law approach: If *D*'s mistake was unreasonable, he is convicted of rape; if he is arrested before the intercourse occurs, and he is charged with the specific-intent offense of assault with intent to commit rape, his unreasonable mistake of fact *will* exculpate him. See subsection [C], *supra*.

[22] It is important here to distinguish between criticisms of the mistake-of-fact rule described in the text, a rule which applies to *all* general-intent crimes, and the particular issue of whether and when a reasonable mistake regarding a female's consent should exculpate in rape prosecutions. There is some movement by the judiciary to make reasonable-mistake-of-fact claims more difficult to present in rape cases. Rosanna Cavallaro, *A Big Mistake: Eroding the Defense of Mistake of Fact About Consent in Rape*, 86 J. Crim. L. & Criminology 815 (1996). See § 33.05, *infra*.

[23] See § 10.04[D][2][c], *supra*.

constitute no more than civil negligence, may be punished as a criminal wrong-doer.

Second, the mistake-of-fact rule permits conviction and punishment of a neg-ligent wrongdoer as if he were guilty of intentional wrongdoing. For example, a male who genuinely, but unreasonably, believes that a female is consenting to intercourse will be convicted of the same degree of offense, and will be subject to the same punishment, as one who has full knowledge that he is acting against the will of the victim. Although the former wrongdoer may be sufficiently cul-pable to merit criminal punishment, his culpability (and, probably, his danger-ousness) is not of the same degree as that of the intentional wrongdoer.

[2] Another Approach: Moral-Wrong Doctrine

[a] The Doctrine Is Explained

As noted in the preceding subsection, the usual approach to a mistake-of-fact claim in the prosecution of a general-intent offense is to determine the actor's culpability for making the mistake — normally, the question to be asked is whether the mistake was reasonable or unreasonable. On occasion, however, common law jurists have measured moral blameworthiness differently. Accord-ing to the "moral wrong" doctrine, one can make a *reasonable* mistake regard-ing an attendant circumstance and yet manifest a bad character or otherwise demonstrate moral culpability worthy of punishment.

The basis of the moral-wrong doctrine is that "there should be no exculpation for mistake where, if the facts had been as the actor believed them to be, his con-duct would still be . . . immoral."[24] Essentially, the intent to commit an act that is immoral furnishes the requisite culpability for the related, but unin-tended, outcome.[25]

Consider the moral-wrong doctrine in light of the classic case of *Regina v. Prince*.[26] In *Prince*, P was prosecuted for "unlawfully tak[ing] or caus[ing] to be taken, any unmarried girl, being under the age of sixteen years, out of the pos-session . . . of her father." The girl in question, V, was only fourteen years old, but the jury found that P honestly and reasonably believed that she was eight-een years of age.

All but one of the seventeen judges ruled that P was guilty of the offense. Judge Blackburn, speaking for a majority of ten, interpreted the offense as one of strict liability as to the statutory element of the girl's age. The remaining judges, however, agreed with Baron Bramwell that *mens rea* had to be proven.

---

[24] Bell v. State, 668 P.2d 829, 833 (Alaska. Ct. App. 1983).

[25] Garnett v. State, 632 A.2d 797, 813 (Md. 1993) (Bell, J., dissenting).

[26] L.R. 2 Cr. Cas. Res. 154 (1875).

The difficulty with this view was that, if the court applied the usual mistake rule pertaining to general-intent offenses, P would have to be acquitted, since it was determined that P's mistake as to V's age was reasonable.

Bramwell voted to affirm P's conviction, however, on the basis of the moral-wrong doctrine. Pursuant to this rule, the first matter to be determined is whether the actor's mistake of fact was reasonable or unreasonable. If it was the latter, the usual mistake rule applies, and he may be convicted.

Here, P's mistake was reasonable, so Bramwell took the second step, which is to look at the factual panorama from the actor's perspective. Suppose that Bramwell had asked P, "What is it that you thought you were doing?" If P had answered candidly, he would have responded, "I thought that I was taking an *eighteen*-year-old girl out of the possession of her father, without his permission."

The third step is for the court to evaluate the morality of the actor's conduct, *based on the facts as the actor reasonably believed them to be*. According to Bramwell, P's conduct as he supposed it to be — "the taking of a female of such tender years [as age eighteen] that she is properly called a *girl*" from the care and possession of her father — was morally wrong. Indeed, this conclusion was self-evident to Bramwell: "no argument is necessary to prove [the immorality of P's conduct]; it is enough to state the case."

In light of Bramwell's belief that P's conduct was self-evidently wrong, he imputed to P knowledge that he was acting immorally. Pursuant to the moral-wrong doctrine, a person who knowingly performs a morally wrong act assumes the risk that the attendant factual circumstances are not as they reasonably appear to be and that, therefore, his conduct is not only immoral but also illegal. In *Prince*, therefore, P knowingly assumed the risk that V, whom he immorally took away from her father, was also underage. P was properly convicted of the offense according to the moral-wrong doctrine.[27]

The moral-wrong doctrine is not triggered unless the defendant's conduct would be immoral had the situation been as he supposed. Suppose, for example, that P had known V's true age, but instead had reasonably believed that she was homeless and, therefore, not in anyone's lawful possession. In these circumstances, P's answer to the question, "What did you think you were doing?" would have been, "I thought I was taking a homeless girl of fourteen off the streets and into my protective possession." Presumably, this conduct is not immoral. If this assumption is correct, P would not assume the risk that he was mistaken about the attendant circumstance that she had a family; as a consequence, he should be acquitted.

---

[27] See also White v. State, 185 N.E. 64, 65 (Ohio Ct. App. 1933) (W abandoned his wife; when he left her she was newly pregnant, although he had no reason to know this; held: W was guilty of the offense of "abandoning one's pregnant wife"; according to the court, "[h]e must make sure of his ground when he commits the simple wrong of leaving her at all").

[b] Criticisms of the Doctrine

The moral-wrong doctrine is deservedly controversial. First, it permits conviction of a person who did not know, and had no reason to know, that his conduct would violate the law. In *Prince*, *P* may have known that his behavior was immoral; immorality and illegality, however, are not identical concepts. Even if all offenses involved immoral conduct, which is not the case, it is not true that all immoral conduct is illegal. The moral-wrong doctrine conflates the two concepts in a manner that runs afoul of the principle of legality.[28] That is, if Parliament had wanted to prohibit the "immoral" act of taking an eighteen-year-old female away from her parents (which is what *P* reasonably thought he was doing and for which, in essence, he was convicted) it could have done so, but it did not. A person should only be punished for conduct that the legislature, the lawmaking branch of government, has prohibited.

Second, the doctrine is founded on the premise that it is fair to punish a person for unintentionally committing the *actus reus* of an offense, if he intentionally committed an immoral act. But, who determines immorality? And, who is to say that the actor *knew* that his conduct was immoral? In *Prince*, Baron Bramwell thought it obvious that taking an eighteen-year-old female from her parents was immoral and, therefore, he *assumed* that *P* must have known he was acting immorally. Perhaps in the English society in which the doctrine developed, this was a fair assumption. In today's culturally heterogeneous American society, however, it does not inevitably follow that, because a court (or jury) believes particular conduct is immoral, the defendant must have known when he acted that he was crossing the nebulous immorality line.

[3] Still Another Approach: Legal-Wrong Doctrine

[a] The Doctrine Is Explained

Some courts apply a less extreme alternative to the moral-wrong doctrine, usually termed the "legal-wrong doctrine." This rule simply substitutes the word "illegal" for "immoral" in the description of the former doctrine, but otherwise is applied similarly. That is, *D* is guilty of criminal offense X, despite a reasonable mistake of fact, if he would be guilty of a different, *albeit less serious*, crime Y, if the situation were as he supposed.[29]

For example, the transportation of a minor across state lines for the purposes of prostitution is a federal offense (call it Crime X); the transportation of an

---

[28] See § 5.01, *supra*.

[29] Judge Brett applied this doctrine in *Regina v. Prince*, L.R. 2 Cr. Cas. Res. 154 (1875), discussed in subsection [D][2], *supra*. *D*'s conduct in that case, as he supposed it to be, did not constitute any other offense, so Brett voted to overturn the conviction.

adult for such purposes is a lesser federal crime (Crime Y).[30] Suppose that *D* procures a seventeen-year-old minor female, *whom he reasonably believes is eighteen*, to perform acts of prostitution. Put somewhat differently, *D* has committed the *actus reus* of crime X, with the *mens rea* of crime Y.

Looking at the facts from *D*'s perspective, he committed crime Y. Under the legal-wrong doctrine, however, he would be convicted of the more serious offense X. *D* intentionally did acts that he knew constituted a crime;[31] therefore, he assumed the risk that, unbeknownst to him or a reasonable person, the attendant circumstance of the female's age was such that his conduct constituted an even greater offense than he realized.[32]

[b] Criticism of the Doctrine

The legal-wrong doctrine authorizes punishment based on the harm that an actor caused — i.e., the *actus reus* of the greater offense — while it ignores the fact that the actor's *mens rea* was at the level of the lesser crime. If a society were concerned only with consequences, this result would follow. In a society that values the importance of *mens rea* in evaluating guilt, however, punishment should be graduated on the basis of the social harm caused *and* the blameworthiness of the person who caused it.

For example, in *Bell v. State*,[33] the offense of promoting prostitution by procuring a person under the age of sixteen was a felony, subject to substantial punishment; the offense of promoting prostitution by procuring someone older constituted a mere misdemeanor. Under the legal-wrong doctrine, the defendant is punished as a felon, although his culpability is that of a misdemeanant. Under some circumstances, this may result in punishment grossly disproportional to the offender's blameworthiness.[34]

[E] *Regina v. Morgan*[35]: Common Law in Transition or an Aberration?[36]

Consider the facts in *Morgan*: *D*s, three men, were convicted of forcibly raping *V*, *X*'s wife. According to *D*s, *X* invited them to have intercourse with *V*,

---

[30] 18 U.S.C. § 2423(a) (2005) (minors); 18 U.S.C. § 2421 (2005) (non-minors).

[31] The common law conclusively presumes that people know and understand the relevant criminal laws. See generally Chapter 13, *infra*.

[32] United States v. Taylor, 239 F.3d 994, 997 (9th Cir. 2001).

[33] 668 P.2d 829 (Alaska Ct. App. 1983).

[34] See People v. Olsen, 685 P.2d 52, 59 (Cal. 1984) (Grodin, J., concurring and dissenting) (discussing the proportionality issue in constitutional terms).

[35] [1976] A.C. 182.

[36] See generally David Cowley, *The Retreat from Morgan*, [1982] Crim. L. Rev. 198; R.A. Duff, *Recklessness and Rape*, 3 Liverpool L. Rev. 49 (1981); James Faulkner, *Mens Rea in Rape: Morgan*

falsely telling them that if she struggled they should not worry, because she "was 'kinky' and this was the only way in which she could be turned on." At trial, the jury was instructed that Ds should only be acquitted if their mistake regarding V's consent was reasonable. On appeal, Ds argued that this instruction was faulty, and that the jury should have been informed that even an unreasonable mistake of fact would exculpate them.

The tendered instruction was proper according to ordinary "mistake" principles. Nonetheless, a majority of the Law Lords ruled that a male who acts on the basis of an honest but unreasonable belief that the female consented is *not* guilty of rape, because the mistake prevents the male from possessing the *mens rea* required for that offense. Lord Cross explained the issue raised in the case this way:

> [T]he . . . question to be answered in this case, as I see it, is whether according to the ordinary use of the English language a man can be said to have committed rape if he believed that the woman was consenting to the intercourse and would not have attempted to have it but for his belief, whatever his grounds for so believing. I do not think that he can. Rape, to my mind, imports at least indifference as to the woman's consent.

Lord Cross seems wrong. The average person using the English language in the "ordinary" way would probably say that V *was* raped, even if Ds believed that she had consented. What Lord Cross may have meant, however, was expressed more clearly by Lord Hailsham:

> [E]ither the prosecution proves that the accused had the requisite intent, or it does not. In the former case it succeeds, and in the latter it fails. Since honest belief clearly negatives intent, the reasonableness or otherwise of that belief can only be evidence for or against the view that the belief and therefore the intent was actually held. . . .

Essentially, Lord Hailsham's remarks demonstrate that he was using the elemental approach to resolve the defendants' mistake claim, a process ordinarily restricted to specific-intent offenses.[37] That is, according to Hailsham, once it is established that the definition of a crime requires proof of "intention," then this *mens rea* term modifies each of the *actus reus* elements, including the attendant circumstance that the intercourse was nonconsensual.[38] Therefore,

---

and the Inadequacy of Subjectivism, or Why No Should Not Mean Yes in the Eyes of the Law, 18 Melbourne U. L. Rev. 60 (1991).

[37] See §§ 10.02[C], 12.03[A] and [C], *supra*.

[38] Notice: If the word "intentional" modifies the attendant circumstance of "without her consent" in the definition of rape, as Lord Hailsham assumes by his remark, rape is effectively converted into a specific-intent crime. It would be as if rape were defined as follows: "nonconsensual sexual intercourse by a male, with a female, not his wife, *with the knowledge or belief* that she is not consenting." If rape *is* a specific-intent offense, of course, the Lords' elemental approach to the mistake issue is correct. Historically, however, rape has been treated as a general-intent crime.

if *Ds* negligently believed that *V* was consenting, they did not possess the requisite *mens rea* of the offense, i.e., the *intention* to act without *V*'s consent.

Morgan seemed at the time to represent an important change in "mistake" law because it ignored the ordinary "general intent"/"specific intent" dichotomy. *Morgan*, however, proved to be a highly controversial decision. The controversy is hardly surprising in light of the fact that the rule announced in *Morgan* would have authorized the acquittal of men who had forcible intercourse with a nonconsenting woman resisting their advances, and who manifested extreme indifference to her wishes.[39]

As a matter of *mens rea* analysis, however, *Morgan* is a sensible decision. In states that have reformed their penal codes, the definitions of most offenses expressly provide for some culpable mental state as to each *actus reus* element of the crime. The dichotomy between "general intent" and "specific intent," therefore, makes no sense in this context: Either a person possesses the mental element required in the definition of the offense (in England, the *mens rea* of intent) or he does not. The elemental approach used by common law jurists in the prosecution of specific-intent offenses, therefore, should be applied to *all* offenses, including rape.

This does not mean that a person who acts on the basis of an unreasonable mistake of fact must be acquitted. The legislature can redefine an offense to permit conviction based on a lesser *mens rea*, as England's Parliament did in reaction to *Morgan*.[40]

§ 12.04 MODEL PENAL CODE[41]

[A] General Rule

The Model Code uses a straightforward elemental approach to matters of *mens rea*, including mistakes of fact. Section 2.02, subsection (1), states the general rule that one is not guilty of an offense unless he acted "purposely, knowingly, recklessly, or negligently, as the law may require, with respect to each material element of the offense." Thus, as to each material element of an offense, there is some *mens rea* requirement, be it purpose, knowledge, recklessness, or negligence. Specifically as to mistakes of fact, Section 2.04(1) pro-

---

[39] The defendants' appeal in *Morgan* was dismissed — their convictions were affirmed — because the Law Lords believed that the trial judge's erroneous instruction did not prejudice *Ds'* rights. In essence, they concluded that *Ds* knew full well that *V* was not consenting, and that a jury would have reached the same outcome, even on the basis of a proper instruction.

[40] See § 1(1) of the Sexual Offenses (Amendment) Act of 1976 (permitting conviction on the basis of knowledge or recklessness as to the victim's lack of consent).

[41] See generally George P. Fletcher, *Mistake in the Model Penal Code: A False False Problem*, 19 Rutgers L.J. 649 (1988); Peter W. Low, *The Model Penal Code, the Common Law, and Mistakes of Fact: Recklessness, Negligence, or Strict Liability?*, 19 Rutgers L.J. 539 (1988).

vides that a mistake is a defense if it negates the mental state required to establish *any* element of the offense. It is irrelevant whether the offense would be identified as general-intent or specific-intent at common law. Put simply, either the actor had the culpable state of mind required in the definition of the offense or he did not.

Consider how the facts in *Morgan*,[42] discussed immediately above in Section 12.03[D], would be analyzed under the Code. Section 213.1 of the Code provides that rape occurs when "a male has sexual intercourse with a female not his wife if he compels her to submit by force. . . ." Because this definition is silent regarding the applicable *mens rea*, the Code provides that each material element is established if the defendant acted purposely, knowingly or recklessly with respect thereto.[43]

Therefore, *D*s in *Morgan* could be convicted of rape if they purposely, knowingly, or recklessly compelled the victim to have sexual intercourse by force, but they could not be convicted on the basis of negligence. For example, if *D*s realized that *X*'s statement to them about his wife's "kinkiness" might be false, and yet they consciously disregarded the substantial and unjustifiable risk that *V* was *not* consenting, then a jury could conclude that they *recklessly* compelled *V*, and their mistaken belief that she was consenting would be no defense.[44] In contrast, if a jury believed that *D*s were so gullible that they were unaware of the risk that her resistance was genuine, then the defendants would not be guilty of rape. In the latter scenario, *D*s negligently compelled *V* by force, but the offense requires proof of recklessness or a more culpable state of mind.

[B] Exception to the Rule

The Model Penal Code provides one exception to the general rule stated above. In a variation on the common law legal-wrong doctrine,[45] the Code provides that the defense of mistake-of-fact is not available if the actor would be guilty of another offense, had the circumstances been as he supposed.[46] However, unlike the common law legal-wrong doctrine, which maintains that the defendant is guilty of the higher offense in such circumstances, the Code only permits punishment at the level of the lesser offense.[47]

---

[42] Regina v. Morgan, [1976] A.C. 182.

[43] Model Penal Code § 2.02(3) and (4). See § 10.07[C], *supra*.

[44] The Model Code definition of rape does not include the element of "non-consent," but the Commentary states that the statutory element of "[c]ompulsion plainly implies non-consent." American Law Institute, Comment to § 213.1, at 306.

[45] See § 12.03[D][3], *supra*.

[46] Model Penal Code § 2.04(2).

[47] American Law Institute, Comment to § 2.04, at 273.

For example, under Model Penal Code Section 221.1, a burglary involves the reckless entry of a building or occupied structure with the purpose of committing a crime inside. The offense is graded as a felony of the third degree, except that it is a felony of the second degree — a more serious crime — if the building entered is a dwelling of another and the entry occurs at night. Suppose that *D* enters the dwelling of another at night with the purpose of committing a felony inside, but he reasonably believes that the building he is entering is a store. That is, he has committed the *actus reus* of the more serious degree of burglary, whereas he has the *mens rea* of the lesser degree of burglary. According to the common law legal-wrong doctrine, *D* is guilty of the higher degree of burglary; under the Model Code, however, in harmony with his lesser *mens rea*, *D* would be punished as if he committed a felony of the third degree.[48]

---

[48] *Id.* at 272.

Chapter 13

MISTAKES OF LAW

§ 13.01 GENERAL PRINCIPLES[1]

[A] General Rule

Subject to two limited exceptions, the common law rule is straightforward: *ignorantia legis neminem excusat*, or ignorance of the law excuses no one.[2] This "dogmatic common-law maxim"[3] is deeply imbedded in Anglo-American jurisprudence.[4]

It is also the case that ignorance or mistake[5] of law does not usually serve as a failure-of-proof defense.[6] That is, neither knowledge nor recklessness or negligence as to whether conduct constitutes an offense, or as to the meaning of an offense, is ordinarily an element of that offense; therefore, it follows that there typically is no *mens rea* capable of being negated by an actor's ignorance or mistake of law.

---

[1] See generally Jerome Hall, General Principles of Criminal Law 382-414 (2d ed. 1960); Ronald A. Cass, *Ignorance of the Law: A Maxim Reexamined*, 17 Wm. & Mary L. Rev. 671 (1976); Fernand N. Dutile & Harold F. Moore, *Mistake and Impossibility: Arranging a Marriage Between Two Difficult Partners*, 74 Nw. U. L. Rev. 166 (1979); Livingston Hall & Selig J. Seligman, *Mistake of Law and Mens Rea*, 8 U. Chi. L. Rev. 641 (1941); Dan M. Kahan, *Ignorance of Law Is an Excuse — But Only for the Virtuous*, 96 Mich. L. Rev. 127 (1997); Gerald Leonard, *Rape, Murder, and Formalism: What Happens if We Define Mistake of Law?*, 72 U. Colo. L. Rev. 507 (2001); Kenneth W. Simons, *Mistake and Impossibility, Law and Fact, and Culpability: A Speculative Essay*, 81 J. Crim. L. & Criminology 447 (1990); Daniel Yeager, *Kahan on Mistakes*, 96 Mich. L. Rev. 2113 (1998).

[2] United States v. Int'l Minerals & Chem. Corp., 402 U.S. 558, 563 (1971); People v. Marrero, 507 N.E.2d 1068, 1069 (N.Y. 1987).

[3] People v. Marrero, 507 N.E.2d at 1069.

[4] Lambert v. California, 355 U.S. 225, 228 (1957).

[5] "Ignorance" and "mistake" involve different states of mind. See § 12.01, Note 2, *supra*. However, the terms will be used interchangeably in this chapter, except when distinguishing between them enhances clarity.

[6] There is a conceptual difference between an "excuse" defense and a "failure-of-proof" defense. Compare § 16.02 with § 16.04, *infra*. However, the immediate point is that, subject to a few exceptions, mistake-of-law constitutes *neither* type of defense.

[B] Rationale of the Rule

[1] Certainty of the Law

According to some common law scholars, the law is "definite and knowable."[7] Therefore, it may be argued that there is no such thing as a *reasonable* mistake of law: Anyone who misunderstands the "definite and knowable" law has simply not tried hard enough to learn it and, consequently, is morally culpable for failing to know the law.

At common law, this claim might have had the ring of plausibility. The courts recognized few criminal offenses, and those that existed involved conduct *malum in se*. Few people could seriously allege surprise in learning that stealing another person's property, intentionally burning another person's house, or unjustifiably taking another person's life was illegal.

However, even at common law, the principle that laws were definite and knowable was often a fiction. Criminal laws were not enacted by legislatures and published, as they are today. Instead, judges shaped the law on a case-by-case basis, which meant that the criminal law changed incrementally with each new decision. Moreover, the definitions of some common law offenses were not models of clarity.[8]

Whatever its plausibility centuries ago, the "definite and knowable" claim cannot withstand modern analysis. There has been a "profusion of legislation making otherwise lawful conduct criminal (*malum prohibitum*)."[9] Therefore, even a person with a clear moral compass is frequently unable to determine accurately whether particular conduct is prohibited. Furthermore, many modern criminal statutes are exceedingly intricate. In today's complex society, therefore, a person can reasonably misunderstand the law, or even fail to know of a particular penal law's existence.

[2] Avoiding Subjectivity in the Law

Jerome Hall once provided a more sophisticated explanation for the common law rule.[10] In stark contrast to the assertion that criminal laws are definite and

---

[7] 1 J. Austin, Lectures on Jurisprudence 497 (4th ed. 1879); see 4 Blackstone, Commentaries on the Laws of England *27 (1769) ("[E]very person of discretion . . . is bound and presumed to know [the law].").

[8] For example, sodomy was considered so shocking an offense that Blackstone not only did not define it with clarity, but he also refused to name it, calling it simply "the infamous *crime against nature*." 4 Blackstone, Note 7, *supra*, at *215. Also, some offenses, e.g., common law larceny, contained exceedingly intricate rules that required judges (and inferentially citizens) to make "hair-splitting distinctions." Rollin M. Perkins & Ronald N. Boyce, Criminal Law 291 (3d ed. 1982).

[9] People v. Marrero, 507 N.E.2d at 1075 (Hancock, J., dissenting).

[10] Hall, Note 1, *supra*, at 382-87.

knowable, Hall claimed that laws are "unavoidably vague" and that persons can "disagree indefinitely regarding the[ir] meaning." At some point, debate regarding the meaning of a law must end. Certain competent officials and institutions, particularly courts, must determine its meaning. Their official declarations provide an objective definition of penal provisions. If mistake-of-law could excuse, Hall argued, the result would be that the law would lose its objective meaning; it would mean whatever a person subjectively (and perhaps incorrectly) thought that it meant.[11] Yet, a "legal order implies the rejection of such contradiction." The legal system favors "objectivity to subjectivity and judicial process to individual opinion."[12]

Hall's thesis, however, misconceives the nature of a mistake-of-law claim. A person who claims mistake-of-law does not assert, nor would her acquittal imply, that the law means whatever she thinks it does. If a defense were recognized, the meaning of the law would remain stable: Mistake-of-law would simply *excuse* the actor for having violated the law, assuming that an ordinary law-abiding person would also have misunderstood the law in question. To punish one whose mistake of law is reasonable "is contrary to 'the [retributive] notion that punishment should be conditioned on a showing of . . . moral blameworthiness.' "[13]

[3] Deterring Fraud

A pragmatic justification for the rule is that recognition of a mistake-of-law defense would provide "opportunities for wrong-minded individuals to contrive [claims of mistake] . . . solely to get an exculpatory notion before the jury."[14] Courts would become hopelessly enmeshed in insoluble questions regarding the extent of a defendant's knowledge of the relevant law. Some false claims would doubtlessly succeed because the truth of the allegations "could scarcely be determined by any evidence accessible to others."[15]

As Holmes observed, however, "it may be doubted whether a man's knowledge of the law is any harder to investigate than many questions which are gone

---

[11] Empirical studies suggest that "citizens show[] no particular knowledge of the laws of their states. But when we asked them to tell us about their state laws, they were able to tell us what they *thought* those laws were." John M. Darley et al., *The Ex Ante Function of the Criminal Law*, 35 Law & Soc. Rev. 165, 181 (2001). According to the Darley study, citizens guessed that the law conformed with *their* moral beliefs: "[P]eople often generate their perceptions of what the law of the state must be from what they think is the morally appropriate form for that law to take. . . . [M]any people are often wrong about what the actual law of their state holds." *Id*. at 183.

[12] Hall, Note 1, *supra*, at 383.

[13] People v. Marrero, 507 N.E.2d at 1074 (Hancock, J., dissenting) (quoting White, *Reliance on Apparent Authority as a Defense to Criminal Prosecution*, 77 Colum. L. Rev. 775, 784 (1977)).

[14] People v. Marrero, 507 N.E.2d at 1073.

[15] 1 Austin, Note 7, *supra*, at 498.

into,"[16] such as a defendant's *mens rea* and whether the actor suffers from the excusing condition of insanity. Moreover, the risk of fraud can be mitigated by allocating to the defendant the burden of persuasion regarding any mistake-of-law excuse claim.

[4] Encouraging Legal Knowledge

The most commonly accepted explanation for the general rule — "frankly pragmatic and utilitarian"[17] — comes from Holmes:

> The true explanation of the rule is the same as that which accounts for the law's indifference to a man's particular temperament, faculties, and so forth. Public policy sacrifices the individual to the general good. . . . It is no doubt true that there are many cases in which the criminal could not have known that he was breaking the law, but to admit the excuse at all would be to encourage ignorance . . . and justice to the individual is rightly outweighed by the larger interests on the other side of the scales.[18]

That is, if a reasonable mistake of law were a defense, this rule would foster lawlessness by encouraging ignorance of the law, rather than respect for and adherence to law. The best way to discourage ignorance is to apply the controversial strict liability doctrine that mistakes of law will *never* be countenanced.[19]

Holmes' explanation, however, is unsatisfactory. As Professor Dan Kahan has persuasively argued, when a person "takes reasonable steps to learn the law, there always remains some residual risk" of error.[20] In the strict liability system Holmes defends, the person who tries to learn the law, but errs, is no better off than one who makes no effort at all — the incentive to learn the law is undermined. If the criminal law permitted a *reasonable* mistake of law to serve as a defense while punishing for negligence (for an *unreasonable* mistake), there would be an incentive to try to learn the law.[21]

---

[16] Oliver Wendell Holmes, The Common Law 48 (1881).

[17] People v. Marrero, 507 N.E.2d at 1074 (Hancock, J., dissenting).

[18] Holmes, Note 16, *supra*, at 48.

[19] For debate regarding strict liability generally, see § 11.02, *supra*.

[20] Kahan, Note 1, *supra*, at 134.

[21] Kahan offers an alternative explanation of the no-excuse rule: Private knowledge of the law is not unambiguously good because, with such knowledge, would-be wrongdoers can search out and exploit legal loopholes. Therefore, the law promotes "purposeful obfuscation" and, in general, punishes reasonable legal mistakes in those cases in which a person who is guided more by morality than legality would be aware that her conduct is, at best, marginally lawful. For a critique of Kahan's position, see Yeager, Note 1, *supra*.

§ 13.02 WHEN MISTAKE-OF-LAW IS A DEFENSE: EXCEPTIONS TO THE GENERAL RULE

[A] Putting the Exceptions in Context

Although the no-defense rule stated in § 13.01 is strict, three categories of mistake-of-law exceptions are recognized. The first two exceptions (reasonable reliance and fair notice) are excuse defenses. (These defenses are sometimes even couched in constitutional terms.) Under the circumstances set out below, the defendant is not guilty of an offense, although all of the essential elements of the crime, including *mens rea*, have been satisfied.

The third exception is a failure-of-proof claim: The defendant claims that because of a mistake of law, she did not have the requisite *mens rea* to be convicted of the offense charged. To the extent that this type of claim is exculpatory, it is like a mistake of *fact* in that the defendant is acquitted for the straightforward reason that the prosecution has failed to meet its constitutional burden of proof regarding an essential element of the offense.

[B] Reasonable-Reliance Doctrine (Entrapment by Estoppel)[22]

[1] Reliance on One's Own Interpretation of the Law

A person is *not* excused for committing a crime if she relies on her own erroneous reading of the law, even if a reasonable person — even a reasonable law-trained person — would have similarly misunderstood the law. For example, in *People v. Marrero*,[23] *M*, a federal corrections officer, was arrested for possession of a loaded .38 caliber automatic pistol, in violation of a statute that prohibited the carrying of a handgun without a permit. *M* sought dismissal of his indictment on the ground that peace officers were expressly exempted from liability under the statute. The statutory definition of "peace officers" included "correction officers of any state correctional facility or *of any penal correctional institution.*" As a federal corrections officer, *M* claimed that he believed that he was exempt under the law.

M's reading of the statute was not self-evidently unreasonable. Indeed, the trial judge agreed with *M*'s interpretation. Nonetheless, an appellate court concluded, by a 3-2 vote, that he was not a "peace officer" within the meaning of the statute. Although this means that three of the six judges who considered the question interpreted the statute as *M* did, *M* was not entitled to claim mis-

---

[22] See generally John T. Parry, *Culpability, Mistake, and Official Interpretations of Law*, 25 Am. J. Crim. L. 1 (1997).

[23] 507 N.E.2d 1068 (N.Y. 1987).

take-of-law at his subsequent trial to the extent that his mistake was founded solely on his own understanding of the law. In such circumstances, the ordinary no-defense rule applies: One is never excused for relying on a personal, even reasonable, misreading of a statute.

[2] Official Interpretation of the Law

Although a person is not excused for relying on her own interpretation of a criminal statute, she will be excused for committing a criminal offense if she reasonably relies on an official statement of the law, later determined to be erroneous, obtained from a person or public body with responsibility for the interpretation, administration, or enforcement of the law defining the offense.[24]

This excuse is sometimes called the "reasonable reliance" or "entrapment by estoppel" doctrine. In a few jurisdictions, the defense is treated as a matter of constitutional due process.[25] Ordinarily, however, the rule is simply labeled a non-constitutional common law or statutory excuse.

This defense may be justified on various grounds. First, the threat of punishment can have little deterrent effect on an individual whose conduct has been authorized by an appropriate party or legal body. Second, a person who acts on the basis of an official, albeit erroneous, interpretation of the law has acted as we would want her to act, i.e., in obedience of the law as it was explained. Third, there is a "clean hands" justification for the rule: It is fundamentally unfair for a government agent to authorize conduct and then seek to have the individual who relied on that authorization prosecuted, even if it later turns out that the original authorization was incorrect.

This defense is very narrowly applied. For a statement of the law to be "official," it must be contained in: (1) a statute later declared to be invalid;[26] (2) a judicial decision of the highest court in the jurisdiction, later determined to be erroneous;[27] or (3) an official, but erroneous, interpretation of the law, secured

---

[24] Commonwealth v. Twitchell, 617 N.E.2d 609, 619 (Mass. 1993). Not all courts explain the rule as stated in the text. See, e.g., United States v. Nichols, 21 F.3d 1016, 1018 (10th Cir. 1994) (stating the defense applies if a government official "misleads a party as to the state of the law and that party proceeds to act on the misrepresentation"; "[f]urther, the defendant's reliance must be reasonable in light of the identity of the agent, the point of law misrepresented, and the substance of the misrepresentation").

[25] E.g., Miller v. Commonwealth, 492 S.E.2d 482, 484-87 (Va. Ct. App. 1997).

[26] See Brent v. State, 43 Ala. 297 (1869); State v. Godwin, 31 S.E. 221 (N.C. 1898).

[27] State v. O'Neil, 126 N.W. 454 (Iowa 1910). The law is divided on whether a person may rely on a lower court ruling. E.g., State v. Chicago, Milwaukee & St. Paul Ry., 153 N.W. 320 (Minn. 1915) (recognizing the excuse); State v. Striggles, 210 N.W. 137 (Iowa 1926) (rejecting the defense); see also Ostrosky v. State, 913 F.2d 590 (9th Cir. 1990) (holding that the Due Process Clause does not necessarily authorize a defendant to rely on a lower court decision, if that decision has been stayed while the state appeals).

from a public officer in charge of its interpretation, administration, or enforcement, such as the Attorney General of the state[28] or, in the case of federal law, of the United States.

According to these narrow principles, *D1*, an ex-felon in possession of a muzzle-loading hunting rifle, who is charged with "possession of a firearm by a person previously convicted of a felony" may defend her actions if she was assured by her probation officer than she could possess the weapon, but she cannot rely on assurances of a state Department of Game and Fisheries official who had no authority to interpret, enforce, or administer the penal law in question.[29] Similarly, *D2*, a motorist charged with disobeying a lawful police order, cannot rely on a 911 telephone operator's advice received by *D2* on a car phone, to ignore a police officer's order to pull over in her car.[30] And, *D3* may clearly not rely on assurances of a private organization that assists aliens that she may re-enter the country despite the fact that she was previously deported.[31]

Even if a person obtains an interpretation of the law from a proper source, that interpretation must come in an "official" manner. For example, a person may rely on an official "opinion letter" from the state Attorney General, formally interpreting the statute in question.[32] However, an informal interpretation of the law will not do. For example, a fisherman may not reasonably rely on a quick interpretation of a fishing regulation, provided by a Fish and Wildlife Patrol Officer at the scene.[33]

[3] Advice of Private Counsel[34]

Reliance on erroneous advice provided by a private attorney is not a defense to a crime.[35] This blanket rejection of a defense can be criticized. Society arguably is far better off if a person acts on the basis of a lawyer's advice, than if she acts on her own untutored reading of the applicable law. A rule that encourages a citizen to seek a lawyer's assistance would likely promote, rather than discourage, knowledge of the law.[36]

---

[28] See Commonwealth v. Twitchell, 617 N.E.2d 609 (Mass. 1993).

[29] Miller v. Commonwealth, 492 S.E.2d 482 (Va. Ct. App. 1997).

[30] State v. DeCastro, 913 P.2d 558 (Haw. 1996).

[31] United States v. Gutierrez-Gonzales, 184 F.3d 1160 (10th Cir. 1999).

[32] Commonwealth v. Twitchell, 617 N.E.2d 609 (Mass. 1993).

[33] Haggren v. State, 829 P.2d 842 (Alaska Ct. App. 1992).

[34] See generally Miriam Gur-Arye, *Reliance on a Lawyer's Mistaken Advice — Should it be an Excuse from Criminal Liability?*, 29 Am. J. Crim. L. 455 (2002).

[35] State v. Huff, 36 A. 1000 (Me. 1897); for an exceptional case to the contrary, see Long v. State, 65 A.2d 489 (Del. 1949).

[36] However, perhaps rejection of the mistake-of-law defense is founded on the belief that we do not always want people to learn the law! See Note 21, *supra*.

Occasionally it is suggested that if reliance on private legal advice could excuse a person's unlawful conduct, she might purposely turn to an unethical lawyer or one of questionable competency in order to obtain advice that authorizes the improper conduct.[37] However, this argument exaggerates the dangers in recognizing an excuse. Unqualified lawyers exist, but courts presume that attorneys are competent, absent evidence to the contrary.[38] Nor is the risk of fraud substantial: An attorney is subject to professional discipline or criminal prosecution for fraudulent conduct.[39]

Probably the most serious problem with permitting the defense in these circumstances is one of line-drawing. Should the advice of any lawyer qualify, or only advice from a specialist in the field? Must a person turn to an experienced lawyer, or may she turn to a new member of the bar? Ultimately, however, any reliance that would result in exculpation would have to be reasonable. A jury could determine whether the defendant made reasonable efforts to obtain accurate legal advice.

[C] Fair Notice and the *Lambert* Principle[40]

At common law, it is said that "every one is *conclusively* presumed to know the law."[41] This means not only that citizens are presumed to understand the law, but more fundamentally to know of the existence of each criminal law. On occasion there may be an exceptional case in which it is so grossly unjust to assume that a citizen is aware of a penal law's existence that one might expect that a court would provide some common law dispensation.[42] And, as it turns out, the Supreme Court held in *Lambert v. California*[43] that, under very limited circumstances, a person who is unaware of a duly enacted and published criminal statute may successfully assert a constitutional defense in a prosecution of that offense.

---

[37] See State v. Downs, 21 S.E. 689, 689 (N.C. 1895); see also Gur-Arye, Note 34, *supra*, at 466 (permitting the excuse "might lead to people purchasing custom-tailored legal opinions in order to acquire immunity from criminal prosecution").

[38] See Strickland v. Washington, 466 U.S. 668, 687-91 (1984).

[39] A lawyer who purposely gives incorrect advice so that her client can assert a mistake-of-law defense could be prosecuted for obstruction of justice, conspiracy with her client to violate the statute in question, and/or be convicted as an accomplice in the criminal act perpetrated by the client.

[40] See generally A.F. Brooke II, Note, *When Ignorance of the Law Became an Excuse: Lambert & Its Progeny*, 19 Am. J. Crim. L. 279 (1992).

[41] State v. Woods, 179 A. 1, 2 (Vt. 1935) (emphasis added).

[42] E.g., Rex v. Bailey, 168 Eng. Rep. 651 (Crown Cases 1800) (affirming *B*'s conviction, but recommending that a pardon be issued, for violating a statute enacted while *B* was in a sailing ship along the coast of Africa and, therefore, without possible knowledge of the statute's existence).

[43] 355 U.S. 225 (1957).

In *Lambert*, *L* was a Los Angeles resident and convicted felon. A local ordinance required felons residing in the city for more than five days to register their presence with the police. Violation of the ordinance was punishable by a maximum sentence of six months in jail, five hundred dollars, or both. *L* never registered and was prosecuted under the ordinance. She was convicted after the trial court barred evidence of her claim that she was unaware of the law.

The Supreme Court ruled that her conviction violated the Due Process Clause of the Constitution. The high court acknowledged that the common law rule that ignorance of the law is no excuse is "deep in our law." Nonetheless, it warned that the Constitution places limits on this doctrine. Specifically, "actual knowledge of the duty to register or proof of the probability of such knowledge" was a constitutional prerequisite to conviction for violation of the registration statute.

Literal application of this language would seem to invite fraudulent claims, and diminish the incentive of citizens to ascertain the laws governing their activities.[44] Therefore, it is important to determine what features of the Los Angeles ordinance troubled the Supreme Court. Perhaps the Court's most significant observation was that *L*'s situation was atypical, because "we deal here with conduct that is wholly passive — mere failure to register. It is unlike the commission of acts, or the failure to act under circumstances that should alert the doer to the consequences of his deed."

Three aspects of the ordinance may have concerned the justices: (1) it punished an omission (failure to register); (2) the duty to act was imposed on the basis of a status (presence in Los Angeles), rather than on the basis of an activity; and (3) the offense was *malum prohibitum*. As a result of these factors, there was nothing to alert *L* or a reasonable person to the need to inquire into the law.

Lambert might require all three factors to be present to entitle a law violator to a constitutional defense. For example, suppose that a statute requires pharmacists to keep written records of all prescription sales of specified dangerous drugs. Suppose that *D*, a pharmacist, is unaware of the law, and consequently fails to keep the requisite records. The *Lambert* doctrine would almost certainly not apply: Although two of the three factors — (1) and (3) — are present, the act of selling dangerous prescription drugs should alert a pharmacist to the possibility of legislation relating to their sale.

What if a legislature enacts an uncommonly silly statute, in which one of the three factors is lacking? For example, suppose that a city enacts and duly publishes an ordinance making it a violation to water the lawn on any February 29th. Assume *D* moves to the city, waters the lawn on the first February 29th that arises, and is prosecuted for violation of the offense. The statute prohibits conduct — watering the lawn — rather than an omission; on the other hand, this conduct is not illegal unless it is February 29 (a status), and the conduct is

---

[44] American Law Institute, Comment to § 2.04, at 276-77.

malum prohibitum, not *malum in se*. In such circumstances, should *D* be permitted to testify that she was unaware of the law?

There was nothing about the fact that it was February 29 that would or should have alerted *D* to the consequences of her deed of watering the lawn. However, if *D* is provided a defense in these circumstances, this would seriously undermine the common law principle that ignorance of the law is no excuse, and would jeopardize the enforcement of many *malum prohibitum* offenses. Therefore, although the Supreme Court has never clarified *Lambert's* meaning, it is doubtful that the current high court would invalidate this or any similar statute.[45]

[D] Ignorance or Mistake that Negates *Mens Rea*[46]

[1] General Approach

As noted in § 13.01[A], neither knowledge nor recklessness or negligence as to whether conduct constitutes an offense, or as to the meaning of an offense, is ordinarily an element of that offense. Therefore, a mistake of law, whether reasonable or unreasonable, will not usually negate any *mens rea* element found in the definition of a crime.

On occasion, knowledge that the prohibited conduct constitutes an offense *is* itself an express element of the crime.[47] Somewhat more often, however, a defendant's lack of knowledge of, or misunderstanding regarding the meaning or application of, *another* law — typically, a nonpenal law — will negate the *mens rea* element in the definition of the criminal offense.

For example, consider these three cases. *D1* takes her automobile to *X*, a mechanic, for repair. Upon receiving what she believes to be an excessive bill, she refuses to pay, whereupon *X* refuses to deliver the car. That night *D1* returns to *X*'s lot, finds her car, and drives it away. She is prosecuted for larceny.[48] *D1*

---

[45] Lower courts have rarely applied *Lambert* to overturn convictions. But see State v. Giorgetti, 868 So. 2d 512 (Fla. 2004) (applying *Lambert*, and holding that *G* could not be convicted of failing to register as a sex offender absent proof he knew of the registration requirement or proof of the probability of such knowledge); State v. Young, 535 S.E.2d 380 (N.C. Ct. App. 2000) (applying *Lambert* in a prosecution of a sex offender for not registering his change of address, reversing the conviction of *Y*, a mentally incompetent individual, because he lacked actual or constructive knowledge of the duty to register).

[46] See generally Sharon L. Davies, *The Jurisprudence of Willfulness: An Evolving Theory of Excusable Ignorance*, 48 Duke L.J. 341 (1998).

[47] For example, the Michigan Campaign Finance Act makes it illegal for any person to make or accept a campaign cash contribution in excess of $20.00. The statute further provides that "[a] person who knowingly violates this section is guilty of a misdemeanor." Mich. Comp. Laws § 169.241 (2005). It is a defense under this statute, therefore, that the defendant, a campaign contributor, did not know it was against the law for her to make a cash contribution in excess of $20.00. People v. Weiss, 479 N.W.2d 30 (Mich. Ct. App. 1991).

[48] See State v. Cude, 383 P.2d 399 (Utah 1963).

is unaware of the fact that a state lien law provides that a mechanic may retain possession of a repaired automobile until the bill is paid.

D2 is charged with rape after he has nonconsensual sexual intercourse with *V*. At the time of his actions, *D2* believed that *V* legally was his wife, thus taking his conduct outside the proscription of common law rape, which prohibits nonconsensual intercourse with a female "not his wife." In fact, the marriage ceremony in which he and *V* participated was legally invalid — *V* was not legally his wife.

D3 is prosecuted for bigamy. She responds that she believed that she had obtained a legally valid divorce before remarrying.

What do these cases have in common? Each defendant presumably was aware of, and understood the meaning of, the criminal statute (larceny, rape, or bigamy) that was the basis of her or his prosecution. At the same time, however, each defendant was unaware of, or misunderstood the import of, another law (mechanics' lien law, marriage law, or divorce law), under circumstances in which this mistake of law arguably is relevant to the defendant's criminal liability. For shorthand purposes, a mistake-of-law claim of the sort described here may be termed a *different-law mistake*, because the claimed mistake relates to a law other than the criminal offense for which the defendant has been charged.

When a defendant seeks to avoid conviction for a criminal offense by asserting a different-law mistake, on the ground that the different-law mistake negates her *mens rea*, the first matter for determination is whether the offense charged is one of specific-intent (as in *D1*'s case), general-intent (*D2*), or strict-liability (*D3*).

[2] Specific-Intent Offenses

A different-law mistake, whether reasonable or unreasonable, is a defense in the prosecution of a specific-intent offense, if the mistake negates the specific intent in the prosecuted offense.[49] This doctrine parallels the rule relating to mistakes-of-*fact* in the prosecution of specific-intent crimes.[50]

For example, in *D1*'s larceny prosecution described in the preceding subsection, the prosecutor must prove that *D1* had the specific intent "to steal the property of another." For purposes of larceny law, the automobile belonged to the mechanic,[51] so *D1* committed the *actus reus* of larceny when she drove away in

---

[49] *Id.*; State v. Varszegi, 635 A.2d 816 (Conn. App. Ct. 1993).

[50] See § 12.03[C], *supra*.

[51] Ownership of property is not determinative in larceny law. The offense is intended to protect the person in lawful possession of personal property. See Chapter 32, *infra*. In this case, the mechanic was in lawful possession of the car.

"X's" car. However, because *D1* was unaware of the lien law, she erroneously believed that she had a right to possession of the vehicle without paying the bill. Therefore, this different-law mistake negated *D1*'s "intent to steal the property of another." As she understood the law, she was simply taking lawful possession of what rightfully was hers. *D1*, therefore, is not guilty of the offense, even if her mistake of law was unreasonable.

Cheek v. United States[52] provides another example of this rule. In *Cheek*, *C*, an anti-tax activist, failed to file federal income tax returns for six years, although he received wages each year as an airline pilot. As a result, *C* was charged with six counts of "wilfully" failing to file federal income tax returns. For purposes of this tax statute, "wilfully" means "a voluntary and intentional violation of a known legal duty."[53]

C testified in his own defense at trial. He admitted that he had not filed personal income tax returns during the years in question, but he explained that during this period he attended seminars sponsored by an anti-tax organization that provided advice on tax matters. *C* introduced evidence that an attorney from that group indicated, among other things, that investment profits ("capital gains"), but not wages, constituted "income," under the Internal Revenue Code. Therefore, *C* testified, he believed that he was not required to report his wages to the Internal Revenue Service. As a consequence, *C* requested the judge to instruct the jury that he was not guilty of the offense if he believed, even unreasonably, that he was not legally required to report his wages.

The trial court did not instruct the jury as *C* requested, but the Supreme Court held that it should have done so: If the jury believed *C*'s testimony, his mistake regarding the meaning of the term "income" under the Internal Revenue Code disproved that he "intentionally violated a *known* legal duty."

[3] General-Intent Offenses

Although there is very little case law on point, a different-law mistake, whether reasonable or unreasonable, apparently is not a defense to a general-intent crime.[54] Thus, in the rape hypothetical described in subsection [1], *D2* may be convicted of *V*'s rape because the *D2-V* marriage was legally invalid. Even if *D2*'s mistake regarding the legality of the marriage was reasonable — and, thus, *D2* did not intend to have intercourse with a "female not his wife" — the common law does not exculpate *D2*.

---

[52] 498 U.S. 192 (1991).

[53] See § 10.04[C], *supra*.

[54] E.g., People v. Snyder, 652 P.2d 42 (Cal. 1982) (*S* was prosecuted for the general-intent offense of "possession of a concealable firearm by a convicted felon"; *S* was denied the opportunity to prove at trial that she believed that her prior conviction for marijuana possession was a misdemeanor; held: the trial court's ruling was correct; *S*'s mistake, i.e., the status of marijuana possession as a felony, was irrelevant to her guilt for the firearm-possession charge).

This result does not conform with the comparable mistake-of-fact rule.[55] Presumably, the difference in result is a function of the strong policy-based presumption against recognizing a mistake-of-law "loophole." However, the outcome is inconsistent with the general principle that people should not be punished in the absence of culpability, since one who acts on the basis of a reasonable mistake of law lacks moral blameworthiness.

[4] Strict-Liability Offenses

A different-law mistake, whether reasonable or unreasonable, is not a defense to a strict-liability offense. This result is sensible: If liability is strict, there is no *mens rea* to negate. Thus, in the bigamy case noted in subsection [1], *D3* will be convicted of bigamy even though she believed, perhaps reasonably, that she had obtained a proper divorce before she remarried.[56]

§ 13.03 MODEL PENAL CODE

[A] General Rule

Unless the definition of a crime so provides, "[n]either knowledge nor recklessness or negligence as to whether conduct constitutes a crime or as to the existence, meaning or application of the law determining the elements of an offense is an element of such offense."[57] Under limited circumstances, a mistake-of-law defense is recognized.

[B] Exceptions to the General Rule

[1] Reasonable-Reliance Doctrine

In nearly all respects, the Model Penal Code codifies the common law reasonable-reliance doctrine. A person's belief that her conduct is lawful constitutes a defense if: (1) she relies on an official, but erroneous, statement of the law; (2) the statement of law is found in a statute, judicial decision, administrative order or grant of permission, or an official interpretation by a public official or body responsible for the interpretation, administration, or enforcement of the law; and (3) the reliance is otherwise reasonable.[58] A person is excused in these circumstances because, according to the Commentary, she has acted in law-

---

[55] See § 12.03[D][1], *supra*.

[56] See State v. Woods, 179 A. 1 (Vt. 1935) (despite *W*'s reasonable belief in the lawfulness of a prior divorce, she may be convicted of violation of a statute prohibiting a person to be "found in bed" with another person's spouse).

[57] Model Penal Code § 2.02(9).

[58] Model Penal Code § 2.04(3)(b).

abiding fashion, the danger of fraud is slight, and her claim is not unduly difficult to prove or disprove.[59]

Because of the danger of collusion, the Model Code, like the common law, does not recognize an excuse for reliance on the advice of a private attorney. The Commentary concedes, however, that cases can "be imagined in which a client is unfairly taxed with his lawyer's bad advice."[60]

[2] Fair Notice

The Model Penal Code provides that a defendant is not guilty of an offense if she does not believe that her conduct is illegal, and the statute defining the offense: (1) is not known to her; and (2) was "not published or otherwise reasonably made available" to her before she violated the law.[61]

The Model Code antedates *Lambert v. California*.[62] The Commentary to the Code, published since *Lambert*, concedes that as a result of that case the Code may require exculpation "in some extraordinary situations not reached by the section."[63] The Code defense applies only if the statute was neither published nor otherwise made reasonably available to the actor before she committed the crime. *Lambert* would apply to a situation in which the statute or ordinance *was* published and available to be read by a citizen, but in which the prohibited conduct itself would not alert an actor to the need to investigate whether there is a relevant published statute.

[3] Ignorance or Mistake that Negates *Mens Rea*

The Model Penal Code requires proof of some culpable state of mind regarding every material element of an offense.[64] Furthermore, Section 2.04(1) provides that a mistake of law is a defense if it negates a material element of the offense, or if the law expressly provides for a mistake-of-law defense.

As noted in subsection [A], however, unless the definition of an offense so provides, "[n]either knowledge nor recklessness or negligence as to whether conduct constitutes a crime or as to the existence, meaning or application of the law

---

[59] American Law Institute, Comment to § 2.04, at 275.

[60] *Id.* at 280.

[61] Model Penal Code § 2.04(3)(a).

[62] 355 U.S. 225 (1957). See § 13.02[C], *supra*.

[63] American Law Institute, Comment to § 2.04, at 276.

[64] Model Penal Code § 2.02(1).

determining the elements of an offense is an element of such offense." Therefore, generally speaking, Section 2.04(1) relates to different-law mistakes.[65] A
claim that a different-law mistake negates the *mens rea* of the offense is handled in the same manner as a claim of mistake-of-*fact* under the Code.[66]

---

[65] For the meaning of "different-law mistakes," see § 13.02[D][1], *supra*.

[66] See § 12.04, *supra*.

Chapter 14

CAUSATION

§ 14.01 GENERAL PRINCIPLES[1]

[A] "Causation": An Element of Criminal Responsibility

D points a gun at *V*, intending to kill *V*. A few seconds before *D* pulls the trigger, *X*, independently[2] of *D*, shoots and instantly kills *V*. The bullet in *D*'s gun strikes the already dead *V*. Is *D* guilty of murder?

The answer, of course, is "no." A crime (here, murder) is composed of an *actus reus* and, usually, a *mens rea*. As described elsewhere,[3] the "*actus reus*" of an offense consists of a voluntary act (or an omission, when there is a duty to act) that results in the social harm prohibited by the offense. The "*mens rea*" is the culpable state of mind.

In the hypothetical, *D*'s conduct included a voluntary act — pulling the trigger of the gun. The social harm of murder — the killing of a human being by another human being — occurred. Moreover, *D* intended to kill *V*, a sufficient *mens rea* for murder. It would appear, then, that everything is in place for *D*'s conviction of murder. Common sense, however, tells us that *D* is only guilty of attempted murder, rather than murder.

Common sense is confirmed by another prerequisite to criminal responsibility: causation. Analytically, "causation" is an ingredient of a crime's *actus reus*.[4] A careful look at the definition of "*actus reus*," provided above, indicates that it contains three rather than two elements. In addition to the voluntary act (or omission) and the social harm, there must be a link between the two: The defendant's voluntary act (or omission) must "result in" — cause — the social harm.

---

[1] See generally Jerome Hall, General Principles of Criminal Law 247-95 (2d ed. 1960); H.L.A. Hart & Tony Honoré, Causation in the Law (2d ed. 1985); Eric A. Johnson, *Criminal Liability for Loss of a Chance*, 91 Iowa L. Rev. 59 (2005); Sanford H. Kadish, *The Criminal Law and the Luck of the Draw*, 84 J. Crim. L. & Criminology 679 (1994); Kimberly D. Kessler, Comment, *The Role of Luck in the Criminal Law*, 142 U. Pa. L. Rev. 2183 (1994); Michael S. Moore, *Causation, in* 1 Encyclopedia of Crime & Justice 150 (Joshua Dressler, ed., 2d ed. 2002); Alan Norrie, *A Critique of Criminal Causation*, 54 Modern L. Rev. 685 (1991); Paul K. Ryu, *Causation in Criminal Law*, 106 U. Pa. L. Rev. 773 (1958); Stephen J. Schulhofer, *Harm and Punishment: A Critique of Emphasis on the Results of Conduct in the Criminal Law*, 122 U. Pa. L. Rev. 1497 (1974); Judith Jarvis Thomson, *The Decline of Cause*, 76 Geo. L.J. 137 (1987).

[2] Throughout this chapter the word "independently" is used to describe a person who is not acting in concert with (i.e., is not an accomplice or co-conspirator of) another actor.

[3] See § 9.01[A], *supra*.

[4] Albin Eser, *The Principle of "Harm" in the Concept of Crime: A Comparative Analysis of the Criminally Protected Legal Interests*, 4 Duq. L. Rev. 345, 386 (1965).

Causation is an implicit element of all crimes,[5] which must be proved by the prosecution beyond a reasonable doubt.[6] As a practical matter, however, "causation" only turns up as an issue in the prosecution of "result" crimes, i.e., when the social harm of an offense is an unwanted result (e.g., the death of another human being).[7] Indeed, causation problems seldom arise outside the context of homicide prosecutions.

Returning to the initial hypothetical, D will not be guilty of murder for the simple reason that X — not D — caused V's death. D is not legally responsible for a result that he did not cause. He may be held responsible, however, for the harm he *did* cause, for example, the social harm that results from the commission of an attempted murder.

[B] "Causation": Its Role in Criminal Law Theory[8]

Causation analysis is so common a part of everyday thought processes that it is easy to ignore or downplay its importance in the criminal law. In fact, however, "causation" is a concept deeply imbedded "in human thought and expressed even among the most [ancient] people in their effort to understand 'the way of things.' "[9]

The role of causality in the criminal law is the same as it is in the evaluation of any everyday event: to determine why something occurred. More specifically, principles of causation assist us in deciding who or what among the various people and forces existing in the world should be held responsible for resulting harm.

The value of "causation" in determining criminal responsibility is virtually irrefutable. Imagine a law that provided that any person in physical proximity to an accident could be punished for the resulting harm, even if he had nothing to do with causing the injury. Such a draconian rule would have immense neg-

---

[5] Moore, Note 1, *supra*, at 151; see State v. Farner, 66 S.W.3d 188 (Tenn. 2001) (holding that causation is an essential element of every homicide offense).

[6] People v. Tims, 534 N.W.2d 675, 680 (Mich. 1995).

[7] Where is the causation requirement with a "conduct" crime? For example, if D is charged with attempted murder of V in the hypothetical shooting episode, isn't D guilty of an attempt precisely because he did *not* cause the social harm of the offense? No. As discussed in § 9.10, *supra*, "social harm" is defined broadly to include the *endangerment* of any socially valuable interest. As discussed more fully in Chapter 27, the social harm of attempted murder might be described as conduct by an actor that brings him in "dangerous proximity" to taking another's life. Thus, an attempt "requires a causing of some further state of affairs beyond simply the moving of one's own body" — here, endangering a life by coming dangerously close to killing another. Michael S. Moore, Act and Crime 218 (1993).

[8] See Joshua Dressler, *Reassessing the Theoretical Underpinnings of Accomplice Liability: New Solutions to an Old Problem*, 37 Hastings L.J. 91, 103-08 (1985).

[9] Hall, Note 1, *supra*, at 248.

ative social consequences. People would rationally fear that the lightning bolt of the law might strike them at any time; therefore, they would be deterred from socially desirable, and not simply unduly dangerous, activities.

This utilitarian argument, however, does not adequately explain the moral importance of the causation requirement in the criminal law. It does not explain why, in the hypothetical at the beginning of this chapter, *D* should not be held responsible for *V*'s death, even though *X* intervened a split second earlier and killed *V*. After all, *D* is *not* an innocent party selected at random for punishment. Presumably, he is as dangerous as *X*; certainly he is no less dangerous than he would have been but for the fortuity of *X*'s involvement in the events. Yet, *D* will only be convicted of attempted murder, a lesser offense than murder. The reason for this is *D*'s lack of causal connection to the death.

The role of causation in the criminal law finds its primary moral justification in retributive concepts of just deserts. Unlike tort law, in which morally innocent people are frequently held vicariously responsible for the wrongful acts of others, the criminal law is wedded to the concept of personal responsibility for crimes. This notion is rooted in the "inarticulate, subconscious sense of justice of the man on the street."[10]

The principle of causation is the instrument society employs to ensure that criminal responsibility is personal. It is the basis that links the actor to the social harm. Moreover, "causation" serves as the mechanism for determining how much the wrongdoer owes society and ought to repay it, i.e., causation principles help quantify his just deserts. According to one school of retributive thought, a wrongdoer's punishment should not exceed the harm that he has caused.[11]

[C] "Causation": Criminal Law versus Tort Law

Causation is a litigated issue in both tort and criminal law. However, causal problems are fewer and often less factually complex in criminal cases. Consequently, much that we think we know about causation in the criminal law springs from tort law and from scholarly literature focused on that area. Nonetheless, "[a]s a matter of historical fact, the rules of causation in criminal cases are not tied to the rules of causation in civil cases."[12] This is particularly the case when one considers issues of "proximate" or "legal" causation.[13]

There is justification for treating criminal law conceptions of causation separately from tort law. Tort law seeks to identify the most suitable party on

---

[10] Francis Bowes Sayre, *Criminal Responsibility for the Acts of Another*, 43 Harv. L. Rev. 689, 717 (1930).

[11] This principle may explain why, for example, an attempted murder is punished less severely than a murder at common law. See § 27.04[B], *infra*.

[12] People v. Tims, 534 N.W.2d 675, 684 (Mich. 1995).

[13] See § 14.03, *infra*.

whom to place financial responsibility for negligently or innocently causing harm. In contrast, the criminal law seeks to determine whether and to what extent a wrongdoer, typically an intentional one, ought to be condemned by the community and have his liberty restricted.

Because of the higher stakes in the criminal law, and its especially strong commitment to personal, rather than vicarious, responsibility, some courts expressly provide that a tort conception of causation is insufficient to impose criminal responsibility.[14] Instead, a stricter test, requiring a closer connection between the defendant's conduct and the resulting harm, should be applied.[15]

§ 14.02 ACTUAL CAUSE (OR "FACTUAL CAUSE")

[A] "But-For" ("*Sine Qua Non*") Test

Causation analysis is divisible into two parts: "actual cause" (also called "factual cause" or "cause-in-fact") and "proximate cause" (or "legal cause"). There can be no criminal liability for resulting social harm "unless it can be shown that the defendant's conduct was a cause-in-fact of the prohibited result."[16] In order to make this determination, courts traditionally apply the "but-for" or "*sine qua non*" test. This test may be stated as follows: "*But for D's voluntary act(s),*[17] *would the social harm have occurred when it did?*" If the answer is "no" — if the social harm would *not* have occurred when it did in the absence of *D*'s voluntary conduct — *D* is an actual cause of the result.

The but-for test serves a limited, but critical, purpose. It functions to *exclude* certain forces, including human ones, from potential responsibility for ensuing harm. That is, subject to one possible and very limited, controversial exception,[18] *D* cannot be held criminally responsible for social harm unless the prosecution proves beyond a reasonable doubt that he is a (not necessarily "the") but-for cause of the harm.

The fact that *D*'s conduct is determined to be an actual cause of a result does not mean that he will be held criminally responsible for the harm. To be guilty, *D* must have acted with the requisite *mens rea*, and he must also be the *proximate* cause of the social harm, the latter issue of which is considered in § 14.03.

---

[14] E.g., Commonwealth v. Rementer, 598 A.2d 1300, 1304 (Pa. Super. Ct. 1991).

[15] Commonwealth v. Root, 170 A.2d 310, 314 (Pa. 1961) (stating that the "tort liability concept of proximate cause has no proper place in prosecutions for criminal homicide and more direct causal connection is required for conviction").

[16] Velazquez v. State, 561 So. 2d 347, 350 (Fla. Dist. Ct. App. 1990).

[17] In the prosecution of a culpable omission, this test would be rephrased to begin "but for *D*'s *omission*."

[18] See § 14.02[C][2][b], *infra*.

[B] "Causes" versus "Conditions"

D pulls the trigger of a gun, and a bullet is propelled from the gun into *V*'s chest, causing *V*'s death. Common sense tells us that *D* was the cause of the death: But for *D*'s voluntary act of pulling the trigger of the gun, *V* would not have died when he did.

In fact, however, there are additional "actual causes" of *V*'s death. For example, *V* would not have died but for the fact that his heart muscle was too weak to withstand the intrusion of the bullet. Other causes of the death are found in certain principles of physics that explain how and why the pulling of the trigger results in a bullet moving at a fast rate of speed. Indeed, if *V*'s mother had not given birth to *V*, *D* could not have killed him.

Usually a court will either ignore these latter "causes" or identify them more realistically as necessary "conditions" for the harm to occur. Although conditions may technically meet the *sine qua non* test of causation, their exclusion from the latter category is consistent with a common sense view of the issue.

In determining causation, people focus on what is interesting in an event. They focus on the abnormal, the matters that seem out of the ordinary.[19] "Conditions" are normal events or circumstances that, although necessary for the result to occur, do not positively contribute to it. *D*'s firing of the gun is the act that is interesting and out of the ordinary. It is *D*'s conduct, therefore, and not the laws of physics, the structure of *V*'s heart, or *V*'s prior birth, that affirmatively contributed to the death.

[C] Special "Actual Cause" Problems

[1] Confusing "Causation" With "*Mens Rea*"

The common law treats "actual causation" and "*mens rea*" as independent concepts, each of which must be proven in a criminal prosecution. Frequently, however, these doctrines are confused.

[a] Causation Without *Mens Rea*

D has a minor argument with her husband, *V*. *V*, upset about the argument, leaves the house, and walks across the street. As he does, he is struck and killed by an automobile driven by *X*. Is *D* an actual cause of *V*'s death? The answer is "yes," unless *V* had planned to cross that street at that precise moment anyway: But for *D* having the argument with *V*, *V* would not have crossed the street at that moment and, therefore, would not have been struck by *X*.

---

[19] Hall, Note 1, *supra*, at 249-50; Hart & Honoré, Note 1, *supra*, at 32-37.

It does not necessarily follow, however, that *D* may be convicted of a crime pertaining to *V*'s death. First, *D* was not the sole cause of the harm. *X*'s conduct was another cause. So, too, was *V*'s decision to leave the house and cross the street. "Actual cause," it will be remembered, serves only to *eliminate* candidates for responsibility; it does not resolve the matter of ultimate causal responsibility, which awaits proximate causation analysis. Second, and more immediately to the point, the facts do not suggest that *D* possessed a culpable state of mind — any *mens rea* — regarding *V*'s death. Thus, this is a case of but-for causation without a *mens rea*.

[b] *Mens Rea* Without Causation

Just as a person may be the actual cause of resulting harm without having a *mens rea*, it is also possible to possess a culpable state of mind without being the actual cause of the harm. For example, suppose that *D1*, intending to kill *V*, shoots *V*, barely nicking him. Simultaneously, *D2*, independently and accidentally, shoots *V* in the heart. *V* dies instantly. Here, *D1* intended to kill *V*, but did not cause the death; thus, *D1* is not legally responsible for *V*'s death.[20] *D2* is the only potential candidate for homicide prosecution, and he may also be acquitted for lack of *mens rea*.

[2] Multiple Actual Causes

[a] Accelerating a Result

D1 intentionally shoots *V* in the stomach. Assume that medical testimony would prove that *V* would have died from the wound in one hour. However, simultaneously and independently of *D1*, *D2* intentionally shoots *V* in the stomach. Medical evidence would show that *V* would have died from the latter wound in one hour. As a result of the two wounds, however, *V* dies in five minutes.

Who is the cause of *V*'s death? At first glance it may appear that application of the but-for test will result in the conclusion that *neither D1* nor *D2* was an actual cause of the death. In fact, however, *both* actors may properly be described as actual causes of *V*'s death.

A careful application of the but-for test supports this conclusion. It must be remembered that this test asks whether, but for the voluntary act of the defendant, the harm would have occurred *when it did*. The italicized words are essential to the correct application of the test. After all, ultimately everyone dies. No act can do more than accelerate the process.

With this point in mind it is evident that *D1* accelerated *V*'s death. Ask the *sine qua non* question: "But for *D1*'s voluntary act [firing the gun], would *V* have

---

[20] Of course, he may be convicted of attempted murder.

died *when he did* [in five minutes]?" The answer is that he would *not* have died *when he did* — he would have died in one hour as the result of the wound simultaneously inflicted by *D2*. Because *D1*'s actions accelerated the death process, *D1* is *an* (not "the") actual cause of the death. One need only substitute *D2* for *D1* in this analysis to reach the same causal conclusion regarding *D2*.

Or, consider the facts in *Oxendine v. State*.[21] *V* was the tragic victim of two separate acts of child abuse: First, he sustained mortal injuries from a beating inflicted by *X*; one day later, *D*, *V*'s father, inflicted additional injuries. *V* died later that day. *X* and *D* were prosecuted for *V*'s death. The government introduced evidence regarding the cause of death: One physician testified that he could not determine whether *V* died as the result of the acts of one person (*X*) or of both; a second doctor stated that the injury inflicted by *X* was the underlying cause of the death and he could not state whether *D*'s subsequent actions accelerated the process.

Based on this evidence, the court ruled that *D* was entitled to a directed verdict of acquittal, because the prosecutor failed to prove beyond a reasonable doubt that *D* hastened *V*'s death. If the state had introduced evidence that the beating inflicted by *D* had shortened his child's life, even by the slightest amount, *D* could properly have been declared an actual cause of the death.

[b] Concurrent Sufficient Causes

D1 shoots *V* in the heart; simultaneously and independently, *D2* shoots *V* in the head. *V* dies instantly. Medical evidence indicates that either attack alone would have killed *V* instantly.

In the real world such events rarely occur. More often, *D1* and *D2* will be acting in concert, so that their joint conduct may be analyzed as if they were one party. Or, one wound will accelerate the result caused by the other. Another possibility in a dual attack is that neither wound will be mortal, but in combination they result in the death. As the facts are described here, however, *D1* and *D2* are *concurrent sufficient causes* of *V*'s death. That is, each act alone was sufficient to cause the result that occurred *when it did*.

Our intuitions probably suggest that both actors should be convicted of murder. Yet, the but-for test *seems* to fail us here: But for *D1*'s act of shooting *V* in the heart, *V* would have died when he did (instantly) as the result of *D2*'s gunshot to *V*'s head. Because *D1* did *not* accelerate *V*'s death, *D1* is not (it seems) the cause of the death. Applying the same test to *D2*'s conduct, *D2* also is relieved of responsibility. If this analysis is correct, and if no other principle applies, *D1* and *D2* could be convicted of attempted murder, but of no more.

---

[21] 528 A.2d 870 (Del. 1987).

There are two ways to avoid this counter-intuitive result. First, some criminal law courts import from tort law its solution in comparable circumstances, which is to rephrase the causation test to ask whether the defendant was a "substantial factor" in causing the prohibited harm.[22] The difficulty with this solution is not only that the critical term — "substantial factor" — is rarely defined,[23] but also that it is difficult to comprehend how a person's conduct can ever be a "substantial factor" in causing a result that was going to occur when it did *even without his contribution*.[24] The only way it may sensibly be said that a concurrent sufficient cause (e.g., *D1*) is a substantial factor in an outcome is to point out that the force *would have been* the cause of the harm if circumstances had been different (i.e., if the *other* sufficient cause, *D2*'s lethal act, had not materialized). However, this is not the way we ordinarily talk about causation. If it were, the would-be killer in the example that began this chapter — *D* shoots to kill *V,* but *X* kills *V* before *D*'s bullet strikes *V* — would be guilty of murder, rather than of attempted murder, but that is not how the example is resolved (nor, sensibly, should it be).

A preferable method of resolving the causal quandary is to retain the but-for test in these circumstances, but to elaborate on it. Two extra words are added, so that the test becomes: "But for *D*'s voluntary act would the social harm have occurred when *and as* it did."[25] In essence, this technique refines the description of the result for which the defendants are prosecuted. Thus, in the present example, the result would not be described as "the death of *V,*" but rather as "the death of *V* by two simultaneous mortal wounds." Applying the but-for test in *this* manner, both *D1* and *D2* satisfy the causation standard, because the result — death from two mortal wounds — could not have occurred without the presence of both actors.

[3] Obstructed Cause

D1 shoots *V* in the stomach. Simultaneously and independently, *D2* shoots *V* three times in the head, killing him instantly.

Although it may appear that *D1* is causally linked to *V*'s death, this might not be the case. A coroner might testify that the wound inflicted by *D1* did not contribute to *V*'s death, i.e., that the three bullets in the head would have killed *V* instantly, even in the absence of the abdominal wound. Under such circum-

---

[22] Anderson v. Minneapolis, St. Paul & Sault Marie Ry., 179 N.W. 45, 46 (Minn. 1920), overruled on other grounds, Borshein v. Great N. Ry., 183 N.W. 519 (Minn. 1921); see also Jeremiah Smith, *Legal Cause in Actions of Tort*, 25 Harv. L. Rev. 223, 229-30 (1912).

[23] According to various torts scholars the phrase "is sufficiently intelligible . . . that it is neither possible nor desirable to reduce it to any lower terms." W. Page Keeton et al., Prosser and Keeton on Torts 267 (5th ed. 1984).

[24] State v. Montoya, 61 P.3d 793, 799 (N.M. 2002) (quoting this Text).

[25] See *id.* at 797 (citing this Text).

stances, *D1* is no more the cause of *V*'s death than if, just a split-second before *D1* fired the gun, *V* had been struck by a bolt of lightning that killed him instantly. In the latter case we would not say that *D1* killed *V*; rather, we would say that he *attempted* to kill *V*, but that his efforts were obstructed by a separate force (the lightning), which actually caused the result. The same analysis applies to *D1* and *D2*: *D1* attempted to take *V*'s life; he was thwarted in this goal because *D2* was a more effective killer.

§ 14.03 PROXIMATE CAUSE (OR "LEGAL CAUSE")

[A] Putting "Proximate Cause" in Context

"Mankind might still be in Eden, but for Adam's biting an apple."[26] The present point of this remark is to remind us that the sole purpose of the but-for test of causation is to identify candidates for responsibility for an event. From this pool, which may include many human actors (and non-human forces) stemming over an extended period of time,[27] the "proximate" or "legal" cause of the social harm must be selected.[28] Thus, we might ask: Is Adam the "proximate cause" of our current state of affairs, or should we hold someone or something else responsible?

The concept of "proximate causation" is obscure.[29] In the process of determining proximate causation, courts and lawyers frequently bandy about conclusory terms like "superseding intervening cause," "direct cause," and "remote cause." An observer might assume from this language that a formula exists to produce uniform and reliable results in proximate causation analysis. Although some scholars believe that causation is a metaphysical concept, it is fair to say that courts and juries don't *discover* the proximate cause of harm — they *select* it. The decision to attach causal responsibility for social harm to one, rather than to another, factor is made in a, hopefully, common sense manner,[30] or by application of moral intuitions, a community sense of justice, and/or public policy considerations.

---

[26] Welch v. State, 235 So. 2d 906, 907 (1970).

[27] E.g., State v. Govan, 744 P.2d 712 (Ariz. Ct. App. 1987) (*G* shot *V*, paralyzing *V* from the neck down; *G* was charged with assault, but the charge was dropped when *V* married *G*; due to her quadriplegia, *V* suffered from various ailments and needed constant care thereafter; five years later, *V* contracted pneumonia and died; *G* was charged with her murder, based on the initial shooting, and convicted of manslaughter; held: a jury could properly find that *G*'s conduct five years earlier was the proximate cause of *V*'s death, despite subsequent events that also affected her health).

[28] Typically, there will be only one proximate cause of a result, but this is not always so. For example, in the case of concurrent sufficient causes, see § 14.02[C][2][b], *supra*, each cause-in-fact is also a proximate cause. Likewise, it is possible for two negligent wrongdoers, acting independently of each other, to be the proximate cause of resulting harm.

[29] American Law Institute, Comment to § 2.03, at 255.

[30] See Roscoe Pound, *The Theory of Judicial Decision*, 36 Harv. L. Rev. 940, 952 (1923) ("[W]e must rely on the common sense of the common man as to common things. . . .").

[B] Direct Cause

In many cases, no serious litigable issue of proximate causation arises. For example, suppose that *D* shoots *V*, and *V* dies instantly. Or, suppose that *D* shoots *V*, and *V* is taken to the hospital where he dies after proper medical care. In both cases, courts are apt to say that *D* was the "direct" cause of the result. That is, no event of causal significance intervened between *D*'s conduct and the social harm for which he is being prosecuted. In the first case, the death occurred instantly; in the second hypothetical, nothing done by the medical personnel aggravated *V*'s injuries or accelerated *V*'s death.

The closest thing to a bright-line rule in the realm of proximate cause is this: *An act that is a direct cause of social harm is also a proximate cause of it.* This makes sense. A "direct cause" is a force already determined to be an "actual cause" of the undesired result. Inasmuch as no other causal factor has intervened, there is no more proximate party to whom to shift legal responsibility for the result.

[C] Intervening Causes

[1] Overview

An "intervening cause" is an independent force — another "but for" cause — that operates in producing social harm, but which only comes into play *after* the defendant's voluntary act has been committed or his omission has occurred.[31] Although not exhaustive of the circumstances in which intervening causes arise, many criminal cases fit the following pattern: *D* gravely harms *V*. Thereafter, another force intervenes. This intervening cause aggravates *V*'s injuries or accelerates the inevitable (i.e., *V*'s death). The intervention usually comes in the form of wrongdoing by a third party, or as the result of the victim's own contributory negligence,[32] or due to a suicidal act by the victim. Sometimes, instead, the intervening cause is a natural force ("an act of God").

The legal issue for consideration in such cases is the following: When is the intervening conduct of a third party, the victim, or a natural force sufficiently out-of-the-ordinary that "it no longer seems fair to say that the [social harm] was 'caused' by the defendant's conduct"?[33] Framing the issue more precisely: Under

---

[31] State v. Marti, 290 N.W.2d 570, 586 (Iowa 1980).

[32] Thus, in the criminal law, a victim's contributory negligence is *not* a defense to a criminal homicide charge, but is a factor in determining whether the defendant's conduct was a proximate cause of the death. State v. Farner, 66 S.W.3d 188, 203 (Tenn. 2001).

[33] State v. Malone, 819 P.2d 34, 37 (Alaska Ct. App. 1991); see also United States v. Main, 113 F.3d 1046, 1049 (9th Cir. 1997) (an intervening cause cuts off the liability of the defendant if it is "'so out-of-the-ordinary' that it is no longer fair to hold the defendant liable") (quoting an earlier edition of this Text).

what circumstances should *D*, who acts with the requisite *mens rea*, and who commits a voluntary act that *is* a cause-in-fact of the social harm, be relieved of criminal responsibility because of an intervening cause? When an intervening cause *does* relieve the defendant of criminal responsibility, the law generally describes that intervening event as the "superseding cause" of the social harm.

One early twentieth century scholar observed that all efforts to set down universal tests that explain the law of causation are "demonstrably erroneous."[34] There are no hard-and-fast rules for rendering the commonsense "community justice" determination of when an intervening cause supersedes the defendant's conduct. However, there are various factors that assist the factfinder in the evaluative process, discussed immediately below.

[2] Factor 1: *De Minimis* Contribution to the Social Harm

Sometimes, a defendant's causal responsibility for ensuing harm is exceptionally insubstantial in comparison to that of an intervening cause. For example, suppose that *D* strikes *V*. Although the injury is not life-threatening, it requires medical attention, so *V* drives himself to the doctor. On the way, his car is struck by lightning. *V* dies instantly.

From a causal perspective, *D* was an actual cause of the ensuing death-by-lightning: But for *D*'s wrongful actions, *V* would not have been in the car, and thus would not have been at the spot where the lightning struck. Nonetheless, the law will very likely treat *D*'s causal connection as *de minimis*, and relieve him of criminal liability for *V*'s death.[35]

This outcome conforms with our commonsense analysis of causal events. If a small pebble is followed immediately by a giant meteor striking Jupiter, our attention focuses on the meteor. Although the pebble may have contributed slightly to the ensuing damage, we treat the giant force as the "real" cause of the harm. The same principle applies in the criminal law: Some wrongdoers have too minor a causal role to justify criminal punishment.[36] The law will treat the substantial, intervening cause as the proximate cause of the social harm.

---

[34] Smith, Note 22, *supra*, at 317.

[35] Of course, *D* may be prosecuted for the original battery.

[36] State v. Montoya, 61 P.3d 793, 799 (N.M. 2002) (citing this Text).

[3] Factor 2: Foreseeability of the Intervening Cause

[a] In General

According to some courts, the "linchpin"[37] of proximate causation is whether the intervening party's acts were reasonably foreseeable. This is an overstatement, but it is certainly true that foreseeability is a matter of considerable significance in proximate-causation analysis.

Cases can be found in which it is said, simply, that the defendant cannot escape liability if the intervening act was reasonably foreseeable,[38] whereas an unforeseeable intervening cause is superseding in nature. Proper analysis, however, is more sophisticated than this. The criminal law tends to distinguish between "responsive" (or "dependent") and "coincidental" (or "independent") intervening causes,[39] as these concepts are clarified below.

[b] Responsive (Dependent) Intervening Causes

A responsive intervening cause is an act that occurs in reaction or response to the defendant's prior wrongful conduct. For example, suppose that *D1* operates his boat at an unsafe speed, causing it to capsize. *V1*, his drunken passenger, drowns foolishly attempting to swim to shore.[40] *V1*'s actions constitute a responsive intervening cause in his own death, i.e., his life-saving efforts were in response to *D1*'s initial improper conduct. Or, suppose that *D2* seriously wounds *V2*. *V2* is taken to a hospital where he receives poor medical treatment by physician *X* and dies. In *D2*'s prosecution for the death, *X*'s negligent conduct constitutes a responsive intervening cause: *X*'s medical actions were in response to *D2*'s act of wounding *V2*.

Generally speaking, a responsive intervening cause does *not* relieve the initial wrongdoer of criminal responsibility, unless the response was not only unforeseeable, but highly abnormal or bizarre.[41] This outcome is justifiable. The defendant's initial wrongdoing caused the response. Since he is responsible for the presence of the intervening force, the defendant should not escape liability unless the intervening force was so out-of-the-ordinary that it is no longer fair to hold him criminally responsible for the outcome.

---

[37] State v. Dunn, 850 P.2d 1201, 1215 (Utah 1993).

[38] *Id.* at 1216.

[39] In his treatise, Professor LaFave use the "responsive/coincidental" terms, Wayne R. LaFave, Criminal Law 344 (4th ed. 2003), whereas Professors Perkins and Boyce describe intervening causes as "dependent/independent." Rollin M. Perkins & Ronald N. Boyce, Criminal Law 791, 809 (3d ed. 1982).

[40] People v. Armitage, 194 Cal. App. 3d 405 (Ct. App. 1987).

[41] E.g., Kibbe v. Henderson, 534 F.2d 493, 498 n.6 (2d Cir. 1976), reversed on other grounds, 431 U.S. 145 (1977); State v. Malone, 819 P.2d 34, 37 (Alaska Ct. App. 1991).

Applying this analysis, case law generally provides that the accused bears criminal responsibility for the death of a person who seeks to extricate himself or another from the dangerous situation created by the defendant, even if the victim was contributorily negligent in his efforts.[42] Similarly, many cases provide that one who wrongfully injures another is responsible for the ensuing death, notwithstanding subsequent negligent medical treatment that contributes to the victim's death or accelerates it.[43] On the other hand, grossly negligent or reckless medical care is sufficiently abnormal to supersede the initial wrongdoer's causal responsibility.[44]

[c] Coincidental (Independent) Intervening Causes

A coincidental intervening cause is a force that does not occur in response to the initial wrongdoer's conduct. The only relationship between the defendant's conduct and the intervening cause is that the defendant placed the victim in a situation where the intervening cause could independently act upon him. For example, suppose that *D1* robs *V1*, a passenger in *D1*'s car, and then abandons *V1* on a rural road. Sometime later, driver *X1* strikes and kills *V1*, who is standing in the middle of the road.[45] *X1*'s conduct is a coincidental intervening cause: *D1*'s actions did not cause *X1* to drive down that road on that particular occasion; *D1* simply put *V1* on the road where *X1*'s independent conduct acted upon *V1*.

Or, suppose that *D2* wounds *V2*. *V2* is taken to a hospital for medical treatment, where he is killed by *X2*, a "knife-wielding maniac" who is running through the hospital killing everyone in sight.[46] Again, *X2* is a coincidental intervening cause: *X2* was going to be running through that hospital killing per-

---

[42] People v. Armitage, 194 Cal. App. 3d 405 (Ct. App. 1987) (see the facts described in the text accompanying Note 40); State v. Wassil, 658 A.2d 548 (Conn. 1995) (*W* is guilty of criminal homicide for delivering heroin to *V*, who injected himself with it and died from an accidental overdose); State v. Leopold, 147 A. 118 (Conn. 1929) (one who knowingly sets fire to a building is responsible for the death or injury of another who enters the building to save his property); People v. Kern, 554 N.E.2d 1235 (N.Y. 1990) (*D*s chased *V* with a baseball bat, with the intention of beating or killing him; *V* attempted to escape by running onto a highway, where he was struck and killed by a third party; held: *D*s are responsible for *V*'s death); State v. Johnson, 615 A.2d 132 (Vt. 1992) (*J* attempted to kill *V*; *V*, fearing for his life, walked into a river to escape, and drowned; held: *J* is guilty of murder).

[43] E.g., State v. Shabazz, 719 A.2d 440 (Conn. 1998); Fairman v. State, 513 So. 2d 910 (Miss. 1987); State v. Baker, 742 P.2d 633 (Or. Ct. App. 1987).

[44] Regina v. Jordan, 40 Crim. App. Rep. 152 (1956). In these circumstances a court may confusingly say that the gross maltreatment was the "sole cause" of the death. E.g., State v. Jacobs, 479 A.2d 226, 229 (Conn. 1984). It is more accurate to say that it was the *superseding* cause.

[45] Kibbe v. Henderson, 534 F.2d 493 (2d Cir. 1976).

[46] This is an embellishment on hypothetical 6(c) in Sanford H. Kadish & Stephen J. Schulhofer, Criminal Law and Its Processes 518 (7th ed. 2001).

sons whether or not *V2* was there. This is a case in which *V2* was in the wrong place at the wrong time, put there by *D2*'s original wrongdoing.

The common law rule of thumb is that a coincidental intervening cause relieves the original wrongdoer of criminal responsibility, unless the intervention was foreseeable. In the present examples, therefore, it would be necessary to determine whether *D1* and *D2*, as reasonable people, should have foreseen, respectively, that *V1* would be struck by another car, and that *V2* would be the victim of a criminal intermediary. In the first case, it may have been foreseeable that another car would drive down that road and strike *V1*. In the second hypothetical, *X2*'s criminal activities were probably abnormal enough to relieve *D2* of liability for the ensuing death, unless, for example, the events occurred in a high-security penal institution.[47]

[4] Factor 3: The Defendant's *Mens Rea* (Intended-Consequences Doctrine)

"The legal eye reaches further in the examination of intentional crimes than in those in which this element is wanting."[48] As two scholars on causation have explained, a voluntary act intended to "bring about what in fact happens, and in the manner in which it happens, has a special place in causal inquiries."[49] That special place is this: *We usually trace the cause of social harm backwards through other causes until we reach an intentional wrongdoer.* Or, as is sometimes said, although too strongly: "Intended consequences can never be too remote."[50]

For example, in a classic case,[51] *M*, intending the death of *V* (her child), furnished poison to *X*, a home nurse, falsely informing *X* that the substance was medicine to be administered to *V*. *X* did not believe that *V* needed the "medicine," so she did not administer it. Instead, she placed the substance on a mantel where, some time later, *C* (a young child) discovered it and gave it to *V*, killing *V*. *M* was prosecuted for murder.

Notice: *D* intended *V*'s death by poisoning. Her voluntary act of providing the poison to *X* was a but-for cause of *V*'s death. On the other hand, at least two

---

[47] One other example: As the result of negligence, *D* strikes *V*'s car, leaving *V* pinned in his car, where he is later eaten by a bear. United States v. Main, 113 F.3d 1046, 1049 (9th Cir. 1997) (suggesting the hypothetical). The bear is a coincidental intervening cause; therefore, barring unusual facts, *D* would not be causally responsible for the death.

[48] State v. Cummings, 265 S.E.2d 923, 927 (N.C. Ct. App. 1980) (emphasis omitted) (Clark, J., dissenting) (quoting Perkins, Criminal Law 693 (2d ed. 1969)).

[49] Hart & Honoré, Note 1, *supra*, at 42.

[50] *Id.* at 170 (emphasis omitted); see Henry T. Terry, *Proximate Consequences in the Law of Torts*, 28 Harv L. Rev. 10, 17 (1914).

[51] Regina v. Michael, 169 Eng. Rep. 48 (1840).

other causes intervened: *X*'s negligent act of placing the "medicine" where it could be reached by *C*; and *C*'s innocent act of administering it to *V*. Despite these intervening acts, *M* was declared to be the proximate cause of *V*'s death.

This outcome is hardly surprising. *M* wanted her child poisoned, which is exactly what she got.[52] As a matter of moral intuitions, the intervening actions — *X*'s possible negligence and *C*'s innocent conduct — should not override *M*'s intentional wrongdoing. It is as if the jurors were to say: "You got *exactly* what you wanted. What right do you have to complain if we hold you responsible for the intended consequence?"[53]

[5] Factor 4: Dangerous Forces That Come to Rest (Apparent-Safety Doctrine)

One scholar has observed that when a "defendant's active force has come to rest in a position of apparent safety, the court will follow it no longer."[54] For example, consider a somewhat simplified version of the facts in *State v. Preslar*:[55] *P* threatened the life of *V*, his spouse. As a consequence, *V* was forced to leave the house on a freezing night in order to protect herself. *V* walked to within 200 yards of her father's home, where she would have been welcome, but she chose to spend the night in the extreme cold, rather than bother her father by entering the house. *V* froze to death during the night. Clearly, *P* was an actual cause of *V*'s death: But for his threatening conduct, *V* would not have gone out into the cold. But, *V*'s decision to sleep outside was also a but-for cause of her own death. Is *P* the proximate cause of *V*'s death? The court in *Preslar* answered this question in the negative.

The result may be explained in terms of the apparent-safety doctrine.[56] *P* did not follow *V* from their home. When *V* reached the vicinity of her father's house, she knew that she could enter and be free from immediate harm. Therefore, her decision to sleep outside constituted a superseding intervening cause.[57]

---

[52] The "intended consequences" doctrine is most often applied when the result *and the means of its commission* were intended by the defendant.

[53] See also State v. Ruane, 912 S.W.2d 766 (Tenn. Crim. App. 1995) (*R* intentionally shot *V* in the neck, intending to kill *V*; *V*'s spinal column was severed, requiring permanent life support; subsequently, *V* requested to be removed from the life support; *V* died minutes later; held: *R* is guilty of murder).

[54] Joseph H. Beale, *The Proximate Consequences of an Act*, 33 Harv. L. Rev. 633, 651 (1920).

[55] 48 N.C. 421 (1856).

[56] Notice that *Preslar* can also be analyzed by applying the foreseeability factor discussed earlier: *V*'s decision to leave the house and seek shelter was a responsive intervening cause. The issue would be whether her decision to sleep out at night was highly abnormal. If, but only if, *V*'s actions are considered bizarre under the circumstances, *P* would be relieved of liability pursuant to *this* "proximate cause" factor.

[57] Compare Commonwealth v. Rementer, 598 A.2d 1300 (Pa. Super. Ct. 1991) (*R* assaulted *V*, his girlfriend, in a bar; *R* continued to pursue *V* when she left; *V* fell to the ground and was run over

[6] Factor 5: Free, Deliberate, Informed Human Intervention

A defendant is far more apt to be relieved of criminal responsibility in the case of a "free, deliberate, and informed"[58] — a voluntary, knowing, and intelligent — intervening human agent than in the case of the intervention of a natural force or the actions of a person whose conduct is not fully free. The result in the *Preslar* case,[59] described in the last subsection, can also be explained in terms of this factor. *V* chose to sleep in the cold rather than to enter her father's home. Her decision was free, deliberate, and with full knowledge of the fact that it was exceedingly cold outside. Under these circumstances, the responsibility for her death is shifted from *P* to *V*. This outcome is consistent with the retributive principle that accords special significance to the free-will actions of human agents.

The same analysis applies if, for example, *D* and *V* operate their vehicles in a reckless manner as part of a drag race, at the end of which race *V* voluntarily turns his car around and speeds through a guardrail, killing himself or another. Regardless of *D*'s initial responsibility for the race, *V*'s decision to "ad lib" by continuing the race after it was over relieves *D* of responsibility for the ensuing harm.[60]

Of course, the critical issue in applying the present factor is whether the human intervention was "free, deliberate, and informed." Frequently, it is not. For example, if *V* escapes *B*, a home-intruder, by jumping out of a second-story window of his house, his actions would not be considered voluntary. Therefore *B* would be liable for *V*'s injuries or death from the jump.[61] Likewise, if *S* kidnaps and rapes *V*, after which despondent *V* commits suicide, *S* may be held responsible for her death.[62] Or, if *R* shoots *V*, requiring *V* to survive on a ventilator, *V*'s decision to be removed from life support and be allowed to die is not sufficiently free to break the causal chain of criminal liability.[63]

---

by a car as she approached *X* for aid; held: *R*'s conduct remained an operative force that justified holding him criminally responsible for *V*'s death).

[58] Hart & Honoré, Note 1, *supra*, at 326.

[59] State v. Preslar, 48 N.C. 421 (1856).

[60] Velazquez v. State, 561 So. 2d 347 (Fla. Dist. Ct. App. 1990).

[61] Rex v. Beech, 23 Cox Crim. Cas. 181 (1912).

[62] Stephenson v. State, 179 N.E. 633 (Ind. 1932).

[63] State v. Ruane, 912 S.W.2d 766 (Tenn. Crim. App. 1995). Compare this, however, to *Regina v. Blaue*, [1975] 1 W.L.R. 1411. In *Blaue*, *B* seriously wounded *V*. *V*, informed that she needed a blood transfusion, which presumably would have saved her, refused it on religious grounds. The court, stating that *D* had to take his victim (including *V*'s religious views) as he found her, concluded that he was the proximate cause of *V*'s death.

This result might be wrong. Arguably, *V*'s decision to refuse medical treatment should be accorded the respect of being treated as a free, deliberate, and informed decision. Although it is often said, as in *Blaue*, that a wrongdoer takes his victim as he finds him, this doctrine is typically applied in

[7] Factor 6: Omissions

"Doing nothing . . . is just that — nothing — so far as the law is concerned.
. . ."[64] Therefore, an omission will rarely, if ever, serve as a superseding intervening cause.[65] For example, if *D* drives his automobile in a negligent manner,
causing the death of *V* (a passenger in *D*'s car or a driver of another vehicle), *V*'s
failure to wear a seat belt, although causally related to his own death,[66] will not
absolve *D* from liability for the death.[67]

This principle operates even if the intervening actor has a duty to act. Therefore, a father's failure to intervene to stop a stranger from beating his child will
not ordinarily absolve the attacker for the ensuing homicide, although the
father may also be responsible for the death on the basis of omission principles.

§ 14.04 MODEL PENAL CODE[68]

[A] Actual Cause

The Model Penal Code applies the but-for (*sine qua non*) rule. To be guilty of
an offense, a person's conduct must cause the prohibited result. "Cause" is
defined under the Code as "an antecedent but for which the result in question
would not have occurred."[69]

The common law principles that clarify the meaning of this test also apply in
Code jurisdictions. In the case of concurrent sufficient causes[70] — e.g., when *D1*

---

cases in which the victim has a pre-existing and hidden medical condition, such as hemophilia or
a weak heart. In such circumstances, it cannot be said that the victim chooses for his blood not to
coagulate, or that he chooses to have a heart attack. In contrast, *V* in *Blaue* chose to "suffer" from
a pre-existing religious "condition," and to act upon it.

[64] Perkins & Boyce, Note 39, *supra*, at 820.

[65] This assertion assumes that the defendant's dangerous conduct has not already come to rest.
For example, in *State v. Preslar*, 48 N.C. 421 (1856), discussed in subsections [5] and [6], *V* failed
to enter her father's home. However, by this time, *V* had reached apparent safety; *P*'s conduct was
no longer operative. Therefore, the omission principle would not come into play.

[66] There is substantial philosophical debate regarding whether an omission can ever "cause" a
resulting event. See Moore, Note 7, *supra*, at 267-78. How can nothing be the "cause" of something?
The criminal law, however, accepts the philosophical view that omissions *can* be causally relevant.
See Model Penal Code § 1.13(5) (defining "conduct" as an "act *or omission* and its accompanying state
of mind"); and § 2.03(1)(a) (providing the circumstances under which "conduct" is the "cause" of a
result).

[67] Bowman v. State, 564 N.E.2d 309 (Ind. Ct. App. 1990), aff'd in part, vacated in part, 577
N.E.2d 569 (Ind. 1991); People v. Clark, 431 N.W.2d 88 (Mich. Ct. App. 1988).

[68] See generally David J. Karp, Note, *Causation in the Model Penal Code*, 78 Colum. L. Rev. 1249
(1978).

[69] Model Penal Code § 2.03(1)(a).

[70] See § 14.02[C][2][b], *supra*.

and *D2* independently inflict immediately-lethal wounds on *V* — the Commentary to the Code states that "the result in question" should be described as "death from two mortal wounds."[71] Thus, the jury would determine whether "but for [*D1*'s]/[*D2*'s] act, the result [death from two mortal wounds] would have occurred when it did." This way, each party is a but-for cause of the result, and a court need not apply the "substantial factor" test.

[B] Proximate Cause (Actually, Culpability)

Unlike the common law, the Model Penal Code treats but-for causation as the exclusive meaning of "causation" in the criminal law. The Code treats matters of "proximate causation" as issues relating instead to the actor's culpability.

Specifically, subsections (2)(b) and (3)(b)[72] of Section 2.03 deal with situations in which the actual result of the defendant's conduct (considering both the precise harm caused and the manner in which it occurred) diverges from that which was designed, contemplated, or risked. In such circumstances, the issue in a Model Code jurisdiction is not whether, in light of the divergences, the defendant was a "proximate cause" of the resulting harm, but rather whether it may still be said that he caused the prohibited result with the level of culpability — purpose, knowledge, recklessness, or negligence — required by the definition of the offense.

Under the Code, the defendant has *not* acted with the requisite culpability unless the actual result, including the way in which it occurred, was not "too remote or accidental in its occurrence to have a [just] bearing on the actor's liability or on the gravity of his offense."[73] Thus, the "varying and sometimes inconsistent"[74] proximate causation factors developed by the common law are replaced with a single standard, which invites the jury to reach a common-sense, or just, result.

In the rare circumstance of an offense containing no culpability requirement,[75] the Code provides that causation "is not established unless the actual result is a probable consequence of the actor's conduct."[76] This would mean that

---

[71] American Law Institute, Comment to § 2.03, at 259.

[72] Subsection (2)(b) applies to crimes in which purposely or knowingly causing a result is the requisite element; subsection (3)(b) applies to crimes of recklessness or negligence.

[73] The word "just" was placed in brackets by the American Law Institute as a possible addition to the formulation. Disagreement existed among its members regarding the desirability of submitting undefined questions of justice to a jury. American Law Institute, Comment to § 2.03, at 261 n.16.

[74] *Id.* at 256.

[75] Under the Code, some element of culpability is required regarding *every* material element of an offense, except in the case of a "violation." Model Penal Code §§ 2.02(1), 2.05. See §§ 10.07[A] and 11.04, *supra*.

[76] Model Penal Code § 2.03(4).

in a jurisdiction that recognizes the felony-murder rule, but which applies Model Penal Code causation principles,[77] a defendant may not be convicted of felony-murder if the death was not a probable consequence of his felonious conduct. For example, if *D* attempted to rob a bank, and the bank teller was accidentally electrocuted pressing the burglar alarm switch, *D* would not be liable for the death because the actual result — death by electrocution — was not a probable consequence of robbing a bank.[78]

---

[77] The felony-murder rule permits a person to be convicted of murder for an accidental (even non-negligent) killing that occurs during the commission of a felony. See § 31.06, *infra*. The Code has rejected this doctrine. See § 31.10[B], *infra*. However, some states have retained the felony-murder doctrine but follow the Code causation approach.

[78] American Law Institute, Comment to § 2.03, at 264.

Chapter 15

CONCURRENCE OF ELEMENTS

§ 15.01 GENERAL PRINCIPLES

A crime contains an *actus reus* and, usually, a *mens rea*. More specifically, a person may not be convicted of an offense unless the prosecutor proves beyond a reasonable doubt that the defendant, with the requisite mental state, performed a voluntary act that actually and proximately caused the proscribed social harm. Implicit in this statement is an additional prerequisite to criminal liability: the *concurrence* of the *actus reus* and the *mens rea*.[1]

The principle of concurrence contains two components, discussed in the next two sections of this chapter. First, there must be temporal concurrence. That is, the defendant must possess the requisite *mens rea* at the same moment that her voluntary conduct (or omission) causes the social harm (the *actus reus*).[2] Second, there must be motivational concurrence: The defendant's conduct that caused the social harm must have been set into motion or impelled by the thought process that constituted the *mens rea* of the offense.

§ 15.02 TEMPORAL CONCURRENCE

Lack of temporal concurrence occurs when the *mens rea* of an offense exists before or after, but not during, the commission of the *actus reus*.

[A] *Mens Rea* Preceding *Actus Reus*

Occasionally, a defendant's *mens rea* will precede the *actus reus* of the offense, but be absent when she acts. For example, suppose that *D* intends to kill *V*, plans the killing, but never has the opportunity to implement the plan. Later, she changes her mind, abandons the scheme, and befriends *V*. Thereafter, *D* and *V* go hunting, during which time *D* innocently (non-negligently) kills *V*. On these facts, *D* is not guilty of criminal homicide. When she had the *mens rea*, there was no *actus reus*. When she subsequently killed *V*, she had no culpable state of mind.

---

[1] The concurrence principle is codified in a few state penal codes. E.g., Cal. Pen. Code § 20 (Deering 2005), which provides that "[i]n every crime . . . there must exist a *union, or joint operation* of act and intent, or criminal negligence" (emphasis added). The Model Penal Code also requires concurrence, albeit inferentially, by defining "conduct" as "an action or omission and *its accompanying* state of mind." Model Penal Code § 1.13(5) (emphasis added).

[2] State v. Cobb, 743 A.2d 1, 62-63 (Conn. 1999).

The concurrence principle is satisfied, however, if the *voluntary act* that causes the social harm concurs with the *mens rea*, although the social harm itself occurs later. For example, suppose that *D*, intending to kill *V*, mortally wounds *V*. *V* dies in the hospital three months later, by which time *D* has expressed genuine remorse, and no longer wants *V* to die. Here, *D* is guilty of murder. The critical issue is whether the lethal act — the firing of the gun — concurred with the *mens rea*, and not whether the *mens rea* was present at the time of the death.

[B] *Actus Reus* Preceding *Mens Rea*

Temporal concurrence is absent if the *actus reus* precedes the *mens rea*. For example, suppose that *D1* breaks into and enters *V1*'s home at night in order to escape the cold. After she enters, *D1* decides to steal *V1*'s property. *D1* is prosecuted for burglary, defined as "breaking and entering the dwelling house of another at night, with intent to commit a felony therein." On these facts, *D1* is not guilty of burglary because the specific intent of the offense ("intent to commit a felony therein") arose *after* the occurrence of the voluntary acts that caused the social harm of burglary ("breaking and entering the dwelling house of another at night").[3] Likewise, *D2* is not guilty of murder if she innocently takes *V2*'s life, after which she decides that she is glad that she killed *V2*.

§ 15.03 MOTIVATIONAL CONCURRENCE

The impelling force or motivation behind the act that causes the social harm must be the *mens rea* of the offense, and not some other thought process, such as the mental state of preparing to commit the offense.

For example, suppose that *D* intends to shoot and kill her domestic partner, *V*, when *V* arrives home. Incorrectly believing the gun is still unloaded, *D* tests the trigger by pulling it. As she does, *V* unexpectedly enters the house and is struck and killed by the bullet. Based on these facts, the requisite motivational concurrence is missing. Although *D* had the intent to kill *V* when she voluntarily performed the act that caused the death (i.e., temporal concurrence existed), the *mens rea* — the intent to kill — was not the actuating force behind the conduct. The lethal act of pulling the trigger was intended as a preparatory act; it was "not done in order to give effect to [the] desire to kill."[4]

---

[3] See Cooper v. People, 973 P.2d 1234 (Colo. 1999), overruled on other grounds, Greigo v. People, 19 P.2d 1 (Colo. 2001) (*C* claimed he broke into his elderly mother's home to get out of the cold; only later, after he got into an altercation with his mother, did he decide to commit a felony; held: if the jury believes *C*'s claim, he is not guilty of burglary).

[4] 1 W. Russell, Crime 54 (12th ed. 1964).

§ 15.04 SPECIAL PROBLEM: TEMPORALLY DIVISIBLE ACTS AND/OR OMISSIONS

In most cases application of the concurrence principle is straightforward. Difficulties arise, however, when a person commits temporally divisible acts only one of which causes the social harm, or when the defendant's *mens rea* concurs with an omission that follows an innocent act.

For example, in *State v. Rose*,[5] *R*, an automobile driver, was prosecuted for negligent homicide, in the death of *V*, a pedestrian. The evidence apparently showed that *R* non-negligently struck *V*, whose body wedged underneath *R*'s car. *R* continued to drive some distance, dragging *V*'s body along. Medical experts could not determine whether *V* died at impact or as the result of being dragged.

Based on this evidence, the court properly reversed *R*'s conviction. Although all of the elements of manslaughter were present — *R* committed a voluntary act; she caused the death of *V*; and as to her post-impact conduct, *R* acted with the requisite *mens rea* — the prosecutor did not prove beyond a reasonable doubt that the elements of manslaughter concurred. Essentially, *R* committed two divisible voluntary acts or series of acts: First, she collided with *V*; second, she dragged *V*'s body after impact. Regarding the first voluntary act, *R* lacked a *mens rea*. Regarding the second voluntary act (or, if you will, *R*'s omission of failing to stop), *R* was criminally negligent. There was insufficient medical testimony, however, to prove beyond a reasonable doubt that *this* negligent conduct/omission caused the death.[6]

In exceptional factual circumstances, courts have been known to ignore the concurrence requirement. In one case *D1*, intending to kill *V1*, poisoned *V1*. Although the poison left *V1* unconscious, it did not kill her. Thereafter, believing that *V1* was dead, *D1* decapitated *V1*, causing her death.[7] In another case, *D2* struck *V2* over the head; thinking that *V2* was now dead, *D2* threw *V2* over a cliff, in order to make it appear that *V2* had died from an accident. *V2* died from exposure after the fall.[8]

In both cases, a defendant, with the intent to kill the victim, performed a voluntary act (poisoning *V1*; striking *V2*) that did *not* cause death, and then committed a second voluntary act (decapitating *V1*; throwing *V2* over a cliff) that *did*

---

[5] 311 A.2d 281 (R.I. 1973).

[6] Sometimes a court can stretch to meet the concurrence requirement by finding a "continuing act." See Fagan v. Commissioner of Metropolitan Police, [1969] 1 Q.B. 439 (*F*, perhaps accidentally, drove his car onto *V*'s toes; thereafter, *F* purposely failed to move his vehicle off *V*'s toes; held: "There was an act constituting a battery which at its inception was not criminal because there was no element of intention but which became criminal from the moment the intention was formed to produce the apprehension [of a battery] which was flowing from the continuing act.").

[7] Jackson v. Commonwealth, 38 S.W. 422 (Ky. 1896).

[8] Thabo Meli v. Regina, [1954] 1 W.L.R. 228, 1 All E.R. 373.

cause death but without the requisite intent to kill (because the defendant thought that the deed had already been completed). Nonetheless, the murder convictions in both cases were affirmed, presumably because the defendant's culpability was that of a murderer, and "[o]rdinary ideas of justice and common sense require that such [cases] . . . be treated as murder,"[9] rather than attempted murder.

---

[9] Glanville Williams, Criminal Law: The General Part 174 (2d ed. 1961).

Chapter 16

DEFENSES: AN OVERVIEW

§ 16.01 DEFENSES: IN CONTEXT[1]

In criminal trials in the United States, the prosecution has the burden of producing evidence, and of persuading the factfinder beyond a reasonable doubt, of the concurrence of four ingredients of criminal responsibility: (1) a voluntary act (or an omission when there is a duty to act) by the defendant; (2) the social harm specified in the definition of the offense; (3) the defendant's *mens rea* (strict-liability crimes aside); and (4) an actual and proximate causal connection between elements (1) and (2).

Even if the prosecution proves the concurrence of these four elements, the defendant may seek to raise one or more defenses, which, if proven, will result in his acquittal of the offense charged.[2] This chapter sets out the various categories of defenses recognized in the criminal law.

Generally speaking, a legislature may allocate to the defendant the burden of persuasion regarding criminal law defenses.[3] When the defendant shoulders the burden, he is usually required to convince the factfinder of his claim by a preponderance of the evidence. But, there is one category of defenses — failure-of-proof defenses — that is a "defense" in only the loosest sense of the term.[4] As to defenses that fall in *this* category, as will be explained, the legislature may *not* properly place the burden of persuasion on the defendant.

Two categories of defenses described briefly below — "justification" and "excuse" defenses — are of such fundamental significance that they are considered in greater detail in Chapter 17.

---

[1] See generally 1 Paul Robinson, Criminal Law Defenses 62-200 (1984). The categorization of defenses set out in this chapter is largely based on the influential work of Professor Robinson.

[2] Some defenses result in the defendant's conviction of a lesser offense. They are sometimes described as "partial defenses." For example, the "heat of passion" (or "provocation") defense to murder, if successfully proven, results in conviction of the defendant for voluntary manslaughter. See § 31.07, *infra*. Partial defenses are complete, however, in the sense that the defendant is acquitted of the crime originally charged, e.g., murder.

[3] See Chapter 7, *infra*.

[4] Loosely speaking, a defense is "any set of identifiable conditions or circumstances that may prevent conviction for an offense." 1 Robinson, Note 1, *supra*, at 70.

§ 16.02 FAILURE-OF-PROOF DEFENSES

A failure-of-proof defense is one in which the defendant introduces evidence at his trial that demonstrates that the prosecution has failed to prove an essential element of the offense charged. For example, suppose that *D1*, charged with an intentional homicide, seeks to prove that he mistakenly believed that the object at which he fired his gun was a tree stump rather than a human being. Or, suppose that *D2* claims that he was unconscious when he killed *V*. Or, *D3* introduces evidence that he was not at the scene of the crime and, therefore, was misidentified as the wrongdoer. Each of these defendants is raising what courts often describe as a "defense." *D1* claims a mistake-of-fact "defense"; *D2* asserts an unconsciousness (or "automatism") "defense"; *D3* alleges an alibi "defense."

Although courts may characterize such claims as defenses, the purpose of the defendants' evidence in these examples is to raise a reasonable doubt regarding an element of the prosecutor's case-in-chief. The mistake-of-fact "defense" for *D1* negates the *mens rea* of the crime; *D2*'s unconsciousness, if believed, demonstrates that the prosecutor has failed to prove beyond a reasonable doubt that *D2*'s conduct included a voluntary act; and the alibi "defense" calls into question whether *D3* performed the *actus reus* of the offense.

The prosecution must shoulder the burden of disproving beyond a reasonable doubt a defendant's failure-of-proof claim. This conclusion follows from the fact that the prosecutor has the constitutional duty to prove every element of a criminal offense.[5]

§ 16.03 JUSTIFICATION DEFENSES

A justification defense is one that defines conduct "otherwise criminal, which under the circumstances is socially acceptable and which deserves neither criminal liability nor even censure."[6] Justified conduct is conduct that is "a good thing, or the right or sensible thing, or a permissible thing to do."[7] That is, a justified act is an act that is right or, at least, not wrong.

For example, killing a human being ordinarily is wrongful conduct. When *D* kills *V* in self-defense, however, society says that *D*'s conduct is "justified." Although *D* has committed the *actus reus* of criminal homicide, the special circumstance of the situation — *D* killed *V* because *V* was unlawfully attacking him — renders the homicide socially acceptable. By providing *D* with the justification defense of self-defense, society announces that *D*'s act of killing *V* was

---

[5] See § 7.03[B], *supra*.

[6] Peter D.W. Heberling, Note, *Justification: The Impact of the Model Penal Code on Statutory Reform*, 75 Colum. L. Rev. 914, 916 (1975).

[7] J.L. Austin, *A Plea for Excuses, in* Freedom and Responsibility 6 (Herbert Morris ed., 1961).

the right or, at least, a permissible, thing to do. Or, put slightly differently, the result of *D*'s conduct — *V*'s death — was not a socially undesirable outcome under the circumstances.

§ 16.04 EXCUSE DEFENSES

An excuse defense, e.g., insanity, differs from a justification defense in a fundamental way. Whereas a justification claim generally focuses upon an *act* (i.e., *D*'s conduct), and seeks to show that the act was not wrongful, an excuse centers upon the *actor* (i.e., *D*), and tries to show that the actor is not morally culpable for his wrongful conduct. Thus, an excuse defense "is in the nature of a claim that although the actor has harmed society, [he] should not be blamed or punished for causing that harm."[8] A defendant who asserts an excuse defense claims, "in essence, 'I admit, or you have proved beyond a reasonable doubt, that I did something that I should not have done, but I [still] should not be held criminally accountable for my actions.'"[9]

An insane actor, for example, does not deny that the prosecutor has proved the essential elements of the crime nor that, all things considered, his conduct was wrongful, intolerable, and censurable (i.e., unjustified). He seeks to avoid criminal liability, however, by demonstrating that, as a result of his mental disease or defect, he lacks the moral blameworthiness ordinarily attached to wrongdoers.

§ 16.05 SPECIALIZED DEFENSES ("OFFENSE MODIFICATIONS")

Justification and excuse defenses apply to all crimes. Some defenses, however, pertain to just one or a few crimes. For example, "legal impossibility" is a common law defense to the crime of attempt. In some jurisdictions "abandonment" or "renunciation" is a defense to the crimes of attempt and conspiracy. And, "Wharton's Rule" is a defense peculiar to the crime of conspiracy.[10]

Crime-specific defenses have a common feature: They authorize acquittal of a defendant, even though his conduct satisfies the elements of the offense, when the underlying purpose for prohibiting the conduct is negated by the conditions that constitute the defense. Professor Paul Robinson terms such defenses "offense modifications."[11]

---

[8] Joshua Dressler, *Justifications and Excuses: A Brief Review of the Concepts and the Literature*, 33 Wayne L. Rev. 1155, 1162-63 (1987).

[9] *Id.* at 1163.

[10] See §§ 27.07[D] (legal impossibility), 27.08 (renunciation of an attempt), 29.09[B] (abandonment of a conspiracy), and 29.09[C] (Wharton's Rule), *infra*.

[11] 1 Robinson, Note 1, *supra*, at 77.

For example, the Model Penal Code crime of criminal attempt serves the utilitarian purpose of providing society with a basis for arresting and punishing a person who has demonstrated his culpability and dangerousness by taking a substantial step toward committing a criminal offense. Suppose, however, *D* purposely takes a substantial step toward committing a murder (i.e., he commits the *actus reus* and *mens rea* of an attempted murder), but then voluntarily and irrevocably abandons his criminal enterprise. In such a case, the Code recognizes the defense of renunciation. This defense applies, although the elements of an attempt have been proven, because the underlying reason for punishing *D* no longer applies. His decision to abandon his criminal goal negates his culpability and dangerousness and, therefore, renders his punishment unnecessary.

§ 16.06 EXTRINSIC DEFENSES ("NONEXCULPATORY DEFENSES")

Justification, excuse, and offense-modification defenses are similar in this regard: These defenses relate to the culpability or dangerousness of the defendant or to the wrongfulness of his conduct. Some defenses, however, bar a defendant's conviction, *or even his prosecution*, for reasons unrelated to these factors. These latter claims, which Professor Robinson terms "nonexculpatory" defenses,[12] involve public policy factors extrinsic to substantive criminal law doctrine. Examples of such defenses are the statute of limitations, diplomatic immunity, and incompetency to stand trial.

Each nonexculpatory defense serves an important public policy interest unrelated to the social harm committed by the actor or to his blameworthiness for causing it. Legislative recognition of such a defense implies that the social interest served by it outweighs the utilitarian and/or retributive reasons for punishing the offender.

---

[12] *Id.* at 102.

Chapter 17

JUSTIFICATIONS AND EXCUSES

§ 17.01 HISTORICAL OVERVIEW[1]

Two categories of criminal law defenses are the subject of this chapter: justifications and excuses. In very early English legal history the distinction between justifications and excuses was a matter of profound practical significance. In the case of felonies, a justified actor was acquitted of the offense; an excused actor, however, was subject to the same punishment as a convicted offender (the death penalty and forfeiture of his property), although he could escape the death sentence with a pardon from the Crown.

This dichotomy blurred over time, as excused actors were pardoned by the Crown on an increasingly *pro forma* basis; and they were allowed to regain their property by means of a writ of restitution.[2] Nonetheless, the excused wrongdoer was not on the same footing as the justified actor, since the former party was subject to incarceration while he petitioned for a pardon and for restitution of his property. The justified actor was free of all legal impediments.

Today, justified and excused actors are treated the same by the criminal courts: Each is acquitted of the offense and neither is punished for her conduct.[3] As a result, many courts, legislatures, and commentators are inattentive to the inherent differences between the two classes of defenses, even to the point of using the terms "justification" and "excuse" interchangeably.[4]

---

[1] There is voluminous literature on the concepts of "justification" and "excuse." The following is just a tiny taste of what is available. See generally George P. Fletcher, Rethinking Criminal Law 759-875 (1978); Marcia Baron, *Justifications and Excuses*, 2 Ohio St. J. Crim. L. 387 (2005); Mitchell N. Berman, *Justification and Excuse, Law and Morality*, 53 Duke L.J. 1 (2003); Joshua Dressler, *Justifications and Excuses: A Brief Review of the Concepts and the Literature*, 33 Wayne L. Rev. 1155 (1987); Albin Eser, *Justification and Excuse*, 24 Am. J. Comp. L. 621 (1976); Kent Greenawalt, *Distinguishing Justifications From Excuses*, 49 Law & Contemp. Probs., Summer 1986, at 89; Jerome Hall, *Comment on Justification and Excuse*, 24 Am. J. Comp. L. 638 (1976); Heidi M. Hurd, *Justification and Excuse, Wrongdoing and Culpability*, 74 Notre Dame L. Rev. 1551 (1999); Eugene R. Milhizer, *Justification and Excuse: What They Were, What They Are, and What They Ought to Be*, 78 St. John's L. Rev. 725 (2004); see also the cites to other literature throughout this chapter.

[2] 4 Blackstone, Commentaries on the Law of England *188 (1838). Forfeiture was statutorily abolished in 1838. 9 Geo. 4, c. 13, § 10 (1838).

[3] However, a person excused on the ground of insanity is subject to civil commitment. See § 25.05, *infra*.

[4] E.g., State v. Cozzens, 490 N.W.2d 184, 189 (Neb. 1992) ("Therefore, the *justification* . . . defense operates to legally *excuse* conduct that would otherwise subject a person to criminal sanctions.") (emphasis added); for citations to other judicial, legislative, and scholarly misuses of the

This inattention has not gone without objection by a cadre of scholars.[5] These writers have sought to clarify the concepts of "justification" and "excuse," to demonstrate how the two defenses differ, and to explain why lawyers should care about the distinctions. Because of renewed interest in the subject, including among courts who are increasingly sensitive to the distinctions, this chapter provides a closer inspection of these concepts.

§ 17.02 UNDERLYING THEORIES OF "JUSTIFICATION"[6]

[A] Searching for an Explanatory Theory

As explained in the last chapter,[7] justified conduct is conduct that under ordinary circumstances is criminal, but which under the special circumstances encompassed by the justification defense is not wrongful and is even, perhaps, affirmatively desirable.[8] A justified act is one that "the law does not condemn, or even welcomes."[9]

The question for consideration in this section is: What makes ordinarily bad conduct justifiable? Why is it, for example, that D is justified in killing V to protect herself from V's unlawful lethal assault or from V's intrusion into her

---

terms, see Joshua Dressler, *New Thoughts About the Concept of Justification in the Criminal Law: A Critique of Fletcher's Thinking and Rethinking*, 32 UCLA L. Rev. 61, 65-66 (1984); Paul H. Robinson, *A Theory of Justification: Societal Harm as a Prerequisite for Criminal Liability*, 23 UCLA L. Rev. 266, 276 (1975).

[5] "Crying in the wilderness . . . are a few possibly prophetic voices, among which the loudest and most eloquent is George Fletcher's." Kent Greenawalt, *The Perplexing Borders of Justification and Excuse*, 84 Colum. L. Rev. 1897, 1897-98 (1984) (footnote omitted).

[6] See generally Fletcher, Note 1, *supra*, at 759-98; Dressler, Note 1, *supra*; R.A. Duff, *Rethinking Justifications*, 39 Tulsa L. Rev. 829 (2004); Douglas N. Husak, *Conflicts of Justifications*, 18 Law & Phil. 41 (1999); Milhizer, Note 1, *supra*; Robinson, Note 4, *supra;* Paul H. Robinson, *Testing Competing Theories of Justification*, 76 N.C. L. Rev. 1095 (1998).

[7] See § 16.03, *supra*.

[8] Notice that "justification," as defined in the text, may imply a positive judgment about conduct (it is right, good, or desirable), or it might constitute a weaker value judgment (that the conduct is tolerable or not wrongful). Some scholars believe that the concept of "justification" necessarily implies the stronger meaning; others favor an interpretation broad enough to include both characterizations. E.g., George P. Fletcher, *The Right and the Reasonable*, 98 Harv. L. Rev. 949 (1985); George P. Fletcher, *Should Intolerable Prison Conditions Generate a Justification or an Excuse for Escape?*, 26 UCLA L. Rev. 1355 (1979) (favoring the view that "justification" implies "right" conduct); Dressler, Note 4, *supra*, and Greenawalt, Note 5, *supra* (favoring the vew that "justification" can mean "permissible" or "not wrongful" conduct).

The significance of this debate is more than semantic. For example, suppose that one's view (or the view of a lawmaking body) is that killing a human being in self-defense is tolerable, but not morally good or desirable. If "justification" necessarily implies the latter concept, then lethal self-defense should not be recognized as a justification defense, but it may be under the former interpretation.

[9] H.L.A. Hart, Punishment and Responsibility 13 (1968) (footnote omitted).

home, but that she is not justified in killing *V* to protect her dog or her television set from theft? Are the justification defenses of self-defense, defense-of-habitation, and defense-of-property, for example, no more than a conglomeration of rules unrelated to one another, or is there a single moral theory that unifies the various justification defenses — some principle that explains why something bad (socially harmful) becomes good or, at least, tolerable?

It would be convenient if there were a single, unifying principle of justification, but there is none. In fact, the ingredients of a single justification defense may reflect the influence of different moral theories. What follows is a brief summary of various justification principles. These principles can and should be considered when evaluating the wisdom of recognizing particular "justificatory" claims.

[B] "Public Benefit" Theory

At early common law, justification defenses had a strong public-benefit cast to them. Generally speaking, conduct was not justified unless it was performed in the public's interest, and in most cases was limited to the actions of public officers.

For example, Blackstone identified three sets of circumstances in which homicides were justifiable:[10] (1) when a public officer was commanded to take a life (e.g., when the warden executed a convicted felon); (2) when a public officer, although not commanded to do so, took a life in order to advance the public welfare (e.g., when an officer killed a felon resisting arrest); and (3) when a private party took a life in order to prevent the commission of a forcible, atrocious felony.[11]

A homicide in these circumstances is considered justifiable because society benefits from the actor's conduct. But, there is more to this justification principle: The benefit to society is not incidental to some self-interested goal of the actor; it is the underlying motivation for the actor's conduct. Although strands of the public-benefit concept remain today, it is no longer the dominant theory of justification.

[C] "Moral Forfeiture" Theory

The public-benefit justification principle discussed in the preceding subsection attaches to conduct that benefits society. Some theories of justification, however, are more limited in their focus: A person's conduct is justified as long as it does

---

[10] 4 Blackstone, Note 2, *supra*, at *177-88.

[11] A person who killed another to prevent a rape, robbery, burglary, or other forcible felony acted justifiably, presumably because she was benefitting others; however, if a person killed in self-defense, this conduct constituted excusable, rather than justifiable, homicide.

not result in a socially undesirable outcome. The moral-forfeiture principle of justification fits this category. It is based on the view that people possess certain moral rights or interests that society recognizes through its criminal laws, e.g., the right to life, but which may be forfeited by the holder of the right.

The *forfeiture* of a right must be distinguished from its *waiver*. Some moral interests are not waivable. For example, a person may not legally consent to her own death. The right to life is inviolable in this sense. Nonetheless, even this nonwaivable right can be *forfeited* — nonconsensually lost — as the result of an actor's voluntary decision to violate the rights of another. In such circumstances, society may determine unilaterally that it will no longer recognize the wrongdoer's interest in her life.

The moral-forfeiture doctrine is frequently called upon to explain why an aggressor or fleeing felon may justifiably be killed: As a result of *V*'s freely-chosen decision to wrongfully threaten *D*'s life or to commit a dangerous felony, *V* forfeits her right to life; consequently, when *D* kills *V* in self-defense or in order to prevent *V*'s escape, no socially recognized harm has occurred. From the law's perspective, *V*'s life is worth no more than that of an insect or inanimate body.[12]

The forfeiture principle, although widespread in the common law, is morally troubling to some people because it involves the nonconsensual loss of a valued right. When the forfeiture principle is applied to the interest in human life, it runs counter to the "good and simple moral principle that human life is sacred."[13] To equate human life with that of an insect or an inanimate object is troubling to those who believe in the sanctity of human life.

[D] "Moral Rights" Theory

Conduct may be justified on the ground that the actor has a right to protect a particular moral interest. This theory of justification differs significantly from the moral-forfeiture principle described in the preceding subsection. The forfeiture doctrine focuses on the wrongdoing of the "victim" (e.g., the aggressor) whereas the moral-rights theory focuses on the interests of the defendant. Whereas forfeiture works in a negative way to deny that there is a socially protected interest harmed when the wrongdoer is injured or killed, the moral-rights theory works in a positive sense to provide the actor with an affirmative right to protect her threatened moral interest.

For example, when *D* kills or seriously injures *V*, a lethal aggressor, her conduct may be justified because she was enforcing a natural right of autonomy

---

[12] Hugo Bedau, *The Right to Life*, 1968 Monist 550, 570 ("[The wrongdoer] no longer merits our consideration, any more than an insect or a stone does.").

[13] Working Party, Board for Social Responsibility, Church of England, On Dying Well — An Anglican Contribution to the Debate on Euthanasia 24 (1975), *quoted in* Sanford H. Kadish, *Respect for Life and Regard for Rights in the Criminal Law*, 64 Cal. L. Rev. 871, 878 (1976).

that V's conduct threatened. D is a right-holder protecting her interest against V, the outlaw who would violate her right. This principle of justification does not treat V's death as socially irrelevant, as the forfeiture doctrine does; rather, it views D's conduct as affirmatively proper.

This concept is not without its critics. Because the theory focuses on the person whose rights are being threatened rather than on the interest of the wrongdoer, some commentators claim that the principle "filters out shades and nuances and transforms all situations into black and white relief."[14] That is, once it is determined that V has intruded on a right belonging to D, it is plausible to contend that D may do whatever is necessary to enforce her right, no matter how minor the intrusion may be. After all, she is in the right, and V is in the wrong, and Right should never give way to Wrong.[15] Unless limits are placed on this justification theory, it could authorize a disproportional response to the harm threatened.

[E] "Superior Interest" (or "Lesser Harm") Theory

Another theory of justification authorizes conduct when the interests of the defendant outweigh those of the person she harms. Pursuant to this principle, the interests of the parties, and, more broadly, the values that they seek to enforce, are balanced. In each case there is a superior, or at least a non-inferior, interest. As long as such an interest is pursued the conduct is justified.

For example, if D trespasses by entering V's house in order to avoid a tornado, her conduct is justified. Protection of human life is more important than property protection. Similarly, the use of nonlethal force upon a lethal aggressor is justifiable because preservation of life is more important than prevention of injury to another. As these examples suggest, the superior-interest theory of justification is consistent with the utilitarian goal of promoting individual conduct that reduces overall harm. It is also consistent with the non-utilitarian concept of weighing moral rights and identifying the superior one.

---

14 George P. Fletcher, *Proportionality and the Psychotic Aggressor: A Vignette in Comparative Criminal Theory*, 8 Isr. L. Rev. 367, 381 (1973).

15 Edmond Coke, Third Institute *55 (1644) (no "man shall [ever] give way to a thief, etc., neither shall he forfeit anything").

§ 17.03 UNDERLYING THEORIES OF "EXCUSE"[16]

[A] Searching for an Explanatory Theory

An excuse defense "is in the nature of a claim that although the actor has harmed society, she should not be blamed or punished for causing that harm."[17] The question that must be answered here is: Is there a single principle that determines when the law will abstain from blaming — and holding legally accountable in a criminal prosecution — a person who has caused social harm?

As with justifications, no single theory explains every excuse defense. Moreover, some of the theories partially overlap. However, unlike the concept of justification, which are often (but need not) be explained on utilitarian grounds, excuses in the criminal law are far more plausibly defended in non-utilitarian terms. As Professor Sanford Kadish has observed, "[s]omething is missing" in the utilitarian account of excuses, namely, "concern for the innocent person who is the object of a criminal prosecution." As Kadish points out:

> To blame a person is to express a moral criticism, and if the person's action does not deserve criticism, blaming him is a kind of falsehood and is, to the extent the person is injured by being blamed, unjust to him. It is this feature of our everyday moral practices that lies behind the law's excuses.[18]

After brief comment on the utilitarian theory of excuses, various nonconsequentialist moral theories are surveyed.

---

[16] See generally Fletcher, Note 1, *supra*, at § 10.3; Peter Arenella, *Convicting the Morally Blameless: Reassessing the Relationship Between Legal and Moral Accountability*, 39 UCLA L. Rev. 1511 (1992); Peter Arenella, *Character, Choice and Moral Agency: The Relevance of Character to Our Moral Culpability*, 7 Soc. Phil. & Pol., Spring 1990, at 59; Michael Corrado, *Notes on the Structure of a Theory of Excuses*, 82 J. Crim. L. & Criminology 465 (1991); Deborah W. Denno, Comment, *Human Biology and Criminal Responsibility: Free Will or Free Ride?*, 137 U. Pa. L. Rev. 615 (1988); Joshua Dressler, *Reflections on Excusing Wrongdoers: Moral Theory, New Excuses and the Model Penal Code*, 19 Rutgers L.J. 671 (1988); Dressler, Note 1, *supra*; John Gardner, *The Gist of Excuses*, 1 Buff. Crim. L. Rev. 575 (1998); Sanford H. Kadish, *Excusing Crime*, 75 Cal. L. Rev. 257 (1987); Anders Kaye, *Resurrecting the Causal Theory of Excuses*, 83 Neb. L. Rev. 1116 (2005); Milhizer, Note 1, *supra*; Michael S. Moore, *Choice, Character, and Excuse*, 7 Soc. Phil. & Pol., Spring 1990, at 29; Michael S. Moore, *Causation and the Excuses*, 73 Cal. L. Rev. 1091 (1985); Stephen J. Morse, *Excusing and the New Excuse Defenses: A Legal and Conceptual Review*, in 23 Crime and Justice: A Review of Research 329 (1998); Stephen J. Morse, *Diminished Rationality, Diminished Responsibility*, 1 Ohio St. J. Crim. L. 289 (2003); Samuel H. Pillsbury, *The Meaning of Deserved Punishment: An Essay on Choice, Character, and Responsibility*, 67 Ind. L.J. 719 (1992); George Vuoso, *Background, Responsibility, and Excuse*, 96 Yale L.J. 1661 (1987).

[17] Dressler, Note 1, *supra*, at 1162-63.

[18] Kadish, Note 16, *supra*, at 264.

[B] Deterrence Theory

Jeremy Bentham, the leading classical utilitarian, explained that excuses are recognized in the criminal law because they identify the circumstances in which conduct is undeterrable, e.g., when a person is insane or coerced to commit an offense. In such situations, punishment of the actor is wrong because it is inefficacious.[19]

This argument has rightly been denounced as a "spectacular *non sequitur.*"[20] The threat of punishment may not deter a person who is suffering from a mental illness or is acting under duress, but its actual infliction may deter misconduct by "normal" persons who might otherwise believe that they could fraudulently convince a jury of their undeterrability. Abolition of all excuses, therefore, might be socially useful: The pain inflicted on the undeterrable actor might be outweighed by the prevention of harm caused by the law's imposition of a stricter form of liability.[21]

Professor H.L.A. Hart has offered a more sophisticated utilitarian account of excuses. He has argued that excuses "function as a mechanism for . . . maximizing within the framework of coercive criminal law the efficacy of the individual's informed and considered choice in determining the future and also his power to predict that future."[22] That is, the rule that criminal liability is limited to voluntary wrongdoing allows each person to derive satisfaction from being able to plan her life with reasonable confidence that she can avoid the sanctions of the law, as long as she chooses to obey society's dictates.

[C] Causation Theory

Perhaps the broadest excuse theory states that a person should not be blamed for her conduct if it was caused by factors outside her control.[23] For example, according to a causal theorist, *D* should be excused if she commits a crime because of a mental illness or a coercive deadly threat: Since she is not to blame for being ill or the victim of coercion — the cause of her actions — she is not to blame for the crime itself. On the other hand, she *is* to blame and punishable if her criminal conduct was caused by *self-induced* intoxication or by any other factor for which she is responsible.

---

[19] Jeremy Bentham, An Introduction to the Principles of Morals and Legislation 160-62 (J. Burns & H.L.A. Hart eds., 1970).

[20] Hart, Note 9, *supra*, at 19.

[21] *Id.* at 19-20; Fletcher, Note 1, *supra*, at 813-17.

[22] Hart, Note 9, *supra*, at 46.

[23] For a full exposition of this theory, which the author ultimately rejects, see Moore, *Causation and the Excuses*, Note 16, *supra*, at 1101-12.

Although this principle is plausible on its face, it does not accurately describe the whole of current excuse law. For example, as is developed elsewhere,[24] only a single, largely discredited, definition of insanity applies the causation principle; most people who commit criminal offenses due to mental disease *are* held criminally responsible. As another example, if a person commits a crime solely because she is threatened with economic ruin, her conduct is nonetheless *not* legally excused.[25]

It is also not evident that the causation principle conforms with our moral intuitions. A person who commits a crime due to self-induced intoxication, for example, may be able to show that her propensity to become intoxicated was the result of genetic or environmental factors over which she had no control; yet we do not consider such a wrongdoer morally blameless. Indeed, acceptance of the causal principle of excuses could threaten to lead society down "the cul-de-sac of . . . determinism,"[26] in which *nobody* can be blamed or punished for her wrongful conduct.

[D] Character Theory

Various theorists treat a person's moral character as central to the concept of deserved punishment. According to one character theory, punishment should be proportional to a wrongdoer's moral desert, and that desert should be measured by the actor's character.[27] Normally, we infer bad character from an actor's wrongful conduct; these character theorists argue that excuses should be recognized in the law in those circumstances in which bad character cannot be inferred from the offender's wrongful conduct.

For example, if *D* robs a bank, we would ordinarily infer that she is a greedy person who lacks concern for the rights of others, i.e., that she possesses a bad character. However, we would not infer bad character if we learned that she robbed the bank because terrorists threatened to kill her child if she did not cooperate. In such circumstances, we assume that even a person of good moral character would probably violate the law. Therefore, we excuse her actions.

This theory may conform with our moral intuitions. We assume that people who commit crimes are "bad people." When a "good person" commits a "bad act" we sometimes say that her act was "out of character." We look for some explanation independent of her character that explains and excuses her conduct.

Nonetheless, critics raise various objections to this and related versions of the character theory of excuses. First, if excuse law were genuinely based on character, a court would need to look at a person's entire life, and not solely at the

---

[24] See § 25.04[C][4], *infra.*

[25] See § 23.01[B], *infra.*

[26] Fletcher, Note 1, *supra*, at 801.

[27] *Id.* at 800.

circumstances surrounding the particular criminal act, in order to evaluate her moral desert. But, as philosopher Jeffrie Murphy has pointed out, "there are staggering obstacles in the way of our making [character] judgments about others." God, it may be argued, can judge our character, but mortals lack "the knowledge required to impute deep character depravity to others with any degree of reliability"; therefore, "we act recklessly in inflicting misery on people as the suffering they deserve for their inner wickedness."[28]

Second, the character theory does not explain why we *do* punish people of *good* character who commit out-of-character offenses. For example, suppose that *D*, unemployed, unjustifiably strikes a stranger in a moment of frustration with her plight. Even if *D* is a person of good character, she has acted in a blameworthy manner and is (and most people would probably say, should be) held accountable for her actions.

Third, causal theorists[29] argue that the character theory assumes that people are responsible for their character — and, thus, may be blamed for their bad character — but this may not be the case. They argue that one's character is shaped by powerful genetic and environmental factors beyond the individual's control. Defenders of the character theory argue, however, that a person *may* properly be held responsible for her character traits, even if she did not initially choose them, because she is responsible for *retaining* them.[30]

[E] "Free Choice" (or Personhood) Theory

Advocates of the free choice theory claim that a person may properly be blamed for her conduct "if, but only if, [s]he had the capacity and fair opportunity to function in a uniquely human way, *i.e.,* freely to choose whether to violate the moral/legal norms of society."[31] According to this account, "free choice" exists if, at the time of the wrongful conduct, the actor has the substantial capacity and fair opportunity to: (1) understand the facts relating to her conduct; (2) appreciate that her conduct violates society's mores; and (3) conform her conduct to the dictates of the law. A person lacking the *substantial capacity* in any of these regards essentially suffers from some serious *internal disability* and, therefore, does not deserve to be punished because she lacks the basic attributes of personhood that qualify her as a moral agent. Alternatively, a person who

---

[28] Jeffrie G. Murphy, *Moral Epistemology, the Retributive Emotions, and the "Clumsy Moral Philosophy" of Jesus Christ, in* The Passions of Law 149, 157-58 (Susan A. Bandes ed., 1999).

[29] See § 17.03[C], *supra*.

[30] Pillsbury, Note 16, *supra*, at 730-31. For variations on the character theory described in the text, see *id.*, at 730-34 (describing, but ultimately rejecting all of the character theories).

[31] Dressler, Note 16, *supra*, at 701 (footnote omitted); see Hart, Note 9, *supra*, at 181 ("Thus a primary vindication of the principle of responsibility could rest on the simple idea that unless a man has the capacity and a fair opportunity . . . to adjust his behaviour to the law its penalties ought not to be applied to him.").

lacks "free choice" under the *no-fair-opportunity* prong does not deserve punishment because some *external* factor is acting upon her on this particular occasion such that it is unjust to blame her for her wrongful conduct.

Critics of the choice theory believe that it is too narrow. Causal theorists argue, for example, that because "free choice" is defined in terms of the actor's capacity and opportunity *at the moment of the criminal act* to obey the law, morally significant events arising earlier are excluded from the picture. For example, although a person may have had free choice regarding whether to rob a particular liquor store on a particular occasion, she may not have had a fair opportunity to avoid the conditions that hardened her character and made committing the crime seem inevitable.

Professor Peter Arenella is also critical, but for a different reason.[32] He contends that the free choice theory provides too "thin" an account of what it means to be a moral agent. He argues that one cannot be a moral decisionmaker, and thus qualify as a morally accountable actor, unless the person possesses certain abilities and attributes, including especially the ability to care for the interests of other human beings, *i.e.*, the capacity to empathize. One who lacks this capacity, Arenella contends, lacks such an important human attribute that she is undeserving of blame, even if she "freely" causes harm, as "free choice" is defined above.

§ 17.04 JUSTIFICATION DEFENSES AND MISTAKE-OF-FACT CLAIMS[33]

[A] General Rule

Consider the following hypothetical: *D* intentionally kills *V*. At trial, *D* claims that she killed *V* because she believed that *V* was about to kill her. In fact, *V* did *not* constitute an imminent unlawful deadly threat to *D*; therefore, *D* did not need to kill *V*. This very common scenario involves the convergence of two "defense" concepts: a traditional justification defense (here, self-defense) and a mistake-of-fact claim (*D*'s erroneous belief that *V* posed an imminent unlawful deadly threat).

Two questions arise when a defendant asserts a justification defense, and yet also claims a mistake of fact: (1) Is a defendant entitled to be acquitted if she

---

[32] See Arenella, *Convicting the Morally Blameless*, Note 16, *supra*; and Arenella, *Character, Choice, and Moral Agency*, Note 16, *supra*.

[33] See generally Fletcher, Note 1, *supra*, at 762-68; 2 Paul H. Robinson, Criminal Law Defenses § 184 (1984); Baron, Note 1, *supra*; Russell L. Christopher, *Mistake of Fact in the Objective Theory of Justification: Do Two Rights Make Two Wrongs Make Two Rights . . . ?*, 85 J. Crim. L. & Criminology 295 (1994); Dressler, Note 4, *supra*; Greenawalt, Note 5, *supra*; Benjamin B. Sendor, *Mistake of Fact: A Study in the Structure of Criminal Conduct*, 25 Wake Forest L. Rev. 707 (1990); Richard Singer, *The Resurgence of Mens Rea: II — Honest But Unreasonable Mistake of Fact in Self-Defense*, 28 B.C. L. Rev. 459 (1987).

was mistaken regarding the facts that would justify her conduct?; and (2) If she *is* entitled to be acquitted, should the law describe her conduct as justified or excused? For current purposes, these questions will be answered in relation to self-defense (considered fully in Chapter 18), *but the principles here have application to the other justification defenses, as well.*

The law is clear-cut in situations of the sort described here. A defendant *is* entitled to be acquitted on the basis of self-defense if her mistake of fact regarding the threat was reasonable. However, she will be convicted of some form of criminal homicide if her mistake was unreasonable.[34] More specifically, the rule is that a defendant is justified — and not merely excused — in using deadly force if, at the time of the homicide, she had reasonable grounds for believing, and did believe, that she was in imminent danger of death or grievous bodily injury, and that deadly force was necessary to repel the threat, *although it turned out later that these appearances were false.*

[B] Criticisms of the General Rule

There is little disagreement with the principle that a defendant who acts on the basis of reasonable appearances should be acquitted,[35] but there is considerable debate about the propriety of treating a mistaken actor's conduct as justifiable, rather than excusable. In the self-defense hypothetical at the beginning of this section, how can it be that *D* is *justified* in taking *V*'s life if, for example, *V* was an innocent person?

Critics of the general rule — the rule that a person is justified in acting on the basis of reasonable, albeit inaccurate, appearances — argue that it confuses the difference between justifications, which go to the propriety of the defendant's *act*, and excuses, which relate to the blameworthiness of the *actor*. The critics maintain that a reasonable-but-mistaken *actor* is morally blameless and, therefore, should be excused; but it is wrong to suggest that the *act* of killing an innocent person or one who does not pose a threat to the life of the actor is justifiable.

These critics are making more than a semantic argument. As discussed more fully in the next section of this chapter, the justification/excuse distinction can have practical implications. Critics of the general rule contend that it is wrong to authorize *D* (in the hypothetical) to kill innocent *V*, because this would seemingly leave *V* without her own right of self-defense against *D*, who is really attacking *her*. Alternatively, the law would have to recognize conflicting justifications: That is, *D* is justified in killing *V*, based on incorrect-but-reasonable appearances; and, meanwhile, *V* is justified in killing *D*, based on the reality

---

[34] Under traditional common law principles, she is guilty of murder; in some jurisdictions today, however, she would be convicted of manslaughter. See §§ 18.01[E] and 18.03, *infra*. Under the Model Penal Code, she is guilty of manslaughter or negligent homicide, depending on whether she was reckless or negligent as to her mistake of fact. See § 18.06[B], *infra*.

[35] But see § 19.01, *infra*, for one potential exception to this proposition.

that D is (justifiably) trying to take V's life! To critics, this is an anomalous outcome: One person, specifically V, should be justified in killing the other. Moreover, critics argue, unless the law properly characterizes D's and V's conduct, a third person who arrives on the scene will not know whether she may come to the aid of D, V, both, or neither.[36]

[C] Defense of the General Rule

Defenders of the general rule point out that "[t]he criminal law does not demand ideal behavior from people."[37] All that the law can fairly expect of a person is that she make a conscientious effort to determine the true state of affairs before acting. If she does this, defenders of the rule claim, her conduct is justifiable, although the result of her conduct (in the hypothetical, V's death) may prove to be tragic.

The defenders of the rule may be right. Consider that a police officer is legally entitled to arrest a person if she has probable cause to believe that the suspect has committed a felony. An officer acting on probable cause is justified in making the arrest, even if the suspect later turns out to be innocent. Critics of the general rule would say that an officer in such circumstances has acted *un*justifiably, no matter how carefully she has investigated the situation. Yet, few would agree that a police officer is acting outside the law, i.e., unjustifiably, simply because her knowledge of the circumstances proves to be humanly imperfect.

Defenders of the general rule argue that there is no inherent anomaly in recognizing incompatible justifications. For example, in the arrest situation, suppose that the innocent person uses nondeadly force to resist her own arrest. If the citizen is later charged with battery upon the police officer, there is no reason why the law must inflexibly deny a justification defense to the aggrieved citizen, even though the officer was also justified in making the arrest. The point here is not that the law *should* permit a justification defense to the citizen in the battery prosecution, but rather that it is not irrational to permit one.

Finally, defenders of the general rule point out that, at least according to some of the justification theories set out earlier in this chapter, a person *can* be justified in acting on the basis of reasonable appearances. For example, it is plausible to argue that a person's natural right to defend her autonomy should apply in any situation in which her life reasonably appears to be in imminent jeopardy, even if later events demonstrate that such appearances were false.

The reader should appraise these competing arguments, and their practical effects, while considering the specifics of the justification defenses, as set out in Chapters 18-22.

---

[36] See § 17.05[E], *infra*.

[37] Greenawalt, Note 5, *supra*, at 1905.

§ 17.05 JUSTIFICATION VERSUS EXCUSE: WHY DOES IT MATTER?[38]

[A] In General

Why should the legal profession care about the conceptual differences between justification and excuse defenses, if they both result in acquittal of a defendant? Not everyone believes that the distinctions are sufficiently important to merit close attention. The drafters of the Model Penal Code, for example, were skeptical that they could draw sensible lines between justifications and excuses; and, even if they could, they concluded that the resulting increased complexity of the statutory system would have outweighed the benefits from drawing distinctions.[39]

Advocates of drawing distinctions offer a number of justifications for their position, a few of which are summarized below.[40]

[B] Sending Clear Moral Messages

The criminal law represents a crude, but nonetheless important, moral compass that can assist people in deciding which of various potential paths they should take in particular circumstances. For example, if a battered woman is considering whether to kill her abusive partner while he is asleep, should the law tell her that her proposed action is justifiable, excusable, or neither?[41] People should take justifiable, rather than wrongful-but-excusable, paths. If the law does not label the paths clearly, the system has failed to provide adequate guidance. Just as importantly, if the justification/excuse distinction is ignored or misapplied, the law may inadvertently express a moral falsity by characterizing improper-but-excusable conduct as proper. In short, the criminal law ought to send the moral messages we intend to send.

[C] Providing Theoretical Consistency in the Criminal Law

Appreciation of the justification/excuse distinction can help lawmakers coherently define criminal defenses. For example, as discussed more fully later in this Text,[42] the common law heat-of-passion defense to murder suffers from a lack

---

[38] See Fletcher, Note 1, *supra*, at 664-70, 759-69; Berman, Note 1, *supra*; Dressler, Note 1, *supra*; Dressler, Note 4, *supra*; Fletcher, *Intolerable Prison Conditions*, Note 8, *supra*; Greenawalt, Note 5, *supra*; Robinson, Note 4, *supra*.

[39] American Law Institute, Comment to art. 3, at 2-4.

[40] See also § 17.04, *supra*.

[41] See § 18.05[B], *infra*.

[42] See § 31.07[C], *infra*.

of proper attention to the differences between justifications and excuses: Some elements of the defense are best explained in justificatory terms, while others seem excuse-based. The law is not well-served when a defense is composed of a set of inconsistent — perhaps even contradictory — principles.

[D] Accomplice Liability[43]

Suppose that D wishes to perform conduct A. D needs assistance to do so, so she turns to X for aid. If X assists, what is *her* criminal responsibility? If conduct A is justified, D has acted properly. X, therefore, should be acquitted as she is an "accomplice" in the commission of a justified — lawful — act.[44] Thus, if X provides D with a gun used to kill V in justifiable self-defense, X should be guilty of no crime.

Suppose, however, that D kills V due to an insane delusion. X, who is sane, provides D with the gun used in the crime. Although D may be acquitted on the basis of insanity, no logical reason precludes the conviction of X for the murder in which she sanely assisted. After all, a wrongful act has occurred, i.e., the death of V. The fact that D is relieved of responsibility due to mental illness should not bar conviction of a sane person who assists in the wrongful act. As one court has explained, "[b]ecause excuses relate to a condition that is peculiar to the actor, such defenses are generally considered to be non-delegable and, thus, unavailable to an accomplice."[45]

[E] Third Party Conduct

Generally speaking, justifications are universalized, whereas excuses are individualized.[46] That is, if D is justified in performing act A to protect her own rights, a third person, X, is also justified in doing A to protect D. As seen in subsection [D], however, an *excuse* may only be invoked by the person who suffers from the excusing condition.

In some cases this generalization works easily and straightforwardly. For example, if D is justified in killing V, an aggressor, in self-defense, it would ordinarily follow that X, an onlooker, is justified in killing V in order to save D. On the other hand, if D is only excused in killing V, e.g., if D is insane, no right attaches to X to kill V. Assuming that X is sane (and is not the victim of any other excusing condition), she is subject to prosecution.

---

[43] See also § 30.06[B][2], *infra*.

[44] United States v. Lopez, 662 F. Supp. 1083 (N.D. Cal. 1987), aff'd, 885 F.2d 1428 (9th Cir 1989).

[45] Taylor v. Commonwealth, 521 S.E.2d 293, 297 (Va. Ct. App. 1999).

[46] See Fletcher, Note 1, *supra*, at 810-13. Some commentators believe that this proposition, although generally accurate, is not true in all circumstances or would lead to undesirable conclusions if it were followed without exception. See Dressler, Note 4, *supra*, at 95-98; Greenawalt, Note 5, *supra*, at 1915-16.

Some cases are far more difficult to resolve. Consider the case of a person who kills a morally innocent aggressor in self-defense:[47] Assume *V*, a very young child (a child too young to understand the consequences of her actions) points a loaded gun at *D* under circumstances in which *D* realizes that her life is in imminent jeopardy and that the only way to protect herself is to take *V*'s life. If *D* kills *V*, *D* will be acquitted, but should her defense be treated as one of justification or excuse? She is *justified* in killing the youth under the moral-right theory of justification,[48] since her right of autonomy is being threatened. She is *not justified*, however, in killing the youth under the moral-forfeiture doctrine,[49] since the child is too young to know what she is doing and, therefore, has not forfeited her right to life.

Arguably, the legal position of *X*, a stranger who comes upon the situation when child *V* is about to kill *D*, depends on the label attached to *D*'s defense. If *D* is justified in killing *V*, it would seemingly follow from the universalization premise[50] that *X* is also justified in killing *V* to save *D*. If *D* is merely excused in killing *V*, however, *X* could be convicted if she killed the youth, unless *X* demonstrates some excuse personal to her.

[F] Retroactivity

Suppose that conduct A constitutes a defense when *D* acts, but that the defense is repealed before *D*'s trial. Is *D* entitled to assert conduct A as a defense at her trial? The answer arguably depends on whether conduct A was a justification or an excuse.

D should be entitled to raise any justification defense recognized at the time of her conduct. A justification defense defines conduct that society wishes to encourage or, at least, tolerate. People should be allowed to rely on these representations. To deny *D* the opportunity at trial to justify her conduct on the basis of the subsequently-repealed defense would be unfair and counter-utilitarian.

The same cannot be said for excuses. Excuse defenses are not directives to would-be actors regarding the permissibility of particular conduct; excuses identify the circumstances under which a person ought to be relieved of criminal responsibility for her conduct because she is undeterrable or is not morally to blame for her conduct. Any person who investigates excuse law and relies on it before she acts, however, is not the type of person to whom the excuses are

---

[47] See generally Fletcher, Note 14, *supra*; Mordechai Kremnitzer, *Proportionality and the Psychotic Aggressor: Another View*, 18 Isr. L. Rev. 178 (1983); Jeff McMaham, *Self-Defense and the Problem of the Innocent Attacker*, 104 Ethics 252 (1994); Michael Otsuka, *Killing the Innocent in Self-Defense*, 23 Phil. & Pub. Aff. 74 (1994).

[48] See § 17.02[D], *supra*.

[49] See § 17.02[C], *supra*.

[50] But see Note 46, *supra*.

meant to apply. Therefore, to the extent that retroactivity principles are based on conceptions of justifiable reliance, it is fair to deny her the opportunity to raise a repealed excuse.

[G] Burden of Proof

As a matter of constitutional law, a legislature may allocate to the defendant the burden of persuasion regarding any justification or excuse defense.[51] Conceptually, however, a strong case can be made for the proposition that the government should carry the burden of persuasion regarding justification defenses, but that the defendant should be required to persuade the factfinder regarding excuses.

The theory behind this distinction would proceed as follows. The prosecutor is allocated the burden of persuasion regarding the elements of a crime because nobody should be punished if a reasonable doubt exists whether the defendant has committed an unlawful act. Justified conduct, in turn, is conduct that society has determined is desirable or, at least, permissible. In short, it is lawful conduct. If the defendant is allocated the burden of persuasion regarding a justification, she may be punished although the jury is not satisfied beyond a reasonable doubt that she has done anything wrong.

In contrast, with excused conduct, all of the elements of the crime have been proven *and* it has been determined that the conduct was unjustifiable. Under these circumstances, it is fair to expect the defendant to persuade the jury that she is not to blame for her wrongful conduct.

---

[51] See § 7.03[B], *supra*.

Chapter 18

SELF-DEFENSE

§ 18.01 GENERAL PRINCIPLES

[A] Overview

Every state in the United States recognizes a defense for the use of force, including deadly force, in self-protection. Although the right to protect oneself from an aggressor has never been declared a constitutional right,[1] one court has observed:

> It is difficult to the point of impossibility to imagine a right in any state to abolish self defense altogether, thereby leaving one a Hobson's choice of almost certain death through violent attack now or statutorily mandated death [or life imprisonment] through trial and conviction of murder later.[2]

Most issues regarding the application of defensive force arise in the context of homicide and attempted murder prosecutions. Therefore, this chapter primarily focuses on the question of when *deadly* force may be used in self-defense.

[B] Elements of the Defense

At common law, a non-aggressor is justified in using force upon another if he reasonably believes that such force is necessary to protect himself from imminent use of unlawful force by the other person.[3] Specifically, however, *deadly* force is only justified in self-protection if the actor reasonably believes that its use is necessary to prevent imminent and unlawful use of *deadly* force by the aggressor.[4]

---

[1] The issue rarely arises. However, at least two federal courts have held or suggested that the right of self-defense is not a constitutional right. White v. Arn, 788 F.2d 338 (6th Cir. 1986); Rowe v. DeBruyn, 17 F.3d 1047 (7th Cir. 1994). And, although the "right to act in self-defense has been regarded as a natural right, taken all but for granted, . . . it was not part of early English common law," which treated self-defense as an excuse, rather than a justification, for homicide. Sydnor v. State, 776 A.2d 669, 672 (Md. 2001).

[2] Griffin v. Martin, 785 F.2d 1172, 1186 n.37 (4th Cir. 1986), aff'd en banc and op. withdrawn, 795 F.2d 22 (4th Cir. 1986).

[3] People v. Dunlap, 734 N.E.2d 973, 981 (Ill. App. 2000); State v. Gheen, 41 S.W.3d 598, 606 (Mo. Ct. App. 2001).

[4] United States v. Peterson, 483 F.2d 1222, 1230-31 (D.C. Cir. 1973); People v. Riddle, 649 N.W.2d 30, 34 (Mich. 2002).

These principles are subject to substantial clarification, as discussed in the next chapter section. However, it should be noted at the outset that the defense of self-defense, as is the case with other justification defenses, contains: (1) a "necessity" component; (2) a "proportionality" requirement; and (3) a reasonable-belief rule that overlays the defense.

[C] The Necessity Component

The *necessity* rule provides that force should not be used against another person unless, and only to the extent that, it is necessary. One aspect of this requirement — one which is increasingly controversial — is that self-defense is limited at common law to *imminent* threats.[5] But, beyond this, a person may not use deadly force to combat an imminent deadly assault if some *non*deadly response will apparently suffice. For example, if *V*, an elderly or infirm aggressor, attempts to stab *D*, *D* may not kill *V* if *D* knows or should know that he could avoid death by disarming *V*, or by using *non*deadly force.[6] And, in some jurisdictions, a person may not use deadly force against an aggressor if he knows that he has a completely safe avenue of retreat.[7]

[D] The Proportionality Component

The *proportionality* rule provides that a person is not justified in using force that is excessive in relation to the harm threatened.[8] Assuming all of the other elements of the defense apply, a person may use nondeadly force to repel a nondeadly threat; he may also use nondeadly force against a deadly threat (and, in some circumstances may be required to do so, as noted above). But a person is *never* permitted to use *deadly* force to repel what he knows is a *non-deadly* attack, even if deadly force is the only way to prevent the battery. For example, if *V* threatens to strike *D* on a public road, and the only way *D* can avoid the battery is to push *V* into the street in front of a fast-moving car, *D* must abstain and seek compensation for the battery after the fact.[9]

---

[5] See § 18.02[D][1], *infra*.

[6] E.g., State v. Garrison, 525 A.2d 498 (Conn. 1987) (*V*, intoxicated, moved menacingly toward *G* with a gun in his waistband; *G* disarmed *V*; *V* then pulled out a knife; *G* shot *V* to death; *G*'s conviction was upheld, in part on the ground that *G* knew, or should have known, that he could have disarmed *V* again); see People v. Riddle, 649 N.W.2d at 34 ("The necessity element of self-defense normally requires that the actor try to avoid the use of deadly force . . . by applying nondeadly force" or by avoiding force altogether).

[7] See § 18.02[C], *infra*.

[8] State v. Warren, 794 A.2d 790, 793 (N.H. 2002).

[9] A lingering issue is what constitutes "deadly force." See § 18.02[A], *infra*.

[E] The "Reasonable Belief" Component

A self-defense claim contains a subjective and an objective component.[10] First, the jury must determine that the defendant subjectively believed that he needed to use deadly force to repel an imminent unlawful attack. Second, the defendant's belief in this regard must be one that a reasonable person in the same situation would have possessed. Notice, however, the implication of the latter component: A defendant is justified in killing a supposed aggressor if the defendant's belief in this regard is objectively reasonable, *even if appearances prove to be false*, i.e., even if the decedent did *not* represent an imminent threat to the defendant.[11]

On the other hand, the defense is unavailable to one whose self-defense belief, although genuine, was *unreasonable*. In such circumstances, the traditional rule is that the *un*reasonably mistaken actor is guilty of murder. However, an increasing number of jurisdictions now permit an unreasonably mistaken actor to assert an "imperfect" or "incomplete" claim of self-defense, which mitigates the offense to manslaughter.[12]

§ 18.02 DEADLY FORCE: CLARIFICATION OF THE GENERAL PRINCIPLES

As stated in § 18.01, a person who is not an aggressor is justified in using deadly force upon another if he reasonably believes that such force is necessary to protect himself from imminent use of unlawful deadly force by the other party. This rule is examined here in detail.

[A] "Deadly Force": Definition

Although statutes today vary slightly in definition, generally speaking "deadly force" may be defined as force intended or likely to cause death or grievous bodily injury.[13] This definition applies whether one is considering the force used by the aggressor or the innocent person threatened.

---

[10] People v. Watie, 100 Cal. App. 4th 866, 877 (2002); State v. Clark, 826 A.2d 128, 134-35 (Conn. 2003).

[11] State v. Simon, 646 P.2d 1119, 1120-21 (Kan. 1982); People v. Goetz, 497 N.E.2d 41, 46-48 (N.Y. 1986); Fresno Rifle & Pistol Club, Inc. v. Van de Kamp, 746 F. Supp. 1415, 1421 (E.D. Cal. 1990); contra, State v. Bradley, 10 P.3d 358 (Wash. 2000) (notwithstanding the general rule, and despite a sharp dissent, the court holds that a jail inmate who uses force against a correctional officer may not successfully claim self-defense unless he is in actual imminent danger of serious injury; a reasonable but mistaken belief is insufficient). For more discussion of the "reasonable belief" topic, see § 17.04, *supra*.

[12] See § 18.03, *infra*.

[13] Commonwealth v. Klein, 363 N.E.2d 1313, 1316 (Mass. 1977).

Notice that under this definition force is characterized as deadly if death or grievous injury is the likely outcome, even if this was not the actor's intention or the actual result. For example, if D stabs V, this constitutes deadly force, even if D intended only to wound V slightly,[14] and regardless of whether V dies from the wounds. Likewise, if D fires a deadly weapon at V, and misses, this constitutes deadly force.

On the other hand, a minor battery does not ordinarily constitute deadly force, even if death unexpectedly results.[15] Even a stranglehold by an actor, if not intended to cause death or serious injury, should constitute nondeadly force if the jury determines that serious injury or death was unlikely.[16] It should follow from this, however, that a serious battery can constitute deadly force if the person being struck is an infirm individual likely to die or be grievously harmed by the force.

[B] The "Non-Aggressor" Limitation

[1] Definition of "Aggressor"

An aggressor "has no right to a claim of self-defense."[17] Although there is no universally accepted definition of the term, an "aggressor" may be defined as one whose "affirmative unlawful act [is] reasonably calculated to produce an affray foreboding injurious or fatal consequences."[18] Or, he is one who threatens unlawfully to commit a battery upon another or who provokes a physical conflict by words or actions calculated to bring about an assault.[19] For example, if D unlawfully brandishes a knife and threatens to kill V, D is not justified in defending himself if V responds to D's threats by use of self-protective force.

---

[14] Of course, if D did not intend to kill V, he would not have the requisite *mens rea* to be convicted of intent-to-kill murder, although he might be guilty of some other form of murder or manslaughter.

[15] E.g., V throws a fist at D; D protects himself by lightly pushing V away. V falls and unexpectedly dies. D may successfully claim self-defense because he used force proportional to the threat — he used nondeadly force (force neither intended nor likely to cause death or serious bodily injury) to repel a nondeadly attack.

[16] See Commonwealth v. Noble, 707 N.E.2d 819 (Mass. 1999).

[17] Bellcourt v. State, 390 N.W.2d 269, 272 (Minn. 1986); see Loesche v. State, 620 P.2d 646, 651 (Alaska 1980) ("The law of self-defense is designed to afford protection to one who is beset by an aggressor and confronted by a necessity not of his own making.") (quoting Bangs v. State, 608 P.2d 1, 5 (Alaska 1980)).

[18] United States v. Peterson, 483 F.2d 1222, 1233 (D.C. Cir. 1973).

[19] State v. Brown, 450 S.E.2d 538, 541 (N.C. Ct. App. 1994); see also People v. Dunlap, 734 N.E.2d 973 (Ill. App. Ct. 2000) (D beat on V's apartment window and threatened V; the court noted that "[e]ven the mere utterance of words may be enough to qualify one as an initial aggressor").

Courts frequently state that a person is not privileged to use force to resist an attack unless he is "free from fault in the difficulty,"[20] but this is an overstatement.[21] In some circumstances, a person *is* justified in using deadly force, although he is not free from fault in creating the situation that results in another person's death. For example, if *D* calls *V*, an acquaintance, "a jerk," to which *V* take such umbrage that he pulls out a gun and menaces *D* with it, *D* is justified in killing *V* (assuming that the other requirements of the defense are met), although *D* was not entirely free from fault in the conflict. *D* was not the aggressor because his mild insult was not an "affirmative unlawful act reasonably calculated to produce an affray foreboding injurious or fatal consequences."

Four features of the concept of "aggression" merit brief attention here. First, a person is an aggressor even if he merely starts a *non*deadly conflict. Second, it is *incorrect* to state that the first person who *uses* force is *always* the aggressor.[22] One who unlawfully brandishes a weapon in a threatening manner, but who does not use it, is an aggressor; the person threatened, who first uses actual force, can still potentially claim self-defense.

Third, a person is *not* an aggressor if he engages in conduct, although provocative, to which he is entitled. For example, if *D*, a police officer, comes upon a fight and threatens to use force against the combatants if they do not desist, his conduct cannot reasonably be interpreted as an aggression.[23] Fourth, the issue of whether a defendant lost the right of self-defense in a conflict is ordinarily a matter for the jury to decide, based on a proper instruction on the meaning of the term "aggressor."[24]

[2] Removing the Status of "Aggressor"

The initial aggressor in a conflict may purge himself of that status and regain the right of self-defense. The issue always is: Who was the aggressor *at the time the defensive — in this context, deadly — force was used*? In this regard, it is important to distinguish between "deadly" (or "felonious") and "nondeadly" aggressors.

---

[20] *Peterson*, 483 F.2d at 1231.

[21] State v. Corchado, 453 A.2d 427, 433 (Conn. 1982) (stating that "[i]t is not difficult to visualize self-defense situations where . . . there is some fault on both sides").

[22] State v. Jones, 665 A.2d 910, 913-14 (Conn. App. Ct. 1995).

[23] An alternative way to reach the same result here is simply to state that the force threatened by the officer does not constitute *unlawful* force. See § 18.02[D][2], *infra*.

[24] Swann v. United States, 648 A.2d 928, 933 (D.C. 1994).

[a] Deadly Aggressor

A "deadly" (or "felonious") aggressor is a person whose acts are reasonably calculated to produce fatal consequences. The only way such a person may regain the right of self-defense is by withdrawing in good faith from the conflict and fairly communicating this fact, expressly or impliedly, to his intended victim.[25]

This rule is strictly applied. For example, suppose that D initiates a deadly attack on V in the street, whereupon V responds with sufficient force that D is now fearful for his own life. If D runs behind a parked car, and V pursues him, D is still not entitled to act in self-defense, unless by actions or words D puts V on actual or reasonable notice that he no longer is a threat to V, i.e., that D's retreat is not simply a temporary strategic act of avoiding V's resistance. In the absence of fair notice to V of the termination of the conflict, D is guilty of murder if he kills V in "self-defense."

[b] Nondeadly Aggressor

Suppose that D wrongfully attempts to slap V. V improperly responds to the threat by pulling out a knife and attempting to kill D. In this conflict, D was the initial aggressor. On the other hand, V's response was disproportional to D's attack, as he wrongfully converted a minor altercation into a deadly one. Thus, V is also an aggressor, indeed, a worse one than D. May D, therefore, now kill V in self-defense?

Case law is split in this regard. Most courts provide that when the victim of a nondeadly assault responds with deadly force, the original aggressor immediately regains his right of self-defense.[26] Thus, in the hypothetical, although D was the initial aggressor — and is subject to prosecution for assault — he may defend himself, including by use of deadly force if required.

Some courts, however, especially in non-recent opinions, do not provide D, the initial nondeadly aggressor, with an automatic right of self-defense.[27] In these jurisdictions, D is not entitled to use deadly force against V unless he avails himself of an obviously safe retreat, if one exists.[28] If no safe place exists, or if D *does* retreat and V pursues him, D may then resort to deadly force. If D does *not* retreat when he could obviously do so, he does *not* lose his status as an aggressor, and is not justified in killing V. However, in such circumstances, D may be convicted in some jurisdictions of manslaughter, rather than of murder.[29]

---

[25] People v. Gleghorn, 193 Cal. App. 3d 196, 200 (Ct. App. 1987); State v. Miller, 868 So. 2d 239, 243 (La. Ct. App. 2004); State v. Morrow, 41 S.W.3d 56, 59 (Mo. Ct. App. 2001).

[26] E.g., Watkins v. State, 555 A.2d 1087, 1088 (Md. Ct. Spec. App. 1989).

[27] See American Law Institute, Comment to § 3.04, at 50-51.

[28] Rollin M. Perkins & Ronald N. Boyce, Criminal Law 1128-29 (3d ed. 1982).

[29] *Id.*

The rationale for reducing the offense to manslaughter in such circumstances is not always explained. Frequently, *D*'s manslaughter verdict can be explained on grounds unrelated to self-defense: *V*'s deadly response to *D*'s nondeadly assault constitutes "adequate provocation," which brings *D*'s conduct within the "sudden heat of passion" doctrine of homicide law.[30] Sometimes, however, a court will treat the nondeadly aggressor as possessing an "imperfect" or "incomplete" right of self-defense, which results in the manslaughter conviction.[31]

[C] Necessity Requirement: The Special Issue of Retreat[32]

[1] Explanation of the Issue

The general rule is that self-defense "is measured against necessity."[33] Thus, as explained earlier,[34] a person under deadly attack should only respond with *non*deadly force, if such lesser force will reasonably prevent the threatened harm. Likewise, one may only use force when a threat has become imminent, a controversial requirement considered later in the Text.[35] At issue in *this* subsection is the question of whether an actor, under attack, must retreat before using deadly force. In other words, if an innocent person is attacked, and if he has only two realistic options — use deadly force or retreat to a place of safety — must he choose the latter option?

[2] Contrasting Approaches

If a person can safely retreat and, therefore, avoid killing the aggressor, deadly force is, objectively speaking, unnecessary. Nonetheless, American jurisdictions are sharply split on the issue of retreat. Perhaps a slim majority of jurisdictions apply the "no retreat" rule,[36] which is that a non-aggressor[37] is per-

---

[30] See § 31.07[B][2], *infra*.

[31] See § 18.03, *infra*.

[32] See generally Richard Maxwell Brown, No Duty to Retreat (1992); Joseph H. Beale, *Retreat from a Murderous Assault*, 16 Harv. L. Rev. 567 (1903); Catherine L. Carpenter, *Of the Enemy Within, the Castle Doctrine, and Self-Defense*, 86 Marq. L. Rev. 653 (2003).

[33] State v. Abbott, 174 A.2d 881, 884 (N.J. 1961).

[34] See § 18.01[C], *supra*.

[35] See § 18.02[D][1], *infra*.

[36] The author has not conducted a state-by-state review of current law. Clearly, however, the trend is away from the "no retreat" rule.

[37] *Aggressors* who wish to defend themselves are required to retreat, even in no-retreat jurisdictions. See § 18.02[B][2], *supra*.

mitted to use deadly force to repel an unlawful deadly attack, even if he is aware of a place to which he can retreat in complete safety.[38]

The rule that a person is not required to retreat is justified on various grounds. First, it is claimed that the law "should not denounce conduct as criminal when it accords with the behavior of reasonable men. . . . [T]he manly thing is to hold one's ground, and hence society should not demand what smacks of cowardice."[39] Second, "Right" should never give way to "Wrong,"[40] yet this is what the retreat doctrine demands of those in the right. Third, the retreat rule may have a counter-utilitarian effect: It might embolden aggressors; and innocent people, if required to retreat, might be killed while fleeing.

Many jurisdictions, with good cause, reject these arguments and provide that an innocent person threatened by deadly force must retreat rather than use deadly force,[41] if he is aware that he can do so in complete safety.[42] Defenders of the retreat rule state that the defense of self-protection — and especially the necessity doctrine — is based on the principle that *all* human life, even that of an aggressor, should be preserved if possible. The retreat requirement properly places protection of human life above the supposedly "manly" response of standing up to aggression.[43]

Moreover, the retreat rule should not increase the risk of harm to innocent persons, because retreat is never demanded when it would imperil the would-be defender.[44] Indeed, in retreat jurisdictions, the duty to retreat is not triggered unless there is a place of *complete* safety to which the non-aggressor can turn.[45]

---

[38] See State v. Anderson, 631 A.2d 1149, 1154, 1155 (Conn. 1993) (stating, but rejecting, what it characterizes as the majority "no retreat" rule); Wayne R. LaFave, Criminal Law 547 (4th ed. 2003) (describing the no-retreat rule as the majority view, but also indicating there is a "strong minority" position).

[39] State v. Abbott, 174 A.2d 881, 884 (N.J. 1961).

[40] See § 17.02[D], *supra*.

[41] Even in retreat jurisdictions, an innocent person is not required to retreat if he can repel the deadly assault with *non*deadly force. State v. Sherman, 18 A. 1040, 1041 (R.I. 1889).

[42] E.g., Sydnor v. State, 776 A.2d 669, 675 (Md. 2001); People v. Riddle, 649 N.W.2d 30, 34 (Mich. 2002).

[43] See Beale, Note 32, *supra*, at 581 (in which the author states that a "really honorable man . . . would perhaps always regret the apparent cowardice of a retreat, but he would regret ten times more . . . the thought that he had the blood of a fellow-being on his hands."). It is worthy of note here, as Professor Susan Estrich has observed, that at least *this* feature of self-defense law (a retreat requirement) is not subject to criticism on the ground that it is biased in favor of the supposedly "male" view of proper conduct. Susan Estrich, *Defending Women*, 88 Mich. L. Rev. 1430, 1431-32 (1990).

[44] State v. Gardner, 104 N.W. 971, 975 (Minn. 1905) ("Self-defense has not, by statute nor by judicial opinion, been distorted, by an unreasonable requirement of the duty to retreat, into self-destruction.").

[45] State v. Anderson, 631 A.2d 1149, 1155 (Conn. 1993) (holding that a judge's "retreat" instruction to the jury was erroneous because it failed to include the word "complete"; "the term 'complete safety' connotes a standard that is more absolute than mere 'safety' ").

Furthermore, the issue is not simply whether a place of such safety exists and that a reasonable person would have been aware of its presence: The duty to retreat only exists if the person under siege is *subjectively* aware of its existence.[46] The practical effect of these conditions is that a person under attack rarely is compelled to retreat, especially when the aggressor is armed with a gun: There is almost never a place of complete safety to which one can turn when confronted by a gun; and even when a place of safety exists, the person is apt to be unaware of it because of the attendant excitement of the situation.[47]

[3] The "Castle" Exception to the Retreat Rule

Even in jurisdictions that ordinarily require a person to retreat to a known place of safety before using deadly force, a universally recognized exception — the so-called "castle doctrine" — exists. This doctrine provides that a non-aggressor is not ordinarily required to retreat from his[48] dwelling,[49] even though he knows he could do so in complete safety, before using deadly force in self-defense.[50]

As one scholar has explained,[51] the castle doctrine is justified on two grounds. Sometimes courts view the rule, although used in self-defense cases, as a form of "defense of habitation,"[52] in that the home-dweller is permitted to kill to protect the sanctity of his home, which has been intruded upon. Second, the home, as castle, is viewed as a person's final sanctuary from external attack. Therefore, "[h]aving retreated as far as possible, the actor should not be compelled to leave the sanctuary."[53]

---

[46] State v. Ash, 651 A.2d 247, 252 (Conn. 1994); Redcross v. State, 708 A.2d 1154, 1158 (Md. Ct. Spec. App. 1998).

[47] State v. Abbott, 174 A.2d 881, 884-86 (N.J. 1961).

[48] Should a social guest also be able to apply the "castle" no-retreat doctrine against an intruding aggressor, although the guest is not in his own dwelling? Case law is split. Compare State v. Brown, 467 S.E.2d 922 (S.C. 1996) (extending the castle doctrine to an invitee), with State v. James, 867 So. 2d 414, 417 (Fla. Dist. Ct. App. 2003) (holding that, given that "[h]uman life is precious," the castle doctrine should not be expanded).

[49] For purposes of the castle doctrine, the "dwelling" typically includes a porch physically attached to the home, *People v. Canales*, 624 N.W.2d 439, 442 (Mich. Ct. App. 2000), but not the lobby or common stairway in a person's apartment building, *People v. Hernandez*, 774 N.E.2d 198, 201-03 (N.Y. 2002). See also State v. Marsh, 593 N.E.2d 35, 38 (Ohio Ct. App. 1990) (*M's* tent at a campground constituted a home, for purposes of the castle doctrine).

Some jurisdictions have also expanded the no-retreat castle doctrine beyond its original rationale (as discussed in the text *infra*) to permit a person to stand his ground in his office. Frazier v. State, 681 So. 2d 824, 825 (Fla. App. 1996).

[50] State v. James, 867 So. 2d 414, 416 (Fla. Dist. Ct. App. 2003).

[51] Carpenter, Note 32, *supra*, at 667.

[52] See generally § 20.03, *infra*.

[53] Carpenter, Note 32, *supra*, at 667; see also Jones v. State, 76 Ala. 8, 16 (1884) ("Why, it may be inquired, should one retreat from his own house, when assailed by . . . a stranger who is . . . upon the premises? Whither shall he flee, and how far, and when may he be permitted to return?").

May a person in his home stand his ground, even if the assailant is a co-dweller, with an otherwise equal right to be there? This is a matter of considerable significance, in view of the fact that "[i]n the great majority of homicides the killer and the victim are relatives or close acquaintances."[54] More to the point, many in-the-home self-defense cases involve a female who needs to defend herself from an abusive domestic partner. As recent courts have increasingly observed, "imposing a duty to retreat from the home may adversely impact victims of domestic violence."[55] Particularly in the case of a battered woman who has attempted to leave her abusive partner — she has tried to retreat *permanently* from the situation — but has been dragged back home, literally or figuratively, it seems especially unjust to deny her the right of self-defense because she did not retreat *again* from her home, when she would have no such legal duty if her assailant was a stranger in the dwelling.[56]

Most retreat jurisdictions, especially in recent years as courts have grown more sensitive to the plight of battered women, have adopted the rule that the assailant's status as a co-dweller is irrelevant, i.e., the innocent person need *not* retreat from the home, even if the aggressor also lives there.[57] The contrary position is that, in the absence of express legislation, it will not conclude that a "legislature intended to sanction the reenactment of the climactic scene from 'High Noon' in the familial kitchens of this state."[58]

[D] Nature of the Threat: "Imminent, Unlawful Deadly Force"

[1] "Imminent"[59]

At common law, a person who wishes to use force in self-defense must reasonably fear that the threatened harm is imminent.[60] In the context of self-

---

[54] State v. Shaw, 441 A.2d 561, 566 (Conn. 1981).

[55] Weiand v. State, 732 So. 2d 1044, 1052 (Fla. 1999).

[56] State v. Gartland, 694 A.2d 564, 570-71 (N.J. 1997) (calling on the state legislature to reconsider its retreat rules in this context).

[57] State v. Glowacki, 630 N.W.2d 392, 400 (Minn. 2001) (characterizing the no-retreat rule among co-dwellers as the majority rule).

[58] State v. Shaw, 441 A.2d at 566. As Professor Carpenter has observed, these jurisdictions may be especially influenced by the defense-of-habitation, rather than home-as-sanctuary self-defense, rationale of the castle doctrine: These courts "choose to emphasize the shared property interest of the deadly aggressor," rather than "the defender's right of protection in the sanctuary." Carpenter, Note 32, *supra*, at 671.

[59] See generally Larry Alexander, *A Unified Excuse of Preemptive Self-Protection*, 74 Notre Dame L. Rev. 1475 (1999); Joshua Dressler, *Battered Women Who Kill Their Sleeping Tormentors: Reflections on Maintaining Respect For Human Life While Killing Moral Monsters*, in Criminal Law: Doctrines of the General Part (A. Simester & S. Shute eds., 2002); V.F. Nourse, *Self-Defense and Subjectivity*, 68 U. Chi. L. Rev. 1235 (2001); Richard A. Rosen, *On Self-Defense, Imminence, and Women Who Kill Their Batterers*, 71 N.C. L. Rev. 371 (1993).

[60] Ha v. State, 892 P.2d 184, 190 (Alaska Ct. App. 1995).

defense, force is said to be "imminent" if it will occur "immediately,"[61] or "at the moment of . . . danger."[62] The danger must be "pressing and urgent."[63] Force is *not* imminent if an aggressor threatens to harm another person at a later time: "'later' and 'imminent' are opposites."[64] Indeed, even if it seems clear that harm at the hands of another is inevitable, use of force is premature until the threat is immediate.[65]

The imminency requirement is controversial. Some scholars advocate its abolition on the ground that "[i]f the concern is to exclude threats of harm that are too remote to require a response, the problem is adequately handled by requiring simply that the response be 'necessary.'"[66] This argument has gathered greater support and attention in recent years because of society's increased awareness of the plight of battered women, who are victims of repeated, seemingly inevitable, but not always imminent, beatings.[67] According to Professor Richard Rosen, because imminency "serves only to further the necessity principle, if there is a conflict between imminence and necessity, necessity must prevail."[68] Therefore, he reasons, if it is truly necessary for a person, such as a battered woman, to use deadly force before a threat is imminent, she should be justified in doing so, just as the law should *disallow* the use of force, even if harm *is* imminent, if it *un*necessary.

There may be good reason to enlarge the defense of self-defense. The Model Penal Code provides an alternative that narrowly expands on the common law.[69] Professor Stephen Morse would take the matter further, however, suggesting that "[i]f death or serious bodily harm in the relatively near future is a virtual certainty *and* the future attack cannot be adequately defended against

---

[61] State v. Norman, 378 S.E.2d 8, 13 (N.C. 1989). According to Professor Holly Maguigan, the terms "imminent" and "immediate" are not precisely interchangeable in the self-defense, particularly battered-woman, context. Holly Maguigan, *Battered Women and Self-Defense: Myths and Misconceptions in Current Reform Proposals*, 140 U. Pa. L. Rev. 379, 414-16 (1991). However, many courts and scholars, even in the latter context, use the terms interchangeably. E.g., State v. Norman, *supra*; State v. Kelly, 478 A.2d 364, 385 n.23 (N.J. 1984); Richard A. Rosen, Note 59, *supra*, at 373 n.4; Robert F. Schopp et al., *Battered Woman Syndrome, Expert Testimony, and the Distinction Between Justification and Excuse*, 1994 U. Ill. L. Rev. 45, 64-65.

[62] Sydnor v. State, 776 A.2d 669, 675 (Md. Ct. App. 2001).

[63] Ha v. State, 892 P.2d at 191 (quoting Perkins & Boyce, Note 28, *supra*, at 1114). Notwithstanding the statement in the text, Professor Nourse's survey of "imminence" cases suggests to her that the "imminence" issue has frequently been "used as a proxy [by courts] for other self-defense factors." Nourse, Note 59, *supra*, at 1255. For discussion of these other factors, see *id.* at 1255-65.

[64] United States v. Haynes, 143 F.3d 1089, 1090 (7th Cir. 1998).

[65] Ha v. State, 892 P.2d at 191.

[66] 2 Paul H. Robinson, Criminal Law Defenses 78 (1984).

[67] The subject of self-defense in the battered-woman context is considered in detail at § 18.05[B], *infra*.

[68] Rosen, Note 59, *supra*, at 380.

[69] See § 18.06[A], *infra*.

when it is imminent *and* if there really are *no* reasonable alternatives, traditional self-defense doctrine ought to justify the pre-emptive strike."[70]

Professor Morse's characterization of the use of deadly force as a "pre-emptive strike" is a valuable one. In some sense, all self-defense cases involve pre-emptive strikes.[71] The real issue is *how prematurely* the perceived aggression may be pre-empted. The difficulty in reforming the law is that when one moves away from an imminency requirement to something less — or to *no* temporal requirement of any kind — the risks of error in predicting the future *and* in predicting whether options less extreme than deadly force may be available are greatly enhanced. Weather forecasters predict the future, but "even funnel clouds sometimes turn around, and human beings sometimes defy predictions."[72] Indeed, because humans have the capacity for free choice — humans are far less predictable than funnel clouds — there is very little "virtual certainty" about human behavior. The benefit of the imminency requirement, or at least of a rule requiring that a threat be fairly close to occurring, is that it reduces the risk of unnecessary use of deadly force.

Current law is premised on an old-fashioned, and perhaps no longer accepted, view: "The life of the good man and the bad stand equal, because how a man has led his life may not affect his claim to continued life."[73] For those who wish to abandon the imminency requirement, the problem is to decide at what point the risk of future harm to a "good person" is sufficiently great to justify the killing of a "bad person" who is not presently threatening another.

[2] "Unlawful Force"

A person may not defend himself against the imposition of *lawful*, i.e., justified, force. For example, a robber may not assert self-defense if he shoots and kills his intended robbery victim when the latter responds with force to the robbery attempt.[74] Likewise, reasonable force applied by a police officer in the performance of his duties is justified. Consequently, a citizen may not use deadly force to resist an officer's proper use of force against him.[75]

---

[70] Stephen J. Morse, *The "New Syndrome Excuse Syndrome"*, 14 Crim. Just. Ethics (Winter/Spring 1995), at 3, 12.

[71] Alexander, Note 59, *supra*, at 1477.

[72] Albert W. Alschuler, *Preventive Pretrial Detention and the Failure of Interest-Balancing Approaches to Due Process*, 85 Mich. L. Rev. 510, 557 (1986).

[73] Sanford H. Kadish, *Respect for Life and Regard for Rights in the Criminal Law*, 64 Cal. L. Rev. 871, 880 (1976).

[74] State v. Amado, 756 A.2d 274, 282-84 (Conn. 2000).

[75] However, in the absence of special legislation restricting his rights, a person may defend himself against excessive (and, therefore, unlawful) police force. See § 18.05[D], *infra*.

Conduct that would constitute a crime or a tort is "unlawful," even if the actor could escape conviction or liability by assertion of an *excuse* defense. For example, if *V*, an insane person or an infant, uses unjustifiable force upon another, this constitutes "unlawful force," notwithstanding *V*'s potential excuse claim.

§ 18.03 DEADLY FORCE: "IMPERFECT" SELF-DEFENSE CLAIMS

In general, the defense of self-defense is a full defense, resulting in exoneration of the person acting in self-protection. Moreover, the traditional common law rule is that if any of the elements of the defense are missing, the defense is wholly unavailable to a defendant,[76] and the defendant may be convicted of murder. Various states, however, now recognize a so-called "imperfect" or "incomplete" defense of self-defense to murder, which results in conviction for the lesser offense of either voluntary or involuntary manslaughter.

There are two versions of imperfect self-defense. First, some courts provide that a *nondeadly* aggressor who is the victim of a *deadly* response must retreat to any known place of complete safety before using deadly force; if he fails to do so, his right of self-defense is considered imperfect.[77]

Second, many states now provide by case law [78] or statute[79] that one who kills another because he *unreasonably* believes that factual circumstances justify the killing, is guilty of manslaughter, rather than murder. That is, *D* is guilty of manslaughter if he kills *V* in either of the following circumstances: (1) *D* unreasonably believes that *V* is about to use deadly force although, in fact, *V* intends no harm or intends only nondeadly harm; or (2) *V* intends to use deadly force, but *D* fails to realize, as a reasonable person, that nondeadly protective force will suffice. In short, "[i]mperfect self-defense consists of the same elements [as "perfect" self-defense], except that the defendant need not have had an *objectively reasonable* belief that he was in . . . imminent danger of death or serious bodily harm . . . , requiring the use of deadly force."[80]

It is unfortunate to characterize cases in this realm as involving "imperfect" self-defense. It is a contradiction in terms to say that a person has a "right" (or "privilege") to use deadly force in self-defense, and yet convict and punish him

---

[76] Ross v. State, 211 N.W.2d 827, 830 (Wis. 1973) (quoting Moreland, The Law of Homicide 91 (1952)) (stating, but rejecting, the historical all-or-nothing rule).

[77] E.g., People v. Amos, 414 N.W.2d 147, 150 (Mich. Ct. App. 1987); State v. McAvoy, 417 S.E.2d 489, 497 (N.C. 1992). See § 18.02[B][2][b], *supra*.

[78] E.g., In re Christian S., 872 P.2d 574, 575 (Cal. 1994); Swann v. United States, 648 A.2d 928, 930-31 (D.C. 1994) (voluntary manslaughter); State v. Peterson, 857 A.2d 1132, 1147-48 (Md. Ct. Spec. App. 2004).

[79] E.g., Kan. Stat. Ann § 21-3403(b) (2005).

[80] State v. Peterson, 857 A.2d at 1148.

for enforcing this "right." Instead, the claim either should be seen as a failure-of-proof defense,[81] on the ground that the defendant's actions demonstrate he lacked a murderous *mens rea* (at common law, malice aforethought),[82] or as a partial *excuse* for the killing, on the ground that the actor's culpability is mitigated by his honest, albeit mistaken, belief.[83]

§ 18.04 DEADLY FORCE IN SELF-PROTECTION: RATIONALE FOR THE DEFENSE[84]

[A] Self-Defense as an Excuse

Although some dispute about the matter exists, use of deadly force in self-defense apparently constituted an excuse, rather than a justification, in early English legal history. It is not difficult to appreciate why the use of deadly force in such circumstances is, at least, excusable.

Each of the three non-utilitarian moral theories of excuse outlined elsewhere[85] can explain self-defense as an excuse. First, under the causation theory of excuses, an innocent person is not responsible for the condition that caused him to commit the crime: But for the aggressor's actions, the defendant would not have taken a life. Therefore, the innocent person is not to blame for the killing. Second, a character theorist would point out that it is the aggressor, and not the innocent person acting in self-defense, whose actions manifest a bad moral character.

Third, the choice theory would support an excuse for self-defense, as the innocent actor finds himself figuratively, if not literally, with his back to the wall, without a fair opportunity to choose *not* to kill. As Blackstone suggested, the common law "respects the passions of the human mind."[86] Killing in self-

---

[81] See § 16.02, *supra*.

[82] In re Christian S., 872 P.2d at 576.

[83] See State v. Abeyta, 901 P.2d 164, 171 (N.M. 1995), overruled on other grounds, State v. Campos, 921 P.2d 1266 (N.M. 1996) (recognizing the inappropriateness of the terminology, and treating the matter as a non-justificatory form of mitigation).

[84] See generally George P. Fletcher, A Crime of Self-Defense: Bernhard Goetz and the Law on Trial (1988); Suzanne Uniacke, Permissible Killing: The Self-Defence Justification of Homicide (1994); Alexander, Note 59, *supra*; A.J. Ashworth, *Self-Defence and the Right to Life*, 34 Camb. L.J. 282 (1975); Russell Christopher, *Self-Defense and Objectivity: A Reply to Judith Jarvis Thomson*, 1 Buff. Crim. L. Rev. 537 (1998); Claire Oakes Finkelstein, *On the Obligation of the State to Extend a Right of Self-Defense to Its Citizens*, 147 U. Pa. L. Rev. 1361 (1999); George P. Fletcher, *Punishment and Self-Defense*, 8 Law & Phil. 201 (1989); George P. Fletcher, *Proportionality and the Psychotic Aggressor: A Vignette in Comparative Criminal Theory*, 8 Isr. L. Rev. 367 (1973); Sanford H. Kadish, Note 73, *supra*; Whitley Kaufman, *Is There a "Right" of Self-Defense?*, 23 Crim. Just. Ethics, Winter/Spring 2004, at 20; Judith Jarvis Thompson, *Self-Defense*, 20 Phil. & Pub. Aff. 283 (1991).

[85] See § 17.03, *supra*.

[86] 3 William Blackstone, Commentaries on the Laws of England *3 (1768).

defense, therefore, may be "excusable from the great universal principle of self-preservation, which prompts every man to save his own life preferably to that of another."[87] The act of killing another person to save one's own life is nearly instinctual; it represents the "the primary law of nature."[88]

The latter argument can also explain self-defense as an excuse according to specific deterrence principles. One who is threatened with immediate death is not deterrable by the threat of criminal sanction. Therefore, his punishment is inefficacious.

[B] Self-Defense as a Justification

[1] Utilitarian Explanations

Killing in self-defense may be socially desirable. A utilitarian may reason that if someone must die in a deadly conflict it is better that the aggressor, whose anti-social nature is manifested by his conduct, be the victim.[89] If it were otherwise, a dangerous person would remain alive and a threat to others, unless and until he is taken into custody.

This argument might somewhat overstate the case. Many self-defense homicidal conflicts occur between mutually intoxicated actors, or start with fisticuffs and escalate into deadly affairs. In many self-defense circumstances, therefore, it is hard to argue convincingly that the aggressor is the "bad" or dangerous person, and the defender is the "good" or more socially desirable individual. Matters are often not so clear-cut.

Another utilitarian claim is that rules of self-defense will function over time to preserve life, because the permission to kill provided to innocent people will operate as a sanction against unlawful aggression.[90] That is, at least in a fair number of cases, the aggressor will be deterred by the fear that his intended victim will resist the attack.

The difficulty with this argument is the basis for *excusing* deadly force in self-defense: It is doubtful that *any* rule of self-defense can successfully affect the actions of parties involved in deadly confrontations. Self-preservation is the "primary law of nature." Therefore, what will deter an aggressor from attacking another person is his expectation that the person being assailed will follow the law of nature, irrespective of the law of society.

---

[87] 4 William Blackstone, Commentaries on the Laws of England *186 (1769).

[88] 3 Blackstone, Note 86, *supra*, at *4.

[89] See Kadish, Note 73, *supra*, at 882.

[90] Herbert Wechsler & Jerome Michael, *A Rationale of the Law of Homicide: I*, 37 Colum. L. Rev. 701, 737 (1937).

[2] Non-Utilitarian Explanations

Various moral theories justify the use of deadly force in self-defense. First, it is frequently said that a defensive killing is justifiable because the aggressor, by his culpable act of threatening an innocent person's life, forfeits his right to life.[91] As a result, the aggressor's death constitutes no cognizable social harm.[92]

Second, "[t]he idea of physical security as one of the 'natural rights' of mankind has a long history."[93] Consequently, when an aggressor "breaches an implicit contract among autonomous agents . . . to respect the living space of all others,"[94] he creates a "state of war" between himself and the person wrongfully threatened,[95] which justifies the innocent person vindicating his autonomy by taking the aggressor's life.[96]

A third rationale of self-defense is that the right of an innocent person to life is morally superior to an aggressor's right to life. Therefore, by balancing moral interests, the safety of the innocent person represents the greater moral good; the aggressor's death is the lesser social evil.[97] Ultimately, however, this argument returns to the principle of forfeiture: Ordinarily, human beings are deserving of equal protection, so this theory only makes sense if the aggressor's interest in life is, at least partially, forfeited by his culpable conduct.

Fourth, self-defense is sometimes justified as a form of private punishment of a wrongdoer, in which the individual being threatened "acts in the place of the state in inflicting on wrongdoers their just deserts."[98] Self-defense as punishment "avoid[s] the injustice of suffering unsanctioned crime."[99]

---

[91] E.g., Ashworth, Note 84, *supra*, at 283; Kadish, Note 73, *supra*, at 883.

[92] For many observers, this is a morally troubling argument. See § 17.02[C], *supra*.

[93] Ashworth, Note 84, *supra*, at 282.

[94] Fletcher, *Proportionality and the Psychotic Aggressor*, Note 84, *supra*, at 380.

[95] John Locke, Second Treatise of Civil Government: An Essay Concerning the True Original, Extent, and End of Civil Government 23 (DeKoster ed., 1978).

[96] Critics of this argument claim that the "state of war" rationale "pushes us toward morally unacceptable results," Kaufman, Note 84, *supra*, at 29, in part because it leads to an absolutist position that can justify the use of deadly force in circumstances that do not require it. See § 17.02[D], *supra*.

[97] Of course, a *utilitarian* balancing of social interests is also possible, as is discussed in subsection [1], *supra*.

[98] Fletcher, A Crime of Self-Defense, Note 84, *supra*, at 27-28.

[99] Fletcher, *Punishment and Self-Defense*, Note 84, *supra*, at 215. This is a troubling explanation to some people because it authorizes a private party to serve as judge, jury, and executioner of one whose guilt, level of culpability, and appropriate sentence has not been determined by due process of law.

§ 18.05 SELF-DEFENSE: SPECIAL ISSUES

[A] The Reasonable-Belief Standard:[100] More Reflections About the "Reasonable Person"[101]

[1] The Issue

The law of self-defense represents a compromise. The right of self-defense is not based on objective reality (whether the person about to be killed represents a real threat to the life of the actor), but neither is it based solely on the actor's subjective impressions: A person may only defend himself if he subjectively believes that deadly force is required *and* a reasonable person would also believe that it is appropriate under the circumstances. The crux of the issue, at least as courts see the matter, is: Who is the "reasonable person" to whom the defendant is compared? Or, put slightly differently, to what extent should courts permit juries, as factfinders, to incorporate the defendant's own characteristics or life experiences in the "reasonable person" standard?[102]

Consider in this regard two controversial self-defense cases. In *People v. Goetz*,[103] *G* shot and wounded four African-American youths on a New York City subway after one or two of them approached him and requested five dollars. *G*, a prior mugging victim, claimed that he shot the youths because he believed that

---

[100] See generally §§ 17.04, 18.01[E], *supra*.

[101] See generally Cynthia Lee, Murder and the Reasonable Man: Passion and Fear in the Criminal Courtroom (2003); Jody D. Armour, *Race Ipsa Loquitur: Of Reasonable Racists, Intelligent Bayesians, and Involuntary Negrophobes*, 46 Stan. L. Rev. 781 (1994); Naomi R. Cahn, *The Looseness of Legal Language: The Reasonable Woman Standard in Theory and in Practice*, 77 Cornell L. Rev. 1398 (1992); Mark Kelman, *Reasonable Evidence of Reasonableness*, 17 Critical Inquiry 798 (1991); V.F. Nourse, *A Comment on Switching, Inequality, and the Idea of the Reasonable Person*, 2 Ohio St. J. Crim. L. 361 (2004); Nourse, Note 59, *supra*; Kenneth W. Simons, *Self-Defense, Mens Rea, and Bernhard Goetz*, 89 Colum. L. Rev. 1179 (1989); Richard Singer, *The Resurgence of Mens Rea: II — Honest But Unreasonable Mistake of Fact in Self Defense*, 28 B.C. L. Rev. 459 (1987). See also §§ 10.04[D][2][d], *supra* ["initial observations" on the topic] and 31.07[B][2][ii], *infra* [the issue in regard to the provocation doctrine in manslaughter cases], and the cites therein.

[102] Some scholars believe that this is a false issue, or at least one that needlessly has "led to heated debates in which otherwise polite scholars have been left trading insults." Nourse, Note 59, *supra*, at 1294. Professor Nourse has raised the "near-heretical question: Would we really lose so much if we were to eliminate the reasonable person" from the law? Nourse, Note 101, *supra*, at 371. She contends that much of the debate — for example, whether a "reasonable woman," "reasonable man," or "reasonable person" standard should be used in particular cases "is a bit of a diversion," *id.*, and that the law ought to "eliminate the implied metaphor of personhood." *Id.* at 373. Nourse argues that the real issue is one of context: "[I]n one situation, the defendant with a particular relation to a victim should be treated differently from a different defendant with a different relation." *Id.* at 373-74. For a fuller discussion of Professor Nourse's position, see her two articles cited here.

[103] 497 N.E.2d 41 (N.Y. 1986).

their request for money was a precursor to an armed robbery. At his trial,[104] *G* claimed that a reasonable person would have believed, as he did, that deadly force was necessary to repel impending use of deadly force by the youths. Among the questions that one may pose about the "reasonable person" in this case are: (1) Like *G*, is the "reasonable person" a prior mugging victim?; (2) Is the "reasonable person" an experienced New York subway user?; and (3) To what extent would a "reasonable person" consider the race, age, sex, body language, and/or wearing apparel of the victims in determining whether deadly force was necessary?

In *State v. Wanrow*,[105] *W*, a 5"4' woman with a broken leg and using crutches, killed *V*, a large and visibly intoxicated man, in her home. Although *V* did not menace *W* at the moment of the shooting, *W* suspected *V* of a prior attempted sexual molestation of her son. Furthermore, a neighbor girl had identified *V* as the man who had molested her, and *W* had previously been told that *V* was a former inmate of a mental institution. At trial, the judge instructed the jury on self-defense, but used the male pronoun "he" in describing the circumstances under which deadly force could properly be used. Among the questions that one may pose in this case are: (1) Is the "reasonable person" male or female?; (2) Is (s)he diminutive and on crutches?; and (3) What knowledge or beliefs would (s)he possess regarding *V*'s background?

These cases pose difficult problems for the law. For example, the traditional description of the "reasonable person" is in male — "reasonable *man*" — terms.[106] Yet, such an approach to self-defense is unfair when the defender is a small woman and the aggressor is a large man, as in *Wanrow*. The effect of a "reasonable man" instruction, if taken literally by a jury, is that a woman in *W*'s situation would be held to the standard of a person whose size, weight, strength, and experience in combat exceeds her own. A strong male, for example, might be able to repel an attack with nondeadly force under circumstances in which a woman might be unable to protect herself except by use of a deadly weapon.[107] Therefore, at first (and, perhaps, later) glance, it seems fairer to test a woman's conduct by the standards of a "reasonable woman." On the other hand, some women are taller, stronger, and better able to defend themselves than some men. Is it fair to hold a diminutive and weak man who lacks self-defense skills

---

[104] *G* originally claimed that his indictment was invalid because the prosecutor instructed the grand jurors to measure the accused's actions against an objective standard. According to *G*, the question under New York law was simply whether he, *G*, subjectively believed that he acted reasonably. The New York Court of Appeals rejected this argument.

[105] 559 P.2d 548 (Wash. 1977).

[106] In light of the subordinate position of women in early Anglo-American society, it is unrealistic to assume that the common law used the gender-specific term "man" in a gender-neutral sense.

[107] State v. Wanrow, 559 P.2d at 558 (footnote omitted) ("In our society women suffer from a conspicuous lack of access to training in and the means of developing those skills necessary to effectively repel a male assailant without resorting to the use of deadly weapons.").

to the standard of a "reasonable man," if the latter standard assumes that males are tall, strong, and experienced in combat?

A few courts permit total subjectivization of the "reasonable person." According to one court, the "accused's actions are to be viewed from the standpoint of a person whose mental and physical characteristics are like the accused's and who sees what the accused sees and knows what the accused knows."[108] Another court has stated that since "guilt is personal, . . . the conduct of an individual is to be measured by that individual's equipment mentally and physically. He may act in self-defense, not only when a reasonable person would so act, but when one with the particular qualities that the individual himself has would so do."[109] Under such a standard, a timid, diminutive male would be judged by the standard of a reasonable timid, diminutive male; and a "strong, courageous and capable female" would be judged by the latter standard.[110]

Subjectivization of the standard sometimes seems morally attractive. For example, in *State v. Hampton*,[111] the defendant used deadly force because, in a confrontation, he was afraid he was going to die. Because he was going to be held to the standard of a reasonable person, he sought to introduce evidence of his "psycho-social history," including the fact that as a six-year-old he had witnessed his mother shoot another person on the way to a bar, later observed her kill the father of three of her children, and was once strung up by his neck by his godfather. Essentially, his argument was that one who had experienced as much trauma and violence as he in growing up could not behave in the same manner as the ordinary "reasonable person." Therefore, he should be measured by a standard of one who has lived *his* life.

But, where does such a subjective standard leave the law? Consider *State v. Simon*:[112] S, an elderly man, fired a weapon at V, a young Asian-American male, although V was not acting aggressively. According to trial testimony, S was a "psychological invalid" who feared persons of Asian ancestry, and who believed that by virtue of V's racial heritage the young man was an expert in martial arts. If a judge were to instruct the jury to incorporate S's beliefs and mental characteristics into the "reasonable person," it would be inviting the jury to measure him by the standard of a "reasonable psychological invalid who fears Asian-Americans and believes that they are all experts in the martial arts." Is this not equivalent to a standard of the "reasonable unreasonable person," "reasonable racist," or "reasonable mentally ill person"?

---

[108] State v. Leidholm, 334 N.W.2d 811, 818 (N.D. 1983).

[109] State v. Thomas, 468 N.E.2d 763, 765 (Ohio Ct. App. 1983) (quoting Nelson v. State, 181 N.E. 448 (Ohio. Ct. App. 1932)).

[110] *Leidholm*, 334 N.W.2d at 818; see also State v. Wheelock, 609 A.2d 972, 976 (Vt. 1992) ("Our law does not hold a nervous coward and fearless bully to an identical reasonable person standard.").

[111] 558 N.W.2d 884 (Wis. Ct. App. 1996).

[112] 646 P.2d 1119 (Kan. 1982).

It is one thing to take into consideration an actor's physical characteristics in determining how a reasonable person would behave; it is quite another to incorporate the actor's mental or emotional characteristics — perhaps the result of a terrible childhood or some other factor beyond his control — into the "reasonable person." The risk is that the normative message of the criminal law will be lost if the reasonableness of an actor's conduct — if, indeed, "reasonableness" is a proper term to use in this context — is measured by the standard of one who may be unreasonable by nature. At some point, a defendant's real claim is not that he is acting *justifiably*, but rather that he should be *excused* because he has done the best he can given his unusual mental or emotional characteristics.

[2] The Law

The law is undergoing significant but uneven change in this area. In general, the law provides that, in determining whether the defendant's self-protective acts were reasonable, the factfinder should hold the accused to the standard of the "reasonable person in the actor's situation." This language derives from the Model Penal Code definitions of the terms "recklessness" and "negligence."[113] As the Commentary to the Code concedes, the word "situation" in this context is ambiguous — inevitably and designedly so.[114]

Most courts have rejected the wholesale subjectivization of the "reasonable person" standard.[115] Nonetheless, in the self-defense context, in determining what a reasonable person in the actor's situation or circumstances would believe or do — that is, in comparing the defendant's conduct and beliefs to that of the "reasonable person" — modern juries typically *are* entitled to consider

> more than the physical movements of the potential assailant. . . . [The] terms ["situation" and "circumstances"] include any relevant knowledge the defendant had about that person [the supposed aggressor]. They also necessarily bring in the physical attributes of all persons involved, including the defendant. Furthermore, the defendant's circumstances encompass any prior experiences he had which could provide a reasonable basis for a belief that another person's intentions were to [harm] . . . him or that the use of deadly force was necessary under the circumstances.[116]

---

[113] See § 10.07[B][3], *supra*.

[114] American Law Institute, Comment to § 2.02, at 242; ("[t]here is an inevitable ambiguity in 'situation'"); *id.*, Comment to § 210.3, at 62 ("[t]he word 'situation' is designedly ambiguous").

[115] E.g., People v. Romero, 69 Cal. App. 4th 846, 848 (1999) (holding that the trial court was correct in refusing to permit expert testimony offered by the defense on "the role of honor, paternalism, and street fighters in the Hispanic culture," because "we are not prepared to sanction a 'reasonable street fighter standard'").

[116] People v. Goetz, 497 N.E.2d 41, 52 (N.Y. 1986).

Thus, arguably, *G*'s prior mugging experience (in *Goetz*) was relevant in determining the reasonableness of his belief that he was about to be attacked again,[117] and *W* was properly measured by a standard of a woman of her height, weight, strength, and physical handicap (in *Wanrow*). And, applying this standard, as well, a battered woman who uses deadly force against her abusive partner should be held to a standard of a reasonable woman who has experienced the same abuse as has the battered woman.

But, this standard still leaves many issues open. For example, would a reasonable person in *W*'s situation consider *V* a child molester and former resident of a mental hospital, although *W* had no first-hand knowledge of these "facts"? The answer should be that a reasonable person would only consider allegations that are based on reliable information. If this is so, to what extent is it appropriate for the reasonable person in *G*'s shoes to take into consideration the race, age, sex, clothing, and body language of the youths in the subway, in order to measure *their* dangerousness? This remains a difficult and sensitive issue,[118] one that the "designedly ambiguous" standard of the "reasonable person in the actor's situation" apparently leaves to jurors to resolve for themselves.

---

[117] If *G*'s prior mugging was in no way similar to the current situation — if he was mugged in quite different circumstances — it would seem that his prior mugging experience should *not* be considered by the jury.

[118] On this subject, see especially the articles by Armour and Kelman, cited in Note 101, *supra*. These articles identify the arguments that a person in *G*'s situation might make at trial. First, *G* could claim that he is a "reasonable racist." That is, he is a "product of a particularly racist subculture that led him to overestimate the risk of violence by young black males." Kelman, *supra*, at 804. This argument must fail. Even if *G* is empirically correct — that his subculture *is* racist — it would defeat the normative message of the criminal law, and would conflict with the fact that self-defense is a justification defense, to treat the "reasonable person" as a racist.

Alternatively, *G* might claim "that his racial fears rest on a valid factual basis, rather than on a racial basis." Armour, *supra*, at 809. That is, it may be that people fitting the victims' description — black young males, dressed in a specific manner, acting in concert — represent a disproportionate threat to New York subway passengers. When reasonable people have to make split-second decisions, *G* might claim, they take race, gender, age, wearing apparel, and body language into account. Professor Armour contends, however, that a defendant should not be allowed overtly to raise race as a factor, in part because it enhances the risk of racial bias in the jury box.

[B] "Battered Woman Syndrome"[119]

[1] Issue Overview

Men are more prone to violence than women are.[120] Although the number of women incarcerated has risen in recent years,[121] it is still true that "[w]omen rarely kill" and, to the extent that they do, "[f]emale homicide is so different from male homicide that women and men may be said to live in two different cultures, each with its own 'subculture of violence.'"[122]

When women *do* kill, their target frequently is an abusive husband or domestic partner.[123] In many of these cases, women have sought exculpation by asserting the defense of self-defense, and have frequently attempted to introduce evidence of "battered woman syndrome."

Battered women cases, and the legal issues that arise in the prosecutions, may be divided into three categories. First, there are "confrontational" homicides, i.e., cases in which the battered woman kills her partner during a bat-

---

[119] See generally Charles Ewing, Battered Women Who Kill: Psychological Self-Defense as Legal Justification (1987); Cynthia Gillespie, Justifiable Homicide: Battered Women, Self-Defense, and the Law (1989); Lee, Note 101, *supra*; Lenore E. Walker, The Battered Woman Syndrome (1984); Elaine Chiu, *Confronting the Agency in Battered Mothers*, 74 S. Cal. L. Rev. 1223 (2001); Anne M. Coughlin, *Excusing Women*, 82 Cal. L. Rev. 1 (1994); Gregory A. Diamond, Note, *To Have Not to Hold: Can "Resistance Against Kidnapping" Justify Lethal Self-Defense Against Incapacitated Batterers?*, 102 Colum. L. Rev. 729 (2002); Dressler, Note 59, *supra*; David L. Faigman & Amy J. Wright, *The Battered Woman Syndrome in the Age of Science*, 39 Ariz. L. Rev. 67 (1997); David L. Faigman, Note, *The Battered Woman Syndrome and Self-Defense: A Legal and Empirical Dissent*, 72 Va. L. Rev. 619 (1986); Kimberly Kessler Ferzan, *Defending Imminence: From Battered Women to Iraq*, 46 Ariz. L. Rev. 213 (2004); Kit Kinports, *Defending Battered Women's Self-Defense Claims*, 67 Or. L. Rev. 393 (1988); Maguigan, Note 61, *supra*; Nourse, Note 59, *supra*; Rosen, Note 59, *supra*; Schopp et al., Note 61, *supra*; Stephen J. Schulhofer, *The Feminist Challenge in Criminal Law*, 143 U. Pa. L. Rev. 2151 (1995).

[120] See James Q. Wilson & Richard J. Herrnstein, Crime & Human Nature 117 (1985); Federal Bureau of Investigation, U.S. Dep't of Justice, Sourcebook of Criminal Justice Statistics — 2002 354 (2003) (Sourcebook) (reporting that males represent 87.5% of arrestees for murder and non-negligent manslaughter in 1997).

[121] Sourcebook, Note 120, *supra*, at 503 (reporting that 44,065 women were incarcerated in prisons or jails in the United States in 1990; that figure has risen to 97,491 in 2002).

[122] Laurie J. Taylor, Comment, *Provoked Reason in Men and Women: Heat-of-Passion Manslaughter and Imperfect Self-Defense*, 33 UCLA L. Rev. 1679, 1680, 1681 (1986) (footnotes omitted); see also Wilson & Herrnstein, Note 120, supra, at 114 ("The male and female style of offending was so different even within crime categories that [criminologists] concluded 'that female criminality is a separate and distinct order of criminal behavior.'").

[123] Although societal attention understandably has focused on the plight of women who are battered by their male partners, some men are victims of recurrent abuse from their female partners. Also, gay men and lesbians are reportedly "as likely [as heterosexual couples], proportionally, to encounter violence in their intimate relationships." Denise Bricker, Note, *Fatal Defense: An Analysis of Battered Woman's Syndrome Expert Testimony for Gay Men and Lesbians Who Kill Abusive Partners*, 58 Brook. L. Rev. 1379, 1383-84 (1993).

tering incident.[124] Most prosecutions fall into this category.[125] The primary issue in these cases is whether the defendant is entitled to introduce history-of-abuse evidence and offer expert battered woman syndrome testimony.

Second, in a relatively few circumstances, the battered woman has killed her abuser while he was asleep[126] or during a significant lull in the violence (a "nonconfrontational" homicide).[127] Two inter-related legal issues commonly arise in these cases. First, in view of the imminent threat requirement,[128] is the defendant entitled to a jury instruction on self-defense in the absence of proof of some aggressive act by the decedent at the time of the killing? Second, in order to cure any problem raised by the first question, may the defendant introduce battered woman syndrome evidence in order to show that she subjectively and reasonably believed that her actions were necessary to combat an imminent deadly assault, notwithstanding the lack of any actual immediate threat?

Finally, in a very few cases, the battered woman has hired[129] or importuned[130] a third party to kill her husband, and then pled self-defense at trial. In these cases, the defendant seeks to introduce evidence of battered woman syndrome in order to show that her response — soliciting a homicide — was reasonable under the circumstances.

Although the primary issues in battered woman cases are those just mentioned, another issue lurks behind the scenes, particularly in the minds of the jurors: In view of his horrific conduct, is the decedent-abuser's death justifiable, even if a traditional self-defense claim is not viable?

---

[124] E.g., State v. Hundley, 693 P.2d 475 (Kan. 1985) (during a long battering incident, the decedent hit, choked, raped, and threatened to kill *H*; *H* picked up a gun and demanded that the decedent leave; decedent laughed and said, "You are dead, bitch, now," and reached for a beer bottle; *H* closed her eyes and fired the gun, killing the decedent).

[125] In one study of appellate court decisions, 75% of the prosecutions involved confrontational homicides. Maguigan, Note 61, *supra*, at 394-97.

[126] E.g., State v. Norman, 378 S.E.2d 8 (N.C. 1989); State v. Leidholm, 334 N.W.2d 811 (N.D. 1987).

[127] E.g., State v. Gallegos, 719 P.2d 1268 (N.M. Ct. App. 1986) (abuser shot while lying in bed); State v. Peterson, 857 A.2d 1132 (Md. Ct. Spec. App. 2004) (abuser shot while watching television).

[128] See § 18.02[D][1]. As discussed there, some advocates for battered women recommend abolition of the imminency rule. See also Chester v. State, 471 S.E.2d 836, 841 (Sears, J., concurring) ("It is incomprehensible to me to permit such severely battered individuals existing in such a deeply troubled state of mind to justifiably use defensive force only when the use or threat of unlawful force against them is in fact 'imminent.'").

[129] E.g., People v. Yaklich, 833 P.2d 758 (Colo. Ct. App. 1991); State v. Leaphart, 673 S.W.2d 870 (Tenn. Crim. App. 1983).

[130] People v. Erickson, 57 Cal. App. 4th 1391 (App. Ct. 1997) (abused woman solicited son to kill her sleeping husband).

[2] Jury Instructions on Self-Defense

A defendant is entitled to an instruction on a defense if he presents some credible evidence in support of the claim. A trial court must give an instruction on a defense, therefore, if it determines that a jury *could* reasonably be persuaded to accept the defense on the basis of the evidence introduced, i.e., that there is evidence to support each element of the defense claim.

In confrontational battered woman cases, an instruction on self-defense is almost always given, as it should be. In these cases, by the very nature of the confrontation, there are sufficient grounds to support a jury instruction,[131] although the jury as factfinder may decide, of course, that one (or more) of the elements of the defense was not satisfactorily proven.

Court are divided on whether self-defense may be claimed if there is no evidence of threatening conduct by the abuser at the time of the homicide, i.e., in nonconfrontational circumstances, but the strong majority position is that a self-defense instruction is unjustified in such cases.[132] And, courts have unanimously refused to permit instructions in third-party hired-killer cases.[133]

[3] Evidentiary Issues

[a] Prior Abuse by the Decedent

Courts do not ordinarily allow a defendant to put the victim of a homicide on trial, because it improperly focuses the jury's attention on the decedent's character, rather than on the events occurring at the time of the homicide. Nonetheless, it is now routine for a court to permit a battered woman to introduce evidence of the decedent's prior abusive treatment of her, in support of her claim of self-defense.[134]

The courts' willingness to allow such evidence makes sense, particularly in those cases in which the decedent's conduct at the time of the homicide was not overtly threatening. A decedent's prior aggressive and violent behavior is rele-

---

[131] For example, consider the facts in *State v. Hundley*, 693 P.2d 475 (Kan. 1985), set out in Note 124, *supra*. A prior victim of domestic violence, in *H*'s shoes, could reasonably have believed that her life was in imminent jeopardy, based on the aggressor's words ("You are dead, bitch, *now*") and actions (reaching for a beer bottle, which could serve as a weapon).

[132] The majority no-instruction position is seen in *State v. Stewart*, 763 P.2d 572 (Kan. 1988), and *State v. Norman*, 378 S.E.2d 8 (N.C. 1989); contra, State v. Leidholm, 334 N.W.2d 811 (N.D. 1982) (permitting a jury instruction on self-defense in non-confrontational circumstances); see also State v. Peterson, 857 A.2d 1132 (Md. Ct. Spec. App. 2004) (permitting an instruction for *imperfect* self-defense).

[133] See People v. Yaklich, 833 P.2d at 762 (discussing the hired-assassin cases to date).

[134] Maguigan, Note 61, *supra*, at 423-24.

vant to show that the actor reasonably feared deadly force at the decedent's hands.[135] A reasonable person in the defendant's shoes would surely take into consideration a decedent's prior violence in determining whether he represents a threat on the present occasion.[136]

[b] Expert Testimony Regarding Battered Woman Syndrome

According to Dr. Lenore Walker,[137] battering relationships go through cycles commencing with comparatively minor incidents of abuse, escalating to the "acute battering incident," followed by a period of time when the abuser expresses contrition and love for the partner, after which the abuse resumes. Dr. Walker also reports that battered women have low self-esteem and suffer from "learned helplessness" as the result of their inability to prevent the abuse. As a consequence of the latter condition, a battered woman is apt to remain in her relationship rather than seek to escape.

In the typical homicide prosecution of a battered woman, defense counsel is apt to seek to introduce expert testimony regarding battered woman syndrome, including testimony that the defendant suffers from the condition and acted pursuant to it. The purpose of such evidence is to enhance the defendant's credibility, explain to jurors why the defendant *subjectively* believed that the decedent was about to kill her (when he may have been asleep or otherwise passive); and to demonstrate that this belief was *objectively* reasonable to a person suffering from the syndrome. Evidence of learned helplessness is especially useful in explaining to jurors why the defendant did not leave the abusive relationship. In the absence of such an explanation, especially in a nonconfrontational homicide, jurors may disbelieve the defendant's claim of prior abuse ("if she really was abused, why didn't she leave?"), blame the woman for her plight, and/or conclude that deadly force was unnecessary given the option of escape.

In most states expert testimony of any sort is inadmissible in a criminal trial unless three conditions are satisfied: (1) the subject matter is beyond the understanding of the average lay-person; (2) the witness has sufficient skill, knowledge, or experience in the field that his testimony will aid the jury in its

---

[135] See People v. Hawkins, 696 N.E.2d 16, 19-20 (Ill. Ct. App. 1998); Ha v. State, 892 P.2d 184, 191 (Alaska Ct. App. 1995) (evidence that the decedent was a violent man who nursed grudges was relevant in a self-defense case).

[136] For example, suppose V, drunk, lurches into the kitchen (where D, his abused wife, is standing) holding an empty beer bottle at the neck, yelling, "Hey, bitch," and raising the bottle above his head. Without evidence of prior abuse, the jury might interpret V's conduct as nothing more than a crude demand that his wife get him another bottle of beer. To previously-abused D, however, his actions might reasonably suggest an impending act of violence. The jury needs to know of the prior abuse in order to appreciate why V's ambiguous conduct could reasonably be interpreted as a threat.

[137] See Walker, Note 119, *supra*, at 75-85; Lenore Walker, Battered Woman 32-51 (1979).

search for the truth; and (3) the state of the pertinent art or scientific knowledge permits a reasonable opinion to be asserted by an expert.[138]

The third prong can be a stumbling block when novel scientific evidence is involved. A rule in many states is that scientific evidence is inadmissible unless the principle upon which it is based is "sufficiently established to have gained general acceptance in the particular field in which it belongs."[139] Initially, many courts doubted that battered woman syndrome met this standard.[140] Today, however, despite some dissenting scholarly opinion,[141] "battered woman's syndrome has . . . gained general acceptance in the scientific community. . . . Equally compelling is the clear trend across the United States towards admissibility of expert testimony on battered woman's syndrome"[142] in appropriate self-defense cases.[143]

Although battered woman syndrome evidence is admissible in most battered woman self-defense cases, states vary as to the purposes for which it may be introduced.[144] Some courts permit evidence of the syndrome, but do not permit the expert to testify as to whether the defendant suffers from the syndrome or regarding what its effect may have been on the defendant at the time of the homicide.[145] Other courts allow the expert to state an opinion as to whether the defendant *subjectively* believed that deadly force was necessary under the circumstances, but will not allow the evidence to be used to show that her conduct was *objectively* reasonable under the circumstances.[146] Still other courts permit syndrome evidence to assist the jury in determining whether the defendant's perceptions were objectively reasonable.[147]

---

[138] Dyas v. United States, 376 A.2d 827, 832 (D.C. 1977).

[139] Frye v. United States, 293 F. 1013, 1014 (D.C. Cir. 1923). Although *Frye* is a federal court opinion, most states adopted this or a similar standard. However, the Supreme Court has announced a new, more liberal, test for use in federal courts: Evidence may be admitted if the expert's testimony rests on a reliable scientific foundation, even if the theory or technique in question lacks general acceptance. Daubert v. Merrell Dow Pharmaceuticals, Inc., 509 U.S. 579 (1993).

[140] E.g., Ibn-Tamas v. United States, 455 A.2d 893, 894 (D.C. App. 1983).

[141] In this regard, see, especially: Schopp, et al., Note 61, *supra*, at 54-55; Faigman, Note 119, *supra*; and Faigman & Wright, Note 119, *supra*.

[142] Rogers v. State, 616 So. 2d 1098, 1098-99 (Fla. Dist. Ct. App. 1993) (footnotes omitted).

[143] A few states have passed legislation expressly providing for the admissibility of battered woman syndrome expert testimony in criminal cases. E.g., Cal. Evid. Code § 1107 (Deering 2005); Md. Code Ann., Cts. & Jud. Proc. § 10-916 (2004).

[144] See Maguigan, Note 61, *supra*, at 429-31.

[145] E.g., People v. Wilson, 487 N.W.2d 822, 825 (Mich. Ct. App. 1992); State v. Hennum, 441 N.W.2d 793, 799 (Minn. 1989).

[146] E.g., State v. Richardson, 525 N.W.2d 378, 382 (Wis. Ct. App. 1994).

[147] See, e.g., People v. Humphrey, 921 P.2d 1, 8-9 (Cal. 1996); State v. Peterson, 857 A.2d 1132, 1150 (Md. Ct. Spec. App. 2004); Boykins v. State, 995 P.2d 474, 476 (Nev. 2000); State v. Kelly, 685 P.2d 564, 570 (Wash. 1984).

The proposition that battered woman syndrome testimony should be admitted to show that the defendant reasonably believed that the decedent was about to kill her is questionable in nonconfrontational cases. Seemingly, such expert testimony shows that the defendant suffers from a condition that renders her unable to appreciate objective reality (namely, that her currently passive, even sleeping, abuser does *not* represent an *imminent* threat, as the law generally requires). Indeed, battered woman syndrome evidence demonstrates the battered woman's abnormal mental condition, which is why courts frequently characterize the battered woman as one "suffering" from battered woman syndrome.[148] As Professor Anne Coughlin has put it, syndrome evidence suggests that "women in battering relationships lose their mental capacity to make rational choices," and the evidence "marks the woman as a collection of mental symptoms and behavioral abnormalities."[149] This evidence might support a claim that the battered woman should be *excused* for her conduct due to her mental condition, or that she is entitled to claim imperfect self-defense (i.e., that she actually but *un*reasonably believed that she was repelling an imminent threat), but it arguably has nothing to do with whether her act of killing her sleeping (or otherwise passive) partner was *justifiable* under the circumstances.

The issue as to whether a battered woman's self-defense claim should be characterized as a justification or excuse is not without deep moral and practical significance, as discussed immediately below.

[4] Nonconfrontational Battered Woman Self-Defense?: Some Reflections

Battered women who kill in confrontational circumstances can assert a relatively traditional self-defense claim. It is worth reflecting, however, on the question of whether a battered women who kills in *non*confrontational circumstances, or who solicits a third party to kill her abuser, should also be able to claim self-defense (or some newly crafted defense). Notice that this question may be asked independent of battered woman syndrome. Perhaps a battered woman, *syndrome or no syndrome*, is justified in killing (or obtaining another to kill) her abuser, independent of any traditional imminent self-defense claim that might be made.

A utilitarian might defend the killing of an abuser on the ground that he constitutes an ongoing danger to the woman and, very possibly, to other persons.

---

[148] E.g., Boykins v. State, 995 P.2d at 476; see also State v. Edwards, 60 S.W.3d 602, 614, 615 (Mo. Ct. App. 2001) (describing "reasonable battered woman" as "something of an oxymoron" because a "battered woman is a terror-stricken person whose mental state is distorted").

[149] Coughlin, Note 119, *supra*, at 71, 76. Some scholars disagree with the "*abnormal* mental condition" characterization. Kinports, Note 119, *supra*, at 417. Essentially, they believe that the syndrome "is more appropriately understood as a normal response to an abnormally stressful situation." Schopp et al., Note 61, *supra*, at 95 (reporting, but rejecting, this view).

Therefore, his immediate death results in a net social benefit. However, ultimately, a more socially acceptable utilitarian solution is for society to offer abused women places of sanctuary from abusers, as well as to devise more efficient mechanisms for bringing abusers to justice. Therefore, from a rule-utilitarian perspective — from the point of what *rule* will result in the best outcome over the course of time — it seems difficult to justify nonconfrontational homicides.

A non-utilitarian justification for killing the abuser, even when he is not an imminent threat, may be found in the principle of moral forfeiture: As a result of the abuser's ongoing culpable conduct, he has forfeited his right to life. This may have been what Justice Harry C. Martin of the North Carolina Supreme Court had in mind when he said about one abuser, who was killed by his wife while he was asleep:

> By his barbaric conduct over the course of twenty years, [he] reduced the quality of the defendant's life to such an abysmal state that, given the opportunity to do so, the jury might well have found that she was justified in acting in self-defense for the preservation of her tragic life.[150]

Even if the controversial moral-forfeiture doctrine is an otherwise acceptable principle,[151] its application here is troubling. First, in the traditional self-defense context, an aggressor only temporarily forfeits his right to life. If he withdraws from the conflict, or once the aggression is thwarted, his right to protect himself is restored. In the case of the abuser, however, the implication is that the constancy of his immoral conduct renders his right to life nearly permanently forfeited. He becomes fair game for killing day or night, awake or asleep, in ambush or otherwise. Second, the *logic* of the forfeiture position is that the abuser is fair game for killing *by anyone*, at least by anyone who acts for the purpose of protecting the woman's autonomy. Does a battered woman, therefore, have a right to solicit her son[152] or another relative to kill her husband? After all, if the abuser has no right to life, why should it matter *who* kills him? It is unlikely that many people would want to take the forfeiture doctrine to its logical conclusion.

An alternative rationale for a battered woman defense starts from the principle that "a state that denies the opportunity for self-defense, that asks its citizens to die rather than protect themselves, [ ]creates the . . . fear that citizens will become the slavish victims of the strong."[153] Therefore, it may be argued, an abused woman should be permitted kill her tormenter whenever the opportunity arises — a pre-emptive strike — in order to protect her natural right of autonomy. This argument, which would justify abolishing the imminency rule

---

[150] State v. Norman, 378 S.E.2d 8, 21 (N.C. 1989) (dissenting opinion).

[151] See § 17.02[C], *supra*.

[152] People v. Erickson, 57 Cal. App. 4th 1391 (Ct. App. 1997).

[153] Nourse, Note 59, *supra*, 1300-01.

(and either replacing it with a different temporal standard, such as that provided by the Model Penal Code, or rejecting any temporal limitation) is considered elsewhere in this chapter.[154]

A different approach to the issue, but one which is criticized by some advocates of abused women, is to provide a full or partial *excuse* to the battered woman who kills her abusive partner, either on traditional grounds of insanity, duress, diminished capacity, or provocation, or by carefully crafting a new excuse defense.[155]

The question of whether a battered woman should be justified or only excused for her actions raises intriguing moral questions, but also practical ones. Suppose that the abused party is about to shoot or set on fire[156] her sleeping husband, when he unexpectedly awakens. What are *his* rights of self-defense at that moment? If she is justified in killing him, the traditional rule would be that he is not justified in killing her, because he would be combating an imminent, *lawful* exercise of deadly force. If she is *excused* (partially or wholly) in killing him, however, he would be *justified* in taking her life in self-defense, assuming that all of the elements of the defense are satisfied. How we feel about *his* rights, therefore, is linked to the question of how we should characterize *her* situation.

Also, how should we deal with the person who helps her commit the crime, such as a person who, knowing her intentions, provides the abused woman with the gasoline? *His* legal position will likely depend on whether *her* actions are justified or merely excused.[157]

[C] Risk to Innocent Bystanders

Assume that *D* is justified in killing *V* in self-defense. *D* fires a gun at *V* but misses him, instead killing or wounding *X*, an innocent bystander. May *D* use his self-defense right against *V* as a basis of exculpation for the harm he inflicted on *X*?

---

[154] See § 18.02[D][1], *supra*.

[155] The concern with the excuse theory is that a battered woman's claim should not be demeaned by suggesting that she is sick or "crazy" for killing her abuser. Ironically, there is some evidence that introduction of battered woman syndrome evidence has the very effect of pathologizing the abused woman in the minds of jurors. Regina A. Schuller & Patricia A. Hastings, *Trials of Battered Women Who Kill: The Impact of Alternative Forms of Expert Evidence*, 20 Law & Human Behavior 167, 169 (1996). For an argument in favor of recognizing an excuse defense that does not run this risk, see Dressler, Note 59, *supra*.

[156] This was the method of killing by Francine Hughes in a famous battered-woman case recounted in an NBC-TV movie, *The Burning Bed*, and in a 1980 book of the same name, written by Faith McNulty.

[157] See § 30.06[B][2], *infra*.

Courts have only infrequently confronted this issue and few non-Model Code jurisdictions have statutes dealing with the problem.[158] In general, however, courts apply a transferred-justification doctrine, similar to the transferred-intent rule:[159] A defendant's right of self-defense "transfers" (just as his intent to kill does) from the intended to the actual victim.[160]

Not all courts treat this rule as absolute. If the defendant, acting justifiably in self-defense against an aggressor, fires a weapon "wildly or carelessly,"[161] thereby jeopardizing the safety of known bystanders, some courts may hold the defendant guilty of manslaughter of a bystander, or of reckless endangerment if no bystander is killed, but not of intent-to-kill murder.[162] Some courts provide an absolute defense in such circumstances.[163]

From a utilitarian perspective, the right to act in self-defense should not be absolute, at least when a defender's conduct jeopardizes multiple innocent bystanders: If the actor's self-protective behavior creates an unjustifiable risk of death to others, it may be socially desirable for him to choose some less dangerous (albeit less protective) means of defending himself.[164]

A non-absolute rule is also consistent with at least one non-utilitarian rationale of self-defense, the moral-forfeiture doctrine: The death of an innocent bystander is unjustified, because he is not guilty of any culpable act that would merit loss of his life. On the other hand, the absolute rule seems consistent with the "moral right" theory that one has a natural right to protect one's own life, even if innocent people are unintentionally harmed.

[D] Resisting an Unlawful Arrest[165]

Suppose that V, a police officer, attempts to arrest D. The arrest is unlawful. Therefore, D uses force to resist the arrest, and is subsequently prosecuted for the harm caused by his resistance, e.g., battery or murder. May D defend his actions on the ground that he had a right to resist the unlawful arrest?

---

[158] The Model Penal Code resolution of this issue is discussed at § 18.06[C], *infra*.

[159] See § 10.04[A][3], *supra*.

[160] People v. Mathews, 91 Cal. App. 3d 1018, 1023-24 (1979); Smith v. State, 419 S.E.2d 74, 75 (Ga. Ct. App. 1992); People v. Adams, 291 N.E.2d 54, 55-56 (Ill. App. Ct. 1972).

[161] People v. Adams, 291 N.E.2d at 56.

[162] See *id*. (dictum); People v. Jackson, 212 N.W.2d 918 (Mich. 1973).

[163] Commonwealth v. Fowlin, 710 A.2d 1130, 1134 (Pa. 1998) ("[W]e do not share the lower court's concern that random wild self-defense shootings will injure large numbers of innocent people.").

[164] It seems unlikely, however, that such a rule would have any deterrent effect on a person "acting within his instinct for self-preservation." *Id*. Therefore, arguably, a utilitarian would favor *excusing* such an actor.

[165] See generally Paul G. Chevigny, *The Right to Resist an Unlawful Arrest*, 78 Yale L.J. 1128 (1969).

An arrest may be unlawful for various reasons. First, an arrest is unlawful if the officer uses excessive force in effectuating it. Under common law doctrine, an officer may use only as much force as necessary to make an arrest, and may never use deadly force to arrest a misdemeanant.[166] Therefore, if a police officer uses excessive force in making an arrest, he is to that extent the aggressor, and the citizen is justified in protecting himself. The rule here is simple: General self-defense doctrines apply. That is, the victim of excessive police force is entitled to use reasonable force to protect himself, including deadly force if his life reasonably appears to be in jeopardy.[167]

Many unlawful arrests, however, do not implicate self-defense concerns. For example, an arrest is unlawful (even if reasonable force is used) if the arresting officer lacks probable cause to believe that the suspect is guilty of the crime for which he is being taken into custody.[168] And, even if an officer has probable cause, he must respect other constitutional and statutory arrest procedures, such as obtaining a warrant to make an arrest in a suspect's home,[169] and knocking and demanding admittance before entering the residence.[170]

The common law rule is that a person may use as much force as is reasonably necessary, *short of deadly force*, to resist an illegal arrest.[171] If the arrestee uses deadly force, he is guilty of manslaughter, rather than murder.[172] However, there is some question as to whether these rules apply to all unlawful arrests, or only to those that occur under provocative circumstances, i.e., in which the person being arrested is aware of the illegality of the police action.[173] For example, there is a split of authority in homicide cases: Some courts treat an unlawful arrest as a trespass to the person, which automatically reduces the homicide to manslaughter, even if the arrestee is unaware of the illegality; other courts refuse to permit reduction of the offense unless the actor is, in fact, aroused to passion by the unlawfulness of the arrest,[174] in which case the heat-of-passion manslaughter doctrine comes into play.

Today, the right to resist an excessive-force arrest remains untrammeled. However, most states by statute[175] or case law[176] have abolished or limited

---

[166] See generally § 21.03, *infra*.

[167] E.g., Commonwealth v. French, 611 A.2d 175, 178 (Pa. 1992).

[168] See Dunaway v. New York, 442 U.S. 200, 207-08 (1969).

[169] Payton v. New York, 445 U.S. 573 (1980).

[170] Wilson v. Arkansas, 514 U.S. 927 (1995).

[171] See People v. Curtis, 450 P.2d 33, 35 (Cal. 1969).

[172] Davis v. State, 102 A.2d 816, 820-21 (Md. 1954).

[173] Chevigny, Note 165, *supra*, at 1129-32 (interpreting early Anglo-American law as requiring provocation).

[174] Davis v. State, 102 A.2d at 820-21 (summarizing the contrasting rules).

[175] E.g., Cal. Penal Code § 834a (Deering 2005) (abolishing the defense).

[176] State v. Wright, 162 S.E.2d 56, 62 (N.C. Ct. App. 1968), aff'd, 163 S.E.2d 897 (N.C. 1968) (no defense if the officer is acting under authority of a warrant, although it is defective or irregular in

the defense in non-excessive-force circumstances.[177] The argument for retrenchment is that the original reasons for the defense no longer apply. At common law, a person who was unlawfully arrested had little hope for early release. Moreover, jail conditions were harsh: Death from disease and maltreatment in jails were not uncommon. When these evils were balanced against the social harm of a battery upon an officer, resistance could be viewed as justifiable.

Today, the balancing process is thought to result in a different conclusion. Jail conditions, although harsh, supposedly "are no longer the pestilential death traps"[178] of old. Bail is easier to obtain than it was centuries ago, and the lawfulness of an arrest can now be determined comparatively rapidly, so that the extent of wrongful incarceration is reduced. Finally, it is much more difficult today than it was in the past to successfully resist an unlawful arrest without using deadly force. In light of these changes, it may be preferable for the arrestee to forego resistance and seek post-custodial remedies.

These arguments for abandonment of the common law rule apply if the defense is perceived as a justification, based on a balancing of utilities. But, the defense can also be justified on the ground that a person should be permitted to use force to protect his autonomy. This right is no less applicable today than it was centuries ago. Moreover, perhaps the common law defense should be understood as an excuse, rather than a justification. That is, the "right" to resist unlawful arrests may be a misnomer; perhaps the underlying basis for the rule is that when one is patently mistreated by government officials, he is apt to become enraged, and that response (expressed in the form of nondeadly resistance to the arrest) is morally blameless under the circumstances.

§ 18.06 MODEL PENAL CODE

[A] General Rules

[1] Force, in General

[a] Permissible Use

Subject to various limitations, a person is justified in using force upon another person if he believes that such force is immediately necessary to protect himself

---

some respect); State v. Valentine, 935 P.2d 1294 (Wash. 1997) (a person may not use force if he is faced only with a loss of freedom).

[177] State v. Valentine, 935 P.2d at 1302 (stating that only 20 states now recognize a defense).

[178] *Id.* at 1301.

against the exercise of unlawful force[179] by the other individual on the present occasion.[180]

This rule diverges from the common law in two noteworthy ways. First, it is drafted in terms of the actor's subjective belief in the need to use force; his belief need not be reasonable. However, nearly all of the Code justification defenses, including the defense of self-protection, are modified by Section 3.09, which re-incorporates a reasonableness component, although not in the fashion of the common law. This feature of the Code is discussed in subsection [B] below.

Second, and quite significantly, the Code substitutes the phrase "immediately necessary . . . on the present occasion," for the common law imminency requirement. This shift in language authorizes self-protective force sooner than may be allowed at common law. This is because the issue under the Code is *not* how soon the aggressor's force will be used, but rather whether the innocent person's *need* to use defensive force exists immediately. For example, suppose that *V*, an abusive husband, tells *D*, his wife who is in the kitchen, that he is going to the bedroom to get a gun and kill her. In response, *V* picks up a kitchen knife and, when *V* turns his back on her to go to the bedroom to obtain the gun, she stabs him to death. Under traditional common law principles, *D*'s self-defense claim would likely fail because *V* did not yet represent an imminent threat: He is unarmed, and she would likely have to wait until he returned with the gun. In contrast, under the Code, *D*'s self-defensive act of stabbing *V* in the back would be justifiable, if she believed that she could not afford to wait until *V* returned with the weapon — i.e., that force was *immediately* necessary.[181]

[b] Impermissible Use: Resisting an Unlawful Arrest

In a departure from common law principles but in accord with the modern trend, a person may not use force to resist an arrest that he knows is being made by a police officer (thus, arrests by undercover officers do not apply), even if the arrest is unlawful (e.g., without probable cause).[182] However, this rule, which

---

[179] The Model Penal Code definition of "unlawful force" (§ 3.11(1)) is cumbersome. The definition, however, does not appreciably differ from the meaning accorded to the phrase at common law. See § 18.02[D][2], *supra*. One difference, however, is that "force" under the Code includes "confinement." That is, if the other provisions of the defense are met, a person may use force to resist an unlawful effort to imprison him, even if he is aware that the imprisoner will not touch him in order to confine him. For example, *D* may use force to prevent *V* from unlawfully locking him in a cellar.

[180] Model Penal Code § 3.04(1).

[181] See American Law Institute, Comment to § 3.04, at 39-40. It must be remembered, however, that if her belief in this regard was wrong, her mistake-of-fact could partially undermine her defense. See § 18.06[B], *infra*.

[182] Model Penal Code § 3.04(2)(a)(I).

was opposed by a substantial minority of the members of the American Law Institute,[183] does *not* prohibit use of force by an arrestee who believes that the officer intends to use excessive force in effectuating the arrest.[184]

[2] Deadly Force, in General

[a] "Deadly Force": Definition

Section 3.11, subsection (2), of the Code provides that "deadly force" is force used for the "purpose of causing or that [the actor] knows to create a substantial risk of causing death or serious bodily injury." The section expressly provides that the act of purposely firing a gun in the direction of a person or of a vehicle that the actor believes is occupied constitutes "deadly force." However, a mere threat (without the purpose) to cause death or serious injury to another is not "deadly force," even if the actor brandishes a weapon to back up his spurious threat.[185]

[b] Permissible Use

Deadly force is unjustifiable unless the actor believes that such force is immediately necessary to protect himself on the present occasion against: (1) death; (2) serious bodily injury; (3) forcible rape; or (4) kidnapping.[186]

The first three categories in which deadly force may be used are not problematic. The provision regarding kidnapping, however, is of questionable legitimacy. As the Commentary concedes,[187] the appropriateness of its inclusion in the Code will depend on how kidnapping is defined by state law. A kidnapping need not involve a threat of death or great bodily injury to the kidnap victim, for example, when a parent abducts a child from the custody of another parent. In such a circumstances, deadly force would be a disproportional (yet, under the Code, permissible) response.

[c] Impermissible Use

Even if deadly force is otherwise permitted, as described immediately above, the Code prohibits its use in two key circumstances.

---

[183] For a summary of the minority's position, see American Law Institute, Comment to § 3.04, at 43.

[184] *Id.*

[185] State v. Moore, 729 A.2d 1021, 1027 (N.J. 1999).

[186] Model Penal Code § 3.04(2)(b).

[187] American Law Institute, Comment to § 3.04, at 48.

[i] Deadly Force by Aggressors

The Code prohibits the use of deadly force by a person who, "with the purpose of causing death or serious bodily injury, provoked the use of force against himself in the same encounter."[188] This concept of aggression is narrower than the common law version because it does not include within its scope the "nondeadly aggressor," i.e., the actor who provokes a *non*deadly conflict. Therefore, in a Model Penal Code jurisdiction, if *D* unlawfully starts a nonlethal conflict, he does not lose his privilege of self-defense if *V* escalates it into a lethal assault.

It should be observed that an actor only loses his privilege to use deadly force in self-protection if he is the aggressor "in the same encounter." This language is consistent with the common law treatment of deadly aggressors.[189] That is, if *D* unlawfully commences a deadly assault upon *V*, he may regain the right of self-protection if he breaks off the struggle, and *V* continues to threaten him. In these circumstances, *V*'s threat is viewed as a "distinct engagement."[190]

[ii] Retreat

The Code comes down on the side of those who favor retreat: A person may not use deadly force against an aggressor if he "knows that he can avoid the necessity of using such force with complete safety by retreating."[191] As a result of policy disagreements among members of the American Law Institute and subsequent compromising,[192] the retreat rule is subject to various exceptions and counter-exceptions.[193] The most significant exception is that, as in common law retreat jurisdictions, retreat is not necessary if the actor would have to retreat from his home, or even from his place of work.

This exception, however, is subject to its own exception, which is that retreat from the home or office *is* required: (1) if the actor was the initial aggressor, and wishes to regain his right of self-protection; or (2) even if he was not the aggressor, if he is attacked by a co-worker in their place of work. However, the Code does not require retreat by a non-aggressor in the home, even if the assailant is a co-dweller, a result beneficial to a battered woman involved in a domestic dispute.[194]

---

[188] Model Penal Code § 3.04(2)(b)(i).

[189] See § 18.02[B][2][a], *supra*.

[190] American Law Institute, Comment to § 3.04, at 52.

[191] Model Penal Code § 3.04(2)(b)(ii).

[192] See generally American Law Institute, Comment to § 3.04, at 52-57.

[193] See Model Penal Code § 3.04(2)(b)(ii).

[194] See § 18.02[C][3], *supra*.

[iii] Summarizing the MPC Deadly-Force Rules

The Code's deadly-force rules add up to this. First, if *D* did not start the unlawful conflict, he may use deadly force against *V* if he believes that such force is immediately necessary on the present occasion to combat an unlawful deadly assault by *V*, assuming one of the following circumstances exists: (1) *D* has retreated, and *V* continues to pursue him; (2) *D* knows of no safe place to retreat; or (3) even if *D* could have retreated, if *D* is in his home or place of work, and *V* is not in his place of work.

Second, if *D did* start the unlawful conflict but did so with*out* the purpose of provoking a deadly conflict — e.g., he lightly struck *V*, but *V* escalated matters by menacing *D* with a knife — *D* may still use deadly force in all of the circumstances noted above. *D* may be prosecuted, however, for the initial unlawful assault or battery that commenced the conflict.[195]

Third, *D* may *not* kill *V* in self-defense if he started the conflict with the intent to cause death or great bodily harm, unless he withdraws from the conflict. If he does so, *D*'s privilege to kill is restored, although he may be charged with a crime pertaining to the initial acts that commenced the conflict.

[B] Mistake-of-Fact Claims and Model Penal Code Justification Defenses[196]

As previously explored, the common law rule is that a person is justified in acting on the basis of reasonable, albeit erroneous, appearances.[197] A justification defense is not available at common law, however, to one who acts on the basis of an unreasonable belief, although some states recognize an "imperfect" defense in such circumstances.[198]

The Model Penal Code recognizes an imperfect defense, but it takes a two-step process to get to this point. Initially each justification defense dealing with the use of defensive force is defined *solely* in terms of the defendant's subjective belief in the necessity of using the force, or in terms of his subjective belief regarding other circumstances that are material to the particular justification claimed.

Each of these defenses, however, is subject to the provisions of Section 3.09, subsection (2), which provides that when the defendant is reckless or negli-

---

[195] American Law Institute, Comment to § 3.04, at 50.

[196] The concepts described in this section apply to the defenses of execution of public duty (§ 3.03), self-protection (§ 3.04), protection of other persons (§ 3.05), protection of property (§ 3.06), law enforcement (§ 3.07), and use of force by persons with special responsibility for care, discipline, or safety of others (§ 3.08).

[197] See §§ 17.04 (justification defenses generally) and 18.01[E] (self-defense), *supra*.

[198] See § 18.03, *supra*.

gent in regard to the facts relating to the justifiability of his conduct, the justi-fication defense is unavailable to him in a prosecution for an offense for which recklessness or negligence suffices to establish culpability. For example, if *D* pur-posely kills *V* because he *unreasonably* (let us assume, negligently) believes that *V* is about to kill him, the defense of self-protection is available to *D* if he is charged with purposely, knowingly, or recklessly killing *V*, but the defense is not available to him if he is prosecuted for negligent homicide, in light of his negligent mistake of fact. Or, if *D* *consciously* disregards a substantial and unjustifiable risk that *V* is not an aggressor, *D*'s recklessness as to the relevant facts would render him guilty of an offense based on a reckless state of mind.

This outcome is sensible. In the hypothetical above, the traditional common law rule, which does not recognize an imperfect defense, authorizes *D*'s convic-tion for a more serious offense than his overall culpability — he may be con-victed of a crime of intent, although he is really a negligent or reckless wrongdoer (in light of his negligent or reckless mistake). The Code approach per-mits conviction of an offense in accord with the culpability of his mistake.[199]

[C] Justification Defenses and Risks to Innocent Bystanders

If a person justifiably uses force against an aggressor, but uses such force in a reckless or negligent manner in regard to the safety of an innocent bystander, the justification defense, which is available to the person in regard to the *aggres-sor*, is *unavailable* to him in a prosecution for such recklessness or negligence as to the *bystander*.[200] For example, if *D* shoots at *A*, an aggressor, in a crowded subway, thereby recklessly causing *X*'s death or recklessly endangering the lives of *X* and others, *D* may successfully assert self-protection as a defense in any prosecution for his actions against *A*, but he is not entitled to use this defense in a prosecution for manslaughter of *X*, or for the offense of reckless endangerment of the bystanders.

However, convictions in this regard are difficult to obtain. In order to show that a defendant acted recklessly or negligently as to a bystander, the prosecu-tion must show that he took an *unjustifiable* risk to others in protecting himself, because "unjustifiability" is an element in the definition of both "recklessness" and "negligence."[201] And, and as the Commentary explains, "in assessing . . . a charge of recklessness or negligence, the actor's justifying purpose [e.g., self-pro-tection] must . . . be given weight in determining whether the risk to innocent persons was sufficient to establish a gross deviation from proper standards of conduct."[202]

---

[199] American Law Institute, Comment to § 3.09, at 151-52.

[200] Model Penal Code § 3.09(3).

[201] See § 10.07[B][3], *supra*.

[202] See American Law Institute, Comment to § 3.09, at 154-55.

Chapter 19

DEFENSE OF OTHERS

§ 19.01 GENERAL RULE

Generally speaking, a person is justified in using force to protect a third party from unlawful use of force by an aggressor.[1] The intervenor's right to use force in such circumstances parallels the third party's right of self-defense;[2] that is, she may use force when, and to the extent that, the third party would apparently be justified in using force to protect herself.[3]

Some potential limits to this rule exist. First, the defense originally was limited to protection of persons[4] related to the intervenor by consanguinity, marriage, or employment relation.[5] This limitation is enforced only infrequently today.

Second, a majority of jurisdictions once applied the "alter ego" rule: An intervenor could only use force to defend a third party if the party being defended would *in fact* have been justified in using force, and force in the same degree, in *self*-defense.[6] This means that D, the intervenor, is placed in the shoes of X, the third party being defended, and *acts at her peril*: If X had no right of self-defense, even though a reasonable person would have believed that X did, D is not justified in using force to protect X. This rule represents an exception to the common law rule that an actor is justified in using force based on reasonable appearances.

Jurisdictions that follow this rule are impressed by the not uncommon circumstance in which the defense is raised: D comes upon an apparently unlawful attack by V on X; D defends X; later D learns that V was an undercover police officer properly using force against an unlawfully resistant X. Permitting D to act on reasonable appearances, it is said, creates "a dangerous precedent . . . that

---

[1] Commonwealth v. Martin, 341 N.E.2d 885, 889-90 (Mass. 1976).

[2] State v. Cook, 515 S.E.2d 127, 133 (W. Va. 1999).

[3] See *id.* at 136-38; State v. Pounders, 913 S.W.2d 904, 907 (Mo. Ct. App. 1996).

[4] May a pregnant mother respond to a threatened punch to her stomach with deadly force to protect the life of her fetus? Courts are split on this, largely depending on whether the state defines a fetus as a "person." Compare People v. Kurr, 654 N.W.2d 651 (Mich. 2002) (permitting the defense), with Ogas v. State, 655 S.W.2d 322 (Tex. App. 1983) (disallowing the defense).

[5] Commonwealth v. Martin, 341 N.E.2d at 891-92.

[6] See People v. Young, 183 N.E.2d 319, 319-20 (N.Y. 1962) (stating and applying the then-majority rule).

plain-clothes police officers attempting lawful arrests over wrongful resistance are subject to violent interference by strangers ignorant of the facts."[7]

Some states retain the alter ego rule. However, largely due to the influence of the Model Penal Code, the modern majority view is that an intervenor may use deadly or nondeadly force to the extent that such force *reasonably appears* to the intervenor to be justified in defense of the third party.[8]

Advocates of the reasonable-appearance rule justify it on utilitarian and retributive grounds. From a utilitarian perspective, a believed consequence of the old alter ego doctrine was that onlookers hesitated to intervene in disputes. As one court explained, "[e]ven if their hearts had been stout enough to enter the fray in defense of a stranger being violently assaulted, the fear of legal consequences chilled their basic instincts."[9] The reasonable-appearance rule seeks "to afford protection to a defender who acts while injury may still be prevented."[10] The alter ego rule also violates concepts of just deserts, because it results in liability and punishment without fault.[11] The reasonable-appearance rule ensures that people who act reasonably, albeit mistakenly, are not punished for their good motives.

§ 19.02 MODEL PENAL CODE

Under the Model Code, subject to retreat provisions discussed in the next paragraph, an intervenor (*D*) is justified in using force upon another person in order to protect a third party (*X*) if three conditions are met: (1) *D* uses no more force to protect *X* than *D* would be entitled to use in *self*-protection, based on the circumstances as *D* believes them to be; (2) under the circumstances as *D* believes them to be, *X* would be justified in using such force in self-defense; and (3) *D* believes that her intervention is necessary for *X*'s protection.[12]

The Code's self-protection retreat rules[13] have limited applicability in the context of the defense of another person. First, if *D* would be required to retreat to a place of known safety if she were protecting *herself* in such circumstances, she is *not* required to retreat before using force in *X*'s protection, except in the unlikely circumstance that she knows that such retreat will assure *X*'s complete safety.[14] Second, *D* is required to attempt to secure *X*'s retreat if *X* would be

---

[7] People v. Young, 210 N.Y.S.2d 358, 367 (App. Div. 1961) (Valente, J., dissenting), rev'd, 183 N.E.2d 319 (N.Y. 1962).

[8] E.g., Alexander v. State, 447 A.2d 880, 885-87 (Md. Ct. Spec. App. 1982); State v. Cook, 515 S.E.2d at 135-37.

[9] Alexander v. State, 447 A.2d at 881.

[10] *Id.* at 887.

[11] American Law Institute, Comment to § 3.05, at 65-66.

[12] Model Penal Code § 3.05(1).

[13] See § 18.06[A][2][c][ii], *supra.*

[14] Model Penal Code § 3.05(2)(a).

required to retreat under the rules of self-protection, but this requirement only applies if D knows that X can reach complete safety by retreating.[15] Third, neither D nor X is required to retreat "in the other's dwelling or place of work to any greater extent than in [her] own."[16]

As with other justification defenses,[17] the applicability of the defense-of-others provision is based on the intervenor's subjective beliefs. Thus, if D is prosecuted for purposely killing V, an undercover officer lawfully pointing a gun at X, D is entitled to raise a defense-of-others claim if she believed that V was an unlawful attacker.[18] However, also as with other justification defenses, if D's belief in this regard was negligent or reckless, the justification would be unavailable to her in a prosecution for negligent or reckless homicide.

---

[15] Model Penal Code § 3.05(2)(b).

[16] Model Penal Code § 3.05(2)(c).

[17] See § 18.06[B], *supra*.

[18] Notice the interesting possibility of conflicting justifications in the police hypothetical in the text: D is justified in using deadly force upon V, based on her reasonable but mistaken belief that she is acting in X's defense; simultaneously, officer V would be justified in killing D in self-protection if *she* (V) reasonably but mistakenly believes that D is X's accomplice. (In such circumstances, V would be acting on the reasonable belief that she is repelling *unlawful* force by D.) Model Penal Code § 3.04(1).

Chapter 20

DEFENSE OF PROPERTY AND HABITATION

§ 20.01 PROPERTY AND HABITATION: COMPARISON AND CONTRAST

This chapter focuses on two related defenses. The first is the defense of property, which is implicated when a person uses force to prevent another person from dispossessing him of real or personal property, or in order to regain possession of the property immediately after dispossession. The second is the defense of habitation, which is involved when the dweller of a home uses force to prevent unlawful entry into the actor's "castle" by an intruder. This defense is distinguishable from the property defense in that its purpose is to safeguard the dweller's bodily security and privacy in his home; dispossession of the home or its contents need not be implicated.

Some courts and statutes treat the habitation defense as part of a broader property defense. It is easy to see why: When *V* enters *D*'s home wrongfully and forcibly in order to dispossess him or to take property from within it, *D* simultaneously has the right to protect his property from dispossession (defense of property) and to protect his right to inhabit his home in privacy and safety (defense of habitation). Realistically, there is often no way to separate the two interests. Nonetheless, it is preferable to distinguish the claims because the common law treats them differently in one significant respect: Deadly force is *never* permitted to protect property, as such; deadly force *is* justified in certain circumstances, however, in order to defend habitation.

These two defenses often overlap other justification claims, as well. For example, one who uses force in his residence might simultaneously claim one or more of the following defenses: defense of property; defense of habitation; crime prevention (which itself subsumes multiple defenses); self-defense; and defense of others. Frequently, some of these defenses overlap nearly completely; sometimes, however, subtle differences exist, so it is important to distinguish between the claims.

§ 20.02 DEFENSE OF PROPERTY

[A] General Rule

Despite the high value placed on property rights in Anglo-American society, the law prefers the resolution of property disputes by nonforcible means, including the use of judicial orders. Forcible self-help is discouraged. Nonetheless, in narrow circumstances, a person may use force to protect his property.

As more fully examined in subsection [B], a person in possession of real or personal property is justified in using nondeadly force against a would-be dispossessor if he reasonably believes that such force is necessary to prevent imminent, unlawful dispossession of the property.[1] Under no circumstances may a person use deadly force to prevent dispossession. And, subject to one exception considered in subsection [B][6] below, once a person is dispossessed of his property, his right to use force to defend his interest in it is extinguished.

[B] Clarification of the Rule

[1] Possession versus Title to Property

The privilege of defense-of-property entitles a person to use necessary force to retain rightful possession of, as distinguished from title to, personal or real property.[2] For example, assuming the other aspects of the defense are satisfied, D, a mechanic repairing X's car, may use nondeadly force against V, a thief, in order to prevent V from taking the vehicle. Similarly, T, a tenant in an apartment, may use nondeadly force, if necessary, to prevent L, the owner of the property, from wrongfully evicting him from the premises.

[2] Necessity for the Use of Force

A person may use no more force than reasonably appears necessary to defend his possessory interest in the property. The necessity component may have two elements. First, some courts specify that a person may not use force until he has sought to avoid a physical conflict by requesting desistance by the would-be dispossessor.[3] A request is unnecessary if it would be futile or would jeopardize the defender's or another person's safety, such as when the wrongdoer attempts to take property by force rather than by stealth.

Second, even if force reasonably appears to be necessary, a defender of property must not use force beyond that which the urgency of the occasion reasonably requires. For example, D may "gently lay hands" on V to force him off D's land or to keep V away from D's personal property,[4] but he may not severely kick V when lesser force would suffice to protect the property.[5]

---

[1] See State v. Trammel, 672 P.2d 652, 654 (N.M. 1983); Pike v. Commonwealth, 482 S.E.2d 839, 840 (Va. Ct. App. 1997).

[2] See State v. Rullis, 191 A.2d 197 (N.J. Super. Ct. App. Div. 1963).

[3] E.g., State v. Elliot, 11 N.H. 540, 544-45 (1841).

[4] 1 Matthew Hale, History of the Pleas of the Crown *485 (1736); *Elliot*, 11 N.H. at 544-45..

[5] Wild's Case, 2 Lewin 214, 168 Eng. Rep. 1132 (1837).

[3] Deadly Force

Deadly force is never permitted in defense of property, even if it is the only means available to prevent the loss.[6] However, the right to use *non*deadly force to protect property is sometimes transformed into an independent right to use *deadly* force in self-protection or defense of a third party. For example, assume this scenario: V threatens to steal D's property; D resists by use of moderate nondeadly force; in an effort to overcome D's lawful resistance, V pulls a knife and attempts to stab D. In these circumstances, D may now use deadly force against V. This right, however, is based on D's privilege to protect himself from an imminent, unlawful deadly attack, and not on the basis of his interest in the property.

[4] Threat to Use Deadly Force

Although a person may not *use* deadly force to protect his property, may he *threaten* it as a way to prevent interference with, or dispossession of, his property? For example, suppose that D discovers V about to steal D's automobile. May D point a gun at V and, although he has no intention of using the weapon (perhaps it is even unloaded), threaten V with it, to prevent the theft? If D is charged with assault on these facts,[7] and asserts the claim of defense-of-property, should he be denied the defense because he threatened perform a forbidden act?

There is relatively little case law directly on point. A few cases, especially old ones, apparently authorize the threatened use of deadly force to prevent unlawful dispossession of property.[8] The prevailing modern position, however, is that a person may not threaten to do that which he is not permitted to do in fact.[9]

Those who would permit the defense in such cases contend that a threat of deadly force will often deter a wrongdoer without harming him. Thus, a *threat* of *deadly* force may be preferable to *implementation* of *non*deadly force, which the common law permits. On the other hand, a threat of deadly force is itself a highly dangerous act because it may provoke a deadly response, so it is desirable to deter threats that the issuer has no right to implement.

---

[6] People v. Ceballos, 526 P.2d 241, 249 (Cal. 1974); Commonwealth v. Alexander, 531 S.E.2d 567, 568 (Va. 2000).

[7] At common law, an assault is an attempted battery. See § 27.02[E], *infra*. D did not intend to batter V, so D is not guilty of common law assault, regardless of the defense-of-property claim. However, most states have redefined the offense of assault to include the tort definition (i.e., intent to place another person in reasonable apprehension of an imminent battery). E.g. Ariz. Rev. Stat. § 13-1203(A)(2) (2004). Under such a statute, D would be guilty of assault, subject to any applicable defense.

[8] State v. Yancey, 74 N.C. 244, 245 (N.C. 1876).

[9] Commonwealth v. Alexander, 531 S.E.2d at 568.

[5] Claim of Right

Occasionally, a person may assert a "claim of right" to possession of property and, therefore, seek to dispossess another person of the disputed property. For example, V, a landlord, may have a right to retake real property from D, a tenant; or V may seek to repossess an automobile from D, who has failed to make timely car payments.

V's claim of right to possession of the property is relevant to D's claim of defense-of-property in one circumstance: If D knows, believes, or as a reasonable person should believe, that V has a legitimate claim of right to possession of the property in question, it follows that D cannot reasonably believe that V represents a threat to dispossess him *unlawfully*. From D's (or the reasonable person's) perspective, V's threatened act of dispossession is *lawful*. Therefore, in these circumstances, D is not privileged to use force against V.

[6] Recapture of Property

In order to discourage self-help and consequent breaches of the peace, a person may not ordinarily use force to recapture property of which he has been unlawfully dispossessed.[10]

One exception to this rule exists. A person who acts *promptly* after dispossession may use nondeadly force, as reasonably necessary, to regain or recapture his property. Thus, a person wrongfully evicted from his land may immediately re-enter the property and attempt to retake it; likewise, one who is unlawfully dispossessed of his personal property may follow the dispossessor in hot pursuit and use nondeadly force, if necessary, to recapture it.[11]

§ 20.03 DEFENSE OF HABITATION[12]

[A] Rationale of the Defense

If jurists have treated the use of force in defense of property with considerable caution, they have always treated the related interest of safe and private habitation of one's home with reverence. The reason for the difference in attitude — as with the rule permitting people to kill in self-defense rather than to retreat from their home — is that the home represents the person's "castle." As with a castle, the home is a dweller's fortress, "as well for his defence against

---

[10] The fourteenth century English Statute of Forcible Entry made it a crime for one entitled to possession of land to regain it by use of force. 5 Rich. 2, ch. 8 (1381). This statute "has been substantially reenacted by nearly all the states." American Law Institute, Comment to § 3.06, at 86.

[11] Woodward v. State, 855 P.2d 423, 428 n.14 (Alaska Ct. App. 1993).

[12] See generally William Wilbanks, The Make My Day Law (1990).

injury and violence, as for his repose."[13] The house serves as a sanctuary from external attack, "for where shall a man be safe if it be not in his house?"[14]

The home is also a source of privacy where the most intimate activities in life are conducted, and from which people seek to exclude the prying eyes and ears of strangers and of the government. The Supreme Court has observed:

> The [Constitution] protects the individual's privacy in a variety of settings. In none is the zone of privacy more clearly defined than when bounded by the unambiguous physical dimensions of an individual's home — a zone that finds its roots in clear and specific constitutional terms: "The right of the people to be secure in their . . . houses . . . shall not be violated."[15]

Although this quotation concerns a person's right to be free from unreasonable intrusions by the government, the constitutional right is itself based on the pre-constitutional common law reverence for the home as a place of security.

When a wrongdoer seeks to enter a person's dwelling, therefore, more than property is invaded. In common law terms, the fortress has been attacked; a person's primary source of safe and private habitation has been jeopardized.

[B] Rules Regarding Use of Deadly Force

A person may use deadly force to defend his home. The scope of this privilege has changed over time, and no single common law or statutory rule universally applies today. Three general approaches will be noted.

[1] Early Common Law Rule

The broadest right to use deadly force is found in the original common law principle that a home-dweller may use deadly force upon another person if he reasonably believes that such force is necessary to prevent an imminent and unlawful[16] entry of his dwelling.[17]

---

[13] Semayne's Case, 5 Co. Rep. 91a, 91b, 77 Eng. Rep. 194, 195 (1620); see State v. Pellegrino, 577 N.W.2d 590, 594 (S.D. 1998) ("The feudal concept of home as castle was borne of an age when inhabitants were compelled to turn their dwellings into fortified strongholds. The idea endures into modern times.").

[14] Edmond Coke, Third Institute *162 (1644).

[15] Payton v. New York, 445 U.S. 573, 589 (1980).

[16] Courts frequently state that the entry must be forcible. E.g., People v. Stombaugh, 284 N.E.2d 640, 643 (Ill. 1972) (the defense applies if the intruder enters in a "violent, riotous or tumultuous manner"). However, other courts require simply that there be an unlawful entry. E.g., State v. Lumpkin, 850 S.W.2d 388 (Mo. Ct. App. 1993). And, at least one court has stated that the right to use deadly force does not even depend on the dweller closing his door. See State v. Bell, 160 N.W. 727 (S.D. 1916). It would seem that, open doors aside, any unlawful entry of a closed door would be considered forcible for purposes of the defense.

[17] See State v. Reid, 210 N.E.2d 142 (Ohio Ct. App. 1965).

A careful look at the elements of this defense demonstrates its wide scope. The right to use deadly force is triggered by the immediacy of the unlawful entry; the unlawful purpose of the intruder, and the degree to which he constitutes a threat to the physical safety of the occupants, is immaterial. For example, *D* may kill *V*, an apparent intruder, whether *V* is an armed burglar intending to kill him or to steal his property, an unarmed intruder seeking to dispossess him of his property, or even an unarmed and intoxicated neighbor mistakenly entering what he thinks is his own home.[18] Indeed, pursuant to this rule, the right to kill exists even if *D knows* that *V* is his intoxicated neighbor, as long as *D* reasonably believes that deadly force is the only way of preventing the entry.

[2] "Middle" Approach

A less broad approach to the defense of habitation provides that a person may use deadly force if he reasonably believes that: (1) the other person intends an unlawful and imminent entry of the dwelling; (2) the intruder intends to injure him or another occupant, or to commit a felony therein; and (3) deadly force is necessary to repel the intrusion.[19]

This rule is narrower than the original common law defense. Under this formulation, for example, *D* may not justifiably shoot *V* if he knows or should know that the intruder is *D*'s intoxicated neighbor mistakenly attempting to enter his own house. Under such circumstances, *V* (presumably) does not represent a threat to an occupant's physical well-being, and *V*'s entry would not constitute a burglary[20] or any other felony.

[3] "Narrow" Approach

A narrow version of the defense provides that a person is justified in using deadly force upon another if he reasonably believes that: (1) the other person intends an unlawful and imminent entry of the dwelling; (2) the intruder

---

[18] Notice the practical irony: Pursuant to the property defense, *D* may *not* use deadly force to prevent *V* from stealing his car in the driveway, nor may he kill a trespasser on his land (but outside the dwelling). *D* may not even use deadly force if he is outside his own dwelling and seeks to prevent *V* from wrongfully boarding up the doors to his house. According to this early common law rule, once *D* is inside the dwelling and *V* is on the outside, however, *D* has the right to use deadly force regardless of *V*'s purpose for the apparently wrongful entry. Technically — but only technically — this is because *D* is protecting his habitation and not his possessory interest in property *per se*.

[19] N.C. Gen. Stat. § 14-51.1 (2004); Falco v. State, 407 So. 2d 203 (Fla. 1981); State v. Pendleton, 567 N.W.2d 265 (Minn. 1997); State v. Pellegrino, 577 N.W.2d 590 (S.D. 1998); see Mondie v. Commonwealth, 158 S.W.3d 203 (Ky. 2005) (statute interpreted to permit use of deadly force, when reasonably necessary, to prevent unlawful entry for any criminal purpose, including petty theft and simple assault).

[20] Burglary requires a specific intent to commit a felony inside the dwelling; *V* does not intend to commit a crime inside.

intends to commit a forcible felony therein or to kill or seriously injure an occupant;[21] and (3) such force is necessary to prevent the intrusion.[22] A "forcible" felony is one "committed by forcible means, violence, and surprise, such as murder, robbery, burglary, rape, or arson."[23]

This version of the defense differs from the immediately preceding one in two significant respects. First, deadly force is impermissible if the occupant knows or should know that the intruder only intends to commit a minor battery. Second, the resident may not use deadly force if he knows or should know that the intruder's purpose is to commit a nonforcible felony, such as larceny.[24]

[C] Looking at the Rules in Greater Depth

[1] May the Occupant Use Force After the Intruder Has Entered?

The defense of defense-of-habitation is triggered when an intruder attempts to enter the dwelling unlawfully. Suppose, however, that *D* awakens at night and finds *V* already in the house, or he returns home and finds *V* on the premises? Does the defense still apply?

Case law is split in this regard. Some courts consider the defense inapplicable once the entry has occurred.[25] In these states, if *D* uses deadly force, he must assert some other defense, such as self-defense (once the threat of unlawful attack is imminent) or crime prevention.

Many jurisdictions permit application of the defense, even after the intruder's[26] forcible entry has taken place.[27] It must be remembered, however, that the fact that entry has already occurred may affect the dweller's right: Once *V* is in the dwelling, *D* may know more about the intruder's intentions than he would have known prior to entry. In some circumstances, e.g., if *D* observes that

---

[21] The rule often is stated in these terms. In fact, however, any effort by the intruder to kill an occupant is itself a forcible felony, e.g., attempted murder, so that the addition of this last phrase is superfluous.

[22] State v. Garrison, 525 A.2d 498 (Conn. 1987); Crawford v. State, 190 A.2d 538 (Md. 1963).

[23] Crawford v. State, 190 A.2d at 542 (quoting 1 F. Wharton, Wharton's Criminal Law and Procedure § 206, at 453-55 (Anderson ed., 1957)).

[24] On the other hand, if the intruder seeks to enter at night in order to commit a larceny, he is guilty of common law burglary, a forcible felony. See 20.03[C][2], *infra*.

[25] E.g., State v. Brookshire, 353 S.W.2d 681 (Mo. 1962).

[26] Some courts have held that the defense of habitation cannot be used against a cohabitant of the dwelling, since such a person is not an "intruder." E.g., State v. Warren, 794 A.2d 790 (N.H. 2002).

[27] E.g., N.C. Gen. Stat. § 14-51.1 (2004) (expanding the prior law to permit the use of the defense to "prevent a forcible entry . . . or to terminate the intruder's unlawful entry"); People v. Stombaugh, 284 N.E.2d 640 (Ill. 1992).

the intruder is his well-meaning but intoxicated neighbor, the occupant's right to use deadly force will no longer be available.

[2] Are the Differences in the Habitation Rules Significant?

The differences among the rules regarding use of deadly force in defense of habitation are more theoretical than real. First, as with all other justification defenses, the right to defend the dwelling is based on reasonable appearances rather than on objective reality. This is an especially significant point in the application of the habitation defense because the right to use force is triggered *before* the intruder's entry of the dwelling and, therefore, often before the occupant is able to determine the intruder's intentions. In these days of ready access to weapons, an occupant can reasonably believe that nearly *any* intruder represents a serious threat to the dwellers' safety. In most cases, therefore, a home-dweller who uses deadly force will be able to satisfy the elements of even the narrowest version of the habitation defense.

Second, even under the narrowest version of the defense, a home-dweller will often be permitted to kill an intruder whom he knows intends to commit a *non*violent felony, such as larceny. This result follows from the inclusion of burglary in the category of forcible felonies. At common law, a person who intends to enter another person's home in order to commit larceny is a burglar if he breaks in at night. Indeed, many modern burglary statutes dispense with the nighttime requirement, thus expanding the right to use deadly force still further.[28]

[3] Relationship of the Defense to Other Defenses

[a] Self-Defense and Defense-of-Others

The defense of habitation is broader than the right to kill in self-defense or to protect a third person. First, under the original common law and "middle" approaches to habitation, a home-dweller may properly use deadly force against an intruder, even if the dweller does not reasonably believe that his life or that of an occupant is jeopardized. The habitation defense, therefore, permits use of force disproportional to the physical harm threatened.

Second, the common law defense of self-defense is not triggered until physical harm to the dweller is imminent. The right to defend the home begins when

---

[28] Contra People v. Ceballos, 526 P.2d 241 (Cal. 1974) (concluding that deadly force is impermissible in order to prevent an intruder from committing a burglary, unless the burglar intends to commit some forcible or dangerous act within the dwelling).

entry of the dwelling is imminent, which may be well before the dweller's physical well-being is in imminent jeopardy.[29]

[b] Law Enforcement Defenses

The privilege to use deadly force to defend one's house will often overlap one of the law enforcement defenses discussed in the next chapter. To the extent that an occupant reasonably believes that the intruder intends to commit a felony inside the home, the resident's right to use deadly force to defend his habitation will coincide with his right to kill in order to prevent commission of a felony (i.e., the defense of "crime prevention").[30]

§ 20.04 SPRING GUNS[31]

[A] The Issue

A "spring gun" or "trap gun" is a mechanical device that is set off when a person opens a door or other entryway into or within a building, equipped with such a device. A spring gun ordinarily has the capacity to kill or seriously injure the intruder. Such devices are frequently placed in unoccupied homes (e.g., while the residents are on vacation) or other structures (e.g., garages, barns, chicken coops on farms). Sometimes they are placed in occupied homes, in order to wound or kill an intruder while the occupant is asleep.

The problem with these devices springs from their advantage: They act mechanically — "without mercy or discretion."[32] A trap gun will as quickly kill an innocent child as an armed robber; it will kill an intoxicated neighbor mistakenly entering the premises, as well as a police officer or firefighter lawfully entering. Moreover, the device cannot determine whether deadly or nondeadly force is needed, or even whether a warning to desist would be sufficient. The lives of innocent people, therefore, may needlessly be lost by use of such devices.

Advocates of spring guns argue that as long as the law permits use of deadly force to protect a dweller of a home, the means used to inflict it — personally or by his "agent," the spring gun — should not matter. Indeed, from the occupant's perspective, a mechanical device may provide special protection: It will stop the intruder immediately upon entry, before a confrontation can occur; in the case of an elderly or infirm resident, or one untrained in firearm use, the

---

[29] State v. Johnson, 54 S.W.3d 598, 603 (Mo. Ct. App. 2001).

[30] Sometimes, however, deadly force in crime prevention is limited to prevention of forcible felonies, whereas the habitation defense may authorize deadly force against intruders intending to commit nonforcible crimes. In these circumstances, the defenses do not perfectly overlap.

[31] The issue discussed in this section applies to the privileges of defense-of-property, defense-of-habitation, self-defense, defense-of-others, and crime prevention.

[32] People v. Ceballos, 526 P.2d 241, 244 (Cal. 1974).

spring gun may be an especially effective mechanism for limiting unlawful entries.

The risks and benefits of spring guns are amply demonstrated by the facts reported in *People v. Ceballos*.[33] *C* placed a spring gun in his garage, a structure in which he kept valuable property and sometimes slept at night, after an unknown intruder attempted unsuccessfully to enter. One afternoon thereafter, while *C* was absent, two unarmed teenagers, after looking in a window to make sure that nobody was present, entered the garage in order to steal property. As they did so, the spring gun fired, striking one youth in the face.

C was charged with assault with a deadly weapon. He raised several claims in support of his right to use the spring gun, including defense-of-property, defense-of-habitation, crime prevention, and apprehension of a felon. The applicability of these defenses are considered below.

[B] Common Law Rule

At common law, a mechanical device may be used "where the intrusion is, in fact, such that the person, were he present, would be justified in taking the life or inflicting the bodily harm with his own hands."[34]

The words "in fact" in this rule are significant. One who deliberately places a spring gun on his property acts at his peril: His right to use force by this means is based on reality, rather than on reasonable appearances. Thus, if *D* is present and reasonably believes that *V*, a police officer, is a felonious intruder, he may kill *V* in defense of his habitation. If *D*'s spring gun kills the same officer, however, *D* is *not* entitled to the defense.

How does the common law rule apply to the events in *Ceballos*, described in subsection [A]? The answer depends on whether *C* would have been justified in using deadly force "by his own hands," when the youths entered the garage. The answer to *that* question depends, in turn, on the nature of the defense being claimed. For example, *C* would not have been justified in using deadly force to defend his property in the garage, so a spring gun, as well, was impermissible for *that* purpose.

C's privilege to use deadly force in defense of habitation was more problematical. Assuming that the garage were determined to be part of his dwelling (on the ground that he sometimes slept in it, or because it was physically connected to the house), he could justifiably have used deadly force by his own hands under the original, "middle," and perhaps "narrow," versions of the habitation

---

[33] *Id.*

[34] *Id.* at 244.

defense.[35] In light of this, *C* had a common law right to use a deadly mechanical device in his absence.[36]

The common law rule regarding spring guns is changing. An increasing number of states now support the proposition that a resident may not justifiably use a mechanical device designed to kill or serious injure an intruder, even if he would be permitted to use deadly force in person.[37]

§ 20.05 MODEL PENAL CODE

[A] Permissible Use of Nondeadly Force

[1] Force to Protect Property

Subject to the limitations described in subsection [B], the Code provides that a person may use nondeadly force upon another person to prevent or terminate an entry or other trespass upon land, or to prevent the carrying away of personal property, if he believes[38] that three conditions exist: (1) the other person's interference with the property is unlawful; (2) the intrusion affects property in the actor's possession, or in the possession of someone else for whom he acts; and (3) nondeadly force is immediately necessary.[39] In general, this provision conforms with the common law.

[2] Force to Recapture Property

Subject to the limitations described in subsection [B], the Code provides that a person may use nondeadly force to re-enter land or to recapture personal property if: (1) he believes that he or the person for whom he is acting was

---

[35] Under the narrow habitation defense, a home-dweller must reasonably believe that the intruder intends to commit a forcible felony upon entry. See § 20.03[B][3], *supra*. The youths intended to commit larceny, a nonforcible crime; and, as it was daytime when they entered, they were not guilty of common law burglary, a forcible felony. Under the law in *C*'s jurisdiction, however, entry of a garage in the daytime constituted statutory burglary; as a result, deadly force by *C* would have been allowed, even under the narrow version of the habitation defense. However, the state supreme court ruled in *Ceballos* that deadly force may not be used unless a burglar's entry creates a reasonable apprehension of serious harm to human life.

[36] The justifiability of the use of spring guns in crime prevention depends on the class of crimes for which deadly force may be used in such circumstances. See § 21.03[B][1], *infra*.

[37] E.g., People v. Ceballos, 526 P.2d 241 (Cal. 1974); Falco v. State, 407 So. 2d 203 (Fla. 1981); State v. Britt, 510 So. 2d 670 (La. Ct. App. 1987).

[38] As with other MPC justification defenses, the Code's "protection of property" defense is based on the actor's subjective beliefs. However, as with other MPC justification defenses, if the actor's relevant beliefs were negligent or reckless, the justification defense is unavailable to him in a prosecution for an offense based on negligence or recklessness. See generally § 18.06[B], *supra*.

[39] Model Penal Code § 3.06(1)(a).

unlawfully dispossessed of the property; and either (2a) the force is used immediately after dispossession; or (2b) even if it is not immediate, he believes that the other person has no claim of right to possession of the property. In the (2b) situation, however, re-entry of land (as distinguished from recapture of personal property) is *not* permitted unless the actor also believes that it would constitute an "exceptional hardship" to delay re-entry until he can obtain a court order.[40]

This recapture provision is broader than the common law. It extends the right to use nondeadly force to circumstances in which hot pursuit of the dispossessor is no longer involved, namely, when the actor believes that he was dispossessed at an earlier time by one who had no claim of right to the property. In this situation, the American Law Institute believes that the law "should not deny a privilege that a well conducted person would expect to have."[41] However, force may *not* be used to regain property if the dispossessed party believes that the dispossessor acted on the basis of a claim of right to the property, even if the dispossessed party believes that the other's claim ultimately will be rejected by the courts. In the latter circumstance, the Institute agrees with the common law that absent immediacy, the best approach is for the parties to resolve their conflicting claims in court.

[B] Impermissible Use of Nondeadly Force

Nondeadly force that is otherwise permitted in defense of property is unjustified in three circumstances. First, force is not "immediately necessary" unless the defender first requests desistance by the interfering party. A request is not required, however, if the defender believes that a request would be useless, dangerous to himself or to another, or would result in substantial harm to the property before the request can effectively be made.[42]

Second, a person may not use force to prevent or terminate a trespass to personal or real property if he knows that to do so would expose the trespasser to a substantial risk of serious bodily injury.[43] For example, it would be impermissible to evict a trespasser from a moving vehicle.[44]

Third, the Code addresses the situation in which both the dispossessor of land or personal property (call him "A") and the person seeking to regain it ("B") believe that they have a right to the property in dispute. For example, suppose

---

[40] Model Penal Code § 3.06(1)(b). "Exceptional hardship" would exist, for example, if the land contained a crop that would be lost if it were not immediately harvested, or if the land were the site of a small business that would suffer substantial economic damage if the owner could not enter to carry on his duties. American Law Institute, Comment to § 3.06, at 87.

[41] American Law Institute, Comment to § 3.06, at 85.

[42] Model Penal Code § 3.06(3)(a).

[43] Model Penal Code § 3.06(3)(b).

[44] American Law Institute, Comment to § 3.06, at 91.

that *A*, believing that he has a lawful right to a television set in *B*'s possession, dispossesses *B* of it. *B*, unaware that *A* claims a right to the set, immediately seeks to recapture his property. Pursuant to the Code's recapture provisions described above, *B* would be justified in using nondeadly force to retake the property. However, since *A*'s original dispossession was based on a claim of right to the property, the Code would appear to authorize *A* to use nondeadly force against *B* to protect his newly-obtained possessory interest in the television set from what *he* (*A*) believes is *B*'s wrongful efforts at recapture. Thus, without a special rule to deal with the situation, the Code seems to allow both parties, justifiably, to fight over the property.

In such circumstances, the Code prefers that the original dispossessor (in the hypothetical, *A*) forego the use of force and permit the recapture to occur. Specifically, the Code provides that *A*, a prior dispossessor, may *not* use force to resist re-entry or recaption of property by *B*, even if he believes that *B* is acting unlawfully, if *B*'s re-entry or recaption is otherwise justifiable.[45]

[C] Use of Deadly Force[46]

[1] In General

Deadly force in defense of property is prohibited except in two circumstances.

[a] Dispossession of a Dwelling

A person may use deadly force upon an intruder if he believes that: (1) the intruder is seeking to dispossess him of the dwelling; (2) the intruder has no claim of right to possession of the dwelling; and (3) such force is immediately necessary to prevent dispossession.[47] The actor may use deadly force although he does not believe that his or another person's physical well-being is jeopardized.

This provision is both broader and narrower than the common law. It is broader in that the right to use deadly force is not predicated on the actor's right to safe and private habitation, but rather is founded on his right to possession of the dwelling. The Commentary to this Code section concedes that "[t]o kill a man is, on a dispassionate view, an evil both more serious and more irrevocable than the loss of possession of a dwelling for a period during which a court order is being obtained."[48] Nonetheless, describing an illegal ouster from one's

---

[45] Model Penal Code § 3.06(3)(c). For further explanation of this complicated provision, see American Law Institute, Comment to § 3.06, at 89-90.

[46] See generally Comment, *The Use of Deadly Force in the Protection of Property Under the Model Penal Code*, 59 Colum. L. Rev. 1212 (1959).

[47] Model Penal Code § 3.06(3)(d)(i).

[48] American Law Institute, Comment to § 3.06, at 93.

home as a "provocation that is not to be depreciated," the Institute determined that the right to use deadly force should be permitted in this class of cases.

On the other hand, this provision does not authorize deadly force merely to prevent an unlawful entry into the home, as the common law originally permitted. The actor must believe two things: that the intruder's purpose for entry is to dispossess him of the dwelling, and that the intruder is acting without a claim of right.

[b] Prevention of Serious Property Crimes

A person may use deadly force in protection of property interests, inside a dwelling *or anywhere else*, if he believes that: (1) the other person is attempting to commit arson, burglary, robbery, or felonious theft or property destruction; (2) such force is immediately necessary to prevent commission of the offense; and either (3a) the other person previously used or threatened to use deadly force against him or another person in his presence, or (3b) use of nondeadly force to prevent commission of the offense would expose him or another innocent person to substantial danger of serious bodily injury.[49]

This provision is highly controversial. It justifies use of deadly force in protection of property, under circumstances that go well beyond any concern relating to habitation. Moreover, the right to kill is not based upon the actor's perceived need to protect his or another person's life. For example, if *F*, a burglar or a robber on the street, uses or threatens to use deadly force against *D* or *X*, but is disarmed by *D* and seeks to flee with the fruits of his crime, *D* may kill *F* if he believes that this is the only way to prevent *F* from successfully consummating the crime. As the Institute puts it, "deadly force may be used in order to prevent [*V*] from capitalizing upon his offense."[50]

The Model Code's position is surprising. Another section of the Code[51] provides that a private person (i.e., one who is neither a law enforcement officer nor a person assisting him) may *not* use deadly force in order to effectuate a felony arrest. Yet, when the actor's justification for using deadly force is protection of personal property — presumably, a less socially valuable interest than law enforcement — the Code authorizes its use. The Commentary recognizes that this result is inconsistent with the judgment underlying the arrest provisions.[52]

---

[49] Model Penal Code § 3.06(3)(d)(ii). This provision in some regards perfectly overlaps the Code's law enforcement provisions discussed in the next chapter. However, in other regards, it is broader. See § 21.05[B][2], *infra*.

[50] American Law Institute, Comment to § 3.06, at 96.

[51] Model Penal Code § 3.07(2)(b). See § 21.05[C][2], *infra*.

[52] American Law Institute, Comment to § 3.06, at 96-97.

[2] Spring Guns

The Model Penal Code prohibits the use of a mechanical device to protect property if it is intended to cause, or is known by the user to create a substantial risk of causing, death or serious bodily injury.[53] Thus, in those circumstances in which deadly force is permitted in defense of property, the actor must personally commit the lethal acts rather than use a spring gun.

---

[53] Model Penal Code § 3.06(5)(a).

Chapter 21

LAW ENFORCEMENT

§ 21.01 WHAT ARE THE "LAW ENFORCEMENT" DEFENSES?

Society wants its criminal laws enforced. Ideally, crimes should be prevented, people involved in criminal activity arrested, and suspects who attempt to flee restrained so that their innocence or guilt can be determined by due process of law. In order to meet these goals, police officers must perform acts that ordinarily would be criminal: They must apply force upon suspected criminals, and deprive them of their liberty or even life in the process.[1] When such acts occur in the reasonable enforcement of the criminal laws, they are legally justified.

The label attached to the defense that authorizes such conduct is problematic. Sometimes, courts speak generically of a "law enforcement" defense. This term, however, encompasses three sub-defenses, which will be described here as: (1) public authority; (2) crime prevention; and (3) effectuation of an arrest. This third defense may itself be sub-divided into two temporal components: (3a) the arrest; and (3b) prevention of the escape of the arrestee.

As considered below, common law "law enforcement" rules (today, typically codified by statute) often differentiate between police officers and private individuals. In general, the law enforcement defenses provide broader authority to police officers than to private persons to make arrests and use force in doing so. In so far as police conduct is concerned, however, the common law and statutory versions of the law enforcement defenses are subject to constitutional limitations.

---

[1] Of course, other harm can occur in the law enforcement context. For example, the police may trespass on land in order to make an arrest, or drive above the posted speed limit on a highway in the apprehension of a fugitive. These comparatively unproblematic issues are not considered in this chapter.

§ 21.02 RESTRAINT ON LIBERTY IN LAW ENFORCEMENT: "PUBLIC AUTHORITY" DEFENSE[2]

[A] By Police Officers

[1] Common Law

At common law, a police officer was authorized to make an arrest, whether for a felony or misdemeanor, if it was based upon "reasonable" or "probable" cause.[3] Felony arrests could be made with or without an arrest warrant.[4] Warrantless misdemeanor arrests, however, were valid only if the offense occurred in the officer's presence.[5]

[2] Constitutional Limits on the Common Law

The Fourth Amendment to the United States Constitution prohibits unreasonable searches and seizures. Generally speaking, this provision protects an individual's legitimate expectations of privacy.[6] Nowhere is the zone of privacy more clearly defined and more rigorously protected than in a person's home. Consequently, in contrast to the common law, warrantless felony arrests in the home are unconstitutional, in the absence of an emergency or consent.[7] Moreover, virtually no emergency will justify a warrantless *misdemeanor* arrest in the home.[8]

---

[2] See generally Rollin M. Perkins, *The Law of Arrest*, 25 Iowa L. Rev. 201 (1940).

[3] "Reasonable cause," a common law term, is equivalent to the Fourth Amendment constitutional term "probable cause." Draper v. United States, 358 U.S. 307, 310 n.3 (1959). "Probable cause" exists when the facts and circumstances within an officer's knowledge and of which she has reasonably trustworthy information are sufficient in themselves to cause a person of reasonable caution to believe that an offense has been committed and that the person to be arrested committed it. Carroll v. United States, 267 U.S. 132 (1925).

[4] See United States v. Watson, 423 U.S. 411, 418-19 (1985); Balt. & Ohio R.R. v. Cain, 31 A. 801 (Md. 1895).

[5] *Watson*, 423 U.S. at 418-19. "Presence" has been broadly construed to mean that commission of the offense is "apparent to the officers' senses." People v. Brown, 290 P.2d 528, 529 (Cal. 1955). For example, this would include hearing the offense committed over a telephone. People v. Cahill, 328 P.2d 995, 998 (Cal. Ct. App. 1958).

[6] Katz v. United States, 389 U.S. 347 (1967).

[7] Payton v. New York, 445 U.S. 573 (1980).

[8] Welsh v. Wisconsin, 466 U.S. 740, 753 (1984).

[B] By Private Persons

Private persons have common law authority to make "citizen arrests" and, therefore, defend against a criminal charge of false imprisonment. The common law provides that a private citizen may arrest another person for a felony, or for a misdemeanor involving a breach of the peace,[9] if: (1) the crime actually occurred; and (2) she reasonably believes that the suspect committed the offense.[10] With misdemeanors, the offense must also occur in the arresting person's presence.[11]

Under this rule, the arresting party acts at her criminal peril regarding the first element of the defense, but is permitted a reasonable mistake of fact regarding the second element. For example, suppose that D observes V flee from a bank as the bank alarm goes off. D believes that V robbed the bank and, therefore, arrests V. If it later turns out that V did not rob the bank, and D is prosecuted for false imprisonment of V, D may not successfully assert a public authority defense unless the bank was robbed. If it was robbed, however, D may successfully claim the defense, although V was not the robber (e.g., she was a customer fleeing the scene), as long as D's belief in V's guilt was a reasonable one.

The Fourth Amendment only applies to the actions of public officers.[12] Therefore, private parties who make arrests are not subject to the constitutional rules discussed above that apply to police officers.

§ 21.03 FORCE USED IN LAW ENFORCEMENT: COMMON AND STATUTORY LAW

[A] Nondeadly Force

A police officer or private citizen may use force in law enforcement, either to prevent the commission or consummation of a crime, or to make an arrest after the offense has been committed. Criminal prosecutions for use of nondeadly force in such circumstances are rare.

The common law rule regarding use of nondeadly force in law enforcement may be summarized simply: A police officer or private person is justified in using nondeadly force upon another if she reasonably believes that: (1) such

---

[9] "Breach of the peace" is conduct that causes or tends to cause a disturbance of the peace and tranquility of other persons. Cantwell v. Connecticut, 310 U.S. 296, 308 (1940). Sometimes, "breach of the peace" is a specific offense; in other cases, it is a general term that encompasses crimes such as "disorderly conduct" and "disturbing the peace."

[10] Rollin M. Perkins & Ronald N. Boyce, Criminal Law 1094-95 (3d ed. 1982).

[11] See State v. Johnson, 930 P.2d 1148, 1154 (N.M. 1996).

[12] Burdeau v. McDowell, 256 U.S. 465 (1921).

other person is committing or has committed a felony, or a misdemeanor amounting to a breach of the peace; and (2) the force used is necessary to prevent commission of the offense, or to effectuate an arrest, i.e., to make the arrest or to prevent the arrestee's escape.[13]

[B] Deadly Force

Deadly force may *never* be used to prevent commission of a misdemeanor offense, or to effectuate an arrest of a misdemeanant.[14] The following discussion relates to use of deadly force in felony cases.

[1] Crime Prevention

Deadly force is permitted to prevent commission of felonies. A split of authority exists regarding the scope of this right.

[a] Broad Defense: Minority Rule

The broad view is that a police officer or private person is justified in using deadly force upon another if she reasonably believes that: (1) such other person is committing any felony; and (2) deadly force is necessary to prevent commission of the crime.[15] This rule is remarkably broad in that it authorizes use of necessary force to prevent nonviolent felonies. Thus, *D* may kill *V*, a would-be felonious thief, if it is the only means to prevent her from taking the personal property of *D* or a third person, even though no life is jeopardized by *V*'s criminal activities.

The right to use deadly force in crime prevention is broader than the scope of the common law justification of defense-of-property, which bars the use of deadly force to protect a person's possessory interest in property.[16] This difference results in an undesirable anomaly: If a defendant kills an intended thief, she may avoid conviction if she claims the defense of crime prevention, but may be convicted of murder if she raises a defense-of-property claim.

[b] Narrow Defense: Majority Rule

Most states do not enforce as broad a defense of crime prevention as that mentioned in the preceding subsection. Usually, the right to use deadly force is limited to the prevention of "forcible" or "atrocious" felonies, i.e., felonies involv-

---

[13] See Durham v. State, 159 N.E. 145 (Ind. 1927); In re C.L.D., 739 A.2d 353, 354-355 (D.C. 1999) (citing a prior edition of this Text); Restatement (Second) of Torts §§ 141-143 (1965).

[14] See Tennessee v. Garner, 471 U.S. 1, 12 (1985); Durham v. State, 159 N.E. at 147.

[15] State v. Rutherford, 8 (1 Hawks) N.C. 457 (1821).

[16] See § 20.02[A], *supra*.

ing the use or threat of physical force of violence against any person.[17] Thus, under this rule, a store owner may shoot a would-be robber, if necessary, to prevent the commission of the offense, but she may not justifiably kill one who takes property and attempts to leave without paying for it, as the latter offense is a misdemeanor or, at most, the nonviolent felony of larceny.[18]

[2] Effectuation of an Arrest

[a] By Police Officers

[i] Early Common Law Rule

Until the fourteenth century, a law enforcement officer had the right (perhaps even the duty) to use deadly force against any person whom the officer reasonably believed had committed *any* felony. The officer was justified in killing the felon *even if deadly force was unnecessary to effectuate the felon's detention.*

This extreme approach was based on the premise that felons were outlaws at war with society.[19] Society was justified, therefore, in treating them as dangerous combatants whose lives could be taken for the community's benefit. This view was strengthened by the fact that all felonies were subject to the penalty of death and forfeiture of property. Thus, it was said, by committing a capital offense, a felon forfeited his right to life;[20] his killing was merely "a premature execution of the inevitable judgment."[21]

[ii] Modification of the Rule

The stark approach of pre-fourteenth century England is no longer followed. Necessity, not part of the original common law rule, is now included as an element of the defense. Thus, deadly force is permitted only as a last resort.[22] Nonetheless, under the modified rule, a person may use deadly force upon another if she reasonably believes: (1) the suspect committed a forcible *or non-*

---

[17] E.g., 4 William Blackstone, Commentaries on the Law of England *180 (1769); 1 Matthew Hale, History of the Pleas of the Crown *488 (1736); Ga. Code Ann. § 16-3-204 (2004).

[18] See Laney v. State, 361 S.E.2d 841 (Ga. Ct. App. 1987), *overruled on other grounds*, Holmes v. State, 543 S.E.2d 688 (Ga. 2001) (upholding *L*'s conviction for manslaughter in the death of *V*, who attempted to leave *L*'s convenience store with a beer without paying for it; but stating that deadly force *would* have been permitted if *L* had reasonably believed that *V* was planning to rob the store).

[19] See Schumann v. McGinn, 240 N.W.2d 525, 532-33 (Minn. 1976).

[20] Petrie v. Cartwright, 70 S.W. 297, 299 (Ky. 1902).

[21] Note, *Legalized Murder of a Fleeing Felon*, 15 Va. L. Rev. 582, 583 (1925).

[22] Schumann v. McGinn, 240 N.W.2d at 533; 4 Blackstone, Note 17, *supra*, at *289; 2 Hale, Note 17, *supra*, at *85.

forcible felony; and (2) such force is necessary to make the arrest or to prevent the suspect from escaping. It should be observed that this rule is broader than the majority common law rule pertaining to the use of deadly force in crime prevention, which only authorizes the use of deadly force to repel *forcible* felonies.

Some jurisdictions have narrowed the scope of the defense still further. In these states, deadly force is only permitted when necessary to effectuate an arrest for a forcible or atrocious felony.[23]

The rules described here are now subject to constitutional dictates, discussed in § 21.04.

[b] By Private Persons

A private person may use deadly force, if reasonably necessary, to arrest or apprehend a felon, but the defense ordinarily is narrower than the comparable right held by police officers. The special limitations are the result of lawmakers' concerns about "uncontrolled vigilantism and anarchistic actions . . . [as well as] the danger of death or injury of innocent persons at the hands of untrained volunteers using firearms."[24]

Although the rules vary among the states, some of the special requirements that often must be satisfied before a private person may justifiably use deadly force in connection with a felony arrest include: (1) the offense must be a forcible felony;[25] (2) the arresting party must give the suspect notice of her intention to make the arrest;[26] and (3) the arresting party must be correct in her belief that the person against whom the force is used actually committed the offense in question, i.e., a reasonable mistake of fact in this regard neither justifies nor excuses the use of deadly force.[27]

§ 21.04 FORCE USED IN LAW ENFORCEMENT: CONSTITUTIONAL LIMITS[28]

[A] Background: The Controversy

Many commentators have criticized the breadth of the common law law-enforcement defense, set out in § 21.03[B][2][a][ii], *supra*, which authorizes the

---

[23] E.g., Storey v. State, 71 Ala. 329, 339 (1882).

[24] Commonwealth v. Klein, 363 N.E.2d 1313, 1317-18 (Mass. 1977).

[25] E.g., *id.* at 1319.

[26] E.g., Commonwealth v. Chermansky, 242 A.2d 237, 240 (Pa. 1968).

[27] E.g., *id.*

[28] See generally Steven E. Barkan & Steven F. Cohn, *Racial Prejudice and Support by Whites for Police Use of Force: A Research Note*, 15 Just. Q. 743 (1998); Kevin P. Jenkins, *Police Use of*

use of deadly force, when reasonably necessary, to arrest or prevent the escape of persons suspected of *non*forcible felonies.

Critics maintain that police officers too often kill or seriously injure innocent people, including suspects innocent of any crime and bystanders caught in the gunfire.[29] Additionally, police use of lethal force may have an undesirable effect on police-community relations. Police shootings can appear to some to be racially motivated,[30] or the result of "trigger-happy" law enforcement officers.[31] Even when these appearances are inaccurate, police use of deadly force can increase tension between them and the communities they serve. In the short run, this may result in disorder; in the long run, it may result in disrespect for the law.

Critics of the common law defense have also claimed that the underlying justifications for the rule no longer apply. The law no longer considers a felon an outlaw whose life may be taken at any time, regardless of necessity. Nor does the forfeiture theory withstand modern scrutiny: Only the crime of murder carries the penalty of death today, and even here it is not mandatory. It cannot be said, therefore, that any felon's "execution" on the street merely speeds up an inevitable process.[32]

Perhaps as a consequence of criticisms of police shootings, law enforcement agencies in many large American cities began in the late 1970s to develop policies restricting police use of firearms to circumstances in which a threat of death or serious bodily injury is posed.[33] In 1985, these changes in depart-

---

Deadly Force Against Minorities: Ways to Stop the Killing, 9 Harv. BlackLetter L.J. 1 (1992); Edward J. Littlejohn, *Deadly Force and its Effects on Police-Community Relations*, 27 How. L.J. 1131 (1984); Abraham N. Tennebaum, *The Influence of the Garner Decision on Police Use of Deadly Force*, 85 J. Crim. L. & Criminology 241 (1994).

[29] Due to a lack of systematic official recordkeeping, there are few statistical studies on bystander victimization in police-criminal gunfire. But, one study based on data obtained from newspaper reports in four cities found substantial increases in reported killings and woundings from 1977 through 1988. In a two-year period, for example, 250 bystanders were killed or wounded in the four cities. The study stated that such shootings "rank[ed] at the top of public outrage." Illinois v. Wardlow, 528 U.S. 119, 131 n.6 (2000) (Stevens, J., concurring in part and dissenting in part) (directly quoting from Sherman et. al, *Stray Bullets and "Mushrooms": Random Shootings of Bystanders in Four Cities, 1977-1978*, 5 J. Quantitative Criminology 297, 303 (1989)).

[30] See The President's Commission on Law Enforcement and Administration of Justice Task Force Report: The Police 183-90 (1967) (documenting the belief among racial minorities that police act abusively on racial grounds, and that such conduct is a principal reason for friction between the police and minority communities); see also Barkan & Cohn, Note 28, *supra* (noting significant attitudinal differences, between white and non-white communities, regarding police use of force).

[31] Eric Lichtblau, *LAPD Officers Faulted in 3 of 4 Shooting Cases*, L.A. Times, Aug. 14, 1994, at A1 (reporting that, according to a review of nearly 700 shooting reports in 1989, officers succumbed to "the John Wayne Syndrome" and, in 75% of the cases, fired their weapons inappropriately).

[32] Of course, the forfeiture justification could never withstand analysis when the suspected felon was innocent of the crime.

[33] Tennessee v. Garner, 471 U.S. 1, 18-19 (1985).

mental policy received the attention of the Supreme Court, as discussed immediately below.

[B] *Tennessee v. Garner*:[34] **The Common Law Restricted**

[1] Facts of the Case

In *Garner*, two officers were dispatched at night to answer a "prowler inside
call." At the scene, a witness told the officers that she had heard glass breaking
and that "they" were, or "someone" was, breaking into the house next door.

One officer investigated while his partner went to the police car to call the dis-
patcher. The investigating officer saw someone run into the backyard of the
apparently-burglarized home. He chased the suspect, *G*, a fifteen-year-old
eighth-grader, to a six-foot high chain-link fence where *G* crouched at the base.
The officer shone a flashlight on *G*'s hands and face, saw no sign of a weapon,
and determined that he was "reasonably sure" that the youth was unarmed.

G began to climb the fence. The officer concluded that if the youth made it
over the fence he would elude capture. The officer called out "police, halt"; when
G did not stop, the officer shot him. The bullet struck the youth in the back of
the head, killing him.

G's suspected conduct constituted burglary. As such, the officer's use of deadly
force was justified under Tennessee law, which authorized the use of deadly
force to arrest a suspect for any felony. Nonetheless, *G*'s family brought a federal action against the police seeking damages for violation of the youth's constitutional rights, on the ground that the use of deadly force against *G* violated
the Fourth Amendment bar on "unreasonable searches and seizures."

[2] Holding of *Garner*

According to the Supreme Court, a police officer violates the Fourth Amendment prohibition on unreasonable searches and seizures if she uses deadly
force to effectuate an arrest, unless: (1) she "has probable cause to believe that
the suspect poses a significant threat of death or serious physical injury to the
officer or others"; and (2) such force is necessary to make the arrest or prevent
escape. In regard to the necessity element, a warning, if feasible, must be given
to the suspect before deadly force is employed. The first condition is satisfied "if
the suspect threatens the officer with a weapon or there is probable cause to
believe that he has committed a crime involving the infliction or threatened
infliction of serious physical harm."

---

[34] 471 U.S. 1 (1985).

[3] **Reasoning of the Supreme Court**

An arrest of a suspect constitutes a "seizure" of that person. Consequently, the Fourth Amendment ban on unreasonable seizures is implicated when a police officer makes an arrest. In order to determine whether *G*'s seizure by deadly force was reasonable, the Supreme Court balanced the suspect's interests against those of society.

According to the Court, the intrusion on a suspect's rights is "unmatched" when an arresting officer uses deadly force — *G*'s fundamental interest in life was jeopardized by the officer's use of deadly force. Such force also frustrates the suspect's and society's interest in obtaining a judicial determination of his guilt and punishment. Consequently, society's interest in the arrest of nonviolent felons is outweighed by the competing interests: "[I]t is not better that all felony suspects die than that they escape." According to Justice White, author of *Garner*, "[a] police officer may not seize an unarmed, nondangerous suspect by shooting him dead."

[4] **Looking Deeper at** *Garner*

A few points of clarification are in order. First, the Court in *Garner* did not need to determine what constitutes "deadly force," since the officer's use of force in the case clearly satisfied any plausible definition of the term. It is not clear, therefore, whether the term will be defined as it is used in the self-defense context[35] or in some other manner. Possibly, however, an officer may *threaten* to use deadly force ("Stop, or I'll shoot") or even shoot her gun into the air well above the head of the fugitive, since the purpose here is not to kill or seriously injure the arrestee.

Does *Garner* bar the use of force that is intended to cause, or is known to create a substantial risk of causing, serious bodily injury, as distinguished from death? Many courts have adopted the Model Penal Code definition of "deadly force," which would treat such force as deadly.[36] Therefore, for example, use of a police dog to subdue an arrestee by biting her might be impermissible.[37]

Second, since the Fourth Amendment only applies to governmental conduct, common law and statutory provisions relating to the use of deadly force by private persons are not directly affected by *Garner*.[38] Third, it is unclear whether the rule of *Garner* has application in *criminal* prosecutions of police officers who

---

[35] See §§ 18.02[A] (common law) and 18.06[A][2][a] (Model Penal Code), *supra*.

[36] E.g., Smith v. City of Hemet, 394 F.3d 689 (9th Cir. 2005); Ryder v. City of Topeka, 814 F.2d 1412 (10th Cir. 1987); Pruitt v. City of Montgomery, 771 F.2d 1475 (11th Cir. 1985).

[37] Smith v. City of Hemet, 394 F.3d 689, 704-07 (9th Cir. 2005).

[38] People v. Couch, 461 N.W.2d 683 (Mich. 1990).

shoot nonviolent felons. Arguably, the rule simply provides a *civil* remedy, as in *Garner*, for use of excessive police force.[39]

Finally, it is evident that deadly force may no longer be used by police officers against persons suspected of nonforcible felonious conduct. Less evident, but also true, is that deadly force is sometimes barred by *Garner*, even when it is necessary to effectuate the arrest of a person suspected of committing a so-called "forcible" or "atrocious" felony. Burglary — the crime that *G* was suspected of committing — is ordinarily deemed a forcible felony; nonetheless, the Court held that the police were not entitled to kill *G*, because *G* was apparently unarmed. The lesson of *Garner* is that the constitutionality of police use of deadly force no longer depends on an abstract characterization of an offense as a "forcible" or "atrocious" felony; instead, it depends on the apparent dangerousness of the suspect and, therefore, the risk the suspect poses to others if she is not imme-diately apprehended, based on the facts of the individual case.

§ 21.05 MODEL PENAL CODE

[A] Authority to Arrest

The Model Penal Code defense of "execution of public duty" provides that conduct is justified when it is required or permitted by: (1) a law defining the duties of a government officer; (2) a law pertaining to the execution of legal process; (3) an order of a court; or (4) any other law imposing a public duty on the actor.[40]

This defense is also available in two circumstances in which an actor *lacks* legal authority to act, but believes that she does. Essentially, these two situa-tions constitute special mistake-of-law rules. First, a law enforcement officer acts justifiably if she believes, albeit incorrectly, that her conduct is authorized "by the judgment or direction of a competent court or tribunal or in the lawful exe-cution of legal process."[41] For example, if *D* makes an arrest based on a warrant (i.e., legal process) that later proves to be defective (e.g., it was issued on less than probable cause), she is not subject to criminal prosecution for restricting the arrestee's liberty in an unlawful manner.

Second, the defense is available to an actor who believes that she is author-ized to assist a public officer in the performance of her duties, although it turns out that the officer was acting beyond her authority.[42] For example, if an offi-

---

[39] State v. Clothier, 753 P.2d 1267 (Kan. 1988) (holding that *Garner* does not apply in criminal prosecutions).

[40] Model Penal Code § 3.03(1).

[41] Model Penal Code § 3.03(3)(a).

[42] Model Penal Code § 3.03(3)(b).

cer requests assistance from a bystander in making an arrest, the private citizen is not subject to prosecution if the officer lacked authority to arrest the suspect, e.g., lacked probable cause for the arrest or did not have a required warrant.

[B] Crime Prevention

[1] Use of Force, In General

A police officer or private person is justified in using force upon another if she believes that: (1) such other person is about to commit suicide, inflict serious bodily injury upon herself, or commit a crime involving or threatening bodily injury, damage to or loss of property, or a breach of the peace; and (2) the force is immediately necessary to prevent commission of the aforementioned act.[43] Deadly force is impermissible except as discussed below.

The Code does not impose any special limitations on the use of nondeadly force in crime prevention. Instead, it provides that the limitations on the use of force imposed by the other justification provisions of the Code apply to the use of force in crime prevention.[44]

[2] Use of Deadly Force

A police officer or private person may not use deadly force to prevent the commission of a crime unless she believes that: (1) a substantial risk exists that the suspect will cause death or serious bodily injury to another person unless she prevents the suspect from committing the offense; and (2) use of deadly force presents no substantial risk of injury to bystanders.[45]

This provision should be compared to the Code's deadly-force provisions in analogous circumstances. First, it largely parallels the effectuation-of-arrest defense discussed below, except that the crime prevention defense applies to all persons, public or private, whereas only public officers and those aiding them may use deadly force in the arrest process. The Institute's justification for this distinction is that "[i]n modern conditions, the arrest of suspected criminals is peculiarly the concern of the police. The prevention of crime, on the other hand, is properly the concern of everybody."[46]

Second, the crime prevention defense is somewhat narrower than the rules regarding defense of property.[47] The present defense, but not the defense of

---

[43] Model Penal Code § 3.07(5)(a).

[44] Model Penal Code § 3.07(5)(a)(i).

[45] Model Penal Code § 3.07(5)(a)(ii)(A).

[46] American Law Institute, Comment to § 3.07, at 132.

[47] Id., Comment to § 3.06, at 95 n.48.

property, prohibits the use of deadly force if it would jeopardize the safety of bystanders. Moreover, deadly force may be used in defense of property in some circumstances in which the safety of the actor is no longer threatened,[48] but deadly force is *not* permitted in crime prevention unless the actor believes that there is a related threat of death or serious bodily injury connected to the commission of the crime.

[C] Effectuation of an Arrest

[1] Use of Force, In General

A police officer or private person is justified in using force upon another to make or assist in making an arrest, or to prevent the suspect's escape, if the actor: (1) believes that force is immediately necessary to effectuate a lawful arrest or to prevent the suspect's escape;[49] and (2a) makes known to such other person the purpose of the arrest or (2b) believes that such other person understands the purpose of the arrest or that notice cannot reasonably be provided.[50] Deadly force is impermissible except as discussed immediately below.

[2] Use of Deadly Force

Deadly force may never be used by a private person, acting on her own, to make an arrest or to prevent a suspect's escape. However, deadly force may be employed by a police officer, or a private person assisting someone she believes is a law enforcement officer, to make an arrest or to prevent the suspect's escape if: (1) the arrest is for a felony; (2) the requirements for the use of force set out in subsection [1] are satisfied; (3) the actor believes that the use of deadly force creates no substantial risk of harm to innocent bystanders; and either (4a) the actor believes that the crime included the use or threatened use of deadly force; or (4b) the actor believes that a substantial risk exists that the suspect will kill or seriously harm another if her arrest is delayed or if she escapes.[51]

This Code provision is considerably narrower than the common law. First, the common law permitted private citizens acting alone to use deadly force in making arrests. Second, deadly force may not be used unless the actor affirmatively believes that its use will not seriously jeopardize the safety of bystanders. For example, assume *D*, a police officer, purposely shoots and kills *V*, a dan-

---

[48] See § 20.05[C][1][b], *supra.*

[49] The defense is not available, however, if the arrest or degree of force used was unlawful and if the actor's belief in its lawfulness was the result of a mistake of law regarding provisions of the criminal law or the law governing the scope of her power to arrest. Model Penal Code § 3.09(1). See generally American Law Institute, Comment to § 3.07, at 107.

[50] Model Penal Code §§ 3.07(1), 3.07(2)(a), 3.07(3).

[51] Model Penal Code § 3.07(2)(b).

gerous fleeing felon, on a crowded street. At common law, *D*'s conduct as to *V* would be justified; under the Code, *D* would be denied the law enforcement defense, and could be convicted of purposely killing *V*, unless she believed that her actions did not jeopardize the bystanders' safety.[52]

Third, unlike the common law, the Code does not permit use of deadly force in making arrests for nonforcible felonies. The Code provision appears to conform to the dictates of *Tennessee v. Garner*.[53] The Code, as required by *Garner*, does not justify use of deadly force in effectuating arrests unless the arrestee appears to pose such a high level of risk to the safety of another that her immediate capture overrides her constitutionally recognized interest in her life.[54]

---

[52] This provision represents a departure from the rule set out in Model Penal Code § 3.09(3), as discussed at § 18.06[C], *supra*. Under § 3.09, a person whose conduct in relation to *V* is justified, but whose conduct recklessly or negligently threatens the safety of *X*, a bystander, is entitled to the defense in a prosecution for use of force against *V*, but may be convicted of an offense based on recklessness or negligence regarding *X*. Under § 3.07, however, *D*'s recklessness regarding the safety of *X* results in the loss of the defense *in relation to V*. The drafters of the Code believed that this was an appropriate way of emphasizing the priority that police officers must accord to the safety of bystanders. American Law Institute, Comment to § 3.07, at 118.

[53] 471 U.S. 1 (1985). See § 21.04, *supra*.

[54] American Law Institute, Comment to § 3.07, at 120.

Chapter 22

NECESSITY

§ 22.01 BASIC NATURE OF THE DEFENSE[1]

This chapter considers the defense of necessity, also called the "lesser evil" or "choice of evils" defense. Unfortunately, "[t]he origins and present status of the defense . . . are shrouded in uncertainty and confusion."[2] Indeed, at the foundational level, there is uncertainty whether the defense should be classified as a justification defense, an excuse, or as having characteristics of both. Also, this defense is often confused with, or is treated as part of, a broader defense encompassing the defense of duress. The excuse characteristics of "necessity" (to the extent that they exist) and the relationship of necessity to the defense of duress, are considered in the next chapter.[3] This chapter considers only necessity as a justification defense.

The defense of necessity can arise in a myriad of circumstances, but it is most often invoked successfully when an actor encounters the following dilemma: As a result of some natural (non-human) force or condition, he must choose between violating a *relatively minor* offense, on the one hand, and suffering (or allowing others to suffer) *substantial harm* to person or property, on the other hand. For example, the necessity defense applies if a seaman violates an embargo by putting into a foreign port due to dangerous and unforeseeable weather conditions,[4] a person drives on a suspended license in order to take a loved one to the hospital in a dire emergency,[5] or a motorist exceeds the speed limit in order to pass another car and move to the right lane, so that an emergency vehicle can pass.[6]

---

[1] See generally George Fletcher, Rethinking Criminal Law § 10.2 (1978); Kent Greenawalt, Conflicts of Law and Morality 286-310 (1987); Glanville Williams, Criminal Law: The General Part §§ 229-239 (2d ed. 1961); Edward B. Arnolds & Norman F. Garland, *The Defense of Necessity in Criminal Law: The Right to Choose the Lesser Evil*, 65 J. Crim. L. & Criminology 289 (1974); P.R. Glazebrook, *The Necessity Plea in English Criminal Law*, 30 Cambridge L.J. 87 (1972); John T. Parry, *The Virtue of Necessity: Reshaping Culpability and the Rule of Law*, 36 Hous. L. Rev. 397 (1999); Rollin M. Perkins, *Impelled Perpetration Restated*, 33 Hastings L.J. 403 (1981); Lawrence P. Tiffany & Carl A. Anderson, *Legislating the Necessity Defense in Criminal Law*, 52 Den. L.J. 839 (1975).

[2] Greenawalt, Note 1, *supra*, at 288; see also Toops v. State, 643 N.E.2d 387, 388 (Ind. Ct. App. 1994) ("The origins of the necessity defense are lost in antiquity.").

[3] See §§ 23.03, 23.05-.06, *infra*.

[4] The William Gray, 29 Fed. Cas. 1300 (D.N.Y.) (No. 17,694) (1810).

[5] State v. Baker, 579 A.2d 479 (Vt. 1990).

[6] State v. Messler, 562 A.2d 1138 (Conn. App. Ct. 1989); see also Toops v. State, 643 N.E.2d 387 (Ind. Ct. App. 1994) (defense is available where *T*, an intoxicated passenger, assumed control of a moving, careening vehicle, when the original driver dove into the back seat in a panic).

Not all litigated necessity cases fit the preceding paradigm. For example, courts have been required to determine whether it is justifiable for a homeless person to violate a city ordinance banning sleeping in designated public areas,[7] or for a person to do any of the following: possess marijuana for use to reduce the effects of a serious disease;[8] to distribute clean hypodermic needles to drug addicts in an effort to combat the spread of acquired immune deficiency syndrome (AIDS);[9] to escape confinement because of intolerable prison conditions;[10] to possess a firearm (otherwise in violation of law) because of an unlawful imminent threat to life;[11] to steal food out of economic necessity;[12] to kidnap a person in order to remove her from the influence of a "religious cult";[13] or to kill an innocent person in order to save several innocent lives.[14] Occasionally, too, the defense is raised when a person commits civil disobedience in order to signal his opposition to a law or governmental policy.[15]

Generally speaking, "necessity" may be characterized as a "residual justification defense." That is, it is a defense of last resort: It legitimizes technically illegal conduct that common sense, principles of justice, and/or utilitarian considerations convince us is justifiable, but which is not dealt with — neither authorized nor disallowed — by any other recognized justification defense. Thus, the necessity defense serves as "a supplement to legislative judgment."[16] It comes into play in relatively unique instances in which it may fairly be assumed that lawmakers *would* have authorized the conduct if they had considered the matter in advance.

The principle of necessity — that, if circumstances require a choice among various evils, an actor is justified if he chooses the least harmful option — is one so "essential to the rationality and justice of the criminal law, [that it] is appropriately addressed in a penal code."[17]

---

[7] In re Eichorn, 69 Cal. App. 4th 382 (Ct. App. 1998) (permitting consideration of the defense).

[8] E.g., Jenks v. State, 582 So. 2d 676 (Fla. Dist. Ct. App. 1991) (permitting a medical necessity defense); State v. Bonjour, 694 N.W.2d 511 (Iowa 2005) (disallowing such a defense); see also United States v. Oakland Cannabis Buyers' Coop., 532 U.S. 483 (2001) (not recognizing the defense in a federal prosecution for manufacturing and distributing marijuana).

[9] Commonwealth v. Leno, 616 N.E.2d 453 (Mass. 1993) (disallowing the defense).

[10] See § 23.05, *infra*.

[11] United States v. Gomez, 92 F.3d 770 (9th Cir. 1996) (allowing the defense).

[12] State v. Moe, 24 P.2d 638, 640 (Wash. 1933) (stating that "[e]conomic necessity has never been accepted as a defense to a criminal charge").

[13] People v. Brandyberry, 812 P.2d 674 (Colo. Ct. App. 1991) (disallowing the defense).

[14] See § 22.04, *infra*.

[15] See § 22.03, *infra*.

[16] Greenawalt, Note 1, *supra*, at 289.

[17] American Law Institute, Comment to § 3.02, at 9.

§ 22.02 GENERAL RULES

Necessity may not have been a common law defense in England,[18] but it is a part of the common law tradition of the United States.[19] Despite this, the defense has no single accepted definition.[20] Indeed, at any given time in history it was exceedingly difficult to determine the standing and scope of the defense in any particular jurisdiction.[21]

Much of this has changed. Largely as the result of the inclusion of a choice-of-evils provision in the Model Penal Code,[22] approximately one-half of the states now statutorily recognize the defense. Some of the statutes define "necessity" in general terms; others are more specific in their descriptions. In states without a statutory defense, the vague contours of the common law seemingly apply.[23]

The parameters of the common law defense may be deduced from its purpose as described in the preceding chapter section. Subject to three potential limitations mentioned below, generally speaking, a person is justified in violating a criminal law if the following six conditions are met.

First, the actor must be "faced with a clear and imminent danger."[24] For example, in *United States v. Paolello*,[25] X, unjustifiably fired a weapon in the air, threatening P, a convicted felon. To protect himself, P wrested the gun from X and ran away with it. P was prosecuted for violation of a statute that made it an offense for a convicted felon to possess a firearm. Based on these facts, however, P was entitled to an instruction on the necessity defense, because the danger to him was clear and imminent. In contrast, in *Commonwealth v. Leno*,[26] L participated in a needle exchange program run by AIDS activists, in which he and others furnished clean needles to drug addicts in order to reduce the spread of the deadly disease. L was charged with possession and distribution of hypodermic needles without a prescription. The Supreme Judicial Court of Massa-

---

[18] Glanville Williams states "somewhat confidently" that it was a defense in England. Williams, Note 1, *supra*, at § 231. Others disagree. See English Law Commission, No. 83, Criminal Law Report on Defences of General Application 20 (1977).

[19] American Law Institute, Comment to § 3.02, at 10.

[20] Toops v. State, 643 N.E.2d 387, 389 (Ind. Ct. App. 1994).

[21] American Law Institute, Comment to § 3.02, at 10-11.

[22] See § 22.05, *infra*.

[23] However, in the *federal* courts, it is now considered "an open question whether federal courts ever have authority to recognize a necessity defense not provided by statute." United States v. Oakland Cannabis Buyers' Coop., 532 U.S. 483, 490 (2001) (dictum).

[24] Commonwealth v. Schuchardt, 557 N.E.2d 1380, 1381 (Mass. 1990) (quoting Commonwealth v. Brugmann, 433 N.E.2d 457 (Mass. App. Ct. 1982)).

[25] 951 F.2d 537 (3d Cir. 1991).

[26] 616 N.E.2d 453 (Mass. 1993).

chusetts held that *L* was not entitled to a jury instruction on the defense necessity because the harm — spread of AIDS — was not imminent in any given case in which the needles were exchanged.

Second, the defendant must expect, as a reasonable person, that his action will be effective in abating the danger that he seeks to avoid, i.e., there must be a direct causal relationship between his action and the harm to be averted.[27] For example, an inmate who flees confinement because of a raging prison fire, has chosen a path that will directly save his life.

Third, there must be no effective *legal* way to avert the harm.[28] For example, in *Nelson v. State*,[29] *N* drove his truck onto a side road off the highway, where it became stuck in a marsh. After spending an hour trying to free the vehicle, *N* and a friend went to a nearby Highway Department Yard where they took a dump truck without permission, and unsuccessfully used it to try to pull *N*'s vehicle out of the mud, damaging the dump truck. *N* was prosecuted for reckless destruction of the Highway Department's property and of driving the truck without consent. The court held that the facts did not support a defense of necessity, in part because *N* had lawful alternatives in his situation — on several occasions strangers offered to help pull the vehicle out of the marsh or by calling for a tow truck or the police.

Fourth, the harm that the defendant will cause by violating the law must be less serious than the harm that he seeks to avoid.[30] Two features of this lesser-harm principle must be understood. First, in balancing the harms, the defendant's actions "should be weighed against the harm reasonably foreseeable at the time, rather than the harm that actually occurs."[31] For example, if *D*'s car loses its brakes and *D* must choose between striking one of two parked automobiles, one of which is occupied by one person (who will likely be injured by the collision) and another that apparently is unoccupied, *D* should choose the latter option. He does not lose the defense, however, if it later turns out that the "unoccupied car" in fact contained two children inside, not visible to *D* when he had to make the emergency decision. Second, given the facts as they reasonably appear, the issue is not whether the *defendant* believes that he made the right choice, but rather is "whether the defendant's value judgment was [in fact] correct,"[32] as determined by the judge or the jury. What is less clear is whether the

---

[27] *Id.* at 455; United States v. Schoon, 971 F.2d 193, 195 (9th Cir. 1991).

[28] Commonwealth v. Leno, 616 N.E.2d at 455; People v. Gray, 571 N.Y.S.2d 851, 853 (N.Y. Crim. Ct. 1991).

[29] 597 P.2d 977 (Alaska 1979).

[30] State v. Warshow, 410 A.2d 1000, 1001-02 (Vt. 1979).

[31] Nelson v. State, 597 P.2d at 980.

[32] *Id.* at 980 n.6.

value judgment should be made on utilitarian grounds[33] or on the basis "of what is [morally] right and proper conduct under the circumstances."[34]

A fifth condition of the necessity defense is that lawmakers must not have previously "anticipated the choice of evils and determined the balance to be struck between the competing values" in a manner in conflict with the defendant's choice.[35] For example, a defendant may not defend his illegal use of marijuana for medical purposes if the legislature previously "weighed the competing value of medical use of marijuana against the values served by prohibition of its use or possession," and rejected the former claim.[36]

The final feature of the necessity defense is that the defendant must come to the situation with clean hands. That is, he must not have "substantially contribute[d] to the emergency"[37] or wrongfully "placed himself in a situation in which he would be forced to engage in criminal conduct."[38] For example, suppose that D recklessly starts a fire. He realizes that the fire is likely to spread quickly and burn down a number of residences, so he purposely burns V's farm land in order to create a "fire line" that will prevent a major conflagration. Although D's act satisfies the other elements of the defense, he may be denied the defense of necessity because he was responsible for creating the emergency.[39]

Even if these elements of the necessity defense are proven, three potential limitations on the application of the necessity defense may come into play. First, some states limit the defense to emergencies created by natural (as distinguished from human) forces.[40] Thus, in these jurisdictions, D may trespass on property in order to avoid a tornado, but not to escape an armed robber. Likewise, D, a prison inmate, may be able to claim necessity if he flees a prison as the result of a fire, but not if another inmate threatens to assault him.

---

[33] United States v. Schoon, 971 F.2d at 196 ("Necessity is, essentially, a utilitarian defense.").

[34] *Id.* at 200 (Fernandez, J., concurring).

[35] State v. Tate, 505 A.2d 941, 946 (N.J. 1986); Commonwealth v. Leno, 616 N.E.2d at 455.

[36] State v. Tate, 505 A.2d at 946. At least eleven states have expressly authorized the use of marijuana for medicinal purposes, see Gonzales v. Raich, 545 U.S. — , 125 S.Ct. 2195, 2198 n.1 (2005), while other state legislatures have considered and rejected such legislation. Defendants who would seek to claim the necessity defense in one of the latter states would be barred under the principle set out in the text above.

[37] People v. Pepper, 41 Cal. App. 4th 1029, 1035 (1996).

[38] United States v. Paolello, 951 F.2d 537, 541 (3d Cir. 1991).

[39] From a utilitarian perspective, this requirement is unwise. The law should provide D with an incentive, i.e., the necessity defense, to save the houses from the fire. D remains liable in tort for his original reckless conduct, and he would be subject to criminal prosecution for any offense (e.g., reckless endangerment) committed by his recklessness, but he should be encouraged to stop the conflagration. From a retributivist perspective, as well, the rule is unsound, for it may result in an actor being punished in excess of his culpability. In the current example, D will be convicted of *purposely* setting fire to V's land, although his true culpability is that of recklessness for setting the original fire. See Paul H. Robinson, *Causing the Conditions of One's Own Defense: A Study in the Limits of Theory in Criminal Law Doctrine*, 71 Va. L. Rev. 1, 3-4, 8-10 (1985).

[40] E.g., Wis. Stat. § 939.47 (2005) ("[p]ressure of natural physical forces").

Assuming that the defendant has chosen the lesser of two evils, and the other elements of the defense are satisfied, this natural-versus-human distinction is indefensible.

Second, the necessity defense may not apply in homicide cases.[41] Third, some states limit the defense to protection of persons and property; in such jurisdictions a person may not act, for example, to protect reputation or economic interests.[42]

§ 22.03 CIVIL DISOBEDIENCE[43]

"Civil disobedience" may be defined as a nonviolent act, publicly performed and deliberately unlawful, that has as its purpose to protest a law, government policy, or action of a private body whose conduct has serious public consequences.[44]

Civil disobedience may be direct or indirect. Direct civil disobedience involves protesting a particular law by breaking it or "by preventing the execution of that law in a specific instance."[45] For example, in the early 1960s civil rights demonstrators "sat-in" all-white lunch counters in the South to protest, and ultimately to prove the unconstitutionality, of segregationist laws that barred their presence. The necessity defense rarely arises in such circumstances, because protesters seek instead to have the protested law declared unconstitutional or otherwise invalidated.

In contrast, indirect civil disobedience involves the violation of a law that is not the object of the protest. In this category, for example, are protesters who violate a trespass statute, although they have no objection to trespass laws, in order to express their opposition to the construction of a nuclear power plant[46] or the performance of abortions in a nearby clinic,[47] or who sit in a Congressman's office in order to protest governmental actions in a foreign country.[48]

---

[41] This is a matter of some doubt and controversy. See § 22.04, *infra*.

[42] E.g., State v. Moe, 24 P.2d 638 (Wash. 1933) (no economic necessity defense).

[43] See generally Carl Cohen, Civil Disobedience (1971); Abe Fortas, Concerning Dissent and Civil Disobedience (1968); Greenawalt, Note 1, *supra*; Steven M. Bauer & Peter J. Eckerstrom, Note, *The State Made Me Do It: The Applicability of the Necessity Defense to Civil Disobedience*, 39 Stan. L. Rev. 1173 (1987); Itzhak Kugler, *On the Possibility of a Criminal Law Defence for Conscientious Objection*, 10 Canadian J. L. & Jurisprudence 387 (1997).

[44] See Cohen, Note 43, *supra*, at 39-40.

[45] United States v. Schoon, 971 F.2d 193, 196 (9th Cir. 1991).

[46] Commonwealth v. Capitolo, 498 A.2d 806 (Pa. 1985) (defense is inapplicable).

[47] E.g., United States v. Lucero, 895 F. Supp. 1421 (D. Kan. 1995) (defense is inapplicable); City of Wichita v. Tilson, 855 P.2d 911 (Kan. 1993) (same); Jones v. City of Tulsa, 857 P.2d 814 (Okla. Crim. App. 1993) (same).

[48] People v. Craig, 585 N.E.2d 783 (N.Y. 1991) (protesting governmental policy in Nicaragua; held: defense is inapplicable); State v. Cram, 600 A.2d 733 (Vt. 1991) (protest of shipment of guns to El Salvador; held: same).

Do the facts alleged in a typical indirect civil disobedience case state a credible claim of necessity, so as to justify a jury instruction on the defense? The issue usually arises prior to trial as part of a prosecutor's motion *"in limine"* ("on or at the threshold") to bar evidence on the necessity claim, or during trial when the prosecutor objects to introduction of such evidence. If the prosecutor's motion or objection is granted, which it nearly always is,[49] the defendant is left without any realistic basis to avoid conviction. Therefore, on appeal from the conviction, the defendant will argue that he was improperly denied the opportunity to raise the necessity claim with the jury.

Appellate courts consistently reject the claim that a defendant is entitled to assert a necessity defense in cases of indirect civil disobedience.[50] Indeed, one federal Circuit Court has ruled that the defense is unavailable as a matter of law in *all* such cases.[51] Typically, the requisites of a traditional necessity claim are lacking in indirect civil disobedience cases: the harm to be avoided is not imminent; the protest cannot directly abate the danger; protesters have legal options, such as the ballot box, to seek change in the disputed policy; and the legislature (or, in the case of issues such as abortion, the judiciary) has calculated the comparative harms differently than the protesters and its value determination may not be overridden.

As a matter of technical application of the necessity defense, the claim should be unavailable to protesters. However, advocates of a "political necessity" defense contend that such a defense should be recognized because it "empowers the individual primarily by presenting a forum in which stifled minority or unheeded majority viewpoints receive a public hearing."[52] Also, the defense empowers the jury, by giving them an opportunity to nullify the law[53] and "weigh in" on a controversial subject. Some would argue, as well, that the criminal law should not be used against those who — in contrast to ordinary criminals — are impelled by conscience and not avarice or some similar improper motive, to nonviolently violate the law.

Opponents of such a defense believe that recognition of a defense would undesirably erode the principle of traditional civil disobedience, which is that people who are compelled by conscience to violate the law, but who also believe

---

[49] On rare occasions, a trial judge permits the defendant to raise the claim. E.g., Terry Wilson, *26 Found Not Guilty of Trespassing At Base*, Chi. Trib., May 18, 1988, at 3 (twenty-six protesters were acquitted of trespassing to dramatize their opposition to United States policy in Central America). If the trial judge allows the defense and the defendant is acquitted, the government has no recourse, because the Fifth Amendment Double Jeopardy Clause prohibits retrial following an acquittal. United States v. Ball, 163 U.S. 662 (1896).

[50] E.g., State v. Warshow, 410 A.2d 1000 (Vt. 1979); United States v. Kroncke, 459 F.2d 697 (8th Cir. 1972); see, also, the citations in Notes 46-48, *supra*.

[51] United States v. Schoon, 971 F.2d 193 (9th Cir. 1991).

[52] Bauer & Eckerstrom, Note 43, *supra*, at 1184.

[53] The jury nullification principle is discussed at § 1.02[C], *supra*.

in a democratic system, should accept their punishment (as Gandhi and Martin Luther King did) as part of their protest.[54] As one philosopher put it, "[w]e must pay a certain price to convince others that our actions have . . . a sufficient moral basis in the political convictions of the community."[55] And, for some critics, a civil disobedient *does* demonstrate his own character flaw, namely, moral arrogance, by believing that his value judgments are better than society's. Therefore, the reasoning goes, the law violator should accept punishment as the price of choosing to break the law, rather than using the democratic process.

§ 22.04 "NECESSITY" AS A DEFENSE TO HOMICIDE[56]

[A] The Issue

Assume for a moment that A, B, and C, are riding in a horse-drawn carriage that is being pursued by a pack of very hungry wolves. If it becomes clear to the passengers that the horse cannot outrun the wolves and that all of them will likely be devoured by the animals, may A push B out of the carriage, so that the wolves devour him, thereby saving the lives of A and C?[57]

Or, suppose that D, a surgeon, wants to save the lives of five critically ill patients, one of whom needs a new heart, two of whom each need a healthy lung, and two of whom require a kidney transplant to survive. Each of his patients is likely to die within twenty-four hours without the needed operation. Along comes E, who possesses two good lungs, two good kidneys, and a very healthy heart. Amazingly, E has the proper blood type and tissue-match to serve as an organ donor for D's patients. May D harvest E's organs, on the ground that he has saved five people at the expense of just one?[58]

Finally, consider the recent tragic British case of conjoined infant twins, Jodie and Mary.[59] Jodie, the stronger twin, provided oxygenated blood to her own body and sister Mary through a shared artery. According to their doctors, Jodie's heart could not continue to support both bodies for longer than a few more months, at which time both would certainly die; if the twins were surgi-

---

[54] Bauer & Eckerstrom, Note 43, *supra*, at 1194.

[55] John Rawls, A Theory of Justice 367 (1971).

[56] See generally A.W. Brian Simpson, Cannibalism and the Common Law (1984); Lon L. Fuller, *The Case of the Speluncean Explorers*, 62 Harv. L. Rev. 616 (1949); John Makdisi, *Justification in the Killing of an Innocent Person*, 38 Clev. St. L. Rev. 85 (1990); S.E. Marshall, *Life or Death on a Plank — Ripstein and Kant*, 2 Ohio St. J. Crim. L. 435 (2005); Arthur Ripstein, *In Extremis*, 2 Ohio St. J. Crim. L. 415 (2005); Tom Stacy, *Acts, Omissions, and the Necessity of Killing Innocents*, 29 Am. J. Crim. L. 481 (2002); Judith Jarvis Thomson, *The Trolley Problem*, 94 Yale L.J. 1395 (1985); Andrew von Hirsch, *Lifeboat Law*, Crim. Just. Ethics, Summer/Fall 1985, at 88.

[57] Perkins, Note 1, *supra*, at 406.

[58] Thomson, Note 56, *supra*, at 1396.

[59] Re A, [2000], 4 All ER 961.

cally separated, however, Jodie could live a full life, but Mary would die immediately. Thus, without surgery, two would die; with surgery, one would die. The parents opposed surgically separating the twins for religious reasons; the physicians sought and secured judicial authorization to conduct the surgery. As expected, Mary died. Jodie survived and is living a relatively normal life.

Each of these circumstances seemingly raises the same issue: Assuming that all of the requirements for a necessity defense are otherwise satisfied, may a person justifiably kill an innocent person in order to save a greater number of innocent lives? Fortunately, this issue rarely arises. Perhaps the most celebrated criminal case involved a lifeboat containing four hungry men.

[B] *Regina v. Dudley and Stephens*[60]

Three adult seamen and a seventeen-year-old youth were forced to survive on an open boat after their sailing vessel sank. After twenty days on the boat, the last nine days of which were without food, and the last seven of which were without water, the seamen were exceedingly weak. The boy was seriously ill, as well, from drinking seawater. As a consequence, two of the men, *D* and *S*, killed *V*, the youth, in order to eat his flesh to survive.[61] Four days later, the three survivors were discovered and saved. *D* and *S* were prosecuted for *V*'s murder. They raised the defense of necessity, arguing that they reasonably believed that, had they not killed *V*, all of the occupants of the boat would have perished.

Their claim was rejected. Lord Coleridge, describing the defense argument as "new and strange," canvassed common law authority and concluded that no decided case or scholar, with one possible exception,[62] supported the claim that "in order to save your own life you may lawfully take the life of another, when that other is neither attempting nor threatening [to take] yours, nor is guilty of any illegal act whatever toward you or any one else."

Lord Coleridge stated that, although "preserv[ing] one's life is generally speaking a duty, . . . it may be the plainest and highest duty to sacrifice it." Thus, he said, it is the duty of a captain to sacrifice his life for the crew, and of the crew to do so for the passengers, and of soldiers to give up their lives for women and children. Although Coleridge conceded that the principle he was espousing was

---

[60] 14 Q.B.D. 273 (1884).

[61] The third man did not approve of, or participate in, the homicide, but he joined in eating the flesh.

[62] Lord Coleridge discounted the views of Lord Bacon, who asserted that one is justified by necessity to thrust another person off a plank in the ocean to save one's own life. Coleridge stated that if Bacon intended "to lay down a broad proposition that man may save his life by killing . . . an innocent and unoffending neighbour, it certainly is not law at the present day." In any case, Bacon's example involves the issue of taking one innocent life to save another (one's own) innocent life. If human lives are equally valued — if, for example, a person is not entitled to weigh his own life or that of a family member above that of a stranger — this becomes an "equal evil," and not a "lesser evil," hypothetical.

harsh, he remarked that "[w]e are often compelled to set up standards that we cannot reach ourselves, and to lay down rules which we could not ourselves satisfy." And, on a more pragmatic level, Coleridge also feared the potential for abuse: "[I]t is quite plain that such a principle [as *D* and *S* were espousing] once admitted might be made the legal cloak for unbridled passion and atrocious crime."

D and *S* were convicted of murder and sentenced to death, although the sentence was commuted by the Crown to six months' imprisonment.

Based on *Dudley and Stephens*, and an American case that also rejected the necessity defense in somewhat similar circumstances,[63] many commentators have concluded that the common law does not recognize the defense of necessity in homicide prosecutions, and some courts and statutes expressly so provide.[64]

[C] What Does *Dudley and Stephens* Really Say?

Some commentators believe that *Dudley and Stephens* did not (or, at least, did not have to) categorically reject the defense of necessity in homicide cases.[65] The argument may be made that *D* and *S* acted precipitously; in necessity terms, the harm they were seeking to avoid was not yet imminent. Lord Coleridge focused on the special finding of the jury that it was only "probable" that the three men would have died had they not killed the youth. As Coleridge weighed the evils, *D* and *S* "with certainty" deprived *V* of his life, merely "upon the chance" of preserving their own lives. Arguably, therefore, had the seamen's plight been more extreme — if Coleridge's concerns about potential abuse had been minimized — the case might have received more favorable treatment.

The weaknesses in the defendants' case are highlighted by comparing it to the following hypothetical:[66] *D* and *V* are mountaineers tied together by a rope. *V* loses his footing, falls off the cliff, and is about to drop to his certain death,

---

[63] United States v. Holmes, 26 F. Cas. 360 (C.C.E.D. Pa. 1842) (No. 15,383), was a case "replete with incidents of deep romance, and of pathetic interest." *Id.* at 363. Holmes and other crew-members of an American ship threw fourteen male passengers of a lifeboat overboard after it began to leak. The trial judge told the jurors that "in applying the law, we must look, not only to the jeopardy in which the parties are, but also to the relations to which they stand." *Id.* at 366. He explained that the sailors were bound to sacrifice their lives to save the passengers. He also expressed the view that when the life of one person must be taken "to appease the hunger of others, the selection is by lot." *Id.* at 367. The defendants were convicted of manslaughter, sentenced to a term of six months, although the maximum potential penalty was three years' imprisonment. President Tyler refused to grant a pardon, despite public pleas on their behalf.

[64] E.g., People v. Trippet, 56 Cal. App. 4th 1532 (App. Ct. 1997); Wis. Stat. § 939.47 (2005) (but reducing the offense to second-degree murder).

[65] E.g., Glazebrook, Note 1, *supra*, at 113-14.

[66] See American Law Institute, Comment to § 3.02, at 15.

pulling D down with him. D holds on as long as he can. When D feels himself about to be pulled over the cliff, may he justifiably cut the rope and permit V to fall?

Dudley and Stephens need not compel a negative answer to this hypothetical. First, unlike the facts in the lifeboat, climber-D's plight is clear: the threat is imminent; he must act now or never. Second, V's status is different from that of the "unoffending" youth in the lifeboat. V may fairly be characterized as an aggressor, albeit an innocent one. That is, by slipping, V threatened D's life.[67]

Third, in *Dudley and Stephens*, the means of selection of the potential victim may have troubled the court. The youth was likely, but not doomed, to die. He died because D and S *chose* to kill him. Selection by lot would have been fairer.[68] Climber-V's death, however, was a certainty. D did not choose for him to die; circumstances did.

Finally, and closely related to the previous point, D and S *caused* the boy to die. They chose him for death, and they shortened his life by more than a *de minimis* amount. In light of the certainty of mountaineer-V's death, however, it seems preferable to say that D's act of cutting the line on the rope merely *permitted* nature to take its course.[69]

Therefore, it is plausible that a court might justify a homicide of an innocent person in necessitous circumstances. But, *should* it *ever*?

[D] Reconsidering the Moral Issue

To repeat, the issue is: Assuming that all of the requirements for a necessity defense are satisfied (which perhaps they were not in *Dudley and Stephens*), may a person justifiably kill an innocent person in order to save a greater number of innocent lives?

---

[67] Although a court might choose to bring this hypothetical within an expansive version of self-defense, a court might instead wish to characterize this as a "lesser harm" necessity case, as the Model Penal Code Commentary does.

[68] On the other hand, the youth was more likely to die than the men, so his selection was not irrational.

[69] Notice, too, differences that can be drawn between *Dudley and Stephens* and the conjoined twin case. As in the mountain-climbing hypothetical, it can be said that "Mary was making use of Jodie's body in a way that put Jodie's life at risk," Stacy, Note 56, *supra*, at 498, so Mary might be characterized as an innocent aggressor, unlike the youth killed in the lifeboat. (See Note 67, *supra*.) Also, the doctors did not choose Mary's life over Jodie's, as D and S chose the youth to be the victim. Mary's death was inevitable; the doctors only accelerated the process. Finally, *Dudley and Stephens* involved four persons in jeopardy determining who amongst themselves would live or die. Lord Coleridge believed that it was better in such circumstances for a person to sacrifice himself than to kill an innocent person. In the conjoined twins case, however, the "killers" — the physicians — were not in jeopardy. They could not sacrifice themselves for the babies, and Mary could not choose to sacrifice herself for Jodie.

A utilitarian might say yes. The calculus would seem simple: One person's life should be taken so that three may survive. Indeed, the calculus may be put more starkly: The choice was between doing nothing, in which case all four occupants of the lifeboat were likely to die, and acting, in which case only one life would be lost. To utilitarians, the end (reduction in aggregate harm) seemingly justifies the means (an intentional homicide).

But this calculus may be too simple. First, if D and S were justified in taking V's life to save three lives, would they not also have been justified in taking the third person's life to save their own, assuming that they were not rescued in time? If so, two lives would be taken to save two lives, although the calculus looked different at each step along the way. Second, even if the killing of an innocent person might be justified in a particular case, a *rule* authorizing such behavior might be abused (as Lord Coleridge feared) or, at least, misapplied, in other cases, thus ultimately resulting in more, not less, social harm. And a rule that justifies killing innocent people in extreme circumstances might weaken general moral strictures against taking human life, which again could have a counter-utilitarian effect. "Rule-utilitarians" — those who look at the big picture, and seek to devise rules that will result in a net reduction of harm over time — would need to consider these possibilities.

A negative answer to the question posed here is more easily made from a non-utilitarian, perhaps Kantian, moral perspective. The imperative would be that each person is an end in himself, and should not be treated merely as a means to an end, as D and S used V. V was "unoffending"; he did not forfeit his moral right to life by any misconduct. Therefore, a non-utilitarian might conclude that an innocent person's life may *never* justifiably be taken, even to save a larger number of lives.[70]

This does not mean that a retributivist would necessarily punish D and S. A very plausible argument can be made that D and S deserved to be *excused*, on the ground that, as a result of the extraordinary natural circumstances in which they found themselves, they were compelled to take a life.[71] Therefore, they should not be blamed for giving in to the coercive circumstances. This points up that "necessity" should sometimes serve as an excuse, rather than a justification.[72]

---

[70] For a contrary Kantian analysis, see Stacy, Note 56, *supra*, at 508-12.

[71] However, if an *excuse* were recognized in these circumstances, V would seemingly have been *justified* in defending himself against D's and S's homicidal assault, because their *excused* conduct would constitute an *unlawful* attack on V!

[72] See § 23.06, *infra*.

§ 22.05 MODEL PENAL CODE

The Model Code recognizes a "choice of evils" defense. A person's conduct is justified if: (1) he believes that his conduct is necessary to avoid harm to himself or another; (2) the harm to be avoided by his conduct is greater than that sought to be avoided by the law prohibiting his conduct; and (3) no legislative intent to exclude the conduct in such circumstances plainly exists.[73] The determination of what constitutes a lesser harm is not left to the actor's evaluation, but rather to the judge or jury at trial. The Code does not resolve whether the balancing-of-harms should be determined by the judge, as a matter of law, or should be submitted to the jury for its evaluation.[74]

This defense is broader than the common law in various respects. First, the Code rejects the common law imminency requirement. Second, a person does not automatically lose the defense because he was at fault in creating the necessitous situation. Instead, the Code provides that the defense is unavailable if the actor is prosecuted for a crime of recklessness or negligence and he acted recklessly or negligently, as the case may be, in bringing about the emergency or in evaluating the necessity of his conduct.[75] For example, in the hypothetical discussed earlier in this chapter,[76] in which D *recklessly* started a fire that threatened to burn down a number of homes, D would be justified in *purposely* burning V's property, although he could be prosecuted for criminal mischief,[77] due to his original reckless act.

Third, the Code provision is one of general applicability. All forms of necessity qualify — the defense is not limited to emergencies created by natural forces, is not limited to physical harm to persons or property, and, most controversially, may be employed in homicide prosecutions. The Commentary states that it would be "particularly unfortunate" to deny the defense in appropriate homicide cases; it contends that the sanctity of human life is promoted by a law that permits an actor to kill to save a larger number of lives.[78]

---

[73] Model Penal Code § 3.02(1).

[74] American Law Institute, Comment to § 3.02, at 12.

[75] Model Penal Code § 3.02(2).

[76] See the text accompanying Note 39, *supra*.

[77] Model Penal Code § 220.3(1) ("damag[ing] tangible property of another . . . *recklessly* . . . in the employment of fire . . .") (emphasis added).

[78] American Law Institute, Comment to § 3.02, at 14-15.

Chapter 23

DURESS

§ 23.01 GENERAL PRINCIPLES[1]

[A] Overview

"Duress" or "coercion" is a common law defense to criminal conduct. As has been written about the defense:

> Our society has a love-hate relationship with the . . . defense. Although "of venerable antiquity," the defense was frequently condemned as illegitimate, narrowly defined at common law, comparatively rarely invoked in criminal prosecutions, and not often successfully pleaded.

> . . . Nonetheless, our society also seems to love the plea or, at least, to be intrigued by it. Despite criticisms, our society has retained the defense, expanded it over the years, and paid close attention to the calls of those who would apply the defense in novel ways.[2]

[B] Elements of the Defense

The contours of the duress defense differ by jurisdiction. However, very generally speaking, a person will be acquitted of any offense *except murder*[3] if the criminal act was committed under the following circumstances: (1) another person threatened to kill or grievously injure the actor or a third party, particularly a near relative, unless she committed the offense; (2) the actor reasonably believed that the threat was genuine; (3) the threat was "present, imminent, and impending" at the time of the criminal act;[4] (4) there was no reasonable escape

---

[1] See generally George Fletcher, Rethinking Criminal Law §§ 10.4.2-10.4.3 (1978); Jerome Hall, General Principles of Criminal Law 436-48 (2d ed. 1960); Glanville Williams, Criminal Law: The General Part §§ 242-50 (2d ed. 1961); Joshua Dressler, *Exegesis of the Law of Duress: Justifying the Excuse and Searching for Its Proper Limits*, 62 S. Cal. L. Rev. 1331 (1989); Herbert Fingarette, *Victimization: A Legalist Analysis of Coercion, Deception, Undue Influence, and Excusable Prison Escape*, 42 Wash. & Lee L. Rev. 65 (1985); Claire O. Finkelstein, *Duress: A Philosophical Account of the Defense in Law*, 37 Ariz. L. Rev. 251 (1995); John Lawrence Hill, *A Utilitarian Theory of Duress*, 84 Iowa L. Rev. 275 (1999); Kyron Huigens, *Duress Is Not a Justification*, 2 Ohio St. J. Crim. L. 303 (2004); Peter Westen & James Mangiafico, *The Criminal Defense of Duress: A Justification, Not an Excuse — And Why It Matters*, 6 Buff. Crim. L. Rev. 833 (2003).

[2] Dressler, Note 1, *supra*, at 1331-32 (footnotes omitted).

[3] Regarding murder, see § 23.04, *infra*.

[4] State v. Crawford, 861 P.2d 791, 797 (Kan. 1993); State v. Toscano, 378 A.2d 755, 760 (N.J. 1977).

from the threat except through compliance with the demands of the coercer; and (5) the actor was not at fault in exposing herself to the threat.[5]

As this description of the common law (and, often, statutory) defense suggests, a person will not be acquitted unless she acts as a result of a very specific type of threat. First, the threat must come from a human being. For example, if *D* breaks into *V*'s home because a rabid dog is threatening her in the street, or a severe lightning storm is underway, she might be able to claim the defense of *necessity* if she is charged with criminal trespass,[6] but the defense of duress is inapplicable.

Second, the coercer must threaten to cause death or serious bodily harm. Force that is likely to cause death *or serious bodily harm* is commonly termed "deadly force" in the criminal law;[7] therefore, it is accurate to state that a person may not claim common law duress unless she is the victim of a threat of "deadly force." A lesser threat, such as a threat to cause property damage, economic hardship, or to damage another person's reputation, is insufficient.[8]

Third, the deadly force threatened must be imminent, or as some courts put it, "present, imminent, and impending." The word "present" suggests that the threat must be operating on the actor's will at the time of the criminal act.[9] The remaining requirement is that the threatened harm will occur immediately, unless the actor complies. Courts rarely explain this requirement any further, except to state that a threat of future harm is insufficient, or that the harm must be likely to occur so quickly that there is no realistic way for the actor to escape the situation.[10] For example, in *State v. Rosillo,*[11] *R*, a police informant, agreed to testify against a suspected drug dealer. Prior to trial, however, armed assailants threatened him, and he was nearly run over on the street. As a consequence of his fear for his life and that of his family, *R* gave false testimony at the trial of the alleged narcotics dealer. *R*, prosecuted for perjury, claimed duress. The court held, however, that the facts did not support the claim, as he was not in fear of *imminent* harm at the moment he testified falsely at the trial. According to the court, a duress claim would have been available if *D* had reasonably feared being shot through a courthouse window!

---

[5] See People v. Merhige, 180 N.W. 418, 422 (Mich. 1920); State v. Toscano, 378 A.2d at 760-63; Dressler, Note 1, *supra*, at 1335-43; Fingarette, Note 1, *supra*, at 67 n.9.

[6] See § 22.02, *supra*.

[7] See § 18.02[A], *supra*.

[8] E.g., United States v. Palmer, 458 F.2d 663 (9th Cir. 1972) ("financial ruin" insufficient threat); People v. Ricker, 262 N.E.2d 456 (Ill. 1970) (threat of loss of job insufficient).

[9] People v. Luther, 232 N.W.2d 184, 187 (Mich. 1975).

[10] See United States v. Contento-Pachon, 723 F.2d 691, 694 (9th Cir. 1984).

[11] 282 N.W.2d 872 (Minn. 1979).

Fourth, the threat must typically be directed at the defendant or a family member.[12]

Even if all of the preceding criteria are satisfied, the duress defense is unavailable to a defendant if she was at fault for finding herself in the coercive situation. For example, if *D* voluntarily joins a criminal organization that she knows or has reason to know is likely to subject her to coercive threats at a later time, she will not be permitted to claim the defense if that foreseeable event arises.[13]

If the elements of the defense *are* satisfied, the coerced actor will be acquitted of the non-homicide offense for which she was prosecuted. The *coercing* party, however, is responsible for the coerced victim's conduct and, therefore, may be convicted of the offense.[14]

[C] Duress: Justification or Excuse?

Some scholars, courts, and statutes characterize duress as a subspecies of the *justification* defense of necessity, or treat the two defenses interchangeably.[15] There is superficial logic in this position: According to common law principles, the duress defense only applies if the coercing party threatens to use deadly force; and the defense is only available if the coerced actor commits a *non*-homicide offense. Therefore, at first blush — but only at first blush — it appears that a coerced party *always* commits the lesser of two evils; therefore, she is *justified* in acceding to the threat. Following this reasoning, the only significant difference between necessity and duress is that the former defense entails natural threats like fires and tornadoes, whereas the latter involves human threats.

---

[12] On occasion courts have suggested that the common law defense is not limited to family members. E.g., United States v. Haney, 287 F.3d 1266, 1272 (10th Cir. 2002) (characterizing a "family members only" limitation as "unprincipled," and stating that "[w]e know of no federal case categorically declining to apply the duress defense in the third party context"), vacated and remanded on rehearing en banc, 318 F.3d 1161 (10th Cir. 2003). States that follow the Model Penal Code *do* extend the defense to threats to all third parties. See § 23.08[B][1], *infra*.

[13] Williams, Note 1, *supra*, at 758-59; American Law Institute, Comment to § 2.09, at 379 n.47.

[14] In common law terminology, the coercer is a "principal in the first degree" who used the coerced party as her "innocent instrumentality" in committing the offense. See § 30.03[A][2][b], *infra*.

[15] E.g., United States v. Haney, 287 F.3d at 1270 (describing duress as a lesser-harm defense); Westen & Mangiafico, Note 1, *supra*, at 947-48 (characterizing the defense as a justification, because "society regards [the coerced actor's conduct] as acceptable under the circumstances"); Wayne R. LaFave, Criminal Law 467, 476-77 (3d ed. 2000) (treating duress as a subspecies of the necessity defense); United States v. Bailey, 444 U.S. 394, 410 (1980) (observing that "[m]odern cases have tended to blur the distinction between duress and necessity," and thereafter treating the two defenses alike); Ariz. Rev. Stat. § 13-412 (2005) (describing duress in justificatory language). In his fourth edition, published in 2003, at 491, Professor LaFave re-characterizes duress as an excuse (quoting Dressler, Note 1, *supra*, at 1367).

It is not true, however, that *every* common law example of duress involves a lesser-evils situation. For example, if C threatens to cut off D's left arm unless D cuts off V's left arm, the harms are of equal severity, yet D is entitled to raise the duress defense if she complies with C's demand.[16]

Furthermore, it is unlikely that the concept of duress as a justification for criminal activity conforms with common moral intuitions. For example, suppose that C orders D to rape V, and backs up the order by threatening grievous harm to X, D's young child — e.g., C threatens to sexually abuse X, cut off X's left hand, or blind X. If D complies with C's threat and rapes V, it is highly unlikely that the decision whether to acquit D of rape would be based on our balancing of the harms threatened and inflicted. Are we *really* prepared to say that V's rape is a lesser harm than X's sexual abuse or loss of an arm or eyesight? More likely, our intuitions suggest that the real issue is whether, in view of the threats, D should be blamed — excused — for the injuries inflicted on V.

In conformity with this analysis, most scholars, courts, and states' criminal codes that draw distinctions between justifications and excuses, treat duress as an excuse defense.[17]

§ 23.02 RATIONALE OF THE DEFENSE (AS AN EXCUSE)

[A] Utilitarian Arguments

The traditional utilitarian argument in support of the duress defense is straightforward: When a person is "in thrall to some [coercive] power" the threat of criminal punishment is ineffective.[18] As Hobbes has reasoned:

> If a man, by the terror of present death, be compelled to do a fact against the law, he is totally excused, because no law can oblige a man to abandon his own preservation. And supposing such a law were obligatory, yet a man would reason thus: *If I do it not, I die presently; if I do it, I die afterwards; therefore by doing it, there is time of life gained.* . . .[19]

Moreover, a utilitarian may argue that the victim of coercion is just that — a victim. The coercing party, and not she, possesses a criminal disposition. Therefore, the coercing party, and not she, requires incapacitation and rehabilitation.

---

[16] It is plausible to argue that a person may properly value her own (and family's) well-being over that of a stranger. Therefore, under this view, the harms are *not* precisely equal in this hypothetical. But, even if one accepts this idea, there will be cases in which the harm threatened is equal to the harm caused, in which case the lesser-harm thesis fails.

[17] E.g., Dressler, Note 1, *supra*; Huigens, Note 1, *supra*; Model Penal Code § 2.09. Professor Wayne LaFave, who used to treat duress as a justification, now considers it an excuse. See Note 15, *supra*. The MPC approach to duress, which has influenced the law, is considered in § 23.08, *infra*.

[18] Williams, Note 1, *supra*, at 756.

[19] Thomas Hobbes, Leviathan, Pt. II, ch. 27 (1651).

Not all utilitarian arguments support the defense. Sir James Stephen has presented the most famous (although not generally accepted) utilitarian argument against the excuse. According to Stephen, recognition of the defense dangerously undermines the moral clarity of the criminal law and invites fraud: "Surely it is at the moment when the temptation to [commit] crime is strongest . . . that the law should speak most clearly and emphatically to the contrary." He conceded that it is unfortunate when an innocent person is "placed between two fires," but he believed that it is a much greater misfortune for society if the coercing party could confer immunity on her "agents by threatening them with death or violence if they refused to execute . . . [her] commands." Such a rule would open "a wide door . . . to collusion, and encouragement would be given to associations of malefactors, secret or otherwise."[20]

[B] Retributive Arguments

Most arguments in support of the duress defense are founded on the retributive principle that a coerced actor does not deserve to be punished for her actions. In order to understand why this is so, it is useful first to consider various incorrect or potentially misleading explanations frequently given in support of the defense.

First, some courts suggest that a coerced actor lacks the requisite *mens rea* to be convicted of an offense.[21] Exceptional circumstances aside, however, this explanation is false.[22] Ordinarily, one who acts under duress *intends* to cause the result in question, for the simple reason that she wants to avoid the harm threatened by the coercer. Thus, a coercive threat *creates* the intent; it does not negate it.[23] The only exception to this proposition is when the coercive threat negates a specific intent or *motive* of the actor that may be required in the definition of an offense.[24]

---

[20] 2 James Stephen, A History of the Criminal Law in England 107-08 (1883).

[21] E.g., State v. Tanner, 301 S.E.2d 160, 163 (W. Va. 1982) ("'[I]n general an act which would otherwise constitute a crime may be excused on the ground that it was done under compulsion or duress, since the necessary ingredient of intention . . . is then lacking.'") (quoting 22 C.J.S. Criminal Law § 44 (1961)).

[22] State v. Rios, 980 P.2d 1068, 1071 (N.M. Ct. App. 1999) ("A defendant pleading duress is *not* attempting to disprove a requisite mental state."); Hibbert v. The Queen, 999 C.C.C.3d 193, 205 (Canada 1995) ("[S]ituations where duress will operate to 'negate' *mens rea* will be exceptional, for the simple reason that the types of mental states that are capable of being 'negated' by duress are not often found in the definitions of criminal offences'.").

[23] People v. King, 1 Cal. App. 4th 288, 298 (Ct. App. 1991).

[24] For example, suppose that *C* coerces *D* to steal a Picasso painting from City Museum. *D* does as she is told, but as soon as the coercion is removed, she contacts the police and leads them to *C*. Under such circumstances, although *D* intended to take and carry away the Picasso, the prosecutor may not be able to prove beyond a reasonable doubt that *D* did do so with the intent to *permanently* deprive the museum of its property. As this motive is an element of larceny, *D* may be acquitted.

Second, courts frequently state that a coerced party should be excused because "commission of the alleged offense was no longer the voluntary act of the accused."[25] In the narrow willed-contraction-of-a-muscle sense of the term "voluntary act,"[26] however, this statement is incorrect. Stephen has correctly observed:

> A criminal walking to execution is under compulsion if any man can be said to be so, but his motions are just as much voluntary actions as if he was going to leave his place of confinement and regain his liberty. He walks to his death because he prefers it to being carried.[27]

That is, the coerced actor wills her muscles to commit the crime, e.g., to strike V or to steal V's automobile. Coercion, therefore, does not negate the voluntary act requirement of the criminal law.

Third, it is not precisely correct to say that a person is excused for violating the law because she "lacked free will." The coerced actor has the capacity to choose, i.e., she is not an automaton controlled by the coercing party. More to the point, the coerced actor *in fact* chooses to violate the law; she chooses to commit an offense rather than to suffer the threatened consequences. She "self-consciously subordinates [the law] to the primacy of the person who is the subject of desire,"[28] i.e., she chooses to make the coercing party's desires her own for present purposes.

Although the free-will explanation is not precisely on target, it brings us very close to understanding why it is unjust to punish one who acts under duress. Although the coerced actor possesses free will, she does not possess a *fair opportunity* to exercise her will to act lawfully.[29] Of course, society does not excuse an actor for violating the law whenever she must make a hard choice. Duress only excuses when the available choices are not only hard but also unfair.[30] Choice-making opportunities are unfair when the alternative to committing an offense is so awful that "judges are not prepared to affirm that they . . . could comply with [the law] if their turn to face the problem should arise."[31] The defense of duress recognizes that all humans have breaking points; society is prepared to excuse a coerced actor's unlawful conduct if she accedes to a

---

[25] Regina v. Hudson, [1971] 2 All E.R. 244, 246.

[26] See § 9.02[C][2], *supra*.

[27] 2 Stephen, Note 20, *supra*, at 102.

[28] Alan Brudner, *A Theory of Necessity*, 7 Oxford J. Legal Stud. 339, 349 (1987).

[29] This is an example of the "free choice" or "personhood" theory of excuses. See § 17.03[E], *supra*.

[30] Dressler, Note 1, *supra*, at 1365.

[31] American Law Institute, Comment to § 2.09, at 374-75.

threat that, upon honest self-reflection, most of us doubt we would have the moral fortitude to resist either.[32]

§ 23.03 DISTINGUISHING DURESS FROM NECESSITY

As noted earlier,[33] some commentators and courts treat duress as a sub-species of the justification defense of necessity, in which case the only true distinction between the defenses is that duress involves human threats, whereas the necessity defense applies to natural forces.

As long as duress is recognized as an excuse defense, which it should be, it is important to see how the two defenses differ.[34] The necessity defense — as one of its alternative names ("lesser evil" defense) reminds us — applies "when a person is faced with a choice of two evils and must then decide whether to commit a crime or an alternative act that constitutes a greater evil,"[35] and the person makes the right choice. In contrast, duress applies even when the coercer's threats overwhelm the actor's will so that she makes the wrong choice, i.e., perpetrates a greater evil.[36]

This potential difference has practical consequences.[37] When a person commits the lesser of two evils, nobody should be subject to prosecution for the outcome, because the outcome is socially desirable or, at least, not undesirable. For example, suppose that *D1* justifiably takes *V*'s parked automobile without permission, in order to drive a gravely injured child to the hospital. Even if it later turns out that the child was in that condition as the result of criminally negligent conduct by *X*, it would be odd to say that *X* is criminally responsible for *D1*'s *justified* act of taking the child to the hospital in *V*'s car.[38] If a defendant is *excused* on the ground of duress, however, the person who coerced her may be prosecuted for the harm caused. For example, if *D2* robs a bank because *C* threatens immediate serious physical harm to *D2*'s husband, *D2* may be excused for the crime; *C*, however, may be prosecuted for the robbery. This

---

[32] Contrast these remarks to Lord Coleridge's observation in *Regina v. Dudley and Stephens*, 14 Q.B.D. 273 (1884), in which he stated that judges "are often compelled to set up standards that we cannot reach ourselves, and to lay down rules which we could not ourselves satisfy." See § 22.04[B], *supra*. In the context of *justification* defenses, this may be an appropriate observation, but here we are talking about *excusing* people: It is wrong to blame and punish people for being unable to live up to standards that nobody but the most "saintly" individual could satisfy.

[33] See § 23.01[C], *supra*.

[34] The assumption here is that necessity is a *justification* defense. Necessity may be an excuse defense in some circumstances. See § 23.06, *infra*.

[35] United States v. Contento-Pachon, 723 F.2d 691, 695 (9th Cir. 1984).

[36] See United States v. Lopez, 662 F. Supp. 1083, 1086 (N.D. Cal. 1987), aff'd, 885 F.2d 1428 (9th Cir. 1989).

[37] The necessity/duress distinction may have additional practical implications. See § 23.05[C][2], *infra*.

[38] Of course, *X* may be prosecuted for any crime she committed in relation to the child.

result follows from the fact that duress is an excuse rather than a justification, and there is a culpable human being who may properly be held responsible for the social harm caused.

§ 23.04 DURESS AS A DEFENSE TO HOMICIDE

[A] General Rule

The common law rule, stemming from antiquity, and expressly adopted by statute in a few states,[39] is that duress is not a defense to an intentional killing.[40] A few states recognize an imperfect duress defense, which reduces the offense of the coerced actor to manslaughter.[41] In contrast, most civil law countries apparently recognize the duress defense to *any* crime, including murder,[42] and, perhaps "the weight of scholarly commentary favors . . . abolition of the common law murder exception to the duress defense."[43]

There is a division of thought regarding whether the duress defense may be raised in a felony-murder prosecution. Some states provide that a person coerced to commit a felony, during which she or an accomplice unintentionally kills the victim, may raise the duress defense as to the felony and, therefore, is not guilty of felony-murder.[44] Other states disallow the defense in all murder prosecutions, regardless of the defendant's *mens rea* regarding the death.[45]

[B] Is the No-Defense Rule Sensible?

What are the arguments for the common law rule that duress does not excuse a murder? Why is a defendant entitled to claim duress if she complies with a gun-to-the-head demand that she steal a car, rob a bank, or sexually assault another person, but the defense is unavailable to her if she kills as the result of precisely the same threat? From a utilitarian perspective, it would seem that the traditional justification for the defense — that a threat of future punishment will not deter an actor confronted by an immediate deadly threat[46] — applies to coerced murderers as it does to coerced thieves, robbers, and assaulter.

---

[39] E.g., Wash. Rev. Code 9A.16.060(2) (2005).

[40] E.g., People v. Anderson, 50 P.3d 368, 370-73 (Cal. 2002); Wright v. State, 402 So. 2d 493, 498 (Fla. Dist. Ct. App. 1981); Jackson v. State, 558 S.W.2d 816, 819-20 (Mo. Ct. App. 1977); see Regina v. Howe, [1987] 2 W.L.R. 568, 575 ("[A]n unbroken tradition of authority dating back to Hale and Blackstone seems to have been . . . that duress was not available to a defendant accused of murder.").

[41] Wentworth v. State, 349 A.2d 421, 427-28 (Md. Ct. Spec. App. 1975); Minn. Stat. 609.20(3) (2004); contra, People v. Anderson, 50 P.3d at 376-79.

[42] People v. Anderson, 50 P.3d at 385 (Kennard, J., concurring and dissenting).

[43] Id.

[44] E.g., id. at 379.

[45] E.g., State v. Ng, 750 P.2d 632, 636 (Wash. 1988).

[46] See § 23.02[A], supra.

Some scholars defend the no-defense rule on utilitarian grounds. According to Jerome Hall, it is wrong to assume that "the drive of self-preservation is irresistible, that conduct in such situation is inexorably fixed for all human beings."[47] Lord Hailsham of the English House of Lords agrees:

> Doubtless in actual practice many will succumb to temptation [and kill]. . . . But many will not. . . . I have known in my own lifetime of too many acts of heroism by ordinary human beings of no more than ordinary fortitude to [reject the common law position].[48]

The California Supreme Court, as well, recently observed:

> [W]hen confronted with an apparent kill-an-innocent-person-or-be-killed situation, a person can always choose to resist. As a practical matter, death will rarely, if ever, inevitably result from a choice not to kill. *The law should require people to choose to resist rather than kill an innocent person.*[49]

But this argument sounds more like a reason not to *justify* a coerced killing. The issue, however, is — or, at least should be[50] — whether a person who accedes to a deadly threat should be *excused* for her actions.

The nonconsequentialist argument for the common law no-defense position is also questionable. Blackstone offered a religious explanation for the rule: Murder is a crime against God; human laws, therefore, can never excuse such a crime.[51] In non-religious terms, the no-defense rule supports the moral imperative that, "if a man be desperately assaulted, and in peril of death, and cannot otherwise escape, unless to satisfy his assailant's fury he will kill an innocent person then present . . . he ought rather to die himself than kill an innocent."[52] The difficulty with this argument is, again, that it supports the proposition that a coerced actor is *unjustified* in taking an innocent life; it does not demonstrate that she should not be *excused* for violating the moral imperative.

From a retributive perspective, the question should come down to "whether a coerced person who unjustifiably violates the moral principle [against taking an innocent life] *necessarily, unalterably,* and *unfailingly* deserves to be pun-

---

[47] Hall, Note 1, *supra*, at 445-46.

[48] Regina v. Howe, [1987] 2 W.L.R. at 579.

[49] People v. Anderson, 50 P.3d at 371 (emphasis added).

[50] Unfortunately, courts are often insensitive to the justification/excuse distinction. It is noteworthy, for example, that the court in *Anderson, id.,* stated that the "basic rationale behind allowing the defense of duress for other crimes 'is that the defendant, faced with a choice of evils, choose to do the lesser evil . . .'" (quoting LaFave, Note 15, *supra*.)

[51] 4 William Blackstone, Commentaries on the Law of England *30 (1769).

[52] 1 Matthew Hale, History of the Pleas of the Crown *51 (1736).

ished as a murderer, as the common law insists."[53] The answer would seem to be that she does not deserve to be treated as a murderer: One who is compelled to kill has no greater opportunity to act freely than one who is ordered to steal, rob, or rape, assuming that the coercive threat is the same in each circumstance. If a person of reasonable moral strength would comply with a kill-or-be-killed threat (or, perhaps more compellingly, a kill-or-I-will-kill-a-loved-one threat), the case for denying the defense, as a matter of law, is weakened considerably.

At a minimum, a person who kills under duress should have her offense mitigated to manslaughter, as a few states recognize.[54] Why should a person who kills in sudden *anger* as the result of adequate provocation be permitted to mitigate her offense to manslaughter,[55] while one who kills out of *fear* for her own or another person's safety receives no formal mitigation? Sometimes this apparent inconsistency is explained in terms of the victims: In the case of duress the homicide victim is innocent; in the provocation case, the homicide victim is to blame for provoking her own death. The difficulty with this reasoning, however, is that by focusing on whether the victim is innocent or not, rather than on the defendant's capacity or opportunity to make the right decision, the law treats the two defenses as if they were justification defenses (focusing on whether the victim deserves to die) rather than excuse defenses (focusing on whether the defendant deserves to be blamed).

§ 23.05 ESCAPE FROM INTOLERABLE PRISON CONDITIONS[56]

[A] The Issue

Supreme Court Justice Harry Blackmun once wrote that "[t]he atrocities and inhuman conditions of prison life in America are almost unbelievable; surely they are nothing less than shocking."[57] Among the conditions that prisoners face are physical and sexual assaults from fellow inmates,[58] brutality at the hands of prison guards, fires in their cells, excessive cold and heat, and inadequate medical attention.

---

[53] Dressler, Note 1, *supra*, at 1372.

[54] See § 23.04[A], *supra*.

[55] See generally § 31.07, *infra*.

[56] See generally David Dolinko, Comment, *Intolerable Conditions as a Defense to Prison Escapes*, 26 UCLA L. Rev. 1126 (1979); Fingarette, Note 1, *supra*; George P. Fletcher, *Should Intolerable Prison Conditions Generate a Justification or an Excuse for Escape?*, 26 UCLA L. Rev. 1355 (1979); Martin R. Gardner, *The Defense of Necessity and the Right to Escape from Prison — A Step Towards Incarceration Free from Sexual Assault*, 49 S. Cal. L. Rev. 110 (1975).

[57] United States v. Bailey, 444 U.S. 394, 421 (1980) (dissenting opinion).

[58] Justice Blackmun stated: "A youthful inmate can expect to be subjected to homosexual gang rape his first night in jail, or, it has been said, even in the van on the way to jail." *Id.*

Occasionally, a prisoner seeks to avoid harsh prison conditions by escaping confinement. She may later be prosecuted for the crime of escape; in such circumstances, the escapee may defend her conduct on the ground that she fled due to intolerable prison conditions. Sometimes such a claim is based on the defense of duress; other times the justification defense of necessity is advanced.

[B] The Law

At the policy level, courts are concerned that if an inmate who flees due to alleged intolerable prison conditions avoids conviction on this ground, other inmates will be emboldened to attempt to escape. As a result, some courts originally refused to recognize a defense in such circumstances.[59] Most modern courts, however, recognize the right of an escapee to assert an intolerable-prison-condition claim. They split, however, on whether the inmate should raise the defense of necessity or of duress.[60]

As either a necessity or duress defense, courts almost always place special restrictions on its use.[61] From a practical perspective, the most significant limitation placed on the defense is the requirement that the escapee make "a bona fide effort to surrender or return to custody as soon as the claimed duress or necessity ha[s] lost its coercive force."[62] That is, once the prisoner attains a point of safety outside the prison, the escapee must turn herself in; if she fails to do so, the defense of duress or necessity is unavailable as a matter of law.[63] A few courts do not go this far, instead treating the actor's failure to turn herself in as merely one factor in assessing the escapee's claim.[64]

---

[59] E.g., State v. Davis, 14 Nev. 439, 444-45 (1880).

[60] E.g., Lacey v. State, 54 P.3d 304 (Alaska Ct. App. 2002) (necessity); People v. Lovercamp, 43 Cal. App. 3d 823 (Ct. App. 1974) (necessity); People v. Unger, 362 N.E.2d 319 (Ill. 1977) (necessity); State v. Reese, 272 N.W.2d 863 (Iowa 1978) (necessity); Spakes v. State, 913 S.W.2d 597 (Tex. Crim. App. 1996) (necessity); State v. Kinslow, 799 P.2d 844 (Ariz. 1990) (duress); People v. Harmon, 220 N.W.2d 212 (Mich. Ct. App. 1974), aff'd, 232 N.W.2d 187 (Mich. 1975) (duress); State v. Tuttle, 730 P.2d 630 (Utah 1986) (duress).

[61] But see Spakes v. State, 913 S.W.2d at 598 (holding that an escapee is entitled to an instruction on necessity if she presents evidence satisfying the ordinary statutory elements of the defense).

[62] United States v. Bailey, 444 U.S. 394, 415 (1980).

[63] According to one recent survey, at least thirty jurisdictions require an escapee to attempt to surrender or report to authorities as a precondition for asserting the defense. See Spakes v. State, 913 S.W.2d at 599 (Keller, P.J., dissenting).

[64] E.g., People v. Mendoza, 310 N.W.2d 860 (Mich. Ct. App. 1981) (duress); State v. Miller, 313 N.W.2d 460 (S.D. 1981) (necessity).

[C] Necessity versus Duress

[1] The Conceptual Problem

Neither necessity nor duress neatly covers all intolerable-prison-condition cases. For example, when an inmate flees as the result of a threatened sexual assault, a necessity claim is inappropriate in jurisdictions that limit that defense to emergencies created by non-human forces. On the other hand, the defense of duress ordinarily is triggered when a coercer orders another person to commit the crime for which the latter individual is prosecuted. In prison cases, however, threats may spur an inmate to flee, but nobody commands her to escape.

[2] Why the Nature of the Defense Is Significant

[a] The Message of Acquittal

An inmate does not care whether she is acquitted on the basis of necessity or duress. Courts, lawyers, and prison officials, however, understandably worry about the message sent in prison escape cases.

The two defenses send different messages. Acquittal on the basis of necessity implies that it is right or, at least, tolerable, for a prisoner to escape confinement in specified circumstances; acquittal on the ground of duress implies only that the escapee should not be blamed for fleeing. A prison official is apt to consider the label of justification unacceptable; advocates of prison reform are likely to prefer this description.

[b] Ability to Obtain Acquittal

A necessity claim may be a harder defense to prove than a claim of duress. With necessity, the prisoner must convince the jury that her flight from confinement was a lesser evil than what was facing her behind bars. Once the balancing process begins, many factors weigh against the inmate. For example, prison escapes jeopardize discipline within the institution, a factor that a jury may weigh against the defendant. Also, if the inmate is an habitual violent criminal, her prior criminal record, which ordinarily would be inadmissible at her trial, arguably is relevant to her lesser-evil defense claim. Juries are likely to conclude that it is better that a dangerous criminal suffer in prison, than that she be free from confinement, even for a short time.

In duress cases, juries are not asked to balance evils. Neither prison discipline nor the inmate's prior criminal record is material. The determinative factor ought to be whether the conditions in the prison that motivated the flight were so extreme and immediate that the jurors could reasonably imagine themselves fleeing under similar circumstances.

[c] Liability of Those Who Assist in the Escape

The line between duress and necessity may be critical in determining the criminal responsibility of persons who assist escapees. Consider *United States v. Lopez*:[65] *L* landed a helicopter on the grounds of a women's prison in order to effect the escape of *X*, his girlfriend, whose life allegedly had been unlawfully threatened by prison officials. *L* and *X* were apprehended ten days later. As a consequence of their actions, *X* was charged with escape, and *L* was charged with aiding in *X*'s escape. The prosecution agreed that *X* was entitled to introduce evidence supporting her claim that her life was threatened in prison; but it sought to bar *L* from introducing the same evidence on his own behalf.

Conceptually, the propriety of a prosecutor's motion to bar such evidence depends on whether *X*'s intolerable-prison-condition claim is properly identified as one of necessity (justification) or of duress (excuse). A justified act is a proper, or at least non-wrongful, act. Therefore, assuming that *X* was justified in escaping, *L* was also justified in assisting in the escape. In such circumstances, *L* should be permitted to raise *X*'s necessity claim on his own behalf.

In contrast, with excuse defenses, the result is wrongful, but the actor is not held responsible for it because she was the victim of an excusing condition. An excuse defense, however, is personal to the actor suffering from the condition. Therefore, since *L*'s life was not threatened — he did not personally experience the excusing condition — he should not be allowed to assert *X*'s duress claim as a basis for exculpation. Under such circumstances — if *X*'s flight from prison was only excusable — *L* may properly be convicted of aiding and abetting *X*'s wrongful-but-excusable act.[66]

[d] Liability of Those Who Resist the Escape

Assume the following scenario: *D* seeks to escape confinement due to intolerable prison conditions; *X*, a prison guard, exercises her authority to prevent the escape. Is *X* acting justifiably? If *X* uses force to stop *D*, should *X* be prosecuted for battery? May *D* use force against *X* in self-defense? The answers to these questions may depend on the nature of *D*'s defense.

If the proper defense to escape is duress, *X* is justified in preventing *D* from committing the wrongful act of escaping. *X* should also be allowed to use reasonable force to prevent the escape, and *D* would not be entitled to use force against her in the conflict.

---

[65] 662 F. Supp. 1083 (N.D. Cal. 1987).

[66] In *Lopez*, the trial court concluded that *X*'s defense "most clearly resemble[d]" a necessity claim. Therefore, it permitted *L* to introduce evidence at his trial regarding the purported threats on *X*'s life.

If *D*'s escape is justifiable, however, the analysis become more complicated. There are two possible solutions. Either the law must recognize incompatible justifications — justify *D*'s escape, yet also justify *X*'s effort to prevent *D*'s justified flight — or it must deny *X*, the prison guard, the right to use force to resist the escape. Following the latter reasoning, *D* would also be justified in using reasonable force, if necessary, to prevent resistance by the guard.[67]

[3] Concluding Comments

There is no reason why a jurisdiction should fit all prison escape cases within just one defense category. Occasionally, an escapee will wish to assert that she (or the person she was assisting) acted properly in escaping, in which case the necessity defense should be permitted, whether or not the threat was human or natural in origin. For example, in *People v. Unger*,[68] *U* was a thief serving his sentence on an honor farm when his life was threatened by a fellow inmate. The *Unger* court considered necessity to be the appropriate defense in the case.

But, why should an inmate always be forced to prove that the escape was the lesser of two evils? An inmate should be permitted to raise a duress claim instead of, or in conjunction with, the necessity claim. If a jury is unwilling to treat an escape as the lesser of two evils, but it does not believe that the inmate should be blamed for escaping, the jury should be allowed this option.

§ 23.06 SITUATIONAL DURESS: BRIEF OBSERVATIONS

[A] The Simplest Case: Necessity as an Excuse[69]

Reconsider *Dudley and Stephens*,[70] in which desperately hungry survivors on a lifeboat killed one of their number — a sick, defenseless youth — in order to eat his remains to survive. The two defendants were denied a necessity defense. One can defend this outcome, although not all do, on the ground that it is never morally justifiable to kill an innocent person or, in a more limited manner, on the ground that no justifiable method was used to choose the victim.

But, even if the defendants in that case acted unjustifiably, does it follow that they should also be denied an *excuse* defense? Under traditional doctrine, the duress defense does not apply. Not only is duress not a common law defense to murder, but even if it were, it would not apply here because the duress defense

---

[67] For discussion of these competing solutions, see Dolinko (arguing for the legitimacy of incompatible justifications) and Fletcher (arguing against such an analysis), Note 56, *supra*.

[68] 362 N.E.2d 319 (Ill. 1977).

[69] See generally Brudner, Note 28, *supra*; Edward M. Morgan, *The Defence of Necessity: Justification or Excuse?*, 42 U. Toronto Fac. L. Rev. 165 (1984).

[70] Regina v. Dudley and Stephens, 14 Q.B.D. 273 (1884). See § 22.04[B], *supra*.

only applies to human threats, whereas *Dudley and Stephens* involved a threat emanating from a natural source.

Is a conviction for murder morally just in such circumstances? If a defense were recognized in the lifeboat case, it might be called "situational duress," to distinguish it from duress claims involving human-induced coercion. Or, the defense of necessity could be enlarged to include an excuse component, to deal with natural forces that compel a person to commit an equal or greater evil, rather than a lesser one.

Opponents of such a new defense argue that in ordinary duress cases "the basic interests of the law may be satisfied by prosecution of the agent of unlawful force,"[71] namely, the coercer. Thus, if *C* compels *D* to rob a bank, *D* is excused, but *C* can be convicted of the crime. However, in a situational duress case — where the "coercer" is a natural force — there is nobody who can be subjected to the law's application. Therefore, critics maintain, society's valid interest in punishing *someone* for wrongful behavior requires that the law not recognize a situational duress defense.[72]

The argument for recognizing such a defense is that natural threats can be as compelling as human ones. Therefore, situational duress should excuse in precisely the same circumstances that human coercion excuses conduct. Of course, at the present time, duress is not available in homicide cases, a highly controversial rule,[73] but if the defense *were* available in human-threat duress cases, it should also apply in natural-threat "situational duress" circumstances. Thus, in a *Dudley-and-Stephens*-type case (or, at least in some exceptionally extreme circumstances), the defendants should be excused because of the compelling natural threat to their lives.[74]

[B] Going Beyond Natural Threats

Assume that a situational duress defense *is* recognized to deal with coercive natural threats. Suppose, then, that *X* uses physically and psychologically coercive techniques over an extended period of time in order to render *D1* submis-

---

[71] American Law Institute, Comment to § 2.09, at 379.

[72] This argument proves too much. If it is accepted, one must also abolish the insanity excuse on the ground that, since the law cannot punish a mental disease, it should punish the insane person acting as a result of the disease.

[73] See § 23.04[B], *supra*. The duress defense *is* available in homicide cases in Model Penal Code jurisdictions. See § 23.08, *infra*.

[74] See Perka v. The Queen, [1984] 2 S.C.R. 232 (Canada Supreme Court) (recognizing a residual excuse defense of necessity, the essential criterion of which is the moral involuntariness of the actor's conduct, as measured by society's expectation of appropriate and normal resistance to pressure).

sive to *X*'s beliefs ("brainwashing"). Later, *X* noncoercively suggests to *D1* that she rob State Bank. *D1* commits the crime. Should *D1* be excused?[75]

Or, suppose that *D2*, whose father has abandoned her and whose mother is a drug addict, lives in a neighborhood dominated by vicious gangs.[76] *D2* spends most of her waking hours with gang members, who teach her a code of conduct including robbery, arson, and murder. One day, *D2* decides to prove her devotion to gang ideals by robbing a liquor store, during which offense she kills the owner. Should *D2* be excused for her crimes?

At common law, of course, neither defendant would be acquitted. *D1* and *D2* knew what they were doing; they intended to violate the law; and their actions were voluntary in the willed-contraction-of-a-muscle sense of that term. More-over, the defense of duress — even situational duress as posited in subsection [A] — is unavailable to them. In the first case, *D1* acted on the basis of *X*'s unco-erced suggestion, rather than a deadly threat. In *D2*'s case, there was no threat or suggestion of any kind; the decision to commit the offense was *D2*'s.

Are the results in these cases morally just? Some would say that they are not. *D1* seems to be of a victim of brainwasher *X*, and not a criminal. *D2*, too, is a victim, if not of a particular person, then of an environment that shaped her attitudes toward the rest of the world. Few people can say with genuine confi-dence that, but for the luck of being born into a better environment, they would not have turned out as *D2* did.

Some commentators believe that the law should recognize new defenses, e.g., "brainwashing" and "rotten social background,"[77] to deal with the particular excusing conditions suggested here. Another solution is to recognize a more general excuse, which would provide that a person is excused for committing a crime if, through no fault of her own, she is placed in a situation so harsh that a person of ordinary moral firmness in her situation would have committed the crime.[78] In essence, this defense would be founded on the principle that a per-son is not responsible for her conduct if it is the result of a condition beyond her control.[79]

Critics argue that recognition of such a defense would undermine the most basic principle of the criminal law, namely, that humans ordinarily possess

---

[75] Compare Richard Delgado, *Ascription of Criminal States of Mind: Toward a Defense Theory for the Coercively Persuaded ("Brainwashed") Defendant*, 63 Minn. L. Rev. 1 (1978) (favoring excul-pation), with Joshua Dressler, *Professor Delgado's "Brainwashing" Defense: Courting a Determin-ist Legal System*, 63 Minn. L. Rev. 335 (1979) (rejecting Delgado's reasoning).

[76] This example is a variation on one provided by Richard Delgado, *A Response to Professor Dressler*, 63 Minn. L. Rev. 361, 365 (1979); see generally Richard Delgado, *"Rotten Social Back-ground": Should the Criminal Law Recognize a Defense of Severe Environmental Deprivation?*, 3 Law & Ineq. 9 (1985).

[77] E.g., Delgado, Notes 75 and 76, *supra*.

[78] See Dressler, Note 75, *supra*, at 359 (suggesting, but not advocating, such a defense).

[79] This is an application of the questionable causation theory of excuses. See § 17.03[C], *supra*.

sufficient free will to be held responsible for their actions. Although we should feel compassion for *D1* and *D2*, critics maintain, there is nothing inconsistent with the claim that victims can also be victimizers who deserve to be blamed and punished for their unjustifiable conduct.[80] According to this view, society may very well have a moral duty to right social wrongs, but jurors have the simultaneous duty to hold individuals responsible for their immediate actions.[81]

§ 23.07 BATTERED WOMEN UNDER DURESS[82]

A battered woman who kills her abusive living partner may seek to defend her actions on the basis of self-defense. Self-defense law has undergone significant change as a result of a flurry of battered-woman self-defense cases that have made their way through the appellate courts in the past decade.[83] Now, a new legal problem is developing: How should the law deal with a battered woman who commits a violent crime[84] or even participates in a crime spree,[85] as the result of domination by her abuser?

Battered women who wish to claim duress typically confront various legal obstacles. First, the abuser may order or simply expect the woman to commit a crime or assist him in its commission, without issuing an immediate (or any) coercive threat. The woman interprets his remarks or actions as threatening, in light of her battering experiences. Second, under ordinary duress principles, a person is not excused for committing a crime if she could have escaped the situation. Likewise, the defense is unavailable to one who is at fault in exposing herself to the coercive situation. In many battered woman cases, the woman has an avenue of escape from committing the crimes, yet she does not take it.

The key issue in most battered-woman duress cases is whether the defendant will be permitted to introduce expert testimony regarding battered woman syn-

---

[80] See Joshua Dressler, *Reflections on Excusing Wrongdoers: Moral Theory, New Excuses and the Model Penal Code*, 19 Rutgers L.J. 671, 682-89 (1988).

[81] Samuel H. Pillsbury, Judging Evil 47-61 (1998).

[82] See generally Alafair S. Burke, *Rational Actors, Self-Defense, and Duress: Making Sense, Not Syndromes, Out of the Battered Woman*, 81 N.C. L. Rev. 211 (2002); Laurie Kratky Doré, *Downward Adjustment and the Slippery Slope: The Use of Duress in Defense of Battered Offenders*, 56 Ohio St. L.J. 665 (1995); Beth I.Z. Boland, *Battered Women Who Act Under Duress*, 28 New Eng. L. Rev. 603 (1994).

[83] See § 18.05[B], *supra*.

[84] State v. Neelley, 531 So. 2d 69 (Ala. Crim App. 1988), aff'd, 642 So. 2d 494 (Ala. Crim. App. 1993) (*N* killed a girl whom she procured for her abusive husband, after he raped and sexually abused her; *N* was convicted and sentenced to death; held: conviction and sentence affirmed).

[85] State v. Dunn, 758 P.2d 718 (Kan. 1988), habeas granted, Dunn v. Roberts, 768 F. Supp. 1442 (D. Kan. 1991), aff'd, 963 F.2d 308 (10th Cir. 1992) (*D* participated with *X* in two-and-a-half-week crime spree involving multiple kidnappings, murder, and a robbery; *D* was convicted; the state supreme court affirmed the conviction; her conviction was overturned by a federal court on the ground that she was entitled to payment for expert psychiatric services in support of her battered woman syndrome claim).

drome to buttress her duress claim. The potential purposes of such testimony are to demonstrate that the battered woman subjectively feared her abuser even in the absence of a direct threat, and that such fear of imminent harm was reasonable; and, in order to explain her failure to escape, the expert can testify regarding "learned helplessness," a common symptom of the syndrome.

Case law is still comparatively slight, and the rulings on battered woman syndrome are mixed, but the trend is to admit the evidence, although the proper purposes for its use vary. Courts are more likely to permit the syndrome evidence to support subjective claims by the battered woman (e.g., lack of intent to assist in a crime, or her subjective fear of imminent harm if she did not cooperate with her abuser)[86] than to support the claim that her fear of imminent harm was reasonable.[87]

§ 23.08 MODEL PENAL CODE

[A] General Rule

Duress is an affirmative defense to unlawful conduct by the defendant if: (1) she was compelled to commit the offense by the use, or threatened use, of unlawful force by the coercer upon her or another person;[88] and (2) a person of reasonable firmness in her situation would have been unable to resist the coercion.[89] The defense of duress is recognized in such circumstances, the Commentary explains, because the "law is ineffective in the deepest sense, indeed . . . it is hypocritical if it imposes on the actor . . . a standard that . . . judges are not prepared to affirm that they should and could comply with. . . ."[90]

The defense is unavailable if the actor recklessly placed herself in a situation in which it was probable that she would be subjected to coercion. If she negligently placed herself in such a situation, however, the defense is available to her

---

[86] E.g., State v. Dunn, 758 P.2d 718 (Kan. 1988), habeas granted, Dunn v. Roberts, 768 F. Supp. 1442 (D. Kan. 1991), aff'd, 963 F.2d 308 (10th Cir. 1992) (BWS evidence relevant to prove D lacked the specific intent to assist in her abuser's crime-spree); People v. Romero, 26 Cal. App. 4th 315, 326 (App. Ct. 1992), rev'd on procedural grounds, 883 P.2d 388 (Cal. 1994) (BWS relevant to R's credibility and to support her testimony she entertained a good faith belief her abuser represented an imminent threat); United States v. Marenghi, 893 F. Supp. 85 (D. Me. 1995) (BWS evidence relevant "to assist the jury in reviewing the evidence").

[87] E.g., United States v. Willis, 38 F.3d 170 (5th Cir. 1994) (BWS testimony demonstrates why W was unusually susceptible to coercion; therefore, it is irrelevant to the issue of whether a person of ordinary firmness would succumb).

[88] Although the Code does not expressly so provide, the defense is also available if the defendant reasonably, but erroneously, believed that a threat to use unlawful force was issued. The defense is unavailable, however, if her mistake in this regard was reckless or negligent, and she is prosecuted for a crime of similar culpability. American Law Institute, Comment to § 2.09, at 380.

[89] Model Penal Code § 2.09(1).

[90] American Law Institute, Comment to § 2.09, at 374-75.

for all offenses except those for which negligence suffices to establish culpability.[91] This provision differs from § 3.02, the MPC choice-of-evils defense, which is available in some circumstances to a person who recklessly causes the emergency.[92]

[B] Comparison to the Common Law

[1] In General

The Code's duress defense is broader than the common law in various respects. First, it abandons the common law requirement that the defendant's unlawful act be a response to an imminent deadly threat. Under the Code, the defendant may plead duress as a result of non-deadly and non-imminent threats — or even as the result of *prior* use of *non*-deadly force — as long as a person of reasonable firmness would have committed the offense in the defendant's circumstances.

Second, the defense is one of general applicability, so the defense may be raised in murder prosecutions.[93] Third, the Code does not require that the imperiled person be the defendant or a member of her family.

The Code defense is similar to the common law in two significant ways. First, the defense is limited to threats or use of "unlawful" force; therefore, it does not apply to coercion arising from natural sources. This results in an anomaly: If *D* is compelled by *X* to run her car over the body of *V*, who is lying on a narrow mountain road, *D* may claim duress; but if she runs over *V* because her brakes give out and she prefers to kill *V* than to die herself by driving over the cliff, *D* may be convicted of criminal homicide.[94]

Second, in conformity with the common law, the Code does not recognize the defense when any interest other than bodily integrity is threatened. The Commentary simply states that other threats, such as to property or reputation, "cannot exercise sufficient power over persons of 'reasonable firmness' to warrant consideration."[95]

---

[91] Model Penal Code § 2.09(2).

[92] See § 22.05, *supra*.

[93] Even if a murder defendant is not acquitted, her duress claim may result in conviction of the lesser offense of manslaughter, on the ground that she committed the crime due to an "extreme emotional disturbance" for which there was a "reasonable explanation or excuse." Model Penal Code § 210.3(1)(b). See § 31.10[C][3], *infra*.

[94] American Law Institute, Comment to § 2.09, at 378.

[95] *Id.* at 375.

[2] Escape from Intolerable Prison Conditions[96]

The common law duress defense applies when the coercer orders another person to commit a specific crime. Under the Code, however, the defense *also* applies if the coercer's use of unlawful force causes the coerced party to perform a different criminal act, one not ordered by the coercer. Therefore, the Model Code defense of duress applies in the typical intolerable-prison-condition escape case.

For example, if X threatens to sexually assault D, a prison inmate, D may be excused for committing the different criminal act of escaping confinement, assuming that a person of reasonable firmness in D's situation would have fled.[97] Moreover, the Code provides that a coerced act may also be *justified* under § 3.02, the Code's choice-of-evils provision.[98] Therefore, a prisoner may be able to assert *both* defenses in an escape prosecution.

[3] "Situational Duress"[99]

Because the duress defense only applies to human threats, "situational duress" claims based on compelling natural circumstances fall outside the scope of the defense. The drafters permitted this gap because they were concerned that if a person were excused as the result of a compelling natural threat, no one would be subject to prosecution for unjustified conduct.[100]

On the other hand, a brainwashing claim of duress might be available in a Model Penal Code jurisdiction. The duress defense applies if the actor commits an offense in response to prior use of unlawful force, assuming that a person of reasonable firmness in the actor's situation would have committed the crime. Therefore, a victim of brainwashing could claim coercion on the ground that prior force by a captor rendered her subconsciously fearful of more force if she did not accede to the suggestion that she commit a crime.[101]

[4] Battered Women and the Nature of the "Person of Reasonable Firmness"[102]

A battered woman should find features of the Code's duress defense helpful to her coercion claim. First, as there is no imminency requirement, she may

---

[96] See § 23.05, *supra*.

[97] American Law Institute, Comment to § 2.09, at 377.

[98] Model Penal Code § 2.09(4).

[99] See § 23.06, *supra*.

[100] American Law Institute, Comment to § 2.09, at 379.

[101] American Law Institute, Comment to § 2.09, at 376-77.

[102] See § 23.07, *supra*.

defend herself on the basis of an earlier threat by the abuser. Second, as with the brainwashing cases discussed immediately above, a person who has suffered from prior abuse — prior unlawful force — may be able to excuse her conduct when she commits a crime at the "suggestion" of her abusive partner.

A battered woman's conduct, however, is measured against the objective standard of a "person of reasonable firmness" in the defendant's situation. Does this mean that the "reasonable person" is a woman suffering from battered woman syndrome? Apparently not, as the Code intends for the overall standard to remain objective.[103] The Commentary provides that a defendant's incapacity should be "based upon the incapacity of men *in general* to resist the coercive pressures."[104] The Code drafters believed that it was impractical to "vary legal norms with the individual's capacity to meet the standards they prescribe." Except when a person suffers from a "gross and verifiable" disability that may otherwise establish irresponsibility, e.g., insanity, the Code leaves consideration of an actor's subjective weaknesses to the discretion of the sentencing judge.

---

[103] E.g., State v. B.H., 870 A.2d 273 (N.J. 2005) (BWS testimony is admissible for the purpose of assisting the factfinder in its assessment of whether the battered woman was reckless in not leaving her abuser, and in understanding her subjective fear of her abuser, but such evidence is properly excluded in determining whether a person of reasonable firmness in her situation would have succumbed); United States v. Willis, 38 F.3d 170 (5th Cir. 1994) (see Note 87, *supra*).

[104] American Law Institute, Comment to § 2.09, at 374 (emphasis added).

Chapter 24

INTOXICATION

§ 24.01 INTOXICATION AND THE CRIMINAL LAW: AN OVERVIEW[1]

[A] "Intoxication": Definition

The term "intoxication" may be defined as a "disturbance of mental or physical capacities resulting from the introduction of any substance into the body."[2] As this definition suggests, the law pertaining to intoxication does not distinguish between alcohol and other foreign substances, including prescribed medications and illegal drugs.

[B] Intoxication Law in Its Social and Historical Context

Intoxicants distort judgment. They also reduce an actor's ability to control his aggressive feelings and anti-social impulses, resulting in criminal conduct, especially of a violent nature.[3] Persons addicted to narcotics, as well, often commit crimes (even when not intoxicated) in order to support their illegal habit.

In light of the social damage caused by intoxicated actors, it is unsurprising that Anglo-American common law has provided wrongdoers very little opportunity to avoid conviction on the basis of intoxication, and the modern legislative trend is to reduce the scope of any intoxication defense still further. Indeed, in a few jurisdictions now, the law has taken on "a certain Alice-in-Wonderland quality," by requiring prosecutors to prove the *mens rea* required in the definition of crimes, but then preventing defendants from introducing evidence of intoxication that might rebut its presence.[4]

---

[1] See generally Jerome Hall, *Intoxication and Criminal Responsibility*, 57 Harv. L. Rev. 1045 (1944); Mitchell Keiter, *Just Say No Excuse: The Rise and Fall of the Intoxication Defense*, 87 J. Crim. L. & Criminology 482 (1997); Monrad G. Paulsen, *Intoxication as a Defense to Crime*, 1961 U. Ill. L.F. 1.

[2] People v. Low, 732 P.2d 622, 627 (Colo. 1987) (quoting Model Penal Code § 2.08(5)(a)).

[3] Montana v. Egelhoff, 518 U.S. 37, 49 (1996); see also Director of Public Prosecutions v. Majewski, [1976] 2 All E.R. 142, 146 ("Self-induced alcoholic intoxication has been a factor in crimes of violence . . . throughout the history of crime in this country."). Some studies, although dated, suggest that as many as one-half of all homicides in the United States are committed by intoxicated persons. *Egelhoff, supra* (citing studies).

[4] Sanford H. Kadish, *Fifty Years of Criminal Law: An Opinionated Review*, 87 Cal. L. Rev. 943, 955 (1999). See § 24.03, *infra*.

[C] Intoxication Cases: Issues to Consider

When a defendant is intoxicated at the time of the alleged criminal conduct, a lawyer must consider at least three questions. First, how did the defendant become intoxicated? Intoxication law is divisible into two general categories: rules pertaining to conduct that was the result of "voluntary" (or "self-induced") intoxication, and the law pertaining to "involuntary" (or "innocent") intoxication. The vast majority of cases concern the former condition.

Second, in what way does the defendant claim that his intoxication affected his culpability? In most cases, the actor claims that he did not form the requisite state of mind to be convicted of the offense. Occasionally, however, the defendant's intoxication is so gross that he may seek to show that he was unconscious when he acted, i.e., that his conduct did not include a voluntary act. Or, the defendant may assert that, although he had the requisite *mens rea* to commit the offense and was conscious when he was acting, the intoxicants rendered him temporarily insane.

Third, of what type of offense is the defendant charged — general intent, specific intent, or strict liability? The common law rules differ considerably depending on the nature of the *mens rea*, if any, that must be proved.

[D] Intoxication Claims: Relationship to Other Defenses

Intoxication claims can confusingly parallel or overlap other defenses. First, as the previous comments suggest, under limited circumstances an *intoxication* defense is recognized when an actor becomes "temporarily insane" as the result of the introduction of drugs, alcohol, or other foreign substances into the body.[5] In other cases, as the result of long-term intoxication, a person may suffer from permanent (or, at least, continuing) insanity; in the latter situation a traditional insanity defense claim may lie.[6]

Second, in some states, the defenses of diminished capacity[7] and intoxication operate similarly, except that the former defense applies when the actor suffers from mental illness rather than intoxication. However, occasionally, a state will permit evidence on one, but not the other, factor.[8]

Third, claims of intoxication and mistake-of-fact[9] frequently overlap. For example, in *Regina v. Cogan and Leak*,[10] L fraudulently convinced C, who was

---

[5] See § 24.06[B], *infra*.

[6] See § 24.05[B], *infra*.

[7] See Chapter 26, *infra*.

[8] State v. Bias, 653 So. 2d 380 (Fla. 1995) (permitting evidence of voluntary intoxication in limited circumstances, but precluding expert testimony on diminished capacity).

[9] See Chapter 12, *supra*.

[10] [1976] Q.B. 217.

intoxicated, that *V*, *L*'s wife, desired intercourse with *C*, despite *V*'s protestations to the contrary. Charged with rape, *C* claimed mistake-of-fact regarding *V*'s lack of consent. Because *C* was intoxicated, however, his claim could also be described as an "intoxicated mistake"[11] claim. Often the two defenses operate similarly, so that the label attached to the claim will not matter. However, in some jurisdictions, the "mistake" defense is broader than the counterpart "intoxication" claim, so that the mixture of the two claims may result in conceptual confusion.

§ 24.02 VOLUNTARY INTOXICATION: GENERAL PRINCIPLES[12]

[A] Definition of "Voluntary Intoxication"

[1] In General

The term "voluntary intoxication" rarely is defined by the courts, which prefer instead to provide examples of the very few circumstances in which intoxication is involuntary. Basically, intoxication is "voluntary" if the actor is culpable for becoming intoxicated. Such culpability exists if the person knowingly ingests a substance that he knows or should know can cause him to become intoxicated, unless the substance was a prescribed medication or he was coerced to ingest it.[13]

Once an actor voluntarily ingests a known intoxicant, courts are unsympathetic to claims that the substance had an unexpected effect on the actor. For example, in *People v. Velez*,[14] *D* knowingly puffed on a marijuana cigarette at a social gathering, unaware that it was laced with phencyclidine (PCP). *D*, while in an unconscious state precipitated by the PCP, assaulted *V* with a deadly weapon. The court held that for purposes of intoxication law, *D* was "voluntarily" intoxicated, because it was "common knowledge that unlawful street drugs do not come with warranties of purity or quality associated with lawfully acquired drugs, such as alcohol."

---

[11] Kenneth L. Campbell, *Intoxicated Mistakes*, 32 Crim. L.Q. 110 (1987).

[12] See generally Derrick Augustus Carter, *Bifurcations of Consciousness: The Elimination of the Self-Induced Intoxication Excuse*, 64 Mo. L. Rev. 383 (1999); Alan R. Ward, *Making Some Sense of Self-Induced Intoxication*, 45 Cambridge L.J. 247 (1986); Peter Westen, *Egelhoff Again*, 36 Am. Crim. L. Rev. 1203 (1999); see also the sources in Note 1, *supra*.

[13] See Model Penal Code § 2.08(5)(b) (defining "self-induced intoxication").

[14] 175 Cal. App. 3d 785 (App. Ct. 1985).

[2] Alcoholism, Drug Addiction, and "Voluntary Intoxication"[15]

The common law treats intoxication resulting from alcoholism or drug addiction as voluntary. In general, "an irresistable [sic] compulsion to consume intoxicants caused by a physiological or psychological disability does not render the ensuing intoxication involuntary."[16] The law treats the alcoholic's first drink of the day, and the drug addict's first use of narcotics on a particular occasion, no differently than it does the actions of the ordinary drinker and casual user of drugs.

As a matter of constitutional law, a state may not punish a person for the *status* — the condition — of being addicted to narcotics[17] or, presumably, of being an alcoholic. On the other hand, an alcoholic may be punished for conduct resulting from intoxication, such as public drunkenness;[18] and a drug addict may not use his condition as a defense to the crime of drug possession or, presumably, offenses committed in support of his drug habit.[19] Constitutional law in this regard is discussed elsewhere in the Text and should be considered at this point.[20]

[B] General Rules

[1] No Excuse

Courts commonly state that voluntary intoxication never excuses criminal conduct.[21] This is a somewhat misleading statement: Although it is true that self-induced intoxication *as such* never excuses wrongdoing, the condition that intoxication causes, e.g., a clouded mental state, unconsciousness, or insanity, may serve as an exculpatory basis in very limited circumstances. Nonetheless, the no-excuse rule is a good starting point from which to appreciate how few are

---

[15] See generally Herbert Fingarette, Heavy Drinking — The Myth of Alcoholism as a Disease (1988); Richard C. Boldt, *The Construction of Responsibility in the Criminal Law*, 140 U. Pa. L. Rev. 2245 (1992); Douglas N. Husak, *Addiction and Criminal Liability*, 18 Law & Phil. 655 (1999); Warren Lehman, *Alcoholism, Freedom, and Moral Responsibility*, 13 Int'l J.L. & Psychiatry 103 (1990); Steven S. Nemerson, *Alcoholism, Intoxication, and the Criminal Law*, 10 Cardozo L. Rev. 393 (1988).

[16] See v. State, 757 S.W.2d 947, 950 (Ark. 1988); see People v. Downey, 515 N.E.2d 362, 371 (Ill. App. Ct. 1987); State v. Bishop, 632 S.W.2d 255, 258 (Mo. 1982).

[17] Robinson v. California, 370 U.S. 660 (1962).

[18] Powell v. Texas, 392 U.S. 514 (1968).

[19] See United States v. Moore, 486 F.2d 1139, 1147-48 (D.C. Cir. 1973).

[20] See § 9.04, *supra*.

[21] E.g., People v. Langworthy, 331 N.W.2d 171, 172 (Mich. 1982) ("Every jurisdiction in this country recognizes the general principle that voluntary intoxication is not any excuse for crime.") (footnote omitted).

the circumstances in which a voluntarily intoxicated actor may avoid criminal conviction.

The early English common law rule was that voluntary intoxication did not serve in any way to exculpate a wrongdoer. Hale wrote that an intoxicated person "shall have no privilege by this voluntarily contracted madness, but shall have the same judgment as if he were in his right senses."[22] Put differently, "a man who by his own voluntary act debauches and destroys his will power [should] be no better situated in regard to criminal acts than a sober man."[23] Indeed, Blackstone viewed intoxication "as an aggravation of the offence, rather than as an excuse for any criminal misbehaviour."[24]

[2] When Voluntary Intoxication May Be Exculpatory

Beginning in the nineteenth century, very narrow exceptions to the early common law no-exculpation rule began to take root.[25] First (and subject to considerable clarification), in most jurisdictions, a person may be acquitted of certain offenses if, as the result of self-induced intoxication, he did not harbor the state of mind provided for in the definition of the offense. Second, there is limited authority for the proposition that one who acts in a state of unconsciousness brought on by voluntary intoxication may seek to avoid conviction on this ground. Third, a person who suffers from long-term intoxication-induced "fixed" insanity may be acquitted. These principles are discussed below.

§ 24.03 VOLUNTARY INTOXICATION: *MENS REA*

[A] In General

The most common voluntary intoxication "defense" raised in criminal trials is not an excuse defense at all, but rather is a failure-of-proof claim,[26] namely that, as a result of the actor's intoxication, he lacked the mental state required in the definition of the offense.

Today, there are as many as seven different common law and statutory approaches to *mens rea* claims, ranging from the rule that voluntary intoxication that negates an actor's *mens rea* is a defense to all crimes, to the opposite

---

[22] 1 Matthew Hale, History of the Pleas of the Crown *32-33 (1736).

[23] Director of Public Prosecutions v. Beard, 1920 A.C. 479, 494 (opinion of Lord Birkenhead); see also People v. Lewis, 36 Cal. 531, 531-32 (1869), overruled in part, People v. Gorshen, 336 P.2d 492 (Cal. 1959) (the law should "not allow [the defendant] to avail himself of the excuse of his own gross vice and misconduct to shelter himself from the legal consequences of [his] crime").

[24] 4 William Blackstone, Commentaries on the Laws of England *25-26 (1769).

[25] Montana v. Egelhoff, 518 U.S. 37, 46-47 (1996).

[26] See § 16.02, *supra*, for a definition of a "failure-of-proof" defense.

and increasingly popular position that it is not recognized for any offense. The traditional common law rule — the rule that took root in the nineteenth century and remains the most common approach — is one that distinguishes between general-intent and specific-intent crimes.[27]

[B] Traditional Common Law Rule

[1] Overview

In matters relating to voluntary intoxication, the common law draws a distinction between general-intent and specific-intent crimes. Indeed, as the California Supreme Court once pointed out, the concepts of "general intent" and "specific intent" "evolved as a judicial response to the problem of the intoxicated offender." The distinction represents the law's "compromise between the conflicting feelings of sympathy and reprobation for the intoxicated offender."[28]

[2] General-Intent Offenses

According to ordinary common law principles, voluntary intoxication is not a defense to general-intent crimes.[29] For example, if *D* rapes *V*, he will not be entitled to claim that, as a result of voluntary intoxication, his mind was so clouded that he did not or could not form the intent to have sexual intercourse with *V*.[30]

This rule made sense when the intoxication doctrine was first formulated. At that time, "general intent" referred to an offense for which the only *mens rea* required was a culpable state of mind.[31] Consistent with this meaning of the term *"mens rea,"* the voluntary act of impairing one's mental faculties with intoxicants is a morally blameworthy course of conduct that renders the actor culpable for the ensuing harm.[32] By this view, a person's voluntary intoxication *proves*, rather than negates, his *"mens rea."*

---

[27] According to one fairly recent survey of statutory and case law, ten states do not admit intoxication evidence as a defense to any crime; two states only admit evidence of intoxication to reduce first-degree murder to a lower degree; in one state, voluntary intoxication is a defense to all crimes; in the remaining thirty-seven states, it is a defense to some, but not all, non-homicide crimes. Twenty-one of these states expressly draw the line on a "specific intent"/ "general intent" basis. Keiter, Note 1, *supra*, at 518-20.

[28] People v. Hood, 462 P.2d 370, 377 (Cal. 1969).

[29] E.g., United States v. Sewell, 252 F.3d 647, 650-51 (2d Cir. 2001); State v. Dwyer, 757 A.2d 597, 604 (Conn. Ct. App. 2000); State v. Erickstad, 620 N.W.2d 136, 144 (N.D. 2000).

[30] See State v. McDaniel, 515 So. 2d 572, 575 (La. Ct. App. 1987); People v. Langworthy, 331 N.W.2d 171, 177 (Mich. 1982).

[31] See §§ 10.02[B] and 10.06, *supra*.

[32] Hendershott v. People, 653 P.2d 385, 396 (Colo. 1982).

In modern language, self-induced intoxication typically constitutes reckless conduct.[33] The effect of alcohol and drugs on the human body is now sufficiently well known that the law can safely assume that when an ordinary person chooses to ingest intoxicating substances, he knows that he will suffer temporary impairment of his powers of perception, judgment, and control; therefore, he knows that he may jeopardize the safety of others while in that condition.

[3] Specific-Intent Offenses

The traditional rule is that voluntary intoxication *is* a defense to specific-intent crimes.[34] That is, a person is not guilty of an offense if, as the result of his intoxication at the time of the crime, he was incapable of forming[35] or did not in fact form,[36] the specific intent required in the definition of the offense.[37]

For example, suppose that *D* becomes intoxicated and sexually assaults *V*, a woman. He is arrested during the assault and charged with the specific-intent crime of assault with intent to rape. Under the common law, *D* is entitled to introduce evidence regarding his intoxication in order to prove that, because of his condition, he lacked the specific intent to rape *V*, either because he was too intoxicated to know what he was doing, or because he mistakenly believed that *V* was consenting.[38] *D* is entitled to introduce this evidence because, the reasoning goes, "[w]here the legislature, in its definition of a crime, has designated a particular state of mind as a material element of the crime, evidence of intoxication becomes relevant if the degree of inebriation has reached that point" where he did not form the required intent.[39]

---

[33] People v. Register, 457 N.E.2d 704, 709 (N.Y. 1983); Director of Public Prosecutions v. Majewski, [1976] 2 All E.R. 142, 150 (Lord Elwyn-Jones, L.C.).

[34] E.g., State v. Dwyer, 757 A.2d at 604; State v. Erickstad, 620 N.W.2d at 143-44.

[35] United States v. Zink, 612 F.2d 511, 515 (10th Cir. 1980); Commonwealth v. Henson, 476 N.E.2d 947, 953 (Mass. 1985); State v. Hicks, 538 N.E.2d 1030, 1034 (Ohio 1989).

[36] Cal. Penal Code. § 22(b) (2005).

[37] The difference in language between "lacking capacity to form" and "not forming" a specific intent is significant. Logically, one who lacks the capacity to form a specific intent does not in fact form it. The converse, however, does not necessarily follow. As a practical matter, acquittal should be more difficult to obtain in an "incapacity" jurisdiction because intoxication rarely renders a person so insensible that he lacks the ability to intend. The "incapacity" language is undesirable, however, because a jury may improperly convict because it determines that the defendant *had* the capacity to form the specific intent, without resolving the pertinent question — *did* the defendant form the intent?

[38] See People v. Guillett, 69 N.W.2d 140, 143 (Mich. 1955), overruled on other grounds, People v. Carines, 597 N.W.2d 130, 140 (Mich. 1999).

[39] Commonwealth v. Graves, 334 A.2d 661, 663 (Pa. 1975), effectively overruled by statute, as noted in Commonwealth v. Pickett, 368 A.2d 799, 801 (Pa. Super. Ct. 1976).

[4] Criticism of the Traditional Approach

[a] Why Draw a Distinction?

Notice the apparent anomaly with the present law. If *D* has nonconsensual sexual intercourse with *V* because he drunkenly believes *V* is consenting, *D* may *not* introduce evidence of his intoxication to support his *mens rea* claim in a prosecution of the general-intent offense of rape. However, if *D* is arrested *before* the intercourse occurs, and he is charged with the specific-intent offense of "assault with intent to rape," *D* may now introduce evidence of his drunkenness in order to negate the specific intent ("intent to rape").

At least in a modern penal code, in which *mens rea* terms are expressly set out in the definition of offenses, nothing commends this dual approach. *D*'s intoxication is the same in both cases. He is equally drunk. He is equally culpable for becoming drunk. His mind is equally clouded. His capacity to form a mental state is equally undermined (or not undermined). And, "neither common experience nor psychology knows of any such phenomenon as 'general intent' distinguishable from 'specific intent.' "[40] Nor do utilitarian concerns favor separate approaches: *D* is equally dangerous in the two cases; and principles of general deterrence demand equal treatment.

[b] Should the Defense Be Abolished?

Most critics of the current law would resolve the perceived anomaly by disallowing *any mens rea*-based voluntary intoxication defense. Supreme Court Justice Antonin Scalia has expressed the arguments for this position as follows:

> Disallowing consideration of voluntary intoxication has the effect of increasing the punishment for all unlawful acts committed in that state, and thereby deters drunkenness or irresponsible behavior while drunk. The rule also serves as a specific deterrent, ensuring that those who prove incapable of controlling violent impulses while voluntarily intoxicated go to prison. And finally, the rule comports with and implements society's moral perception that one who has voluntarily impaired his own faculties should be responsible for the consequences.[41]

Justice Scalia's utilitarian arguments are based on the proposition that "the aim of the law is to protect the innocent from injury by the sick as well as the bad."[42] Therefore, it follows, the intoxication defense is detrimental to the wel-

---

[40] People v. Kelley, 176 N.W.2d 435, 443 (Mich. Ct. App. 1970).

[41] Montana v. Egelhoff, 518 U.S. 37, 49-50 (1996).

[42] State v. Maik, 287 A.2d 715, 720 (N.J. 1972), overruled on other grounds by State v. Krol, 344 A.2d 289 (N.J. 1975).

fare and safety of the citizenry. Unlike insane people, who are usually institu-tionalized on the basis of an insanity acquittal,[43] intoxicated persons who are acquitted, many of whom are alcoholics and drug addicts, return to the street where they may commit new offenses.

Those who favor a defense[44] disagree with Scalia's "moral perception" argu-ment. Even if an intoxicated actor is dangerous, they contend, this fact does not prove that he possessed the state of mind required in the definition of the offense. When a lawmaking body expressly includes a mental state in the def-inition of a crime, as common law courts did with specific-intent offenses and which legislatures now do with most non-strict-liability crimes, it does so because it believes that the particular *mens rea* incorporated therein renders the actor more deserving of punishment than if that mental state were absent.

Supreme Court Justice Sandra O'Connor has explained the pro-defense posi-tion on the ground that there is a "fundamental incompatibility" with imposing a mental-state requirement in the definition of an offense, and then disallow-ing "consideration of evidence that might defeat establishment of that mental state."[45] It is not that voluntary intoxication excuses commission of a crime, but, as she explains, "rather, an element of the crime, the requisite mental state, was not satisfied and therefore the crime [has] not been committed." Put simply, "where a subjective mental state [is] an element of the crime to be proved, the defense must be permitted to show, by reference to intoxication, the absence of that element."[46] Notwithstanding the latter arguments, statutes that bar evi-dence of voluntary intoxication apparently do not inevitably offend constitu-tional principles.[47]

[C] Special Problem: Intoxication and Homicide

The voluntary intoxication rules pertaining to criminal homicide merit spe-cial attention. Many jurisdictions separate murder into degrees, in which first-degree murder includes "wilful, deliberate, premeditated" killings.[48] In virtually all states with this type of statutory system, a defendant may introduce evidence that, because his mental faculties were clouded by intoxicants, he did not pre-

---

[43] See § 25.05, *infra*.

[44] Some persons who favor a defense contend that voluntary intoxication should serve as a potential basis for exculpation for *any* offense, regardless of its characterization as "general" or "spe-cific" intent. Others would retain the common law distinction between general-intent and specific-intent offenses.

[45] Montana v. Egelhoff, 518 U.S. at 69 (dissenting opinion).

[46] *Id.* at 70.

[47] Montana v. Egelhoff, 518 U.S. 37 (1996). See § 7.03[B][4][b], *supra*.

[48] See §§ 31.02[D] and 31.03[C], *infra*.

meditate and deliberate the killing.[49] In such circumstances, the defendant is entitled to have his crime reduced to second-degree murder.[50]

A defendant's intoxication may also arise as an issue in a felony-murder prosecution.[51] For example, suppose that D, in an extremely intoxicated condition, takes property from V by force. V dies of a heart attack brought on by the robbery. Robbery is a specific-intent offense. In a jurisdiction that recognizes the voluntary intoxication defense in specific-intent prosecutions, what should happen if D is so intoxicated that he does not form the specific intent to steal V's property? The answer should be that D is not guilty of robbery and, therefore, not guilty of felony-murder.[52]

§ 24.04 VOLUNTARY INTOXICATION: VOLUNTARY ACT

Occasionally, a person will become so intoxicated that he is rendered unconscious, in which condition his body may move in an automatic, i.e., unwilled, manner and cause harm to others. If so, may a defendant seek to avoid conviction by asserting the general principle of criminal responsibility that a person may not be convicted of a crime unless his conduct includes a voluntary act, i.e., a willed, conscious, muscular contraction?[53]

There are few cases that deal directly with this issue, since an unconscious person will almost certainly also assert a voluntary-intoxication *mens rea* defense as well, assuming the jurisdiction permits such claims. Where courts have spoken to the issue, some have stated that, although unconsciousness ordinarily precludes criminal liability, it is not a defense if the condition was itself brought on by voluntary consumption of alcohol or drugs.[54] Others courts, incorporating the *mens rea* rules to claims of involuntariness, allow evidence of

---

[49] E.g., State v. Ludlow, 883 P.2d 1144, 1147-50 (Kan. 1994); Commonwealth v. Henson, 476 N.E.2d at 953; State v. Stasio, 396 A.2d 1129, 1131 (N.J. 1979).

[50] Even if the intoxication also negates the element of "wilfulness" — intent to kill — the crime is typically only reduced to second-degree murder because a person who becomes so intoxicated that he cannot form the requisite intent for first-degree murder has acted recklessly in becoming so insensible. Therefore, his actions fall within the recklessness or "depraved heart" form of murder that typically constitutes second-degree murder. See § 31.05, *infra*. "Thus, the erosion, through voluntary intoxication, of the specific intent to kill . . . moves the crime *down and over* from a murderous *mens rea* requiring a specific intent to a different murderous *mens rea* not requiring such specific intent." Cirincione v. State, 540 A.2d 1151, 1153 n.1 (Md. Ct. Spec. App. 1988); but see State v. Brown, 931 P.2d 69, 73-75 (N.M. 1996) (in a state in which depraved-heart murder is *first*-degree, held: excessive consumption of alcohol can negate the statutory requirement of subjective or actual knowledge of the high degree of risk involved in the actor's conduct).

[51] The felony-murder doctrine is considered at § 31.06, *infra*.

[52] E.g., Commonwealth v. Parker, 522 N.E.2d 924, 926 (Mass. 1988).

[53] See § 9.02[A], *supra*.

[54] E.g., Lewis v. State, 27 S.E.2d 659 (Ga. 1943); State v. Utter, 479 P.2d 946 (Wash. Ct. App. 1971).

intoxication-based involuntariness as a defense to specific-intent offenses, but not to general-intent crimes.[55]

Unconsciousness may serve as a basis for acquittal in another manner. Courts sometimes state that evidence of unconsciousness produced by voluntary intoxication may be introduced by a defendant when "his defense is that he did not physically accomplish the act of which he is accused."[56] In other words, the defendant may use his intoxication-induced unconsciousness to prove that he did not commit the criminal act at all, as distinguished from claiming that he committed it involuntarily.

§ 24.05 VOLUNTARY INTOXICATION: INSANITY[57]

[A] "Temporary" Insanity

Suppose that a person becomes so intoxicated that, at the time he commits an offense, he is so out of touch with reality that he does not appreciate the wrongfulness of his conduct, or he cannot conform his conduct to the law. Assume further that if his state of mind were caused by a mental disease, rather than by intoxication, he could raise the excuse of insanity.[58] As mental illness is not involved, however, the defendant may wish to claim that because of his voluntary ingestion of drugs or alcohol, he experienced something like "temporary insanity," or what Hale called "temporary phrenzy."[59]

The common law does not recognize such a defense. To the extent that an actor's intoxication was voluntary, "any degree of insanity thus produced would be a part of the consequences of such voluntary intoxication."[60] In contrast to mental illness, which is a condition that ordinarily is contracted involuntarily, one who voluntarily introduces alcohol or drugs into his system is the victim of "artificial voluntarily contracted madness."[61] As such, he is not entitled to the law's dispensation.[62]

---

[55] E.g., People v. Chaffey, 25 Cal. App. 4th 852, 855 (Ct. App. 1994).

[56] Linehan v. State, 442 So. 2d 244, 250 (Fla. 1983).

[57] See generally Andrew M. Levine, Note, *Denying the Settled Insanity Defense: Another Necessary Step in Dealing with Drug and Alcohol Abuse*, 78 B.U. L. Rev. 75 (1998); Lawrence P. Tiffany, *The Drunk, the Insane, and the Criminal Courts: Deciding What to Make of Self-Induced Insanity*, 69 Wash. U. L.Q. 221 (1991).

[58] The definition of "insanity" varies by jurisdiction. See § 25.04[C], *infra*.

[59] 1 Hale, Note 22, *supra*, at *32.

[60] Roberts v. People, 19 Mich. 401, 422 (1870); see Evans v. State, 645 P.2d 155, 158-60 (Alaska 1982); State v. Wicks, 657 P.2d 781, 782 (Wash. 1983).

[61] 4 Blackstone, Note 24, *supra*, at *25.

[62] However, a person suffering from such a mental condition may be incapable of forming a required *mens rea*, and be able to avoid conviction on that ground, as considered in § 24.03, *supra*.

[B] "Fixed" Insanity

Habitual use of intoxicants can result in a substance-induced mental disorder that persists, i.e., the disorder remains even when the actor is not under the influence of intoxicants.[63]

The law distinguishes between mental impairment that does not extend beyond the period of voluntary intoxication, for which no defense is available, and insanity resulting from long-term use of drugs or alcohol. If the unsoundness of mind, although produced by long-term alcohol or drug abuse, has become "fixed" or "settled," the general, but not universal, rule is that the defendant may assert a traditional insanity defense.[64] Although the defense is usually asserted when the defendant was not intoxicated at the time of the offense, the insanity defense applies even if the actor was intoxicated at the time of the crime.[65]

In light of the unsympathetic view of common law jurists regarding intoxication-caused criminal conduct, it is surprising that "madness . . . contracted by the vice and will of the party"[66] would excuse. Indeed, one court that has rejected the defense has asserted:

> There is no principled basis to distinguish between the short-term and long-term effects of voluntary intoxication by punishing the first and excusing the second. If anything, the moral blameworthiness would seem to be even greater with respect to the long-term effects of many, repeated instances of voluntary intoxication occurring over an extended period of time.[67]

The law's general willingness to recognize the defense is sometimes defended on the theory that it would constitute an impossible task to trace the chain of causation back to the original misconduct of abusive drinking or narcotics usage.[68] More likely, however, the law recognizes the fact that at some point a person's earlier voluntary decisions become morally remote.[69] One should not be blamed for every harmful act that can be linked to a much earlier transgression.

---

[63] See American Psychiatric Association, Diagnostic and Statistical Manual of Mental Disorders 209 (4th ed. Text Revision 2000).

[64] 1 Hale, Note 22, *supra*, at *32; Jones v. State, 648 P.2d 1251, 1255 (Okla. Crim. App. 1982); State v. Wicks, 657 P.2d at 782.

[65] People v. Chapman, 418 N.W.2d 658, 659 (Mich. Ct. App. 1987).

[66] 1 Hale, Note 22, *supra*, at *32.

[67] Bieber v. People, 856 P.2d 811, 817 (Colo. 1993); see also People v. Robinson, 72 Cal. App. 4th 421 (Ct. App. 1999) (interpreting Cal. Penal Code § 25.5).

[68] Paulsen, Note 1, *supra*, at 23.

[69] See Parker v. State, 254 A.2d 381, 388 (Md. Ct. Spec. App. 1969) (distinguishing between "the direct results of drinking, which are voluntarily sought after, and its remote and undesired consequences").

§ 24.06 INVOLUNTARY INTOXICATION[70]

[A] Definition

Intoxication is "involuntary" (or "innocent") if the actor is not to blame for becoming intoxicated.[71] According to one scholar, if we judge the state of legal affairs from court opinions, involuntary intoxication is "simply and completely non-existent."[72] Although this is an exaggeration, cases of involuntary intoxication are exceedingly uncommon.

As described in *City of Minneapolis v. Altimus*,[73] intoxication is characterized as "involuntary" in four circumstances. First, if the person is coerced to ingest an intoxication, such as when *B*, a youth, was told that he would be left in the desert if he did not drink alcohol.[74] Second, if the person ingests an intoxicant by innocent mistake, e.g., *X* fraudulently induces *P* to ingest cocaine by telling him that it is a "breath freshener."[75]

Third, blame is inappropriate if the actor becomes unexpectedly intoxicated from a prescribed medication, i.e., he does not know, and has no reason to know, that the medication is likely to have an intoxicating effect.[76] However, if the actor purposely takes more than the prescribed medication, the jury may find that the intoxication is voluntary.[77]

---

[70] See generally Lawrence P. Tiffany & Mary Tiffany, *Nosologic Objections to the Criminal Defense of Pathological Intoxication: What Do the Doubters Doubt?*, 13 Int'l J. L. & Psychiatry, 49 (1990).

[71] Mendenhall v. State, 15 S.W.3d 560, 565 (Tex. App. 2000) (involuntary intoxication is an affirmative defense when "the accused has exercised no independent judgment or volition in taking the intoxicant").

[72] Jerome Hall, General Principles of Criminal Law 539 (2d ed. 1960).

[73] 238 N.W.2d 851, 856 (Minn. 1976).

[74] Burrows v. State, 297 P. 1029, 1035 (Ariz. 1931), overruled on other grounds by State v. Hernandez, 320 P.2d 467, 469 (Ariz. 1958).

[75] People v. Penman, 110 N.E. 894, 900 (Ill. 1915).

[76] City of Minneapolis v. Altimus, 238 N.W.2d at 856-57; Commonwealth v. Darch, 767 N.E.2d 1096, 1098-99 (Mass. App. Ct. 2002); e.g., Brancaccio v. State, 698 So. 2d 597 (Fla. Dist. Ct. App. 1997) (*B* took Zoloft, a drug for depression, and suffered from side effects of the drug, including hallucinations and aggression); Mendenhall v. State, 15 S.W.3d 560, 565 (Tex. App. 2000) (*M*, a diabetic, failed to eat appropriately in conjunction with a self-administered prescribed insulin injection; he had not been provided sufficient information from medical personnel on the appropriate diet for his condition and the effects of taking insulin on an empty stomach).

[77] People v. Chaffey, 25 Cal. App. 4th 852 (Ct. App. 1994) (taking an overdose of prescription medicine in order to commit suicide may be deemed *voluntary* intoxication); contra People v. Turner, 680 P.2d 1290 (Colo. Ct. App. 1983) (as in the past, *T* took more than the prescribed medication for migraine headaches; in the past, he suffered drowsiness from the overdose; on the present occasion it had an intoxicating effect; held: because the doctor had never warned him that an overdose might cause intoxication, and it had not caused this effect in the past, a jury could find that the intoxication was *involuntary*).

Fourth, "pathological intoxication" is involuntary. Pathological intoxication "is a temporary psychotic reaction, often manifested by violence, which is triggered by consumption of alcohol by a person with a pre-disposing mental or physical condition,"[78] e.g., temporal lobe epilepsy, encephalitis, or a metabolic disturbance. The defense only applies if the actor had no reason to know that he was susceptible to such a reaction.

[B] General Rule

A person who is involuntarily intoxicated is entitled to acquittal in all of the circumstances in which *voluntary* intoxication is a defense. Although there is exceedingly little case law on the matter, it would seem that because the actor's intoxication was contracted in a nonculpable manner, he should also be acquitted of any general-intent offense.[79]

In contrast to the principles relating to voluntary intoxication,[80] a defendant is also excused for his conduct if, as the result of involuntary intoxication, he is "temporarily insane," i.e., he suffers from a temporary intoxication-induced mental condition that satisfies that jurisdiction's definition of insanity.[81]

§ 24.07 MODEL PENAL CODE

[A] General Rule

The Code distinguishes between three types of intoxication:[82] (1) self-induced intoxication; (2) pathological intoxication; and (3) intoxication that is not self-induced (i.e., involuntary intoxication).[83]

---

[78] Tiffany & Tiffany, Note 70, *supra*, at 49.

[79] To the extent that involuntary intoxication is a defense because it negates the required *mens rea* of an offense, it should not be a defense to a strict-liability crime, because there is no *mens rea* to negate. E.g., State v. Miller, 788 P.2d 974 (Or. 1990) (*M* drank coffee fixed for him by *X*, without knowledge that it had been spiked with alcohol; held: *M* may *not* claim involuntary intoxication in a strict-liability prosecution for driving under the influence of alcohol); Aliff v. State, 955 S.W.2d 891 (Tex. App. 1997) (same holding, driving while intoxicated); contra, Commonwealth v. Darch, 767 N.E.2d 1096 (Mass. App. Ct. 2002) (driving while intoxicated); People v. Koch, 294 N.Y.S. 987 (App. Div. 1937) (driving while intoxicated).

[80] See § 24.05[A], *supra*.

[81] People v. Caulley, 494 N.W.2d 853, 859 (Mich. Ct. App. 1992); State v. Bauman, 689 A.2d 173, 182 (N.J. Super. Ct. App. Div. 1997); State v. Voorhees, 596 N.W.2d 241, 250 (Minn. 1999); Mendenhall v. State, 15 S.W.3d 560, 565 (Tex. App. 2000); State v. Gardner, 870 P.2d 900, 901-02 (Utah 1993); State v. Gardner, 601 N.W.2d 670, 673 (Wis. Ct. App. 1999).

[82] For the MPC definition of "intoxication," see the text accompanying Note 2, *supra*.

[83] Model Penal Code § 2.08(4)-(5).

An actor's intoxicated condition at the time of a crime may exculpate him in two circumstances. First, any form of intoxication is a defense to criminal conduct if it negates an element of the offense.[84] Second, pathological intoxication and intoxication that was not self-induced are affirmatives defenses, if the intoxication causes the actor to suffer from a mental condition comparable to that which constitutes insanity under the Code.[85] These exculpatory claims are explained below.

[B] Negation of an Element of an Offense

[1] Mental State

[a] In General

The Code does not distinguish between "general intent" and "specific intent" offenses.[86] Consequently, with one exception, a person is not guilty of an offense — regardless of whether it would be characterized as "general intent" or "specific intent" at common law — if, as the result of intoxication, he lacked the state of mind required in respect to an element of the crime.

For example, assume that under state law "rape" occurs when a male "knowingly has nonconsensual sexual intercourse with a female not his wife." Under this statute, D would be entitled to acquittal if, because of self-induced intoxication, he did not have the knowledge required for the offense, e.g., he did not know that he was having intercourse, he did not know that the female did not consent, or he did not know that the victim was a "female not his wife."

[b] Exception to the Rule

The Code recognizes one exception to the rule described above. The exception relates to crimes defined in terms of recklessness. Ordinarily, a person acts "recklessly" as defined by the Code if "he consciously disregards a substantial and unjustifiable risk that the material element of the offense exists or will result from his conduct."[87] However, the Code provides that if a person "due to self-induced intoxication is unaware of a risk of which he would have been aware had he been sober, such unawareness is immaterial" in a prosecution for which recklessness establishes criminal liability.[88] In other words, in a prosecution for recklessness, a voluntarily intoxicated defendant cannot negate proof

---

[84] Model Penal Code § 2.08(1).

[85] Model Penal Code § 2.08(4).

[86] See § 10.07[A], *supra*.

[87] Model Penal Code § 2.02(2)(c).

[88] Model Penal Code § 2.08(2).

of recklessness by introducing evidence of his intoxication-caused lack of aware-ness of a risk. As a practical matter, this means that a negligent actor may be convicted of a crime of recklessness, in violation of ordinary Model Penal Code culpability principles.

The Commentary to the Code concedes that criticism of this rule is "worthy of respect," but the drafters concluded:

> [A]wareness of the potential consequences of excessive drinking on the capacity of human beings to gauge the risks incident to their conduct is by now so dispersed in our culture that it is not unfair to postulate a general equivalence between the risks created by the conduct of the drunken actor and the risks created by his conduct in becoming drunk. Becoming so drunk as to destroy temporarily the actor's powers of per-ception and judgment is conduct that plainly has no affirmative social value to counterbalance the potential danger.[89]

[2] Voluntary Act

The Code provides that a person is entitled to acquittal if his intoxication negates *any* element of the offense. Under the Code, a person is not guilty of an offense unless his conduct includes a voluntary act (or an omission in limited cir-cumstances).[90]

Conduct during unconsciousness is involuntary. Therefore, a person who is unconscious as the result of intoxication, even if the intoxication is self-induced, may raise an involuntariness claim. However, the requisite voluntary act may sometimes be found in conduct prior to the unconsciousness.[91]

[C] Intoxication as an Affirmative Defense

Even if all of the elements of a crime are proved, the Code recognizes an affir-mative defense based on intoxication if, at the time of his conduct: (1) the actor suffered from pathological intoxication or intoxication that was not self-induced; and (2) the actor's condition qualifies under the American Law Institute's test of insanity.[92]

If the criteria for the defense are satisfied, the actor's defense is that of intox-ication, rather than insanity. The Code expressly provides that intoxication

---

[89] American Law Institute, Comment to § 2.08, at 359.

[90] Model Penal Code § 2.01(1). See § 9.05[A], *supra*.

[91] American Law Institute, Comment to § 2.08, at 353.

[92] For the Code definition of insanity, see Model Penal Code § 4.01(1), discussed at § 25.04[C][3], *infra*.

does not "in itself, constitute mental disease."[93] As is the case in common law jurisdictions, however, an actor is entitled to raise an *insanity* claim if, at the time of his conduct, he suffered from a mental disease caused by long-term use of alcohol or drugs.[94]

---

[93] Model Penal Code § 2.08(3). The key words here are "in itself." The Institute does not preclude the possibility that experts will someday conclude that there is a disease giving rise to an uncontrollable urge to drink, in which case, an alcoholic whose intoxicated conduct meets the Code test of "insanity" would be entitled to raise the latter defense. American Law Institute, Comment to § 2.08, at 361.

[94] American Law Institute, Comment to § 2.08, at 362.

Chapter 25

INSANITY

§ 25.01 INSANITY: AN OVERVIEW[1]

Few doctrines of criminal law engender more controversy than the defense of insanity. Since the time of Edward III in the fourteenth century, when "madness" became a complete defense to criminal charges,[2] English and American courts and, more recently, legislatures have struggled to define "insanity." No sooner is a definition propounded than critics, often from conflicting philosophical vantage points, attack it. Some criticism runs deeper, in the form of calls for outright abolition of the defense.

The issue of the proper relationship of mental disease to criminal responsibility is controversial for various reasons. First, although the insanity defense is rarely raised,[3] it is offered in some unusually heinous and well-publicized cases — in attacks upon public officials (such as when John Hinckley attempted to kill President Ronald Reagan[4]), in mass and serial killings, and in especially bizarre homicides.[5] These crimes shock the community and create a conflict between society's desire to punish aggravated wrongdoing and its intuitive sense that punishment — as distinguished from psychiatric treatment — of such persons may be inappropriate, because people who commit such awful acts probably are mentally ill.

---

[1] See generally Herbert Fingarette, The Meaning of Criminal Insanity (1972); Herbert Fingarette & Ann Fingarette Hasse, Mental Disabilities and Criminal Responsibility (1979); Abraham S. Goldstein, The Insanity Defense (1967); Michael S. Moore, Law and Psychiatry: Rethinking the Relationship (1984); Norval Morris, Madness and the Criminal Law (1982); Michael L. Perlin, The Jurisprudence of the Insanity Defense (1994).

[2] Rollin M. Perkins & Ronald N. Boyce, Criminal Law 950 (3d ed. 1982).

[3] See § 25.06[A][1], *infra*.

[4] Hinckley v. United States, 163 F.3d 647 (D.C. Cir. 1999) (summarizing the facts of the much-litigated case stemming from the 1981 attempted assassination of the President and subsequent insanity acquittal of John Hinckley).

[5] Remarkably, "data concerning such a fundamental issue as frequency of insanity pleas and acquittals" have historically been exceptionally hard to obtain, because states have failed to keep suitable records. Carmen Cirincione & Charles Jacobs, *Identifying Insanity Acquittals: Is It Any Easier?*, 23 Law & Hum. Behav. 487, 487 (1999). Data collection is improving, albeit slowly. *Id.* at 495. However, contrary to the common impression that the insanity defense is raised virtually exclusively in homicide cases, it has been estimated that as many as 86% of insanity pleas occur in the prosecution of nonviolent felonies and misdemeanors. National Mental Health Association, Myths & Realities: A Report of the National Commission on the Insanity Defense 20-21 (1983).

Second, the insanity defense suffers from the conceptual intermingling of psychiatry and the law, or of what one mental health professional has called the "war between lawyers and psychiatrists."[6] The two groups, it is said, "speak two different languages in regard to professional matters."[7] A *legal* defense based at its core on a *medical* conception, therefore, is inevitably difficult to administer, because the legal standard must satisfy several sometimes conflicting objectives. It must reflect underlying principles of criminal responsibility, comport with the current scientific understanding of mental disease, permit mental health experts reasonable opportunity to provide their insights to the court, and yet also preserve to the trier of fact the ultimate and full authority to render a verdict on criminal responsibility.[8]

This chapter addresses the principal issues regarding the insanity defense in its various forms, and considers the underlying arguments regarding its abolition or reform.

§ 25.02 INSANITY DEFENSE: PROCEDURAL CONTEXT

[A] Competency to Stand Trial[9]

[1] General Rule

The criminal trial of an incompetent defendant violates the Due Process Clause of the United States Constitution.[10] A person is incompetent if, during the criminal proceedings, she: (1) lacks the capacity to consult with her attorney "with a reasonable degree of rational understanding"; or (2) lacks "a rational as well as factual understanding of the proceedings" against her.[11] Incompetency may be the result of a physical handicap (e.g., an inability to speak) or temporary or permanent mental disability (e.g., mental illness, mental retardation, or amnesia).

Competency to stand trial is constitutionally required because an incompetent person is unable to provide needed assistance to her attorney, e.g., to discuss strategy, explain her side of the case, and provide the names of potential witnesses. She is also unable meaningfully to confront her accusers at trial, and

---

[6] Karl Menninger, The Crime of Punishment ch. 4 (1966). See § 25.06[A][3], *infra*.

[7] *Id.* at 96.

[8] State v. Johnson, 399 A.2d 469, 471 (R.I. 1979).

[9] See generally Bruce J. Winick, *Presumptions and Burdens of Proof in Determining Competency to Stand Trial: An Analysis of Medina v. California and the Supreme Court's New Due Process Methodology in Criminal Cases*, 47 U. Miami L. Rev. 817 (1993); Bruce J. Winick, *Restructuring Competency to Stand Trial*, 32 UCLA L. Rev. 921 (1985).

[10] Medina v. California, 505 U.S. 437, 453 (1992).

[11] Dusky v. United States, 362 U.S. 402, 402 (1960).

rationally to testify in her own behalf.[12] Moreover, two justifications for punishment of offenders, retribution and some aspects of specific deterrence, may be frustrated if an incompetent defendant does not understand the nature of the proceedings against her.[13]

[2] Procedures for Determining Competency

The issue of competency to stand trial may be raised by the prosecutor, the defense, or by the trial judge on her own motion,[14] and is independent of any insanity plea that the defendant might later raise.[15]

Typically, a defendant's competency to stand trial is treated as an issue of law to be determined by the trial judge, rather than a question of fact for jury consideration.[16] Whenever the issue of competency is raised, the defendant is required to submit to a psychiatric examination during which time she may be committed to a mental facility. The report of the examination is filed with the court.

If the findings of the report are not disputed by the parties, the judge may act on it. If the findings are disputed, a hearing is held at which the parties may present evidence on the matter of competency. State laws vary on the burden of proof at the hearing: some states require the prosecutor to demonstrate the defendant's competency once the issue is credibly raised; other states place the burden on the defendant to prove by preponderance of the evidence[17] that she is not competent to stand trial; and still other jurisdictions allocate the burden of proof to whichever party raised the competency issue.[18]

---

[12] Riggins v. Nevada, 504 U.S. 127, 139-40 (1992) (Kennedy, J., concurring).

[13] American Law Institute, Comment to § 4.04, at 230 n.1. Assaultive retribution (see § 2.03[B][2], *supra*) is frustrated if the person against whom vengeance is sought cannot understand why society is bringing the proceedings against her. Specific deterrence by intimidation (see § 2.03[A][2], *supra*) will fail if the party is so irrational that she cannot see the cause-and-effect relation between her conduct and the pain that would be inflicted.

[14] The defendant's competency must be investigated, even over her objection, if the trial judge believes that she may be incompetent. Pate v. Robinson, 383 U.S. 375, 385-86 (1966).

[15] The insanity defense pertains to a defendant's mental condition at the time of the crime, rather than during the criminal proceedings.

[16] Model Penal Code § 4.06(1). Prior to the promulgation of the Code, most states allowed a jury trial on the issue. American Law Institute, Comment to § 4.06, at 241-42.

[17] See Cooper v. Oklahoma, 517 U.S. 348 (1976) (state law requiring the defendant to prove incompetency by clear and convincing evidence violates due process).

[18] Medina v. California, 505 U.S. 437, 447 (1992) (summarizing state laws).

[3] Effect of an Incompetency Finding

If it is determined that the defendant is incompetent to stand trial, criminal proceedings must be suspended until she is competent.[19] In some cases, particularly if the defendant's incompetency is based on a permanent condition, such as severe mental retardation, a criminal trial may never be held.

An incompetency ruling usually results in the defendant's commitment to a mental facility. The Supreme Court has held, however, that the Due Process Clause is violated when a criminal defendant is committed indefinitely solely on the basis of her incompetency to stand trial.[20] A person may not be restrained "more than the reasonable period of time necessary to determine whether there is a substantial probability that [s]he will attain . . . capacity in the foreseeable future."[21] If it is determined that this is likely, her continued commitment "must be justified by progress toward that goal." If not, the defendant must be released or committed pursuant to customary civil procedures.[22] Even with these protections, the length of pretrial commitment will frequently extend beyond the possible maximum sentence for the crime.[23]

[B] Pre-Trial Assertion of the Insanity Plea

Many states and federal rules require a defendant to provide the prosecutor with notice prior to trial of her intention to raise the defense of insanity.[24] She may also be required to provide the prosecutor with a list of witnesses who will testify on behalf of her insanity claim. The purpose of these rules is to provide the prosecutor adequate time to prepare a rebuttal to the defense at trial, and to allow the court an opportunity to require the defendant to submit to a psychiatric examination, as described in the next subsection.

In virtually all states, a trial court has statutory authority to order a defendant to submit to a pretrial psychiatric examination if she plans to raise an insanity defense.[25] Under such rules, the defendant is committed to a mental facility for a specified period of time, usually sixty to ninety days, during which period the examination is conducted. In some states, a psychiatrist retained by the defendant may witness or even participate in the examination process.[26] In

---

[19] Model Penal Code § 4.06(2).

[20] Jackson v. Indiana, 406 U.S. 715, 731 (1972).

[21] *Id.* at 738.

[22] As a result, Model Penal Code § 4.06(2), which authorizes indefinite commitment without a civil hearing, is unconstitutional. American Law Institute, Explanatory Note to § 4.06, at 241; see Foucha v. Louisiana, 504 U.S. 71, 83 n.6 (1992).

[23] Winick, *Restructuring Competency to Stand Trial*, Note 9, *supra*, at 926.

[24] E.g., Model Penal Code § 4.03(2); Fed. R. Crim. Proc. 12.2(a).

[25] Model Penal Code § 4.05(1); Fed. R. Crim. Proc. 12.2(c).

[26] Model Penal Code § 4.05(1).

order to avoid the possibility of violating the defendant's constitutional privilege against compelled self-incrimination at trial, some jurisdictions prohibit the introduction at trial of the defendant's statements to the government's psychiatrist, except on the matter of insanity.[27] If the court-ordered psychiatric report supports the defendant's claim of insanity, the prosecutor will frequently dismiss the charges against the defendant, on the condition that the accused agrees to civil commitment to a mental facility.

[C] Jury Verdicts

In most states, the factfinder may return one of three verdicts in a criminal trial in which the defendant pleads insanity: "not guilty" (NG); "not guilty by reason of insanity" (NGRI); or "guilty."[28]

A verdict of NGRI implies that the prosecution proved all of the elements of the crime, including the defendant's *mens rea*, beyond a reasonable doubt, that all of the defendant's non-insanity defenses were rejected, but that the accused was insane at the time of the crime.

Logically, a jury should consider a NG verdict before it considers a NGRI verdict. Indeed, an instruction to the jury to consider the insanity defense *before* it considers the accused's guilt or innocence should be considered inappropriate[29] because it permits the jury to reach a NGRI verdict, which usually results in civil commitment of the insanity acquittee,[30] without determining whether the prosecution has satisfied its constitutional responsibility of proving every element of the crime beyond a reasonable doubt.

[D] Bifurcated Trial

A few states[31] require, and most states permit, a trial court to bifurcate a criminal trial in which the insanity defense is raised. In a bifurcated system, all aspects of the case except the defendant's sanity are litigated at the first phase of the trial. At the completion of this first phase, the factfinder deliberates and returns a verdict of guilty or not guilty (NG). If the verdict is NG, the defendant is acquitted and the trial is over.

If the defendant is found guilty, the second phase is conducted. Here, the sole issue is the accused's insanity claim. After introduction of the testimony, most

---

[27] Model Penal Code § 4.09; Fed. R. Crim. Proc. 12.2(c).

[28] The jury may return a fourth verdict, "guilty but mentally ill," in a few states. See § 25.07, *infra*.

[29] At least one court has so indicated. State v. McMullin, 421 N.W.2d 517 (Iowa 1988).

[30] See § 25.05, *infra*.

[31] E.g., Cal. Penal Code § 1026(a) (Deering 2005); Wis. Stat. § 971.165 (2004).

notably expert psychiatric evidence, the factfinder deliberates and returns a second verdict of guilty or, instead, not guilty by reason of insanity.[32]

The purpose of bifurcation is four-fold. First, time may be saved. If the jury returns a NG verdict in the first phase, time consuming psychiatric testimony is avoided. Second, confusion may be reduced. The jury can reach a verdict in the first phase without considering complicated psychiatric evidence.

Third, the bifurcated system may decrease the possibility of compromise verdicts. In a unitary system, the jury deliberates once. If it has reasonable doubts regarding the defendant's involvement in the crime, but is convinced that she is insane, the jury may improperly compromise and find her insane, rather than acquit her outright, as it should.

Finally, the bifurcated system protects a defendant's privilege against compelled self-incrimination. In a unitary system, she may be forced to testify about her mental condition at the time of the crime in order to support her insanity defense. In the process, she opens herself up to questioning on issues unrelated to her mental condition. In a bifurcated system she may remain silent during the first phase, and force the prosecutor to prove her participation in the crime by independent evidence.

The bifurcated system has not worked as intended. The primary problem is that evidence of mental illness sometimes needs to be introduced by the defense at the first phase in order to demonstrate that the defendant lacked the mental state required in the definition of the offense. The same evidence, therefore, is introduced twice, although the testimony is phrased slightly differently at each stage. In the first phase, the psychiatrist may testify regarding whether, as the result of a mental disease or defect, the defendant was capable of forming or did form the requisite intent for the criminal offense, e.g., whether *D* intended to kill *V*. In the second phase, the same witness is questioned regarding whether the accused was insane at the time of the crime, e.g., whether *D* knew right from wrong when she intentionally killed *V*. The effect of this process is that time is wasted, not saved; and juries are apt to be confused, not benefitted, by the system.

[E] Burden of Proof

Insanity is an affirmative defense. The defendant has the initial burden of producing evidence regarding her mental condition in order to raise the insan-

---

[32] Although psychiatric testimony, frequently conflicting, typically dominates a trial during the insanity phase, the jury as factfinder not only may disregard the testimony of some experts in favor of others, but may disregard *all* of the expert testimony. Thus, although exceedingly uncommon, an insanity verdict can be justified solely on the basis of non-expert testimony of the defendant's mental condition. Pacheco v. State, 770 S.W.2d 834, 835 (Tex. App. 1989). Conversely, a jury may disregard psychiatric testimony that a defendant is insane and rely entirely upon lay testimony of sanity. Dashield v. State, 110 S.W.3d 111, 115 (Tex. App. 2003); Bonham v. State, 644 N.E.2d 1223, 1227 (Ind. 1994).

ity defense. Furthermore, the legislature may constitutionally require the defendant to persuade the jury that she was insane at the time of the crime.[33]

Until the 1980s, most states and the federal courts required the prosecutor to prove the defendant's sanity beyond a reasonable doubt.[34] However, as the result of the insanity acquittal of John Hinckley for the attempted murder of President Ronald Reagan,[35] a majority of states and the federal system now require the defendant to shoulder the burden of persuasion regarding her insanity claim.[36]

Most states that require a defendant to prove her insanity provide that she must do so by a preponderance of the evidence. Since 1984, however, defendants in federal courts have been required to prove insanity by clear and convincing evidence.[37] No state presently requires the defendant to prove her insanity beyond a reasonable doubt, although such a burden may be constitutional.[38]

§ 25.03 RATIONALE OF THE INSANITY DEFENSE[39]

The insanity defense is controversial. The arguments for abolition of the defense are set out in Section 25.06 of this chapter. But, what are the arguments *for* the defense that explain its recognition and retention?

[A] Utilitarian Theory

To the extent that the insanity defense is limited to persons who suffer from serious cognitive or volitional disorders,[40] punishment of an insane person may be "pointless or counter-productive."[41] A person who does not know what she is doing or who cannot control her conduct cannot be deterred by the threat of criminal sanction.

---

[33] Leland v. Oregon, 343 U.S. 790, 799 (1952); see generally § 7.03[B], *supra*.

[34] 2 Paul H. Robinson, Criminal Law Defense 284-85 (1984); e.g., Model Penal Code § 4.03(1).

[35] See Note 4, *supra*.

[36] As of 1998, only twelve states place the burden of persuasion on the prosecution in insanity claims. U.S. Dept. of Justice, State Court Organization 1998 (NCJ 178932 2000), at 257-259.

[37] 18 U.S.C. § 17(b) (2005).

[38] Leland v. Oregon, 343 U.S. at 798-99 (upholding such a burden); but see Jones v. United States, 463 U.S. 354, 368 n.17 (1983) (describing the law in somewhat more cautious terms: "A defendant [may] be required to prove his insanity *by a higher standard than a preponderance of the evidence.*") (emphasis supplied).

[39] See generally R.B. Brandt, *The Insanity Defense and the Theory of Motivation*, 7 Law & Phil. 123 (1988); Stephen J. Morse, *Excusing the Crazy: The Insanity Defense Reconsidered*, 58 S. Cal. L. Rev. 777 (1985); Benjamin B. Sendor, *Crime as Communication: An Interpretive Theory of the Insanity Defense and Mental Elements of Crime*, 74 Geo. L.J. 1371 (1986).

[40] A *cognitive* disorder is one that undermines a person's ability to perceive reality accurately. A *volitional* disorder is one that undermines a person's ability to control her conduct.

[41] American Law Institute, Comment to § 4.01, at 168 n.12.

Incapacitation of an insane person normally is socially desirable, but acquittal by reason of insanity need not, and ordinarily does not, result in her liberty, inasmuch as the acquittal almost always serves as the basis for civil commitment.[42] There is no need, therefore, to convict and stigmatize an insane person in order to ensure her segregation from society.

Similarly, rehabilitation is not furthered by convicting an insane person and sending her to prison. It is more rational to separate her from the penal system and treat her condition as a medical problem.

[B] Retributive Theory

Although utilitarian arguments are sometimes posited in support of the insanity defense, the underlying rationale of the defense is primarily retributive in nature. As one scholar has observed, "[w]e . . . put up with the bother of the insanity defense because to exclude it is to deprive the criminal law of its chief paradigm of free will."[43]

The role that free will plays in recognition of the insanity defense can be appreciated by focusing on our feelings and intuitions. First, we make judgments about people, based on their actions. We condemn people who commit crimes, and blame them for their wrongdoing. At the same time, we applaud courage; we praise those who perform acts of benevolence. These reactions, however, are unjustifiable unless we acknowledge the concept of free will — that people can and do choose to do good or to do evil, that human behavior is not scripted by other persons or by non-human forces.

Another human feeling cannot be denied — severely mentally ill people do not appear to be like the rest of us. They seem odd or "crazy." We pity them (sometimes, too, we fear them), because they lack the capacity to do what other humans are able to do: to act rationally or to control their behavior. Ordinarily, we do not blame the "crazy" person for her wrongdoing or, if we do, we sense that such negative expressions are wrong. To blame such an individual for her acts is much like blaming a sick person for sneezing or an infant for dropping her glass of milk.

Our impressions of the mentally diseased actor reinforce our basic belief in human free will. The exception of the insane person serves as proof of the general rule. The fact that we do not blame the insane person serves to justify the fact that we blame the sane wrongdoer. The insanity defense, therefore, serves as a distinguishing point between the bad and the mad, between evil and sickness, between those who possess free choice and those whose free choice is seriously undermined.

---

[42] See § 25.05, *infra*.

[43] Herbert L. Packer, The Limits of the Criminal Sanction 132 (1968).

We can place these feelings into a rational set of retributivist premises: just punishment is dependent on moral desert; moral desert is dependent on moral responsibility for one's actions; and moral responsibility for one's actions is dependent on the essential attributes of personhood, namely rationality and self-control.[44] Insane people, however, lack essential attributes of personhood. Therefore, they are "no more the proper subjects of moral evaluation than are young infants, animals, or even stones."[45] Or, as one court put it: "To punish a man who lacks the power to reason is as undignified and unworthy as punishing an inanimate object or an animal. A man who cannot reason cannot be subject to blame. Our collective conscience does not allow punishment where it cannot impose blame."[46]

§ 25.04 DEFINITIONS OF "INSANITY"[47]

[A] Putting the Insanity Tests in Historical and Legal Context

Generally speaking, five tests of insanity, discussed in subsection [C], *infra*, have gained support at one time or another in the United States: the *M'Naghten*[48] rule; the "irresistible impulse" (or "control") test; the "product" standard; the American Law Institute's (ALI) Model Penal Code definition; and the federal statutory definition of insanity.

The first insanity test of modern relevance was enunciated by the English House of Lords in the *M'Naghten* case. It quickly became the generally accepted standard in this country. Criticism of the *M'Naghten* rule, however, was immediate[49] and has been unending. As a result of the perceived narrowness of the

---

[44] Morse, Note 39, *supra*, at 783.

[45] Michael S. Moore, *Causation and the Excuses*, 73 Cal. L. Rev. 1091, 1137 (1985).

[46] Holloway v. United States, 148 F.2d 665, 666-67 (D.C. Cir. 1945).

[47] See generally Jodie English, *The Light Between Twilight and Dusk: Federal Criminal Law and the Volitional Insanity Defense*, 40 Hastings L.J. 1 (1988); Stephen J. Morse, *Crazy Behavior, Morals, and Science: An Analysis of Mental Health Law*, 51 S. Cal. L. Rev. 527 (1978); Christopher Slobogin, *The Integrationist Alternative to the Insanity Defense: Reflections on the Exculpatory Scope of Mental Illness in the Wake of the Andrea Yates Trial*, 30 Am. J. Crim. L. 315 (2003); see also the sources in Note 1, *supra*.

For discussion of juror responses to insanity instructions, see generally Norman J. Finkel & Sharon F. Handel, *How Jurors Construe "Insanity"*, 13 Law & Hum. Behav. 41 (1989); James R.P. Ogloff, *A Comparison of the Insanity Defense Standards on Juror Decision Making*, 15 Law & Hum. Behav. 509 (1991); Michael L. Perlin, *Psychodynamics and the Insanity Defense: "Ordinary Common Sense" and Heuristic Reasoning*, 69 Neb. L. Rev. 3 (1990); Caton Roberts & Stephen Golding, *The Social Construction of Criminal Responsibility and Insanity*, 15 Law & Hum. Behav. 349 (1991).

[48] *M'Naghten's Case*, 10 Cl. & F. 200, 8 Eng. Rep. 718 (1843).

[49] See Isaac Ray, A Treatise on the Medical Jurisprudence of Insanity 42 (Winfred Overholder ed., 1962) (originally published in 1833).

test, a few courts expanded the standard of insanity, by coupling the *M'Naghten* rule with the irresistible impulse test.

In 1954, the influential United States Court of Appeals for the District of Columbia promulgated the "product" or *Durham* rule of insanity.[50] Based on an 1870 New Hampshire case,[51] the *Durham* test was exceedingly broad, and was intended to bring insanity law more in accord with modern psychiatric knowledge. *Durham* represented a dramatic departure in the jurisprudence of insanity, and consequently received tremendous scholarly attention. No other court, however, adopted the standard.

The *Durham* court itself encountered problems with the product rule, which it struggled to resolve. In 1972, it abandoned the rule and substituted for it a version of the ALI insanity defense, originally promulgated by the Institute in 1962. The ALI test quickly attracted support from courts and legislatures. In less than two decades, it was adopted by ten of the eleven federal circuit courts and by a majority of the states.[52]

The trend in favor of the ALI test seemed unstoppable until the attempted assassination of President Ronald Reagan. Public fury following John Hinckley's acquittal on the ground of insanity[53] resulted in pressure to abolish the defense.[54] Although the abolitionist movement generally failed, it had a significant effect on the law. Courts and legislatures began to reconsider their support for the comparatively broad ALI rule. "When the dust cleared, the sun of the Model Penal Code test had set."[55] For example, California, which originally adopted the *M'Naghten* test, and then shifted to the ALI standard, reversed itself again and returned to *M'Naghten*.[56] Congress, too, enacted a *M'Naghten*-like definition of insanity, thereby overriding the nearly unanimous adoption of the ALI test in the federal system. A few states abolished the insanity defense.[57]

---

[50] Durham v. United States, 214 F.2d 862 (D.C. Cir. 1954), overruled by United States v. Brawner, 471 F.2d 969 (D.C. Cir. 1972).

[51] State v. Pike, 49 N.H. 399 (1870).

[52] Michael L. Perlin, Mental Disability Law: Civil and Criminal 302 (1989); American Law Institute, Comment to § 4.01, at 175-76.

[53] See Note 4, *supra*.

[54] For example, an Associated Press-National Broadcasting Company poll found that 69% of the respondents favored abolition of the insanity defense. Minneapolis Trib., Oct. 25, 1981, at 9a. See generally Daniel S. Bailis et al., *Community Standards of Criminal Liability and the Insanity Defense*, 19 Law & Hum. Behav. 425 (1995); Valerie P. Hans, *An Analysis of Public Attitudes Toward the Insanity Defense*, 24 Criminology 393 (1986).

[55] Sanford H. Kadish, *Fifty Years of Criminal Law: An Opinionated Review*, 87 Cal. L. Rev. 943, 960 (1999).

[56] Cal. Penal Code § 25(b) (Deering 2005). The saga of California's insanity law, culminating in the passage of a statewide initiative designed to eliminate the ALI standard, is chronicled in *People v. Skinner*, 704 P.2d 752 (Cal. 1985).

[57] See § 25.06[B], *infra*.

One must put the controversy over the insanity tests in context. There is social science literature suggesting that jurors either do not consider or fail to understand the insanity instructions they are given. Jurors apparently come to a trial with their own implicit standards of criminal responsibility. These standards involve a mixtures of factors, such as the defendant's motive for her conduct, history of mental illness, degree of remorse, and the specific psychiatric diagnosis.[58] According to one empiricist, "jurors apply their own sense of justice when determining whether a defendant" should be found not guilty by reason of insanity.[59] And, according to him, the insanity test most consistent with jurors' intuitions is one that has never been accepted by a court, namely, the so-called "justly responsible" test suggested by one federal judge.[60]

[B] "Mental Disease or Defect"[61]

[1] In General

The terms "mental illness," "mental disorder," and "mental disease or defect," on the one hand, and "insanity," on the other hand, are not synonymous. The first set of terms is used by the mental health community; the word "insanity" is a legal term. Thus, it is incorrect to say that "mental illness" is a criminal defense; "insanity" is the excusing defense.

"Mental illness" is a more encompassing term than "insanity." A person can be mentally ill without being insane; insanity, however, presupposes a mental disease or defect.

[2] Medical Definition of "Mental Disorder"

The American Psychiatric Association's manual of mental disorders concedes that "no definition adequately specifies precise boundaries for the concept of 'mental disorder.'"[62] A mental disorder is not a discrete entity. There are no sharp boundaries between "mental disorder" and "no mental disorder." And, as the manual admits, "[a] compelling literature documents that there is much

---

[58] See Jocelyn A. Lymburner & Ronald Roesch, *The Insanity Defense: Five Years of Research (1993-1997)*, 22 Int'l J. L. & Psychiatry 213, 293-94 (1999) (and studies cited therein).

[59] Ogloff, Note 47, *supra*, at 527.

[60] United States v. Brawner, 471 F.2d 969, 1032 (D.C. Cir 1972) (Bazelon. C.J., concurring in part and dissenting in part) (proposing the follow instruction: "[A] defendant is not responsible *if at the time of his unlawful conduct his mental or emotional processes or behavior controls were impaired to such an extent that he cannot justly be held responsible for his act.*").

[61] See generally Bruce J. Winick, *Ambiguities in the Legal Meaning and Significance of Mental Illness*, 1 Psychology, Pub. Pol'y & L. 534 (1995).

[62] American Psychiatric Association, Diagnostic and Statistical Manual of Mental Disorders xxx (4th ed. Text Revision 2000).

'physical' in 'mental' disorders and much 'mental' in 'physical' disorders."[63] That being said, the manual defines a "mental disorder" as a:

> clinically significant behavioral or psychological syndrome or pattern that occurs in an individual and that is associated with present distress (e.g., a painful symptom) or disability (i.e., impairment in one or more important areas of functioning) or with a significantly increased risk of suffering death, pain, disability, or an important loss of freedom. In addition, this syndrome or pattern must not be merely an expectable and culturally sanctioned response to a particular event. . . .[64]

Notice that this conceptualization of the term "mental disorder" treats mental illness in an atheoretical manner: Whereas symptoms may point to the existence of a *physical* disease, a symptom or a cluster of symptoms resulting in distress, disability, etc., is itself a mental disorder. Also, unlike physical disorders, the concept of "mental disorder" is culture-bound, i.e., one cannot identify a cluster of symptoms as a disorder without also considering the society in which the behavior pattern arises.

[3] Legal Definition of "Mental Disease or Defect"

All of the insanity tests presuppose that the actor suffers from a "mental disease or defect" or "disease of the mind," yet courts rarely define the terms.[65] The Model Penal Code insanity defense, as well, provides no general definition of the critical phrase, preferring instead to leave the issue "open to accommodate developing medical understanding."[66]

Only the now-defunct *Durham* test of insanity included a definition of the term: It defined a mental disease or defect as "any abnormal condition of the mind which substantially affects mental or emotional processes and substantially impairs behavior controls."[67] Under this definition, a "disease" is a condition capable of improving or deteriorating; a "defect" is a condition incapable of changing, which may be congenital (e.g., retardation), the result of injury to the brain, or the residual effect of a physical or mental illness.[68]

---

[63] *Id.*

[64] *Id.* at xxxi.

[65] See Goldstein, Note 1, *supra*, at 47-48.

[66] American Law Institute, Explanatory Note to § 4.01, at 164.

[67] McDonald v. United States, 312 F.2d 847, 851 (D.C. Cir. 1962).

[68] Durham v. United States, 214 F.2d 862, 875 (D.C. Cir. 1954), overruled by United States v. Brawner, 471 F.2d 969 (D.C. Cir. 1972).

[C] The Tests

[1] *M'Naghten* Test[69]

[a] Rule

The *M'Naghten* test of insanity is cognitive-based. According to *M'Naghten*, a person is insane if, at the time of her act,[70] she was laboring under such a defect of reason, arising from a disease of the mind, that she: (1) did not know the nature and quality of the act that she was doing; or (2) if she did know it, she did not know that what she was doing was wrong, i.e., the accused at the time of doing the act did not know the difference between right and wrong.

Various features of the test should be observed. First, the word "know" used in both prongs of the test may be defined narrowly or broadly. Some courts apply the word narrowly: A person may be found sane if she can describe what she is doing ("I was strangling her") and can acknowledge the forbidden nature of her conduct ("I knew I was doing something wrong"). This may be referred to as "formal cognitive knowledge." Some courts, however, require a deeper meaning of "knowledge" ("affective knowledge"), which is absent unless the actor can evaluate her conduct in terms of its impact on others and appreciate the total setting in which she acts, i.e., can "internalize the enormity of the[ir] criminal act" and, thus, "emotionally appreciate its wrongfulness."[71]

Second, the phrase "nature and quality of the act" in the first prong of the *M'Naghten* test potentially is an exceedingly narrow concept. If *D* squeezes *V*'s neck, believing that she is squeezing a lemon, she does not know the nature and quality of her act. However, if she knows that she is squeezing the neck of a human being, but does not appreciate that her act is causing pain, she is sane insofar as the first prong of *M'Naghten* is concerned in jurisdictions that apply a narrow meaning of the word "knowledge," as discussed immediately above. Frequently, this prong is omitted from jury instructions, because anyone who does not know what she is doing (e.g., cannot distinguish a neck from a lemon) will also "fail" the right-and-wrong test, the second prong of the insanity definition.

Third, a question exists whether the word "wrong" in the right-and-wrong prong refers to legal or moral wrongdoing. There is language in *M'Naghten* to support either interpretation. Lord Tindal, for example, stated early in the opinion that M'Naghten could be punished if he "knew . . . that he was acting

---

[69] M'Naghten's Case, 10 Cl. & F. 200, 8 Eng. Rep. 718 (1843).

[70] The issue with *any* definition of insanity is whether the actor was insane at the time of the offense. Theoretically, at least, an actor may be sane before and after the crime, and yet be insane at the time of the criminal act and, therefore, be entitled to acquittal on the basis of insanity. See Miller v. State, 911 P.2d 1183, 1185-87 (Nev. 1996). Realistically, such "temporary insanity" is rare.

[71] Slobogin, Note 47, *supra*, at 324.

contrary to law; by which expression we . . . mean the law of the land." Subsequently, however, he stated that if the jury were instructed "exclusively with reference to the law of the land it might tend to confound the jury by inducing them to believe that an actual knowledge of the law was essential." Rather, Lord Tindal stated, the question is whether M'Naghten knew that his "act was one which he ought not to do, and if the act was at the same time contrary to the law of the land, he is punishable." England has removed the ambiguity in the test by declaring that the *M'Naghten* prong refers to awareness that an act is legally wrong.[72] American law, however, is divided on the moral-versus-legal distinction.[73]

The distinction between legal and moral right-and-wrong will rarely affect the outcome of a trial. However, suppose that *D*, due to mental illness, believes that God has personally given her permission to kill *V*, an act that *D* knows violates the secular law. In view of God's permission, however, *D* believes that it is morally proper to kill *V*. On these facts, *D* is sane if the right-and-wrong test is based on awareness of the *illegality* of an act. However, subject to one clarification noted in the next paragraph, *D* is insane if *M'Naghten* requires knowledge of the *immorality* of her actions.

In American jurisdictions that apply a "moral right-and-wrong" standard, the issue is not whether the defendant personally believed that her conduct was morally proper. Rather, the question is whether she knowingly violated *societal* standards of morality.[74] That is, *D* is sane under this prong of *M'Naghten* if she commits an offense that she knows society will condemn, even if (as a result of mental illness) she is personally convinced her conduct is morally proper.[75]

Fourth, a few *M'Naghten* jurisdictions that apply the "moral right-and-wrong" standard also apply the so-called "deific decree" doctrine. Under this principle, a mentally disordered individual who believes that she is acting on the direct command of God (not simply with God's approval) is deemed legally insane. Sometimes this doctrine is treated as an *exception* to the general rule, i.e., it applies when "a party performs a criminal act, knowing it is morally and legally wrong, but believing, because of a mental defect, that the act is ordained by God."[76] However, other courts believe that the doctrine "is not so much an

---

[72] R. v. Windle, [1952] 2 All E.R. 1, 2.

[73] See People v. Serravo, 823 P.2d 128, 135 (Colo. 1992) (noting the division of American courts).

[74] *Id*. at 137; Wallace v. State, 766 So. 2d 364, 367 (Fla. Dist. Ct. App. 2000); People v. Stress, 205 Cal. App. 3d 1259, 1274 (Ct. App. 1988).

[75] Notice, however, that the line drawn in the text can be blurred to near extinction. Presumably, in determining whether the defendant knew that society would consider her actions morally wrong, we have to look at the circumstances as she believes them (in her mentally disturbed mind) to be. See State v. Wilson, 700 A.2d 633, 653 (Conn. 1997). For example, a mentally disturbed person is apt to know that society considers it morally wrong to kill, but if she is acting pursuant to a delusionary belief that God wants her to kill, she might believe that society would agree with her God-endorsed actions.

[76] State v. Crenshaw, 659 P.2d 488, 494 (Wash. 1983).

exception to the right-wrong test measured by the existing societal standards of morality as it is an integral factor in assessing a person's cognitive ability to distinguish right from wrong with respect to the act charged."[77] That is, a person who believes that God has commanded her act is likely to believe that society would approve of her conduct.[78]

[b] Criticisms of the Rule

The *M'Naghten* rule has been subject to persistent criticism. First, the test is considered "grossly unrealistic" because, by its terms, it does not recognize degrees of incapacity. A person must wholly lack cognition. Yet, "our mental institutions, as any qualified psychiatrist will attest, are filled with people who *to some extent* can differentiate between right and wrong,"[79] or who can tell the difference between a human neck and a lemon, but who still are significantly out of touch with reality. Because of the apparent absolutism of the test, some psychiatrists are tempted to shape their testimony to fit the definition of insanity, although few of them believe that incapacity is ever complete.

Second, some critics believe that *M'Naghten* places "unrealistically tight shackles"[80] upon expert psychiatric testimony. If a trial court refuses to permit a psychiatrist to testify on any matter that falls outside the narrow confines of the test, the jury is unable to learn the full background of the defendant's state of mind.

Third, the test is outdated in that it disregards mental illnesses that affect *volition*.[81] By focusing solely on cognitive disability, the rule disregards the possibility that a person may be able to distinguish right from wrong, and yet be unable to control her behavior.

Finally, closely tied to the latter point, is the suggestion that the test is too narrow in terms of penological theory. If a person knows what she is doing but cannot control her conduct, she is undeterrable; therefore, punishment is inefficacious. Moreover, it is morally wrong to punish a person who, due to mental illness, lacks sufficient free will to control her conduct.

---

[77] People v. Serravo, 823 P.2d at 139; see also State v. Potter, 842 P.2d 481, 486-89 (Wash. Ct. App. 1992) (concluding that notwithstanding language in prior Washington cases treating the deific-decree doctrine as an "exception," the doctrine is instead an "elaboration[] of the second prong of the insanity rule").

[78] See also Note 75, *supra*.

[79] United States v. Freeman, 357 F.2d 606, 618 (2d Cir. 1966) (emphasis added).

[80] *Id.* at 619.

[81] See United States v. Pollard, 171 F. Supp. 474, 478 (E.D. Mich. 1959) (but convicting the defendant on the facts), conviction reversed, Pollard v. United States, 282 F.2d 450 (6th Cir. 1960).

[2] "Irresistible Impulse" Test

[a] Rule

In order to broaden the scope of *M'Naghten*, some states (and, for a while, federal courts) formulated a third prong to the insanity test, which encompasses mental illnesses affecting volitional capacity. The latter prong has come to be known as the "irresistible impulse" test.

The precise language of the test varies by jurisdiction. Generally speaking, a person is insane if, at the time of the offense: (1) she "acted from an irresistible and uncontrollable impulse";[82] (2) she "lost the *power to choose* between the right and wrong, and to avoid doing the act in question, as that [her] free agency was at the time destroyed";[83] or (3) the "[defendant's] will . . . has been otherwise than voluntarily so completely destroyed that [her] actions are not subject to it, but are beyond [her] control."[84]

[b] Criticisms of the Rule

Criticisms of this rule run in both directions — that it is too narrow and, to the contrary, that it should be abolished. Those who believe the test is too narrow state that it is improper to exclude from its coverage non-impulsive behavior (i.e., behavior that is the result of brooding and reflection), and that it is psychologically naive to require total incapacity (i.e., an *irresistible* impulse).[85] These criticisms are not ordinarily relevant in practice. The label "irresistible impulse" has proven to be a misnomer.[86] Many courts permit use of the test even if the defendant planned her behavior, as long as the defendant lacked the ability to control her conduct; and most courts do not require proof of total volitional incapacity.

Both principled and pragmatic arguments have been made for abolition of any test based on an actor's lack of volition. Some abolitionists argue that if an exceptionally strong urge to commit a crime should excuse, it should excuse whether the person suffers from a mental illness or not:

> [T]he psychotic individual who hears voices telling him to kill may experience a powerful urge to commit crime. But that claim is also true of pedophiles, repeat rapists, . . . serial murderers . . . , and thieves who steal to feed an addiction. It may even be true of the greedy corporate

---

[82] Commonwealth v. Rogers, 48 Mass. 500, 502 (1844).

[83] Parsons v. State, 2 So. 854, 866 (Ala. 1887).

[84] Davis v. United States, 165 U.S. 373, 378 (1897).

[85] United States v. Pollard, 171 F. Supp. at 478.

[86] Goldstein, Note 1, *supra*, at 67-79.

executive who manipulates accounts, or of the teenage boy who, on Friday night, wants to have intercourse with an underage girlfriend. The subjectively experienced urges of a person with mental illness are not provably greater than the urges of people we would never think of excusing.[87]

The pragmatic criticism of the "irresistible impulse" test is that "a majority of psychiatrists now believe that they do not possess sufficient accurate scientific bases for measuring a person's capacity for self-control or for calibrating the impairment of that capacity."[88] According to the American Psychiatric Association, "[t]he line between an irresistible impulse and an impulse not resisted is probably no sharper than between twilight and dusk."[89]

[3] American Law Institute (Model Penal Code) Test

[a] Rule

The Model Penal Code provides that a person is not responsible for her criminal conduct if, at the time of the conduct, as the result of a mental disease or defect, she lacked substantial capacity to: (1) appreciate the "criminality" (or, in the alternative, at the option of the legislature adopting the Code, the "wrongfulness") of her conduct;[90] or (2) to conform her conduct to the requirements of the law.[91] This is a revised version of the *M'Naghten* and irresistible-impulse tests. It consists of the second, and more significant, cognitive prong of the former test, and restates the volitional aspects of the latter standard.

Notice the differences between the ALI test and its antecedents. First, it uses the term "appreciate" rather than "know," in order to avoid a narrow interpretation of the *M'Naghten*-like cognitive prong.[92] Second, the test avoids the word "impulse," in order to sidestep the potential pitfalls arising from using that word. Third, both prongs of the test are modified by the words "lacks substantial capacity." This avoids the criticism that the earlier tests unrealistically required total incapacity.

[b] Criticisms of the Rule

The ALI test has received little criticism independent of the objections raised regarding the earlier tests on which it is founded. Those who favor a broader test

---

[87] Slobogin, Note 47, *supra*, at 322 (footnotes omitted).

[88] United States v. Lyons, 731 F.2d 243, 248 (5th Cir. 1984).

[89] American Psychiatric Association, Statement on the Insanity Defense 11 (Dec. 1982).

[90] Thus, the *M'Naghten*-like issue of moral-versus-legal right-and-wrong is resolved by the legislature at the outset of the adoption of the test.

[91] Model Penal Code § 4.01(1).

[92] See § 25.04[C][1][a], *supra*.

and who believe that psychiatric knowledge is unduly restricted in the court-room have criticized the ALI definition because they believe that it is based on an outdated psychological assumption that the human mind is divisible into "volitional" and "cognitive" functions. In contrast, persons who favor a narrow definition of insanity are critical of the fact that the ALI standard includes a volitional prong, even though psychiatrists now question their ability to provide reliable data on the subject.

[4] The Product Test

[a] Rule

The product test of insanity, first adopted in New Hampshire,[93] gained national attention when David Bazelon, one of the country's most respected judges, announced recognition of the product rule in the District of Columbia.[94] This standard provided, quite simply, that a person should be excused if her unlawful act was the product of a mental disease or defect. Pursuant to this rule, the jury would determine whether the defendant was suffering from a mental disease or defect at the time of the offense and, if so, whether the disease caused the criminal conduct in a but-for sense.

Advocates of this test believed that it brought the insanity standard into modern times. The test was intended to permit mental health professionals to testify without the volitional/cognitive strictures of the other insanity standards. In turn, the product rule would give jurors the critical information they needed to decide whether to hold a defendant criminally accountable for her actions.

These observations about the product test are stated in the past tense because difficulties with, and criticisms of, the test (as discussed below) led the *Durham* court ultimately to abandon it.[95] No jurisdiction today applies the product rule.[96]

[b] Criticisms of the Rule

An early criticism of *Durham* was that the test failed to define the critical phrase "mental disease or defect." As such, it left the matter solely in the hands of mental health professionals. If a psychiatrist testified that the condition

---

[93] State v. Pike, 49 N.H. 399 (1870).

[94] Durham v. United States, 214 F.2d 862 (D.C. Cir. 1954).

[95] United States v. Brawner, 471 F.2d 969 (D.C. Cir. 1972).

[96] New Hampshire no longer applies the rule. State v. Hall, 808 A.2d 55, 61 (N.H. 2002), aff'd, 883 A.2d 319 (N.H. 2005) (stating that the insanity rule applies to "evidence 'of a mental *disease* or *defect* that deprives the defendant of the ability to form a specific intent'") (quoting State v. James, 663 A.2d 83, 84 (N.H. 1995)).

that caused the defendant's behavior was a mental disease, the accused was entitled to acquittal; if the expert stated that the same condition fell outside the parameters of any recognized disease model, the defendant lost her insanity claim. Yet, the causal connection between the condition and the conduct was the same in both circumstances. After an embarrassing situation, in which a psychiatrist "flip-flopped" on whether a particular condition was a mental illness,[97] the Court of Appeals for the District of Columbia provided a working definition, set out elsewhere in this Chapter.[98]

Second, some lawyers criticized the test because they believed it allowed psychiatrists to usurp the jury's authority. As the *Durham* rule was applied, psychiatrists were called by the defense and the prosecution; the competing psychiatrists would testify that D suffered (or did not suffer) from condition X, that condition X was (or was not) a mental disease or defect, and that D would not (or would) have committed the crime but for condition X. Essentially, the expert's testimony "proved" that D was (or was not) insane. There was nothing for the jury to do other than to decide which expert to believe. The jury's moral judgment regarding D's conduct was suppressed. The federal court later acknowledged this problem and set limits on psychiatric testimony by preventing experts from testifying directly in terms of "products," "results" or "causes."[99] Thus, a test intended to let experts testify freely now was restricting them.

A third and more basic criticism of the product test was that it excluded from criminal responsibility deterrable and morally blameworthy actors. For example, assume that Alice suffers from a delusion (brought on by a mental disease) that Bob will marry her if Carla, Bob's wife, is dead. As a result, Alice kills Carla. Pursuant to the product rule, Alice is insane: but for her delusion, she would not have killed Carla. Alice's acquittal on these facts, however, is penologically indefensible. Alice knew what she was doing, knew that her conduct was legally and morally wrong, and, presumably, could have controlled her conduct. Therefore, Alice was deterrable. From a retributive perspective, as well, she may be blamed for her conduct. At least under the free-choice theory of excuses,[100] a person who appreciates the illegality or immorality of her conduct, and is able to control her behavior, is a moral agent who may properly be held accountable for her actions.

---

[97] In re Rosenfield, 157 F. Supp. 18 (D.D.C. 1957) (a psychiatrist testified on Friday that R's condition was not a mental disease; over the weekend, as the result of an administrative change in the witness' hospital policy, the condition was reclassified as a mental disease).

[98] See § 25.04[B][3], *supra*.

[99] Washington v. United States, 390 F.2d 444, 455-56 (D.C. Cir. 1967).

[100] See § 17.03[E], *supra*.

[5] Federal Test

The United States Congress enacted a statutory definition of insanity in 1984. In federal courts, a person is excused if she proves by clear and convincing evidence that, at the time of the offense, as the result of a severe mental disease or defect, she was unable to appreciate: (1) the nature and quality of her conduct; or (2) the wrongfulness of her conduct.[101]

Various features of the federal test are noteworthy. First, unlike prior standards, the federal law requires proof that the actor suffers from a "severe" mental disease or defect. However, this word may be superfluous, since any mental disease or defect that satisfies either of the two prongs of the test is apt to be severe. Second, like *M'Naghten*, but unlike the ALI standard, cognitive incapacity must be total.

One feature of the federal rule is patterned on the ALI test — the word "appreciate," rather than "know," modifies both prongs of the defense. This should render the test broader than *M'Naghten* in this regard.

§ 25.05 EFFECT OF AN INSANITY ACQUITTAL

[A] Mental Illness Commitment Procedures

[1] Automatic Commitment

Contrary to a common conception,[102] a person found not guilty by reason of insanity (NGRI) is rarely released upon acquittal. One scholar has gone so far as to state that the defense of insanity is not an excuse in the ordinary sense, but is actually a direction to punish the insane person in a noncriminal context.[103]

In many states, a person found NGRI is automatically committed to a mental facility on the basis of the verdict.[104] Under automatic-commitment laws, the NGRI-acquittee is not entitled to a hearing to determine whether she continues to suffer from a mental illness,[105] or to determine whether her institutionalization is necessary for her protection or for that of society.

---

[101] 18 U.S.C. § 17(a) (2005).

[102] National Mental Health Association, Note 5, *supra*, at 24-25.

[103] Packer, Note 43, *supra*, at 134; see also Joseph Goldstein & Jay Katz, *Abolish the "Insanity Defense" — Why Not?*, 72 Yale L.J. 853, 868 (1963) ("[T]he insanity defense is not a defense, it is a device for triggering indeterminate restraint.").

[104] E.g., Model Penal Code § 4.08(1).

[105] See Note 70, *supra*.

In this respect, NGRI-acquittees are provided fewer procedural rights than are granted to people who may otherwise be subjected to civil commitment. The Supreme Court has held that a person may *not* be committed to a mental institution in a civil proceeding unless the state proves by clear and convincing evidence that she is presently mentally ill and that she is dangerous to herself or others.[106] In contrast, with NGRI-acquittees in automatic-commitment jurisdictions, the insanity verdict at the criminal trial is considered a sufficiently reliable finding of current mental illness and dangerousness to dispense with a hearing.[107]

[2] Discretionary Commitment

In some jurisdictions, commitment of an insanity-acquittee is not automatic. Instead, the trial judge has authority to require a person found NGRI to be detained temporarily in a mental facility for observation and examination, in order to determine whether she should be committed indefinitely.

Under federal law, a commitment hearing must be held within forty days of an NGRI verdict, during which time the acquittee is detained in a mental hospital.[108] If the offense for which the defendant was acquitted involved bodily injury to another, serious damage to property, or a substantial risk to either, she must prove by clear and convincing evidence that she is entitled to release, i.e., that "release would not create a substantial risk of bodily injury to another person or serious damage of property of another due to a present mental disease or defect."[109] With less serious crimes, she must meet the same standard by a preponderance of the evidence.

[B] Release After Commitment for Mental Illness

[1] Criteria for Release

An insanity-acquittee may be detained as long as she is *both* mentally ill and dangerous to herself or others. Put differently, she is constitutionally entitled to release from a mental facility if she is no longer mentally ill (even if she remains dangerous to herself or others[110]) or is no longer dangerous (even if she continues to suffer from a mental illness).[111] In this regard, state laws based on

---

[106] Addington v. Texas, 441 U.S. 418, 426-27 (1979).

[107] Jones v. United States, 463 U.S. 354, 363-64 (1983).

[108] 18 U.S.C. § 4243(c) (2005).

[109] 18 U.S.C. § 4243(d) (2005).

[110] But see § 25.05[C], *infra*, in regard to sexual predators.

[111] Foucha v. Louisiana, 504 U.S. 71, 80-83 (1992).

the Model Penal Code,[112] which authorizes the continued commitment of dangerous persons who are *not* mentally ill, violate the Due Process Clause of the United States Constitution.[113]

[2] Length of Confinement

An insanity-acquittee's commitment is of an indeterminate length, i.e., until she meets the criteria for release. In practice and as a constitutional matter,[114] she may remain in a mental hospital for a longer period of time than she would have served in a prison had she been convicted of the crime that triggered her commitment. The concept of proportionality between a criminal offense and the length of detention is irrelevant in such circumstances, because the purpose of her confinement is "treatment," rather than "punishment."

[3] Release Procedures

Release procedures vary by jurisdiction.[115] In many states, the court that ordered the insanity-acquittee's commitment retains jurisdiction over her. She or the mental facility may petition the court to release her based on that jurisdiction's criteria for release.[116] In most jurisdictions, the acquittee may not petition for release for a specified period of time, ranging from ninety days to one year after initial commitment.[117] Thereafter, subsequent petitions for release may be limited to stated time intervals.

The institutionalized party is entitled to a hearing on her petition for release. In nearly all states, the burden of proof is placed on the committed party to demonstrate that she is either no longer mentally ill or dangerous. The burden of proof varies from a preponderance of the evidence to clear and convincing evidence.

[C] A Different Form of Commitment: Sexual Predator Laws[118]

In recent years, at least fifteen states have adopted exceedingly controversial so-called "sexual predator" statutes, which authorize civil commitment of indi-

---

[112] Model Penal Code § 4.08.

[113] See Foucha v. Louisiana, 504 U.S. at 83 n.6.

[114] Jones v. United States, 463 U.S. 354, 370 (1983).

[115] See generally American Law Institute, Comment to § 4.08, at 262-65.

[116] Model Penal Code § 4.08(2)-(3).

[117] E.g., Model Penal Code § 4.08(5) (providing a six-month waiting period).

[118] See generally John Q. La Fond, *Can Therapeutic Jurisprudence Be Normatively Neutral? Sexual Predator Laws: Their Impact on Participants and Policy*, 41 Ariz. L. Rev. 375 (1999); see also 4 Psych. Pub. Pol'y & L. 1-576 (1998) (special issue on "Sex Offenders: Scientific, Legal and Policy Perspectives").

viduals who are dangerous but who do not necessarily suffer from a mental disease or defect.

Sexual predator laws vary in scope and procedure by jurisdiction, but a brief overview is possible. For example, the State of Kansas has established procedures for the "long-term care and treatment" of "sexually violent predators."[119] A "sexually violent predator" was defined as "any person who has been convicted of or charged with a sexually violent offense and who suffers from a mental abnormality or personality disorder which makes the person likely to engage in repeat acts of sexual violence." A "mental abnormality" was defined as a "congenital or acquired condition affecting the emotional or volitional capacity which predisposes the person to commit sexually violent offenses in a degree constituting such person a menace to the health and safety of others."

Notice that this statute applies to any one "convicted of or charged with" specific sexual offenses. Thus, the law covers those who have been convicted of a sexual offense, but also encompasses those who have been acquitted on the ground of insanity, *those acquitted generally*, and even those who, although charged with an offense, have not been brought to trial. Also, a "mental abnormality or personality disorder" is a broader concept than "mental disease or defect," the triggering mechanism for an insanity defense.

To invoke the law, a prosecutor files a petition in a state court seeking the individual's involuntary commitment.[120] If there is probable cause to believe that the person is a sexual predator, the individual is transferred to a mental facility for evaluation, after which a full hearing is held. If the court determines beyond a reasonable doubt that the individual is a sexually violent predator, he is civilly committed until he "is safe to be at large." Currently, such persons are not generally thought to be amenable to existing mental health treatment modalities, so the practical effect of sexual predator laws may be the life-long commitment of the person.

§ 25.06 ABOLITION OF THE INSANITY DEFENSE[121]

[A] Abolitionist Arguments

Opponents of the insanity defense (abolitionists, for short) come from different ideological and philosophical vantage points. Some abolitionists are political "hawks" who favor abolition of the defense as part of a broader effort to

---

[119] Kan. Stat. Ann. § 59-29a01 to -29a21 (2005).

[120] This may occur, for example, as a person convicted of a sexual offense is about to be released from prison after serving the criminal sentence, or immediately after acquittal or dismissal of charges for a sexual offense.

[121] See generally Morris, Note 1, *supra*; National Mental Health Association, Note 5, *supra*; Goldstein & Katz, Note 103, *supra*; Norval Morris, *The Criminal Responsibility of the Mentally Ill*, 33 Syracuse L. Rev. 477 (1982); Morse, Note 39, *supra*; Stephen J. Morse, *Justice, Mercy, and*

reduce the number of excuse defenses recognized in the criminal law. In contrast, "dove" abolitionists would like to *expand* the law of excuses, but for reasons of equity do not want to treat mentally ill people more leniently than others the critics consider similarly morally blameless but who are punished for their wrongdoing. Public opinion surveys also suggest that abolitionism is founded on both retributive and utilitarian grounds.[122]

[1] Abuse

Abolitionists assert that the insanity defense results in abuse of the criminal justice system. They claim that the defense is frequently asserted and too often successful.[123] Implicit in this argument is that insanity claims, including successful ones, are often fraudulent in nature. As a result, wrongdoers "walk free" because they are able to persuade psychiatrists and gullible juries of their non-existent madness.

There is little or no empirical support for this proposition.[124] According to one team of commentators, "[a]ll empirical analyses . . . have been consistent: the public, legal profession and . . . legislators 'dramatically' and 'grossly' overestimate both the frequency and the success rate of the insanity plea."[125]

Although statistics regarding use of the insanity plea are sketchy,[126] it appears that the defense is rarely invoked; when it is invoked, there is often agreement among the experts that the defendant suffers from a mental illness; and the success rate for the insanity plea, although variable, is usually extremely low.[127] For example, in one reported New Jersey study, NGRI verdicts were secured in only ½ of 1 percent of all cases handled by the Office of Public Defenders.[128] In a survey of 36 states for the years 1970-1995, there were only 16,379 insanity acquittals, or an average of 33.4 acquittals per state per year in the many hundreds of thousands of felony and misdemeanor prosecutions during that period, including a modest decline in such acquittals beginning in the

---

Craziness, 36 Stan. L. Rev. 1485 (1984); Michael L. Perlin, *Unpacking the Myths: The Symbolism Mythology of Insanity Defense Jurisprudence*, 40 Case W. Res. L. Rev. 599 (1990); Jonas Robitscher & Andrew Ky Haynes, *In Defense of the Insanity Defense*, 31 Emory L.J. 9 (1982); Ernest van den Haag, *The Insanity Defense*, Criminal Just. Ethics, Winter-Spring 1984, at 3.

[122] See Hans, Note 54, *supra*.

[123] See National Mental Health Association, Note 5, *supra*, at 14-15. A national survey in 1981 found that 87% of the public believed that the defense was over-used and too often successful. Minneapolis Trib., Oct. 25, 1981, at 9a.

[124] American Law Institute, Comment to § 4.01, at 182.

[125] Joseph H. Rodriguez et al., *The Insanity Defense Under Siege: Legislative Assaults and Legal Rejoinders*, 14 Rutgers L.J. 397, 401 (1983) (footnotes omitted).

[126] See Note 5, *supra*.

[127] See Perlin, Note 121, *supra*, at 648-49, 651-53.

[128] National Mental Health Association, Note 5, *supra*, at 15.

late 1980s.[129] As a result of jury antipathy to insanity claims, many criminal defense lawyers view the defense as a plea of last resort.

[2] Counter-Deterrence

Although the insanity defense may serve a valid utilitarian purpose with genuinely insane people,[130] abolitionists fear that the defense may have a negative impact on those who are *not* mentally ill, and on those whose illnesses are not severe enough to qualify for acquittal. They reason that awareness by such people that the law recognizes an insanity defense may reduce the deterrent effect of the criminal sanction. A would-be wrongdoer may believe, although perhaps inaccurately, that if she is caught for her crime she will be able to avoid conviction or commitment by raising the insanity defense.

Defenders of the insanity plea contend that even if this argument is correct, the solution is not to abolish the defense, but instead is to educate the public regarding the true effect of the insanity defense (e.g., that long-term civil commitment usually follows the rare acquittal), and/or place the burden of proof on the defense to prove insanity, rather than on the prosecution to prove the defendant's sanity.[131]

[3] Conflict of Perspectives

Some abolitionists contend that the criminal law and psychiatry cannot mix any more than oil and water does. They point out that the criminal law and psychiatry look at human conduct from different philosophical perspectives.[132] The law is premised on the concept of free will, whereas psychiatry typically is deterministic regarding human conduct. From the psychiatric point of view, "[t]he study of man . . . has an undoubted tendency to make him, in the eyes of his investigator, a creature of forces beyond its control. . . . Law, on the other hand, stands pre-eminently for the freedom of the will."[133] The distinction the criminal law seeks to draw between the mad and the bad, therefore, is an illusion.

Psychiatrist Karl Menninger agrees with the claim that lawyers and psychiatrists have conflicting perspectives on human conduct. He states that "[t]he Law — with a capital L — has no real relation to the affairs of men." He observes disparagingly that lawyers are interested in placing or rebutting

---

[129] See Cirincione & Jacobs, Note 5, *supra*, at 490, 494.

[130] See § 25.03[A], *supra*.

[131] Most states do not place the burden of persuasion on the prosecution in insanity claims. See § 25.02[E], *supra*.

[132] United States v. Pollard, 171 F. Supp. 474, 479 (E.D. Mich. 1959).

[133] Gino C. Speranza, *The Medico-Legal Conflict over Mental Responsibility*, 13 Green Bag 123, 125 (1901).

"blame," and that "the word *justice*, which is so dear to lawyers, is one which the doctor *qua* scientist simply does not use or readily understand."[134]

The conflict-of-perspectives argument has much to commend it, but it arguably proves too much. Although psychiatrists are less apt to blame wrong-doers than are lawyers and the general public, the idea that some people are too sick to be blamed for their conduct is not antithetical to the criminal law, nor does it endanger the paradigm of free will. The criminal law is based on the view that, although humans *generally* possess free will, some people are so ill that they lack the basic attributes of personhood that make them morally account-able for their actions. Therefore, the present claim is more an argument for lim-iting the scope of psychiatric testimony at trial than it is for abolishing the insanity defense.

[4] "Mental Illness": Merely a Deviation from a Cultural Norm

Some abolitionists[135] believe that the term "mental illness" is little more than a pseudo-scientific term for describing abnormal behavior. And, the argu-ment proceeds, "abnormality" means no more than that the conduct is unusual or odd in a particular cultural environment. Ultimately, the term "mental dis-ease" is attached to behavior that society considers strange, frightening, or dis-agreeable.

Historical support for this premise can be found. For example, when slavery was the norm in the Southern U.S.A., slaves who fled where characterized as mentally ill.[136] Likewise, before feminism became socially acceptable, some Freudian psychologists described female advocates of women's rights as "neu-rotics . . . compensating for masculine trends . . . [or] more or less successfully sublimating sadistic and homosexual [trends]."[137] Also, the psychiatric estab-lishment labeled homosexuality as a mental disease until 1973, at which time the Board of Trustees of the American Psychiatric Association voted to remove homosexuality from that category. Politics and changing social attitudes, not new science, is credited for the change — "[a] more recent moral judgment sim-ply replaced an older one."[138]

---

134 Menninger, Note 6, *supra*, at 96.

135 E.g., Thomas S. Szasz, The Myth of Mental Illness (1961); Thomas S. Szasz, Ideology and Insanity (1970).

136 Emily Eakin, *Bigotry as Mental Illness or Just Another Norm*, N.Y. Times, Jan. 15, 2000, at A9 (quoting from an 1851 report of Dr. Samuel A. Cartwright, a Louisiana psychologist).

137 See Mary P. Ryan, Womanhood in America 276 (1975) (quoting H.W. Frink).

138 Van den Haag, Note 121, *supra*, at 4; see also Eakin, Note 136, *supra* (quoting the views of Dr. Alvin Poussaint, a professor of psychiatry at Harvard Medical School).

Advocates of the insanity defense assert that even if the preceding criticism of psychiatry is valid, it is beside the point. In the typical case in which the insanity defense is raised in a criminal proceeding, e.g., in which the defendant hallucinates or experiences exceeding strong urges to commit criminal acts, there is little doubt that she is suffering from an aberrant mental or physical condition, and is not simply a person out of place in her culture.

[5] Equity

Some abolitionists contend that various conditions, e.g., abuse as a child or growing up in a bad social environment, are equally or more criminogenic than psychoses, and yet they are not considered legitimate bases for exculpation. Advocates of the equity position concede that a defense based on such factors is politically unacceptable at this time. Therefore, since morally similar cases should be treated alike, they contend that until society recognizes an excuse for persons suffering from non-medical criminogenic factors, insane people should also be punished.[139]

Advocates for an insanity defense believe that critics are comparing apples with oranges. "Identification of the correlates of crime . . . does not mean the crime is compelled";[140] "[c]ausation is not compulsion."[141] A person from a bad social environment knowingly commits a crime and could choose to act otherwise; in contrast, one who suffers from a mental disease or defect that prevents her from knowing right from wrong lacks the basic attributes of a moral agent and, therefore, should be declared morally blameless.

[B] Legislative Efforts to Abolish the Defense[142]

After the attempted assassination of President Ronald Reagan in the 1980s,[143] four state legislatures abolished the insanity defense.[144] A fifth state, by judicial action, has reached the same outcome.[145] These states, however, permit a defendant to introduce evidence of her mental disease or defect in

---

[139] Norval Morris & Gordon Hawkins, The Honest Politician's Guide to Crime Control 179 (1970).

[140] Slobogin, Note 47, *supra*, at 321-22.

[141] Moore, Note 45, *supra*, at 1131; see generally § 17.03[C], *supra*.

[142] Daniel J. Nusbaum, Note, *The Craziest Reform of Them All: A Critical Analysis of the Constitutional Implications of "Abolishing" the Insanity Defense*, 87 Cornell L. Rev. 1509 (2002).

[143] See the text to Note 4, *supra*.

[144] A fifth state, Nevada, abolished the defense in 1995, but this legislative action was declared violative of the Due Process Clauses of the federal and state constitutions. Finger v. State, 27 P.3d 66 (Nev. 2001).

[145] The New Hampshire legislature never enacted an insanity defense. The state used to recognize the common law "product" test of insanity, see § 25.04[C][4], *supra*, but no longer does so.

order to rebut the prosecution's claim that she possessed the mental state required in the definition of the crime.[146]

For example, if *D* is prosecuted for intentionally killing *V*, *D* may introduce evidence that, due to mental illness, she believed that she was squeezing a lemon rather than strangling *V* and, therefore, that she lacked the intent to kill a human being. Evidence of *D*'s mental condition would be inadmissible, however, to show that she did not realize that taking a human life is morally or legally wrong, that she acted on the basis of an irresistible impulse to kill, or even that she killed *V* because she hallucinated that *V* was about to kill her.

These state laws have been declared constitutional.[147] Although defendants have argued that "the insanity defense is so embedded in our legal history that it should be afforded status as a fundamental right,"[148] the United States Supreme Court has stated that:

> The doctrines of *actus reus, mens rea*, insanity, . . . justification, and duress have historically provided the tools for a constantly shifting adjustment of the tension between the evolving aims of the criminal law and changing religious, moral, philosophical, and medical views of the nature of man. This process of adjustment has always been thought to be the province of the States.[149]

Since the federal Due Process Clause does not prohibit a legislature from abandoning the basic requirement of *mens rea*,[150] it would seem to follow that a state may take the less drastic approach of retaining the element of *mens rea*, while repealing the *defense* of insanity, as long as the prosecution is required to prove beyond a reasonable doubt that the defendant had the requisite mental state. Nor does abolition of the defense currently constitute unconstitutionally disproportionate punishment because, except in death penalty cases, legisla-

---

[146] Idaho Code § 18-207 (Michie 2005); Kan. Stat. Ann § 22-3220 (2005); Mont. Code Ann. § 46-14-102 (2004); Utah Code Ann. § 76-2-305(1) (2005); State v. Hall, 808 A.2d 55, 61 (N.H. 2002) (see Note 96, *supra*).

[147] State v. Searcy, 798 P.2d 914 (Idaho 1990) (abolition of the defense does not violate the Due Process Clause); State v. Korell, 690 P.2d 992 (Mont. 1984) (abolition does not violate Due Process Clause or Eighth Amendment bar on cruel and unusual punishment); State v. Herrera, 895 P.2d 359 (Utah 1995) (abolition does not violate due process or equal protection rights of the defendant); State v. Mace, 921 P.2d 1372 (Kan. 1996) (abolition does not constitute cruel and unusual punishment); but see Note 148, *infra*.

[148] State v. Korell, 690 P.2d at 998 (stating, but rejecting, the argument); but see Finger v. State, 27 P.3d 66, 84 (Nev. 2001) ("We conclude that legal insanity is a well-established and fundamental principle of the law of the United States. It is therefore protected by the Due Process Clauses of both the United States and Nevada Constitutions."); State v. Joyner, 625 A.2d 791, 800 (Conn. 1993) (stating in dictum that "[w]e agree with the defendant that our common law tradition provides considerable support for the proposition that . . . the state could not entirely eradicate such a defense from the penal code").

[149] Powell v. Texas, 392 U.S. 514, 536 (1968).

[150] See § 11.03, *supra*.

tures have almost unfettered discretion in determining appropriate penalties for serious crimes.[151]

These rulings by the Supreme Court are controversial and may be unwise, but unless and until the Supreme Court reverses itself on these matters, state legislatures are not barred by the federal[152] constitution from abolishing the insanity defense, as long as the defendant is entitled to a *mens rea* "defense."

§ 25.07 "GUILTY BUT MENTALLY ILL"[153]

In response to criticisms of the insanity defense, at least twenty-two states have adopted an alternative verdict, "guilty but mentally ill" (GBMI).[154] In all but two of these states, the insanity defense has been retained, but a jury may now choose from among four, rather than the usual three, verdicts: guilty, not guilty, not guilty by reason of insanity (NGRI), and GBMI.[155] In these states, the jury returns a NGRI verdict if the defendant was insane at the time of the crime; it returns a GBMI verdict if she is guilty of the offense, was sane at the time of the crime, but is "mentally ill" at the time of trial, as the latter term is defined by statute.

The effect of a GBMI verdict is that the convicted party receives the sentence that would otherwise be imposed if she were found guilty; after sentencing, however, she may receive psychiatric care in the prison setting or in a mental institution. If she is cured while in custody, she must complete her prison sentence.

Proponents of the GBMI verdict claim the following benefits of the system: (1) inappropriate insanity findings will be reduced; (2) treatment of mentally ill, but sane, offenders is provided; and (3) the public receives greater protection from mentally disordered and dangerous offenders.

Critics of the verdict raise the following objections. First, the distinction between mental illness and insanity may be too fine for a jury to distinguish. Second, the GBMI verdict is unnecessary: Any person convicted of a crime may receive psychiatric care if the state wishes to provide it. Third, persons who are found GBMI are not guaranteed treatment. Especially during state budgetary

---

[151] See § 6.05, *supra.*

[152] This does not preclude a state from enforcing its own constitution in a manner more protective of defendants' rights. See Note 148, *supra.*

[153] See generally Ingo Keilitz et al., The Guilty But Mentally Ill Verdict: An Empirical Study (1984); R.D. MacKay & Jerry Kopelman, *The Operation of the "Guilty But Mentally Ill" Verdict in Pennsylvania,* 16 J. Psych. & L. 247 (1988); Donald W. Morgan et al., *Guilty But Mentally Ill: The South Carolina Experience,* 16 Bull. Am. Acad. Psychiatry & L. 41 (1988); Gare A. Smith & James A. Hall, Project, *Evaluating Michigan's Guilty But Mentally Ill Verdict: An Empirical Study,* 16 U. Mich. J.L. Ref. 77 (1982).

[154] Bradford Charles, *Pennsylvania's Definitions of Insanity and Mental Illness: A Distinction with a Difference?,* 12 Temp. Pol. & Civ. Rts. L. Rev. 265, 268 (2003).

[155] E.g., Mich. Comp. Laws § 768.36 (2005).

crises, insufficient funds may be allocated to mental health agencies. Finally, juries may compromise and return GBMI verdicts when NGRI verdicts should be reached, i.e., the GBMI alternative may reduce the number of *appropriate* insanity acquittals.[156]

---

[156] With one exception, however, studies have found that the GBMI option has not resulted in a decrease in NGRI verdicts. See MacKay & Kopelman, Note 153, *supra* (reviewing four previous studies that found no reduction in insanity acquittals, but reporting a reduction in Pennsylvania).

Chapter 26

DIMINISHED CAPACITY

§ 26.01 "DIMINISHED CAPACITY": A TERM OF CONFUSION[1]

The term "diminished capacity" is used and misused by courts and commentators alike to describe two different concepts, neither one of which is adequately characterized by the term. Although the problem is less severe than in the past,[2] one scholar has aptly depicted the state of affairs in this field as "undiminished confusion in diminished capacity."[3] Because of the confusion pervading this area of the law, any generalization about it is just that — a generalization subject to exceptions and inconsistencies.

With this caveat in mind, it may be said that "diminished capacity" is a term used to describe two categories of circumstances in which an actor's abnormal mental condition, short of insanity, will occasionally exonerate him or, more often,[4] result in his conviction of a less serious crime or degree of crime than the original charge.

First, there is a *mens rea* form of diminished capacity. As explained below, the *mens rea* model of diminished capacity functions as a failure-of-proof defense. That is, evidence of mental abnormality is *not* offered by the defendant to partially or fully *excuse* his conduct, but rather as evidence to negate an element of the crime charged,[5] almost always the *mens rea* element.[6]

---

[1] See generally Peter Arenella, *The Diminished Capacity and Diminished Responsibility Defenses: Two Children of a Doomed Marriage*, 77 Colum. L. Rev. 827 (1977); Joshua Dressler, *Reaffirming the Moral Legitimacy of the Doctrine of Diminished Capacity: A Brief Reply to Professor Morse*, 75 J. Crim. L. & Criminology 953 (1984); Stephen J. Morse, *Diminished Capacity*, in Action and Value in Criminal Law 239 (Stephen Shute et al., eds. 1993); Stephen J. Morse, *Undiminished Confusion in Diminished Capacity*, 75 J. Crim. L. & Criminology 1 (1984).

[2] Morse, *Diminished Capacity*, Note 1, *supra*, at 240 n.8.

[3] Morse, *Undiminished Confusion*, Note 1, *supra*.

[4] State v. Joseph, 590 S.E.2d 718, 723 (W. Va. 2003).

[5] State v. Mott, 931 P.2d 1046, 1050 (Ariz. 1997).

[6] In rare circumstances, mental condition evidence may be introduced to prove that the defendant acted in an unconscious state, thereby negating the voluntary act requirement of a criminal offense. Of course, proof of lack of a voluntary act will also demonstrate lack of *mens rea*, but the "voluntary act" approach will result in a different outcome in prosecutions of strict liability offenses, as well as in jurisdictions that (as discussed in the text *infra*) bar evidence of mental abnormality to negate *mens rea*. E.g., Reed v. State, 693 N.E.2d 988, 992 n.6 (Ind. Ct. App. 1998).

The second form of diminished capacity, which partially excuses or mitigates a defendant's guilt even if he has the requisite *mens rea* for the crime, will be called here "partial responsibility."[7] This version of the defense is now recognized in only a few states, and only for the crime of murder, to mitigate the homicide to manslaughter.

§ 26.02 DIMINISHED CAPACITY: *MENS REA* DEFENSE

[A] Nature of the Defense

Consider three hypothetical cases. First, *D1* is charged with first-degree murder based on the claim that he intentionally killed *V*. *D1* wishes to introduce expert testimony that at the time he killed *V* he was suffering from a mental illness. Although the testimony will not show that *D1* was insane at the time of the crime, it is intended to prove that, as a result of his abnormal mental condition, he did not form the intent to kill *V*.

Second, suppose that *D2* is prosecuted for rape and wishes to introduce evidence that as a result of mental retardation, he genuinely believed that the female with whom he was having intercourse consented.

Finally, suppose that *D3* is prosecuted for assault with intent to commit rape, but wishes to prove that due to a delusion he believed that the woman he was forcibly attacking was his wife.

In each of these cases, the proffered expert testimony forms the basis of the *mens rea* version of the diminished capacity defense. The testimony that each defendant seeks to introduce speaks to the "question of whether the defendant in fact possessed a particular mental state [intent to kill, by *D1*; intent to have nonconsensual intercourse, by *D2*; intent to rape, by *D3*] which is an element of the charged offense."[8]

The word "defense," as used here, is a "legal colloquialism," because the doctrine "is not designed to defeat a case the State has otherwise established."[9] Indeed, it is potentially "confusing to refer to [the *mens rea* version of] diminished capacity as a 'defense.'"[10] This is because "the 'diminished capacity defense' . . . does not provide any grounds for acquittal not provided in the definition of the offense. Properly understood, [diminished capacity] is . . . not a defense at all but merely a rule of evidence."[11] As one court put it, "[f]or the pur-

---

[7] It is also called "diminished responsibility." See Arenella, Note 1, *supra*.

[8] United States v. Pohlot, 827 F.2d 889, 896 (3d Cir. 1987).

[9] State v. Humanik, 489 A.2d 691, 697 (N.J. Super. Ct. App. Div. 1985).

[10] State v. Joseph, 590 S.E.2d 718, 723 (W. Va. 2003).

[11] United States v. Pohlot, 827 F.2d at 897.

pose of determining criminal guilt, diminished capacity either negates the state of mind required for a particular offense, if successful, or it does not."[12]

[B] Law

[1] Overview

Because of judicial confusion regarding the concept of diminished capacity,[13] and legislative imprecision in the enactment of relevant statutes, the law of "diminished capacity" is unclear in many states. However, certain observations and a general summary are possible.

American law is sharply divided regarding the extent to which evidence of an abnormal mental condition not amounting to legal insanity may be introduced for the purpose of negating the *mens rea* of an offense. As examined below, some states, primarily those that follow the Model Penal Code, permit introduction of such evidence, when relevant,[14] to negate the *mens rea* of *any* crime. Other states limit the admissibility of such evidence to some or all specific-intent offenses. A third group bars "diminished capacity" evidence in prosecutions of all offenses.

[2] Defense-to-All-Crimes (Model Penal Code) Approach

Perhaps as many as fifteen states, consistent with the Model Penal Code,[15] provide that evidence that the defendant suffered from a mental disease or defect at the time of his conduct is admissible if it is relevant to prove that he lacked a mental state that is an element of the charged offense.[16] The Col-

---

[12] State v. Breakiron, 532 A.2d 199, 208-09 (N.J. 1987).

[13] See § 26.01, *supra*.

[14] Even in jurisdictions that recognize a defense of diminished capacity, a jury instruction on the subject is inappropriate unless the proffered evidence is legally relevant, i.e., evidence of the defendant's abnormal mental condition must tend to support the claim that it "impaired the defendant's ability to form the culpable mental state to commit the crime charged." State v. Atsbeha, 16 P.3d 626, 632 (Wash. 2001). For example, in State v. Guillot, 22 P.3d 1266 (Wash. Ct. App. 2001), *G* was not entitled to a diminished capacity instruction, although he offered to prove that he suffered from narcissistic personality traits, because this mental condition, even if supported by expert testimony, would not have prevented *G* from forming the mental state required to be convicted of murder.

[15] Model Penal Code § 4.02(1).

[16] According to Professor Paul Robinson, in 1984, twelve states followed the rule set out in the text. 1 Paul H. Robinson, Criminal Law Defenses § 64(a)-(b) (1984). The 2004-2005 Pocket Part to the Robinson treatise reports that since then some states seemingly have joined this list, while others may have dropped off. Because of ambiguities in judicial opinions and dicta, it is uncertain how many jurisdictions now apply the equivalent of the Model Penal Code standard, but the figure seems to be between eleven and fifteen states.

orado Supreme Court in *Hendershott v. People*[17] has succinctly explained the reasoning behind this rule:

> Once we accept the basic principles that an accused is presumed inno-
> cent and that he cannot be adjudicated guilty unless the prosecution
> proves beyond a reasonable doubt the existence of the mental state
> required for the crime charged, it defies both logic and fundamental
> fairness to prohibit a defendant from presenting reliable and relevant
> evidence that, due to a mental impairment beyond his conscious control,
> he lacked the capacity to entertain the very culpability which is indis-
> pensable to his criminal responsibility in the first instance.

Applying the Model Penal Code rule to the hypotheticals posited in subsection [A], the defendants in each case would be entitled to introduce evidence of their respective mental abnormalities. The effect of the evidence, if believed, would be to acquit the defendants of the crimes charged, although they might still be guilty of lesser offenses.[18] In contrast, a murder defendant who seeks to show, for example, that he is very mildly retarded and, as a consequence, is a follower of stronger-willed persons, would not be permitted to introduce expert evidence in *this* regard in an intent-to-kill prosecution, because such testimony, even if believed, would not negate the required element of intent.[19]

[3] Limited-Use Approach

A few states arbitrarily limit the introduction of mental-condition evidence to murder prosecutions.[20] Thus, in the hypotheticals in subsection [A], *D1* would be permitted to introduce evidence of his mental illness in order to reduce the degree of murder of which he could be convicted, but *D2* and *D3* would not be allowed to introduce evidence of their abnormal mental conditions.

A more common distinction is one drawn between specific-intent and general-intent offenses: Evidence of an abnormal mental condition may be introduced if it tends to show that the defendant could not, or did not, form a *specific* intent specified in the offense, but such evidence is inadmissible in the prose-

---

[17] 653 P.2d 385, 393-94 (Colo. 1982).

[18] *D1* could be convicted of any form of criminal homicide for which intent to kill is not an ele-ment. *D2*'s situation is more problematic: Because of his mental condition *D2* believed he was hav-ing consensual intercourse; probably, therefore, he would be guilty of no offense, unless the state recognizes an offense of fornication. *D3* would be guilty of assault or battery since, as he perceived the situation, he was sexually attacking his own wife. Only the specific intent to rape would be negated by his mental condition. (This latter analysis assumes that rape is defined as it was at com-mon law, namely as sexual intercourse by a man with a woman, *not his wife*, without her consent. See generally Chapter 33, *infra*.)

[19] State v. Watson, 618 A.2d 367, 372 (N.J. Super. Ct. App. Div. 1992).

[20] E.g., Commonwealth v. Garcia, 479 A.2d 473, 476 (Pa. 1984) (evidence admissible to negate the first-degree murder requirement of specific intent to kill).

cution of a *general*-intent crime.[21] Thus, *D1* could raise his diminished capacity claim to prove that he lacked the capacity to form, or did not in fact form,[22] the specific intent to kill. *D3*, as well, could introduce evidence to prove that he lacked the specific intent to rape *V*. *D2*, however, would not be permitted to introduce evidence of his mental condition to disprove rape, because rape is a general-intent crime.[23]

As a practical matter, this version of diminished capacity functions only as a partial defense, because there is almost always a crime for which a person with diminished capacity can be convicted, even if he succeeds in proving that he lacked a specific intent.[24] Thus, the defense will reduce a defendant's guilt from one degree of murder to a lower degree of criminal homicide, or from a non-homicide specific-intent offense to a general-intent crime, e.g., from burglary to criminal trespass. Outright acquittal is exceedingly rare.

[4] No-Defense Approach

Some jurisdictions permit introduction of evidence of a defendant's mental illness or defect in order to prove insanity, but refuse to admit such evidence for the purpose of negating the *mens rea* of the offense charged, regardless of whether the crime is one of "specific intent" or "general intent."[25]

In some states, this rule leads to an anomaly: A defendant may introduce evidence of his self-induced, and thus culpable, *intoxication* in order to show that he lacked the specific intent to commit an offense, but he is barred from introducing expert testimony regarding an abnormal mental condition — which he did not culpably contract — for the same purpose.[26] The stated justification for this distinction is that "[u]nlike the notion of partial or relative insanity, con-

---

[21] E.g., State v. Jacobs, 607 N.W.2d 679, 684 (Iowa 2000); State v. Lancaster, 527 S.E.2d 61, 66-67 (N.C. Ct. App. 2000); State v. Eakins, 902 P.2d 1236, 1242 (Wash. 1995).

[22] In a manner reminiscent of the law pertaining to voluntary intoxication, see § 24.03[B][3], *supra*, some jurisdictions speak of the defense in "lack of capacity" terms, e.g., *State v. Galloway*, 628 A.2d 735, 743 (N.J. 1993) ("[T]he claimed deficiency . . . affect[ed] the defendant's cognitive capacity to form the mental state necessary for the commission of the crime."), whereas other states are concerned with whether the actor *actually* formed the state of mind in question.

[23] See State v. Lopez, 892 P.2d 898 (Idaho Ct. App. 1995).

[24] Some courts expressly limit the defense in this regard. E.g., State v. Doyon, 416 A.2d 130, 137 (R.I. 1980) ("Acceptance of the doctrine requires that there must be some lesser-included offense which lacks the requisite specific intent of the greater offense charged.").

[25] E.g., State v. Mott, 931 P.2d 1046, 1050-51 (Ariz. 1997); Chestnut v. State, 538 So. 2d 820, 820 (Fla. 1989); People v. Carpenter, 627 N.W.2d 276, 283 (Mich. 2001); Bethea v. United States, 365 A.2d 64, 89-90 (D.C. 1976).

[26] State v. Joseph, 590 S.E.2d 718, 724 (W. Va. 2003) (quoting State v. Simpson, 309 S.E.2d 89, 98 n.18 (1983) (characterizing such an approach as illogical and unjust).

ditions such as intoxication, medication, epilepsy, infancy, or senility are, in varying degrees, susceptible to quantification or objective demonstration."[27]

Intoxication issues aside, why would a legislature require the prosecutor to prove an element of an offense — *mens rea* — and yet bar the defendant from introducing evidence to disprove that very same element?[28] Advocates of the no-defense rule offer various explanations for their position. First, some observers contend that the *mens rea* version of the diminished capacity defense is unneeded.[29] They reason that forming an intent is such a simple, basic, process that even insane people almost always can form the requisite *mens rea* of an offense. For example, a mentally ill person may kill on orders from God, or because of a compelling urge to do so. In both cases, the defendant may be insane, but in both circumstances he has the requisite intent to kill, so the diminished capacity *mens rea* defense would do him no good. On the other hand, if a person lacks the capacity to form a required intent to kill due to a mental disease or defect and, therefore, would be entitled to raise a diminished capacity claim — e.g., *D* strangles *V*, believing that he is squeezing a lemon — he is also insane (i.e., he does not appreciate the nature and quality of his conduct).

A second reason given for barring psychiatric testimony to prove a lack of *mens rea* is, quite simply, that psychiatrists are not up to the task. Thus, according to critics of the defense, a legislature may reasonably "find psychiatric testimony to be a useful tool in the determination of insanity, yet not be convinced that the sciences of psychiatry and psychology are advanced enough to 'fine-tune' among sane defendants and find whether they possess[] the specific intent necessary for commission of a crime."[30] A related argument is that diminished capacity evidence, if permitted, is likely to confuse jurors. As one court explained, "the ability [of jurors] to assimilate and apply the finely differentiated psychiatric concepts associated with diminished capacity demands a sophistication (or as critics would maintain, a sophistic bent) that jurors (and officers of the court) ordinarily have not developed."[31]

---

[27] Bethea v. United States, 365 A.2d at 88. Based on this purported distinction, Florida bars "mental abnormality" evidence, *Chestnut v. State*, 538 So. 2d 820 (Fla. 1989), but permits evidence of epilepsy, *Bunney v. State*, 603 So. 2d 1270, 1273 (Fla. 1992), to prove lack of specific intent.

[28] Various courts have upheld the constitutionality of such a rule. E.g., State v. Mott, 931 P.2d 1046, 1051-52 (Ariz. 1997); State v. Wong, 641 N.E.2d 1137, 1150-51 (Ohio Ct. App. 1994); see also Montana v. Egelhoff, 518 U.S. 37 (1996) (in which a four-justice plurality held that a statute barring evidence of voluntary intoxication to negate an element of an offense does not offend the Constitution); but see State v. White, 109 P.3d 1199, 1209 (Kan. 2005) (holding that, although the state legislature abolished the insanity defense, expert testimony that *W* suffered from a mental disease or defect that made him unable to form the intent to kill, is admissible, and that failure to permit such testimony violated the defendant's constitutional right to a fair trial).

[29] E.g., Arenella, Note 1, *supra*, at 833-35; see also United States v. Pohlot, 827 F.2d 889, 903 (3d Cir. 1987).

[30] State v. Wong, 641 N.E.2d at 1150-51.

[31] State v. Wilcox, 436 N.E.2d 523, 530 (Ohio 1982).

§ 26.03 DIMINISHED CAPACITY: "PARTIAL RESPONSIBILITY" DEFENSE

[A] Rule

[1] In General

Few states recognize the "partial responsibility" defense. Where it does apply, it is only a defense to murder to mitigate the offense to manslaughter. As discussed below, the California Supreme Court promulgated the United States judicial version of the doctrine in the 1960s.[32] Only four other state courts adopted the defense.[33] The drafters of the Model Penal Code developed a different version of the partial responsibility doctrine. Although legislatures and courts only rarely recognize the doctrine as a partial defense, "it has long been applied, at least implicitly, by judges during sentencing."[34]

[2] The Largely Discredited California Approach

The partial responsibility defense was adopted "through the judicial back door,"[35] in order to allow mitigation of some homicides from first-degree to second-degree murder. Later the mitigation process extended to reducing murder to manslaughter. California courts led the judicial movement.

In order to avoid the appearance of encroaching on legislative authority, the California Supreme Court dressed the partial responsibility defense in *"mens rea* clothing."[36] That is, the judges developed strained definitions of *mens rea* terms; then the courts concluded that mentally impaired actors lacked the requisite mental state (under the new definitions) to be convicted of first-degree or second-degree murder. In fact, however, the true rationale of the partial responsibility doctrine was — and is — that a person who does not meet the state's definition of insanity, but who suffers from a mental abnormality, is less blameworthy, and therefore less deserving of punishment, than a killer who acts with a normal state of mind.[37]

---

[32] The common law defense was first recognized in the nineteenth century in Scotland, to reduce the offense of the "partially insane" from murder to the non-capital offense of "culpable homicide." Arenella, Note 1, *supra*, at 830 n.16. It was codified in England in the Homicide Act of 1957, 5 & 6 Eliz. 2, ch. 11, Part I, § 2.

[33] American Law Institute, Comment to § 210.3, at 70 n.77.

[34] United States v. Leande, 132 F.3d 796, 802 (D.C. Cir. 1998).

[35] Morse, *Undiminished Confusion*, Note 1, *supra*, at 24.

[36] Arenella, Note 1, *supra*, at 831.

[37] See United States v. Skodnek, 896 F. Supp. 60, 63 (D. Mass. 1995) ("[M]ental illness is not like a spigot, to be turned on and off, but exists in varying degrees in different individuals. . . .").

For example, in *People v. Conley*,[38] *C* shot his ex-lover and her husband after planning their deaths over a weekend. According to psychiatric testimony, *C* suffered from "personality fragmentation" and was in a "dissociative state" on the fatal weekend. Nonetheless, the jury found that at the time of the crime, *C* killed the victims intentionally and with premeditation and deliberation. In short, the *mens rea* variant of the diminished capacity defense apparently did not apply.

The California Supreme Court overturned *C*'s first-degree murder conviction, although it accepted the jury's findings. It stated that the judge had failed to instruct the jury properly on the element of "malice aforethought," the mental element of murder that distinguishes that offense from manslaughter. To act with "malice aforethought," the court stated, a person must be aware of his "obligation to act within the general body of laws regulating society." If *C*, although sane, lacked this awareness, he did not act with malice aforethought and, therefore, lacked the required *mens rea* of murder. Under such circumstances, *C* was guilty only of manslaughter. Of course, a person who is unaware of his obligation to act within the law because he suffers from a mental disease or defect is probably insane because he does not know right from wrong. What the court really was doing was creating a mini-insanity defense, so that a jury could mitigate a defendant's guilt when it was unwilling to find insanity.

Subsequently, the California Supreme Court extended the doctrine. Probably because the state legislature had not codified the irresistible-impulse test of insanity, the court further redefined "malice," by including a volitional feature. According to the court, "malice" is absent if, as the result of a mental abnormality, the defendant is "unaware of or *unable to act* in accordance with the law."[39]

In response to controversial verdicts involving the diminished capacity defense, the California legislature and the state's electorate abolished the partial responsibility form of the diminished capacity doctrine in the 1980s.[40]

[3] The Model Penal Code Approach

The Model Penal Code provides that a homicide that would otherwise constitute murder is manslaughter if it is committed as the result of "extreme mental or emotional disturbance for which there is a reasonable explanation or excuse." The reasonableness of the actor's explanation or excuse for the "extreme mental or emotional disturbance" (EMED) is "determined from the viewpoint of

---

[38] 411 P.2d 911 (Cal. 1966).

[39] People v. Poddar, 518 P.2d 342, 348 (Cal. 1974) (emphasis supplied).

[40] Cal. Penal Code §§ 28(b), 188 (Deering 2005). For a thorough discussion of California law, including the abandonment of the doctrine, see People v. Saille, 820 P.2d 588 (Cal. 1991).

a person in the actor's situation under the circumstances as he believes them to be."[41]

The EMED provision has two purposes: (1) it codifies and expands on the common law "sudden heat of passion" doctrine;[42] and (2) it permits, but does not require, courts in states that adopt the EMED language to recognize a partial responsibility defense.[43] It is unclear how many states that have codified the EMED provision allow for a partial responsibility defense, but courts in at least two jurisdictions expressly recognize the defense.[44] The Commentary to the Code explains the partial responsibility doctrine this way:

> [The defense] looks into the actor's mind to see whether he should be judged by a lesser standard than that applicable to ordinary men. It recognizes the defendant's own mental disorder or emotional instability as a basis for partially excusing his conduct. . . . To the extent that the abnormal individual is judged as if he were normal, to the extent that the drunk man is judged as if he were sober, to the extent, in short, that the defective person is judged as if he were someone else, the moral judgment underlying criminal conviction is undermined.[45]

> As a practical matter, the EMED provision is very difficult to apply in the context of diminished capacity, because the latter concept is subjective — the defendant is not like an ordinary person because he suffers from an abnormal mental condition — yet the EMED standard is partially objective, i.e., the provision includes the *"reasonable* explanation or excuse" language. More specifically, the issue in partial responsibility cases is not whether there is a reasonable explanation or excuse for the defendant's homicidal act, but rather whether there is a reasonable explanation or excuse for the defendant's EMED that caused him to take a life.[46]

To see how the EMED doctrine works in the context of mental abnormalities, consider *State v. Dumlao*:[47] *D* introduced testimony at his trial that he suffered from "paranoid personality disorder," a condition that caused him to experience "unwarranted suspiciousness" of other people's actions and to be hypersensitive to criticism. As a result of his condition, *D* irrationally believed that his wife was being unfaithful to him, and he became enraged when his

---

[41] Model Penal Code § 210.3(1)(b).

[42] See §§ 31.07 (common law) and 31.10[C][3] (Model Penal Code), *infra*.

[43] American Law Institute, Comment to § 210.3, at 72-73.

[44] State v. Perez, 976 P.2d 379 (Haw. 1999); State v. Counts, 816 P.2d 1157 (Or. 1991).

[45] American Law Institute, Comment to § 210.3, at 71.

[46] See People v. Casassa, 404 N.E.2d 1310, 1316 n.2 (N.Y. 1980).

[47] 715 P.2d 822 (Haw. Ct. App. 1986).

brother-in-law and father sought to counsel him about his suspicions. *D* took a life while in the preceding emotional state.

According to the appellate court, this evidence was sufficient to justify an instruction on EMED manslaughter. In determining whether there was a reasonable explanation or excuse for *D*'s disturbance, the court concluded that the jury should consider "the subjective, internal situation in which the defendant found himself and the external circumstances as he perceived them at the time, however inaccurate that perception may have been, and assess[] from that standpoint whether the explanation . . . for his emotional disturbance was reasonable."[48]

To summarize: The issue is not whether there was a reasonable explanation or excuse for the homicide *or* for *D*'s paranoid condition.[49] Instead, the issue is whether there was a reasonable explanation or excuse, *based on D's psychological characteristics*, for his emotional disturbance (here, his suspicion-based rage) at the time of the crime. *D*'s psychological makeup is relevant because the Code provides that the reasonableness of the actor's explanation for his rage should be considered "from the viewpoint of a person *in the actor's situation*," which includes his paranoid delusions and hypersensitivity, "under the circumstances as he believes them to be," which includes his paranoid belief that his wife was unfaithful to him.

The Commentary to the Code warns that the fact that an actor suffers from a mental disorder does not preclude a finding that he is morally depraved. Moreover, it states that "surely" cases will exist (although it offers no examples) in which a defendant's mental condition, although abnormal, "should be regarded as having no just bearing on his liability" for the intentional homicide.[50]

[B] Controversy Regarding the Defense[51]

As the American Law Institute concedes, the partial responsibility defense "brings formal guilt more closely into line with moral blameworthiness, but only at the cost of driving a wedge between dangerousness and social control."[52] Indeed, the very factor that mitigates an actor's blameworthiness — his mental abnormality — aggravates his dangerousness.[53]

---

[48] *Id.* at 830 (quoting People v. Casassa, 404 N.E.2d at 1316).

[49] As to the latter condition, unless a defendant can be blamed for "contracting" a mental abnormality, there will *always* be a reasonable explanation or excuse.

[50] American Law Institute, Comment to § 210.3, at 72.

[51] Stephen J. Morse, *Diminished Rationality, Diminished Responsibility*, 1 Ohio St. J. Crim. L. 289 (2003); see also the articles cited in Note 1, *supra*.

[52] *Id.* at 71-72.

[53] Arenella, Note 1, *supra*, at 857.

Critics of psychiatry are troubled by the recognition of this defense. Even if agreement exists that at some gross level mental disease can be so severe that it is fair to excuse the defendant, they believe that the subtle gradations that this defense implies — the distinction between full, partial, and no mental abnormality — cannot be reliably determined.

As a normative matter, as well, it has been argued that the partial responsibility doctrine is unjustified. A leading law and mental health scholar, Professor Stephen Morse, once opposed the defense. He reasoned that it is easy not to offend the law: The criminal law does not require people to live up to a high moral standard; all it demands of citizens is that they *not* rob, rape, kill, and commit other serious offenses. Morse reasoned that even if a person has a mental health problem (short of insanity), it is not difficult for him to avoid offending society's laws. Therefore, Morse called for abolition of *all* partial excuses to murder (e.g., heat of passion and partial responsibility). He would have treated *all* sane intentional killers alike, "without regard to differences in background, mental or emotional condition, or other factors often thought to necessitate mitigation."[54]

However, even though it is true that it is not hard to avoid killing persons, it remains true that it *is* harder for some people to avoid violating the law than it is for others. For example, in *Fisher v. United States*,[55] *F*, an African-American of subnormal intelligence and a victim of an abnormal condition that made him highly aggressive, intentionally strangled *V* to death, after *V* uttered a racial epithet. *F* was convicted of murder. An advocate of the partial responsibility defense might respond that, although *F* assuredly deserved to be punished for his conduct, his mental condition, for which he was not culpable, rendered him less blameworthy than a "normal" person, because it was harder for *F* to avoid taking a life than for an ordinary person.[56] In the case of murder, in which the most severe penalties are imposed (in *Fisher*, *F* was executed), it may be appropriate to investigate an actor's mental condition with great care, and mitigate the offense when justice seems to require it, i.e., when the defendant's choice-making capacities are undermined by a mental disease or defect.

And, indeed, on further reflection, Professor Morse now believes "that the moral claim [for a partial responsibility defense] is sufficiently weighty to justify bearing the potential practical costs."[57] Indeed, he now "proposes that the criminal law . . . include a generic, doctrinal mitigating excuse of partial respon-

---

[54] Morse, *Undiminished Confusion*, Note 1, *supra*, at 30.

[55] 328 U.S. 463 (1946).

[56] For a fuller exposition of this argument see Dressler, Note 1, *supra*.

[57] Stephen J. Morse, *Excusing and the New Excuse Defenses: A Legal and Conceptual Review*, 23 Crime & Just. 329, 397 (1998).

sibility that would apply to all crimes," and not simply murder.[58] Morse now agrees that such an excuse "is a moral imperative for a just criminal law that attempts never to punish defendants more than they deserve."[59]

---

[58] Morse, Note 51, *supra*, at 289 (and thereafter laying out the specifics of the defense).

[59] *Id*. at 290. Morse continues, however, to oppose the specific partial excuse of "heat of passion." *Id*.

Chapter 27

ATTEMPT

§ 27.01 CRIMINAL ATTEMPTS: AN OVERVIEW TO INCHOATE CONDUCT[1]

When a person intentionally commits a crime, it is the result of a six-stage process.[2] First, the actor conceives the idea of committing a crime. Second, she evaluates the idea, in order to determine whether she should proceed. Third, she fully forms the intention to go forward. Fourth, she prepares to commit the crime, for example, by obtaining any instruments necessary for its commission. Fifth, she commences commission of the offense. Sixth, she completes her actions, thereby achieving her immediate criminal goal.[3] In some cases, of course, this process takes only seconds to transpire; in other circumstances, the six stages may take days, weeks, or even years, to complete.

Anglo-American law does not punish a person during the first three stages of the process. Until the third step occurs, the actor lacks a *mens rea*. Even after the *mens rea* is formed, she is not punished if there is no *actus reus* — people are not punished for thoughts alone.

Activity in the middle ranges, i.e., after the formation of the *mens rea* but short of attainment of the criminal goal, is described as "inchoate" — imperfect or incomplete — conduct. Anglo-American law recognizes various inchoate offenses, the most notable of which are attempt, solicitation, and conspiracy. This chapter focuses on the inchoate crime of attempt.

Criminal attempts are of two varieties: "complete" (but "imperfect"); and "incomplete."[4] A complete-but-imperfect attempt occurs when the actor per-

---

[1] See generally R.A. Duff, Criminal Attempts (1996); Jerome Hall, General Principles of the Criminal Law 558-99 (2d ed. 1960); Glanville Williams, Criminal Law: The General Part §§ 197-209 (2d ed. 1961); Thurman W. Arnold, *Criminal Attempts — The Rise and Fall of an Abstraction*, 40 Yale L.J. 53 (1930); Joseph H. Beale, Jr., *Criminal Attempts*, 16 Harv. L. Rev. 491 (1903); Douglas N. Husak, *The Nature and Justifiability of Nonconsummate Offenses*, 37 Ariz. L. Rev. 151 (1995); Rollin M. Perkins, *Criminal Attempt and Related Problems*, 2 UCLA L. Rev. 319 (1955); Francis Bowes Sayre, *Criminal Attempts*, 41 Harv. L. Rev. 821 (1928).

[2] See Hall, Note 1, *supra*, at 576.

[3] The actor may not have achieved her *ultimate* goal. For example, *D1* may hit *V1* in the eye in order to give her a black eye, but the eye does not bruise; or *D2* may kill *V2*, her business rival's husband, to cause the rival to sell her business, but the rival refuses to do so. In these cases, the actors have failed in their ultimate goals but the crimes of battery and murder have been committed. For criticism of this six-stage analysis, see Husak, Note 1, *supra*, at 166-67.

[4] Andrew Ashworth, *Criminal Attempts and the Role of Resulting Harm Under the Code, and in the Common Law*, 19 Rutgers L.J. 725, 734 (1988).

forms all of the acts that she set out to do, but fails to attain her criminal goal. For example, if *D*, intending to kill *V*, purchases a gun, loads it, drives to *V*'s home, waits for *V* to arrive, and then fires the weapon at *V*, but misses her target, this is a complete attempt. In contrast, an incomplete attempt occurs when the actor does some of the acts necessary to achieve the criminal goal, but she quits or is prevented from continuing, e.g., a police officer arrives before completion of the attempt.

Inchoate conduct, including attempts, raise special enforcement issues that do not arise with successfully completed offenses. The earlier the police intervene to arrest for inchoate conduct, the greater the risk that suspicious looking, but innocent, conduct will be punished, or that a person with a less than fully-formed criminal intent will be arrested before she has had the opportunity to reconsider and voluntarily desist. On the other hand, the longer the law requires police officers to abstain from intervention, the greater the risk that an actor will successfully complete an offense.[5]

§ 27.02 GENERAL PRINCIPLES

[A] Historical Background

Although language favoring punishment of inchoate conduct can be found in judicial opinions as early as the middle of the fourteenth century, the general offense of attempt was not recognized until 1784.[6] Until then, "in those forthright days, a miss was as good as a mile."[7]

A common law attempt was a misdemeanor, regardless of the nature or seriousness of the offense that the person sought to commit (i.e., the "target" or "substantive" offense).

[B] Definition of "Attempt"

Until the Model Penal Code was drafted, most states punished, but did not define, criminal attempts.[8] However, subject to substantial clarification in this chapter, a criminal attempt occurs when a person, with the intent to commit an offense, performs any act that constitutes a substantial step, beyond mere preparation, toward the commission of that offense.[9] The term "substantial step" is a term of art in the Model Penal Code,[10] but for current purposes, the

---

[5] See § 27.06[A].

[6] Rex v. Scofield, Caldecott 397 (1784).

[7] Hall, Note 1, *supra*, at 560.

[8] American Law Institute, Comment to § 5.01, at 300.

[9] Dabney v. State, 858 A.2d 1084, 1089 (Md. Ct. Spec. App. 2004).

[10] See § 27.09[D], *infra*.

"substantial step" required for a criminal attempt is, simply, any conduct that has reached the fifth stage of criminality described in § 27.01, i.e., conduct that has passed the preparatory stage and moved to the point of perpetration of the target offense.

In common law parlance, attempt is a specific-intent crime.

[C] Punishment of Attempts

As noted in subsection [A], a criminal attempt was a misdemeanor at common law, even when the target offense was a felony. Thus, an attempt to commit a felony was punished less severely than the target crime.

Today, an attempt to commit a felony is graded as a felony, but typically is treated as a lesser offense than the substantive crime.[11] Almost always, the penalty for an attempt to commit a capital crime or an offense for which the penalty is life imprisonment is set at a specific term of years of imprisonment. An attempt to commit a less serious felony is usually punished at one-half of the maximum allowed for the target crime (or by some similar formula).

[D] Relationship of an Attempt to the Target Offense

A criminal attempt is "an adjunct crime; it cannot exist by itself, but only in connection with another crime,"[12] the so-called "target" offense.

A few statutes and court opinions expressly provide that failure to consummate the target offense is an essential element of a criminal attempt.[13] The implication of this statement is that a criminal attempt and the substantive offense are mutually exclusive crimes: A wrongdoer may commit a crime or, perhaps, unsuccessfully attempt to commit it, but she can never do both.

In contrast to the preceding analysis, most jurisdictions provide that a "person is guilty of a criminal attempt when, with intent to commit a crime, the person engages in conduct which constitutes a substantial step toward the commission of that crime *whether or not his intention is accomplished*."[14] The implication of *this* definition is that, with crimes of intent, the successful commission of the target crime logically involves an attempt to commit it. This

---

[11] This is not generally the case in jurisdictions that follow the lead of the Model Penal Code. See § 27.09[F][1], *infra*.

[12] Lane v. State, 703 A.2d 180, 186 (Md. 1997) (quoting Cox v. State, 534 A.2d 1333, 1335 (Md. 1988)).

[13] E.g., Cal. Penal Code § 664 (Deering 2005) ("Every person who attempts to commit any crime, but fails, . . . is punishable . . ."); People v. Lardner, 133 N.E. 375, 376 (Ill. 1921) ("The essentials of the attempt are the intent to commit the crime, the performance of some overt act towards its commission, and a failure to consummate the crime.").

[14] Grill v. State, 651 A.2d 856, 857 (Md. App. 1995) (emphasis added); Crump v. State, 287 N.E.2d 342, 345 (Ind. 1972) (criticizing *Lardner*, Note 13, *supra*).

point is significant for two reasons: (1) in a prosecution for a crime of intent, a jury may properly return a guilty verdict for the lesser offense of an attempt to commit the substantive crime; and (2) in every case where an attempt is charged, proof of its actual commission establishes the attempt.[15]

If a person commits the target offense, she may *not* be convicted of both it and the criminal attempt.[16] If she was charged with the target offense, and the jury convicts her of this offense, the criminal attempt "merges" with the substantive crime; the lesser offense of attempt is absorbed by the greater offense.

[E] "Assault": "Attempt" in Different Clothing

[1] "Assault" versus "Attempt"

In the early common law, a criminal assault was defined as an attempted battery.[17] Today, most states have broadened the offense to include the tort version of assault, i.e., intentionally placing another in reasonable apprehension of an imminent battery.[18] Thus, today an assault ordinarily is proved if D attempts to batter V or, even if she does not, if she intentionally places V in apprehension of an imminent battery. Today, as at common law, a simple assault is a misdemeanor. Aggravated assaults, e.g., "assault with the intent to kill" and "assault with the intent to rape," are felonies.

Although a common law assault is an attempted battery, the law pertaining to criminal attempts does not apply to assaults. This is the result of an historical accident — assault law developed earlier and, therefore, independently of the crime of attempt. Specifically, for a criminal assault to occur, a greater degree of proximity to completion of the offense is required than in the case of non-assault attempts. For example, although an attempted murder may occur before the victim is in the would-be assailant's sights, a common law assault does not occur until the defendant is within apparent reach of the victim.[19]

Another difference between assault and attempt pertains to the doctrine of "impossibility." As described more fully below,[20] a person may be convicted of an attempt even if consummation of the target offense is factually impossible. For

---

[15] Townes v. State, 548 A.2d 832, 834 (Md. 1988); Berry v. State, 280 N.W.2d 204, 209 (Wis. 1979).

[16] United States v. York, 578 F.2d 1036, 1040 (5th Cir. 1978).

[17] Rollin M. Perkins & Ronald N. Boyce, Criminal Law 159 (3d ed. 1982). A battery is any unlawful application of force to the person of another. American Law Institute, Comment to § 211.1, at 175.

[18] Carter v. Commonwealth, 594 S.E.2d 284, 288 (Va. Ct. App. 2004), aff'd, 606 S.E.2d 839 (Va. 2005).

[19] E.g., State v. Boutin, 346 A.2d 531 (Vt. 1975) (in a scuffle, B walked toward V with a bottle raised over his head, apparently with the intention of striking V with it; the police intervened when B and V were ten feet apart; held: assault conviction was reversed).

[20] See § 27.07, *infra*.

example, *D* may be convicted of attempted murder if, with the intention of killing *V*, she pulls the trigger of an unloaded gun. In contrast, some statutes define "assault" as "an unlawful attempt, *coupled with a present ability*, to commit [a battery]."[21] Under this definition, *D* would not be guilty of *assault* if she fired an unloaded weapon at *V*.

[2] Attempted Assault

Inasmuch as a criminal attempt is a substantial step, beyond mere preparation, toward the commission of any offense, and assault is a criminal offense, the question arises whether a person may be convicted of "attempted assault." Since a common law assault is an attempted battery, an attempted assault would be an attempt to attempt to commit a battery, i.e., a substantial step beyond mere preparation toward committing a substantial step beyond mere preparation toward committing a battery!

Some courts have upheld convictions for attempted common law assault.[22] They reason that because an assault does not occur unless the assailant is near enough to the victim that she can immediately batter her, it should be possible to convict a person of *attempted* assault if she endeavors to place herself in such a position, but fails to do so.[23]

Most courts, however, do not recognize the offense of an attempted (common law) assault.[24] Such jurisdictions fear "a perversion of the law of attempt":[25] If an attempt to commit an attempt were permitted, "there could be a never ending domino effect backward from the targeted crime. . . . [T]here might then be urged upon [a court] an attempted attempted attempt, and so on *ad infinitum* until the *actus reus* would completely disappear into the bare *mens rea*."[26] Or, if such a "double inchoate" offense were permitted, a person might be convicted on the basis of innocent, albeit suspicious appearing, conduct.[27]

---

[21] E.g., Cal. Penal Code § 240 (Deering 2005) (emphasis added).

[22] E.g., State v. Wilson, 346 P.2d 115, 121 (Or. 1959) (applying state law since superseded by statute).

[23] People v. O'Connell, 14 N.Y.S. 485, 485-86 (1891).

[24] Wilson v. State, 53 Ga. 205, 206 (1874) (suggesting that such an offense "is like conceiving of the beginning of eternity or the starting place of infinity"). An attempted assault of the tort variety is recognized, however. E.g., People v. Jones, 504 N.W.2d 158, 164 (Mich. 1993).

[25] American Law Institute, Comment to § 211.1, at 179.

[26] Dabney v. State, 858 A.2d 1084, 1097 (Md. 2004).

[27] E.g., McQuirter v. State, 63 So. 2d 388, 390 (Ala. Ct. App. 1953) (*M* was convicted of "attempted assault with intent to rape," based on evidence that he, a black man, followed *V*, a white woman, somewhat closely down the street; the court affirmed the conviction, stating that "the jury may consider social conditions and customs founded upon racial differences, such as that the prosecutrix was a white woman and defendant was a Negro man").

[F] Inchoate Crimes in Disguise

Some common law and statutory offenses, although defined as if they were complete crimes, are inchoate offenses in disguise. Indeed, some such offenses prohibit conduct less proximate to completion than is required for a criminal attempt. For example, common law burglary is defined as "breaking and entering the dwelling house of another at night with the intent to commit a felony therein." Thus, a fully consummated burglary is "inchoate to a theft or to some other crime intended to be committed on the inside" of the dwelling.[28]

The crime of burglary serves the purpose of compensating for stringencies found in the law of attempt. The act of breaking into another person's home in order to commit a felony inside may fall short of a criminal attempt to commit the in-dwelling crime. For example, suppose D intends to break into V's residence, obtain a kitchen knife, and then enter V's second-floor bedroom and kill her. On these facts, D may not be guilty of attempted murder when she enters the home. Recognition of the substantive crime of burglary, therefore, allows a police officer who observes D's conduct to arrest her as she enters the house, while she still is within the practical reach of the officer. Indeed, recognition of the crime of burglary allows for preventive law enforcement even before D enters, when she is guilty of an *attempted* burglary.

The common law offense of larceny, as well, has an inchoate aspect to it. A person is guilty of larceny if she takes and carries away the personal property of another with the intent to permanently deprive the other of the property.[29] In essence, larceny occurs the instant the thief wrongfully moves the property even an inch, long before the permanent loss — the *ultimate* harm — results.

Other offenses of a statutory nature include such double or triple inchoate crimes as possession of burglars' tools,[30] stalking,[31] and child luring.[32]

---

[28] Dabney v. State, 858 A.2d at 1098.

[29] See Chapter 32, *infra*.

[30] E.g., Cal. Penal Code § 466 (Deering 2005).

[31] E.g., Ala. Code § 13A-6-90(a) (2005) ("A person who intentionally and repeatedly follows or harasses another person and who makes a credible threat . . . with the intent to place that person in reasonable fear of death or serious bodily harm is guilty of the crime of stalking.").

[32] E.g., N.J. Stat. Ann. 2C:13-6 (2005) ("A person commits a crime . . . if he attempts . . . to lure or entice a child . . . into a motor vehicle . . . with a purpose to commit a criminal offense . . . against the child.").

§ 27.03 "SUBJECTIVISM" AND "OBJECTIVISM"[33]

According to Austin, "[g]enerally, attempts are perfectly innocuous, and the party is punished . . . in respect of what he intended to do."[34] In other words, a person who attempts a crime is punished for possessing a *mens rea*; no harm is required.

On its face, Austin's perception seems correct. Many incomplete attempts, and even some complete but imperfect ones,[35] appear to be harmless. For example, suppose that *D1* lies in wait with a loaded gun outside *V1*'s house, intending to kill *V1* when she returns home. Just as *V1* shows up, a police officer drives by and arrests *D1* for attempted murder. Or, suppose that *D2*, intending to kill spouse *V2*, who is asleep in bed, points a gun at *V2* and pulls the trigger, only to discover that the gun is unloaded. *V2* sleeps through the attempt, and goes on with his life oblivious of *D2*'s efforts. *D1* and *D2* are guilty of attempted murder, but *V1* and *V2* have suffered no apparent harm.

But, this does not end the analysis. As earlier defined,[36] there is social harm whenever a person "negates, *endangers* or destroys" an individual, group, or state interest that is socially valuable. When a person lies in wait in order to kill another, or pulls the trigger of a gun, she endangers another person's bodily security, jeopardizes the interests of loved ones of the intended victim, and impairs society's interest in a safe community in which to live. Likewise, when a person comes close to violating one of society's moral and legal commandments, she tears the fabric of society, if only slightly. Contrary to Austin's assertions, therefore, criminal attempts are *not* innocuous; criminal attempts *do* cause social harm.

Notwithstanding the deficiency, Austin's statement serves as a useful starting point for considering two conflicting perceptions of the proper roles of social harm and personal culpability in criminal attempt law. The competing philosophies may be characterized as "subjectivism" and "objectivism." As will become evident in later sections of this chapter, the criminal attempt provisions of the Model Penal Code are largely based on subjectivist conceptions of inchoate lia-

---

[33] See generally George P. Fletcher, Rethinking Criminal Law 115-22, 135-84 (1978); Ashworth, Note 4, *supra*; Lawrence Crocker, *Justice in Criminal Liability: Decriminalizing Harmless Attempts*, 53 Ohio St. L.J. 1057 (1992); Paul H. Robinson & John M. Darley, *Objectivist Versus Subjectivist Views of Criminality: A Study in the Role of Social Science in Criminal Law Theory*, 18 Oxford J. Legal Studies 409 (1998); Stephen J. Schulhofer, *Harm and Punishment: A Critique of Emphasis on the Results of Conduct in the Criminal Law*, 122 U. Pa. L. Rev. 1497 (1974); Thomas Weigend, *Why Lady Eldon Should Be Acquitted: The Social Harm in Attempting the Impossible*, 27 DePaul L. Rev. 231 (1977).

[34] 1 John Austin, Lectures on Jurisprudence 523 (4th ed. 1873).

[35] For the definition of "incomplete" and "complete" attempts, see § 27.01, *supra*.

[36] See § 9.10[B], *supra*.

bility, whereas the common law of attempts includes many strands of objectivist thought, as well as some subjectivism.

Subjectivists assert that, in determining guilt and calibrating punishment, the criminal law in general, and attempt law in particular, should focus on an actor's subjective intentions (her *mens rea*), which simultaneously bespeak her dangerousness and bad character, rather than focus on her conduct (the *actus reus*), which may or may not result in injury on a particular occasion. With inchoate offenses, a subjectivist believes that "the act of execution is important [only] so far as it verifies the firmness of the [actor's] intent."[37] In a purely subjectivist system, therefore, any act — no matter how innocuous — that verifies the actor's commitment to carry out a criminal plan, or which corroborates her confession or other incriminating evidence, is sufficient to justify punishment for an inchoate offense.

In contrast, objectivists believe that conduct should not be punished unless its criminality is "objectively discernible at the time that it occurs,"[38] i.e., the defendant's "acts performed, without any reliance on the accompanying *mens rea*, [must] mark [her] . . . conduct as criminal in nature."[39] According to George Fletcher, under objectivism, "[t]he assumption is that a neutral third-party observer could recognize the activity as criminal even if [she] had no special knowledge about the offender's intention."[40] For an objectivist, criminal liability only occurs when the inchoate conduct manifests criminality and, therefore, causes social harm by "disturb[ing] the public repose,"[41] "unnerving . . . the community,"[42] or by causing apprehension, fear or alarm in the community because the actor has patently "set out to do serious damage . . . and to break the accepted rules of social life."[43] Once this social harm has been identified, the actor's *mens rea* is relevant in order to determine whether she should be held accountable for the societal harm that she has caused. If she did not intend to commit a crime, she should not be punished.

Subjectivists and objectivists will frequently reach the same result regarding criminal liability, but for different reasons. For example, reconsider the two hypotheticals at the beginning of this chapter section. Subjectivists and objectivists alike would convict *D1* and *D2* of attempted murder. Subjectivists would favor conviction on the basis of the defendants' *mens rea*. The actors' conduct would be of limited significance, i.e., to verify the fact that their homicidal

---

[37] Fletcher, Note 33, *supra*, at 138.

[38] *Id.* at 116.

[39] United States v. Oviedo, 525 F.2d 881, 885 (5th Cir. 1976).

[40] Fletcher, Note 33, *supra*, at 116.

[41] Clark v. State, 8 S.W. 145, 147 (Tenn. 1888).

[42] Fletcher, Note 33, *supra*, at 144.

[43] Weigend, Note 33, *supra*, at 264 (footnote omitted).

intentions were genuine and fixed. Conduct considerably less proximate to the outcome could be sufficient to justify punishment.

From an objectivist perspective, the criminality of the defendants' conduct is easily discernible to a hypothetical observer on the basis of their conduct alone. Therefore, assuming sufficient evidence of the actors' *mens rea*, objectivists would also punish *D1* and *D2*. However, if the actors' conduct had terminated at an earlier stage — e.g., while *D1* was driving to *V1*'s house, or after *D2* loaded the gun but before she pointed it at her husband[44] — the criminality of their conduct might not have been manifest, in which case objectivists would not have favored conviction.

The difference between subjectivism and objectivism may be seen more dramatically if one considers the following simple event: *D3* puts sugar in spouse-*V3*'s coffee. Is this attempted murder? Of course not. Suppose, however, that we learn that *D3* had told a friend a day earlier that she intended to put a lethal dose of poison in *V3*'s coffee the next morning, and suppose further that *D3* thought that the sugar was arsenic. If we are convinced beyond a reasonable doubt from this new information that *D3* intended to kill *V3*, and that the act of putting sugar in the coffee was a misguided act in execution of this murderous plan, the subjectivist would punish *D3* for attempted murder. The innocuous conduct of putting sugar in *V3*'s coffee verifies *D3*'s criminal intent.

An objectivist seemingly would *not* convict *D3*. An objectivist would look at the conduct, without consideration of *D3*'s prior incriminating statements or subjective belief that the substance was arsenic. Based on conduct alone, the act of placing sugar in coffee does not demonstrate criminality. Therefore, in the absence of knowledge of *D3*'s intentions and beliefs, her conduct would not cause public alarm or unnerve the hypothetical observer.[45] Notwithstanding other evidence of *D3*'s *mens rea* — and thus of her dangerousness and moral culpability — the objectivist would not punish *D3*, for want of social harm from the conduct itself.

---

[44] Since *D2* and *V2* live in the same house together, as wife and husband, there is nothing manifestly criminal about one spouse loading a firearm in their home.

[45] Of course, the issue will not always be as simple for the objectivist as is described in the text. How does the hypothetical observer know that the white substance put in the coffee is sugar, rather than arsenic? Suppose that the sugar is spooned into the coffee cup from a container labeled "poison," but which strangely contains sugar? Would the hypothetical observer know that the substance is sugar, or would she believe that it is poison? Objectivists do not have a settled answer to questions of this sort, but one scholar has suggested that "our hypothetical observer, if he is to be of any help at all, must be thought of as having a correct notion of all objective circumstances of the defendant's act which can be observed from outside." Weigend, Note 33, *supra*, at 267. Under this view, the observer would know that the substance is sugar, although it is being removed from a poison container.

§ 27.04 PUNISHING ATTEMPTS: WHY, AND HOW MUCH?[46]

[A] Rationale for Punishing Attempts

[1] Utilitarian Analysis

Professor H.L.A. Hart has written that "[i]t is not obvious . . . on some versions of utilitarian theory, why attempts should be punishable, as they are, in most legal systems."[47] After all, an attempt is merely conduct targeted at commission of a substantive crime. Those who set out to commit a crime expect to succeed. Therefore, any deterrent effect of threatened punishment emanates from the target offense; the penalty threatened for an attempt has no additional influence. As it is inefficacious, it should not be inflicted.

As Hart has demonstrated, this argument is fallacious. First, a person may assume that if she is successful in her conduct she will avoid detection, so she will be willing to risk the penalty for the targeted crime. On the other hand, she may figure that if she fails in her attempt it will be because she executed the crime poorly, in which case her poor execution may result in arrest. Therefore, she may be deterred by the punishment imposed for an attempt.

Second, applying subjectivist theories,[48] anyone who attempts to commit a crime is dangerous. Whether or not she succeeds in her criminal venture, she is likely to represent an ongoing threat to the community. Therefore, her incapacitation and/or rehabilitation is justifiable, even if she fails in her criminal plans.

Third, criminal attempt laws serve a valuable preventive law enforcement purpose: If there were no inchoate offenses in a penal code, police officers would lack legal authority to stop criminal activities before they are consummated.

---

[46] See generally Fletcher, Note 33, *supra*, at 472-83; H.L.A. Hart, Punishment and Responsibility 125-35 (1968); Ashworth, Note 4, *supra*; Theodore Y. Blumoff, *A Jurisprudence for Punishing Attempts Asymmetrically*, 6 Buff. Crim. L. Rev. 951 (2003); Björn Burkhardt, *Is There a Rational Justification for Punishing an Accomplished Crime More Severely Than an Attempted Crime?*, 1986 B.Y.U. L. Rev. 553; Russell Christopher, *Does Attempted Murder Deserve Greater Punishment than Murder? Moral Luck and the Duty to Prevent Harm*, 18 Notre Dame J.L. Ethics & Pub. Pol'y 419 (2004); Michael Davis, *Why Attempts Deserve Less Punishment Than Complete Crimes*, 5 Law & Phil. 1 (1986); Joel Feinberg, *Equal Punishment for Failed Attempts: Some Bad But Instructive Arguments Against It*, 37 Ariz. L. Rev. 117 (1995); Barbara Herman, *Feinberg on Luck and Failed Attempts*, 37 Ariz. L. Rev. 143 (1995); Sanford H. Kadish, *The Criminal Law and the Luck of the Draw*, 84 J. Crim. L. & Criminology 679 (1994); Stephen J. Morse, *Reasons, Results, and Criminal Responsibility*, 2004 U. Ill. L. Rev. 363; Craig A. Stern, *Crime, Moral Luck, and the Sermon on the Mount*, 48 Cath. U. L. Rev. 801 (1999); Gary Watson, *Closing the Gap*, 37 Ariz. L. Rev. 135 (1995).

[47] Hart, Note 46, *supra*, at 128.

[48] See § 27.03, *supra*.

[2] Retributive Analysis

Punishment of attempts makes sense under retributive theory, although retributivists differ in their basis for defending attempt laws. Some retributivists focus on the culpability of criminal attempters. These culpability-retributivists argue that a person who, for example, shoots but misses her intended victim is as morally culpable as one who succeeds in her endeavor. The only difference is the actor's aim or the fortuity of the victim's movement. The attempter, therefore, deserves to be punished. It would be "unthinkable" that the law would allow the lucky attempter off, while it punishes the successful wrongdoer.[49]

A second group of retributivists, harm-retributivists, focus instead on the harm caused by at attempter. A person who attempts to commit a crime, by her actions, "disturbs the order of things ordained by law."[50] By disturbing the public's repose and causing other social harm,[51] "punishment is necessary so as to restore, at least symbolically," the public order.[52]

[B] Less or Equal Punishment?

[1] Overview to the Issue

Once it is determined that inchoate conduct should be punished, the question turns to one of grading. At common law and in most jurisdictions today, an attempt to commit a felony is considered a less serious crime and, therefore, is punished less severely, than the target offense. Is this traditional rule justifiable, or should an attempt be graded and punished at the same level as a successful criminal enterprise, as is generally the case in states following the Model Penal Code?[53] It is here that the subjectivist/objectivist debate[54] comes into clearer focus. As the discussion below suggests, in general subjectivists favor equal punishment; objectivists do not.

Social science studies suggest that most persons in the United States are "objectivist-grading subjectivist[s]."[55] That is, people tend to be subjectivist — they focus on an actor's state of mind — in determining what the minimum criteria should be for holding an actor criminally responsible for her inchoate conduct, but once it is determined that punishment is appropriate and the issue

---

[49] American Law Institute, Comment to Article 5, at 294.

[50] Ashworth, Note 4, *supra*, at 735.

[51] There is social harm in an unsuccessful criminal attempt. See § 27.03, *supra*.

[52] Ashworth, Note 4, *supra*, at 735.

[53] See § 27.09[F][1], *infra*.

[54] See § 27.03, *supra*.

[55] Robinson & Darley, Note 33, *supra*, at 430.

turns to punishment, they tend to become objectivist — they focus on resulting harm — and favor the common law lesser-punishment result.

[2] Utilitarian Analysis

Utilitarian advocates of equal punishment argue that a person who attempts to commit a crime is no less dangerous or in need of rehabilitation than one who succeeds in her criminal endeavor. Assume three persons, A, B, and C, each intending to kill another person. A aims a gun at V1, but is arrested before she pulls the trigger. B shoots V2, but through the heroic efforts of hospital personnel, V2 survives the attack. C kills V3. Utilitarian advocates for equal punishment, applying subjectivist criteria, say that nothing distinguishes the actors here except simple luck. The actors' intentions are the same; their criminal resolve is the same; they are equally dangerous. Punishment, therefore, should be the same.

This argument may prove too much. Blackstone has reasoned that "[f]or evil, the nearer we approach it, is the more disagreeable and shocking, so that it requires more obstinacy and wickedness to perpetrate an unlawful action, than barely to entertain the thought of it."[56] If it takes more "obstinacy" and "wickedness" — which can also be characterized as dangerousness — to come closer to committing an offense than to "barely entertain the thought of it," it may follow that "from the moment the defendant's conduct crosses the threshold of an attempt [and, therefore, merits punishment], up until the completion of the attempt, the punishments should ideally be graded with increasing severity."[57] In other words, a complete, but imperfect, attempt should be punished at the same level as the target offense, whereas incomplete attempts are apt to require less punishment. But, this argument may itself fail, since the only reason that an attempt is incomplete may be factors outside the actor's control (e.g., the presence of a police officer and/or absence of the victim), and not factors that demonstrate a less dangerous character.

The better utilitarian argument for lesser punishment is that mitigated punishment provides "an encouragement to repentance and remorse,"[58] i.e., reduced punishment serves as an incentive to an actor to desist before completing the attempt. For example, if a person entering a bank to rob it already is subject to the punishment imposed for a successful robbery, she has one less reason to stop short. The same reasoning would apply to some completed attempts: If D sends V a mail bomb which is set to explode the next day, the attempt is complete (she has done every act in her power to commit the offense); but if punishment for attempted murder is less than for murder, D has a powerful incentive to prevent detonation of the bomb.

---

[56] 4 William Blackstone, Commentaries on the Laws of England *14 (1769).

[57] Ashworth, Note 4, *supra*, at 739.

[58] 4 Blackstone, Note 56, *supra*, at *14.

[3] Retributive Analysis

Culpability-retributivists[59] generally believe that a failed attempt should be punished as severely as an accomplished crime. They reason that luck — whether the attempt succeeds or fails — should have no role to play in setting the punishment of a wrongdoer. A person should be punished depending on her moral desert; and "desert [is] the same whether or not the harm occurs."[60] A person deserves punishment proportional to her culpability, and "fault depends on [the] choice to do the wrongful action, not on what is beyond [her] control,"[61] namely, whether the harm intended occurs.

Harm-retributivists disagree. They reason that **punish**ment should be apportioned according to culpability *and* harm. After all, the criminal law punishes for external results, not merely for culpable thoughts; it is the harm that an actor culpably causes that generates the debt that she must repay through her punishment. Put another way, the criminally successful actor and the unsuccessful one "have done different things. They are indeed equally morally blameworthy, but that fact determines not the degree of punishment that is appropriate, but their equal eligibility for penal sanction."[62] Since the harm caused by a failed attempt is less than that caused by the successful commission of the targeted crime, the debt owed by the attempter is less than that of the successful wrongdoer. Therefore, the traditional approach to attempt law is correct: A criminal attempt should always be a lesser offense than the consummated crime.

§ 27.05 *MENS REA* OF CRIMINAL ATTEMPTS[63]

[A] General Rule

It is sometimes said that the mental state required for a criminal attempt is "the intent to commit some other crime."[64] This is an accurate statement, as far as it goes. It is more complete to say, however, that a criminal attempt involves two "intents": the actor (1) must intentionally commit the acts that constitute the *actus reus* of an attempt (as the latter concept is explained in § 27.06), that is, she must intentionally perform acts that bring her in proximity to commis-

---

[59] See § 27.04[A][2], *supra*, for the definition of this term (and that of "harm-retributivism," discussed *infra* in the text).

[60] Kadish, Note 46, *supra*, at 688.

[61] *Id.*

[62] Herman, Note 46, *supra*, at 149.

[63] See generally Larry Alexander & Kimberly D. Kessler, *Mens Rea and Inchoate Crimes*, 87 J. Crim. L. & Criminology 1138 (1997); R.A. Duff, *Attempted Homicide*, 1 Legal Theory 149 (1995); Arnold N. Enker, *Mens Rea and Criminal Attempt*, 1977 Am. B. Found. Res. J. 845.

[64] State v. Green, 480 A.2d 526, 534 (Conn. 1984).

sion of a substantive offense; and (2) she must perform these acts with the specific intention of committing the target crime. As the latter intent suggests, an attempt is a specific-intent offense,[65] *even if the target offense is a general-intent crime.*

To see how the dual "intents" work, suppose that *D*, a hunter, fires a gun in the woods, wounding *V*. *D* is guilty of attempted murder of *V* if: (1) she intentionally pulled the trigger of the gun (as this would satisfy the first "intent" required above); and (2) she did so intending to kill *V* (the second, and specific, intent). If *D* intentionally pulled the trigger of the gun, but she did *not* intend to kill *V* by her intentional acts, then *D* is *not* guilty of attempted murder.

Although this rule seemingly is straightforward, various issues arise that require clarification.

[B] "Result" Crimes

[1] In General

A "result" crime is an offense defined in terms of a prohibited result. For example, the offense of murder prohibits the result of the death of a human being at the hands of another. For crimes of this nature, the ordinary rule is that a person is not guilty of an attempt unless her actions in furtherance of the prohibited result are committed with the specific purpose[66] of causing the unlawful result.

Because of the specific-intent nature of a criminal attempt, the prosecutor in an attempt prosecution is sometimes required to prove that the actor possessed a higher degree of culpability than is required to commit the target offense. For example, if *D* blindfolds herself and fires a loaded pistol into a room that she knows is occupied, she may be convicted of murder if someone is killed. Such a killing, although unintentional, is malicious (the *mens rea* of murder), because it evinces a reckless disregard for the value of human life.[67] However, if *D*'s

---

[65] State v. Earp, 571 A.2d 1227, 1230 (Md. 1990).

[66] Suppose that a person does not want the result to occur but knows that it will take place. Is knowledge, rather than purpose, sufficient *mens rea* to be convicted of attempt? Reconsider a hypothetical discussed earlier in the Text at § 10.04[A][1], *supra*: *D* plants a bomb in an airplane so that it will explode in air and kill *V*, *D*'s spouse. *D* knows that, short of a miracle, every other passenger on the airplane will also die. At common law, a person causes a result "intentionally" if it is her conscious object to cause the result (she causes it "purposely") or if she knowingly causes the result. Therefore, if the bomb explodes, *D* may be convicted of "intentionally" killing each passenger. If the bomb fails to go off, however, is *D* guilty of *attempted* murder of the passengers? (*D* is clearly guilty of attempted murder of *V*, as *V*'s death was *D*'s conscious object.) The common law answer to this question is uncertain. American Law Institute, Comment to § 5.01, at 305. The Model Penal Code resolution of this hypothetical is described at § 27.09[C], *infra*.

[67] See § 31.05, *infra*.

reckless act does *not* kill anyone in the room, she is *not* guilty of *attempted* murder: *D* purposely aimed and fired the gun — she intentionally performed the acts that brought her close to taking human life — but she lacked the specific intent to kill anyone in the room.[68]

Similarly, if *D* intends to severely injure *V*, *D*'s state of mind constitutes malice, so she may be convicted of murder if she unintentionally kills *V*. If *V* does not die from the attack, however, *D* is not guilty of attempted murder, as she lacked the specific intent to kill.[69]

[2] Rationale of Intent Requirement

Why does the law not punish unintentional "attempts"? One answer could be etymological: The word "attempt" means "to try," which in turn means "to seek to do." This basis for the common law intent requirement, however, cannot take us very far. If the only obstacle to permitting guilt for unintentional "attempts" is the meaning of the word "attempt," legislators can simply change the name of the crime. The more important question is whether the requirement of specific intent makes good penal sense. Or, restating the question: Should the law be changed to permit a person to be convicted of an attempt as long as she acts with the *same* level of culpability regarding the prohibited result as would be sufficient to convict her for the completed offense?

Those who would answer the preceding question in the affirmative contend that the policies underlying the target offense should apply to criminal attempts. Advocates for change "emphasize[] the illogic of requiring the state to prove an intent for successful prosecution of an attempt to commit a crime when no such degree of proof is necessary for successful prosecution of the completed crime."[70] Thus, for example, since the common law considers reckless indifference to the value of human life a sufficiently culpable frame of mind to justify a murder conviction when a person dies, it should also be adequate for conviction of attempted murder, if nobody dies.[71]

Those who defend the intent requirement focus on the supposed heightened dangerousness of intentional wrongdoers. One who intends to commit an offense, takes substantial steps in that direction, but fails in its commission or is required temporarily to desist, remains a threat, i.e., "the actor's unspent

---

[68] Thacker v. Commonwealth, 114 S.E. 504, 506 (Va. 1922) (shooting into a tent without the specific intent to kill does not constitute attempted murder); People v. Lee, 738 P.2d 752, 754 (Cal. 1987) (specific intent to kill is a required element of attempted murder; lesser forms of malice are insufficient); People v. Gentry, 510 N.E.2d 963, 966 (Ill. App. Ct. 1987) (same); State v. Casey, 82 P.3d 1106, 1115 (Utah 2003) (same).

[69] State v. Hawkins, 631 So. 2d 1288, 1290 (La. Ct. App. 1994).

[70] Gentry v. State, 437 So. 2d 1097, 1098 (Fla. 1983).

[71] This is apparently the rule in Florida. *Id.* at 1098-99; State v. Brady, 745 So.2d 954, 957 (Fla. 1999).

intent is itself a source of harm independent of his conduct."[72] The danger is that after the failed attempt or involuntary desistance, the actor will try again to commit the crime.

In contrast, one who acts recklessly or negligently is less apt to represent an ongoing threat. For example, one who drives recklessly in order to get to the airport for a flight, but who fortunately kills nobody in the process, has no "unspent" intent to kill that is apt to recur. Although the law may choose to punish the driver for her reckless driving, her conduct should not be equated with an attempted — intentional — harmdoer.

[3] Special Homicide Problems

[a] Attempted Felony-Murder

Suppose that *D* intentionally commits a felony, during the perpetration of which another person unintentionally dies. At common law, *D* is guilty of murder as the result of the felony-murder rule.[73] Suppose, however, *D* accidentally fires a gun during the felony, and *V* is wounded. May *D* be convicted of *attempted felony-murder*?

All but two states[74] that have considered this issue have held that attempted felony-murder is not a cognizable offense.[75] This is consistent with the principle that the offense of attempted murder requires a specific intent to kill; the defendant's intent to commit a felony does not substitute for the intent to kill. Even if a person by committing a felony acts recklessly thereby, it is illogical to say that "a defendant intended to kill the victim by being reckless."[76]

If a jurisdiction is going to recognize the offense, it is difficult to determine at what instant an attempted felony-murder occurs. Presumably, the doctrine would apply if the actor unintentionally wounds a person during the commission of the felony. But, in one state in which the offense is recognized, an attempted felony-murder conviction was allowed when a rapist fired his weapon but struck nobody.[77] Indeed, one may ask whether firing of a weapon is necessary. Suppose that an attempted rapist displays a gun or knife and *V* suffers an

---

[72] Enker, Note 63, *supra*, at 855.

[73] See § 31.06, *infra*.

[74] White v. State, 585 S.W.2d 952 (Ark. 1979); Fla. Stat. ch. § 782.051 (2005).

[75] Among the states that have recently ruled that attempted felony-murder is not a cognizable offense are State v. Robinson, 883 P.2d 764, 767 (Kan. 1994); State v. Lea, 485 S.E.2d 874, 877 (N.C. Ct. App. 1997); State v. Kimbrough, 924 S.W.2d 888, 892 (Tenn. 1996); and Goodson v. Commonwealth, 467 S.E.2d 848, 855 (Va. Ct. App. 1996).

[76] State v. Kimbrough, 924 S.W.2d 888, 892 (Tenn. 1996).

[77] White v. State, 585 S.W.2d 952 (Ark. 1979).

unforeseeable non-lethal heart-attack? In Florida, "attempted felony murder" occurs when one "commits, aids or abets an intentional act that is not an essential element of the felony and that could, but does not, cause the death of another."[78] It would seem that conviction under this remarkable statute would be possible in the latter hypothetical. Indeed, it is not clear that the victim would have to suffer the cardiac attack in order for an attempted felony-murder conviction to be allowed.

[b] Attempted Manslaughter

A person who intentionally kills another in sudden heat of passion, as the result of adequate provocation, is guilty of voluntary manslaughter.[79] If a person in such an emotional state attempts to kill the provoker, but fails, the actor may properly be convicted of attempted voluntary manslaughter.[80] No reason of logic precludes this result, as the provoked actor possesses the specific intent to kill.

A person may not be convicted of attempted *involuntary* manslaughter, when the latter offense is based on a *mens rea* of criminal negligence or some other state of mind other than intent-to-kill.[81] It is illogical to say that a person can intentionally commit an unintentional crime.[82]

[C] "Conduct" Crimes

The problems described in the preceding subsection should be distinguished from those pertaining to "conduct" crimes, i.e., crimes whose *actus reus* are defined in terms of conduct rather than injurious results. For example, the offense of "reckless endangerment" punishes dangerous conduct, even if such endangering conduct does not result in further harm to others.

Although very little case law exists on the point, it is submitted that there is no logical reason why a person should not be convicted of an attempt to commit such a conduct crime, as long as she possesses the specific intent to engage in the conduct which, if performed, constitutes the substantive offense. For example, suppose that *D* drives her car blindfolded, as a practical joke. This conduct, it may be assumed, would constitute reckless endangerment. Therefore, if *D* enters her car, blindfolds herself, turns on the ignition, and is arrested at that

---

[78] Fla. Stat. ch. § 782.051(1) (2005).

[79] See § 31.07[B][2], *infra*.

[80] E.g., Cox v. State, 534 A.2d 1333, 1336 (Md. 1988); State v. Robinson, 643 A.2d 591, 597 (N.J. 1994).

[81] Cox v. State, 534 A.2d at 1336.

[82] Commonwealth v. Griffin, 456 A.2d 171, 177 (Pa. Super. Ct. 1983).

moment, she should be convicted of attempted reckless endangerment: She has intentionally committed the *actus reus* of the attempt by purposely blind-folding herself and turning on the car ignition; and she has the specific intent to drive the car on the road, the conduct that a jury could conclude was reck-less.[83]

[D] Attendant Circumstances

Suppose that *D*, believing that *V* is eighteen years of age, has sexual inter-course with her. In fact, *V* is 16, under the age of legal consent for intercourse. In a prosecution for statutory rape, *D*'s mistake of fact, even if reasonable, will not excuse him in most jurisdictions. This is because most statutory rape laws are interpreted to be strict-liability in nature in regard to the attendant cir-cumstance of the girl's age.

Suppose, however, that *D* is arrested immediately before intercourse occurs. Is *D* guilty of *attempted* statutory rape? That is, what *mens rea* regarding an attendant circumstance is required for the offense of attempt? Virtually all commentators agree that the ordinary specific-intent requirement of attempt law should not apply to attendant circumstances.[84] Some commentators favor the proposition that a person should be convicted of a criminal attempt if she is reckless with regard to any attendant circumstance.[85] Thus, in the statutory rape case, *D* would not be guilty of attempted statutory rape unless he knew that there was a substantial risk that the girl was underage.

Other commentators would not impose a special *mens rea* requirement regarding attendant circumstances in attempt prosecutions.[86] For them it is suf-ficient that the actor is as culpable regarding the attendant circumstance as is required for that element of the completed offense. These scholars reason that as long as the actor has the specific intent to engage in the conduct, or to cause the result, that is prohibited by the statute defining the substantive crime, the law should not artificially require culpability greater than is necessary to com-mit the target offense. The policy supporting the latter offense should preempt attempt doctrines. Following this reasoning, *D* would be guilty of attempted statutory rape: The target offense is one of strict liability with regard to the girl's age, so the same analysis would apply to the attempt.[87]

---

[83] Contra, Minshew v. State, 594 So. 2d 703, 713 (Ala. Crim. App. 1991) (holding that the offense of attempted reckless endangerment "is legally impossible").

[84] See Enker, Note 63, *supra*, at 867 n.58.

[85] E.g., Williams, Note 1, *supra*, at 619-20.

[86] E.g., J.C. Smith, *Two Problems in Criminal Attempts Reexamined — I*, 1962 Crim. L. Rev. 135, 143.

[87] Simmons v. State, 10 So. 2d 436, 438 (Fla. 1942)

§ 27.06 *ACTUS REUS* OF CRIMINAL ATTEMPTS[88]

[A] Policy Context

Neither the common law nor most statutes provide a clear vision of the *actus reus* of a criminal attempt. Unhelpful conclusory statements are frequently expressed. For example, an attempt involves "perpetration" rather than "preparation"; or the defendant's conduct must be "proximate" to completion, rather than "remote." Beyond this, courts have developed a myriad of sometimes overlapping rules or tests meant to identify the point, or line, past which conduct constitutes a criminal attempt. One court has conceded "that the line of demarkation [sic] is not a line at all but a murky 'twilight zone.' "[89] Indeed, the crime of attempt "expands and contracts and is redefined commensurately with the substantive offense"[90] — the more serious the offense, the sooner a criminal attempt will likely be found.

A major difficulty in drawing a line between noncriminal preparation and a criminal attempt is that courts are torn by competing policy considerations. On the one hand, there is the understandable desire of courts and legislators to ease the burden on the police, whose goal is to prevent crimes from occurring. Thus, as one court has candidly put it, an attempt occurs when "acts of preparation when coupled with intent have reached a point at which they pose a danger to the public so as to be worthy of law's notice."[91] On the other hand, if courts authorize too early police intervention, innocent persons, as well as those with still barely formed criminal intentions — persons who might voluntarily turn back from criminal activity — may improperly or needlessly be arrested.

The struggle to find the proper demarcation line is also a function of the debate between subjectivists and objectivists.[92] Generally speaking, subjectivists favor an *actus reus* test of attempt that allows for early attachment of guilt. This generalization follows from the underlying premises of the doctrine. For subjectivists, proof of an actor's dangerousness, as evidenced by her *mens rea*, is paramount. Intention, however, can be proved through confessions, independent evidence of the actor's motive to commit the offense, and third-party testimony regarding the defendant's state of mind. It follows from this that any conduct, no matter how slight, that corroborates the defendant's alleged *mens rea*, should suffice for a criminal attempt.

---

[88] See generally Robert Batey, *Minority Report and the Law of Attempt*, 1 Ohio St. J. Crim. L. 689 (2004); Herbert Wechsler et al., *The Treatment of Inchoate Crimes in the Model Penal Code of the American Law Institute: Attempt, Solicitation, and Conspiracy [Pt. 1]*, 61 Colum. L. Rev. 571, 586-592 (1961).

[89] United States v. Williamson, 42 M.J. 613, 617 n.2 (N.M. Ct. Crim. App. 1995).

[90] Cox v. State, 534 A.2d 1333, 1335 (Md. 1988).

[91] State v. Otto, 629 P.2d 646, 653 (Idaho 1981) (Bakes, C.J., dissenting).

[92] For an explanation of these doctrines, see § 27.03, *supra*.

For objectivists, the *actus reus* element has independent significance, because adherents to this theory do not believe that society should use its coercive power against inchoate conduct unless the actor has caused some social harm, at least in the form of societal apprehension of criminal activity. Often, however, conduct does not lose its ambiguity and result in societal apprehension until far into the criminal transaction.

Objectivists believe that unchecked subjectivism, with its emphasis on *mens rea* and de-emphasis on conduct, endangers civil liberties, and too easily results in conviction of innocent persons. They fear that subjectivism may result in criminal liability for little more than bad thoughts. Moreover, guilt may too often be based on unreliable confessions, and other circumstantial evidence of an actor's alleged motivations. In contrast, subjectivists reason that if a society must wait until conduct unambiguously demonstrates its criminality, crime prevention will be frustrated.

[B] The Tests

[1] General Observations

"Much ink has been spilt in an attempt to arrive at a satisfactory standard for telling where preparation[] ends and attempt begins."[93] Generally speaking, the "attempt" tests that have developed over the years fall into two categories: those that focus on how much remains to be done before the crime is committed; and those that consider how much has already occurred.

In light of the conflicting policy considerations relating to attempt law, there is little or no way to predict with certainty where a court will draw the critical line between preparation and perpetration in a particular case. However, various factors come into play, including: (1) whether the act in question appears to be dangerously close to causing tangible harm, so that police intervention cannot realistically be delayed;[94] (2) the seriousness of the threatened harm, i.e., "the more serious the crime attempted . . . , the further back in the series of acts leading up to the consummated crime should the criminal law reach in holding the defendant guilty for an attempt"[95] and (3) the strength of the evidence of the actor's *mens rea*, i.e., the more clearly the intent to commit the offense is proven, the less proximate the acts need to be to consummation of the offense.[96]

---

[93] Mims v. United States, 375 F.2d 135, 148 (5th Cir. 1967).

[94] Arnold N. Enker, *Impossibility in Criminal Attempts — Legality and the Legal Process*, 53 Minn. L. Rev. 665, 674 (1969).

[95] Sayre, Note 1, *supra*, at 845.

[96] See People v. Berger, 280 P.2d 136, 138 (Cal. Ct. App. 1955).

The most frequently used common law tests or factors are described below. (The "substantial step" test, formulated by the American Law Institute and included in the Model Penal Code, is described at § 27.09, *infra*.) It should be noted at the outset, however, that: (1) most states rarely adopt a single test as the exclusive basis for determining when an attempt has occurred;[97] and (2) the names of the tests (if, indeed, they are provided) and their precise descriptions vary by jurisdiction.

[2] "Last Act" Test

Some courts used to state that a criminal attempt only occurred when the person performed all of the acts that she believed were necessary to commit the target offense.[98] Applying this standard, an attempted murder-by-shooting does not occur until *D* pulls the trigger of the gun; an attempted theft of a museum painting does not take place until *D* begins to remove the property from the wall; and an attempted arson does not occur unless *D* sets fire to the dwelling that she hopes to destroy. Today, there is general agreement that an attempt occurs *at least* by the time of the last act, but no jurisdiction *requires* that it reach this stage on all occasions.

Little commends the last-act standard, except for its bright-line nature. As the examples of its application suggest, the police would be stymied by such a rule; it would virtually be impossible to prevent commission of a substantive crime.[99] To the extent that subjectivist principles are important, an actor's dangerousness can be identified well before the last act; and, from an objectivist viewpoint, social harm can occur, and the criminality of an actor's conduct can often be discerned, before the final act.

[3] "Physical Proximity" Test

Some courts state that, while an actor's conduct need not reach the last act, it must be "proximate" to the completed crime, in that "it must approach sufficiently near to it to stand either as the first or some subsequent step in a *direct movement* towards the commission of the offense after the preparations are made."[100] Or, as another court has explained, for an act to be indicted as an attempt, "it must go so far that it would result, or apparently result in the

---

[97] E.g., Hudson v. State, 745 So. 2d 997, 1000 n.3 (Fla. Dist. Ct. App. 1999) (noting that Florida has not expressly adopted a particular "attempt" test, and stating that "[a]dopting one approach to the exclusion of the other[s] . . . may not be advisable").

[98] E.g., Regina v. Eagleton, 6 Cox Crim. Cas. 559, 571 (1855).

[99] "[T]he law of attempts would be largely without function if it could not be invoked until the trigger was pulled, the blow struck, or the money seized." People v. Dillon, 668 P.2d 697, 703 (Cal. 1983).

[100] State v. Dowd, 220 S.E.2d 393, 396 (N.C. Ct. App. 1975) (emphasis added).

actual commission of the crime it was designed to effect, if not extrinsically hindered or frustrated by extraneous circumstances."[101]

In essence, according to this test, an attempt does not arise unless an actor has it within her power to complete the crime almost immediately. For example, *D* would be guilty of attempted robbery if, weapon in hand, she has her victim in view and can immediately proceed to rob her, absent external factors, such as the intervention of the police. On the other hand, applying this test, an attempt does not occur if two men, intending to trick the victim out of his money, convince him to go to the bank and withdraw some of his cash, but the culprits are arrested before the victim withdraws the cash, and before they can make overtures to secure the money from him.[102]

[4] "Dangerous Proximity" Test

In a series of cases,[103] Justice Oliver Wendell Holmes formulated a test that incorporates the just-discussed "physical proximity" standard, but in somewhat more flexible form: According to this standard, a person is guilty of an attempt when her conduct is in "dangerous proximity to success,"[104] or when an act "is so near to the result that the danger of success is very great."[105] There is no clear point of proximity — "[e]very question of proximity must be determined by its own circumstances"[106] — but Holmes observed that courts consider three factors: the "nearness of the danger, the greatness of the harm, and the degree of apprehension felt."[107] Thus, in a prosecution for attempted murder by poisoning, Holmes observed that

> the gravity of the crime, the uncertainty of the result, and the seriousness of the apprehension, coupled with the great harm likely to result from poison, even if not enough to kill, would warrant holding the liability for an attempt to begin at a point more remote from the possibility of accomplishing what is expected than might be the case with lighter crimes.[108]

---

[101] Commonwealth v. Kelley, 58 A.2d 375, 377 (Pa. Super. Ct. 1948); see also People v. Buffum, 256 P.2d 317, 321 (Cal. 1953), overruled on other grounds by People v. Morante, 975 P.2d 1071 (Cal. 1999) ("[I]t must be in such progress that it will be consummated unless interrupted by circumstances independent of the will of the attempter. . . .").

[102] Commonwealth v. Kelley, 58 A.2d 375 (Pa. Super. Ct. 1948).

[103] Commonwealth v. Kennedy, 48 N.E. 770 (Mass. 1897); Commonwealth v. Peaslee, 59 N.E. 55 (Mass. 1901); Hyde v. United States, 225 U.S. 347 (1912) (dissenting opinion).

[104] Hyde v. United States, 225 U.S. at 388 (Holmes, J., dissenting).

[105] People v. Rizzo, 158 N.E. 888, 889 (N.Y. 1927).

[106] Commonwealth v. Kennedy, 48 N.E. at 771.

[107] Oliver Wendell Holmes, Jr., The Common Law 68 (1881).

[108] Commonwealth v. Kennedy, 48 N.E. at 771.

Applying the dangerous-proximity standard, one state court has held that a person who, with intent to possess cocaine, orders contraband from a supplier, meets a courier at her home, examines the goods, but rejects them on quality grounds, is guilty of attempted possession of a controlled substance;[109] in contrast, a person who tells the courier that she will buy the drugs once she obtains sufficient funds, and schedules a later meeting to consummate the sale, but who is arrested immediately, is not guilty of an attempt.[110]

One of the most famous — and controversial — applications of this standard occurred in *People v. Rizzo*,[111] in which four armed men drove around looking for V, whom they expected would be withdrawing a large sum of money from the bank. They entered various buildings looking for their victim. Suspicious, two police officers placed the men under surveillance. Finally, the suspects were arrested when one of them entered another building. V was not present where the arrest occurred.

With apparent embarrassment, the court overturned the conviction. While commending "[t]he police of the city of New York [for their] excellent work in this case by preventing the commission of a serious crime," and expressing their "great satisfaction to realize that we have such wide-awake guardians of our peace," the court concluded that in the absence of a victim, the armed suspects were not dangerously close to success. It is submitted here, however, that the result in this case, although correct under the physical-proximity standard, is probably wrong under the dangerous-proximity standard, in view of the seriousness of the planned offense and the degree of reasonable apprehension experienced in this case by the officers who observed the defendants' conduct.

The beneficial feature of Holmes' test is its flexibility in comparison to the potentially more strict physical-proximity standard. On the other hand, the test provides little guidance to police officers on the street, who must determine at what point they may properly arrest a suspect.

[5] "Indispensable Element" Test

In determining proximity, some courts "emphasize[] any indispensable aspect of the criminal endeavor over which the actor has not yet acquired control."[112] For example, according to this standard, an actor who does not yet possess a necessary instrumentality for the crime, e.g., a gun for a murder or the equipment needed to manufacture illegal drugs, has not yet crossed the line from prepa-

---

[109] People v. Acosta, 609 N.E.2d 518, 519 (N.Y. 1993).

[110] People v. Warren, 489 N.E.2d 240, 241-42 (N.Y. 1985).

[111] 158 N.E. 888 (N.Y. 1927).

[112] Wechsler et al., Note 88, *supra*, at 587.

ration to perpetration;[113] and an offense that requires action by an innocent person cannot be attempted until such action is completed.[114]

This test, although easier to apply than the dangerous-proximity standard, is arbitrary. The presence or absence of an indispensable element often says little regarding the actor's culpability, the firmness of her intentions, or the degree to which prior conduct may have disturbed the public's repose.

[6] "Probable Desistance" Test

The preceding tests focus on the actor's proximity to successful completion of the crime, i.e., on how much remains to be done. In contrast, the Commentary to the American Law Institute has described (but not endorsed) another standard, which it terms the "probable desistance" test, that centers on how far the defendant has already proceeded. Specifically, a court will not find an attempt unless, in the ordinary course of events, "the actor . . . reached a point where it was unlikely that he would have voluntarily desisted from his effort to commit the crime."[115]

According to this standard, a man who induced a youth to come to his house for improper sexual relations and met the intended victim as the latter exited a taxicab, was guilty of attempted lewd and lascivious acts on a minor.[116] But a woman who altered a prescription form for "Tylenol 3" (containing codeine) so that she could obtain "11" refills rather than the "1" specified by the doctor, and who brought it to a pharmacy to fill the prescription for the first time, was not guilty of attempted fraudulent acquisition of a controlled substance, because there existed reasonable doubt whether she would have returned twice more (once to get the refill to which she was entitled, and then to obtain a refill to which she was *not* entitled).[117]

Factfinders called upon to make the necessary judgment do not try to determine whether the defendant reached her own psychological point of unlikely desistance; instead they try to identify the "point of no return" of an ordinary person in the actor's shoes.[118] What is unclear is how a jury, presumably com-

---

[113] See also State v. Addor, 110 S.E. 650 (N.C. 1922) (there was no attempt to manufacture "spiritous liquors" because the defendants did not yet possess a still, necessary for production of the illegal whiskey).

[114] E.g., In re Schurman, 20 P. 277 (Kan. 1889) (S, with the intent to defraud a life insurance company, feigned death; X, the beneficiary under the policy, and an innocent party to the scheme, had not yet filed a claim; held: S is not guilty of an attempt to defraud the company).

[115] American Law Institute, Comment to § 5.01, at 325.

[116] Hudson v. State, 745 So. 2d 997, 1000 n.3 (Fla. Dist. Ct. App. 1999).

[117] State v. Henthorn, 581 N.W.2d 544, 547 (Wis. Ct. App. 1998).

[118] Berry v. State, 280 N.W.2d 204, 209 (Wis. 1979) ("The defendant's conduct must pass that point where most men, holding such an intention as the defendant holds, would think better of their conduct and desist.").

posed of law-abiding persons, determine when an ordinary would-be criminal would or would not desist.

[7] "Unequivocality" Test

According to the unequivocality (or *res ipsa loquitur*) test, an act does not constitute an attempt until it ceases to be equivocal. That is, an attempt occurs when a person's conduct, standing alone, unambiguously manifests her criminal intent.[119] It is as if the jury observed the conduct in video form with the sound muted (so as not to hear the actor's potentially incriminating remarks), and sought to decide from the conduct alone whether the accused was attempting to commit the offense for which she was prosecuted.[120]

For example, in *People v. Miller*,[121] *M* threatened to kill *V*, whom *M* accused of harassing his wife. Later that day, *M* went armed with a rifle to a field where *C*, the local constable, and *V*, standing approximately thirty yards further away, were working. *M* walked in the direction of *C* and *V*, stopped, loaded his rifle but did not aim it, and resumed his approach. At some point either before or after *M* loaded his weapon, *V* fled at a right angle from *M*'s line of approach. *C* took possession of *M*'s rifle without resistance. The court remarkably held that *M* was not guilty of attempted murder, because "up to the moment the gun was taken from the defendant, no one could say with certainty whether [he] had come into the field to carry out his threat to kill [*V*] or merely to demand his arrest by [*C*]."

The unequivocality test is in general harmony with the objectivist goal of reserving criminal liability for those whose conduct manifests criminality and, as a consequence, causes social apprehension. The test, however, has been attacked as impractical. For example, in a leading case in support of the doctrine,[122] the court stated that buying a box of matches to burn a haystack is too ambiguous to justify conviction for attempted arson, but that "he who takes matches to a haystack and there lights one of them," acts unambiguously. However, as one scholar has shown,[123] the unequivocality standard fails to work in this case, because a person who lights a match near a haystack may only intend to light a pipe. Thus, in this example, either we must say that the actor's conduct is equivocal (in which case, police intervention would be improper until the last act occurs, e.g., when the match is tossed into the hay), or we must concede

---

[119] People v. Staples, 6 Cal. App. 3d 61, 67 (1970) (an attempt occurs "when it becomes clear what the actor's intention is and when the acts done show that the perpetrator is actually putting his plan into action").

[120] See J.W. Cecil Turner, *Attempts to Commit Crimes*, 5 Cambridge L.J. 230, 236-38 (1934); Hamiel v. State, 285 N.W.2d at 645 n.4 (quoting Turner); State v. Henthorn, 581 N.W.2d 544, 547 (Wis. Ct. App. 1998) (applying the Turner test to the facts set out in the text at Note 117).

[121] 42 P.2d 308 (Cal. 1935).

[122] King v. Barker, [1924] N.Z.L.R. 865.

[123] Williams, Note 1, *supra*, at 630.

that after conduct manifests criminality, a later act may render it ambiguous again (in which case the standard may not adequately protect the innocent from arrest).

§ 27.07 DEFENSE: IMPOSSIBILITY[124]

[A] The Issue

D wants to kill *V*. Standing outside *V*'s house, she fires a gun at the bed in which she believes *V* is sleeping. *V* is not killed because she is not at home. Is *D* guilty of attempted murder, even though it was impossible for *D* to kill *V* under these circumstances?

Our intuitions almost certainly tell us that *D* should be convicted of an attempt. She has the requisite *mens rea*, and she has performed every act in her power to kill *V*. From a policy perspective, too, *D* merits punishment — she is dangerous, culpable, and has acted in a manner that would cause societal apprehension. The law seemingly confirms our moral intuitions and legal analysis: *D* almost certainly is guilty of attempted murder.[125]

However, suppose that we change the facts slightly. Suppose that when *D* fires the gun, *V* is in the bed, but is already dead from a coincidental heart attack. That is, *V* is a corpse, rather than a "human being," as defined by homicide law. Is *D* *now* guilty of attempted murder? No, according to dicta in various court opinions.[126] Is this dicta wrong, or can this example be distinguished in a principled manner from the "empty bed" case?

---

[124] See generally Larry Alexander, *Inculpatory and Exculpatory Mistakes and the Fact/Law Distinction: An Essay in Memory of Myke Bayles*, 12 Law & Phil. 33 (1993); Fernand N. Dutile & Harold F. Moore, *Mistake and Impossibility: Arranging a Marriage Between Two Difficult Partners*, 74 Nw. U. L. Rev. 166 (1979); Enker, Note 94, *supra*; Norman J. Finkel et al., *Lay Perspectives on Legal Conundrums: Impossible and Mistaken Act Cases*, 19 Law & Human Behav. 593 (1995); George P. Fletcher, *Constructing a Theory of Impossible Attempts*, Crim. Just. Ethics, Winter/Spring 1986, at 53; John Hasnas, *Once More unto the Breach: The Inherent Liberalism of the Criminal Law and Liability for Attempting the Impossible*, 54 Hastings L.J. 1 (2002); Graham Hughes, *One Further Footnote on Attempting the Impossible*, 42 N.Y.U. L. Rev. 1005 (1967); Ira P. Robbins, *Attempting the Impossible: The Emerging Consensus*, 23 Harv. J. on Legis. 377 (1986); Kenneth W. Simons, *Mistake and Impossibility, Law and Fact, and Culpability: A Speculative Essay*, 81 J. Crim. L. & Criminology 447 (1990); Weigend, Note 33, *supra*.

[125] E.g., State v. Mitchell, 71 S.W. 175, 177 (Mo. 1902). The words "seemingly" and "almost certainly" are used in the text because one English trial judge, in giving instructions to a jury in a case *not* involving these facts, suggested a contrary conclusion. Rex v. Osborn, 84 J.P. 63, 63 (Central Crim. Ct. 1919) (suggesting that if *O*, intending to kill *V*, enters *V*'s bedroom and strikes the pillow with a hatchet, but *V* is not in bed and miles away, *O* is *not* guilty of attempted murder because *O* "has not yet got at the thing near enough to attempt it"). It should be noted that when the actor is arrested prior to completing all of the requisite acts, courts are apt to consider the issue in terms of the physical-proximity or dangerous-proximity standards. See § 27.06[B][3]-[4], *supra*.

[126] State v. Taylor, 133 S.W.2d 336, 341 (Mo. 1939); State v. Guffey, 262 S.W.2d 152, 156 (Mo. Ct. App. 1953); see State v. Logan, 656 P.2d 777, 778 (Kan. 1983).

Or, suppose that we move our case to a forest. *D* and *V* are hunting together; *D* wants to use this opportunity to kill *V*, so she shoots at *V* in the woods. As it turns out "*V*" — the object at which she aimed — is a tree stump. Or *V*, sensing danger, displays a wax facsimile of herself, and it is this object that hunter-*D* shoots. Attempted murder? No, according to dicta and a holding in equivalent circumstances.[127]

Now, consider an increasingly frequent Internet scenario.[128] Suppose that *D* enters an Internet chat room and "converses" with *V*, whom *D* believes is an underage female, but who actually is an undercover male decoy. If *D* sends *V* an obscene photograph by electronic mail, he cannot be convicted of distribution of obscene materials to a minor, since *V* was not a minor, but may he be convicted of *attempted* distribution?[129] Or, if *D* makes plans with *V* to meet for sexual relations, may *D* be convicted of "attempted sexual performance upon a child" when he arrives at the planned site only to learn that the 13-year-old female turned out to be a 47-year-old male Internet undercover officer?[130]

Finally consider these two cases. In each one, a male has sexual intercourse with a 17-year-old female in a jurisdiction that sets the age of consent for intercourse at sixteen. In other words, in both cases statutory rape has *not* occurred. *D1*, however, believed that the girl was fifteen, so he thought that he was committing statutory rape.[131] *D2* knew that the girl was seventeen, but he incorrectly believed that the lawful age of consent was eighteen.[132] Should either or both of these cases constitute *attempted* statutory rape?

The real cases, and imaginative hypotheticals, go on and on. In each of these cases, the actor presumably has the requisite *mens rea*, and has done everything in her power to commit the target offense. But, in each of these cases, the desired outcome is predestined to fail — for one reason or another, it was impossible for the actor to succeed in consummating the offense Therefore, these cases raise the same issue: whether a person should be convicted for an attempt that cannot succeed. In other words, is "impossibility" a defense to the crime of attempt?

---

[127] See State v. Guffey, 262 S.W.2d 152, 156 (Mo. Ct. App. 1953) (*G*, a hunter, was not guilty of attempting to kill a deer out of season when he shot at a wax-dummy deer); Regina v. M'Pherson, 7 Cox Crim. Cas. 281, 284 (1857) (dictum, tree stump); Rex v. Osborn, 84 J.P. at 64 (same).

[128] See generally Audrey Rogers, *New Technology, Old Defenses: Internet Sting Operations and Attempt Liability*, 38 U. Rich. L. Rev. 477 (2004).

[129] People v. Thousand, 631 N.W.2d 694 (Mich. 2001).

[130] Chen v. State, 42 S.W.3d 926 (Tex. Crim. App. 2001).

[131] Notice that this is a mirror image of the typical mistake-of-fact case, in which *D* believes that the female is old enough to consent, but she is not. In the typical case, therefore, the *actus reus* of statutory rape is committed; at issue is *D*'s *mens rea*. In the present case, however, the *actus reus* of statutory rape did not occur, but *D* possessed a culpable mental state.

[132] Notice that this is a mirror image of the usual mistake-of-law case, in which an actor believes that her conduct is lawful, but it is not; here, *D* believed that he was violating a law, but he was not. If ignorance of the law does not ordinarily exculpate, may it nonetheless inculpate?

[B] General Rule

The common law rule regarding impossible attempts is easy to state. It distinguishes between two types of impossibility: "factual impossibility" and "legal impossibility." *At common law, legal impossibility is a defense; factual impossibility is not.*[133]

When one moves from the hornbook rule to specific cases, however, the law becomes exceedingly complex. Many pages of court opinions and scholarly literature have been filled in a largely fruitless effort to explain and justify the difference between factual and legal impossibility. Perhaps no aspect of the criminal law is more confusing and confused than the common law of impossible attempts.

In part because of the confusing nature of the law, and as a result of the influence of the Model Penal Code,[134] most jurisdictions no longer recognize legal impossibility as a defense.[135] However, as discussed below,[136] some arguments exist for retaining the defense in some form.

[C] Factual Impossibility

[1] In General

"Factual impossibility" exists when a person's intended end constitutes a crime, but she fails to consummate the offense because of an attendant circumstance unknown to her or beyond her control.[137] Examples of factual impossibility are: (1) a pickpocket putting her hand in the victim's empty pocket;[138] (2) an abortionist beginning the surgical procedure on a nonpregnant woman;[139] (3) an impotent male trying to have nonconsensual sexual intercourse;[140] (4) an assailant shooting into an empty bed where the intended victim customarily sleeps;[141] or (5) an individual pulling the trigger of an unloaded gun aimed at a person who is present.[142]

---

[133] American Law Institute, Comment to § 5.01, at 307-17; Williams, Note 1, *supra*, at §§ 206-07; Bandy v. State, 575 S.W.2d 278, 279-80 (Tenn. 1979); United States v. Oviedo, 525 F.2d 881, 883 (5th Cir. 1976).

[134] See § 27.09[E][1], *infra*.

[135] United States v. Hsu, 155 F.3d 189, 199 (3d Cir. 1998) (stating that "the great majority of jurisdictions" have abolished the defense).

[136] See § 27.07[D][3][b], *infra*

[137] United States v. Berrigan, 482 F.2d 171, 188 (3d Cir. 1973); see Robbins, Note 124, *supra*, at 380 n.13 (quoting similar definitions).

[138] E.g., People v. Twiggs, 223 Cal. App. 2d 455 (Ct. App. 1963).

[139] E.g., State v. Moretti, 244 A.2d 499 (N.J. 1968).

[140] E.g., Waters v. State. 234 A.2d 147 (Md. Ct. Spec. App. 1967).

[141] E.g., State v. Mitchell, 71 S.W. 175 (Mo. 1902).

[142] E.g., State v. Damms, 100 N.W.2d 592 (Wis. 1960).

In each of these examples the actor was mistaken regarding some fact relating to the actor, the victim, and/or the method of commission. More specifically, the target offense was not consummated because the actor chose the wrong victim (the pickpocket and abortion cases), the victim was not present (the empty bed case), the actor was not physically capable of committing the offense (the impotency case), or inappropriate means were used to commit the crime (the unloaded gun case). Had the circumstances been as the actors believed them to be, or hoped that they were (e.g., the pocket contained property; the woman was pregnant; the victim was in the bed; the actor was physically capable of having intercourse; the gun was loaded), the crimes would have been consummated.

It should not be surprising that lawmakers are unsympathetic to claims of factual impossibility. In each of the cases described above, the actor has demonstrated dangerousness (critical to subjectivists) and manifested criminality (important to objectivists). No good reason exists to recognize a defense merely because a person chooses her victim badly, does not use proper means to commit the crime, or for some other reason unrelated to her culpability does not successfully commit the offense.

[2] "Inherent" Factual Impossibility

Although factual impossibility is not a defense to a criminal attempt, "inherent impossibility" (or, more completely, "inherent *factual* impossibility") *may* be a defense. The doctrine of inherent impossibility has arisen primarily in scholarly literature and judicial dictum, but it is recognized as a statutory defense in at least one state.[143] To the extent that the defense is recognized, it applies if the method to accomplish the crime was one that "a reasonable person would view as completely inappropriate to the objectives sought."[144]

What is an example of an inherently impossible attempt? In one of the earliest cases to discuss the topic, an example was suggested: a " 'voodoo doctor' . . . [who] actually believed that his malediction would surely bring death to the person on whom he was invoking it."[145] However, this is a poor example, as an incantation is not a "completely inappropriate" means of killing another if the intended victim believes in hexes and, as a consequence, could die of fright. A better example of the doctrine is attempting "to sink a battleship with a popgun."[146]

---

[143] Minn. Stat. Ann. § 609.17(2) (2004) (providing an impossibility defense, if "such impossibility would have been clearly evident to a person of normal understanding"). For the Model Penal Code approach, see § 27.09[F][2], *infra*.

[144] State v. Bird, 285 N.W.2d 481, 482 (Minn. 1979).

[145] Commonwealth v. Johnson, 167 A. 344, 348 (Pa. 1933) (Maxey, J., dissenting).

[146] State v. Logan, 656 P.2d 777, 779 (Kan. 1983).

Should the law recognize an inherent-impossibility defense? For an objectivist, the answer is clear: If conduct is harmless and would appear so to a person of normal understanding, no societal apprehension will occur and, therefore, punishment is unjustified. For subjectivists, the defense is harder to support: The actor is no less morally blameworthy because she has chosen an inherently impossible way to consummate the offense; on the issue of dangerousness, one who is so far out of touch with reality that, for example, she believes that she can sink a battleship with a pop-gun, may later commit some other irrational and dangerous act, or such a person may come upon a more sensible way to accomplish her criminal task.

[D] Legal Impossibility

[1] Introductory Comments

"Legal impossibility" is an unfortunate term, for two reasons. First, there are two different categories of attempts that have been identified by courts as implicating "legal impossibility." Those two versions may be termed "pure" and "hybrid" legal impossibility. The failure of courts generally to distinguish between them creates confusion.[147]

Second, neither version of legal impossibility should be identified as such. As is developed below, hybrid legal impossibility cannot be distinguished from factual impossibility in any principled manner, and may properly be merged with it. On the other hand, pure legal impossibility may as accurately be identified as an application of the general principle of legality.[148]

The modern trend is to abolish legal impossibility (more accurately, "hybrid legal impossibility") as a defense.[149] However, "pure legal impossibility" remains a basis for exculpation.

[2] Pure Legal Impossibility

"Pure legal impossibility" arises "when the law does not proscribe the goal that the defendant sought to achieve."[150] The simplest case of pure legal impossibility occurs when a person performs a lawful act with a guilty conscience, i.e., she believes that she is committing a crime, but she is not. For example, as Jerome Hall has observed, "it is not a crime to throw even a Kansas steak into

---

[147] But see People v. Thousand, 631 N.W.2d 694, 698-700 (Mich. 2001) (recognizing the distinction).

[148] See § 5.01, *supra*.

[149] State v. Logan, 656 P.2d at 779; United States v. Hsu, 155 F.3d 189, 199 (3d Cir. 1998).

[150] Robbins, Note 124, *supra*, at 389.

a garbage can."[151] If *D* commits this dastardly act, she is guilty of no offense. And, even if she believes that there is such an offense, she is not guilty of *attempting* to commit this fanciful crime. Just as a person may not ordinarily escape punishment on the ground that she is ignorant of a law's existence,[152] it is also true that "we cannot punish people under laws that are purely the figments of their guilty imaginations."[153] Similarly, *D* is not guilty of a criminal attempt if, unknown to her, the legislature has repealed a statute that *D* believes that she is violating. For example, if *D* attempts to sell "bootleg" liquor after the repeal of the Prohibition laws, she is not guilty of an attempt even though she is unaware of their repeal.[154]

A more problematic situation occurs when an actor's conduct *is* prohibited, but cannot legally constitute the offense charged. *Wilson v. State*[155] is commonly (but not universally) treated as a "pure legal impossibility" case.[156] In *Wilson*, *W* was prosecuted for forgery because he added the number "1" to a check made out to him in the sum of "$2.50," so that he could receive "$12.50." Under state law, however, *W*'s actions did not constitute forgery because he tampered with a legally "immaterial" part of the check.[157] Consequently, the trial judge informed the jury that it could not convict *W* of forgery, but that it could convict him of the lesser offense of attempted forgery, which it did.

W's conviction was reversed. Although *W*'s actions may have constituted some offense,[158] they did *not* constitute the crime of forgery. Wisely or not, state lawmakers had excluded his conduct from the ambit of the crime of forgery. Therefore, *W* was not guilty of *attempted* forgery: Put simply, an actor's mistaken belief that she is committing Crime X does not make her guilty of *attempted* violation of Crime X, even if she might be guilty of Crime Y. This is no different than if a male touches a woman on her breasts without consent, believing this constitutes rape or, even more crazily, forgery. What the male did is *not* rape or forgery, although it constitutes a battery; therefore, the male is not guilty of *attempted* rape or *attempted* forgery simply because he may believe he has "raped" or "forged" his victim.

---

[151] Hall, Note 1, *supra*, at 595.

[152] See § 13.01[A], *supra*.

[153] Alexander, Note 124, *supra*, at 46.

[154] Thus, too, in the hypothetical described in the text at Note 132, *supra*, in which *D2* knew the age of the female with whom he had intercourse, but he mistakenly believed that his conduct constituted statutory rape, he would not be guilty of attempted statutory rape.

[155] 38 So. 46 (Miss. 1905).

[156] E.g., Robbins, Note 124, *supra*, at 390-91.

[157] Under state law at the time, when a discrepancy existed between the written words and the figures on a check, the words took precedence. As a result, *W*'s alteration of the numbers without changing the words constituted an immaterial change.

[158] *W* may have been guilty of attempted receiving property by false pretenses.

Although courts may treat the *Wilson* case, and the Kansas steak, bootleg-liquor, and breast-touching hypotheticals, as "legal impossibility" (more accurately, "pure legal impossibility") cases, the better basis for acquittal is the principle of legality. The legality principle provides that we should not punish people — no matter culpable or dangerous they may be — for conduct that does not constitute the charged offense at the time of the action. Therefore, it is similarly wrong to convict a person of an *attempt* to violate a law that is not, in fact, encompassed by the defendant's conduct.

[3] Hybrid Legal Impossibility

[a] In General

Hybrid legal impossibility (or what courts typically call, simply, "legal impossibility") exists if the actor's goal is illegal, but commission of the offense is impossible due to a *factual* mistake (and not simply a misunderstanding of the law) regarding the *legal* status of some attendant circumstance that constitutes an element of the charged offense.[159] As the preceding definition implies and as is clarified immediately below, this is a hybrid version of impossibility: The actor's impossibility claim includes both factual and legal aspects to it.

Courts have recognized a defense of legal impossibility or have stated that it would exist if *D*: (1) receives *un*stolen property believing that it was stolen;[160] (2) tries to pick the pocket of a stone image of a human;[161] (3) offers a bribe to a "juror" who is not a juror;[162] (4) tries to hunt deer out of season by shooting a stuffed animal;[163] (5) shoots a corpse believing that it is alive;[164] (6) shoots at a tree stump believing that it is a human;[165] or (7), in a prosecution for distribution of obscene literature to a minor, sends pornography to an adult, believing that she is a minor.[166]

Notice that in each of the preceding examples of hybrid legal impossibility, *D* was mistaken about a fact: whether the property had been stolen; whether a person was a juror; whether the victims were living human beings; whether the victim was an animal subject to being hunted out of season; or whether the victim was a minor.

---

[159] See Robbins, Note 124, *supra*, at 389-90.

[160] E.g., People v. Jaffe, 78 N.E. 169 (N.Y. 1906); Booth v. State, 398 P.2d 863 (Okla Crim. App. 1964).

[161] Trent v. Commonwealth, 156 S.E. 567, 569 (Va. 1931) (dictum).

[162] E.g., State v. Taylor, 133 S.W.2d 336 (Mo. 1939).

[163] E.g., State v. Guffey, 262 S.W.2d 152 (Mo. Ct. App. 1953).

[164] State v. Taylor, 133 S.W.2d 336 (Mo. 1939) (dictum).

[165] See the citations at Note 127, *supra*.

[166] People v. Thousand, 631 N.W.2d 694 (Mich. 2001).

But, what distinguishes these cases from simple "factual impossibility" is that these factual mistakes relate to the *legal* status of the defendant's conduct. A person is not guilty (and *cannot* be guilty) of "receiving stolen property with knowledge that it is stolen" unless the property is "stolen" in character. Likewise, one cannot legally bribe a juror unless the person bribed is a juror. The status of a victim as a "human being" — rather than as a corpse, tree stump, or statue — legally is necessary to commit the crime of murder or to "take and carry away the personal property *of another*." Putting a bullet into a stuffed deer cannot legally constitute the crime of killing a deer out of season. And, it cannot constitute the crime of distribution of obscene materials to a minor if the person to whom the materials are sent is not a minor.[167]

Ultimately any case of hybrid legal impossibility may reasonably be characterized as factual impossibility.[168] That is, by skillful characterization, one can describe virtually any case of hybrid legal impossibility, which is a common law defense, as an example of factual impossibility, which is *not* a defense. For example, if *D* shoots a corpse, believing that it is a human being, *D* would describe this as one of legal impossibility: "As a matter of law, shooting a corpse is not, and never can, constitute murder, because the offense of criminal homicide, by definition, only applies to the killing of human beings." The prosecutor, however, would couch the claim in factual impossibility terms: "If the factual circumstances had been as *D* believed them to be — that the 'victim' had been alive when *D* shot him — he would be guilty of murder."

Something is amiss when semantics alone, and not underlying policy, determines whether a defense will be recognized.

[b] Modern Approach: Abolition of the Defense

Most states have abolished the defense of hybrid legal impossibility on the subjectivist ground that an actor's dangerousness is "plainly manifested"[169] in such cases. In most jurisdictions, therefore, lawyers and courts no longer have to distinguish between hybrid legal impossibility and factual impossibility.

Is abolition a good idea? Two objectivist objections to the modern trend deserve attention. First, some (certainly not all) cases of hybrid legal impossibility involve objectively innocuous conduct. For example, putting one's hands

---

[167] The latter case is similar in principle to the hypothetical set out at Note 131, *supra*, in which *D1* had intercourse with a female old enough to consent, although he believed that she was underage. This example involves hybrid legal impossibility: *D1* was mistaken about a fact (the girl's age); but the attendant circumstance of her age is of legal significance in that sexual intercourse with a 17-year-old female (her true age) does not constitute statutory rape.

[168] People v. Thousand, 631 N.W.2d at 699 (quoting this treatise). The converse of the statement in the text is not necessarily true. For example, there is no realistic issue of legal impossibility when *D* tries to fire an unloaded gun or puts her hand in an empty pocket in order to pick it.

[169] American Law Institute, Comment to § 5.01, at 309.

near the "pocket" of a statue, shooting a tree stump, or receiving unstolen property are innocuous acts. These acts, by themselves, do not manifest criminality of any kind, so they should not induce societal apprehension of impending crime (punishable social harm, to an objectivist). What converts these harmless actions into crimes are the actors' criminal thoughts. For objectivists, punishment based essentially on criminal thoughts is objectionable, and represents a troubling feature of the "impossibility defense" abolitionist movement.

Second, when conduct is objectively innocent, there exists "a significant risk of enforcement error or abuse."[170] That is, a conviction may be obtained of an entirely innocent person (one who does not even have a criminal thought) or one whose "guilt" constitutes little more than a passing guilty thought — someone who isn't even dangerous in subjectivist terms. Although abolitionists contend that the risk of punishment of such a person "is more theoretical than practical,"[171] prosecutions of this sort *do* occur.

For example, in *Anderton v. Ryan*,[172] R purchased a video recorder at a deep discount. Because of its price, R believed that it had been stolen and, therefore, she believed that she was guilty of the offense of "handling stolen property." Later, her house was burglarized. When the police routinely questioned her about the lost goods, including the video recorder, R admitted to the officers that she had purchased what she believed at the time was a stolen recorder. Based on her admission, she was prosecuted for *attempted* handling of stolen property.[173] She was convicted, based exclusively on her guilty feelings, truthfully admitted to police officers.[174]

As one scholar has observed, what the defendant in *Anderton* did is hardly unusual: "Almost all of us jump at the chance to purchase an item we want at a bargain price, often from non-retail sources."[175] Few of us, however, fear, prosecution if the bargain turns out to be just that — a lawful bargain. So, why was R prosecuted in *Anderton*? Perhaps overzealousness or prosecutorial abuse explains her case. But, more often, those who will be prosecuted in the absence

---

[170] Hasnas, Note 124, *supra*, at 60.

[171] American Law Institute, Comment to § 5.01, at 319-20.

[172] [1985] 2 All E.R. 355 (House of Lords).

[173] Because the recorder was never retrieved, no effort was made at trial to prove that it actually was stolen property when R purchased it. The court assumed, therefore, she had purchased *un*stolen property.

[174] In *Anderton*, the House of Lords ruled that R was not guilty of the offense, although it had to provide a very strained interpretation of a statute that appeared to abolish the defense of legal impossibility. Subsequently, the House of Lords overruled *Anderton*. Regina v. Shivpuri, [1986] 2 All E.R. 334. Much as in *Anderton*, the defendant in *Shivpuri* was convicted on the basis of an admission to customs officers that the suitcase he was attempting to bring into the country contained prohibited drugs, when in fact the substance in the suitcase turned out to be harmless vegetable matter. His conviction was upheld.

[175] Hasnas, Note 124, *supra*, at 60.

of an impossibility defense will be people with a "bad" background: "How secure can those of us with criminal records or other associations or characteristics that reduce our credibility with a jury be if a prosecutor can obtain a conviction for [attempted] receiving stolen property merely by convincing a jury that we believed the property to be stolen?"[176]

§ 27.08 DEFENSE: ABANDONMENT[177]

Once a person crosses the line from preparation to perpetration of an offense, i.e., once a criminal attempt has commenced, may the actor avoid conviction for the attempt if she abandons her criminal conduct before consummation of the target offense? For example, in *People v. McNeal*,[178] *M*, with the intention of raping *V*, grabbed *V* from a bus stop, took her at knifepoint to his home, pushed her onto a couch, and then began to fondle *V*. In an effort to prevent her rape, *V* begged *M* to let her go, explaining that she was trying to finish her education and that she was on the way to school to take two examinations. After *V* promised not to report him if he let her go, *M* apologized, took her to the bathroom so that she could fix her hair, and then walked her back to the bus stop. Clearly, *M*'s acts satisfied any reasonable test of attempted rape, but should he be entitled to defend his actions on the ground that he abandoned the rape before consummation?

Although there is disagreement on the matter, most scholars believe that abandonment was not a common law defense to attempt,[179] and many courts today continue to decline to recognize the defense.[180] To the extent that a defense of abandonment is recognized today, however, it applies only if the defendant *voluntarily* and *completely* renounces her criminal purpose. Abandonment by the defendant is voluntary when it is the result of repentance or a

---

[176] *Id.*

[177] See generally Paul R. Hoeber, *The Abandonment Defense to Criminal Attempt and Other Problems of Temporal Individuation*, 74 Cal. L. Rev. 377 (1986); Daniel G. Moriarty, *Extending the Defense of Renunciation*, 62 Temple L. Rev. 1 (1989).

[178] 393 N.W.2d 907 (Mich. Ct. App. 1986) (affirming a conviction for attempted criminal sexual conduct).

[179] Hoeber, Note 177, *supra*, at 381; Williams, Note 1, *supra*, at § 199; United States v. Smauley, 39 M.J. 853, 855 (N-M.C.M.R. 1994) (citing numerous treatises); but see American Law Institute, Comment to § 5.01, at 356-57 (stating that there is uncertainty on the matter, but suggesting that the prevailing rule favored a limited defense).

[180] E.g., United States v. Shelton, 30 F.3d 702, 706 (6th Cir. 1994). Even when abandonment is not recognized as a defense, however, a court may still find a defendant's abandonment relevant in an attempt prosecution. For example, in *Commonwealth v. McCloskey*, 341 A.2d 500 (Pa. Super. Ct. 1975), *M*, a prison inmate, scaled the fence leading to the prison recreation yard, but he then returned because he did not want to shame his family by escaping. *M* was convicted of attempted prison escape, but his conviction was overturned on the ground that *M*'s actions demonstrated that he was still only contemplating an escape, but had not yet begun attempting the act.

genuine change of heart.[181] Abandonment is not voluntary if the actor is motivated by unexpected resistance, the absence of an instrumentality essential to the completion of the crime, or some other circumstance that increases the likelihood of arrest or unsuccessful consummation of the offense.[182] And, the abandonment is not complete if the actor merely postpones the criminal endeavor until a better opportunity presents itself.[183]

There is also support for the proposition that a person may not claim abandonment as a defense, even if the actor's desistance is motivated by genuine remorse and is complete, once she has performed the last act necessary to commit the offense, or has already caused serious harm to the victim. For example, in one case,[184] S stabbed V, his uncle, became remorseful, and rushed V to a hospital. In an ensuing attempted murder prosecution, the court held that S's abandonment could not be claimed in these circumstances.

The common law no-defense rule is motivated by objectivist principles, namely, that once the social harm of an attempt has occurred, a person should no more be able to avoid conviction for the harm caused than if a thief were to repent for her actions and return the property after the crime has transpired. Although abandonment of an attempt, like voluntary restitution by a thief, may be relevant in sentencing, renunciation of a criminal purpose cannot undo the harm already inflicted.

Jurisdictions that recognize the defense do so on subjectivist grounds. First, the defense encourages desistance by the attempter. Second, by voluntarily and completely abandoning an offense, an actor demonstrates that she possesses a less dangerous character than an ordinary attempter or person who quits the offense out of fear of arrest.[185]

§ 27.09 MODEL PENAL CODE[186]

[A] Introductory Comments

According to the Commentary to Section 5.01 of the Model Penal Code, which is the Code provision on criminal attempts:

---

[181] Pyle v. State, 476 N.E.2d 124, 126 (Ind. 1985) (permitting a defense on the basis of repentance or "rising revulsion for the harm intended").

[182] People v. Cross, 466 N.W.2d 368, 369-70 (Mich. Ct. App. 1991); State v. Mahoney, 870 P.2d 65, 71 (Mont. 1994).

[183] American Law Institute, Comment to § 5.01, at 356.

[184] State v. Smith, 409 N.E.2d 1199, 1202 (Ind. Ct. App. 1980); accord, State v. Mahoney, 870 P.2d at 71.

[185] Sheckles v. State, 501 N.E.2d 1053, 1056 (Ind. 1986); People v. Taylor, 598 N.E.2d 693, 699 (N.Y. 1992).

[186] See generally Wechsler et al., Note 88, *supra*.

The literature and the decisions dealing with the definition of a criminal attempt reflect ambivalence as to how far the governing criterion should focus on the dangerousness of the actor's conduct, measured by objective standards, and how far it should focus on the dangerousness of the actor, as a person manifesting a firm disposition to commit a crime.[187]

That is, the law has struggled with the competing principles of objectivism and subjectivism. The drafters of the Code, however, are not ambivalent: "[T]he proper focus of attention is the actor's disposition. The Model Code provisions are accordingly drafted with this in mind."[188]

The Model Code's approach to criminal attempts — indeed, to all of the inchoate offenses — is subjectivist nearly throughout. It defines a criminal attempt in a manner that "make[s] amenable to the corrective process those persons who have manifested a propensity to engage in dangerous criminal activity."[189] Its treatment of defenses to criminal attempts (it abolishes the defense of hybrid legal impossibility, but recognizes the defense of abandonment), and the punishment it imposes for inchoate offenses (in general, it grades an inchoate crime at the same level as the completed offense), are similarly motivated by subjectivist goals.

Section 5.01 has had significant impact on American attempt law. Most of the federal courts apply the doctrines of Section 5.01, although Congress has not enacted the provision; and a large number of states have adopted the Code provision in its entirety or in part.[190]

[B] Criminal Attempt: In General

[1] Elements of the Offense

Generally speaking, a criminal attempt under the Code contains two elements: (1) the purpose to commit the target offense; and (2) conduct constituting a "substantial step" toward the commission of the target offense. These elements are explained more fully in subsections [C] and [D] below.

[2] Explaining Subsection (1)

Section 5.01, subsection (1), which defines a criminal attempt, is a complicated provision. It reads:

---

[187] American Law Institute, Comment to § 5.01, at 298 (footnote omitted).

[188] *Id.* (footnote omitted).

[189] United States v. Dworken, 855 F.2d 12, 16 (1st Cir. 1988).

[190] By the author's own research, at least twenty-five states have codified the Model Penal Code's "substantial step" standard, discussed in subsection [D], *infra*. As noted earlier, see § 27.07[B],

A person is guilty of an attempt to commit a crime if, acting with the kind of culpability otherwise required for commission of the crime, he:

> (a) purposely engages in conduct that would constitute the crime if the attendant circumstances were as he believes them to be; or
>
> (b) when causing a particular result is an element of the crime, does or omits to do anything with the purpose of causing or with the belief that it will cause such result without further conduct on his part; or
>
> (c) purposely does or omits to do anything that, under the circumstances as he believes them to be, is an act or omission constituting a substantial step in a course of conduct planned to culminate in his commission of the crime.

To analyze an attempt issue under subsection (1), it is necessary to ask and answer one or two questions. First, does the case involve a complete or incomplete attempt? Second, if the case involves a complete attempt, is the target offense a "result" crime (e.g., murder) or a "conduct" crime (e.g., driving an automobile under the influence of alcohol)?

Subsections (1)(a) and (1)(b) pertain to *completed* attempts. Specifically, subsection (1)(a) should be considered when the target offense of the completed attempt involves conduct; subsection (1)(b) applies to results. If the prosecution involves an *incomplete* attempt, subsection (1)(c) is used. However, this subsection must be read in conjunction with subsection (2), which elaborates on the meaning of "substantial step."

[C] *Mens Rea*

In general, a person is not guilty of a criminal attempt unless it was her purpose, i.e., her conscious objective, to engage in the conduct or to cause the result that would constitute the substantive offense.

There are two exceptions to the requirement of purpose. First, subsection (1)(b) expressly and subsection (1)(c) implicitly[191] provide that a person is guilty of an attempt to cause a criminal result if she *believes* that the result will occur, even if it were not her conscious object to cause it. For example, if *D* plants a bomb on an airplane in order to kill *V*, her husband, and the bomb fails to go off or is defused, she is guilty of attempted murder of *V*, because it was *D*'s conscious objective to take *V*'s life; but she would also be guilty of attempted

---

supra, the overwhelming trend is to abolish the legal impossibility defense, as the Code provides. At least twenty-two states statutorily recognize a Model Penal Code renunciation (abandonment) defense.

[191] American Law Institute, Comment to § 5.01, at 305 n.17.

murder of the other passengers in the airplane if she believed that they would die in the bombing.[192] The common law outcome in this case is uncertain.[193]

Second, the Commentary to Section 5.01 explains that the prefatory phrase in subsection (1) — "acting with the kind of culpability otherwise required for the commission of the crime" — means that the *mens rea* of "purpose" or "belief" does not necessarily encompass the attendant circumstances of the crime.[194] For "attendant circumstance" elements, it is sufficient that the actor possesses the degree of culpability required to commit the target offense. For example, if *D* may be convicted of statutory rape on proof that he was reckless as to the girl's age (the attendant circumstance), then he may convicted of *attempted* statutory rape if he was reckless, but not if he was negligent or innocent, as to the girl's age. If the material element of the girl's age is one of strict liability, i.e., *D* may be convicted of statutory rape although he reasonably believed that she was old enough to consent, then he may also be convicted of *attempted* statutory rape although he lacked a culpable mental state as to this attendant circumstance. The common law rule on this matter is uncertain.[195]

[D] *Actus Reus*

[1] In General

In a significant departure from the common law, the Model Penal Code shifts the focus of attempt law from what remains to be done, i.e., the actor's proximity to consummation of the offense, to what the actor has already done.[196] Subsection (1)(c) provides that, to be guilty of an offense, an actor must have done or omitted to do something that constitutes a "substantial step in a course of conduct planned to culminate in his commission of the crime." The premise of the Code is that one who engages in such purposive conduct is sufficiently dangerous to justify state intervention, even if she is not yet close to consummation of the offense. The "substantial step" standard is intended to "broaden the scope of attempt liability."[197]

Section 5.01(2) provides further content to the imprecise term "substantial step." First, it indicates that conduct is not a substantial step unless it strongly corroborates the defendant's criminal purpose. This language is meant to reduce the risk of conviction of innocent persons. It incorporates some aspects of the common law unequivocality test of attempt,[198] without including its potential

---

[192] *Id.* at 304-05.

[193] See Note 66, *supra*.

[194] American Law Institute, Comment to § 5.01, at 301-03.

[195] See § 27.05[D], *supra*.

[196] American Law Institute, Comment to § 5.01, at 329.

[197] *Id.*

[198] See § 27.06[B][7], *supra*.

stringencies. Specifically, this subsection does not require that the defendant's conduct *by itself* manifest criminality, as objectivists favor. Rather, the key words in the provision are "strongly corroborative": The actor's conduct, considered in light of all the circumstances, must add significantly to other proof of her criminal intent, such as a confession or other incriminating evidence.[199]

Second, subsection (2) provides a list of recurrent factual circumstances in which an actor's conduct, if strongly corroborative of her criminal purpose, "shall not be held insufficient as a matter of law." That is, if any of the enumerated instances are established, the jury as factfinder is entitled to evaluate whether the defendant has taken a substantial step;[200] and if the jury convicts the defendant of an attempt, this verdict may not be overturned on the ground that the defendant's conduct was insubstantial. The circumstances set out in subsection (2), drawn primarily from common law decisions in the field, include: lying in wait; searching for or following the contemplated victim of the crime; reconnoitering the contemplated scene of the crime; unlawful entry into a structure or building in which the crime will be committed; and possession of the materials to commit the offense, if they are specially designed for a criminal purpose.

[2] Attempt to Aid

Suppose that *D1* furnishes a gun to *X1* so that *X1* can kill *V1*. If *X1* attempts to kill *V1*, *X1* is guilty of attempted murder, and *D1* is also guilty of attempted murder, as an accomplice.[201]

Compare the preceding example with the following: *D2* furnishes a gun to *X2* so that *X2* can kill *V2*. *X2*, however, does *not* attempt to commit the offense. In this example, *X2* is not guilty of attempted murder. *D2*, in turn, is not guilty of aiding and abetting an attempted murder, since *X2* committed no such offense. Is *D2* guilty of *any* offense?

Conceptually, *D1* aided and abetted an attempt; *D2* attempted to aid and abet. Although *D1*'s liability for attempted murder is clear at common law, *D2* is guilty of no common law offense.[202] The Model Penal Code, however, takes a different approach: Under Section 5.01(3), a person may be convicted of a criminal attempt, *although a crime was neither committed nor attempted by another*, if: (1) the purpose of her conduct is to aid another in the commission of the

---

[199] American Law Institute, Comment to § 5.01, at 331.

[200] The jury is *not* informed that any of the enumerated factual circumstances, if proven, does, or may, constitute a substantial step. This list is used exclusively by the judge: If the prosecution has presented evidence of one or more of these subsection (2) factual circumstances, then the judge must permit the jury to consider whether the defendant's conduct constituted a "substantial step" (not otherwise defined), if such conduct is "strongly corroborative of the actor's criminal purpose."

[201] See generally Chapter 30, *infra*.

[202] See § 30.02[A][2], *infra*.

offense; and (2) such assistance *would* have made her an accomplice in the commission of the crime under the Code's complicity statute[203] if the offense had been committed or attempted.

In the hypothetical above, *D2* would be guilty under the Code of attempted murder (conceptually, she is guilty of attempting to aid and abet a murder), although *X2* did not attempt to commit the murder. *D2* is guilty because, if *X2* *had* attempted the crime, *D2 would have been* an accomplice in the attempt, by furnishing the gun for the purpose of the homicide.

The rationale of the rule is straightforward: A person who attempts to aid in the commission of an offense is as dangerous as one who successfully aids in its commission or attempted commission.[204] Therefore, under subjectivist principles, her conduct justifies punishment.

[E] Defenses

[1] Impossibility

[a] Hybrid Legal Impossibility

Section 5.01(1), reprinted in subsection [B] above, is designed to abolish the defense of hybrid legal impossibility. This outcome may be seen by considering three examples. First, assume that *D1* receives unstolen property, believing that it was stolen, and is prosecuted for attempting to receive stolen property. As this case involves a completed attempt, and the offense charged is a conduct crime, subsection (1)(a) applies. Based on the language of subsection (1)(a), *D1* is guilty if she purposely engaged in conduct (receiving the property) that would constitute a crime *"if the attendant circumstances were as [s]he believes them to be."* In this case, the attendant circumstance is the "stolenness" of the property. *D1* believed that the property was stolen. Had the circumstance been as she believed it to be, she *would* have been guilty of the offense of receiving stolen property. Therefore, she is guilty of attempting to receive stolen property.

Second, suppose that *D2* shoots to kill *V*, unaware that *V* is already dead. Although this might constitute hybrid legal impossibility, and a defense at common law,[205] *D2* is guilty of attempted murder under the Model Penal Code.[206] Because this involves a completed attempt, and criminal homicide is a result crime, subsection (1)(b) applies. Here, *D2* performed an act — firing a gun at *V* — "with the purpose of causing or with the belief that it [would] cause such result [*V*'s death] without further conduct on [*D2*'s] part." The fact that *V* was a corpse rather than a human being does not exculpate *D2*.

---

[203] Model Penal Code § 2.06. See § 30.09, *infra*.

[204] American Law Institute, Comment to § 5.01, at 356.

[205] See § 27.07[D][3][a], *supra*.

[206] People v. Dlugash, 363 N.E.2d 1155 (N.Y. 1977).

Finally, suppose that in either of these examples, the defendant is arrested prior to completion of the last act, but after commission of a substantial step. For example, suppose that *D1* prepares to receive the property but is arrested immediately before she takes possession; or, suppose that *D2* is arrested with the gun aimed at the corpse. Because further actions were intended in these cases, subsection (1)(c), rather than (1)(a) or (1)(b), applies. Still, *D1* and *D2* will be convicted because they performed acts that, "under the circumstances as [they] believe[d] them to be" — the property was stolen, *V* was alive — consti- tuted "a substantial step in a course of conduct planned to culminate in . . . com- mission of the crime[s]."

The abrogation of the impossibility defense conforms with subjectivist prin- ciples. One who intends to commit a crime, but who fails to consummate it because of a circumstance of which the person is unaware, is as dangerous (and culpable) as one who successfully commits the crime or who does not com- mit it because of police intervention.

One aspect of the Code's treatment of impossibility cases deserves special attention. Observe that only in subsection (1)(c) cases, i.e., in cases of *incomplete* attempts, does the Code require that the actor's conduct be strongly corrobora- tive of her criminal purpose. The typical impossibility case, however, involves a *completed* attempt, in which event subsection (1)(a) or (1)(b) applies. In the usual impossibility case, therefore, corroboration of the actor's criminal purpose is *not* required under the Code.

This feature of the Code is objectionable to advocates of objectivism. As dis- cussed earlier,[207] some impossibility cases involve objectively innocuous conduct. Thus, if *D* buys unstolen electronic equipment on the street believing that it is stolen, her conduct objectively is innocent. Nonetheless, she may be convicted under the Code of an attempt to receive stolen property, although the radio was not stolen, on the basis of circumstantial evidence of criminal purpose. The dan- ger of conviction of an innocent person, therefore, is unmitigated.[208]

[b] Pure Legal Impossibility

Although the Code does not expressly so provide, the American Law Institute did not intend to abolish the defense of pure legal impossibility. The Commen- tary states that "it is of course necessary [pursuant to the principle of legality] that the result desired or intended by the actor constitute a crime."[209]

---

[207] See § 27.07[D][3][b], *supra*.

[208] The Commentary's response to this criticism is that it is "unlikely . . . that persons will be prosecuted on the basis of admissions alone." American Law Institute, Comment to § 5.01, at 319- 20. However, as discussed earlier, prosecutions of this sort do occur on occasion.

[209] American Law Institute, Comment to § 5.01, at 318.

[2] Renunciation (Abandonment)

The Code recognizes an affirmative defense of "renunciation of criminal purpose." A person is not guilty of an attempt if: (1) she abandons her effort to commit the crime or prevents it from being committed; and (2) her conduct manifests
a complete and voluntary renunciation of her criminal purpose.[210]

Under this provision, renunciation is not complete if it is wholly or partially
motivated "by a decision to postpone the criminal conduct until a more advan-
tageous time or to transfer the criminal effort to another but similar objective
or victim." For example, D is guilty of attempted bank robbery, if she arrives at
the bank, but leaves without committing the offense because she determines
that it is too risky to go ahead until she secures the assistance of an accomplice.[211] D would also be guilty of an attempt if, after taking a substantial step
toward robbing Bank A, she shifted her efforts to Bank B.[212]

Renunciation is not voluntary if it is partially or wholly motivated by "circumstances, not present or apparent at the inception of the actor's course of conduct, that increase the probability of detection or apprehension or that make
more difficult the accomplishment of the criminal purpose." Under this provision, an actor is not entitled to the defense if she desists from a theft because
she is aware that she is being observed by a police officer. Similarly, a person is
guilty of attempted rape if he desists due to the victim's resistance.

[F] Grading of Criminal Attempts and Other Inchoate Crimes

[1] In General

In a significant departure from common law tradition, the Code provides
that, with one exception, the crimes of attempt, solicitation, and conspiracy
are offenses of the same grade and degree, i.e., subject to the same punishment,
as the offense attempted, solicited, or that is the object of the conspiracy.[213] This
is consistent with the Code's subjectivist view of inchoate crimes.

The only exception to this grading system relates to "felonies of the first
degree,"[214] which are crimes that carry a maximum penalty of life imprison-

---

[210] Model Penal Code § 5.01(4).

[211] E.g., United States v. Jackson, 560 F.2d 112 (2d Cir. 1977).

[212] If D proceeded to rob Bank B, she would be guilty of attempted robbery of Bank A *and* of robbery of Bank B. If she were arrested before completing the Bank B robbery, D would be guilty of two
counts of attempted robbery.

[213] Model Penal Code § 5.05(1).

[214] Model Penal Code § 6.01(1)(a).

ment.[215] An attempt (or solicitation or conspiracy) to commit a felony of the first degree constitutes a felony of the *second* degree,[216] the maximum penalty of which is ten years.[217]

[2] Special Mitigation

The Model Penal Code grants a trial judge the authority to dismiss a prosecution of an inchoate offense, or to impose a sentence for a crime of a lower degree than is otherwise allowed, if the actor's conduct was so inherently unlikely to result in a crime that neither she nor her conduct represents a danger to society justifying her conviction and punishment at ordinary levels.[218] This provision provides flexibility to a judge in the rare case of an inherently impossible attempt, e.g., when *D* attempts to sink a battleship with a pop-gun.[219]

---

[215] Model Penal Code § 6.06(1). Felonies of the first degree are expressly designated as such by the Code. Murder (§ 210.2), kidnapping (§ 212.1), rape (§ 213.1(1)), and robbery (§ 222.1) are felonies of the first degree.

[216] Model Penal Code § 5.05(1).

[217] Model Penal Code § 6.06(2).

[218] Model Penal Code § 5.05(2).

[219] See § 27.07[C][2], *supra*.

Chapter 28

SOLICITATION

§ 28.01 GENERAL PRINCIPLES[1]

[A] Definition

[1] In General

Subject to clarification below, "solicitation" occurs when a person invites, requests, commands, hires, or encourages another to engage in conduct constituting any felony, or a misdemeanor relating to obstruction of justice or a breach of the peace. Solicitation is a common law misdemeanor, regardless of the grade of the offense solicited. Although there is very little case law on point, "impossibility" apparently is not a defense to the crime of solicitation.[2]

Until the adoption of the Model Penal Code, most state penal codes did not contain a general criminal solicitation statute.[3] Instead, solicitations to commit specific offenses, such as murder and prostitution, were prohibited. As a result of the Code's influence, many states now have a general solicitation statute that covers all crimes or, at least, all felonies. However, many of these states have followed the common law approach of treating solicitation as a lesser offense than the crime solicited.[4]

[2] *Mens Rea*

Common law solicitation is a specific-intent crime. A person is not guilty of solicitation unless he intentionally commits the *actus reus* of the inchoate offense — he intentionally invites, requests, commands, hires, or encourages another to commit a crime — with the specific intent that the other person consummate the solicited crime. For example, *D1* is not guilty of solicitation if

---

[1] See generally Glanville Williams, Criminal Law: The General Part §§ 193-95 (2d ed. 1961); Larry Alexander & Kimberly D. Kessler, *Mens Rea and Inchoate Crimes*, 87 J. Crim. L. & Criminology 1138 (1997); John W. Curran, *Solicitation: A Substantive Crime*, 17 Minn. L. Rev. 499 (1933).

[2] Benson v. Superior Court, 368 P.2d 116, 118 (Cal. 1962); Commonwealth v. Jacobs, 91 Mass. 274 (1864). Neither of the cited cases drew a distinction between factual and legal impossibility, but both involved hybrid legal impossibility, as that term is explained at § 27.07[D][3], *supra*.

[3] American Law Institute, Comment to § 5.02, at 367.

[4] Commonwealth v. Barsell, 678 N.E.2d 143, 145 (Mass. 1997) (summarizing statutory law).

he jokingly suggests to *X1* that *X1* steal *V1*'s television set, even if *X1* takes the suggestion seriously and commits the crime.

Or, suppose that *D2* encourages *X2* to pick *V2*'s pocket. *D2* knows that *V2*'s pocket is empty, but *X2* is unaware of this. If *X2* follows *D2*'s suggestion and puts his hand in *V2*'s empty pocket, *X2* is guilty of attempted larceny, as the factual impossibility of committing the larceny does not serve as a defense to *X2*'s conduct.[5] *D2*, however, should *not* be guilty of common law solicitation, because he knew that *X2* could not succeed in the larceny; therefore, *D2* lacked the specific intent required for solicitation.[6]

In contrast to the last example, suppose that *D2*, like *X2*, is *unaware* of the fact that *V2*'s pockets are empty when he encourages *X2* to pick *V2*'s pocket. Under these changed circumstances, *D2 is* guilty of solicitation, because he *believed* that the crime (larceny) could be committed.

[3] *Actus Reus*

The *actus reus* of a solicitation takes place when one person invites, requests, commands, hires, or encourages[7] another to commit a particular offense. For a solicitation to occur, neither the solicitor nor the solicited party needs to perform any act in furtherance of the target offense.[8] The solicitation is complete the instant the actor communicates the solicitation to the other person.[9] Thus, a solicitation occurs if *D* asks *X* to commit a crime but *X* refuses, or even if *X* agrees but does not intend to commit the crime (e.g., if *X* is an undercover police officer feigning intent).

In the absence of clarifying statutory language, courts have struggled to determine how to deal with uncommunicated solicitations. For example, in *State v. Cotton*,[10] *C*, a jail inmate, wrote letters to *X*, his wife, in which he solicited criminal activities on her part. Although *C* attempted to mail or forward the letters to *X*, there was no evidence that they actually reached her. The court held that, on this evidence, *C* could not be convicted of solicitation,[11]

---

[5] See § 27.07[C][1], *supra*.

[6] Williams, Note 1, *supra* at 611. Conceptually, *D2* has solicited an *attempted* larceny, but the common law apparently did not recognize such an offense.

[7] The idea of the offense need not originate with the solicitor; it is enough that he encourages another to commit an offense, even if the other person already plans to commit the crime. In light of the *mens rea* requirement, however, a person is not guilty of solicitation if his comments are not uttered for the purpose of encouraging the commission of the crime. American Law Institute, Comment to § 5.02, at 371.

[8] People v. Cheathem, 658 N.Y.S.2d 84, 85 (App. Div. 1997).

[9] United States v. Carroll, 43 M.J. 487, 489 (C.A.A.F. 1996).

[10] 790 P.2d 1050 (N.M. 1990).

[11] The same analysis would apply if a solicitor sends a message in a language that the other party does not understand, or if the solicitor communicates the message orally, but the solicitee does not hear the words.

although it suggested that a charge of *attempted* solicitation might have been allowed.[12]

[B] Relationship of the Solicitor to the Solicited Party

[1] In General

A typical solicitation occurs when *D* importunes *X* to perpetrate the substantive offense. In common law terms,[13] *D* intends for *X* to be the "principal in the first degree" of the solicited crime; *D* wishes to be the "principal in the second degree" or "accessory before the fact." Put less technically, "the essence of criminal solicitation is an attempt [by the solicitor] to *induce another to commit a criminal offense*";[14] the solicitor intends to be in the background — to "hide behind his hireling(s)"[15] — as an accomplice in the commission of the crime. Although there is relatively little case law on point, it also appears that a "solicitation of a solicitation" is itself a common law solicitation, e.g., if *D* importunes *X* to procure *another* person to kill *V*.[16]

No common law solicitation occurs if the solicitor intends to commit the substantive offense himself, but requests assistance by another. For example, if *D* requests *X* to kill *V*, *D* has solicited a murder. However, if *D* asks *X* to supply a gun so that he (*D*) can kill *V*, a common law solicitation has *not* transpired.

[2] Use of an Innocent Instrumentality

A person may sometimes use another as his "innocent instrumentality"[17] in the commission of an offense. It is critical to appreciate the difference between solicitation of another to commit an offense, on the one hand, and use of an innocent instrumentality, on the other hand.

For example, if *D1* suggests to *X1* that the latter steal *V1*'s television set, *D1* is guilty of solicitation. This fits the solicitation paradigm: If *X1* does as requested, *X1* is the perpetrator of the offense; *D1* is an accomplice. In contrast, suppose that *D2* fraudulently says to *X2*: "My television set is at *V2*'s house. He

---

[12] State v. Cotton, 790 P.2d at 1054; Laughner v. State, 769 N.E.2d 1147 (Ind. Ct. App. 2002) (recognizing the offense of attempted solicitation of a child to engage in sexual intercourse); American Law Institute, Comment to § 5.02, at 380-81 (recognizing such an approach at common law).

[13] See § 30.03[A], *infra*.

[14] People v. Herman, 97 Cal. App. 4th 1369, 1381 (2002).

[15] People v. Kauten, 755 N.E.2d 1016, 1019 (Ill. App. Ct. 2001).

[16] Ganesan v. State, 45 S.W.3d 197, 201 (Tex. App. 2001); see also People v. Bloom, 133 N.Y.S. 708 (App. Div. 1912) (*B* attempted to bribe *X* to solicit *Y* to commit perjury at *B*'s trial); People v. Terrell, 792 N.E.2d 357, 361 (Ill. App. Ct. 2003) (dictum).

[17] See § 30.03[A][2][b], *infra*.

asked me to pick it up. Would you do me a favor and get it for me?" In this example, *D2* is *not* guilty of solicitation to commit larceny, because *D2* is not requesting *X2* to engage in conduct that would constitute a crime *by X2*. Instead, *D2* is attempting to perpetrate the offense himself, by using *X2* as his dupe. *X2* is *D2*'s "innocent instrumentality" because, if *X2* believes *D2*'s representations and takes *V2*'s property, *X2* is not guilty of larceny since he lacks the specific intent to steal.

[C] Relationship of a Solicitation to the Target Offense

Solicitation is not only an inchoate offense but is also a basis for accomplice liability. That is, one who intentionally assists in an offense is, by way of accomplice law, guilty of the offense in which he assisted. Solicitation of a substantive offense is one way of assisting in an offense and, therefore, of being held accountable for the other's criminal acts.[18]

To see how this works, assume that *D* solicits *X* to murder *V*. In Scenario 1, *X* kills *V* because of the request. *D* is guilty of murder via his solicitation. However, *D* will not be punished for the crime of solicitation, *as the latter offense merges with the murder*.[19] In Scenario 2, *X* attempts to murder *V* at *D*'s request, but fails in the effort. *D* is now guilty, along with *X*, of attempted murder. *D* is not guilty of solicitation, *as this offense again merges with the attempt*. In Scenario 3, *D* solicits *X* to murder *V*, and *X* agrees but takes no action in furtherance of their agreement. Here, as a result of the agreement, *D* is guilty with *X* of conspiracy to murder *V*.[20] As before, *the solicitation merges with the conspiracy*. Finally, in Scenario 4, *X* refuses to commit the crime solicited. *X* is guilty of no offense; *D* is guilty of solicitation.

[D] Policy Considerations

Solicitation is a controversial offense. Some commentators believe that solicitations should not be punished because the offense suppresses conduct at too early a stage.[21] Indeed, no common law crime (except an *attempted* solicitation) punishes conduct more preparatory to a substantive offense than the crime of solicitation. According to Glanville Williams, the purpose of the offense is to enable police to "nip criminal tendencies in the bud."[22] In fact, however, his

---

[18] See § 30.04, *infra*.

[19] Lewis v. State, 404 A.2d 1073, 1083 (Md. 1979).

[20] See § 29.01[A], *infra*.

[21] Solicitation statutes, unless carefully drafted and applied circumspectly, may also raise First Amendment free speech concerns. See generally Kent Greenawalt, *Speech and Crime*, 1980 Am. B. Found. Res. J. 645; State v. Robertson, 649 P.2d 569, 573-77 (Or. 1982)

[22] Williams, Note 1, *supra*, at 609.

metaphor would be more accurate if he had stated that its purpose is to nip criminal tendencies at the stem.

The extremely inchoate nature of the crime of solicitation is evident if one carefully analyzes the offense. Essentially, solicitation is an attempted conspiracy.[23] That is, when D solicits X to commit an offense, he wants X to agree to commit the offense solicited; if X agrees, they have formed a conspiracy. In turn, a conspiracy can exist long before a crime is attempted. Thus, solicitation is an attempt to conspire to commit an offense — a *double* inchoate crime. And, thus, an *attempted* solicitation is a *triple* inchoate offense.

The contrasting view is that solicitations are dangerous precisely because they *are* attempted conspiracies. As discussed more fully elsewhere,[24] one rationale for punishing conspiracies is that there is more danger in two persons agreeing to commit a crime than in one or two persons separately planning to commit the same offense. Therefore, when a solicitor attempts to create such a dangerous grouping, his conduct represents a threat that advocates of the offense believe society has a legitimate interest in deterring. Moreover, it has been argued that "solicitation poses special dangers not inherent in conspiracy, one of which is that the instigator will be a sophisticated operator, such as a gang leader, who will hide behind his hireling(s),"[25] therefore justifying more severe penalties for a solicitation than for a conspiracy or a criminal attempt.[26]

§ 28.02 COMPARISON OF SOLICITATION TO OTHER INCHOATE OFFENSES

[A] Conspiracy

A conspiracy is an agreement between two or more persons to commit an unlawful act or series of unlawful acts.[27] As noted in the preceding subsection, a solicitation is an attempted conspiracy. However, it is possible to have a conspiracy without a prior solicitation. For example, suppose that A, intending to kill V, requests B's assistance in the crime. If B agrees to help, they have formed a conspiracy; however, as A did not request B to perpetrate the offense, no common law solicitation has occurred.[28]

---

[23] People v. Saephanh, 80 Cal. App. 4th 451, 460 (Ct. App. 2000); State v. Sexton, 657 P.2d 43, 44 (Kan. 1983).

[24] See § 29.02[B], *infra*.

[25] People v. Kauten, 755 N.E.2d 1016, 1019 (Ill. App. Ct. 2001).

[26] *Id*. 1018-20.

[27] See § 29.01[A], *infra*.

[28] See § 28.01[B][1], *supra*.

Or, suppose that C informs D that he (C) intends to kill V. D tells C that, he, too, wishes V dead. As a consequence of their common goal, they form a pact to kill V. The latter agreement would constitute a conspiracy, although C never solicited the offense.[29]

[B] Criminal Attempt[30]

An issue that has perplexed courts is whether or when a solicitation can constitute an attempt to commit the crime solicited. That is, if D solicits X to rob V, under what circumstances, if any, may D be convicted of attempted robbery, rather than of solicitation? The matter is of considerable significance in jurisdictions in which a criminal attempt is punished more severely than a solicitation.

Courts have taken various approaches to this issue.[31] First, a substantial majority of courts state that the act of solicitation cannot, by itself, constitute an attempt to commit the offense solicited.[32] Some courts, however, provide that a solicitation can constitute an attempt, subject to ordinary attempt doctrines.[33] On this basis, a solicitation that is proximate to the target offense may constitute an attempt to commit it. For example, if D solicits unarmed X to murder V when V returns to town in a week, D's conduct does not constitute an attempt because the crime is too remote. On the other hand, if D solicits X, who is already armed and in V's presence, to commit the offense immediately, D's solicitation could constitute an attempt.[34]

Second, some courts hold that solicitation coupled with a "slight act" in furtherance of it *by the solicitor* is an attempt.[35] For example, in jurisdictions that follow this rule, if D solicits X to sell him an illegal drug, and then displays or proffers the money, the solicitation has matured into an attempt.[36] Likewise, if D pays X money to murder V, or furnishes X with a weapon to commit the offense, D is guilty of an attempt even if X does nothing further, and even if X is an undercover police officer who would never have committed the crime.[37]

---

[29] Monoker v. State, 582 A.2d 525, 528 (Md. Ct. Spec. App. 1990); see People v. Stroner, 449 N.E.2d 1326, 1328 (Ill. 1983).

[30] See Williams, Note 1, *supra*, at § 198.

[31] American Law Institute, Comment to § 5.02, at 368-69 (and citations therein).

[32] State v. O'Neil, 782 A.2d 209, 216 (Conn. App. Ct. 2001).

[33] State v. Sunzar, 751 A.2d 627, 632 (N.J. Super. Law. Div. 1999) (adopting the "minority" position that "mere solicitation, even when unaccompanied by any other act in furtherance, can constitute an attempt").

[34] See Mettler v. State, 697 N.E.2d 502, 503 (Ind. Ct. App. 1998) (a solicitation does not constitute an attempt unless the solicitation urges *immediate* commission of a crime).

[35] Stokes v. State, 46 So. 627, 629 (Miss. 1908).

[36] People v. York, 60 Cal. App. 4th 1499, 1506 (1998).

[37] E.g., State v. Gay, 486 P.2d 341, 347 (Wash. Ct. App. 1971); contra State v. Otto, 629 P.2d 646, 650 (Idaho 1981).

Third, some courts hold that a solicitation is not an attempt unless the solicitor's overt acts would constitute an attempt if he had intended to commit the crime himself. For example, if D pays X money to commit a crime or furnishes him with an instrumentality to commit a future offense, D is *not* guilty of attempt. However, if D solicits X to burglarize V's home, and then opens a window at V's house for X's later entry, D would be guilty of attempted burglary, even if X never arrives at the scene.

Finally, other courts hold that "no matter what acts the solicitor commits, he cannot be guilty of an attempt because it is not his purpose to commit the offense personally."[38]

These situations must be distinguished from the case in which a person seeks to use another as his innocent instrumentality to commit an offense. Suppose, as hypothesized earlier,[39] D fraudulently says to X: "My television set is at V's house. He asked me to pick it up. Would you do me a favor and pick it up for me?" In this circumstance, D is *not* guilty of solicitation because he is not requesting X to commit larceny, but instead is trying to commit the offense himself through an innocent instrumentality, X. Although D's request is not a solicitation, it may constitute an *attempt* by D to commit the offense solicited. D has committed the last act in his power to cause the property to be taken. Moreover, his conduct is more proximate to the theft than a solicitation, because X is more apt to agree to take the property when he believes that he is acting lawfully than when he is asked to knowingly commit a criminal act.

§ 28.03 MODEL PENAL CODE[40]

[A] In General

The Model Penal Code provides that a person is guilty of solicitation to commit a crime if: (1) the actor's purpose is to promote or facilitate the commission of a substantive offense; and (2) with such purpose, he commands, encourages, or requests another person to engage in conduct that would constitute the crime, an attempt to commit it, or would establish the other person's complicity in its commission or attempted commission.[41] The Code grades nearly all inchoate crimes, including solicitation, at the same level as the target offense.[42]

---

[38] American Law Institute, Comment to § 5.02, at 369.

[39] See § 28.01[B][2], *supra*.

[40] See generally Herbert Wechsler et al., *The Treatment of Inchoate Crimes in the Model Penal Code of the American Law Institute: Attempt, Solicitation, and Conspiracy (Pt. 1)*, 61 Colum. L. Rev. 571 (1961).

[41] Model Penal Code § 5.02(1).

[42] Model Penal Code § 5.05(1). See § 27.09[F][1], *supra*.

The Code definition of solicitation is broader than the common law version in four key respects. First, it applies to the solicitation of all crimes and not simply of felonies and serious misdemeanors.

Second, unlike the common law, the Code recognizes a solicitation to commit an attempt. Reconsider the case discussed earlier,[43] in which D solicits X to put his hand in what D knows is an empty pocket of V. If X does as requested, X is guilty of attempted larceny; D would be guilty of no common law offense, however, because he did not intend for X to commit larceny. Under the Code, however, D would be guilty of solicitation of an *attempted* larceny. In the language of Section 5.02, D solicited X to "engage in specific conduct [picking V's empty pocket] that would constitute . . . an attempt to commit such crime [of larceny]."

Third, the relationship of the solicitor to the solicited party need not be that of accomplice to perpetrator. Suppose that D asks X to provide him with a weapon so that D may kill V. At common law, D has not solicited a murder, because he has not requested X to perpetrate the offense. Under the Code, D is guilty of solicitation because, applying the Code, D has requested X to "engage in specific conduct [provide a weapon] that would . . . establish [X's] complicity [as an accomplice] in its commission or attempted commission."[44]

Finally, an uncommunicated solicitation, i.e., an attempted solicitation at common law, is itself a solicitation under the Code.[45]

[B] Defense: Renunciation

The Model Code establishes a defense to solicitation of "renunciation of criminal purpose." A person is not guilty of solicitation if he: (1) completely and voluntarily renounces his criminal intent; and (2) either persuades the solicited party not to commit the offense or otherwise prevents him from committing the crime.[46]

This defense is recognized for the same reason that it applies to the other inchoate offenses of attempt and conspiracy: A person who abandons his criminal purpose and thwarts the commission of the offense demonstrates thereby that he is no longer dangerous. Establishment of the defense also serves as an incentive to the solicitor to prevent commission of the crime.

---

[43] See § 28.01[A][2], *supra*.

[44] Model Penal Code § 5.02(1).

[45] Model Penal Code § 5.02(2).

[46] Model Penal Code § 5.02(3).

Chapter 29

CONSPIRACY

"Conspiracy" is both an inchoate offense and a complicity doctrine (a basis for holding a person accountable for the *consummated* offenses of another). The crime of conspiracy is the subject of this chapter. Complicity doctrine is considered in the next chapter.

§ 29.01 CONSPIRACY: IN GENERAL[1]

[A] Common Law

A common law conspiracy is an agreement between two or more persons to commit a criminal act or series of criminal acts, or to accomplish a legal act by unlawful means.[2] Formulated by the English Star Chamber in 1611,[3] conspiracy was a common law misdemeanor. As discussed below,[4] the offense is punished more severely today than it was at common law.

Conspiracy is a frequently prosecuted,[5] but extremely controversial, crime. Some courts and many scholars have called for its reform or abolition.[6] The nature of the controversies become evident in subsequent sections of this chapter. Three interrelated criticisms of the crime, however, may be emphasized

---

[1] See generally Peter Buscemi, Note, *Conspiracy: Statutory Reform Since the Model Penal Code*, 75 Colum. L. Rev. 1122 (1975); *Developments in the Law — Criminal Conspiracy*, 72 Harv. L. Rev. 920 (1959); Abraham S. Goldstein, *Conspiracy to Defraud the United States*, 68 Yale L.J. 405 (1959); Phillip E. Johnson, *The Unnecessary Crime of Conspiracy*, 61 Cal. L. Rev. 1137 (1973); Neil Kumar Katyal, *Conspiracy Theory*, 112 Yale L.J. 1307 (2003); Paul Marcus, *Criminal Conspiracy Law: Time to Turn Back from an Ever Expanding, Even More Troubling Area*, 1 Wm. & Mary Bill Rts. J. 1 (1992); Herbert Wechsler et al., *The Treatment of Inchoate Crimes in the Model Penal Code of the American Law Institute: Attempt, Solicitation, and Conspiracy (Pt. 2)*, 61 Colum. L. Rev. 957 (1961).

[2] People v. Carter, 330 N.W.2d 314, 319 (Mich. 1982); United States v. Jimenez Recio, 537 U.S. 270, 274 (2003) ("[T]he essence of a conspiracy is 'an agreement to commit an unlawful act.'") (quoting Ianelli v. United States, 420 U.S. 770, 777 (1975)).

[3] Poulterers' Case, 9 Co. Rep. 55b, 77 Eng. Rep. 813 (1611).

[4] See § 29.03[A], *infra*.

[5] United States v. Reynolds, 919 F.2d 435, 439 (7th Cir. 1990) (Easterbrook, J.) ("[P]rosecutors seem to have conspiracy on their word processors as Count I; rare is the case omitting such a charge."). This is, of course, an exaggeration, but it is true that perhaps "more than one-quarter of all federal criminal prosecutions and a large number of state cases involve prosecutions for conspiracy." Katyal, Note 1, *supra*, at 1310 (and accompanying supporting citations).

[6] For an example of the abolitionist position see Johnson, Note 1, *supra*; see also Katyal, Note 1, *supra*, at 1309 (noting that critiques of conspiracy law, "[f]or more than 50 years . . . have [unfortunately, to the author] successfully permeated the criminal law").

here. First, it has been said that the "crime of conspiracy is so vague that it almost defies definition."[7] The formlessness of the crime of conspiracy has served as a powerful tool of prosecutors to suppress inchoate conduct that they consider potentially dangerous or morally undesirable. Indeed, Judge Learned Hand once described the offense as the "darling of the modern prosecutor's nursery."[8]

Second, some see the offense as undesirable because of the highly inchoate nature of the offense: A person may be convicted of the common law offense before she commits any act in perpetration of a substantive crime. Third, and closely related to the last point, the crime "is always 'predominantly mental in composition' because it consists primarily of a meeting of minds and an intent."[9] Because of conspiracy law's emphasis on *mens rea*, and its consequent de-emphasis on conduct, critics maintain that there exists a greater than normal risk that "persons will be punished for what they say rather than for what they do, or [simply] for associating with others who are found culpable."[10] Histori-cally, conspiracy laws have been used to suppress controversial activity, such as strikes by workers and public dissent against governmental policies.[11]

[B] Model Penal Code

Section 5.03, subsection (1), of the Model Penal Code defines "conspiracy" as follows:

> A person is guilty of conspiracy with another person or persons to com-mit a crime if with the purpose of promoting or facilitating its com-mission he:
>
> (a) agrees with such other person or persons that they or one or more of them will engage in conduct that constitutes such crime or an attempt or solicitation to commit such crime; or

---

[7] Krulewitch v. United States, 336 U.S. 440, 446 (1949) (Jackson, J., concurring). Justice Jack-son also described the crime as "chameleon-like." *Id.* at 447. Another critic has compared the crime to Einstein's theory of relativity, stating that the concept is "so far removed from ordinary human experience or modes of thought . . . [that] it escapes just beyond the boundaries of the mind." Jes-sica Mitford, The Trial of Dr. Spock 61 (1969).

[8] Harrison v. United States, 7 F.2d 259, 263 (2d Cir. 1925). An additional reason why "conspir-acy" is a "darling" of prosecutors is that they can use the threat of a conspiracy prosecution against a relative "small fry" in a criminal transaction as a means to induce the individual to provide infor-mation and testimony against others. See Katyal, Note 1, *supra*, at 1328 (noting that one federal study "found that flipping [i.e., assisting in the prosecution of a colleague in crime] helped the gov-ernment obtain guilty pleas of co-defendants, prosecution of new defendants, additional convictions and arrests, recovery of assets, cooperation of known and new co-defendants, and deportations").

[9] *Krulewitch*, 336 U.S. at 447-48 (Jackson, J., concurring) (footnote omitted).

[10] Johnson, Note 1, *supra*, at 1139.

[11] See Mitford, Note 7 *supra*, at 61-72.

  (b) agrees to aid such other person or persons in the planning or commission of such crime or of an attempt or solicitation to commit such crime.

This definition and other features of the Code's treatment of criminal conspiracies are explored throughout this chapter.

§ 29.02 PUNISHING CONSPIRACIES: WHY?

[A] "Conspiracy" as an Inchoate Offense: Preventive Law Enforcement

As with other inchoate offenses, criminal conspiracy laws provide police officers with a basis for arresting persons whom they believe intend to commit other criminal offenses.

Conspiracy laws allow police intervention at a much earlier point than is permitted under attempt law. As is explained below,[12] a common law conspiracy is formed the moment two or more persons agree that one of them will later commit an unlawful act. At common law, no conduct in furtherance of the conspiracy is required. Even when an overt act in furtherance of the conspiracy is statutorily required, the act may be trivial and wholly preparatory to the commission of the target offense. Consequently, advocates of conspiracy laws believe that the offense unfetters police and fills in the gaps in the "unrealistic" law of criminal attempts.

Conspiracy law is also justified on the ground that an agreement to commit a criminal act is concrete and unambiguous evidence of the actors' dangerousness and the firmness of their criminal intentions.[13] However, the agreement that serves as "concrete" and "unambiguous" evidence of the defendants' dangerousness and culpability is often proved inferentially. Moreover, even if an agreement is conclusively proved to exist, the potential temporal remoteness of the agreement to the target offense increases the likelihood that some conspirators who might later renounce their intentions will be punished.

[B] Special Dangers of Group Criminality

The combination that constitutes a conspiracy is said to represent a "distinct evil."[14] According to advocates of conspiracy laws, two people united to commit a crime are more dangerous than one or both of them independently planning to commit the same offense: "[T]he strength, opportunities and

---

[12] See § 29.04, *infra*.

[13] American Law Institute, Comment to § 5.03, at 387-88.

[14] United States v. Jimenez Recio, 537 U.S. 270, 274 (2003) (quoting Salinas v. United States, 522 U.S. 52, 65 (1997)).

resources of many is obviously more dangerous and more difficult to police than the efforts of a lone wrongdoer."[15]

The purported dangers inherent in collective criminal action are many. First, out of fear of co-conspirators, loyalty to them, or enhanced morale arising from the collective effort, a party to a conspiracy is less likely to abandon her criminal plans than if she were acting alone.[16] Other special dangers are said to inhere in conspiracies: Collectivism promotes efficiency through division of labor; group criminality makes the attainment of more elaborate crimes possible; and the "[c]ombination in crime makes more likely the commission of crimes unrelated to the original purpose for which the group was formed."[17]

Almost a half century ago, Professor Abraham Goldstein questioned whether these "special danger" claims were empirically correct.[18] He reasoned that it was plausible to argue that conspiracies will frustrate rather than promote crime: With more people involved, there is an enhanced risk that someone will leak information about the offense, turn against others, or try to convince colleagues to desist from their criminal endeavor. According to Professor Neal Katyal, however, there is psychological and economic research supporting many of the traditional claims of special dangers inherent in group behavior.[19]

§ 29.03 PUNISHING CONSPIRACIES: HOW MUCH?

[A] In General

[1] Common Law and Non-Model Penal Code Statutes

At common law, a conspiracy to commit a felony or a misdemeanor was a misdemeanor.[20] Modern statutory treatment of the offense varies widely among the states. Some states continue to treat all conspiracies, regardless of the seriousness of their objectives, as misdemeanors. More often, however, the sanction for conspiracy is graded in relationship to the contemplated crime. Many states punish conspiracies to commit felonies as felonies, and conspiracies to commit

---

[15] Krulewitch v. United States, 336 U.S. 440, 448-49 (1949) (Jackson, J., concurring) (footnote omitted).

[16] United States v. Jimenez Recio, 537 U.S. at 275 (the combination "decreases the probability that the individuals involved will depart from their path of criminality") (quoting Callanan v. United States, 364 U.S. 587, 593-94 (1961)).

[17] Callanan v. United States, 364 U.S. 587, 593-94 (1961).

[18] Goldstein, Note 1, *supra*, at 414.

[19] For a review of the literature the author believes justifies the "special danger" claim, see Katyal, Note 1, *supra*, at 1315-28.

[20] Glanville Williams, Criminal Law: The General Part § 221 (2d ed. 1961).

misdemeanors as misdemeanors. In most states, a conspiracy to commit a felony is punished less severely than the target offense.[21]

[2] Model Penal Code

As with other inchoate offenses, the Model Penal Code grades a conspiracy to commit any crime other than a felony of the first degree at the same level as the object of the conspiracy.[22] If a conspiracy has multiple objectives, e.g., to rape and to steal,[23] the conspiracy is graded on the basis of the more or most serious target offense. The Code takes the subjectivist view[24] that people who agree to commit crimes but are arrested before consummation are as dangerous as those who commit the target offenses.

[B] Punishment When the Target Offense Is Committed

[1] Common Law

Unlike the crimes of attempt and solicitation, the offense of conspiracy does *not* merge into the attempted or completed offense that was the object of the conspiracy.[25] For example, if *D1* and *D2* conspire to rob *V*, and later consummate or attempt to commit the robbery, they may be convicted and punished for both the conspiracy and the robbery or its attempt.[26]

The non-merger doctrine is unsupportable if the main purpose of conspiracy law is to provide the police with an opportunity to prevent commission of the target offense. Once the object of the conspiracy is committed or attempted, this purpose of conspiracy law evaporates. Similarly, if the focus of the offense is on the dangerousness of the individual conspirator, her punishment should be calibrated to the crime that she threatened to commit; punishing her for both crimes is duplicative. The non-merger rule makes sense, however, if one focuses

---

[21] At least one state authorizes *more severe* punishment of a conspiracy than of the substantive offense. People v. Tatman, 20 Cal. App. 4th 1 (Ct. App. 1993) (applying a state statute, upholding a *felony* conviction for conspiracy to commit a *misdemeanor* offense relating to unlawful possession of red abalone).

[22] Model Penal Code § 5.05(1). See § 27.09[F][1], *supra*.

[23] As is explained more fully at § 29.08, *infra*, an agreement to commit multiple crimes constitutes only one conspiracy.

[24] See § 27.03, *supra*.

[25] Callanan v. United States, 364 U.S. 587, 593-94 (1961).

[26] E.g., People v. Jones, 601 N.E.2d 1080, 1088 (Ill. App. Ct. 1992) (upholding conviction of attempted armed robbery and conspiracy to commit armed robbery); United States v. Boykins, 966 F.2d 1240, 1245 (8th Cir. 1992) (upholding against constitutional attack, punishment for conspiracy to possess cocaine and attempted possession, based on the same incident).

on the alternative rationale of conspiracy law, i.e., to attack the special dangers thought to inhere in conspiratorial groupings.[27]

[2] Model Penal Code

The Model Penal Code diverges from the common law. It provides that a person may not be convicted and punished for both conspiracy and the object of the conspiracy or an attempt to commit the target offense, unless the prosecution proves that the conspiratorial agreement involved the commission of additional offenses not yet committed or attempted.[28]

For example, if *D1* and *D2* conspire to rob Bank *V* and then do so, they may be convicted and punished for robbery or conspiracy, but not for both offenses. In contrast, if *D1* and *D2* conspire to rob Banks *V1*, *V2*, and *V3*, and they are arrested after robbing Bank *V1* — thus, before their other criminal objectives were fully satisfied — the conspiracy does *not* merge with the completed offense. The drafters of the Code believed that, in these circumstances, the special dangers inherent in collective action justify independent punishment of the conspiracy.

§ 29.04 CONSPIRACY: THE AGREEMENT

[A] In General

The gist — or "essence"[29] — of a conspiracy is the agreement to commit an unlawful act or series of such acts.[30] An express agreement, however, need not be proved.[31] Indeed, a physical act of communication of an agreement (e.g., a nod of the head or some verbal exchange) is not required. Furthermore, an agreement can exist although not all of the parties to it have knowledge of every detail of the arrangement, as long as each party is aware of its essential nature.[32] Moreover, a "conspiracy may exist even if a conspirator does not agree to commit or facilitate each and every part of the substantive offense."[33] It is

---

[27] "That [conspiratorial] agreement is 'a distinct evil,' which 'may exist and be punished whether or not the substantive crime ensues.'" United States v. Jimenez Recio, 537 U.S. 270, 274 (2003) (quoting Salinas v. United States, 522 U.S. 52, 65 (1997)). The special dangers are discussed in § 29.02[B], *supra*.

[28] Model Penal Code § 1.07(1)(b). See American Law Institute, Comment to § 1.07, at 109.

[29] United States v. Jimenez Recio, 537 U.S. 270, 274 (2003).

[30] Cuellar v. State, 13 S.W.3d 449, 453 (Tex. App. 2000).

[31] United States v. James, 528 F.2d 999, 1011 (5th Cir. 1976).

[32] Blumenthal v. United States, 332 U.S. 539, 557-58 (1947); People v. Mass, 628 N.W.2d 540, 549 n.19 (Mich. 2001) (but also stating that the agreement need "not rise to the level of the 'meeting of the minds' concept from contract law").

[33] Salinas v. United States, 522 U.S. 52, 63 (1997).

enough that each person agrees, at a minimum, to commit or facilitate some of the acts leading to the substantive crime.

Nonetheless — and this is the essence of the agreement — there must be present "on the part of each conspirator communion with a mind and will outside [herself]."[34] In this very limited sense, the conspiracy is externalized; that is, the agreement takes the law beyond the individual mental states of the parties, in which each person separately intends to participate in the commission of an unlawful act, to a shared intent and mutual goal, to a spoken or unspoken understanding by the parties that they will proceed in unity toward their shared goal.

How does a prosecutor prove the existence of this amorphous yet critical agreement? "Conspiracy is by nature a clandestine offense,"[35] one in which the agreement that constitutes the crime "is seldom born of 'open covenants openly arrived at.'"[36] Ironically, the difficulty in demonstrating an agreement has proven to be the prosecutor's greatest advantage because, "in their zeal to emphasize that the agreement need not be proved directly, the courts sometimes neglect to say that it need be proved at all."[37]

A conspiratorial agreement may be established directly or through entirely circumstantial evidence of a mutual, implied understanding.[38] As one court has acknowledged, "because of the clandestine nature of a conspiracy and the foreseeable difficulty of the prosecution's burden of establishing the conspiracy by direct proof, the courts have permitted broad inferences to be drawn . . . from evidence of acts, conduct, and circumstances."[39]

A conspiracy "may be inferred from a 'development and a collocation of circumstances.'"[40] A crime committed as the result of a prior agreement is apt to look choreographed.[41] For example, in one case,[42] the prosecution proved the following: *D1* was driving an automobile in which *D2* and *D3* were passengers; as

---

[34] *Developments in the Law*, Note 1, *supra*, at 926.

[35] *Id.* at 933.

[36] Lacaze v. United States, 391 F.2d 516, 520 (5th Cir. 1968); see also Cuellar v. State, 13 S.W.3d 449, 453 (Tex. App. 2000) ("[C]onspirators' work is often done in secrecy and under cover.").

[37] *Developments in the Law*, Note 1, *supra*, at 933 (footnote omitted).

[38] State v. Merrill, 530 S.E.2d 608, 611 (N.C. Ct. App. 2000).

[39] People v. Persinger, 363 N.E.2d 897, 901 (Ill. App. Ct. 1977).

[40] Glasser v. United States, 315 U.S. 60, 80 (1942) (quoting United States v. Manton, 107 F.2d 834, 839 (2d Cir. 1939)); Commonwealth v. Murphy, 844 A.2d 1228, 1238 (Pa. 2004) ("Direct evidence of the . . . conspiratorial agreement . . . is rarely available. . . . Consequently, . . . the agreement is almost always proven through circumstantial evidence, such as by 'the relations, conduct or circumstances of the parties or overt acts on the part of the co-conspirators.'") (quoting Commonwealth v. Wayne, 720 A.2d 456, 464 (1998)).

[41] Garner v. State, 6 P.3d 1013, 1020 (Nev. 2000) ("Evidence of a coordinated series of acts . . . is sufficient to infer the existence of an agreement."), overruled in part by Sharma v. State, 56 P.3d 868 (Nev. 2002).

[42] Commonwealth v. Azim, 459 A.2d 1244 (Pa. Super. Ct. 1983).

the car drove by *V*, a pedestrian, *D1* stopped the car; *D2* called *V* over to the curb; *D2* and *D3* got out of the vehicle leaving their car doors open, and robbed *V*; *D2* and *D3* re-entered the car; and *D1* drove away. Based on these facts, the court held that a jury could rationally find, beyond a reasonable doubt, that a conspiracy to rob *V* had been formed, and that *D1*, the driver of the vehicle, was a party to the agreement. Countless cases based on far less evidence than this have found conspiratorial agreements.[43]

When the choreography is missing, however, a court is somewhat less likely to find an agreement, absent more direct evidence. For example, in *Commonwealth v. Cook*,[44] *D1* and *D2*, brothers, conversed with *V*, a female, on a street. When *D1* said he was out of cigarettes, the three began walking toward a nearby convenience store. Along the way, *V* slipped and fell to the ground, at which moment *D1* jumped on top of *V* in order to rape her. *D1* handed his trouser belt to *D2*, who encouraged *D1* in the rape. *D2*'s conduct — holding the belt and encouraging *D1* — constituted assistance in the rape. As such, he was properly charged as an accomplice in the commission of the rape. Based on this evidence, however, an appellate court concluded that *D2* was *not* properly convicted of conspiracy with *D1* to rape *V*.

The court's conclusion was sound. It was a chance meeting of the two men with the victim; the rape occurred in an apparently spontaneous, unplanned manner, i.e., *V* slipped and *D1* suddenly attacked her. As the court reasoned, it is as likely that *D2* became involved as an accomplice (rather than a co-conspirator) after the rape began as it is "to infer that the minds of the parties had met in advance" as part of an agreement to commit the rape.

[B] Distinguishing the Agreement from the Group That Agrees

The term "conspiracy" describes the agreement that constitutes the offense for which the parties may be punished. However, a common but misleading use of the word "conspiracy" is as a description of *the group itself* that intends to commit the unlawful acts.

These two different uses of the term — "conspiracy" as the agreement, and "conspiracy" as the people who have formed the agreement — are often blurred by commentators and courts. Thus, one treatise states that "the gist of a conspiracy is the combination which is formed."[45] Some courts repeat the unfortu-

---

[43] E.g., People v. Persinger, 363 N.E.2d 897 (Ill. App. Ct. 1977) (*O*, an undercover officer, purchased barbiturates from *D1* at the latter's residence; during the meeting, *D1* turned to *D2*, her husband, and requested a pocket knife to scratch the prescription label off the container in which the pills were enclosed; *D2* was also present at other illegal purchases; held: there was sufficient evidence of a *D1-D2* conspiracy).

[44] 411 N.E.2d 1326 (Mass. App. Ct. 1980).

[45] Rollin M. Perkins & Ronald N. Boyce, Criminal Law 682 (3d ed. 1982).

nate characterization of a conspiracy as a "combination" of people.[46] Holmes, too, has described a conspiracy as "a partnership in criminal purposes."[47]

The crime of conspiracy should not be described in this fashion. One danger in failing to distinguish between the agreement and the group is that conspiracy convictions may improperly be affirmed. For example, suppose that X and Y agree (conspire) to commit a robbery. Suppose that D, a stranger to X and Y, assists in the robbery at the scene in some spur-of-the-manner way. On these facts, as explained in the next chapter, D may be convicted of the robbery as an accomplice of X and Y. If X and Y were conspirators, however, may D also be convicted of the crime of conspiracy? If "conspiracy" is the X-Y group rather than their agreement, then it follows logically that when D aids X and Y she aids the "conspiracy" (i.e., the group). Therefore, pursuant to complicity law, D would be an accomplice of the "conspiracy" and, consequently, guilty of the crime of conspiracy.

This analysis is wrong.[48] The essence of a conspiracy is the agreement itself, and not the group of conspirators. On the hypothesized facts, just as in *Commonwealth v. Cook* described in subsection [A], D's last-moment participation in the offense does not mean that she "agreed" with X and Y to rob the bank. Therefore, to properly convict D of conspiracy, it would be necessary (since she did not form an agreement with X and Y to rob the bank) to prove that she aided and abetted the conspiracy — that D intentionally aided in the *formation* of the agreement, such as by arranging the meeting at which X and Y formed the agreement. D did not aid in this manner and, therefore, ought not be convicted of conspiracy.

[C] Object of the Agreement

At common law, the object[49] of a conspiracy must be "to do either an unlawful act or a lawful act by criminal or unlawful means."[50] As this quote may suggest, the contemplated act that is the basis of the conspiratorial agreement need not constitute a crime; "it will be enough if the acts contemplated are corrupt, dishonest, fraudulent, or immoral."[51] Thus, it is possible for *two* people to be guilty of the common law offense of conspiracy because they have agreed to perform an act that is not criminal if performed in the absence of agreement by *one* of them. For example, it is a common law conspiracy for two or more persons

---

[46] E.g., Commonwealth v. Cook, 411 N.E.2d at 1328.

[47] United States v. Kissel, 218 U.S. 601, 608 (1910).

[48] *Developments in the Law*, Note 1, *supra*, at 934-35; American Law Institute, Comment to § 5.03, at 420-21.

[49] For purposes of clarity it is assumed here that the conspirators have a single objective. However, a single agreement may include multiple objectives. See § 29.08, *infra*.

[50] State v. Parker, 158 A. 797, 799 (Conn. 1932).

[51] *Id.*

to agree to perform a civil wrong (i.e., an act that would subject them to civil damages),[52] or to agree to perform an act that is not a civil wrong but is otherwise considered immoral or dangerous to the public health or safety.[53]

This feature of common law conspiracy, followed in many pre-Model Penal Code statutes,[54] has been strongly criticized by commentators as violative of the principle of legality.[55] People are entitled to fair notice that their planned conduct is subject to criminal sanction. In an age in which legislatures rather than courts define criminal conduct, people should be able to turn to a written code for reasonable guidance in the conduct of their lives. If the legislature has not made a specified act criminal it is unfair to surprise people by punishing the *agreement* to commit the *non*criminal act.

Fair notice is also a constitutional requirement. Although the Supreme Court has never ruled on the validity of this feature of conspiracy law, it once hinted that the breadth of the "unlawfulness" element violates due process.[56] State court rulings on the subject are mixed.[57]

Following the Model Penal Code,[58] many states have avoided the unfairness of the common law rule by limiting the offense of conspiracy to agreements to commit criminal acts.

[D] Overt Act

A common law conspiracy is complete upon formation of the unlawful agreement. No act in furtherance of the conspiracy need be proved.[59] Nonetheless, many statutes diverge from the common law and require an allegation in the indictment and proof at trial of the commission of an overt act in furtherance of the conspiracy.

In jurisdictions requiring an overt act, the act need not constitute an attempt to commit the target offense.[60] Any act, no matter how trivial, is sufficient, if

---

[52] E.g., State v. Loog, 179 A. 623 (N.J. 1935) (conspiracy to defame another).

[53] E.g., Shaw v. Director of Public Prosecutions, [1962] A.C. 220 (H.L.) (affirming a conviction for conspiracy to corrupt public morals, based on the publication of a lawful "Ladies' Directory" that contained the names and telephone numbers of prostitutes); Commonwealth v. Donoghue, 63 S.W.2d 3 (Ky. Ct. App. 1933) (affirming a conviction for conspiracy to exact usurious rates of interest, although usury was not a crime).

[54] American Law Institute, Comment to § 5.03, at 395.

[55] Commonwealth v. Bessette, 217 N.E.2d 893, 896 n.5 (Mass. 1966) (noting the criticism).

[56] Musser v. Utah, 333 U.S. 95, 96-97 (1948).

[57] E.g., compare State v. Bowling, 427 P.2d 928, 932 (Ariz. Ct. App. 1967) (unconstitutional), with People v. Sullivan, 248 P.2d 520, 526 (Cal. Ct. App. 1952) (constitutional).

[58] See § 29.04[E][2], *infra*.

[59] State v. Merrill, 530 S.E.2d 608, 611 (N.C. Ct. App. 2000) ("As soon as the union of wills for the unlawful purpose is perfected, the crime . . . is complete, . . . and no overt act is required.").

[60] State v. Heitman, 629 N.W.2d 542, 553 (Neb. 2001).

performed in pursuance of the conspiracy. Furthermore, the overt act need not be illegal.[61] For example, the act of writing a letter or making a telephone call pursuant to the unlawful agreement, the lawful purchase of an instrumentality to commit the offense, or attendance at a lawful meeting,[62] can qualify as the overt act.

In "overt act" jurisdictions, the allegation and proof of a single overt act by *any* party to a conspiracy is sufficient basis to prosecute *every* member of the conspiracy,[63] including those who may have joined in the agreement *after* the act was committed.[64]

To the extent that an overt act is an element of the offense of conspiracy,[65] it "serves to make certain that society does not intervene prematurely."[66] The overt act requirement, "like the substantial-step component of the law of attempt, helps to separate truly dangerous agreements from banter and other exchanges that pose less risk."[67] It shows "that a conspiracy has moved beyond the talk stage and is being carried out,"[68] that the conspiracy is "at work."[69]

[E] Model Penal Code

[1] In General

Section 5.03, subsection (1) — the Model Penal Code definition of conspiracy[70] — "rests on the primordial conception of agreement as the core of the conspiracy idea."[71] The American Law Institute rejected the misleading[72] conception of conspiracy as a "combination" or as a "partnership."

---

[61] *Id.*

[62] Yates v. United States, 354 U.S. 298, 333-34 (1957), overruled on other grounds in Burks v. United States, 437 U.S. 1 (1978) (attendance at a meeting of the Communist Party may constitute the overt act in furtherance of a conspiracy to overthrow the government).

[63] Bannon v. United States, 156 U.S. 464, 469 (1895).

[64] Kaplan v. United States, 7 F.2d 594, 596 (2d Cir. 1925).

[65] In some jurisdictions, an overt act, although required to convict, is not a formal element of the offense. Instead, the act "merely affords a *locus penitentiae*, so that before the act done either one or all of the parties may abandon their design, and thus avoid the penalty prescribed by the statute." United States v. Britton, 108 U.S. 199, 205 (1883). Thus, it gives a conspirator "an opportunity to repent." People v. Russo, 25 P.3d 641, 645 (Cal. 2001).

[66] People v. Mass, 628 N.W.2d 540, 559 (Mich. 2001) (Markman, J., concurring).

[67] United States v. Sassi, 966 F.2d 283, 284 (7th Cir. 1992).

[68] People v. Abedi, 595 N.Y.S.2d. 1011, 1020 (N.Y. Sup. Ct. 1993).

[69] State v. Heitman, 629 N.W.2d at 553 (quoting State v. Hansen, 562 N.W.2d 840, 849 (1997)).

[70] The definition is set out in full in § 29.01[B], *supra.*

[71] American Law Institute, Comment to § 5.03, at 421.

[72] See § 29.04[B], *supra.*

Four types of agreement fall within the definition of conspiracy. A person is guilty of conspiracy if she agrees to: (1) commit an offense (i.e., "engage in conduct that constitutes such crime"); (2) attempt to commit an offense;[73] (3) solicit another to commit an offense;[74] or (4) aid another person in the planning or commission of the offense.[75]

[2] Object of the Agreement

In a significant departure from the common law, the Model Penal Code provides that the object of the conspiratorial agreement must be a criminal offense. All but three state penal code revisions since the adoption of the final draft of the Code in 1962 have agreed with the American Law Institute in this regard.[76]

[3] Overt Act

The Code provides that a person may not be convicted of conspiracy to commit a misdemeanor or a felony of the third degree[77] unless she or a fellow conspirator performed an overt act in furtherance of the conspiracy. With felonies of the first and second degree, however, no overt act is required.[78]

As a result of this feature of the Code, the overt-act requirement has gained wide acceptance among the states. Most penal code revisions, however, have gone beyond the Code and apply the overt-act rule to all crimes.[79]

§ 29.05 CONSPIRACY: *MENS REA*

[A] In General

Common law conspiracy is a specific-intent offense. A criminal conspiracy does not occur unless two or more persons: (1) intend to agree; *and* (2) intend that the object of their agreement be achieved.[80] Absence of either intent renders the defendants' conduct non-conspiratorial. Thus, if *O*, an undercover police officer, agrees with *D* to murder *V*, *O* has the requisite intent to form an agreement with

---

[73] The purpose of this aspect of the definition is examined at § 29.09[A][2], *infra*.

[74] E.g., *D1* may be convicted of conspiracy if she agrees with *D2* that *D2* will solicit *X* to steal *V*'s painting.

[75] E.g., *D1* agrees to provide *D2* with a gun to be used to kill *V*. *D1* is guilty of conspiracy to commit murder, although she did not agree to commit the offense herself.

[76] American Law Institute, Comment to § 5.03, at 397.

[77] All felonies under the Model Penal Code are of the third degree unless another degree is specified. Model Penal Code § 6.01(1).

[78] Model Penal Code § 5.03(5).

[79] American Law Institute, Comment to § 5.03, at 455-56.

[80] People v. Cortez, 960 P.2d 537, 542 (Cal. 1998).

D (the first intent noted above), but she lacks the specific intent that the murder be consummated. As a result, *O* is not guilty of conspiracy. And, as discussed more fully elsewhere,[81] since *O* is not guilty of conspiracy, *D* cannot be convicted, because there are not "*two* or more persons" with the requisite intent.

It follows from the specific-intent nature of conspiracy that the culpability required for conviction of conspiracy at times must be greater than is required for conviction of the object of the agreement. For example, suppose that *D1* and *D2* agree to set fire to an occupied structure in order to claim the insurance proceeds. If the resulting fire kills occupants, they may be convicted of murder on the ground that the deaths, although unintentional, were recklessly caused. They are *not* guilty of conspiracy to commit murder, however, because their objective was to destroy the building, rather than to kill someone. Put another away, as a matter of logic, one "cannot agree to accomplish a required specific result unintentionally."[82]

[B] Special Issues

[1] "Purpose" versus "Knowledge": The Meaning of "Intent"

The specific intent of conspiracy is the "intent" that the object of the agreement be achieved. In most cases, the word "intent" suffices to describe the state of mind required. Sometimes, however, it does not.

It will be remembered that the common law term "intent" encompasses two different mental states, namely, what the Model Penal Code describes as "purpose" and "knowledge."[83] That is, *D* "intends" a result to occur if it is her conscious object (*purpose*) to cause the result or, even if it not her purpose, if she *knows* that it will occur from her conduct. The question that lurks, therefore, is whether the specific mental state of conspiracy is proved if either form of "intent" exists, or whether conspiracy can be demonstrated only if each party has as her *purpose* that the conspiratorial objective be achieved.

---

[81] See § 29.06[A], *infra*.

[82] State v. Beccia, 505 A.2d 683, 684 (Conn. 1986) (holding that conspiracy to commit reckless arson is not a cognizable offense); see also People v. Cortez, 960 P.2d 537, 538 (Cal. 1998) (holding that all conspiracies to commit murder are necessarily *first*-degree [premeditated] murders, and not *second*-degree [intentional, spur-of-the-moment] murders); State v. Donahue, 834 A.2d 253, 257 (N.H. 2003) (holding that a person may not be convicted of conspiracy to commit a reckless assault). Similarly, it seems impossible as a matter of law for two people to conspire to commit a *sudden* heat-of-passion intentional killing, which constitutes common law voluntary manslaughter (see § 31.07, *infra*), since the formation of an agreement to kill demonstrates premeditation, which is the antithesis of sudden, provoked homicide.

[83] See § 10.04[A][1], *supra*.

Usually this issue arises in a narrow context: A person or business furnishes goods or services to another person or group *knowing* that the goods or services will be used for illegal purposes. For example, consider these cases: *F* sells sugar to persons whom she knows are producers of illicit whiskey;[84] *L*, the operator of a telephone answering service, provides telephone messages to known prostitutes;[85] and *D*, a drug wholesaler, sells large quantities of legal drugs to *X*, knowing that *X* is using them for unlawful purposes.[86] In each of these cases, the person furnishing goods or services is aware of the customer's criminal intentions, but may not care whether the crime is committed.

The argument for requiring proof of criminal purpose, rather than mere knowledge — and, thus, potentially letting the defendants in the preceding cases off the criminal hook — is that conspiracy laws should be reserved for those with criminal motivations, rather than "seek to sweep within the drag-net of conspiracy all those who have been associated in any degree whatever with the main offenders."[87] In particular, it is argued, the law should not be broadened to punish those whose primary motive is to conduct an otherwise lawful business in a profitable manner. Indeed, in extending liability to merchants who *know* harm will occur from their activities, there is a risk that merchants who only suspect their customers' criminal intentions (thus, are merely *reckless* in regard to their customers' plans) will also be prosecuted, thereby seriously undermining lawful commerce.

The argument in favor of **permitting** conviction on the basis of knowledge is that society has a compelling interest in deterring people from furnishing their wares and skills to those whom they know are practically certain to use them unlawfully. Free enterprise should not immunize an actor from criminal responsibility in such circumstances; unmitigated desire for profits or simple moral indifference should not be rewarded at the expense of crime prevention.

Case law is divided on this purpose-versus-knowledge issue.[88] However, even in jurisdictions in which purpose is required, it may often be inferred from a defendant's knowledge of the customer's plans.[89] The requisite purpose may be inferred if the person furnishing the service or instrumentality promotes the venture and has a "stake in its outcome,"[90] such as when she furnishes the goods or services at a grossly inflated price. Similarly, purpose may be inferred from knowledge if a grossly disproportionate share of *D*'s business is with *X*,[91]

---

[84] United States v. Falcone, 109 F.2d 579 (2d Cir.), aff'd, 311 U.S. 205 (1940).

[85] People v. Lauria, 251 Cal. App. 2d 471 (Ct. App. 1967).

[86] Direct Sales Co. v. United States, 319 U.S. 703 (1943).

[87] United States v. Falcone, 109 F.2d at 581.

[88] American Law Institute, Comment to § 5.03, at 404 (and cases cited therein).

[89] See People v. Lauria, 251 Cal. App. 2d at 477-81.

[90] United States v. Falcone, 109 F.2d at 581.

[91] E.g., Direct Sales Co. v. United States, 319 U.S. 703 (1943) (*D*, a drug wholesaler, sold morphine sulfate to *X*, a physician, in quantities 300 times the amount required for lawful purposes).

or with separate customers whose planned conduct is illegal.[92] Finally, purpose may be inferred from knowledge if *D* provides goods or services for which there is no lawful use.

[2] *Mens Rea* Regarding Attendant Circumstances

The specific-intent element of conspiracy applies to the proscribed conduct or results of conduct that are the object of the agreement, but what mental state is required regarding attendant circumstances of an offense? For example, consider the essential facts of *United States v. Feola*:[93] *D1* and *D2*, drug dealers, agreed to attack *V*, a federal officer disguised as a drug customer. Clearly, *D1* and *D2* intended the prohibited result (battery), but were they guilty of the more serious federal offense of conspiracy to assault a federal officer in the performance of his official duties? That is, does the specific-intent requirement of conspiracy apply to the attendant circumstance of *V*'s status as a law enforcement officer?

As explained in *Feola*, the substantive offense of "assault upon a federal officer" requires no culpable state of mind regarding the attendant circumstance. That is, a person may be convicted of "assault upon a federal officer" as long as she has the requisite intent to commit the assaultive acts, even if she does not know or even have reason to know that the intended victim is an officer engaged in official duties. In light of this, the prosecution in *Feola* argued for symmetry: The *mens rea* required for conviction of *conspiracy* to assault a federal officer should be the same — neither more nor less — as that which is required for conviction of the substantive offense itself. Thus, in this case, to convict *D1* and *D2* of conspiracy, no *mens rea* would be required as to *V*'s status as a federal officer.

The *Feola* defendants argued that even if a person may be convicted of assault upon a federal officer without knowledge of the victim's federal status, one can hardly *conspire* to assault a federal officer without knowing the victim's identity. In support of this proposition they quoted the reasoning of Judge Learned Hand, who provided this example:

> While one may, for instance, be guilty of running past a traffic light of whose existence one is ignorant, one cannot be guilty of conspiring to run past such a light, for one cannot agree to run past a light unless one supposes that there is a light to run past.[94]

Although Judge Hand's "attractive, but perhaps seductive"[95] reasoning "seems difficult to overcome,"[96] the Supreme Court in *Feola* rejected his rea-

---

[92] E.g., Shaw v. Director of Public Prosecutions [1962] A.C. 220 (H.L.) (*S* sold space in a telephone and address directory to prostitutes).

[93] 420 U.S. 671 (1975).

[94] United States v. Crimmins, 123 F.2d 271, 273 (2d Cir. 1941).

[95] *Feola*, 420 U.S. at 689.

[96] American Law Institute, Comment to § 5.03, at 413.

soning, and held that the federal conspiracy statute does not require any greater *mens rea* as to an attendant circumstance than is embodied in the substantive offense itself.

Was the Court correct in rejecting Hand's traffic light analogy? Arguably, the circumstances in *Feola* were distinguishable from it. First, Hand's traffic offense was a *malum prohibitum* strict-liability crime, whereas an assault requires a wrongful intent to injure another. A court might wish to be more protective of defendants when the underlying offense is of the *malum prohibitum* variety.

Second, the moral-wrong doctrine[97] supports a distinction. As the Supreme Court said in *Feola*:

> This interpretation [that no *mens rea* is required as to the victim's status as a law enforcement officer] poses no risk of unfairness to defendants. It is no snare for the unsuspecting. Although the perpetrator of a narcotics [offense], such as the one involved here, may be surprised to find that his intended victim is a federal officer in civilian apparel, he nonetheless knows from the very outset that his planned course of conduct is wrongful.

The same cannot be said in the case of Judge Hand's hypothetical traffic violator, who was not committing a wrongful act based on the facts as she reasonably believed them to be.

Third, in *Feola* the attendant circumstance was a so-called "jurisdictional" element of the crime. That is, the fact that a victim is a federal officer performing her official duties is not a material element of the offense: It is included in the definition of the crime solely to provide the federal courts with authority to prosecute assaults that would otherwise constitute a state crime only. According to *Feola*, Congress did not intend for this jurisdictional-only feature of the law to stand in the way of conspiracy prosecutions based on the federal assault statute. In Hand's traffic light example, however, the issue of federal jurisdiction was not implicated.

Feola is not a constitutionally based decision. As such, states are not required to follow the principles of that case in interpreting their own conspiracy statutes. Thus, it remains an open question, on a state-by-state, offense-by-offense, basis, whether the crime of conspiracy may require a higher level of culpability regarding an attendant circumstance than is embodied in the underlying offense.

---

[97] See § 12.03[D][2], *supra*.

[3] Corrupt-Motive Doctrine

Some jurisdictions apply what has come to be known as the "corrupt-motive doctrine."[98] This doctrine states that in addition to the usual *mens rea* requirements of conspiracy (i.e., intent to agree and intent to commit the substantive offense), the parties to a conspiracy must also have a corrupt or wrongful motive for their actions.[99]

When the objective of a conspiracy is a *malum in se* offense, e.g., murder, rape, or larceny, the effect of this requirement is minimal, in that it only requires that the parties have sufficient knowledge of the relevant facts that they can appreciate that their conduct is wrongful. Thus, if we reconsider *Feola*,[100] in which *D1* and *D2* agreed to assault *V*, an undercover police officer, the parties had the requisite corrupt motive to commit a wrongful act (assault a human being), although they did not realize the degree of seriousness of their wrongful plan (i.e., they did not know that *V* was a law enforcement officer).

When the criminal objective is a *malum prohibitum* offense, however, the corrupt-motive doctrine serves as an exception to the usual rule that ignorance of the law is no excuse. Thus, in a jurisdiction that applies this doctrine, if *D1* and *D2* agree to do X, a morally innocent but illegal act, they cannot be convicted of conspiracy to commit X if they did not realize that X was illegal. In the absence of knowledge of the law, the parties lack a corrupt motive.[101]

Assuming the propriety of the ignorance-of-the-law-is-no-excuse rule, is this exception to it justifiable? The best argument for the exception is that, in light of the highly inchoate nature of the offense of conspiracy, "breathing space" should be given to those who lack a corrupt motive for their planned conduct: We may reasonably predict that, unlike those animated by criminal intent, those who agree to commit actions that constitute a *malum prohibitum* offense would voluntarily abandon their efforts if they were aware of its illegality. On the other hand, if the *malum prohibitum* statute in question is strict liability in nature,

---

[98] At one time, the doctrine was said to have "won general acceptance." *Developments in the Law*, Note 1, *supra*, at 936. In part because the issue only rarely arises today, the current status of the doctrine in most jurisdictions is uncertain, but the trend is to reject the doctrine, especially in the federal courts. United States v. Cohen, 260 F.3d 68 (2d Cir. 2001) (refusing to apply the corrupt motive doctrine).

[99] E.g., Commonwealth v. Benesch, 194 N.E. 905, 910 (Mass. 1935); State v. Jacobson, 697 N.W.2d 610, 615 (Minn. 2005) (requiring proof that the parties possessed a "conscious and intentional purpose to break law"); People v. Powell, 63 N.Y. 88, 92 (1875).

[100] United States v. Feola, 420 U.S. 671 (1975). See § 29.05[B][2], *supra*.

[101] E.g., Commonwealth v. Gormley, 77 Pa. Super. 298 (Pa. Super. Ct. 1921) (*D1* and *D2*, election officials, were not guilty of conspiracy to violate a *malum prohibitum* election law when they agreed to commit acts that violated the substantive offense, because they were unaware that their activities were encompassed by the statute); State v. Jacobson, 697 N.W.2d at 615 (holding that, in a conspiracy prosecution, a defendant's mistake of law, based on a lawyer's wrongful advice and/or an official misinterpretation of the law, is sufficient to prove a lack of requisite intent to convict).

as is often the case, there may be no justification for requiring more culpability for the conspiracy charge than for the target offense.

[C] Model Penal Code

A person is not guilty of conspiracy under the Model Penal Code[102] unless the conspiratorial agreement was made "with the purpose of promoting or facilitating" the commission of the substantive offense. As at common law, this means that a person is not guilty of conspiracy unless the object of the agreement was to bring about the prohibited result or to cause the prohibited conduct to occur, even if such purpose is not an element of the target offense. For example, suppose that *D1* and *D2* agree to burn down an occupied building for the insurance proceeds and, in the ensuing fire, an occupant dies. The defendants are guilty of murder, based on their reckless indifference to the value of human life.[103] However, they are not guilty of conspiracy to commit murder, unless another object of their agreement was to take human life.[104] The express requirement of purpose also resolves a common law debate: A conspiracy does *not* exist if a provider of goods or services is aware of, but fails to share, another person's criminal purpose.[105]

The Model Penal Code does not recognize the corrupt-motive doctrine.[106] Section 2.04, subsection (3), of the Code specifies the circumstances in which ignorance of the law is a defense. The drafters of the Code did not believe that a special ignorance defense in the case of conspiracy was justified. They reasoned that the real purpose of the corrupt-motive doctrine was to "import fair mens rea requirements into [strict liability] statutes."[107] Although the drafters agreed with this goal, they favored promoting it directly through changes in general culpability rules, rather than through conspiracy doctrine.

The Code does not determine what culpability, if any, regarding an attendant circumstance of a substantive offense is required to convict for the offense of conspiracy.[108] The Commentary states that this issue is "best left to judicial resolution."[109]

---

[102] For the full Code definition of "conspiracy," see § 29.01[B], *supra*.

[103] Model Penal Code § 210.2(1)(b).

[104] American Law Institute, Comment to § 5.03, at 407-08. However, *D1* and *D2* may be convicted of conspiracy to recklessly endanger the occupants of the building. Model Penal Code § 211.2. This result is possible because their *purpose*, in the language of § 5.03(1)(a), was to "engage in conduct [setting fire to the building] that constitutes such crime [placing another person in danger of death or serious bodily injury, the offense of reckless endangerment]."

[105] See generally American Law Institute, Comment to § 5.03, at 403-04. The issue is raised in 29.05[B][1], *supra*.

[106] See § 29.05[B][3], *supra*.

[107] American Law Institute, Comment to § 5.03, at 417 (footnote omitted).

[108] This issue is raised in § 29.05[B][2], *supra*.

[109] See American Law Institute, Comment to § 5.03, at 413.

§ 29.06 "PLURALITY" REQUIREMENT

[A] Common Law

According to Justice Cardozo, "[i]t is impossible . . . for a man to conspire with himself."[110] This observation follows from the fact that a conspiracy is an agreement, and an agreement is a group act. Unless two or more people form an agreement, no one does. As a consequence, a prosecution of common law conspiracy must fail in the absence of proof that at least two persons possessed the requisite *mens rea* of a conspiracy, i.e., the intent to agree and the specific intent that the object of their agreement be achieved.[111] This is the so-called "plurality" requirement; it is founded on the premise that "conspiracy" is a bilateral concept.

As a result of the plurality principle, there can be no common law conspiracy if one of two parties to an agreement lacks the specific intent to commit the substantive offense. For example, no conspiracy conviction is possible — although, perhaps, an *attempted* conspiracy charge might lie[112] — if one of the two persons is an undercover agent feigning agreement,[113] or lacks the capacity to form the agreement due to mental illness.[114] Indeed, although the rule is break-

---

[110] Morrison v. California, 291 U.S. 82, 92 (1934).

[111] People v. Justice, 562 N.W.2d 652, 658 (Mich. 1997).

[112] Can one *attempt* to conspire? There is little case law on this issue, but most courts have rejected the concept. Ira P. Robbins, *Double Inchoate Crimes*, 26 Harv. J. on Legis. 1, 54-55 (1989); United States v. Yu-Leung, 51 F.3d 1116, 1122 n.3 (2d Cir. 1995) ("an attempted conspiracy — a creature unknown to federal criminal law"); Hutchinson v. State, 315 So. 2d 546, 547-48 (Fla. Dist. Ct. App. 1975), overruled on other grounds by Gentry v. State, 422 So. 2d 1072 (Fla. Dist. Ct. App. 1982); State v. Eames, 365 So. 2d 1361, 1364 (La. 1978). Contra Llorente v. Commissioner, 649 F.2d 152 (2d Cir. 1981) (indicating that *L* pleaded guilty in state court to attempted conspiracy to criminally possess cocaine); United States v. Riddle, 44 M.J. 282, 284-85 (C.A.A.F. 1996) (recognizing the offense); People v. Anderson, 509 N.W.2d 548 (Mich. Ct. App. 1993) (*A* convicted of attempted conspiracy to deliver cocaine).

Conceptually, there is no reason why a jurisdiction could not recognize such an offense. Some courts, however, may be troubled on policy grounds about recognizing such a highly inchoate offense: A conspiracy can occur far sooner than an attempt; an attempted conspiracy, therefore, takes the process to an even earlier stage. The difficulty with this argument is that most states have enacted general solicitation statutes, and a *solicitation, by definition, is an attempted conspiracy*. See § 28.02[A], *supra*. Thus, the reason for not recognizing the defense may simply be that the prosecutor has mischarged the defendant. It is noteworthy, for example, that one court, *United States v. Riddle, supra*, in upholding an attempted conspiracy charge, observed that no general solicitation statute existed in that jurisdiction.

Although a solicitation is always an attempted conspiracy, an attempted conspiracy does not always constitute a solicitation. See § 28.02[A], *supra*. Thus, inchoate policy issues aside, there is reason for recognizing such an offense.

[113] E.g., State v. Pacheco, 882 P.2d 183, 186 (Wash. 1994); Palato v. State, 988 P.2d 512, 515-16 (Wyo. 1999); United States v. Escobar de Bright, 742 F.2d 1196, 1199-1200 (9th Cir. 1984).

[114] See Regle v. State, 264 A.2d 119 (Md. Ct. Spec. App. 1970) (the prosecutor alleged a four-person conspiracy, but one party was a police informant, the second was a police officer, and the third was insane, leaving only one defendant with the requisite *mens rea*; held: conspiracy conviction could not stand).

ing down, in a joint trial of a two-person conspiracy, the acquittal of one alleged conspirator traditionally requires the discharge of the remaining defendant, regardless of the jury's reasons for acquittal.[115]

The plurality rule does not require, however, that two persons be prosecuted and convicted of conspiracy. It is enough that the prosecutor proves beyond a reasonable doubt that two persons are guilty of conspiracy. Thus, the conviction of a conspirator is not in jeopardy simply because the other person involved in the arrangement is unapprehended, dead, or unknown, or cannot be prosecuted because he has been granted immunity.[116] And, although the rule used to be to the contrary,[117] the modern rule is that a convicted conspirator is not automatically entitled to relief because of the acquittal of the remaining conspirators in a *separate* trial.[118] As long as the evidence at the first trial was "sufficient unto itself to support its verdict"[119] — that is, the prosecutor proved that there was a conspiratorial agreement between two or more persons, one of whom was the defendant — the failure to convince the second jury of the conspiracy does not impair the validity of the first conviction, since the acquittal at the second trial may have been the result of a multitude of factors, such as the unexpected absence of a critical state witness.

---

[115] State v. Valladares, 664 P.2d 508, 512-13 (Wash. 1983). As noted in the text, this rule is breaking down. For example, in *Commonwealth v. Campbell*, 651 A.2d 1096 (Pa. 1994), the Supreme Court of Pennsylvania turned away from earlier law and ruled that "acquittal of the sole alleged co-conspirator does not per se preclude the conviction of the remaining defendant, even if the defendants are jointly tried." *Id.* at 1099. In *Campbell*, the prosecutor presented sufficient evidence that a jury could conclude beyond a reasonable doubt that: (a) a two-person conspiracy existed; and (b) *C* was one of the two conspirators. The jury acquitted *C*'s co-defendant, but the apparent reason for this acquittal was that the jury had a reasonable doubt that the acquitted individual was, in fact, *C*'s co-conspirator — the government may have arrested the wrong person. The *Campbell* court held that *C*'s conviction could stand under these circumstances.

The California Supreme Court, as well, has rejected the traditional rule. In *People v. Palmer*, 15 P.3d 234 (Cal. 2001), *D1* and *D2* were accused of attempted murder and conspiracy to commit murder. They were tried jointly but in front of separate juries. *D1* was convicted of all charges; the second jury convicted *D2* of attempted murder but acquitted him of conspiracy. *D1* argued that, as a result of *D2*'s conspiracy acquittal, his conviction for that offense had to be reversed. The state supreme court, while conceding that the verdicts were logically inconsistent and that a person cannot conspire with himself, ruled that *D1*'s conspiracy conviction should stand. It reasoned that a jury can acquit a defendant for any reason or for no reason at all. It speculated that the jury may have acquitted *D2* out of compassion for the fact that he was fifteen years old, while *D1* was twenty-nine years old. As there was substantial evidence supporting *D1*'s conspiracy conviction, the court determined he should not receive a windfall as a result of the jury's compassionate (or simply legally mistaken) decision to acquit *D2* of conspiracy.

[116] See Commonwealth v. Byrd, 417 A.2d 173, 176-77 (Pa. 1980).

[117] E.g., Sherman v. State, 202 N.W. 413, 414 (Neb. 1925), overruled by Platt v. State, 8 N.W.2d 849, 855 (Neb. 1943); *Developments in the Law*, Note 1, *supra*, at 972-73.

[118] E.g., State v. Colon, 778 A.2d 875, 883 (Conn. 2001); State v. Johnson, 788 A.2d 628, 632-33 (Md. 2002) (also stating that this rule "is well-accepted in most state jurisdictions").

[119] Gardner v. State, 408 A.2d 1317, 1322 (Md. 1979).

The plurality requirement has been criticized. First, the rule undermines the law enforcement purpose of conspiracy laws. For example, if *O*, an undercover police officer, feigns willingness to assist *D* in the commission of a murder, the plurality rule supposedly prevents *O* from arresting *D* until the latter's conduct reaches the more dangerous stage of an attempt.[120] Second, one who fails to conspire because her "partner in crime" is an undercover officer feigning agreement is no less personally dangerous or culpable than one whose colleague in fact possesses the specific intent to go through with the criminal plan.[121]

On the other hand, the plurality doctrine is consistent with the "special dangers in group criminality" rationale of conspiracy.[122]

[B] Model Penal Code

The Model Code departs significantly from the common law by establishing a unilateral approach to conspiracy liability. Unlike the common law definition of conspiracy, which is phrased in terms of "two or more persons," the Code "focuses inquiry on the culpability of the actor whose liability is in issue, rather than on that of the group of which [she] is alleged to be a part."[123] That is, although the gist of the offense, as at common law, is the agreement, "conspiracy" is defined in terms of the guilt of a single party. This is evident from the Code's definition of "conspiracy,"[124] which starts, "*A person* is guilty of conspiracy with another person" if "*he agrees* with such other person" to commit an offense.

The unilateral nature of the Code's conspiracy provision affects legal analysis in various ways, some of which are discussed later in this chapter.[125] Its effect regarding the plurality doctrine, however, is straightforward. Although the prosecution may not convict a person of conspiracy in the absence of proof of an agreement, it is no defense that the person with whom the actor agreed: (1) has not been or cannot be convicted; or (2) is acquitted in the same or subsequent trial on the ground that she did not have the intent to go forward with the

---

[120] This criticism is overstated. Even with the plurality doctrine, *D* may be guilty of solicitation. Furthermore, if a jurisdiction recognizes the offense of *attempted* conspiracy, *D* could be arrested for the latter offense. See Note 112, *supra*.

[121] Miller v. State, 955 P.2d 892, 897 (Wyo. 1998).

[122] See § 29.02[B], *supra*.

[123] American Law Institute, Comment to § 5.03, at 393; see generally *id*. at 398-402.

[124] See § 29.01[B], *supra*, for the full definition.

[125] See §§ 29.07[E], 29.09[D][2], *infra*.

criminal plan (e.g., she feigned agreement in an effort to frustrate the endeavor,[126] or is insane[127]).

The unilateral approach has been adopted in all but a very few recent revisions of state penal codes.[128]

§ 29.07 PARTIES TO A CONSPIRACY

[A] The Issue

Frequently, the facts surrounding an incident demonstrate that a conspiracy is afoot, but what is unclear is whether there is a single conspiracy involving many defendants, or multiple conspiracies involving fewer persons in each group. Four well-known cases illustrate the issue. They will be discussed throughout this section.

[1] *Kotteakos v. United States*[129]

Brown served as a broker for thirty-one persons in obtaining fraudulent loans from the government. He and the loan recipients were indicted on one count of conspiracy. The evidence at trial demonstrated that the loan recipients were part of eight or more independent groups, none of which had any connection with any other group except that each used Brown as its broker.

The issue in the case was whether the thirty-two defendants were parties to a single conspiracy (as the prosecutor contended), or whether there existed eight or more smaller conspiracies, each consisting of a different group of loan recipients and Brown (as the loan recipients asserted).

[2] *Blumenthal v. United States*[130]

In *Blumenthal*, the unnamed owner of a liquor wholesale agency distributed whiskey through two men, Weiss and Goldsmith, who arranged with Feigen-

---

[126] E.g., State v. Heitman, 629 N.W.2d 542 (Neb. 2001) (*H* conversed on the Internet with a police officer posing as a 14-year-old; "the child" agreed to have sexual relations with *H*; held: *H* was guilty of conspiracy to commit sexual assault on a child).

[127] Model Penal Code § 5.04(1)(b) expressly provides that it is no defense that the person with whom the defendant conspired is "irresponsible or has an immunity to prosecution or conviction." However, this result is already implicit in the unilateral conception. American Law Institute, Comment to § 5.03, at 399-400.

[128] *Id.* at 398-99; see Miller v. State, 955 P.2d 892, 897 (Wyo. 1998) ("[T]he modern trend in state courts is to rule that a conspiracy count is viable even when one of the participants is a government agent or is feigning agreement.").

[129] 328 U.S. 750 (1946).

[130] 332 U.S. 539 (1947).

baum and Blumenthal to sell the whiskey to local tavern owners at a price in violation of the law.

The prosecutor alleged one conspiracy, the parties being the unidentified owner, the two distributors, and the salesmen. The salesmen claimed, however, that they never dealt with the owner or knew his identity. If they participated in a conspiracy, they asserted, it was one with the distributors alone; in turn the distributors were supposedly in a separate conspiracy with the owner.

[3] *United States v. Peoni*[131]

Peoni sold a small quantity of counterfeit money to Regno, who in turn sold the money to Dorsey, who passed the money in commerce to innocent persons. The prosecutor alleged that the three men were parties to a single conspiracy. Peoni contended that if he was a party to any conspiracy it was with Regno alone, who in turn conspired with Dorsey.

[4] *United States v. Bruno*[132]

Bruno and eighty-seven others were prosecuted for conspiracy to import, sell, and possess narcotics. The evidence showed that a group of persons whose object it was to smuggle narcotics into the country through the Port of New York distributed the drugs through middlemen to retailers in New York and other retailers serving the Texas-Louisiana region. The retailers distributed the drugs to individual addicts.

No communication between the importers and any of the retailers or between the New York retailers and the Texas-Louisiana retailers was proved. The importers did know, however, that the middlemen dealt with retailers, and the retailers knew that the middlemen obtained their drugs from importers.

On appeal, the petitioners claimed that instead of a single conspiracy, there were at least three conspiracies — one between the importers and the middlemen; a second between the middlemen and the New York retailers; and a third between the middlemen and the Texas-Louisiana retailers.

[B] Why the Issue Matters

[1] Liability for Conspiracy

The most obvious reason why the structure of a conspiracy is important is that it will affect the number of counts of conspiracy for which a particular per-

---

[131] 100 F.2d 401 (2d Cir. 1938).

[132] 105 F.2d 921 (2d Cir. 1939), rev'd on other grounds, 308 U.S. 287 (1939).

son may be prosecuted and convicted. For example, in *Kotteakos*, as the prosecutor conceived of the case, Brown was guilty of one count of conspiracy with thirty-one loan recipients; alternatively, Brown was potentially guilty of eight or more counts of conspiracy, each involving a smaller number of parties.

[2] Liability of Parties for Substantive Offenses

As is discussed more fully elsewhere,[133] a conspirator is guilty of every offense committed by every other conspirator in furtherance of the unlawful agreement. The structure of the conspiracy, therefore, may dramatically affect an individual conspirator's liability for the substantive crimes of others.

For example, if the prosecutor in *Kotteakos* was correct in treating the thirty-two defendants as parties to a single conspiracy, each party could be convicted of thirty-one separate counts of fraud (assuming that the fraudulent loans were obtained); if the loan recipients' theory was correct, however, each of them was guilty of only a few fraudulently obtained loans, namely those obtained by the group composing the smaller conspiracy.

Similarly, in *Bruno* the prosecutor's theory could result in New York retailers being held accountable for every drug sale on the Texas-Louisiana streets (and vice-versa); their liability would be considerably less if the defense theory of the structure of the conspiracy was correct.

[3] Use of Hearsay Evidence

"Hearsay evidence" is evidence of a statement made other than by a witness while testifying at the hearing, which is offered to prove the truth of the matter stated. Subject to many exceptions, hearsay testimony is inadmissible at trial. Thus, under this rule, W, a witness, may not testify that X told her that she (X) saw D commit an offense.[134]

The hearsay rule is subject to two exceptions relevant here. First, an out-of-court admission by a defendant, e.g., an assertion by D that she killed V, may be introduced at D's trial through the hearsay testimony of W, someone to whom D made the statement or who overheard the remarks. Second, an out-of-court statement of a conspirator made while participating in the conspiracy may be introduced in evidence against her co-conspirators. Thus, a statement by $D1$ to W that she and $D2$ murdered V may be introduced against both $D1$ and $D2$ and any other co-conspirators.

---

[133] See § 30.08, *infra*.

[134] Hearsay testimony is inadmissible because if it were allowed, a defendant would be denied her constitutional right to cross-examine her accuser (X in the example in the text), and because it would render the trial less reliable than if the accuser were required to testify directly.

The structure of the alleged conspiracy, therefore, is critical to determination of the admissibility of hearsay testimony. For example, under the prosecutor's theory of the conspiracy in *Bruno*, an out-of-court statement made by a New York retailer that "we and the Texans and Louisianans are getting a rotten deal from the importers and middlemen," could be used against the importers, middlemen, Texas and Louisiana retailers, and every other New York retailer. Applying the retailers' theory of the conspiracy, however, the New York retailer's remarks would be inadmissible against the Texas-Louisiana retailers, because they were not parties to the New York conspiracy.

[4] Joint Trial

Generally speaking, prosecutors prefer to bring every member of an alleged conspiracy to trial in a single proceeding, rather than to prosecute the conspirators in separate trials. Joint trials are more efficient (e.g., all of the evidence may be introduced once to a single jury). Perhaps equally importantly, a joint trial makes it more difficult for innocent or barely culpable defendants to separate themselves from guilty co-defendants. As Justice Jackson has observed:

> A co-defendant in a conspiracy trial occupies an uneasy seat. There generally will be evidence of wrongdoing by somebody. It is difficult for the individual to make his own case stand on its own merits in the minds of jurors who are ready to believe that birds of a feather are flocked together.[135]

Thus, in *Bruno*, the most culpable importers were joined with comparatively small-time street retailers. Even if some of the eighty-eight persons charged with conspiracy were innocent of wrongdoing, they faced substantial difficulties of proof.

[5] Overt-Act Requirement

The structure of a conspiracy is critical in jurisdictions recognizing an overt-act requirement.[136] In these jurisdictions, an act of one conspirator in furtherance of the agreement renders a prosecution permissible against every other party to the same agreement.

For example, in *Kotteakos* proof of a single overt act by one person, for example by Brown, pertaining to a single fraudulent loan, would be sufficient to bring the conspiracy prosecution against all thirty-two defendants. If the loan recipients' argument was correct, however, at least eight separate conspiracies were involved, and proof of an overt act in each of these cases would be required.

---

[135] Krulewitch v. United States, 336 U.S. 440, 454 (1949) (concurring opinion).

[136] See generally § 29.04[D], *supra*.

[6] Venue

In general, a trial may be held in any jurisdiction in which the crime was committed. With conspiracies, a trial may be brought not only where the agreement was formulated, but also in any jurisdiction in which any member performed any act in its furtherance.

The effect of this venue rule is especially dramatic in federal cases. The larger the conspiracy alleged by the prosecutor, the greater are the number of federal districts in the country in which it is permissible to bring the prosecution. The prosecutor, therefore, has an incentive to shape the conspiracy in a manner that will allow her to bring the case in a sympathetic venue. It also permits her to compel a defendant in a conspiracy prosecution "to defend at a great distance from any place he ever did any act because some accused confederate did some trivial and by itself innocent act in the chosen district."[137]

[C] Structure of Conspiracies

In conspiracy prosecutions involving multiple layers of actors, it is useful for a lawyer to conceptualize the alleged conspiracy in diagrammatic fashion. Usually the diagraming will demonstrate that a conspiracy looks something like a wheel, a chain, or a combination of the two.

[1] Wheel Conspiracies

Some conspiracies look like wheels. In the center of the wheel (*the hub*) is one person or group who transacts illegal dealings with various other persons or groups (*the spokes*). As the prosecutor conceptualized it, *Kotteakos* was a wheel conspiracy. Brown was the hub. Each of the persons for whom he obtained loans or, at least, each of the eight groups of persons with whom he dealt, was a spoke.

However, for a wheel conspiracy to be complete, i.e., for it to be fair to say that there exists a single conspiracy that includes the hub and all of the spokes, there must be a rim around the wheel. That is, one must be able to draw a line around the wheel connecting the spokes. If this cannot be done, then there is no wheel conspiracy; rather there exist as many chain conspiracies (see below) as there are spokes, with the membership of each conspiracy consisting of the person/group in the hub and the individual at the other end of the spoke. The process of how the spokes are connected together to create a genuine wheel conspiracy is considered in subsection [D].

---

[137] Krulewitch v. United States, 336 U.S. at 453 (Jackson, J., concurring).

[2] Chain Conspiracies

A chain conspiracy ordinarily involves "several layers of personnel dealing with a single subject matter, as opposed to a specific person."[138] These conspiracies most often occur in business-like criminal activities, in which each person or group in the conspiracy has specialized responsibilities that link together the various aspects of the unlawful conduct.

As the prosecutors alleged the facts, *Blumenthal* and *Peoni* were three-link chain conspiracies. In *Blumenthal* the unidentified owner of the wholesale agency was linked to Weiss and Goldsmith, the distributors, who in turn were linked to Feigenbaum and Blumenthal, who sold the whiskey to taverns. In *Peoni*, Peoni was linked to Regno who was linked to Dorsey.

The issue with chain conspiracies is how many people or groups may properly be linked together. The longer the chain, the more tenuous the relationship between the distant links.

[3] Chain-Wheel Conspiracies

It is not unusual to find that the structure of a very large conspiracy has features of both a wheel and a chain. *Bruno* potentially fits this description. Notice that it was basically a chain consisting of smugglers, middlemen, and retailers. However, there existed at least two geographically disparate groups of retailers. It is possible, therefore, to conceptualize the conspiracy either as two chain conspiracies (in which the importers, middlemen, and the separate state retailers are linked) or as a chain conspiracy with spokes at the end (thus, the importers are linked to the middlemen, at which point the various retail groups become spokes connected to the middlemen).[139]

[D] Common Law Analysis

[1] In General

There is no simple method for determining the proper structure of a conspiracy. Many factors, including the nature of the criminal activity, the number of defendants, the size of the business, and the extent of contact between the parties, will affect the ultimate result. One matter is clear, however: To be regarded as a co-conspirator, a person does not need to know the identity, *or even*

---

[138] People v. Macklowitz, 514 N.Y.S.2d 883, 886 (N.Y. Sup. Ct. 1987).

[139] Of course, the New York and Texas-Louisiana spokes consisted of many individual retailers no more likely to be connected to one another than one state group was connected to the retailers in the other region. Thus, if one were inclined to do so, one could break up the two spokes into many more individual spokes.

the existence, of every other member of the conspiracy, nor must she participate in every detail or event of the conspiracy.[140] It follows, therefore, that a prosecutor's theory of a conspiracy is not fatally flawed solely because one party to the alleged agreement never communicated with certain other members. However, to be a co-conspirator, a defendant must "have a general awareness of both the scope and the objective of the enterprise";[141] in general, there must be a "community of interest [among the parties] or reason to know of each other's existence."[142]

[2] Wheel Conspiracies

Hubs and spokes frequently perceive events differently. The hub views each spoke as part of a broader criminal enterprise; the spokes, however, often interpret the situation more narrowly. For example, in *Kotteakos*, Brown was in the business of obtaining fraudulent loans for his customers. He sought each customer — each spoke — as a part of a broader plan. The customers, however, were interested only in their own loans.

A rim does not exist — there is no wheel conspiracy — unless the prosecutor demonstrates that the spokes viewed their contacts with the hub as part of a plan broader than any individual spoke's relationship with the hub: "What is required is a *shared*, single criminal objective, not just similar or parallel objectives between similarly situated people."[143]

In *Kotteakos*, the appellate court concluded that the spokes lacked this shared objective. No community of interest existed among the spokes: Each loan recipient wanted a loan, received it, and moved on. Each loan was independent of the others. Each fraudulent application stood or fell on the basis of the false claims asserted in that particular application. Thus, the spokes were correct in concluding that, rather than one wheel conspiracy, there existed multiple chain conspiracies involving Brown and each spoke.

An example of a genuine wheel conspiracy is *Anderson v. Superior Court*:[144] A, an illegal abortionist, hired as many as seventeen persons, to whom he paid "finder's fees," to refer pregnant women to him. The court upheld an indictment charging the eighteen persons (A, the hub; and the seventeen spokes) as parties to a single conspiracy. Here, unlike in *Kotteakos*, the spokes had an ongoing rela-

---

[140] United States v. Sophie, 900 F.2d 1064, 1080-81 (7th Cir. 1990).

[141] United States v. Evans, 970 F.2d 663, 670 (10th Cir. 1992).

[142] Kilgore v. State, 305 S.E.2d 82, 90 (Ga. 1983).

[143] United States v. Evans, 970 F.2d at 670; United States v. Shorter, 54 F.3d 1248, 1254 (7th Cir. 1995) (there is a single conspiracy if there is a shared design; there are separate conspiracies "if there are distinct illegal ends and no overlapping interest between parties").

[144] 177 P.2d 315 (Cal. Ct. App. 1947), overruled on other grounds by People v. Weiss, 327 P.2d 527 (Cal. 1958).

tionship with the hub. And, arguably, each of the spokes shared a common objective, since their continued employment depended on the success of the broader illegal venture.

[3] Chain Conspiracies

Large chain conspiracies are easier to prove than wheel conspiracies. This follows from the fact that chain conspiracies ordinarily involve unlawful plans that cannot succeed unless each link successfully performs her responsibilities in the arrangement.

Thus, in *Blumenthal*, the Supreme Court found that the prosecutor properly charged a single conspiracy. Although the salesmen claimed that they did not know of the owner's existence (much less his identity), the Court pointed out that they knew that the persons with whom they dealt were not the true owners of the wholesale agency. Therefore, the "salesmen knew or must have known that others unknown to them were sharing in so large a project." Each salesman "by reason of [his] knowledge of the plan's general scope, if not its exact limits, sought a common end, to aid in disposing of the whiskey."

This does not mean that every chain is a single conspiracy. *Peoni*, for example, was not a single conspiracy. Here, Peoni apparently sold only a small number of counterfeit bills to Regno. Peoni did not care whether Regno passed the money himself or, as he did, sold it to another person to pass. Peoni had no common interest, therefore, with Dorsey. Instead, there were two independent conspiracies, one between Peoni and Regno and a second one between Regno and Dorsey. If larger numbers of bills had been involved — enough that Peoni needed Regno to obtain assistance in passing the money — a single conspiracy might have been proved.[145]

[4] Chain-Wheel Conspiracies

Quite arguably, *Bruno* involved a chain-wheel conspiracy. The court ruled that the importers, middlemen, and geographically disparate retailers were all part of a single chain conspiracy. The retailers knew that smugglers existed (and vice-versa). More importantly, each link had a stake in the larger venture. The court failed to explain, however, why and how the retailers — the separate spokes — were drawn together. The court properly analyzed the chain feature of the conspiracy, but it ignored the wheel aspect.

---

[145] E.g., United States v. La Vecchia, 513 F.2d 1210 (2d Cir. 1975).

[E] Model Penal Code

[1] Relevant Provisions

The Model Penal Code provides a complex but potentially fairer approach to the party dimension of a conspiracy. Two aspects of the Code are relevant. First, Section 5.03(1), as reprinted above,[146] and discussed earlier,[147] adopts the unilateral approach to conspiracy, and provides that a person is guilty of conspiracy if, with the purpose of promoting or facilitating the commission of a crime, she agrees with another to commit the offense.

Second, Section 5.03(2) provides additional guidance in determining when parties to separate agreements to commit the same crime may be linked together:

> *Scope of Conspiratorial Relationship.* If a person guilty of conspiracy . . . knows that a person with whom he conspires to commit a crime has conspired with another person or persons to commit the same crime, he is guilty of conspiring with such other person or persons, whether or not he knows their identity, to commit such crime.

[2] Example of the Code Approach: *United States v. Bruno*[148]

The Commentary to the Code explains how some of the cases discussed earlier in this section would be analyzed under the Model Penal Code.[149] The most interesting questions arise regarding *Bruno*, in which the Code would require a different mode of analysis and, very likely, would reach a different outcome. In order to understand how the Code provisions are applied, we may simplify the *Bruno* facts by assuming the existence of a single importer, a single middleman, and one retailer each in New York and Texas-Louisiana; also, for sake of clarity, certain facts not clear in *Bruno* will be assumed.[150]

Here is the *Bruno*-inspired hypothetical scenario: Importer meets with Middleman and agrees that Importer will smuggle narcotics into the country, in violation of Statute X. In their meeting, they further agree that Middleman will find retailers to sell the narcotics in their states, which sales would violate Statute Y. Middleman proceeds to meet with New York Retailer and, on another date, with Texas-Louisiana Retailer, and agrees with each of them that the

---

[146] See § 29.01[B], *supra.*

[147] See §§ 29.04[E], 29.05[C], 29.06[B], *supra.*

[148] 105 F.2d 921 (2d Cir. 1939), rev'd on other grounds, 308 U.S. 287 (1939). See § 29.07[A][4], *supra.*

[149] See American Law Institute, Comment to § 5.03, at 425-35.

[150] As a consequence of the potentially different facts being assumed here, a precise comparison between *Bruno* and the Model Penal Code approach is not possible.

retailers will sell drugs in their respective states, in violation of Statute Y. Neither retailer knows that Middleman is dealing with another retailer, nor do the retailers know the details of the Importer-Middleman dealings.

Based on these facts a lawyer would start by applying Section 5.03(1), in order to identify each agreement to commit a crime that occurred. Doing this, the evidence supports the existence of four agreements: (1) Importer and Middleman, to violate Statute X; (2) Importer and Middleman, to violate Statute Y; (3) Middleman and New York retailer, to violate Statute Y; (4) Middleman and Texas-Louisiana retailer, to violate Statute Y.

Based on Section 5.03(1) alone, therefore, we have four two-person agreements. At this point, however, Section 5.03(2) may be applied to add additional links to the conspiracies. Importer knew that Middleman, with whom she had conspired to violate Statute Y, would also conspire with New York Retailer and Texas-Louisiana Retailer to commit the same offense. Consequently, Importer is guilty of conspiring with both retailers to violate Statute Y.

The retailers, however, did not know that Middleman, with whom they dealt, had conspired with Importer to violate Statute Y; therefore, in light of the Code's unilateral approach to conspiracy, the retailers are not guilty of conspiring with Importer to violate Statute Y (although, as just seen, Importer is guilty of conspiring *with them* to commit the same offense). Moreover, there is probably no basis for finding that the New York and Texas-Louisiana retailers had the requisite purpose of promoting or facilitating the commission of the sales in the other region, so neither retailer should be joined in any conspiracy relating to the violation of Statute Y outside their own area.

Thus, we reach this conclusion. Importer conspired with Middleman to violate Statute X; and she conspired with Middleman, New York Retailer, and Texas-Louisiana Retailer to violate Statute Y. The same result applies to Middleman. New York Retailer is guilty of conspiring with Middleman to violate Statute Y, but is guilty of no other offense. Similarly, Texas-Louisiana Retailer conspired with Middleman to violate Statute Y.

Notice the difference between this analysis and the common law. The *Bruno* court described the conspiracy broadly to be "to smuggle narcotics into the Port of New York and distribute them to addicts both in [New York] and Texas and Louisiana." That was a fair description of the situation from the viewpoint of Importer and Middleman, but it was not either retailer's perception. Given the bilateral nature of common law conspiracy, however, if it is concluded that Importer and Middleman conspired with the retailers to import and sell drugs, the retailers are necessarily guilty of conspiring with them to violate the same laws.

The result under the Code, however, more accurately represents the divergent culpabilities of the parties: Importer and Middleman, who were deeply involved in the events, are guilty of conspiring with everyone; the retailers, who cared little about anything other than the sales in their respective region, would be guilty of conspiracy with Middleman to sell drugs in their region, but no more.

§ 29.08 OBJECTIVES OF A CONSPIRACY

[A] The Issue

Suppose that *D1* and *D2* rob *V1* on Day 1, rob *V2* on Day 2, and rob and rape *V3* on Day 3. Assuming that these crimes were committed as the result of a conspiratorial relationship between *D1* and *D2*, a critical question remains: How many conspiracies were there? That is, do we say that there were four conspiracies, one for each crime (to rob *V1*, to rob *V2*, to rob *V3*, and to rape *V3*)? Or were there three conspiracies, one for each victim? Are there two conspiracies based on the statutes violated (robbery and rape)? Or, is there just one conspiracy to commit all of the criminal acts?

[B] Common Law Analysis

Although various approaches to the issue have developed, the Supreme Court in *Braverman v. United States*[151] announced the following rule regarding federal conspiracy prosecutions:

> [T]he precise nature and extent of the conspiracy must be determined by reference to the agreement which embraces and defines its objects. Whether the object of a single agreement is to commit one or many crimes, it is in either case that agreement which constitutes the conspiracy which the statute punishes. The one agreement cannot be taken to be several agreements and hence several conspiracies because it envisages the violation of several statutes rather than one.

It follows in the case discussed above, therefore, that the fact that *D1* and *D2* planned to violate two criminal statutes, or to violate a particular statute multiple times, does not in itself convert a single conspiracy with multiple objectives into multiple conspiracies with a single objective each.

Ultimately, under *Braverman*, the issue is whether a single agreement or many distinct ones were formed. In the hypothetical, for example, it is possible that *D1* and *D2* got together once and agreed to commit each of the offenses, in which case there was one conspiracy. On the other hand, they may have met various times, each time reaching a new and independent agreement to rob, and the rape may have been a spur-of-the moment group decision, in which case *D1* and *D2* are guilty of four conspiracies. It is also possible that the co-conspirators originally agreed to conduct robberies together (without specifying the number or identity of the victims), and (as in the last scenario) the rape of *V3* was a last-moment decision. Under these circumstances, there were two conspiracies.

Because of inherent difficulties of proof, and in order not to "place a premium upon foresight in crime,"[152] many courts avoid careful inquiry into the events,

---

[151] 317 U.S. 49, 53 (1942).

[152] *Developments in the Law*, Note 1, *supra*, at 930.

and instead treat the initial agreement between the parties as one that implicitly incorporated the later objectives.

[C] Model Penal Code

The Model Penal Code provides that a person with multiple criminal objectives is guilty of only one conspiracy if the multiple objectives are: (1) part of the same agreement; or (2) part of a continuous conspiratorial relationship.[153] Thus, in the *D1-D2* example discussed in subsection [A], each person would be guilty of only one count of conspiracy if the crimes were part of a single agreement (the *Braverman* approach) or, even if the crimes resulted from multiple agreements, if the crimes were committed as a result of "a single and continuous association [by *D1* and *D2*] for criminal purposes."[154]

§ 29.09 DEFENSES

[A] Impossibility

[1] Common Law

Issues of factual and legal impossibility, matters of considerable complexity in the realm of criminal attempts,[155] also arise in conspiracy prosecutions. For example, are *D1* and *D2* guilty of conspiracy if they agree to: (1) perform an abortion on a nonpregnant woman;[156] (2) kill or have unlawful sexual intercourse with a non-existent person;[157] (3) receive stolen property that was not actually stolen;[158] or (4) steal trade secrets that turn out not to be trade secrets?[159]

Case law on the subject is thin. Some courts affirm or reverse convictions in this area without expressly identifying the issue as one of "impossibility." When

---

[153] Model Penal Code § 5.03(3).

[154] American Law Institute, Comment to § 5.03, at 439.

[155] See § 27.07, *supra.*

[156] E.g., People v. Tinskey, 228 N.W.2d 782 (Mich. 1975) (impossibility defense is recognized); State v. Moretti, 244 A.2d 499 (N.J. 1968) (defense is not recognized).

[157] State v. Houchin, 765 P.2d 178 (Mont. 1988) ("factual impossibility" defense rejected in conspiracy to murder case); United States v. Roeseler, 55 M.J. 286, 291 (C.A.A.F. 2001) (the language of Military Code of Justice "does not support an argument that the impossibility of the crime conspired upon is a valid defense to a charge of conspiracy" to murder); State v. Heitman, 629 N.W.2d 542 (Neb. 2001) (see the facts in Note 126, *supra*; conviction affirmed).

[158] United States v. Petit, 841 F.2d 1546 (11th Cir. 1988) (defense not recognized).

[159] United States v. Yang, 281 F.3d 534 (6th Cir. 2002) (defense rejected); United States v. Hsu, 155 F.3d 189 (3d Cir. 1998) (legal impossibility is not a defense).

identification of the issue is made, the stated majority rule is that neither factual impossibility nor legal impossibility is a defense to a criminal conspiracy.[160]
To the extent that there are special dangers inherent in group criminality,[161] the
factual or legal impossibility of committing a particular offense does not negate
the dangerousness of the conspiratorial agreement.[162]

[2] Model Penal Code

The Model Penal Code does not recognize a defense of impossibility in conspiracy cases. The Code's definition of conspiracy states that a person is guilty
of an offense if she agrees with another person that "they or one of them will
engage in conduct that constitutes . . . *an attempt* . . . to commit such crime," or
if she "agrees to aid such other person or persons in . . . *an attempt* . . . to commit such crime."[163]

Of course, people do not conspire to attempt crimes; they conspire to commit
them. This language is meant to take account of the impossibility situation.[164]
Thus, as the Commentary suggests, if *D1* and *D2* agree to rob a bank that they
incorrectly believe is federally insured, they may be convicted of conspiracy to
rob a federally insured bank, although commission of such offense is impossible, because they would have been guilty of criminal attempt had they proceeded with the plan.

[B] Abandonment

[1] Common Law

The crime of conspiracy is complete the moment the agreement is formed or,
in some jurisdictions,[165] once an overt act is committed in furtherance of a
criminal objective. Once the offense is complete, abandonment of the criminal
plan by a party to the conspiracy is not a defense to the conspiracy.[166] The reasoning is the same as with attempts: Once a crime has occurred, a person cannot undo that offense.[167]

---

160 State v. Houchin, 765 P.2d at 179-80 (stating the majority rule, but interpreting the state's
conspiracy statute as allowing for a defense of legal impossibility); United States v. Hsu, 155 F.3d
at 203 (no legal impossibility defense to conspiracy charge, although such a defense was previously
recognized for criminal attempts).

161 See § 29.02[B], *supra*.

162 Katyal, Note 1, *supra*, at 1376-77.

163 Model Penal Code § 5.03(1) (emphasis added).

164 American Law Institute, Comment to § 5.03, at 421.

165 See § 29.04[D], *supra*.

166 American Law Institute, Comment to § 5.03, at 457; Gray v. Commonwealth, 519 S.E.2d 825,
829 (Va. Ct. App. 1999).

167 United States v. Rogers, 102 F.3d 641, 644 (1st Cir. 1996).

An actor's abandonment of the conspiratorial objective, however, is not without relevance. If a person withdraws from a conspiracy, she may avoid liability for subsequent crimes committed in furtherance of the conspiracy by her former co-conspirators. Also, once a person withdraws, the statute of limitations for the conspiracy begins to run in her favor.[168]

Courts are strict in their requirement of proof of abandonment. Usually they require that the abandoning party communicate her withdrawal to each of her fellow co-conspirators.[169] Some courts go further and require her successfully to dissuade the others from pursuing their criminal objectives.[170]

[2] Model Penal Code

Contrary to the common law, the Model Penal Code provides an affirmative defense to the crime of conspiracy if the conspirator renounces her criminal purpose, and thwarts the success of the conspiracy under circumstances demonstrating a complete and voluntary renunciation of her criminal intent.[171]

The drafters of the Code rejected the no-defense rule on the same ground that it recognizes the abandonment defense to other inchoate offenses,[172] namely, that a voluntary renunciation of a criminal purpose negates the actor's dangerousness. On the other hand, in light of the special dangers inherent in conspiratorial groupings, it is insufficient for a conspirator merely to withdraw — she must also negate the danger of the group she joined.

[C] Wharton's Rule

[1] Common Law

[a] In General

According to the common law "Wharton's Rule," an agreement by two persons to commit an offense that *by definition* requires the voluntary concerted criminal participation of two persons cannot be prosecuted as a conspiracy.[173]

The offenses of adultery, bigamy, and incest classically fall within the scope of Wharton's Rule. These offenses, by definition, require the willing participa-

---

[168] *Id.*; see also Gray v. Commonwealth, 519 S.E.2d at 829 n.2 (hearsay statement of co-conspirator is inadmissible if it is made after withdrawal).

[169] People v. Sconce, 228 Cal. App. 3d 693, 701 (Ct. App. 1991).

[170] See Eldredge v. United States, 62 F.2d 449, 451-52 (10th Cir. 1932).

[171] Model Penal Code § 5.03(6).

[172] See §§ 27.09[E][2], 28.03[B], *supra*.

[173] 2 Francis Wharton, Criminal Law § 1604 (12th ed. 1932); Iannelli v. United States, 420 U.S. 770, 773 n.5 (1975); *Developments in the Law*, Note 1, *supra*, at 954.

tion of two persons; there is no way one person can commit these offenses. Other examples of crimes for which Wharton's Rule applies are: dueling; sale of contraband;[174] and receipt of a bribe.[175] A person cannot duel with herself, sell contraband in the absence of a willing buyer, or receive a bribe without a briber.

On the other hand, Wharton's Rule is not a common law bar to a conspiracy prosecution for: (1) possession of a controlled substance with the intent to deliver;[176] (2) "bartering, exchanging, or offering" an illegal narcotic to another;[177] or (3) unlawfully "receiving or disposing" of another person's property.[178] In each of these cases it is possible for the offense to be committed in the absence of an agreement.[179]

The rationale of Wharton's Rule is that if a substantive offense cannot be committed in the absence of an agreement, the added dangers inherent in group criminality are absent. This reasoning ignores the other rationale of conspiracy: the concern regarding inchoate conduct. That is, even if there is no increased danger resulting from, for example, two persons agreeing to duel, a pure application of Wharton's Rule prevents the police from arresting the would-be duelers until they reach the more dangerous stage of an attempt.

Because Wharton's Rule can frustrate law enforcement, many courts limit the applicability of the doctrine to cases in which the substantive offense has been consummated or attempted.[180] For example, if *D1* agrees to sell *D2* heroin, the conspirators may be arrested, convicted, and punished for conspiracy to sell heroin, notwithstanding Wharton's Rule. However, if the offense is attempted or completed before arrest, *D1* and *D2* may not be convicted and punished for the conspiracy. Instead, contrary to the usual rule,[181] the conspiracy merges into the substantive offense.

Although Wharton's Rule was described in 1959 as "firmly entrenched"[182] in American common law jurisprudence, the Supreme Court in 1975 ruled that the doctrine in the federal courts "has current vitality only as a judicial presump-

---

[174] People v. Urban, 553 N.E.2d 740, 741-42 (Ill. App. Ct. 1990).

[175] People v. Wettengel, 58 P.2d 279, 281 (Colo. 1935).

[176] Johnson v. State, 587 A.2d 444, 452-53 (Del. 1991).

[177] State v. Cavanaugh, 583 A.2d 1311, 1314 (Conn. App. Ct. 1990).

[178] Guyer v. State, 453 A.2d 462, 466 (Del. 1982).

[179] In (1), it takes only one person to *possess* a controlled substance, and actual delivery (as distinguished from the intent) is not an element of the crime. In (2), it requires two persons to *barter* or *exchange*, but it takes only one willing person to *offer* an illegal narcotic. As the offense is defined in the disjunctive, Wharton's Rule does not apply. In (3), a person can *receive* property by finding it on the street; likewise, she can *dispose* of property by throwing it away.

[180] See, e.g., State v. Miller, 929 P.2d 372, 378 (Wash. 1997); United States v. Kohne, 347 F. Supp. 1178, 1185-86 (W.D. Pa. 1972).

[181] See § 29.03[B][1], *supra*.

[182] *Developments in the Law*, Note 1, *supra*, at 955.

tion, to be applied in the absence of legislative intent to the contrary."[183] Many state courts, too, now treat the rule as only a presumption.

[b] Exceptions to the Rule

Even when Wharton's Rule otherwise applies, two exceptions are recognized. First, the "third-party exception" provides that if more than the minimum number of persons necessary to commit an offense agree to commit the crime, Wharton's Rule is not triggered.[184] For example, if *D1*, *D2*, and *D3* agree on the sale of illegal narcotics, one person more than is statutorily necessary to perform the sale is involved in the conspiracy. Now, the added dangers of collective criminality return, so that all three persons may be convicted of conspiracy to sell narcotics.[185]

Second, Wharton's Rule does not apply if the two persons involved in the conspiracy are not the two people necessarily involved in committing the substantive offense. For example, if *D1* and *D2*, two males, conspire for *D2* to commit adultery with *X*, a conviction of *D1* and *D2* for conspiracy to commit adultery is proper.[186]

[2] Model Penal Code

Wharton's Rule is not recognized under the Code. The drafters believed that the doctrine improperly "overlooks the functions of conspiracy as an inchoate crime."[187] On the other hand, as described earlier in this chapter,[188] a conspirator may not ordinarily be convicted and punished for both a conspiracy to commit a crime and for its attempt or successful commission. Therefore, the absence of a "Wharton's Rule" defense does not result in additional punishment of a conspirator who implements her criminal objectives.

---

[183] Iannelli v. United States, 420 U.S. 770, 782 (1975).

[184] Gebardi v. United States, 287 U.S. 112, 122 n.6 (1932); Brown v. Commonwealth, 390 S.E.2d 386, 389 (Va. Ct. App. 1990).

[185] Wharton's Rule can combine with the plurality doctrine to cause anomalous results. For example, in the three-person drug-conspiracy example, if one of the three is acquitted because she was insane or for some other reason lacked the requisite specific intent, only two guilty persons remain in the conspiracy. In such a case, Wharton's Rule re-emerges, and neither of the remaining drug-sale co-conspirators may be convicted of conspiracy.

[186] State v. Martin, 200 N.W. 213, 214 (Iowa 1924).

[187] American Law Institute, Comment to § 5.04, at 482-83.

[188] See § 29.03[B][2], *supra*.

[D] Legislative-Exemption Rule

[1] Common Law

A person may not be convicted of conspiracy to violate an offense if her conviction would frustrate a legislative purpose to exempt her from prosecution for the substantive crime.

A classic example of the application of the legislative-exemption rule is *Gebardi v. United States*.[189] *Gebardi* involved a prosecution under the Mann Act, which made it an offense to "knowingly transport . . . any woman or girl [in interstate commerce] for the purpose of prostitution . . . or for any other immoral purpose."[190] Although violation of this law can involve the willing concurrence of the female in her transportation across interstate boundaries, the offense can also occur as the result of transportation of the female against her will. The Mann Act, therefore, does not come within the ambit of Wharton's Rule, discussed immediately above.[191]

This does not end the analysis, however. As *Gebardi* explained, the purpose of the Mann Act is to protect females from sexual exploitation. Thus, a female who willingly or unwillingly crosses state lines for immoral purposes is perceived by the legislature as the victim of the transporter's conduct. It would frustrate this purpose if a female were subject to prosecution as an accomplice in the Mann Act violation of her own rights, or if she were convicted of conspiracy in her own transportation. The legislative-exemption rule precludes such a prosecution.[192]

The legislative-exemption rule can result in an anomaly when it is applied in conjunction with the plurality doctrine. In *Gebardi*, for example, one defendant (a male) conspired with a female for her to cross interstate boundaries for immoral purposes. The female was not subject to prosecution for conspiracy under the legislative-exemption rule. Therefore, the court treated the male as if he had conspired with himself, a logical impossibility. Because "two or more persons" were not involved in the offense, the plurality doctrine precluded conviction of the *non*-immunized male defendant.

---

[189] 287 U.S. 112 (1932).

[190] 18 U.S.C. § 2421 (2005) (as since amended to make it gender-neutral).

[191] *Gebardi*, 287 U.S. at 122-23.

[192] The same analysis applies to statutory rape. This offense is meant to protect young unmarried females from a less-than-fully informed decision to have sexual intercourse. It would frustrate legislative intent, therefore, if the girl could be convicted as an accomplice in her own statutory rape, or if she were subject to prosecution for conspiracy in her own victimization. See Queen v. Tyrrell, [1894] 1 Q.B. 710.

[2] Model Penal Code

Unless the legislature otherwise provides, a person may not be prosecuted for conspiracy to commit a crime under the Model Code if she would not be guilty of the consummated substantive offense: (1) under the law defining the crime; or (2) as an accomplice in its commission.[193] In turn, a person is not guilty as an accomplice in the commission of an offense if she was the victim of the prohibited conduct, or if her conduct was "inevitably incident to its commission."[194]

For example, in the absence of express legislative authority to the contrary, if a male and an underage female have sexual intercourse, the female may not be convicted as an accomplice in her own "victimization." Similarly, in the absence of contrary legislative intent, a pregnant woman may not be convicted as an accomplice in a criminal abortion of her own fetus, because her conduct is "inevitably incident" to the commission of the crime. And, because underage females and pregnant women cannot be convicted as *accomplices* in these offenses, they are also immune from prosecution for *conspiracy* to commit these offenses upon themselves.

However, because conspiracy is a unilateral offense under the Model Code, one who conspires with the immunized party remains subject to conviction for conspiracy.[195]

---

[193] Model Penal Code § 5.04(2).

[194] Model Penal Code § 2.06(6)(a)-(b).

[195] Model Penal Code § 5.04(1)(b).

Chapter 30

LIABILITY FOR THE ACTS OF OTHERS: COMPLICITY

§ 30.01 COMPLICITY: OVERVIEW TO ACCOMPLICE AND CONSPIRATORIAL LIABILITY[1]

This chapter considers multi-party criminal conduct or, more specifically, the circumstances under which a person who does not personally commit a proscribed harm may be held accountable for the conduct of another person with whom he has associated himself.

Two bases of complicity are considered here. First and foremost, a person may be held accountable for the conduct of another person if he assists[2] the other in committing an offense. Liability of this nature is called "accomplice" or "accessory" liability. Second, in most jurisdictions, a person may be held accountable for the conduct of a co-conspirator who commits a crime in furtherance of their agreement. In the latter case, the mere existence of the conspiracy is sufficient to justify liability for the other's conduct; assistance in commission of the crime is not required.

The common law of complicity uses special terms to distinguish between parties to offenses.[3] For purposes of clarity, however, two general terms will also be used in this chapter — the "primary party" (P, for short), and the "secondary party" (S). The "primary party" is the person who personally commits the physical acts that constitute an offense. For example, in a criminal homicide, P is the one whose conduct directly causes the death of V, e.g., the person who shoots or poisons V.[4] Any person who is *not* the primary party, but who is associated with him in commission of an offense, is a "secondary party." Generally speaking, S is the person who assists P to commit the offense. S's liability for P's acts is the focus of this chapter.

---

[1] See generally George P. Fletcher, Rethinking Criminal Law §§ 8.5-8.8 (1978); Glanville Williams, Criminal Law: The General Part §§ 118-41 (2d ed. 1961); Joshua Dressler, *Reassessing the Theoretical Underpinnings of Accomplice Liability: New Solutions to an Old Problem*, 37 Hastings L.J. 91 (1985); Sanford H. Kadish, *Complicity, Cause and Blame: A Study in the Interpretation of Doctrine*, 73 Cal. L. Rev. 323 (1985); Rollin M. Perkins, *Parties to Crime*, 89 U. Pa. L. Rev. 581 (1941); Francis Bowes Sayre, *Criminal Responsibility for the Acts of Another*, 43 Harv. L. Rev. 689 (1930); Robert Weisberg, *Reappraising Complicity*, 4 Buff. Crim. L. Rev. 217 (2000).

[2] The word "assists" is used here in a very general sense. For more specifics, see § 30.04, *infra*.

[3] See § 30.03, *infra*.

[4] More than one person can be a primary actor, e.g., if *P1* and *P2* each shoot V, who dies as the result of both wounds.

§ 30.02 ACCOMPLICE LIABILITY: GENERAL PRINCIPLES

[A] General Rules

[1] Definition of an "Accomplice"

Subject to substantial clarification below, S ("secondary party") is an accomplice of P ("primary party") in the commission of an offense if he intentionally assists P to engage in the conduct that constitutes the crime, i.e., if S intends to assist in the crime and, in fact, assists.[5] The term "assists" is used here as a general term to encompass many forms of conduct, including aiding, abetting, encouraging, soliciting, advising, and/or procuring the commission of the offense.

[2] Criminal Responsibility of an Accomplice: Derivative Liability

Accomplice liability is derivative in nature.[6] That is, an accomplice is not guilty of an independent offense of "aiding and abetting";[7] instead, as the secondary party, he derives his liability from the primary party with whom he has associated himself.[8] The primary party's acts become *his* acts. In general, the accomplice may be convicted of any offense committed by the primary party with the accomplice's intentional assistance.[9]

For example, if S intentionally assists P to rob V, S is liable for the robbery committed by P. If P fails in his effort to rob V, but is guilty of attempted robbery, S is also guilty of attempted robbery.[10] If P's conduct does not proceed sufficiently far to constitute any offense, S is guilty of no offense as an accomplice.[11]

---

[5] Commonwealth v. Murphy, 844 A.2d 1228, 1236 (Pa. 2004).

[6] Kadish, Note 1, *supra*, at 337; People v. Perez, 113 P.3d 100, 104 (Cal. 2005).

[7] State v. Estrada, 603 A.2d 1179, 1189 (Conn. App. Ct. 1992); Sanquenetti v. State, 727 N.E.2d 437, 441 (Ind. 2000); People v. Carter, 330 N.W.2d 314, 322 (Mich. 1982).

[8] Weisberg, Note 1, *supra*, at 225 ("In cases of complicity, . . . liability for wrongdoing flows from the accomplice's relationship to the *perpetrator*.").

[9] As described in § 30.05[B][5], *infra*, there is considerable authority for the view that S is also liable for any crime committed by P that was a natural and probable consequence of the criminal activity in which S intentionally assisted.

[10] See People v. Rehkopf, 370 N.W.2d 296, 298 n.3 (Mich. 1985).

[11] E.g., People v. Genoa, 470 N.W.2d 447 (Mich. Ct. App. 1991) (S furnished money to X, an undercover police agent, so that X would purchase drugs for him; X did not purchase or attempt to purchase the drugs; held: S cannot be convicted as an accomplice in a drug purchase, as the underlying crime was not committed or attempted by X); see also People v. Perez, 113 P.3d at 105 ("[A]iding and abetting liability cannot attach unless the substantive elements of a predicate offense [or its attempt] are met.").

Since P committed no substantive crime, there is no liability for S to derive from P.[12]

[B] Theoretical Foundations of Accomplice Liability

The doctrine of accomplice liability is such an old and now accepted part of American criminal law jurisprudence that few observers focus on why a person who does not directly engage in conduct that constitutes an offense should be held accountable for the wrongful behavior of others.

At first glance, the premise that a person may be held criminally responsible for the conduct of another should prove surprising, if not also disturbing.[13] After all, the concept of personal, as distinguished from vicarious, responsibility is "deeply rooted" in criminal law jurisprudence.[14] Yet Anglo-American courts impute the acts of the primary party to the secondary actor. That is, once a person is deemed to be an accomplice of another, his identity as a person subject to criminal punishment is subsumed in that of the primary party.

There are at least two ways to defend accomplice liability. First, accomplice liability is analogous to civil agency law. In civil law, a person may be held accountable for the actions of another if he "consent[s] to be bound by the actions of his agent, whom he vests with authority for this purpose."[15] In criminal law, an accomplice is held accountable for the conduct of the primary party because, by intentionally assisting the primary party, the accomplice voluntarily identifies himself with the other. His intentional conduct, therefore, is "equivalent to manifesting consent to liability under the civil law."[16]

Second, accomplice liability may be perceived in terms of "forfeited personal identity."[17] That is, we may euphemistically describe accomplice liability in agency terms, but underlying this language is the belief that "she who chooses to aid in a crime forfeits her right to be treated as an individual."[18] In essence,

---

[12] McKnight v. State, 658 N.E.2d 559, 561 (Ind. 1995) ("Logic alone would . . . require that one cannot be convicted of assisting a [crime] if there is no [crime] to assist."). However, S and P may be guilty of the offense of conspiracy to commit robbery. See Chapter 29, *supra*.

[13] State v. Burney, 82 P.3d 164, 169 (Or. Ct. App. 2003):

> [T]he law does not always flow logically from stated premises. It is sometimes a product of accidents of history that cannot be squared with bare reason. Indeed, for over a century down to the present day, the law of accomplice liability has been subject to the criticism that it reflects no coherent set of criminal law principles or policies.

[14] Sayre, Note 1, *supra*, at 702.

[15] Kadish, Note 1, *supra*, at 354.

[16] *Id.* at 355.

[17] Dressler, Note 1, *supra*, at 111; People v. Prettyman, 926 P.2d 1013, 1018 (Cal. 1996) (quoting this treatise).

[18] Dressler, Note 1, *supra*, at 111.

the accomplice authorizes the primary party's conduct: The accomplice says, as it were, "your acts are my acts." The law treats the accomplice, therefore, as if he were no more than an incorporeal shadow of the primary party.

§ 30.03 ACCOMPLICE LIABILITY: COMMON LAW TERMINOLOGY

[A] Parties to a Felony

[1] General Comments

Except for the offense of treason,[19] the common law created two categories of parties to crime — principals and accessories — each of which category was further divided into two subgroups,[20] discussed below.

As discussed in subsection [B], the distinctions between the parties were of considerable practical significance. Today, however, almost every state has legislatively repealed the common law distinctions, in whole or in part. Nonetheless, many courts persist in using common law language. Therefore, knowledge of common law terminology remains valuable.

[2] Principal in the First Degree

[a] In General

A "principal in the first degree" is the person who, with the requisite *mens rea*: (1) physically commits the acts that constitute the offense; or (2) as described in subsection [b] below, commits the offense by use of an "innocent instrumentality" or "innocent human agent."[21] The principal in the first degree is "the criminal actor"[22] or "perpetrator" of the offense. It is *his* conduct from which all secondary parties' liability derives.

In most cases, the principal in the first degree is the individual who personally commits the crime. He is the one who strangles *V1*, has sexual intercourse with *V2*, or takes and carries away the personal property of *V3*, i.e., he is the person who performs the proscribed physical acts.

---

[19] The common law treated all parties to treason as "principals."

[20] McKnight v. State, 658 N.E.2d 559, 560 (Ind. 1995).

[21] State v. Ward, 396 A.2d 1041, 1046 (Md. 1978), overruled in part on other grounds by Lewis v. State, 404 A.2d 1073 (Md. 1979).

[22] State v. Burney, 82 P.3d 164, 166 (Or. App. 2003).

[b] Innocent-Instrumentality Rule

[i] In General

The innocent-instrumentality rule provides that a person is the principal in the first degree if, with the *mens rea* required for the commission of the offense, he uses a non-human agent or a non-culpable human agent to commit the crime.

For example, suppose that *D* trains his dog to pick up his neighbor's newspaper every morning from the front lawn and bring it to *D*, who keeps the newspaper as his own. *D* is guilty of petty larceny: He is the principal in the first degree of the theft. Because the dog is not a human being and, therefore, does not have the capacity to form a culpable mental state, the animal is *D*'s innocent instrumentality. We no more treat the dog as the perpetrator of the theft than we would say that a gun is the "perpetrator" of a murder and that the person pulling the trigger is the gun's "accomplice."

A human being may also be an innocent instrumentality. A person is the principal in the first degree of an offense if he uses or manipulates another to commit an offense, such that the other person is acquitted on the basis of lack of *mens rea* or the existence of an excusing condition. For example, suppose that *D* falsely informs *X* that *V*'s lawn mower belongs to *D*. Based on the false representation, *D* convinces *X* to "retrieve" the property from *V*'s front lawn. On these facts, *X* is not guilty of larceny, because he lacked the specific intent to steal. Instead, *D* is guilty of the theft as the principal in the first degree. In this example, *X* is like the dog in the preceding hypothetical: He is a non-culpable agent being manipulated — like the strings on a marionette — by a culpable party to commit an offense.

A party is also the principal in the first degree if he causes *X*, an insane person[23] or a child,[24] to commit an offense, or if he coerces *X* to commit the crime.[25] In these circumstances, *X* is innocent of the offense as the result of an excuse (insanity, infancy, or duress).

---

[23] 4 William Blackstone, Commentaries on the Laws of England *35 (1769) (a party is a principal if he kills another by "inciting a madman to commit murder").

[24] Queen v. Manley, 1 Cox Crim. Cas. 104 (1844) (by dictum, *M* is the principal in the first degree if he convinces a child to take money from his father).

[25] People v. Hack, 556 N.W.2d 187 (Mich. Ct. App. 1996) (*H* forced a three-year-old to perform a sex act on a one-year-old; held: *H* was guilty of criminal sexual conduct through the innocent-instrumentality doctrine).

[ii] Difficulties in Application of the Rule

Occasionally, the innocent-instrumentality doctrine creates problems for courts when dealing with what has been characterized as a "nonproxyable"[26] offense. A "non-proxyable" offense is one that, by definition, can only be perpetrated by a designated class of persons.

For example, as ordinarily defined, perjury can only be committed by one who intentionally falsely testifies under oath as a witness in an official proceeding. Suppose that *D*, by deception, causes *W*, a witness in a judicial proceeding, to unintentionally give false testimony as to certain material facts. In these circumstances, *W* is not guilty of perjury, due to lack of *mens rea*. Ordinarily, therefore, *D* would be guilty of perjury as a principal in the first degree through the innocent-instrumentality doctrine. But, can someone, never under oath in a judicial proceeding, be said to have perjured himself?

Or, suppose a twist on the Biblical story: Adam gives Eve an apple to eat, which Adam alone knows is a forbidden act. Are we prepared to hold Adam guilty, through his innocent instrumentality, of "eating the apple," which he did not do?[27]

More seriously, consider the offense of rape. As the offense is defined at common law, a husband cannot be convicted of raping his own wife, nor can a woman be convicted of raping another woman, although either can be convicted as accomplices in a rape.[28] In short, the prohibited action of "rape" only applies to a designated class of persons — men who have sexual intercourse with women not their wives. What happens, then, if *D* coerces *X* to rape *D's* wife? To convict *D* through the innocent-instrumentality doctrine would mean that he is guilty of raping his own wife, a legal impossibility.

In such "nonproxyable" cases, some,[29] but by no means all,[30] courts refuse to convict a person as a principal in the first degree through the innocent-instru-

---

[26] Kadish, Note 1, *supra*, at 374.

[27] See Glanville Williams, Textbook on Criminal Law 317 (1978) (finding it improbable that a court would convict Adam as the principal in the first degree).

[28] E.g., Cody v. State, 361 P.2d 307, 319 (Okla. Crim. App. 1961), aff'd, 376 P.2d 625 (Okla. Crim. App. 1962) (a husband may be an accomplice in the rape of his wife); People v. Reilly, 381 N.Y.S.2d 732, 739 (County Ct. 1976) (a woman may be convicted as an accessory in the rape of another woman).

[29] E.g., People v. Enfeld, 518 N.Y.S.2d 536, 537-38 (Sup. Ct. 1987) (*E*, a private party, fraudulently induced *X*, a public servant, to issue a false certificate; due to lack of *mens rea*, *X* was not guilty of violating a statute that prohibited public servants from issuing false certificates; held: *E* could not be convicted of the offense); Dusenbery v. Commonwealth, 263 S.E.2d 392, 394 (Va. 1980) (*D*, who coerced *X* and *Y* to have sexual intercourse with each other, was prosecuted for rape of the female (*Y*); the court overturned *D's* conviction as a principal in the first degree of *Y's* rape because prior state rulings "establish[ed] that one element of rape is the penetration of the female sexual organ by the sexual organ of the principal in the first degree").

[30] E.g., People v. Hernandez, 18 Cal. App. 3d 651, 656 (Ct. App. 1971) (*H* compelled her husband to have sexual intercourse with a nonconsenting woman; held: *H's* conviction for rape may be

mentality doctrine. In such circumstances, a court must either stretch to interpret the facts in a manner that allows the defendant to be treated as a secondary party,[31] or it must permit the culpable party to escape punishment for the offense.

[3] Principal in the Second Degree

A "principal in the second degree" is one who is guilty of an offense by reason of having intentionally assisted in the commission of the crime in the presence, either actual or constructive, of the principal in the first degree.[32] A person is "constructively" present if he is situated in a position to assist the principal in the first degree during the commission of the crime, e.g., if S serves as a "lookout" or "getaway" driver outside a bank that P robs.

[4] Accessory Before the Fact

An "accessory before the fact" does not differ appreciably from a principal in the second degree, except that he is *not* actually or constructively present when the crime is committed. An accessory before the fact often is the person who solicits, counsels, or commands (short of coercing[33]) the principal in the first degree to commit the offense.

[5] Accessory After the Fact

An "accessory after the fact" is one who, with knowledge of another's guilt, intentionally assists the felon to avoid arrest, trial, or conviction.[34] The line between a principal in the second degree, on the one hand, and accessory after the fact, on the other hand, can be a factually thin one: For purposes of accomplice liability, the commission of an offense continues — and, therefore, those who aid are principals in the second degree — until all of the acts constituting the crime have ceased. For example, in a bank robbery, the offense is not complete until the principal in the first degree takes possession of another's property and carries it to a place of temporary safety.[35] Therefore, the driver of the

---

upheld either as an accomplice or as a principal in the first degree); Morrisey v. State, 620 A.2d 207, 210-11 (Del. 1993) (*M* forced a couple to engage in sexual intercourse; held: *M* was guilty of unlawful sexual intercourse through the "innocent intermediary" doctrine); People v. Hack, 556 N.W.2d at 189-90 (see Note 25); United States v. Walser, 3 F.3d 380, 387-88 (11th Cir. 1993) (by deception, *W* caused *X* to testify falsely at a trial; held: *W* may be convicted of perjury).

[31] See § 30.06[B][3][a], *infra*.

[32] State v. Burney, 82 P.3d 1645, 167 (Or. Ct. App. 2003).

[33] If D coerces X to commit the offense, D is the principal in the first degree through an innocent instrumentality. See § 30.03[A][2][b], *supra*.

[34] State v. Ward, 396 A.2d 1041, 1047 (Md. 1978).

[35] People v. Cooper, 811 P.2d 742, 747-48 (Cal. 1991).

"getaway" car is a principal in the second degree rather than an accessory after the fact; once the property has reached a point of temporary safety, however, anyone who intentionally assists the robber to avoid prosecution is an accessory after the fact.[36]

At common law, an accessory after the fact was derivatively liable for the original felony, although he did not assist in its commission.[37] His knowing involvement after the fact "tainted him with guilt of that very offense."[38] Today, nearly all jurisdictions treat accessoryship after the fact as an offense *separate* from, and often *less* serious than, the felony committed by the principal in the first degree.[39] As a result, this chapter does not consider further the liability of accessories after the fact.

[B] Principals versus Accessories: Procedural Significance[40]

[1] General Comments

Although the common law distinguished between principals in the first and second degree, no matter of procedural significance depended on this dichotomy. However, the line between principals and accessories was of profound significance, as discussed below.

Why did the distinctions develop? As with other areas of substantive criminal law, the specter of the death penalty distorted legal doctrine. At common law, all felons were subject to the death penalty. As the number of felonies expanded, courts invented devices for reducing the number of people subject to execution. According to Professor Perkins, "[w]ithout doubt, the principal-accessory distinction was one of those devices, and because of this it is not surprising to find the development along lines which tended to prevent conviction in spite of clear evidence of guilt."[41] In short, the procedural devices served to protect many accomplices from the fate suffered by principals.

---

[36] People v. Montoya, 874 P.2d 903, 912-13 (Cal. 1994) (for purposes of accomplice liability, a burglary remains underway as long as the principal in the first degree remains inside the dwelling; therefore, one who joins the scene after the initial entry and intentionally aids at that time is an accomplice to burglary).

[37] State v. Allred, 995 P.2d 1210, 1213 (Or. Ct. App. 2000).

[38] Perkins, Note 1, *supra*, at 589.

[39] E.g., Ind. Code § 35-44-3-2 (2004) ("Assisting a Criminal"); Or. Rev. Stat. § 162.325 (2003) ("Hindering Prosecution"); Wash. Rev. Code § 9A.76.050 (2005) ("Rendering Criminal Assistance"); Model Penal Code § 242.3 ("Hindering Apprehension or Prosecution").

[40] See generally Perkins, Note 1, *supra*, at 607-14.

[41] *Id.* at 607.

[2] Jurisdiction

At common law, a principal was prosecuted in the jurisdiction in which the crime was perpetrated. An accessory had to be tried in the jurisdiction in which the accessorial acts occurred. If the prosecutor was unsure where the acts took place, he ran the risk of losing the conviction of the accessory. For example, assume that S solicited P to murder V. If the prosecutor believed that the solicitation and homicide both occurred in jurisdiction X — and, therefore, he brought S and P to trial in X — S's conviction could not stand, even though the murder occurred in X, if the evidence at trial showed that S solicited the crime while he and P were eating lunch in neighboring jurisdiction Y.

[3] Rules of Pleading

At common law, an indictment had to state correctly whether the party charged was a principal or an accessory. If the prosecutor alleged that X was the principal in the first degree and that Y was the principal in the second degree, but evidence at trial demonstrated that the roles of the parties were reversed, both defendants could still be convicted. On the other hand, if the evidence demonstrated that Y was not the principal in the second degree as alleged in the indictment, but was an accessory before the fact, his conviction could not stand. Likewise, if a person was indicted as an accessory, but it was proved at trial that he was a principal, acquittal was required.[42]

[4] Timing of the Trial of Accessories

At common law, principals and accessories could be tried jointly (assuming that the court had jurisdiction over all of the parties) or separately. However, under no circumstances could the accessory be tried in advance of the principal's trial. Consequently, if the principal could not be brought to trial, for example, because he had died, fled the jurisdiction, or was immune from prosecution, the accessory could not be brought to justice.

[5] Effect of the Acquittal of a Principal

Closely related to the preceding point, an accessory could not be convicted of a crime unless and until the principal was convicted. If the principal was acquitted in a separate trial, the accessory could not be prosecuted; if they were prosecuted jointly, the accessory could not be convicted if the jury failed to convict the principal. This rule applied regardless of the reason for the principal's acquittal, even if it was based on a jury finding that, although the crime

---

[42] Today, a defendant may virtually always be convicted as an accessory although indicted as a principal (or vice versa), *State v. Burney*, 82 P.3d 164, 168-69 (Or. Ct. App. 2003), as long as the defendant was put on adequate notice before or during trial that the prosecution might pursue alternative theories of liability. Commonwealth v. Spotz, 716 A.2d 580, 588 (Pa. 1998).

occurred and the accessory assisted in it, the principal was not guilty of the offense due to insanity or because another person committed the crime.

[6] Degree of Guilt of the Parties

The common law rule was that an accessory could not be convicted of a more serious offense, or higher degree of an offense, than his principal. For example, if P were convicted of assault, the accessory could not be convicted of the more serious offense of assault with intent to kill.

One exception to this rule existed: An accessory could be convicted of a higher degree of criminal homicide than the principal.[43] For example, an accessory could be convicted of murder, although the principal was guilty of the lesser offense of voluntary manslaughter. This outcome was possible if the principal killed in sudden heat of passion,[44] but the accomplice acted with malice aforethought, i.e., he calmly and intentionally assisted the enraged principal to kill the victim.[45]

§ 30.04 ACCOMPLICE LIABILITY: ASSISTANCE

[A] Types of Assistance

[1] In General

An accomplice is a person who, with the requisite *mens rea*, assists the primary party in committing an offense. Generally speaking, there are three forms of assistance: (1) assistance by physical conduct; (2) assistance by psychological influence; and (3) assistance by omission (assuming that the omitter has a duty to act).

[2] Physical Conduct

The most straightforward cases of assistance involve physical conduct. For example, S may assist P by furnishing him with an instrumentality to commit an offense,[46] "casing" the scene in advance,[47] locking the door to keep an assault victim from escaping,[48] or driving a "getaway" car from the scene of the crime.

---

[43] Williams, Note 1, *supra*, at § 130; 1 Matthew Hale, History of the Pleas of the Crown *438 (1736).

[44] See § 31.07, *infra*.

[45] Parker v. Commonwealth, 201 S.W. 475, 478 (Ky. 1918).

[46] E.g., Hensel v. State, 604 P.2d 222, 239 (Alaska 1979) (furnishing fuses used to destroy a structure as part of a burglary).

[47] E.g., State v. Arillo, 553 A.2d 281, 283 (N.H. 1988).

[48] E.g., Commonwealth v. Hatchin, 709 A.2d 405, 410 (Pa. Super. Ct. 1998).

[3] Psychological Influence

Assistance by psychological influence occurs if S incites, solicits, or encourages P to commit the crime. The most controversial cases involve assistance by *encouragement*, because juries and courts must often speculate as whether the secondary party has psychologically influenced the primary party by his presence or words.

May mere presence at the scene of a crime constitute encouragement? It is said that presence at a crime scene, even when coupled with a private determination not to interfere[49] or passive acquiescence,[50] is insufficient to convict a person as an accomplice.[51] Presence at the scene, coupled with the hidden intent to aid if necessary, is also not enough.[52] Thus, it has been held that an indictment founded simply on the allegation that S accompanied P to the location of a crime and watched as the offense occurred, was insufficient to sustain an accomplice prosecution.[53] And, a conviction was reversed where the evidence showed that S, the driver of a car containing his wife and two children, said and did nothing while P, a back seat passenger, robbed a hitchhiker whom S had previously picked up.[54]

The latter holding is surprising in light of a line of cases that suggest that, while presence alone is insufficient to justify conviction as an accomplice, presence coupled with *very little else* will justify (although not require) a finding of accomplice liability based on psychological encouragement. For example, encouragement may be found from the *expressed* assurance of a bystander that he will not interfere with the perpetrator's plans.[55] Likewise, proof of presence, *coupled with a prior agreement to assist*, will support a claim of encouragement, even if such assistance is not rendered.[56] Thus, assistance-by-encouragement serves as a powerful, and yet highly speculative, basis for allowing accomplice liability.

---

[49] See State v. Richardson, 923 S.W.2d 301, 317 (Mo. 1996).

[50] E.g., Pace v. State, 224 N.E.2d 312, 313 (Ind. 1967); State v. Flint H., 544 A.2d 739, 741 (Me. 1988); State v. Vaillancourt, 453 A.2d 1327, 1328 (N.H. 1982).

[51] State v. V.T., 5 P.3d 1234, 1236 (Utah Ct. App. 2000) ("Passive behavior, such as mere presence — even continuous presence — absent evidence that the defendant affirmatively did something to instigate, incite, embolden, or help others in committing a crime is not enough to qualify as 'encouragement' as that term is commonly used.").

[52] State v. Noriega, 928 P.2d 706, 709 (Ariz. Ct. App. 1996); see Hicks v. United States, 150 U.S. 442, 450 (1893).

[53] State v. Vaillancourt, 453 A.2d 1327 (N.H. 1982).

[54] Pace v. State, 224 N.E.2d 312 (Ind. 1967).

[55] State v. Doody, 434 A.2d 523, 530 (Me. 1981).

[56] Hicks v. State, 150 U.S. at 450. The prior agreement to assist will also justify liability on the basis of conspiratorial, as distinguished from accomplice, liability, in jurisdictions that recognize this separate form of complicity. See § 30.08, *infra*.

[4] Assistance by Omission

Although there is relatively little case law on point, the failure of a person to try to prevent the commission of an offense can justify a finding of passive assistance through omission, if the omitter has a duty to intervene. For example, a parent is an accomplice in the commission of a criminal homicide if, with the requisite *mens rea*, he allows another person to kill his child.[57] Likewise, a property owner may have a legal duty to prevent the commission of a crime on his property, e.g., *S*'s knowing failure to prevent the commission of a drug offense on his property would justify a finding of assistance-by-omission.[58] Similarly, the failure of a police officer to stop a crime, *if coupled with the requisite mens rea*, would support a conviction on the basis of accomplice liability.

[B] Amount of Assistance Required

[1] In General

A person is not an accomplice unless his conduct (or omission) in fact assists in the commission of the offense. Thus, *S* is not an accomplice in the commission of a robbery if he is present at the scene of the crime in order to aid *P* if necessary, but his assistance is not called upon, and there are no additional facts to support a claim of assistance by encouragement.[59] Likewise, *S* is not an accomplice of *P* if he performs an act to assist *P*, but his conduct is wholly ineffectual. For example, *S* is not an accomplice if he utters words of encouragement to *P* who fails to hear them, or if *S* opens a window to allow *P* to enter a dwelling unlawfully, but *P* (unaware of the open window) enters through a door.[60]

Once it is determined that *S* assisted *P*, however, the degree of aid or influence provided is immaterial.[61] Any aid, *no matter how trivial*, suffices.[62] For example, *S* may be deemed an accomplice of *P* if, acting with the requisite *mens rea*, he: (1) applauds *P*'s criminal activities;[63] (2) holds *P*'s child while *P* commits the crime;[64] (3) prepares food for *P* to give *P* sustenance during the

---

[57] See State v. Walden, 293 S.E.2d 780, 786-87 (N.C. 1982) (crime of assault). Guilt in such circumstances may also be founded on *direct*, rather than accomplice, liability. See generally § 9.07[A], *supra*.

[58] Porter v. State, 570 So. 2d 823, 826-27 (Ala. Crim. App. 1990).

[59] See Hicks v. United States, 150 U.S. 442, 450 (1893).

[60] Kadish, Note 1, *supra*, at 358-59.

[61] Fuson v. Commonwealth, 251 S.W. 995, 997 (Ky. 1923).

[62] State v. Noriega, 928 P.2d 706, 709 n.2 (Ariz. Ct. App. 1996); Commonwealth v. Murphy, 844 A.2d 1228, 1234 (Pa. 2004).

[63] See Wilcox v. Jeffery, [1951] 1 All E.R. 464, 465 (*S* met *P* at the airport and was present and applauded when *P*, a saxophonist, performed at an illegal concert; the court noted that *S*'s presence was not accidental, but was meant to encourage *P*; it opined that the result might have been different had *S* booed at the concert).

[64] See State v. Duran, 526 P.2d 188 (N.M. Ct. App. 1974).

planning or commission of the crime;[65] or (4) provides moral support by asking *P* to bring home bananas from the grocery store that *P* plans to rob.[66]

[2] Accomplice Liability and the Doctrine of Causation[67]

[a] The Law

A secondary party is accountable for the conduct of the primary party even if his assistance was causally unnecessary to the commission of the offense. That is, *S* is guilty of an offense as an accomplice even if, but for his assistance, *P* would have committed the offense anyway.[68] Thus, it would be immaterial to *S*'s liability in each of the examples of trivial assistance noted in the preceding subsection, that *P* would have committed the crime when he did without *S*'s minor aid or encouragement. To be an accomplice, *S* must help, but need not cause, the crime.

The absence of a causation requirement is consistent with the underlying rationale of accomplice liability. It will be remembered that accomplice liability is derivative in nature:[69] *S* is not guilty of an independent, substantive offense of "aiding and abetting"; instead, his guilt is derived from that of *P*. Therefore, once it is determined that *S* assisted *P* with the requisite *mens rea* (i.e., *S* is *P*'s accomplice), "proof that the *principal* [*P*] caused the [social harm] satisfies the requirement of establishing the causal relationship of the *accomplice*."[70] Since *S* is an accomplice and, as such, forfeits his personal identity in the criminal transaction,[71] it is no longer relevant whether *S*'s assistance caused the harm. It is enough that he assisted someone else who caused the harm.

[b] Criticism of the Law

The requirement of a causal relationship between a person's conduct and the social harm for which he is being punished is a fundamental feature of criminal responsibility.[72] Its irrelevance to accomplice liability, therefore, is troubling.

---

[65] See Alexander v. State, 102 So. 597 (Ala. Ct. App. 1925).

[66] See State v. Helmenstein, 163 N.W.2d 85, 89 (N.D. 1968).

[67] See generally Dressler, Note 1, *supra*.

[68] State ex rel. Martin, Att'y Gen. v. Tally, 15 So. 722, 738–39 (Ala. 1894); Weisberg, Note 1, *supra*, at 228.

[69] See § 30.02[A][2], *supra*.

[70] Commonwealth v. Smith, 391 A.2d 1009, 1011 (Pa. 1978) (emphasis added).

[71] See § 30.02[B], *supra*.

[72] See § 14.01, *supra*.

Causality serves two important functions in the criminal law. First, it guarantees that criminal liability will be personal rather than vicarious. Second, causation is a tool by which to calibrate the appropriate level of a wrongdoer's punishment.

The element of causation could serve the same valuable purposes in the field of accomplice law. First, as previously shown,[73] a person whose connection to a crime is exceedingly remote can be ensnared as an accomplice. If a causal connection between S's assistance and P's criminal conduct were required, however, the risk of attenuated liability would be greatly reduced.

Second, accomplice law can result in disproportionate punishment. At common law and under modern statutes, accomplices are treated alike in terms of punishment: One whose participation in an offense is substantial and one whose conduct is trivial are subject to the same punishment. This approach, however, may be inconsistent with the retributive principle of just deserts. In this context, recall how the common law treats inchoate conduct: Although one who unsuccessfully attempts to commit a crime is as dangerous and morally culpable as one who commits the offense, the unsuccessful criminal is punished less severely than the successful one. One reason for this outcome is that the harm actually caused by the would-be murderer, robber, or rapist is less than the harm caused by the successful murderer, robber, or rapist.[74]

The same principle arguably ought to apply to accomplices. The accomplice whose assistance was a *sine qua non* factor in the harm caused by the primary party should be punished proportionally to the harm that he and the primary party intentionally caused. Thus, if S solicits P to commit an offense that P would not otherwise have committed, S should be punished at the same level as P. Similarly, if S provides essential assistance to P — aid but for which the crime would not have occurred when it did — S may fairly be punished as severely as P is punished. Non-causal accomplices, however, should be punished less than causal accomplices and primary parties.[75] For example, if S provides encouragement to P, but P would have committed the crime when he did notwithstanding the psychological aid, S should be punished less than P.

§ 30.05 ACCOMPLICE LIABILITY: *MENS REA*

[A] In General

Courts frequently state that a person is an accomplice in the commission of an offense if he intentionally aids the primary party to commit the offense

---

[73] See § 30.04[B][1], *supra*.

[74] See § 27.04[B][3], *supra*.

[75] See United States v. Hansen, 256 F. Supp. 2d 65, 67 n.3 (D. Mass. 2003) (sentencing H more leniently because of his lesser contribution to the offense, and citing Dressler, Note 1, *supra*, at 86, 92, which distinguishes between causal and non-causal assistance).

charged.[76] This statement is sometimes broken down into "dual intents": (1) the intent to assist the primary party; and (2) the intent that the primary party commit the offense charged.[77]

These formulations are adequate to deal with many cases, since many offenses are defined in terms of "intent." However, in some cases, particularly when a person is charged as an accomplice in the commission of an offense for which recklessness or negligence suffices for liability,[78] it is necessary to be somewhat more precise about the mental state. Therefore, although not all courts and commentators agree on the matter, it is more precisely correct to state that an accomplice must possess two states of mind: (1) the intent to assist the primary party to engage in the conduct that forms the basis of the offense; and (2) the mental state required for commission of the offense, as provided in the definition of the substantive crime.[79]

Almost always,[80] the second mental state may be inferred upon proof of the first and, likewise, the *absence* of proof of the first mental state will demonstrate the *lack* of the second mental state. For example, suppose that S is a customer in a bank when P enters and announces that he is robbing it. S, startled, unthinkingly exclaims, "You'll never succeed because the guard is right behind you." Alerted, P disarms the guard and robs the bank. Based on these facts, S *in fact* assisted P in the robbery by providing a warning to P that facilitated him in the commission of the crime.

Nonetheless, S is not an accomplice of P because he lacked both mental states required of an accomplice. First, he did not intend for his words to assist P to engage in the robbery. At most, he was reckless in this regard. Second, and following almost inextricably from the first point, S did not want the bank robbed, i.e., it was not his objective to have the bank deprived permanently of its property, the specific intent required for the offense.[81]

---

[76] E.g., Commonwealth v. Murphy, 844 A.2d 1228, 1234 (Pa. 2004); see Kadish, Note 1, *supra*, at 346 ("[H]e must act with the intention of influencing or assisting the primary party to engage in the conduct constituting the crime.").

[77] State v. Harrison, 425 A.2d 111, 113 (Conn. 1979); State v. Neal, 14 S.W.3d 236, 239 (Mo. Ct. App. 2000).

[78] See § 30.05[B][3], *infra*, for further discussion.

[79] State v. Foster, 522 A.2d 277, 283 (Conn. 1987).

[80] But see § 30.05[B][1], *infra*.

[81] See People v. Tewksbury, 544 P.2d 1335, 1341 (Cal. 1976) ("Although it is undisputed that Mary aided appellant [in a robbery] by calling the restaurant, by supplying Sheila with pencil and paper, and by driving some of the principals to a point of rendezvous in the vicinity of the crimes, such actions do not confer upon her accomplice status unless she also acted with the requisite guilty intent.").

[B] Significant *Mens Rea* Issues

[1] The Feigning Accomplice

It is frequently said that, to be an accomplice, a person "must not only have the purpose that someone else engage in the conduct which constitutes the particular crime charged, but the accomplice must also *share in the same intent which is required for commission of the substantive offense.*"[82] It is almost always reasonable to infer that when a person intentionally assists another to engage in the conduct that constitutes an offense, he does so because he wants the other person to succeed in his endeavor, i.e., he shares the criminal intent of the primary party. Sometimes, however, this inference is inaccurate. Matters of complexity arise, for example, when a police officer or private person joins a criminal endeavor as an "accomplice" and feigns a criminal intent in order to obtain incriminating evidence against the primary party or in order to ensnare the other in criminal activity.

Consider the classic case of *Wilson v. People*.[83] S and P, drinking partners, got into an argument over S's assertion that P had stolen his watch. A conversation followed in which the two men agreed to steal property from V's drugstore. In furtherance of the agreement, S assisted P to enter V's store. While P was inside, S called the police and then returned to the drugstore and took property handed to him by P. Before the parties could leave, the police arrived and arrested S and P for burglary and larceny.

S's conviction as an accomplice was overturned by the state supreme court. Some of its reasoning was unpersuasive. It analogized S's conduct to that of a detective who enters an existing criminal endeavor in order to "explode" it. S, however, hardly fit that characterization. He did not join a crime already in play; he helped devise the plan, apparently in order to set up P for arrest, in retaliation for the latter's alleged theft of S's watch.

So, was S properly acquitted as an accomplice? S had the intent to assist P to engage in the conduct that (on P's part) constituted burglary and larceny; that is, he intended to assist P to enter V's store and to take property out of it. But, did S possess the second (and, ultimately, key) *mens rea* of an accomplice, namely, the mental states required for commission of the offenses of larceny and burglary?

Larceny requires a specific intent to deprive another person of his property permanently. Although P possessed this intent (and, therefore, was guilty of larceny as the perpetrator), S's act of calling the police demonstrated that he did not intend for V to be deprived of the property permanently. Consequently, S

---

[82] State v. Williams, 718 A.2d 721, 723 (N.J. Super. Ct. Law Div. 1998) (emphasis added).

[83] 87 P.2d 5 (Colo. 1939).

lacked the specific intent of larceny, and was properly acquitted as an accomplice of this offense.

The burglary charge is a more difficult issue. Plausibly, S should have been convicted of burglary as an accomplice. The argument would run as follows: S knew that P intended to enter V's drugstore for the purpose of committing larceny (which made P guilty of burglary), and with that knowledge and for the very purpose of securing P's conviction for burglary, S assisted P to go inside V's drugstore — the *actus reus* of the burglary. Therefore, S *did* want a burglary (as distinguished from a larceny) to occur, and thus should be convicted for assisting in that offense.

But, there is a strong — this author contends, better — case for relieving S of responsibility for the burglary. The reason goes back to the *mens rea* requirement, as stated in subsection [a]: an accomplice must possess two states of mind: (1) the intent to assist the primary party to engage in the conduct that forms the basis of the offense; and (2) the mental state required for commission of the offense, as provided in the definition of the substantive crime. Here, S possessed the first intent: As noted in the preceding paragraph, he intended to assist P to engage in the conduct (entering the drugstore) that constituted the social harm of burglary. But, S did not possess the second mental state: Because S did not intend for a larceny to occur, he personally lacked the "specific intent" requirement of burglary. He did not share with P the felonious intent that constitutes the "specific intent" that converts a criminal trespass into a burglary.[84]

The latter analysis does not provide a ready-made escape hatch for persons to join crimes in order to arrest or ensnare suspects. *Wilson* was an unusual case because both of the offenses charged are "inchoate offenses in disguise,"[85] and also required proof of specific states of mind that S lacked. However, if S had intentionally assisted P to kill V, S would be guilty of murder because he shared with P the intent for the latter to kill V. The fact that S's motive for wanting V dead was to set up P for arrest would not negate the requisite *mens rea*.

[2] "Purpose" versus "Knowledge": The Meaning of "Intent"

The *mens rea* of accomplice liability is usually described in terms of "intention." As with the crime of conspiracy, however, there is considerable debate regarding whether a person may properly be characterized as an accomplice if he *knows* that his assistance will aid in a crime, but he lacks the *purpose* that the crime be committed. For example, suppose that S rents his house to P, the manager of an illegal gambling enterprise.[86] Is S an accomplice in P's illegal

---

[84] Conceptually and uncontroversially, S *was* an accomplice in P's criminal trespass.

[85] See § 27.02[F], *supra*.

[86] United States v. Giovannetti, 919 F.2d 1223, 1227 (7th Cir. 1990) (holding that a person may not be convicted as an accomplice unless he participates in something that he wishes to bring about).

activities if he rented the property with knowledge of his tenant's intended activities, or must it be proved that he shared P's criminal purpose?

The policy arguments for and against imposing liability on the basis of knowledge, rather than purpose, have been summarized elsewhere in the context of conspiracy law.[87] As in that area, the case law is mixed. Most courts, however, hold that a person is not an accomplice in the commission of an offense unless he "share[s] the criminal intent of the principal; there must be a community of purpose in the unlawful undertaking."[88] In the words of Judge Learned Hand, the complicity doctrine requires that the secondary party "in some sort associate himself with the venture, that he participate in it as in something that he wishes to bring about, that he seek by his action to make it succeed. All the words used — even the most colorless 'abet' — carry an implication of purposive attitude towards it."[89]

[3] Liability for Crimes of Recklessness and Negligence[90]

Courts and statutes frequently express the culpability requirement for accomplice liability in terms of "intent," e.g., the "intent to promote or facilitate the commission of the offense."[91] The implication of these words is that the secondary party must want the crime to be committed by the primary party (or, at least, know that it will take place). If so, it is logically impossible for a person to be an accomplice in the commission of a crime of recklessness or negligence. For example, suppose that S encourages P to drive at an exceedingly high rate of speed on a busy public road near a school. While speeding, P loses control of his car and strikes and kills V, a child leaving school for the day. We may assume that P is guilty of manslaughter as the result of his criminal negligence. Of what is S guilty? Based on a statute interpreted to require an intent to commit the substantive office, S cannot be convicted as an accomplice in the negligent manslaughter. If S must "intend that the offense be committed," then he must "intend that the offense [of negligent manslaughter] be committed." However, how can one *intend* a *negligent* killing? Essentially, that would mean that S intended V to die in a negligent manner, which means that S intended P to kill V. In the latter case, the offense would be murder, not negligent homicide.

---

[87] See § 29.05[B][1], *supra*.

[88] State v. Duran, 526 P.2d 188, 189 (N.M. Ct. App. 1974); see People v. Beeman, 674 P.2d 1318, 1326 (Cal. 1984); State v. Gladstone, 474 P.2d 274, 278 (Wash. 1970); Weisberg, Note 1, *supra*, at 239 (stating that "the majority of jurisdictions . . . require a showing of purpose").

[89] United States v. Peoni, 100 F.2d 401, 402 (2d Cir. 1938).

[90] See generally Sanford H. Kadish, *Reckless Complicity*, 87 J. Crim. L. & Criminology 369 (1997); Audrey Rogers, *Accomplice Liability for Unintentional Crimes: Remaining Within the Constraints of Intent*, 31 Loy. L.A. L. Rev. 1351 (1998).

[91] E.g., Alaska Stat. § 11.16.110(2) (2005).

In the past, some courts analyzed accomplice liability in this manner,[92] but the overwhelming majority rule now is that accomplice liability *is* allowed in such circumstances. Conviction of an accomplice in the commission of a crime of recklessness or negligence is permitted as long as the secondary party has the two mental states described in the second paragraph of subsection [A]: (1) the intent to assist the primary party to engage in the conduct that forms the basis of the offense; and (2) the mental state — intent, recklessness, or negligence, as the case may be — required for commission of the substantive offense.[93]

In the present hypothetical, S should be treated as an accomplice in the negligent death. First, he intended to encourage P to engage in the conduct that formed the basis of the offense, i.e., he intended to encourage P to drive at a high rate of speed on a public road near a school, which speeding resulted in V's death. Second, S was criminally negligent in relation to V's death by encouraging P to drive in this manner. This outcome is sensible:

> [B]ecause accessorial liability is not a distinct crime, but only an alternative means by which a substantive crime may be committed, it would be illogical to impose liability on the perpetrator of the crime, while precluding liability for an accessory, where both possess the mental state required for the commission of the crime.[94]

On the other hand, if P, while speeding at S's encouragement, had negligently turned the wrong way on a one-way street, thereby striking and killing V, S might not be an accomplice in *this* negligent homicide. It is quite arguable that the conduct that formed the basis of *this* homicide was the act of wrong-way driving, and not the conduct that S intentionally encouraged, i.e., the speeding.

---

[92] E.g., Echols v. State, 818 P.2d 691, 694-95 (Alaska Ct. App. 1991) (overturning accomplice conviction for reckless assault on the ground that such an offense does not exist), overruled by Riley v. State, 60 P.3d 204 (Alaska Ct. App. 2002); State v. Etzweiler, 480 A.2d 870, 874-75 (N.H. 1984) (quashing an indictment of S as an accomplice of P in a negligent homicide), superseded by statute as recognized in State v. Anthony, 861 A.2d 773, 775 (N.H. 2004).

[93] E.g., Ex Parte Simmons, 649 So. 2d 1282, 1284-85 (Ala. 1994) (S may be convicted of reckless murder as an accomplice if he purposely aided or encouraged another to fire a weapon on a public street, recklessly resulting in the death of a child); State v. Garnica, 98 P.3d 207, 209 (Ariz. Ct. App. 2004) (affirming conviction of an accomplice for second-degree, reckless murder; held: an accomplice need only have the kind of culpability with respect to the result that is sufficient for commission of the crime); People v. Wheeler, 772 P.2d 101, 103 (Colo. 1989) (affirming S's conviction as an accomplice in a negligent homicide, as long as S intended to promote or facilitate the conduct of P that negligently resulted in the death); State v. Anthony, 861 A.2d 773, 776 (N.H. 2004) (affirming conviction of an accomplice to the crime of negligent cruelty to animals: held: conviction is permitted if the secondary party (1) intended to promote or facilitate the other person's dangerous *conduct*; and (2) acted with the culpable mental state regarding the *result* specified in the underlying statute); State v. Chaney, 989 P.2d 1091, 1101 (Utah Ct. App. 1999) (S may be convicted as an accomplice in rape of a child, in which S may not have possessed the specific intent that P have intercourse with the child, as long as he was at least reckless as to the possibility of intercourse, since recklessness was the minimum level of culpability required for rape).

[94] Weisberg, Note 1, *supra*, at 225.

[4] Attendant Circumstances

Suppose that S intentionally assists P to have sexual intercourse with V, a nonconsenting female. P realizes that V is not consenting (and, therefore, is guilty of rape), but S negligently believes that V is consenting. Is S guilty of rape as P's accomplice? Notice the unusual situation: S intended to assist P in the conduct, i.e., sexual intercourse, that constituted the rape; however, S did not intend to assist in a *nonconsensual* act of intercourse, i.e., he did not share P's knowledge of the attendant circumstance of V's lack of consent.

The issue here — whether the intent requirement of accomplice liability applies as well to attendant circumstances — is one that courts have rarely considered. It is submitted that the better rule is that, as long as the secondary party acts with the purpose of assisting the principal in the conduct that constitutes the offense — and has the level of culpability required as to the prohibited *result*, if any, of the offense — he should be deemed an accomplice if his culpability as to the attendant circumstance would be sufficient to convict him as a principal. Put simply, the *mens rea* policies regarding the substantive offense should control the accomplice's situation. For example, in a jurisdiction in which the rape statute is interpreted to require proof of recklessness regarding the female's lack of consent, the secondary party should be held responsible for the rape if he acted with at least that level of culpability as to the attendant circumstance, but not if his culpability was less than that of recklessness.[95] Or, in a prosecution for the rape of a child, in which the age element is one of strict liability,[96] a secondary party should be convicted even if he lacked any culpability as to the victim's age.

[5] Natural-and-Probable-Consequences Doctrine

At common law, and today in most jurisdictions, "a person encouraging or facilitating the commission of a crime [may] be held criminally liable not only for that crime, but for any other offense that was a 'natural and probable consequence' of the crime aided and abetted."[97] That is, if S is an accomplice in the commission of *a* crime (call it Crime A), he is also responsible for every other crime (e.g., Crimes B and C) perpetrated by the primary party that was a natural and probable consequence of Crime A, the target offense.

One court[98] has explained the meaning of "natural and probable consequences" in this context as follows: An accomplice to Crime A is also an accom-

---

[95] Bowell v. State, 728 P.2d 1220, 1222-23 (Alaska Ct. App. 1986), overruled on other grounds by Echols v. State, 818 P.2d 691 (Alaska Ct. App. 1991).

[96] E.g., State v. Chaney, 989 P.2d at 1101.

[97] People v. Prettyman, 926 P.2d 1013, 1019 (Cal. 1996); State v. Richmond, 90 S.W.3d 648, 654 (Tenn. 2002).

[98] Roy v. United States, 652 A.2d 1098, 1105 (D.C. 1995).

plice in Crime B, if "in the ordinary course of things," Crime B might "reasonably ensue from the planned events." It is not enough that Crime B "might conceivably ensue" from Crime A. Crime B must be "within the normal range of outcomes that may be expected to occur if nothing unusual has intervened."

To apply the natural-and-probable-consequences doctrine, one should ask four questions: (1) Did P commit target Crime A?;[99] (2) If yes, did S culpably assist in the commission of Crime A, i.e., was S an accomplice in the commission of that offense?; (3) If yes, did P commit any other crimes?; and (4) If yes, were these crimes, although not contemplated or desired by S, reasonably foreseeable consequences of Crime A?[100]

For example, suppose that S intentionally aids P in the commission of an armed bank robbery, by driving P to the bank and serving as a lookout from that position. During the robbery, P forcibly moves bank teller V to a back room (kidnapping), and intentionally kills police officer X, who is attempting to prevent the robbery. On these facts, P is guilty of robbery; and S is guilty as an accomplice. P is also guilty of the offenses of kidnapping and murder. And, in a jurisdiction applying the natural-and-probable-consequences doctrine, S is *also* guilty of these offenses, because they were reasonably foreseeable consequences of the armed bank robbery in which S assisted. In contrast, if P had taken the opportunity of the robbery to sexually assault a customer in the bank, S would not be guilty of the latter offense, as this was not a reasonably foreseeable consequence of the bank robbery. The rape would be treated as separate and distinct from the robbery in which S assisted.[101]

Likewise, if S encourages P to hit V (a simple battery), which P does by obtaining a steel pipe and beating V to death, S arguably is *not* an accomplice in the resulting murder, but he would be an accomplice if he encourages P to commit the offense of assault with a deadly weapon.[102] The homicide is a natural and probable consequence of attacking another with a deadly weapon, but is remote in the case of a simple assault.

The natural-and-probable-consequences doctrine has been subjected to substantial justifiable criticism.[103] Notice the effect of the rule: An accomplice may be convicted of a crime of intent although his culpability regarding its commission may be no greater than that of negligence. Thus, the effect of the rule

---

[99] But see People v. Prettyman, 926 P.2d at 1020 n.4 (raising, but leaving open, the issue of "whether a defendant may be convicted under the 'natural and probable consequences' doctrine when the target criminal act was not committed").

[100] People v. Woods, 8 Cal. App. 4th 1570, 1586 (Ct. App. 1992).

[101] See also 4 Blackstone, Note 23, *supra*, at *37 ("But if A. commands B. to burn C.'s house and he, in so doing, commits a robbery; now A., though accessory to the burning, is not accessory to the robbery, for that is a thing of a distinct and unconsequential nature.").

[102] People v. Prettyman, 926 P.2d at 1024.

[103] E.g., American Law Institute, Comment to § 2.06, at 312 n.42 (characterizing the rule as "incongruous and unjust"); Rogers, Note 90, *supra*, at 1361 & 1361 n.33 (stating that "most commentators" are critical of the doctrine, and citing scholarly criticism of the rule).

is to permit conviction of an accomplice whose culpability as to the non-target offense is *less* than is required to prove the guilt of the primary party.[104] And yet, in view of the relative roles of the primary and secondary parties, one would assume that an accomplice should not be convicted of an offense unless he has the same or higher degree of culpability required to convict the perpetrator.[105]

§ 30.06 LIABILITY OF THE SECONDARY PARTY IN RELATION TO THE PRIMARY PARTY[106]

[A] General Principles

At common law, an accessory could not be convicted of the crime in which he assisted until the principal was convicted and, with the limited exception of criminal homicide, could not be convicted of a more serious offense or degree of offense than that of which the principal was convicted.[107] Nearly all states have abrogated these rigid common law rules. It does not follow from this, however, that issues regarding the relationship between the primary party and secondary parties no longer arise, for they often do.

Accomplice liability is derivative in nature.[108] This means that for an accomplice to be liable for an offense, there must be a primary party. It is still true that "a defendant may not be convicted as an [accomplice] where the guilt of a principal has not been shown."[109] Or, put another way, logically, for an accomplice to be guilty of a crime, there must have been a crime committed by another person from whom the accomplice's liability originates.[110]

What does it mean, however, to say that the primary party "has committed a crime" for which the accomplice may be held accountable? Some cases are straightforward. For example, ordinarily it is no longer a procedural bar to the conviction of a secondary party that the primary party was not prosecuted for the offense. The non-prosecution of the alleged perpetrator of an offense does not in itself suggest that a crime did not occur. His non-prosecution might be the

---

[104] Sharma v. State, 56 P.3d 868, 872 (Nev. 2002) ("reevaluat[ing] the wisdom of the doctrine," the court rejects as "unsound" the use of the natural-and-probable-consequences doctrine in cases involving specific-intent offenses).

[105] American Law Institute, Comment to § 2.06, at 312 n.42.

[106] See generally Peter Alldridge, *The Doctrine of Innocent Agency*, 2 Crim. L.F. 45 (1990); David Lanham, *Accomplices, Principals and Causation*, 12 Melb. U. L. Rev. 490 (1980).

[107] See § 30.03[B][5]-[6], *supra.*

[108] See § 30.02[A][2], *supra.*

[109] People v. Vaughn, 465 N.W.2d 365, 369 (Mich. Ct. App. 1990).

[110] See McKnight v. State, 658 N.E.2d 559, 561 (Ind. 1995) ("Logic alone would seem to require that one cannot be convicted of assisting a criminal if there is no criminal to assist.").

result of any one of countless factors extraneous to his guilt (e.g., death, flight from the jurisdiction, or immunity from prosecution).

Difficulties arise, however, when the primary party is acquitted of the offense. Does an acquittal imply that a crime was not committed? Not necessarily. For example, if P and S are charged with raping V, and V is unable to identify her attacker, but provides a clear identification of his accomplice, a jury could logically acquit P and convict S. P's acquittal does not imply that a crime did not occur, only that the jury had a reasonable doubt that P was the perpetrator of the crime.[111]

Some acquittals do suggest that a crime has not occurred. For example, if P is charged with stealing V's car, and he proves at trial that V consented to the taking, then no larceny occurred. Conceptually, P's acquittal precludes the conviction of an accomplice to this *non*-offense.[112]

The next subsection deals with other acquittal-based circumstances in which it may be argued that a "crime" has not occurred in some sense: The *actus reus* of the offense was committed, but P did not have the requisite *mens rea*; or all of the elements of the crime were proven, but P has a valid claim of defense to his conduct. Under which of these circumstances, if any, should S be allowed to escape conviction?

An additional question considered below, in subsection [C], is this: Under what circumstances, if any, may S derive *more* guilt than arises from P's conviction?

[B] Liability When the Primary Party Is Acquitted

[1] "Primary Party" as an Innocent Instrumentality

If D coerces X to commit a theft by threatening X's life, X will be acquitted of larceny on the ground of duress. Today, and according to common law principles, D may be convicted of larceny. X was D's innocent instrumentality. Therefore, at common law, D was the principal in the first degree of the offense.[113] Conceptually, as D and X "were enemies in an adversarial relationship"[114] and

---

[111] People v. Vaughn, 465 N.W.2d at 369 (although there must be a principal for there to be an accomplice, the "evidence need not show that a specifically named individual was the guilty principal").

[112] Courts hesitate to disapprove of inconsistent jury verdicts, because it is rarely possible to determine why the jury acquitted one defendant while convicting another. This hesitancy is particularly strong when the accomplice is convicted in a separate trial — in front of a different jury, potentially based on different evidence — after the acquittal of the principal. E.g., People v. Wilkins, 26 Cal. App. 4th 1089 (Ct. App. 1994) (permitting the conviction of an accomplice following the acquittal of the primary party). See also § 29.06[A], *supra*, regarding the similar issue in conspiracy cases in which one of two alleged co-conspirators is acquitted.

[113] See § 30.03[A][2][b], *supra*.

[114] Commonwealth v. Gaynor, 648 A.2d 295, 298 (Pa. 1994).

shared no common criminal intent, *D's guilt is not founded on accomplice liability principles.* Instead, *D* is *directly* liable for committing the crime through
the instrumentality; *D's* guilt is not derived from another culpable person. *X's*
acquittal, therefore, presents no bar to the conviction of the only culpable party.

[2] Acquittal on the Basis of a Defense

[a] Justification Defenses

Suppose that *V* unlawfully and imminently threatens *P's* life. *S* assists *P* to
kill *V*. *P* is acquitted of murder on the ground of self-defense. Is *S* guilty in the
homicide? Although case law in this area is understandably sparse, the proper
result seems evident: As *P* was acquitted because his actions were justified, *S*
should also be acquitted.[115] Although *V* was killed, recognition of the justification defense of self-defense implies that no crime has occurred, or even that a
positive good has resulted. In the absence of wrongdoing by *P*, there is no crime
to impute to *S*.[116]

[b] Excuse Defenses

When the primary party is acquitted on the basis of an excuse (e.g., insanity,
involuntary intoxication, or duress), his acquittal should *not* bar a successful
prosecution of a secondary party to whom the excuse does not extend. An acquittal on the ground of an excuse means that the actions of the primary party *were*
wrongful, but that he was not responsible for them because of the excusing
condition.[117] If the primary party is guilty of all of the elements of the crime,
and his conduct is otherwise wrongful, there is no reason why the secondary
party should not be convicted of assisting in the wrongful conduct, assuming
that he has no personal excuse of his own.[118]

---

[115] Some scholars would limit the statement in the text to cases in which *S* was aware of the justificatory condition when he assisted. This subject — whether justification defenses should be limited to persons who act for the right reason or, at least, act with knowledge of the justifying
circumstance — has been the subject of rich debate. See, e.g., Paul H. Robinson, *A Theory of Justification: Societal Harm as a Prerequisite for Criminal Liability*, 23 UCLA L. Rev. 266 (1973)
(favoring the defense even when the actor lacks knowledge of the justifying condition); George P.
Fletcher, *The Right Deed for the Wrong Reason: A Reply to Mr. Robinson*, 23 UCLA L. Rev. 293 (1975)
(responding to Robinson).

[116] See Patton v. State, 136 S.W. 459, 460 (Tex. Crim. App. 1911); see also United States v.
Lopez, 662 F. Supp. 1083 (N.D. Cal. 1987) (discussed in subsection [b], *infra*).

[117] See §§ 16.04 and 17.03, *supra*.

[118] See Fletcher, Note 1, *supra*, at 664-67; Kadish, Note 1, *supra*, at 380-81; accord, United States
v. Azadian, 436 F.2d 81, 82-83 (9th Cir. 1971).

For example, in *United States v. Lopez*,[119] *S* assisted *P* to escape from prison. *P* sought to show at her trial that she fled the prison because of unlawful threats on her life. The prosecution did not object to *P* seeking to defend her actions on this ground, but it did resist *S*'s efforts to introduce evidence of the threats as a basis for acquittal in *S*'s prosecution as an accomplice.

The court held that *S*'s right to introduce such evidence depended on whether *P*'s defense claim was founded on necessity (justification) or duress (excuse).[120] As the court explained, and as considered in subsection [a], "[a] third party has the right to assist an actor in a justified act." Therefore, if *P*'s claim was that she did the right thing by escaping, *S* was entitled to show that he assisted in this justified act. On the other hand, excuses "are always personal to the actor."[121] If *P*'s claim was that she did the wrong thing by escaping, but that she was not to blame because she was coerced, this was *her* personal excusing condition. As *S* was not personally coerced, he was *not* entitled to avoid conviction for assisting in an *unjustified* escape.[122]

[3] Acquittal on the Basis of Lack of *Mens Rea*

[a] In General

Suppose that a culpable secondary party assists a primary party to commit a wrongful act, but the primary actor is acquitted because he lacked the requisite *mens rea*. For example, consider *Regina v. Cogan and Leak*.[123] Leak convinced Cogan to have sexual intercourse with Leak's wife by falsely telling him that she would agree to the intercourse. In fact, Leak compelled his wife to submit to Cogan. Cogan was acquitted of rape on the basis of English precedent[124] that his unreasonable mistake of fact regarding the wife's consent negated the *mens rea* of the offense.

In light of Cogan's acquittal, was Leak guilty of rape? The court answered the question affirmatively, providing two alternative theories. First, since Leak caused Cogan to misunderstand the attendant circumstances, Cogan was Leak's innocent instrumentality. Thus, Leak was the principal in the first degree who used Cogan's "body as the instrument for the necessary physical act."[125] The dif-

---

[119] 662 F. Supp. 1083 (N.D. Cal. 1987).

[120] See § 23.05, *supra*.

[121] *Lopez*, 662 F. Supp. at 1086; see also Taylor v. Commonwealth, 521 S.E.2d 293, 297 (Va. App. 1999).

[122] In *Lopez*, the court concluded that *P*'s defense more nearly resembled a justification claim; therefore, *S* was permitted to raise *P*'s defense. But see Taylor v. Commonwealth, 521 S.E.2d 293 (Va. Ct. App. 1999) (*S* was convicted as an accomplice of *P*, her fiancé, who abducted his son from his son's mother; held: whatever excuse *P* might claim did not apply to *S*).

[123] [1976] Q.B. 217.

[124] Regina v. Morgan, [1976] App. Cas. 182 (H.L.). See § 12.03[D][4], *supra*.

[125] *Cogan and Leak*, Q.B. at 223.

ficulty with this analysis, however, is that it makes Leak guilty of raping his own wife, a conclusion that some courts are unwilling to reach, on the ground that rape is a "nonproxyable" offense.[126]

Second, the court opined that there was no reason why Leak should not be viewed as an accomplice of Cogan: "The fact that Cogan was innocent . . . does not affect the position that she was raped." It said further, "[n]o one outside a court of law would say that she had not been [raped]." In essence, the *actus reus* of rape was committed: The victim was forced to have sexual intercourse against her will. Therefore, a "crime" occurred. Cogan committed it. Leak encouraged it. Cogan's "crime" may be imputed to Leak.

This analysis, however, has serious conceptual difficulties. Can we truly say that the "crime" of rape occurred? As Professor Glanville Williams has observed, "this will not do at all. [The court] uses popular . . . language, on the question whether the *fact* of 'rape' has occurred, instead of legal language, on the question whether the *crime* of rape has occurred."[127] Certainly, the most common legal understanding of the term "crime" is that it involves an *actus reus and* a *mens rea* — that is, after all, what the prosecutor must prove (beyond a reasonable doubt) against a perpetrator. But, Cogan did not commit "rape" in *that* sense, as he lacked the requisite *mens rea*. Therefore, this case is not like that of a party who commits the *actus reus* with the requisite *mens rea* (i.e., commits all of the elements of a crime), but is acquitted on the ground of an excuse. Since Leak's liability must be derived from that of Cogan, and Cogan committed no "crime" on *this* understanding of the term, it is highly questionable whether Leak should have been convicted of rape as an accomplice.

Some scholars would permit conviction of a secondary party, as long he assists in the commission of the *actus reus* of an offense. For example, Professor Peter Alldridge, while disagreeing with the *Cogan and Leak* court's use of the innocent-instrumentality doctrine in that case,[128] sees no difficulty in treating Leak as an accomplice:

> The answer appropriate to the case . . . is to say that the norm laid down by the law relating to rape is that it is wrongful for a man to have intercourse with a woman who does not in fact consent. *That wrongful act is rape.* The excuse [lack of *mens rea* of Cogan] . . . is personal to [Cogan], and there is no reason why there should not be liability [of Leak] as an accessory.[129]

---

[126] See § 30.03[A][2][b][ii], *supra*.

[127] Williams, Note 27, *supra*, at 320 (emphasis added).

[128] He viewed rape as nonproxyable: "[T]o allege . . . that [Leak] had intercourse with his wife without her consent . . . is not what happened and . . . , had this been what had happened, it would not have constituted a crime." Alldridge, Note 106, *supra*, at 52.

[129] *Id*. (emphasis added) (footnote omitted).

Thus, under this view, the "wrongful act" (as distinguished from a "crime") of the primary party is imputed to the secondary party, which when coupled with the secondary party's own *mens rea*, creates the "crime."

But, this analysis seems misguided. It is one thing to impute a crime to the accomplice, and then measure the culpability of the respective parties on the basis of each person's *mens rea*;[130] it is quite another matter to derive criminal liability from a person *who has committed no offense*. It would be sensible, applying Alldridge's reasoning, to convict Leak *as a perpetrator, rather than an accomplice*, of a new crime, such as "causing or encouraging a wrongful act by another."[131] But, it is inaccurate to say that there was a *crime* committed by Cogan that may be imputed to Leak.

[b] Special Problem: The Feigning Primary Party

Earlier in this chapter we considered the liability of a putative accomplice to a crime whose purpose for participation with the primary party was to ensnare the latter in criminal activity.[132] Suppose that the converse occurs: Consider the classic case of *State v. Hayes*.[133]

S proposed to *P* that he join *S* in the burglary of *V*'s store. *S* was unaware of the fact that *P* was a relative of *V*. With *V*'s approval, *P* agreed to the plan. *S* assisted *P* into the building, and took possession of property handed to him by *P*. Before they could leave the scene, *S* was arrested for burglary. *S* was convicted of the offense, but the state supreme court overturned the conviction.

At first glance the court's ruling seems incorrect: *S* intentionally assisted *P*; and *S* had the requisite felonious intent. On a closer look, however, the result is unexceptionable. *P* was the primary party: He committed the acts that arguably constituted the burglary. *S*'s liability, therefore, had to derive from *P*. Yet, *P* was not guilty of burglary, because he entered the building with the express approval of the owner, with no intention to commit a felony (theft) therein.

Is there any way to justify *S*'s conviction? One possible theory would be to suggest that *he* was the primary party, who used *P* as his innocent instrumentality. The innocent-instrumentality doctrine, however, does not apply here because that rule is limited to circumstances in which the instrumentality is used or manipulated by another person. In this case *P* was not *S*'s puppet; if anything, *S* was duped by *P*.

---

[130] See § 30.06[C], *infra*.

[131] See Kadish, Note 1, *supra*, at 382.

[132] See § 30.05[B][1], *supra*.

[133] 16 S.W. 514 (Mo. 1891), overruled on other grounds by State v. Barton, 44 S.W. 239 (Mo. 1898).

Alternatively, we could say that *P* committed the *actus reus* of burglary. Therefore, a crime occurred for which *S* may be held accountable. This argument, however, is subject to the criticism noted in subsection [a], namely that it is inappropriate to say that a burglary has occurred when a person commits the *actus reus* of an offense without the requisite *mens rea*.[134] This criticism is especially compelling here since *P* not only lacked the requisite *mens rea* of burglary, but he had an antagonistic mental state, i.e., the intent to cause *S*'s arrest.

[C] Liability of an Accomplice When the Primary Party Is Convicted

At common law and today, there is no bar to convicting an accessory before the fact or a principal in the second degree of a *lesser* offense or degree of offense than is proven against the primary party/perpetrator, if the secondary party's culpability is less than that of the primary actor. For example, even if *P* is guilty of first-degree premeditated murder, *S* is properly convicted of second-degree murder if he did not premeditate or if he lacked the specific intent to kill, required elements of first-degree murder.[135] Or, suppose that *S* and *P* walk into *S*'s house and discover *S*'s spouse in an act of adultery with *V*. If *S*, in sudden heat of passion, provides a gun to *P*, who calmly kills *V*, *S* may be guilty of voluntary manslaughter,[136] although *P* is guilty of murder.

The more difficult issue is whether a secondary party may be convicted of a *more serious* offense or degree of offense than the primary party. At common law, the general rule was that an accessory (as distinguished from a principal in the second degree) could *not* be so convicted. The one apparent exception to this rule was in criminal homicide prosecutions. Now that the distinctions between principals and accessories have largely been abandoned, many commentators have concluded that there is no conceptual obstacle to convicting *any* secondary party — even an accessory — of a more serious offense than is proved against the primary party. The reasoning is that once it is agreed that a crime has occurred, each person's level of guilt should be assessed according to his own *mens rea*.[137]

---

[134] It is not even clear that we can say that the *actus reus* of the offense was committed by *P*: In view of the owner's permission for *P* to enter, there arguably was no unlawful breaking and entering of the building by *P*.

[135] State v. O'Brien, 857 S.W.2d 212, 217-18 (Mo. 1993) (the element of deliberation or premeditation cannot be imputed from the principal to the accomplice); Commonwealth v. Huffman, 638 A.2d 961, 962 (Pa. 1994) (stating the general principle that an accomplice's liability must be found on his own mental state and "cannot depend upon proof of the intent to kill only in the principal").

[136] See § 31.07[B][2], *infra*.

[137] People v. McCoy, 24 P.3d 1210, 1214, 1215 (Cal. 2001) (quoting this treatise, and observing that the accomplice's "mental state is her own; she is liable for her mens rea, not the other person's").

In homicide prosecutions, an accomplice may be convicted of first-degree murder, even though the primary party is convicted of second-degree murder or of manslaughter.[138] This outcome follows, for example, if the secondary party premeditates and calmly assists in a homicide, while the primary party kills without premeditation or in provocation. Likewise, it is possible for a primary party negligently to kill another (and, thus, be guilty of involuntary manslaughter), while the secondary party is guilty of murder, because he encouraged the primary actor's negligent conduct, with the intent that it result in the victim's death.

This approach makes sense as long as we view "criminal homicide" as a single offense — that of causing the death of another with a culpable mental state — involving multiple levels of blameworthiness. It is fair to say, then, that when P commits the offense of criminal homicide, this crime is imputed to S, whose own liability for the homicide should be predicated on his own level of *mens rea*, whether it is greater or less than that of the primary party.

It does not necessarily follow that this analysis should be applied in all non-homicide circumstances.[139] Consider, for example, the English case of *Regina v. Richards*:[140] S procured two men — we will call them, together, P — to severely beat up her husband, V. In American terms, S solicited an aggravated battery or, perhaps, the offense of mayhem. However, P did not do as procured, but instead committed the lesser offense of "unlawful wounding" (in American terms, a simple misdemeanor battery). Of what is S guilty? Is it "unlawful wounding" (the crime committed by P) or, as the jury concluded, the more serious offense of "unlawful wounding with the intent to commit grievous bodily harm"?

The *Richards* court held that S could be convicted only of the lesser offense of which P was convicted, although she concededly had a more culpable state of mind than P. *Richards* was the subject of both ardent criticism and support by commentators.[141] Ultimately, it was overruled.[142]

At first glance, the problem in *Richards* seems indistinguishable from the homicide cases. Although the crimes of "wounding" and "wounding with the intent to cause grievous bodily harm" were separate offenses, they could have

---

[138] *Id.* at 1215 (holding that even if the primary party is convicted of voluntary manslaughter, the secondary party may be convicted of murder).

[139] *Id.* at 1217 n.3 (in a homicide prosecution, holding that a secondary party may be convicted of a greater offense than the primary party, but concluding that "[b]ecause we cannot anticipate all possible non-homicide crimes or circumstances, we express no view on whether or how these principles apply outside the homicide context").

[140] [1974] Q.B. 776.

[141] Compare Williams, Note 27, *supra*, at 322-23, and J.C. Smith & Brian Hogan, Criminal Law 132-36 (5th ed. 1983) (criticizing the decision), with Kadish, Note 1, *supra*, at 388-91, and Fletcher, Note 1, *supra*, at 672-73 (providing support for the court's analysis).

[142] Regina v. Howe, [1987] App. Cas. 417 (H.L.).

been treated as different degrees of the same offense, much as criminal homi-cide is divided into degrees and/or separate offenses severable only in terms of *mens rea*. Therefore, we can say that *P* committed the crime — not just the *actus reus* of the offense — of wounding, and we can then treat *S* and *P* as guilty of different degrees of this offense, based on their respective levels of culpability. So interpreted, *Richards* was properly overruled.

But, notice this: What *S* wanted *P* to do was to commit a *different* social harm than was actually perpetrated. If *P* had done as *S* had wanted, she would have been guilty as an accomplice of an aggravated battery (e.g., "battery caus-ing grievous bodily harm") or mayhem. That is, *S* wanted one offense to occur (one with a more serious *actus reus*), which she attempted to cause by procur-ing *P* to commit that greater offense, *but the greater harm never occurred*. Thus, this is *not* like a homicide case, in which the secondary party wants precisely what has occurred — the wrongful death of another — and in which the only dif-ference between the parties is their degree of culpability *as to the harm that has been inflicted*.

As already seen, a person cannot be an accomplice to a crime that never occurred, as there is no crime for which to derive liability. In *Richards*, if we per-mit conviction of *S* for the greater offense, are we not effectively convicting her for a non-existent crime? The crime that occurred was a simple battery. What *S* wanted to occur, but which did not, was an aggravated battery or mayhem. At least in a legal system in which attempts are punished less severely than com-pleted offenses because less harm has occurred, it is submitted that a person who assists in a "mini-crime" (unlawful wounding), with the intent that it result in a "maxi-crime" (mayhem or aggravated battery), should *not* be convicted of the greater offense simply because she desired its commission. Here, too, *S* should be guilty of the crime that occurred (unlawful wounding) and not an offense that did not (unlawful wounding with the intent to cause grievous bod-ily harm). *S*'s heightened culpability (and dangerousness) can be handled through an additional solicitation charge.

§ 30.07 LIMITS TO ACCOMPLICE LIABILITY

[A] Legislative-Exemption Rule

A person may not be prosecuted as an accomplice in the commission of a crime if he is a member of the class of persons for whom the statute prohibit-ing the conduct was enacted to protect. For example, the statutory rape law was enacted to protect young females from immature decisions to have sexual inter-course; the legislature considers her to be the victim of the offense. It would con-flict with legislative intent, therefore, if she could be prosecuted as a secondary party to her own statutory rape.[143]

---

[143] In re Meagan R., 42 Cal. App. 4th 17 (Ct. App. 1996) (R cannot legally be an accomplice in her own statutory rape; therefore, she is also not guilty of burglary based on the intent to commit

[B] Abandonment

As with the law of conspiracy,[144] many courts hold that a person who provides assistance to another for the purpose of promoting or facilitating the offense, but who subsequently abandons the criminal endeavor, can avoid accountability for the subsequent criminal acts of the primary party.

A spontaneous and unannounced withdrawal will not do.[145] Instead, the accomplice must communicate his withdrawal to the principal and make bona fide efforts to neutralize the effect of his prior assistance. For example, one who provides an instrumentality for use in the crime must regain possession of it or otherwise neutralize its effect. Thus, a person who provides a fuse for dynamiting a building, must remove the fuse; and, "if [it] has been set, he must step on the fuse."[146] On other hand, one who has offered nothing more than mild encouragement may be able to neutralize his effect by communicating his objection to the crime, unless he provides it at the point at which the event is virtually unstoppable.

§ 30.08 CONSPIRATORIAL LIABILITY: THE *PINKERTON* DOCTRINE

[A] "Accomplice" versus "Conspiratorial" Liability

Courts and lawyers frequently fail to distinguish between *accomplice* liability, the subject of the preceding sections of this chapter, and *conspiracy* liability — complicity based solely on a *conspiratorial* relationship — which is the topic of this chapter section. This is because the two concepts "normally go hand-in-hand."[147] However, it is sometimes critical to distinguish between the two forms of complicity liability. As discussed in subsections [B] and [C], many jurisdictions hold that a person, *simply because he is a party to a conspiracy*, may be held responsible for the actions of his "partner[s] in crime."[148] And, as will be seen, conspiratorial liability is potentially a broader form of liability than accomplice doctrine.

The distinction between the two forms of accountability is this: An agreement between two or more persons to participate in the commission of a crime is the

---

the felony of statutory rape). The legislative-exemption rule is discussed more fully at § 29.09[D], *supra*.

[144] See § 29.09[B], *supra*.

[145] State v. Thomas, 356 A.2d 433, 442 (N.J. Super. Ct. App. Div. 1976), rev'd on other grounds, 387 A.2d 1187 (N.J. 1978).

[146] See Eldredge v. United States, 62 F.2d 449, 451 (10th Cir. 1932) (discussing withdrawal from a conspiracy).

[147] Rollin M. Perkins & Ronald N. Boyce, Criminal Law 703 (3d ed. 1982).

[148] Pinkerton v. United States, 328 U.S. 640, 647 (1946).

key to a conspiracy and, therefore, to conspiratorial liability. Actual assistance in the crime is not required. Accomplice liability requires proof that an actor at least indirectly participated (assisted) in the crime; an agreement to do so is not needed.[149]

In most circumstances, an accomplice is also a conspirator with the primary party in the commission of the crime. For example, if *S* drives *P* to a bank, which *P* robs with *S*'s weapon, and *S* drives *P* away from the bank, it is reasonable to infer a conspiratorial agreement between accomplice *S* and perpetrator *P*. Indeed, even when a conspirator does not actively participate in the planning or commission of an offense, the sheer act of agreeing may serve as encouragement to the primary party, and thereby render the conspirator an accomplice in the commission of the crime.

Nonetheless, one can be a conspirator without being an accomplice. For example, in *Pinkerton v. United States*,[150] *S* and *P* conspired to violate certain provisions of the Internal Revenue Code. Thereafter, *P* violated the Revenue Code provisions. However, he did so while *S* was in prison for unrelated reasons. The prosecutor did not claim that *S* assisted *P* in the planning or commission of the substantive offenses. And, *S*'s presence in prison negated any reasonable inference that his earlier act of agreeing encouraged *P* when he committed the crimes. *S*'s responsibility in *P*'s conduct, therefore, was not based on accomplice principles, and had to find its source exclusively in conspiracy law.

Accomplice liability in the absence of a conspiracy is also possible. For example: *P* enters a bank to rob it; *S*, a customer, observes *P*'s actions and silently assists in the crime by disabling a bank security camera. Here, *P* and *S* never agreed to commit the robbery together. But, *S* is *P*'s accomplice in light of his assistance.[151]

Thus, in most cases an accomplice is a co-conspirator (and vice-versa). Sometimes, only one theory of complicity will apply.

[B] Rule of Conspiratorial Liability

According to the so-called "*Pinkerton* doctrine," a party to a conspiracy is responsible for any criminal act committed by an associate if it: (1) falls within the scope of the conspiracy; or (2) is a foreseeable consequence of the unlawful agreement.[152]

---

[149] Chisler v. State, 553 So. 2d 654, 664 (Ala. Crim. App. 1989); State v. Roldan, 714 A.2d 351, 360 (N.J. Super. Ct. App. Div. 1998).

[150] 328 U.S. 640 (1946).

[151] See also State ex rel. Martin, Att'y Gen. v. Tally, 15 So. 722 (Ala. 1894) (*S*, aware that *P1* and *P2* have set out to kill *V*, independently prevents a warning from reaching *V*; *S* may be an accomplice in the subsequent homicide even though he did not conspire with the others). For another example of accomplice liability in the absence of a conspiracy, see *Commonwealth v. Cook*, 411 N.E.2d 1326 (Mass. App. Ct. 1980), discussed at § 29.04[A], *supra*.

[152] Pinkerton v. United States, 328 U.S. at 647-48.

It has been said that the *Pinkerton* rule, adopted in the federal courts, is the majority rule in states that have considered the issue.[153] However, one should be cautious in measuring the strength of the *Pinkerton* rule: Many courts that have expressed approval of the rule have done so in cases in which the result would have been the same had traditional accomplice rules been invoked.[154]

[C] Comparison of Liability

Accomplice and conspiracy liability often overlap completely. For example, suppose that S and P agree to commit an armed robbery and work together in its planning stages. P commits the offense. On these facts, S will be held accountable for the robbery under either theory of liability: He intentionally assisted P to rob the bank; and, as the robbery was the object of the conspiracy, he is liable for it under conspiracy rules. And, if P kills bank teller V during the same robbery, S is accountable for the death under either theory: The killing was a natural and probable consequence of the crime in which S intentionally assisted; and the homicide was a foreseeable consequence of the conspiracy to commit the robbery.

The rules potentially diverge in dramatic ways, however, when the P-S conspiracy is broad or open-ended. Notice that under *Pinkerton*, a person may be held accountable for the natural and probable consequences of the conspiracy, which may result in extensive liability if the agreement is a broad one; under accomplice law, however, a person is only responsible for the natural and probable consequences of the particular crimes in which the person has intentionally assisted.

To see the difference, suppose that $D1$ and $D2$ conspire to run a prostitution ring and live off the earnings of the prostitutes.[155] Assuming that the conspiracy includes the individual prostitutes, $D1$ and $D2$ would clearly be guilty under *Pinkerton*, and less clearly under doctrines of accomplice liability, of every act of prostitution committed by every prostitute.[156]

But, consider the prostitutes' position in the far-flung conspiracy. It is unlikely that any prostitute assisted in the acts of prostitution by other women. Under accomplice liability doctrine, therefore, a prostitute would not be guilty of any substantive offenses except her own. Pursuant to *Pinkerton*, however, once it is determined that a prostitute was a party to an open-ended agreement to com-

---

[153] State v. Walton, 630 A.2d 990, 998 (Conn. 1993). States that do not apply the *Pinkerton* doctrine include State ex rel. Woods v. Cohen, 844 P.2d 1147 (Ariz. 1992); Commonwealth v. Stasiun, 206 N.E.2d 672 (Mass. 1965); People v. McGee, 399 N.E.2d 1177 (N.Y. 1979); State v. Small, 272 S.E. 2d 128 (N.C. 1980), superseded by statute as recognized in State v. Woods, 272 S.E.2d 128 (N.C. 1980); and State v. Stein, 27 P.3d 184, 185 (Wash. 2001).

[154] *Developments in the Law — Criminal Conspiracy*, 72 Harv. L. Rev. 920, 993-95 (1959).

[155] People v. Luciano, 14 N.E.2d 433 (N.Y. 1938).

[156] In *id*., Luciano was convicted of sixty-two counts of prostitution.

mit prostitution, she would be liable for every act of prostitution performed by every other prostitute, *and of every other offense committed by D1 and D2 and by any other prostitute that was committed in furtherance of the broad conspiracy*. Rigid application of the *Pinkerton* rule, therefore, may result in extensive liability of comparatively minor parties to a criminal agreement.

Critics of the *Pinkerton* doctrine assert that the law "lose[s] all sense of just proportion if simply because of the conspiracy itself each [conspirator is] held accountable for thousands of additional offenses of which he was completely unaware and which he did not influence at all."[157] Defenders of the rule state that "such harshness may be considered as an occupational hazard confronting those who might be tempted to engage in a criminal conspiracy within a jurisdiction that adheres to the so-called *Pinkerton* rule."[158]

§ 30.09 MODEL PENAL CODE

[A] Forms of Liability

[1] In General

Under the Model Penal Code a person is guilty of an offense if he commits it "by his own conduct or by the conduct of another person for which he is legally accountable, or both."[159] In other words, a person can be convicted of an offense if he personally commits the crime, or if his relationship to the person who commits it is one for which he is legally accountable. Three forms of accountability for the acts of others are recognized by the Code and are described below.

[2] Accountability Through an Innocent Instrumentality

The Code adopts the accepted principle that one is guilty of the commission of a crime if he uses an innocent instrumentality to commit the crime. A person (*D*) is legally accountable for the conduct of "an innocent or irresponsible person" (*X*) if he (*D*): (1) has the mental state sufficient for commission of the offense; and (2) causes the innocent or irresponsible person to engage in the criminal conduct.[160]

It should be observed that the Code is explicit where the common law is implicit: The innocent-instrumentality doctrine applies only if *D causes X* to

---

[157] American Law Institute, Comment to § 2.06, at 307.

[158] State v. Barton, 424 A.2d 1033, 1038 (R.I. 1981).

[159] Model Penal Code § 2.06(1).

[160] Model Penal Code § 2.06(2)(a).

engage in the conduct in question. Thus, this section does not apply merely because X is insane or otherwise "innocent or irresponsible." D must have done something to manipulate or otherwise use X, so that it may fairly be said that, but for D's conduct, X would not have engaged in the conduct for which D is being held accountable.

If D causes X, an innocent or irresponsible person, to engage in criminal conduct, D is responsible for X's conduct if, but only if, D possessed the mental state sufficient for the commission of the crime. For example, if D coerces X to have nonconsensual sexual intercourse with V, D is guilty of rape because he possessed the mental state required for that offense.[161] Or, suppose that D provides his car to X, an insane person with a known "penchant for mad driving."[162] If X proceeds to drive D's car in a dangerous manner, D may be convicted of reckless endangerment, on the basis of D's recklessness in providing the car to a known mad driver. However, if D is unaware of X's dangerous tendencies, D would not be guilty of reckless endangerment: He has caused X to engage in the conduct, but he does not possess the mental state (recklessness) sufficient for commission of the offense.

[3] Miscellaneous Accountability

A person may be held accountable for another person's conduct if the law defining an offense so provides.[163] This provision is not of broad importance, but it does recognize that a legislature may wish to enact special laws of accomplice liability, as, for example, when it prohibits aiding and abetting a suicide attempt,[164] or knowingly causing or facilitating a prison escape.[165]

[4] Accomplice Accountability

A person is legally accountable for the conduct of another person if he is an accomplice of the other in the commission of the criminal offense.[166]

Two features of accomplice liability should initially be observed. First, it is a form of liability independent of the innocent-or-irresponsible-person doctrine described in subsection [2], i.e., the rules of accomplice liability described below have no bearing on the situation in which a person uses an innocent instrumentality.

---

[161] Morrisey v. State, 620 A.2d 207, 211 (Del. 1993).

[162] American Law Institute, Comment to § 2.06, at 302.

[163] Model Penal Code § 2.06(2)(b).

[164] Model Penal Code § 210.5(2).

[165] Model Penal Code § 242.6.

[166] Model Penal Code § 2.06(2)(c).

Second, accomplice liability is dependent on the relationship of the parties in the commission of a *specific offense*. In other words, if *S* is prosecuted for robbery because he allegedly served as *P*'s accomplice, the issue that must be resolved is whether *S* was *P*'s accomplice *in that robbery*, and not whether *S* was *P*'s accomplice in the commission of some other crime or of crimes in general.

[5] Rejection of Conspiratorial Liability

The Model Code rejects the *Pinkerton*[167] doctrine of conspiratorial liability. That is, under the Code, a person is not accountable for the conduct of another solely because he conspired with that person to commit an offense. The liability of one who does not personally commit an offense must be based on one of the preceding forms of accountability, most often on the basis of accomplice liability. The drafters of the Code rejected the *Pinkerton* doctrine because they believed there was "no better way to confine within reasonable limits the scope of liability to which conspiracy may theoretically give rise."[168]

[B] Nature of an "Accomplice"

[1] Conduct

[a] In General

S is an accomplice of *P* in the commission of an offense if, with the requisite *mens rea*, he: (1) solicits *P* to commit the offense; (2) aids, agrees to aid, or attempts to aid *P* in the planning or commission of the offense; or (3) has a legal duty to prevent the commission of the offense, but makes no effort to do so.[169]

[b] Accomplice Liability by Solicitation

S is an accomplice of *P* in the commission of an offense if he solicits *P* to commit the crime. The complicity section does not define the term "solicits." Rather, accomplice liability exists if *S*'s conduct would constitute criminal solicitation, as that offense is defined elsewhere in the Code.[170]

[c] Accomplice Liability by Aiding

The Code dispenses with the many common law and statutory terms used to describe the conduct that may constitute assistance in the commission of an

---

[167] Pinkerton v. United States, 328 U.S. 640 (1946). See § 30.08, *supra*.

[168] American Law Institute, Comment to § 2.06, at 307.

[169] Model Penal Code § 2.06(3)(a).

[170] Model Penal Code § 5.02. See generally § 28.03, *supra*.

offense, and replaces them with the single word "aids." It should be observed, however, that in the Model Code, "soliciting" a crime is *not* a form of "aiding"; it is an independent basis for accomplice liability. This distinction can prove significant, as discussed in the next two subsections.

[d] Accomplice Liability by Agreeing to Aid

S is an accomplice of *P* if he agrees to aid *P* in the planning or commission of an offense. This requirement is met, for example, if *S* tells *P* that he will help to plan the commission of the offense, or if he agrees to provide *P* with an instrumentality for the commission of the crime, *even if S does not fulfill his promise*. However, because this form of accomplice liability is based on "aiding," rather than "soliciting," *S* is *not* an accomplice of *P* merely because he agrees to *solicit* the commission of an offense but fails to do so.

This feature of the Code differs at least in form from the common law. In most cases, *S*'s agreement to aid in the commission of an offense serves as encouragement to *P* and, therefore, functions as a basis for common law accomplice liability. The Code does not require proof of such encouragement, however; it is enough that *S* manifested his participation in the offense by agreeing to aid.

On the other hand, "agreeing to aid" is *not* equivalent to conspiring to commit an offense. That is, this is not the *Pinkerton* doctrine in disguise. One can conspire to commit an offense (and, therefore, be guilty of conspiracy) and yet not "agree to aid" another person in a particular offense (and, therefore, not be an accomplice of a co-conspirator in the commission of that crime). For example, suppose that *S* agrees to aid *P* to rob Bank A. In furtherance of their conspiracy, *P* steals a "getaway" car. Under *Pinkerton* doctrine, *S* is guilty of the theft, as that offense was committed in furtherance of their conspiracy to rob Bank A. However, under the Code, *S* is *not* guilty of the car theft, as he did not agree to aid (or, for that matter, solicit, aid, or attempt to aid) *P* in the commission of *that* offense.

[e] Accomplice Liability by Attempting to Aid

[i] In General

In a significant departure from the common law,[171] the Code provides that *S* may be held accountable as an accomplice of *P* in the commission of an offense if he attempts to aid in the planning or commission of the crime, even if his aid proves ineffectual. For example, if *S* opens a window so that *P* may enter to commit a felony inside the building, *S* is an accomplice in the burglary, even if *P* enters by the door. In such circumstances, *S* has "attempted" to aid *P*, i.e., he has

---

[171] See § 30.04[B][1], *supra*.

taken a substantial step in a course of conduct intended to culminate in assistance in the commission of an offense.

[ii] The Relationship of § 2.06 (Complicity) to § 5.01 (Criminal Attempt)

It is useful to see how Section 2.06, the Model Penal Code's complicity provision, relates to Section 5.01, which prohibits criminal attempts. In particular, Section 5.01(3), discussed elsewhere in this Text,[172] should be considered here.

Suppose that S provides P a gun in order to assist P in the commission of a robbery. If P performs the robbery, S is guilty as an accomplice of P in its commission. Similarly, if P, in the midst of the robbery, is arrested before he can complete it, P is guilty of *attempted* robbery under the Code's criminal attempt provision. In turn, S would be guilty of the attempt under the Code's complicity statute.

However, suppose that P is arrested *before* he takes a substantial step in a course of conduct intended to result in the robbery. Under these circumstances, P is not guilty of attempted robbery.[173] In this case, S is not accountable under the complicity statute, because the person from whom he would derive his liability committed no crime. Nonetheless, S is guilty of a criminal attempt by *his own conduct* (i.e., *not* through the doctrine of complicity), by application of Model Penal Code Section 5.01(3), which provides that a person who engages in conduct designed to aid[174] in the commission of an offense "that would establish complicity under Section 2.06 if the crime were committed by such other person, is guilty of an attempt . . . although the crime is not committed or attempted by such other person."[175]

Notice the irony in this result: S is guilty of attempted robbery; P, the primary participant, is not guilty of attempt.

[f] Accomplice Liability by Omission

Ordinarily, one cannot be an accomplice in the commission of an offense by failing to act. The rule is to the contrary, however, if the omitter has a duty to

---

[172] See § 27.09[D][2], *supra*.

[173] He may be guilty of another offense, e.g., conspiracy to commit robbery.

[174] Notice that Section 5.01(3) uses the word "aid" in relationship to the complicity statute; thus, this provision does not apply if S *solicits* another to commit an offense, which offense is neither committed nor attempted.

[175] This provision also comes into play when a person, with criminal intent, provides aid to one whom he believes will commit an offense, but who actually is an undercover officer who does not attempt to commit the offense. E.g., United States v. Washington, 106 F.3d 983 (D.C. Cir. 1997) (based on the M.P.C., W was convicted of attempted possession of cocaine with intent to distribute, when he "assisted" an undercover officer whom he believed to be a drug dealer to possess what he believed was cocaine).

prevent the commission of the offense, for example, if he is a police officer standing by while a crime is committed in his presence.

It should be remembered, however, that the omitter must possess the mental state required of an accomplice, i.e., he must have failed to act with the purpose of promoting or facilitating the commission of the offense. An omission that is the result of fright or ignorance, rather than dereliction of duty, would not result in accomplice liability.

[2] Mental State

[a] In General

A person is an accomplice if he assists "with the purpose of promoting or facilitating the commission of the offense."[176] This provision conforms with common law precedent. For example, if S drives P to a liquor store where P commits a robbery, S is guilty of robbery if his act of assistance (driving the automobile) was committed with the purpose of facilitating the robbery; however, he is not guilty if he did not know what P intended to do in the store.

After considerable debate, the American Law Institute rejected the argument that complicity liability should apply to one who knowingly, but not purposely, facilitates the commission of an offense.[177] For example, if S, a merchant, sells dynamite to P, with knowledge that P intends to use the explosives to blow open a safe, S is not an accomplice in the subsequent crime, unless it was his conscious object to facilitate the commission of the offense.

[b] Liability for Crimes of Recklessness and Negligence

The requirement of purposeful conduct set out in Section 2.06 triggers the same question that confronts courts interpreting the common law and pre-Model Code statutes: Under what circumstances, if any, is a person an accomplice in the commission of a crime of recklessness or negligence?

The Code expressly deals with this issue. Section 2.06(4) provides that, when causing a particular result is an element of a crime, a person is an accomplice in the commission of the offense if: (1) he was an accomplice in the *conduct* that caused the *result*; and (2) he acted with the culpability, if any, regarding the *result* that is sufficient for commission of the offense.

Reconsider an earlier hypothetical:[178] S encourages P to speed on a public road near a school. P loses control of the car and strikes and kills V, a child.

[176] Model Penal Code § 2.06(3)(a).
[177] See American Law Institute, Comment to § 2.06, at 314-19.
[178] See § 30.05[B][3], *supra*.

S and P are prosecuted for negligent homicide. On these facts, S may be held accountable for the death caused by P.

To see this, one must go through a three-step process. First, determine P's potential responsibility. For sake of discussion, assume that P is guilty of negligent homicide. Second, ask whether S was an accomplice in the *conduct* that caused the *result* (rather than asking the ordinary question of whether S was an accomplice in the commission of the charged offense). The answer is that S was an accomplice in the *conduct*: He assisted by encouraging the conduct (speeding) that caused the result (the death); and he uttered the words of encouragement with the purpose of promoting the conduct (the speeding). Third, ask whether S acted with the culpability in regard to the *result* (the death) that is sufficient for commission of the offense. In this case, S quite arguably acted with the requisite culpability (negligence).

This provision has special significance in states that recognize the common law doctrines of felony-murder and misdemeanor-manslaughter.[179] These common law rules allow the primary party in a homicide to be convicted if the death occurs accidentally while he is committing a felony or misdemeanor. The effect of Section 2.06(4) is to make the accomplice in the *conduct* (the underlying felony or misdemeanor) that causes the result strictly liable for the ensuing death, on the ground that he possessed the level of culpability in regard to the *result* that is sufficient for commission of the offense, i.e., no culpability.

[c] Attendant Circumstances

Reconsider an earlier case:[180] S purposely assists P to have sexual intercourse with V, a nonconsenting female. P realizes that V is not consenting (and, therefore, is guilty of rape), but S unreasonably believes that V is consenting. Is S guilty of rape as P's accomplice?

The Code does not address this question. The Commentary states that "[t]here is deliberate ambiguity"[181] in this regard. Thus, a court might determine that the requirement of purpose extends to the attendant circumstances, in which case S is not guilty of the rape. Alternatively, the policy of the substantive offense might control, i.e., S would be guilty of the offense if he has the culpable state of mind regarding the victim's nonconsent that is sufficient to convict the perpetrator of that offense.

---

[179] See §§ 31.06 and 31.09, *infra*. Although the Code rejects these doctrines, a state could adopt Section 2.06(4) and yet retain one or both of these homicide rules.

[180] See § 30.05[B][4], *supra*.

[181] American Law Institute, Comment to § 2.06 at 311 n.37.

[d] Natural-and-Probable-Consequences Doctrine

The Code rejects the common law natural-and-probable-consequences rule.[182] As a result, the liability of an accomplice does not extend beyond the purposes that he shares. For example, suppose that S aids P in the commission of a bank robbery by furnishing P with the details of the bank's security system. Later, P steals an automobile, which he uses as his "getaway" vehicle in the robbery. Although S is an accomplice of P in the commission of the robbery (he aided P with the purpose of promoting that offense), he is *not* an accomplice in the commission of the theft: Although the theft may have been a foreseeable consequence of the offense in which he was an accomplice, he did not purposely aid in the car theft.

[C] Liability of the Accomplice in Relation to the Perpetrator

The Model Code provides that an accomplice in the commission of an offense may be convicted of a crime, upon proof of its commission by another person, regardless of whether the other person is convicted, acquitted, or not prosecuted. Furthermore, an accomplice may be convicted of a different offense or different degree of offense than the primary party is convicted.[183] Thus, the fact that P is acquitted of an offense does not preclude the conviction of S for that offense, as long as the prosecutor shows that *someone* committed the crime in question, and that S aided that person.[184] It is also possible to convict S of assault with intent to kill, and P of simple assault, if S has a more culpable frame of mind regarding the attack.

The Code also expressly provides that a person who is legally incapable of committing an offense personally may be held accountable for the crime if it is committed by another person for whom he is legally accountable.[185] For example, although a husband cannot legally rape his own wife at common law or under the Model Penal Code,[186] he may be convicted as an accomplice in her rape.

---

[182] See § 30.05[B][5], *supra*. However, with homicides, the natural-and-probable-consequences rule can come in the back door as the result of the convergence of the felony-murder and misdemeanor-manslaughter rules and Model Penal Code Section 2.06(4), as described at § 30.09[B][2][b], *supra*.

[183] Model Penal Code § 2.06(7).

[184] Although the acquittal of the perpetrator is not a bar to conviction of an accomplice, as noted, the Code does require proof of "the commission of the offense." The Code does not indicate, however, what it means by the word "offense" in this context. Thus, the Code does not expressly resolve the issues raised in § 30.06[B][2]-[3], *supra*.

[185] Model Penal Code § 2.06(5).

[186] Model Penal Code § 213.1.

[D] Limits to Accomplice Liability

Section 2.06(6) states that, unless the Code expressly provides to the contrary, a person is not an accomplice in the commission of an offense if any one of three circumstances exist. First, S may not be convicted as an accomplice if he is the victim of the offense. For example, the parent of a kidnapped child who pays a ransom may not be convicted as an accomplice in the kidnapping of his own child.

Second, S is not an accomplice of P if S's conduct is "inevitably incident" to the commission of the offense. For example, a purchaser of narcotics is not an accomplice in the commission of the sale or delivery of the controlled substance to himself.[187]

Third, the Code establishes a defense of abandonment. A person is not an accomplice in the commission of a crime if he terminates his participation before the crime is committed, and if he: (1) neutralizes his assistance; (2) gives timely warning to the police of the impending offense; or (3) in some other manner attempts to prevent the commission of the crime.[188]

---

[187] State v. Celestine, 671 So. 2d 896 (La. 1996); Robinson v. State, 815 S.W.2d 361 (Tex. App. 1991).

[188] See § 30.07[B] for general discussion of how the defense is applied.

Chapter 31

CRIMINAL HOMICIDE

§ 31.01 HOMICIDE[1]

[A] Definition of "Homicide"

At very early common law, "homicide" was defined as "the killing of a human being by a human being."[2] This definition includes suicide within its compass. However, the later common law definition of "homicide," followed in modern statutes, is "the killing of a human being by *another* human being." Suicide, therefore, is no longer a form of homicide.[3]

"Homicide" is a legally neutral term. That is, a homicide may be innocent or criminal. The duly authorized execution of a convicted felon, for example, is no less a homicide than the most "cold-blooded" murder.

[B] Definition of "Human Being"

[1] The Beginning of Human Life[4]

At common law, a fetus must be born alive to constitute a "human being" within the meaning of that term in criminal homicide law.[5]

This rule is anomalous. Following the common law approach, a homicide occurs when one causes the death of a being that is not considered human at the time of the death-producing act, as long as it is "human" when it dies.[6] Thus, if *D* strikes *V*, a pregnant woman, in the abdomen causing lethal injury to the

---

[1] See generally Herbert Wechsler & Jerome Michael, *A Rationale of the Law of Homicide* (Pts. I & II), 37 Colum. L. Rev. 701 (1937), 37 Colum. L. Rev. 1261 (1937).

[2] Royal Commission on Capital Punishment Report, (Cmd. 8932) ¶ 72 (1953).

[3] Attempted suicide was a common law misdemeanor. Today, a person who assists another to commit suicide may be charged with aiding and abetting a suicide, an independent statutory offense in many jurisdictions. E.g., Model Penal Code § 210.5.

[4] See generally Clarke D. Forsythe, *Homicide of the Unborn Child: The Born Alive Rule and Other Legal Anachronisms*, 21 Val. U. L. Rev. 563 (1987); Alan S. Wasserstrom, Annotation, *Homicide Based on Killing of Unborn Child*, 64 A.L.R.5th 671 (1998) (and Supp. 2005).

[5] See Meadows v. State, 722 S.W.2d 584, 585 (Ark. 1987); Keeler v. Superior Court, 470 P.2d 617, 622 (Cal. 1970); State v. Beale, 376 S.E.2d 1, 3 (N.C. 1989); Commonwealth v. Booth, 766 A.2d 843, 844 (Pa. 2001).

[6] E.g., State v. Cotton, 5 P.3d 918 (Ariz. Ct. App. 2000) (*C* shot *V*, his pregnant girlfriend, in the head; *V* died at the hospital, her daughter was delivered alive but died shortly thereafter; held: *C* may be convicted of two counts of criminal homicide).

fetus, a homicide occurs if the fetus is expelled from the womb alive and dies from the blow seconds after birth. Yet, if the same act is more efficient, in that it causes immediate death of the fetus in the womb, a homicide has not occurred.

Critics of the common law rule have declared it outdated. The stated basis of the "born alive" rule was that a live birth was needed to prove that the "unborn child" was alive at the time of the accused's actions, and that these acts were the cause of its death.[7] In light of advances in modern medical technology, it is now possible to determine whether a fetus is alive in the mother's womb, to determine with much greater likelihood of accuracy its chances of being born alive, and to identify the cause of its death if it is born dead. Therefore, it is reasoned, the definition of "human being" should include unborn fetuses.

Although the original common law rule remains intact in most jurisdictions, an increasing number of states now define a viable (and, at times, even nonviable) fetus as a "human being," protected by that jurisdiction's homicide laws.[8]

[2] The End of Human Life[9]

When does a person cease to be a "human being" for purposes of homicide law, i.e., what constitutes the legal death of a human being? The traditional rule, based on then-prevailing medical standards, recognized a cardiopulmonary definition of "death": A human being was dead when there was a complete and permanent stoppage of the circulation of the blood and the "cessation of the animal and vital functions consequent thereon, such as respiration, pulsation, etc."[10]

Since the development of life-support devices and procedures, this definition has proven unsatisfactory. It is now possible artificially to maintain the

---

[7] Commonwealth v. Cass, 467 N.E.2d 1324, 1328 (Mass. 1984); Hughes v. State, 868 P.2d 730, 732 (Okla. Crim. App. 1994); cf. Keeler v. Superior Court, 470 P.2d at 633 (Burke, Acting C.J., dissenting) ("The common law reluctance to characterize the killing of a quickened fetus as a homicide was based solely upon a presumption that the fetus would have been born dead.").

[8] E.g., Commonwealth v. Morris, 142 S.W.3d 654 (Ky. 2004) (viable fetus); State v. Holcomb, 956 S.W.2d 286 (Mo. Ct. App. 1997) (any unborn child); Hughes v. State, 868 P.2d 730 (Okla Crim. App. 1994) (viable fetus); State v. Horne, 319 S.E.2d 703 (S.C. 1984) (viable fetus).

California has amended its murder statute to prohibit the unlawful killing of a human being *or fetus*. Cal. Penal Code § 187 (Deering 2005). As such, a fetus is *not* a human being, but it receives similar protection. See People v. Davis, 872 P.2d 591, 597-600 (Cal. 1994) (the statute covers any fetus that has progressed beyond the embryonic stage of seven to eight weeks). Because the California legislature did not similarly amend its manslaughter statute, the common law rule persists and there is no crime of manslaughter of a fetus. People v. Dennis, 950 P.2d 1035, 1055 (Cal. 1998).

[9] See generally Alexander Morgan Capron & Leon R. Kass, *A Statutory Definition of the Standards for Determining Human Death: An Appraisal and a Proposal*, 121 U. Pa. L. Rev. 87 (1972); Report of the Ad Hoc Committee of the Harvard Medical School to Examine the Definition of Brain Death, *A Definition of Irreversible Coma*, 205 J.A.M.A. 337 (1968).

[10] Smith v. Smith, 317 S.W.2d 275, 279 (Ark. 1958) (quoting Black's Law Dictionary 488 (4th ed. 1951)).

heart and lung activities of persons who have lost the spontaneous capacity to perform these "animal and vital functions." As one court put it, "human bodies can be made to breathe and blood to circulate even in the utter absence of brain function."[11] The effect of the machinery, therefore, is to keep some people legally "alive" long after their capacity for independent life has ceased. Furthermore, in an era of sophisticated organ transplant technology, the traditional definition prevents medical personnel from "harvesting" healthy organs from "artificially alive" persons, resulting in the death of patients in desperate need of healthy organs.

In 1968, an influential Harvard Medical School committee reported that the medical conception of death was changing.[12] It concluded that cessation of brain function is a more suitable measure of death, especially when a patient's respiration and circulation are being supported artificially. The committee set forth a multi-step test designed to identify "brain death syndrome."

As is now understood, the brain anatomically is divided into three parts. The cerebrum (the "higher brain") controls cognitive functions, including consciousness. The cerebellum ("middle brain") controls motor coordination. And the brain stem ("lower brain") provides the "animal functions," i.e., reflexive and spontaneous activities such as breathing and swallowing.[13] "Brain death" exists when the whole brain — all three portions — irreversibly cease to function. The fact that respiration and pulsation can be or are artificially induced by machinery does not affect the conclusion.

In 1970, the Kansas legislature enacted the first statute recognizing termination of brain functions as a basis for determining legal death. The law provided that death occurs when, according to accepted medical standards, the individual experiences an irreversible cessation of breathing and heartbeat (the common law definition) *or* there is an absence of spontaneous brain activity.[14] Since then, a majority of states, by statute or judicial decision,[15] have incorporated "brain death" — more accurately, "whole brain death"[16] — in their definition of "death."[17]

---

[11] In re T.A.C.P., 609 So. 2d 588, 591 (Fla. 1992).

[12] See Report of the Ad Hoc Committee of the Harvard Medical School, Note 9, *supra*.

[13] People v. Eulo, 472 N.E.2d 286, 291-92 (N.Y. 1984).

[14] Kan. Stat. Ann. § 77-202 (repealed in 1984).

[15] E.g., State v. Guess, 715 A.2d 643, 651-52 (Conn. 1998); People v. Eulo, 472 N.E.2d at 288-89.

[16] E.g., Kan. Stat. Ann. § 77-205 (2005) ("An individual who has sustained either (1) irreversible cessation of circulatory and respiratory functions, or (2) irreversible cessation of all functions of the entire brain, including the brain stem, is dead.").

[17] See also Uniform Determination of Death Act § 1, 12 U.L.A. 340 (Supp. 1991) (stating that death occurs when there is either irreversible cessation of circulatory and respiratory functions or of "all functions of the entire brain, including the brain stem"). For philosophical objections to the "whole brain death" definition, see F.K. Kamm, *Brain Death and Spontaneous Breathing*, 30 Phil. & Pub. Aff. 297 (2002).

[C] Year-and-a-Day Rule[18]

The common law provides that a defendant may not be prosecuted for criminal homicide unless the victim dies within a year and a day of the act inflicting the fatal injury.[19] That is, if *D* shoots *V* on January 1, 2000 and *V* dies on January 1, 2001 a homicide has resulted; but, if *V* dies on or after January 2, 2001, a criminal homicide prosecution is barred, although a non-homicide prosecution, such as for assault with intent to kill,[20] is permitted.

The year-and-a-day rule dates back to 1278,[21] and is "well established"[22] in Anglo-American common law. The rule apparently "reflects the judgment that proof of causation for murder 'should not be unduly speculative.'"[23] In light of the inexactitude of medical science at the time the rule originated, there was virtually no way to ensure that a death after an extended passage of time was attributable to human rather than to natural causes. Consequently, the arbitrary time limitation was devised.

The year-and-a-day-rule is now considered "an outdated relic of the common law."[24] As a result of advances in medical technology, an assault victim can be kept alive indefinitely, well past the year-and-a-day line. And, medical science can now determine the cause of death with considerable precision, even if the person suffers a lingering death. As a consequence, the overwhelming trend is to abrogate the rule or apply a longer time limitation.[25]

---

[18] See generally D.E.C. Yale, *A Year and a Day in Homicide*, 48 Cambridge L.J. 202 (1989).

[19] 4 William Blackstone, Commentaries on the Laws of England *197 (1769) ("In order . . . to make the killing murder, it is requisite that the party die within a year and a day after the stroke received, or cause of death administered. . . .").

[20] E.g., Commonwealth v. Pinnick, 234 N.E.2d 756 (Mass. 1968), overruled on other grounds by Commonwealth v. Lewis, 409 N.E.2d 771 (Mass. 1980).

[21] Statutes of Gloucester, 6 Edward 1, ch. 9 (1278).

[22] People v. Stevenson, 331 N.W.2d 143, 145 (Mich. 1982); see State v. Picotte, 661 N.W.2d 381, 385 (Wis. 2003).

[23] United States v. Jackson, 528 A.2d 1211, 1216 (D.C. 1987) (quoting State v. Young, 390 A.2d 556, 562 (N.J. 1978)).

[24] Rogers v. Tennessee, 532 U.S. 451, 462 (2001).

[25] *Id.* at 463 (stating that the rule "has been legislatively or judicially abolished in the vast majority of jurisdictions recently to have addressed the issue"); see also, e.g., Cal. Penal Code § 194 (Deering 2005) (creating a rebuttable presumption that a killing after three years and a day is not criminal).

§ 31.02 CRIMINAL HOMICIDE: GENERAL PRINCIPLES

[A] "Murder" and "Manslaughter": Common Law Definitions

A criminal homicide is one committed without justification or excuse. In very early English legal history, "criminal homicide" was a single offense, punishable by death; later, it was divided by statute into "murder" and the lesser non-capital offense of "manslaughter." These two offenses are part of the American common law.

The common law definition of "murder" is "the killing of a human being by another human being with malice aforethought."[26] Manslaughter is "an unlawful killing of a human being by another human being *without* malice aforethought."[27] Thus, as Blackstone has put it, "malice aforethought" is the "grand criterion which now distinguishes murder from other killing."[28]

At common law, there were no degrees of murder or manslaughter. However, for purpose of clarity, judges often distinguished between "voluntary" (really, "intentional") and "involuntary" ("unintentional") manslaughter. These terms have persisted to this day. Originally, the punishment for the two forms of manslaughter was the same;[29] today, voluntary manslaughter is a statutorily more serious crime than involuntary manslaughter.[30]

[B] Murder: Definition of "Malice Aforethought"

[1] "Aforethought"

In very early English history, the word "aforethought" probably required that a person think about, or premeditate, the homicide long before the time of the killing.[31] It gradually lost this meaning, so that the term "aforethought" is now superfluous in English homicide law.[32]

---

[26] United States v. Wharton, 433 F.2d 451, 454 (D.C. Cir. 1970); American Law Institute, Comment to § 210.2, at 13-14. Coke defined murder as follows: "When a man of sound memory and of the age of discretion unlawfully kills any reasonable creature in being, and under the King's peace, with malice aforethought, either express or implied by the law, the death taking place within a year and a day." Quoted in *id.* at 14 n.1.

[27] 4 Blackstone, Note 19, *supra*, at *191 (emphasis added).

[28] *Id.* at *198-99; see People v. Mendoza, 664 N.W.2d 685, 692 (Mich. 2003) ("[T]he only element distinguishing murder from manslaughter is malice.").

[29] Rollin M. Perkins & Ronald N. Boyce, Criminal Law 83 (3d ed. 1982).

[30] See § 31.02[D][1], *infra*.

[31] Perkins & Boyce, Note 29, *supra*, at 57.

[32] Royal Commission, Note 2, *supra*, at ¶ 74.

The word "aforethought" has always been superfluous to the definition of murder in American law. Therefore, unless a statute modifies the common law by requiring proof of premeditation,[33] a spur-of-the-moment killing may constitute murder.[34]

[2] "Malice"

"Malice" is a legal term of art with little connection to its non-legal meaning. As the term has developed, a person who kills another acts with "malice" if she possesses any one of four states of mind: (1) the intention to kill a human being; (2) the intention to inflict grievous bodily injury on another; (3) an extremely reckless disregard for the value of human life (so-called "depraved heart" murder); or (4) the intention to commit a felony during the commission or attempted commission of which the death results (so-called "felony murder"). These four mental states are discussed in detail in subsequent sections of this chapter.

These disparate mental states have one feature in common: In the absence of justification (e.g., self-defense), excuse (e.g., insanity), or mitigating circumstance (e.g., adequate provocation), each mental state manifests the actor's extreme indifference to the value of human life. In the first case — intent-to-kill murder — the malice is said to be "express"; the other forms involve so-called "implied" malice.

[C] Manslaughter: Types of "Unlawful Killings"

Manslaughter is an unlawful killing that does not involve malice aforethought or, as the Commentary to the Model Penal Code puts it, it is a "homicide without malice aforethought on the one hand and without justification or excuse on the other."[35]

Traditionally, three types of unlawful killings constitute manslaughter, described more fully in subsequent sections of this chapter. First, an intentional killing committed in "sudden heat of passion" as the result of "adequate provocation" is voluntary manslaughter.

Second, an unintentional killing that is the result of "an act, lawful in itself, but [done] in an unlawful manner, and without due caution and circumspection"[36] is involuntary manslaughter. In modern terminology, this is a homicide committed in a criminally negligent manner.

---

[33] Frequently, such a requirement exists. See generally § 31.03[C], *infra*.

[34] State v. Heidelberg, 45 So. 256, 258 (La. 1907).

[35] American Law Institute, Comment to § 210.3, at 44.

[36] 4 Blackstone, Note 19, *supra*, at *192.

Third, an unintentional killing that occurs during the commission or attempted commission of an unlawful act may constitute involuntary manslaughter. If the killing occurs during the commission of an unlawful act amounting to a felony, the homicide is murder, "but if no more was intended than a mere trespass [i.e., a non-felony], [the homicide] will amount only to manslaughter."[37] This type of manslaughter is sometimes dubbed "unlawful-act manslaughter" or "misdemeanor-manslaughter."

[D] Statutory Reformulation of Criminal Homicide Law

[1] In General

At common law, murder was a capital offense. Over time, efforts were made to ameliorate the harshness of homicide law: The general judicial and legislative consensus was that not every homicide committed with malice aforethought merited the death penalty.

American reform of homicide law began in Pennsylvania in 1794, when that State's legislature passed a statute dividing murder into two degrees: murder in the first degree, for which the death penalty remained intact; and murder in the second degree, for which a lesser sentence was imposed. Pennsylvania did not materially change the nature of manslaughter law, although it formally divided the offense into "voluntary" and "involuntary" components; whereas the common law graded both forms of manslaughter equally, Pennsylvania imposed a more severe penalty for voluntary manslaughter than for involuntary manslaughter. By 1953, thirty-seven states and the District of Columbia had divided murder into degrees, with most of them adopting verbatim the "Pennsylvania Model" of murder and manslaughter.[38]

In more recent years, reform of the common law has taken three separate paths. Many states continue to follow the Pennsylvania approach, discussed immediately below. A few states have modified the Pennsylvania Model by dividing murder into *three* degrees.[39] And, some states have followed the path of the Model Penal Code, discussed later in this chapter,[40] which rejects the degrees-of-murder approach, divides criminal homicide into three crimes (murder, manslaughter, and negligent homicide), and significantly reformulates these offenses.

---

[37] *Id.* at *193.

[38] Smith v. State, 398 A.2d 426, 434 (Md. Ct. Spec. App. 1979).

[39] In fact, Pennsylvania now divides murder into three degrees. 18 Pa. Cons. Stat. § 2502 (2005).

[40] See generally § 31.10, *infra*.

[2] The Division of Murder Into Degrees ("Pennsylvania Model")

The common law of murder remains relevant in the twenty-first century, particularly in states that apply the Pennsylvania Model of murder. This is because such statutes either do not expressly define "murder" (in which case the common law definition is assumed to apply) or, more often, they define "murder" in common law terms. The murder statute's role is to divide common law murder into statutory degrees of the offense.

To apply a murder statute modeled on the Pennsylvania system, a lawyer must first determine whether a murder (as distinguished from a lesser offense or no offense) has occurred. That is, a lawyer cannot logically determine what statutory *degree* of murder is involved until she determines that the killing is properly characterized as "murder" in the first place. Ultimately, this means that a lawyer must decide whether the homicide was committed with any one of the four mental states that constitutes common law "malice aforethought."[41]

Assuming that a murder *has* occurred, three types of murder fall within the first-degree category in the Pennsylvania model. First, murders that are committed in a statutorily specified manner (in the original Pennsylvania statute, there were two: by means of poison; or lying in wait) are considered sufficiently morally heinous to merit the stiffest penalty. Second, a "wilful, deliberate, and premeditated" killing constitutes first-degree murder.[42] Third, a homicide that occurs during the perpetration or attempted perpetration of a statutorily enumerated felony (in the original Pennsylvania statute: arson, rape, robbery, and burglary) is murder in the first degree.

All other forms of murder constitute second-degree murder. That is, within the class of homicides that constitute murder under common law principles, any killing that is *not* specified as first-degree murder necessarily constitutes the

---

[41] Collman v. State, 7 P.3d 426, 444 (Nev. 2000) ("It must be emphasized . . . that a *killing* . . . is not murder of the first degree unless it is first established that it is *murder*. If the killing was not murder, it cannot be first degree murder, and a killing cannot become murder in the absence of malice aforethought.") (quoting People v. Mattison, 481 P.2d 193, 196 (Cal. 1971)).

[42] The original Pennsylvania statute read: "all murder, which shall be perpetrated by means of poison, or by lying in wait, or *by any other kind of wilful, deliberate and premeditated killing*. . . ." On the face of it, poisoning and lying-in-wait are examples of a "wilful, deliberate, premeditated" killing, and do not constitute an independent form of first-degree murder. Nonetheless, courts have typically interpreted this language to mean that any murder that occurs by means of poison or lying in wait (or in any other manner specified in the homicide statute) is first-degree murder, *even if the actor did not intend to kill the victim.*

For example, one who lies in wait in order to inflict serious bodily injury, but who inadvertently kills the victim, is guilty of first-degree murder according to the following reasoning: (1) the defendant's *mens rea* (intent to inflict serious bodily injury) constitutes one of the four common law forms of "malice"; (2) as a consequence, the killing constitutes "murder"; and (3), since the murder occurred by lying-in-wait, it is first-degree murder. E.g., see People v. Laws, 12 Cal. App. 4th 786 (Ct. App. 1993) (holding *L* guilty of first-degree murder for a "depraved heart" lying-in-wait homicide).

lesser form of murder. In general, this means that the following murders would constitute second-degree murder: intentional killings that are *not* premeditated and deliberate; intent-to-inflict-grievous-bodily-injury killings; reckless ("depraved heart") killings; and deaths that occur during the commission of any felony *not* specifically listed in the first-degree section of the murder statute.

§ 31.03 MURDER: INTENT TO KILL

[A] In General

One who intentionally kills another human being without justification (e.g., self-defense), excuse (e.g., insanity), or mitigating circumstance (e.g., sudden heat of passion) is guilty of killing with "malice aforethought" — "express malice" — and, therefore, is guilty of common law murder.[43] Typically, a murder involving the specific intent to kill is first-degree murder in jurisdictions that grade the offense by degrees if the homicide was also "deliberate" and "premeditated," as these terms are defined in subsection [C].

[B] Proving the Intent to Kill

[1] In General

[a] Natural-and-Probable-Consequences Rule

An intentional killing involves subjective fault. That is, the prosecutor must prove beyond a reasonable doubt that the defendant formed the actual intent to kill another person, rather than that, simply, a reasonable person would have known that the conduct would result in death.

How is this subjective fault proved? How does the factfinder "get into the head" of the accused? Often "intent to kill" is proved by means of a syllogism: (1) ordinary people intend the natural and probable (or "foreseeable") consequences of their actions; (2) the defendant is an ordinary person; and (3) therefore, she intended the natural and probable consequences of her actions.

When the probable consequence of a defendant's conduct is that another person will die, the preceding syllogism invites the jury to infer the requisite specific intent. For example, if *D* savagely beats *V* over the head with a steel pipe, which actions cause *V*'s death, the prosecution may seek to prove that *D* intended to kill *V* by demonstrating to the jury (and emphasizing in closing arguments) that the probable consequence of such a beating was *V*'s death; therefore, in the absence of evidence that *D* was not an ordinary person, the jury

---

[43] 4 Blackstone, Note 19, *supra*, at *199.

may infer that *D* intended the natural and probable consequence of her conduct, i.e., *V*'s death.

[b] Deadly-Weapon Rule

When a person kills another with a deadly weapon, proof of intent-to-kill is buttressed further. The more general proposition that a person intends the natural and probable consequences of her actions is supported by the somewhat more specific proposition that when she intentionally uses a deadly weapon[44] or, more precisely, intentionally uses a deadly weapon directed at a vital part of the human anatomy, an intention to kill may properly be inferred.[45] This is sometimes called the "deadly-weapon rule."

[2] Constitutional Limitation

In the past, judges instructed juries on the rules described above, by stating that, in essence, "the law *presumes* that a person intends the natural and probable consequences of her voluntary acts," or that "the law *presumes* that a person intends to kill another if she intentionally uses a deadly weapon on another."

Although it is permissible, even desirable, for jurors to draw common sense *inferences* from objective circumstances, a jury instruction of the sort just described violates the Due Process Clause of the United States Constitution. It is violative because the instruction requires or might cause a reasonable juror to believe that she should shift the burden of persuasion regarding an element of the offense — here, intent — to the defendant, notwithstanding the constitutional rule that the prosecutor must prove every element of the crime beyond a reasonable doubt.[46]

[C] "Wilful, Deliberate, Premeditated" Killings[47]

[1] Overview of the Issue

Nearly all states that grade murder by degrees provide that a "wilful, deliberate, premeditated" killing is murder in the first degree. Unfortunately, courts have had great difficulty agreeing on the meaning of this phrase. One matter

---

[44] A "deadly weapon" is variously defined as anything "designed, made, or adapted for the purpose of inflicting death or serious physical injury," Ala. Code § 13A-1-2(11) (2005), or that is "likely to produce," People v. Rodriquez, 50 Cal. App. 3d 389, 396 (Ct. App. 1975), or is "capable of causing," Alaska Stat. § 11.81.900(b)(15) (2004), such harm. The Model Penal Code defines it broadly as an animate or inanimate substance that, as used or intended, is capable of causing death or serious physical injury. Model Penal Code § 210.0(4).

[45] Glenn v. State, 511 A.2d 1110, 1126-28 (Md. Ct. Spec. App. 1986); Commonwealth v. O'Searo, 352 A.2d 30, 35-37 (Pa. 1976).

[46] Sandstrom v. Montana, 442 U.S. 510, 524 (1979). See § 8.02, *supra*, for further details.

[47] See generally Samuel H. Pillsbury, *Judging Evil: Rethinking the Law of Murder and Manslaughter* 98-124 (1998); Mordechai Kremnitzer, *On Premeditation*, 1 Buff. Crim. L. Rev. 627

is fairly clear: Although the term "wilful" has various definitions in the criminal law,[48] in this context it means, simply, "a specific intent to kill."[49]

But, what do the other two words — "deliberate" and "premeditated" — add to this? A few courts treat both terms as if they were superfluous, i.e., the phrase "wilful, deliberate, and premeditated" is a single mental state amounting, simply, to the intent to kill.[50] Other courts, on occasion, treat "premeditation" as an independent term, but underemphasize or ignore the element of "deliberation."[51]

Most jurisdictions understand "wilful, deliberate, premeditated" to mean more than an intention to kill. They understand that the division of murder into degrees is meant to separate the most heinous forms of murder, which deserve the most severe penalties, from "those which, although 'intentional' in some sense, lack the gravity associated with first degree murders."[52] However, some courts draw such a razor thin line between a "wilful" (intentional) killing, on the one hand, and a "wilful, deliberate, premeditated" one, on the other hand, that the distinction loses practical significance: If, as has been claimed, that a premeditated and deliberate killing "can be accomplished very quickly or even in the proverbial 'twinkling of an eye,'" nearly every intentional killing constitutes first-degree murder.[53]

In contrast, some states treat the terms "wilful," "deliberate," and "premeditated" as genuinely independent elements of first-degree murder.[54] In these states, a significant line is drawn between a spur-of-the-moment, albeit inten-

---

(1998); Suzanne Mounts, *Premeditation and Deliberation in California: Returning to a Distinction Without a Difference*, 36 U.S.F. L. Rev. 261 (2002); Matthew A. Pauley, *Murder by Premeditation*, 36 Am. Crim. L. Rev. 145 (1999).

[48] See § 10.04[C], *supra*.

[49] Byford v. State, 994 P.2d 700, 713 (Nev. 2000).

[50] See Smith v. State, 398 A.2d 426, 443 (Md. Ct. Spec. App. 1979) ("This is not a series of distinct mental states but a repetitive stressing of the same mental state — the requirement that the killing itself and not merely the murder-producing act, be intentional."); Powell v. State, 838 P.2d 921, 927 (Nev. 1992), vacated on other grounds, 511 U.S. 79 (1994) (stating that "[o]ther jurisdictions have held that the terms . . . are a single phrase, meaning simply that the actor intended to commit the act and intended death to result").

[51] Byford v. State, 994 P.2d at 713 (conceding that it had previously underemphasized the element of deliberation, and abandoning this previous line of authority).

[52] State v. Garcia, 837 P.2d 862, 865 (N.M. 1992).

[53] State v. Schrader, 302 S.E.2d 70 (W. Va. 1982) (accepting the twinkling-of-eye approach); but see State v. Brown, 836 S.W.2d 530, 540 (Tenn. 1992) (conceding that the line between first- and second-degree murder had been "substantially blurred," and seeking to remedy that failing); State v. Guthrie, 461 S.E.2d 163, 181 (W. Va. 1995) (conceding that prior definitions of "premeditation" and "deliberation" had been "confusing, if not meaningless" in that they "completely eliminate[d] the distinction between the two degrees of murder," and seeking to remedy that failing).

[54] E.g., People v. Morrin, 187 N.W.2d 434, 436 (Mich. Ct. App. 1971); Byford v. State, 994 P.2d at 713-15; but see Mounts, Note 47, *supra*, at 263-65 (concluding that, although state courts may pay lip service to the need to distinguish between degrees of murder, "[v]irtually every jurisdiction" has treated the two degrees of murder indistinguishably).

tional, killing, and what lay people might describe as a "cold-blooded" killing, i.e., a homicide committed after calm and careful reflection by the wrongdoer. The view of these jurisdictions is that one who acts "cold-bloodedly" is "more dangerous, more culpable[,] or less capable of reformation than one who kills on . . . impulse."[55]

But, *is* it true that a person who intentionally kills upon careful reflection is a more dangerous or culpable person than one who acts on impulse? Premeditation and deliberation might only reflect "the uncertainties of a tortured conscience rather than exceptional depravity."[56] Contrast, for example, the case of one who impulsively pushes a small child sitting on a bridge into the river with another person who kills her terminally ill parent after long and careful consideration, in order to end the parent's physical torment.[57] Under current law, if "premeditation" means anything, the impulsive killer is guilty of second-degree murder, and the mercy killer could be convicted of first-degree murder. Yet, as a function of depravity or dangerousness, most people would reverse the results. Therefore, some commentators believe that the current dividing lines between degrees of murder should be abandoned in favor of another line.[58] Others advocate returning to the common law no-degree approach.[59]

[2] "Deliberate"

Some courts treat "deliberate" as a synonym for "intentional," as when the statement "I *deliberately* did X" means "I *intentionally* did X."[60]

The better view is that "deliberate" — as in "to deliberate" — means "to measure and evaluate the major facets of a choice or problem."[61] It is "the process of determining upon a course of action to kill as a result of thought, including weighing the reasons for and against the action and considering the consequences of the action."[62] As such, deliberation presupposes a "*cool* pur-

---

[55] Bullock v. United States, 122 F.2d 213, 214 (D.C. Cir. 1941).

[56] American Law Institute, Comment to § 210.6, at 127-28.

[57] See State v. Forrest, 362 S.E.2d 252 (N.C. 1987) (upholding a conviction for first-degree murder in a "mercy killing").

[58] E.g., Tom Stacy, *Changing Paradigms in the Law of Homicide*, 62 Ohio St. L.J. 1007 (2001) (proposing a draft statute containing aggravating and mitigating circumstances that a jury would weigh in determining whether a criminal homicide constitutes first-degree murder, second-degree murder, or voluntary manslaughter).

[59] E.g., Mounts, Note 47, *supra*, at 332 ("[A] persuasive argument could be made that the degrees of murder no longer play any essential role in the larger homicide scheme."). This is the position of the Model Penal Code. See § 31.10, *infra*.

[60] E.g., Commonwealth v. Carroll, 194 A.2d 911, 917 (Pa. 1963) (in which the state supreme court found adequate evidence that the killing was wilful, deliberate, and premeditated from the fact that C testified that he "remembered the gun, *deliberately* took it down, and *deliberately* fired two shots into the head of his sleeping wife") (emphasis added).

[61] People v. Morrin, 187 N.W.2d 434, 449 (Mich. Ct. App. 1971).

[62] Byford v. State, 994 P.2d 700, 714 (Nev. 2000).

pose."[63] This state of mind is "free from the influence of excitement, or passion."[64] It is the term "deliberation" that brings to first-degree murder the idea that the most heinous killings are those that are "cold-blooded."

It takes time to deliberate. Therefore, it is impossible for a person to deliberate unless she premeditates.[65] Nonetheless, it is possible to premeditate (as that concept is explained below) without possessing the frame of mind characteristic of the concept of "deliberation." Whereas "premeditation" involves the *quantity* of time that a person put into formulating her design, "deliberation" speaks — or, at least, *ought* to speak — to the *quality* of the thought processes.

Thus, one who kills in a sudden rage may be guilty of manslaughter if her anger is the result of adequate provocation.[66] But, even if her anger does not mitigate the homicide to manslaughter, it may reduce the degree of murder because the killing is "hot-blooded," rather than "cold-blooded." Similarly, a severely intoxicated person might not be able to act with sufficient depth of reflection to be guilty of first-degree murder, no matter how long she premeditates.[67]

[3] "Premeditated"

To "premeditate" means "to think about beforehand."[68] The law is sharply divided, however, on how much prior thought must go into a homicide before it is considered premeditated. At one extreme is a line of cases that finds its origins in an 1868 court opinion that stated that "if sufficient time be afforded to enable the mind fully to frame the design to kill, and to select the instrument, or to frame his plan . . . , it is premeditated."[69] Specifically, "*no* time is too short for a wicked man to frame in his mind the scheme of murder."[70]

Courts following this line of reasoning state that the time required to premeditate is not "days or hours, or even minutes."[71] It may be no more than "a

---

[63] State v. Brown, 836 S.W.2d 530, 538 (Tenn. 1992) (emphasis added).

[64] Clarke v. State, 402 S.W.2d 863, 868 (Tenn. 1966) (quoting Lewis v. State, 40 Tenn. 127, 148 (1859)).

[65] Smith v. State, 398 A.2d 426, 444 (Md. Ct. Spec. App. 1979).

[66] See § 31.07, *infra*.

[67] This might explain the outcome in *Midgett v. State*, 729 S.W.2d 410, 413 (Ark. 1987), in which *M*, while disciplining his child, beat the youth to death. *M* was convicted of first-degree murder. The state supreme court overturned the conviction. It stated that even if *M* intended to kill his child in the "overheated" and "drunken disciplinary beating . . . , there [was] still . . . no evidence whatever of a premeditated and deliberate killing." What presumably was missing was the calm (not "overheated" or "drunken") reflection implicit in the concept of "deliberation."

[68] People v. Morrin, 187 N.W.2d 434, 449 (Mich. Ct. App. 1971).

[69] Commonwealth v. Drum, 58 Pa. 9, 16 (1868).

[70] *Id*.

[71] Bostic v. United States, 94 F.2d 636, 639 (D.C. Cir. 1937).

brief moment of thought."[72] Indeed, according to this view, "[a]ny interval of time between the forming of the intent to kill and the execution of that intent, which is of sufficient duration for the accused to be fully conscious of what he intended" is sufficient.[73] Premeditation "may be as instantaneous as successive thoughts of the mind."[74]

This approach essentially equates premeditation with any intentional killing. "Deliberation" loses its independent status. It undermines the principle underlying the legislative division of murder into degrees, namely, that a carefully considered and planned killing is worse than a spur-of-the-moment homicide. As one court has stated, "if the only difference between first and second degree murder is the mere passage of time, and that length of time can be 'as instantaneous as successive thoughts of the mind,' then there is no meaningful distinction between first and second degree murder."[75]

In order to ensure that the elements of premeditation and deliberation retain independent significance, some courts provide that it takes "some appreciable time" to premeditate.[76] No specific period of time is required, but the essence of the term is preserved by requiring proof that the killer had time not only to form the intent, but also to turn the matter over in her mind and to give the matter at least a second thought.[77] Obviously, the greater the substance of the deliberation requirement, the longer the period of premeditation must be. It is not possible to conduct unhurried, careful, thorough, and cool calculation and consideration of effects and consequences — the essence of the deliberative process — in a matter of a split second.

§ 31.04 MURDER: INTENT TO INFLICT GRIEVOUS BODILY INJURY

Malice aforethought is implied if a person intends to cause grievous bodily injury to another, but death results.[78] In states that grade murder by degree, this form of malice nearly always constitutes second-degree murder.

The term "grievous bodily injury" (or, equivalently, "great bodily harm" or "serious bodily injury") is not often defined in the murder context, but the term

---

[72] Government of Virgin Islands v. Lake, 362 F.2d 770, 776 (3d Cir. 1966); Watson v. United States, 501 A.2d 791, 793 (D.C. 1985) ("as brief as a few seconds").

[73] State v. Guthrie, 461 S.E.2d 163, 182-83 (W. Va. 1995).

[74] Kazalyn v. State, 825 P.2d 578, 583 (Nev. 1992).

[75] State v. Thompson, 65 P.3d 420, 427 (Ariz. 2003); see also People v. Plummer, 581 N.W.2d 753, 757 (Mich. Ct. App. 1998) ("To speak of premeditation and deliberation being instantaneous . . . destroys the statutory distinction between first- and second-degree murder.").

[76] State v. Moore, 481 N.W.2d 355, 361 (Minn. 1992).

[77] People v. Morrin, 187 N.W.2d 434, 449 (Mich. Ct. App. 1971).

[78] 3 James Stephen, A History of the Criminal Law in England 80-81 (1883).

is often explained in case law or statutes in relation to other offenses, such as "assault with intent to commit grievous bodily harm," and these definitions typically are carried over to "implied malice" murder prosecutions.

"Grievous bodily injury" is sometimes judicially defined, e.g., "such injury as is grave and not trivial, and gives rise to apprehension of danger to life, health, or limb."[79] Some states define the term by statute. For example, California law provides that it is an injury involving "serious impairment of physical condition, including, but not limited to the following: loss of consciousness; concussion; bone fracture; protracted loss or impairment of function of any bodily member or organ; a wound requiring extensive suturing; and serious disfigurement."[80]

Depending on the state law, a person who must be treated in a hospital emergency room for abrasions to her hands and knees and for a fracture of the jawbone,[81] or who experiences a broken rib, a black eye, and a two-and-a-half inch cut in the back of her head requiring stitches,[82] is likely to have experienced serious bodily injury. It follows, therefore, that a person who unjustifiably and inexcusably *intends* to cause these injuries is guilty of murder if the victim dies as a result of the attack.

Serious issues regarding this form of malice rarely arise in murder prosecutions. If the defendant intentionally used a deadly weapon on the victim, it is likely that the jury will find express malice, i.e., intent to kill, unless the injuries or wounds were directed at a non-vital part of the body, in which case implied malice is easily proven. Also, virtually any time a person intends to imperil life (but does not intend to kill) she acts with "extreme recklessness," still another version of malice, discussed immediately below.

---

[79] State v. Bogenreif, 465 N.W.2d 777, 780 (S.D. 1991); see also Jackson v. State, 323 S.W.2d 442, 443 (Tex. Crim. App. 1959).

[80] Cal. Penal Code § 243(f)(4) (Deering 2005) (defining "serious bodily injury" in the context of a battery statute); see also Tenn. Code Ann. § 39-11-106(a)(34)(A)-(E) 2005) (a "substantial risk of death, [p]rotracted unconsciousness; [e]xtreme physical pain; [p]rotracted or obvious disfigurement; [p]rotracted loss or substantial impairment of a function of a bodily member, organ, or mental faculty").

[81] State v. Miller, 491 P.2d 481, 483 (Ariz. Ct. App. 1971).

[82] State v. Perry, 426 P.2d 415, 418 (Ariz. Ct. App. 1967).

§ 31.05 MURDER: EXTREME RECKLESSNESS ("DEPRAVED HEART" MURDER)[83]

[A] In General

[1] Terminology

Malice aforethought is implied if a person's conduct manifests an extreme indifference to the value of human life. In states that separate murder into degrees, this type of murder almost always constitutes second-degree murder.

At common law, this state of mind is often described colorfully — or, as one court put it, "more visceral[ly] than intellectual[ly]"[84] — as conduct demonstrating "an abandoned heart,"[85] "an abandoned and malignant heart,"[86] a "depraved heart,"[87] or (to change bodily organs) "a depravity of mind."[88] Some courts have characterized this form of malice in terms of both the heart and the mind: "wickedness of disposition, hardness of heart, cruelty, recklessness of consequences, and a mind regardless of social duty."[89] For current purposes, it will be described as "depraved heart" murder.

In less colorful, but more precise and modern, terms, a depraved-heart murder is a "reckless" or "extremely reckless" homicide. The addition of the adverb "extremely" is useful because many court opinions antedating the Model Penal Code used the word "recklessness" as a synonym for "criminal negligence," the mental state required for one form of involuntary manslaughter.[90] If "recklessness" (as in "criminal negligence") is required for guilt of manslaughter, then "extreme recklessness" is the form of risk-taking that constitutes murder.

[2] Facts Supporting a Finding of Extreme Recklessness

With depraved-heart murder, the accused does not intend to kill her victim, but malice is implied because there is a "wanton and wilful disregard of the likelihood that the natural tendency of [the] defendant's behavior is to cause death or great bodily harm."[91]

---

[83] See generally Pillsbury, Note 47, *supra*, at 161-88.

[84] People v. Love, 111 Cal. App. 3d 98, 105 (Ct. App. 1980).

[85] 4 Blackstone, Note 19, *supra*, at *200.

[86] Cal. Penal Code § 188 (Deering 2005).

[87] Windham v. State, 602 So. 2d 798, 800 (Miss. 1992).

[88] People v. Register, 457 N.E.2d 704, 706 (N.Y. 1983).

[89] Commonwealth v. Malone, 47 A.2d 445, 447 (Pa. 1946) (quoting Commonwealth v. Drum, 58 Pa. 9, 17 (1868)).

[90] See § 31.08, *infra*.

[91] People v. Goecke, 579 N.W.2d 868, 879 (Mich. 1998).

Cases falling within the depraved-heart category of murder "are not stereo-typed";[92] "extreme recklessness" or "depraved heart" is a factual matter determined on the basis of the specific circumstances of each case.[93] However, each case involves risk-taking serious enough that "it might be fairly said that the actor 'as good as' intended to kill his victim and displayed . . . unwillingness to prefer the life of another person to his own objectives."[94]

For example, a jury may find implied malice if a person, without intending to kill or seriously injure another: (1) intentionally shoots a firearm in or into a crowded room, killing a person;[95] (2) drives her car at a high rate of speed in inclement weather and while intoxicated, killing a pedestrian or car occupant;[96] (3) purchases Rottweiler dogs, fosters their aggression through improper training, and places them in an unsecured yard, resulting in the mauling death of a child;[97] or (4) plays "Russian roulette" by loading a gun with one "live" and four "dummy" shells, spinning the revolver, and intentionally firing it at another person, killing her.[98] Malice may also be manifested by a lethal omission, such as when a parent, out of indifference, fails to feed her infant for two weeks.[99]

[B] Distinguishing Murder from Manslaughter

There is no common law bright line between "negligence" and "recklessness,"[100] complicated by the fact there is no universally accepted common law definition of "recklessness."[101] Consequently, the line between unjustified risk-taking that constitutes involuntary manslaughter (based on criminal negligence) and that which constitutes depraved-heart, reckless murder has never been drawn with clarity.

In general, however, most present-day courts provide that implied malice is proven if the actor's conduct involves "the deliberate perpetration of a *knowingly* dangerous act with . . . unconcern and indifference as to whether anyone is

---

[92] People v. Love, 111 Cal. App. 3d 98, 105 (Ct. App. 1980).

[93] People v. Hall, 999 P.2d 207, 218 (Colo. 2000).

[94] Lloyd Weinreb & Dan M. Kahan, *Homicide: Legal Aspects, in* 2 Encyclopedia of Crime and Justice 790 (Joshua Dressler ed., 2d ed. 2002).

[95] E.g., People v. Register, 457 N.E.2d 704 (N.Y. 1983); People v. Jernatowski, 144 N.E. 497 (N.Y. 1924).

[96] E.g., Davis v. State, 593 So. 2d 145 (Ala. Crim. App. 1991); see also State v. Fuller, 531 S.E.2d 861 (N.C. Ct. App. 2000) (*F*, with high blood-alcohol content, led police on a seventeen-mile chase, driving at speeds in excess of ninety miles per hour, driving through stop signs and stop lights).

[97] E.g., State v. Davidson, 987 P.2d 335 (Kan. 1999).

[98] E.g., People v. Roe, 542 N.E.2d 610 (N.Y. 1989).

[99] People v. Burden, 72 Cal. App. 3d 603 (Ct. App. 1977).

[100] See § 10.04[D][1], *supra*.

[101] See § 10.04[D][3], *supra*.

harmed or not,"[102] or "where the killing was proximately caused by an act, the natural consequences of which are dangerous to [human] life, which act was deliberately performed by a person who *knows* that his conduct endangers the life of another and who acts with *conscious* disregard for life."[103]

In more precise terms, a person kills "recklessly" if she *consciously* disregards a *substantial* and *unjustifiable* risk to human life. When such recklessness is extreme — when the risk of death is great and the justification for taking the risk is weak or non-existent — the actor is guilty of murder.[104] In such circumstances, she has acted with a "depraved heart."

In contrast, when a person *should be*, but is not, aware that her conduct is very risky (and unjustifiably so) — the risk-taking is inadvertent — her behavior may justify the appellation of "criminal negligence," but the callousness that connotes "implied malice" is lacking. In these less culpable circumstances, a killing constitutes involuntary manslaughter.

§ 31.06 MURDER: FELONY-MURDER RULE[105]

[A] The Rule

"The classic formulation of the felony-murder doctrine declares that one is guilty of murder if a death results from conduct during the commission or attempted commission of any felony."[106] This so-called "felony-murder rule" was abolished by statute in England in 1957.[107] It never existed in France or

---

[102] DeBettencourt v. State, 428 A.2d 479, 484 (Md. Ct. Spec. App. 1981) (emphasis added).

[103] People v. Nieto-Benitez, 840 P.2d 969, 975 (Cal. 1992) (quoting People v. Phillips, 414 P.2d 353 (Cal. 1966)) (internal quotations omitted) (emphasis added).

[104] This is *not* to suggest that the risk of death must be more like than not to occur. The risk of death may be well below fifty percent, especially if there is no meaningful justification for taking the risk, such as in "Russian roulette" cases (see the text to Note 98, *supra*). People v. Hall, 999 P.2d 207, 217 (Colo. 2000).

[105] See generally David Crump & Susan Waite Crump, *In Defense of the Felony Murder Doctrine*, 8 Harv. J.L. & Pub. Pol'y 359 (1985); Norman J. Finkel & Kevin B. Duff, *Felony-Murder and Community Sentiment: Testing the Supreme Court's Assertions*, 15 Law & Hum. Behav. 405 (1991); George P. Fletcher, *Reflections on Felony-Murder*, 12 Sw. U. L. Rev. 413 (1981); Nelson E. Roth & Scott E. Sundby, *The Felony-Murder Rule: A Doctrine at Constitutional Crossroads*, 70 Cornell L. Rev. 446 (1985); James J. Tomkovicz, *The Endurance of the Felony-Murder Rule: A Study of the Forces That Shape Our Criminal Law*, 51 Wash. & Lee L. Rev. 1429 (1994).

[106] American Law Institute, Comment to § 210.2, at 30; see 4 Blackstone, Note 19, *supra*, at *200-01 ("And if one intends to do another felony, and undesignedly kills a man, this is also murder."); State v. Williams, 24 S.W.3d 101, 110 (Mo. Ct. App. 2000).

Professor Guyora Binder has recently asserted, however, that this classical formulation is false. According to Binder, historical research indicates that "the harsh 'common law' felony murder rule [is] a myth," and, specifically, that "the draconian doctrine of strict liability for all deaths resulting from all felonies was never enacted into English law or received into American law." Guyora Binder, *The Origins of American Felony Murder Rules*, 57 Stan. L. Rev. 59, 63 (2004). His careful research and revisionist account is set out fully in *id.*

[107] Homicide Act, 1957, 5 & 6 Eliz. 2, ch. 11 § 1.

Germany. The rule is richly criticized in this country.[108] Nonetheless, the rule, at least in limited form, "still thrives"[109] in the United States, and is retained in some form in nearly every state.[110]

Most modern murder statutes provide that a death that results from the commission of an enumerated felony (such as arson, rape, robbery, or burglary) constitutes first-degree murder for which the maximum penalty is death or life imprisonment. If a death results from the commission of an unspecified felony, it is second-degree murder.

The felony-murder rule applies whether a felon kills the victim intentionally, recklessly, negligently, or accidentally and unforeseeably. Thus, the felony-murder rule authorizes strict liability for a death that results from commission of a felony. Although some courts have candidly suggested that the felony-murder rule dispenses with the requirement of malice,[111] the more usual explanation is that the intent to commit the felony constitutes the implied malice required for common law murder.

In light of the strict-liability nature of the rule, *D1*, a robber, is guilty of murder if *V1* dies from fright caused by the robbery.[112] Similarly, *D2* is guilty of felony-murder if she accidentally shoots *V2* in the chest during the commission of a felony, and *V2* dies years later from a heart attack during a backyard basketball game, as the result of permanent damage to the heart produced by

---

[108] In general, the felony-murder rule is criticized because, as discussed *infra*, it authorizes conviction for murder, sometimes first-degree murder, for an unintentional, even accidental, death. As a consequence, "legal scholars have criticized the rule for incorporating 'an artificial concept of strict criminal liability that "erodes the relationship between criminal liability and moral culpability." '" People v. Howard, 104 P.3d 107, 111 (Cal. 2005) (quoting People v. Patterson, 668 P.2d 697 (Cal. 1989), and People v. Washington, 402 P.2d 130 (Cal. 1965)).

For example, in *People v. Robertson*, 95 P.3d 872 (Cal. 2004), the California Supreme Court upheld a second-degree murder conviction for a death predicated on the felony of discharging a firearm in a grossly negligent manner. Thus, a negligent killing, which would ordinarily constitute involuntary manslaughter, see § 31.08, *infra*, is converted into the far more serious offense of murder as a consequence of the underlying felony. As Justice Janice Brown, in dissent in *Robertson* observed, "[i]t takes no genius to discern that a rule that relieves the People of the need to prove malice *because* the defendant asserts he did not harbor any is problematic." *Id.* at 894.

The justifications for the felony-murder rule and critics' rebuttal are developed more fully at § 31.06[B], *infra*.

[109] State v. Maldonado, 645 A.2d 1165, 1171 (N.J. 1994).

[110] The rule is not recognized by statute in Hawaii, see Haw. Rev. Stat. §§ 707-701; 707-701.5 (2004); Kentucky, see Ky. Rev. Stat. Ann. § 507.020 (Lexis Nexis 2004); and Michigan, see People v. Aaron, 299 N.W.2d 304, 321 (Mich. 1980) (interpretation of a statute). In New Mexico, the state supreme court imposed a *mens rea* requirement for felony-murder. State v. Ortega, 817 P.2d 1196, 1204 (N.M. 1991).

[111] E.g., People v. Howard, 104 P.3d at 110-11.

[112] People v. Stamp, 2 Cal. App. 3d 203 (Ct. App. 1969) (*S* ordered *V* and others to lie down on the floor during a robbery; *V*, who had heart disease, died from fright); see State v. Dixon, 387 N.W.2d 682 (Neb. 1986) (*D* broke into *V*'s house; *V* suffered cardiac arrhythmia and died from the emotional trauma of the burglary).

the original wound.[113] And, since the rule in its classical form[114] applies to a homicide that occurs during the commission of *any* felony, in the absence of any special limitation[115] *D3* is guilty of murder if she attempts to steal *V3*'s watch from *V3*'s purse and a gun concealed in it discharges, killing *V3*. Furthermore, the felony-murder rule extends implicitly (and often expressly by statute) to accomplices in the commission of felonies. Therefore, if *S* were an accomplice in any of the hypothesized felonies, she would be guilty of murder, *without regard to her own state of mind relating to the death*.

[B] Rationale of the Rule

[1] Initial Observations

Consider these observations: (1) "[p]rincipled argument in favor of the felony-murder doctrine is hard to find";[116] (2) the "ancient rule . . . has been bombarded by intense criticism and constitutional attack";[117] and (3) "[c]riticism of the rule constitutes a lexicon of everything that scholars and jurists can find wrong with a legal doctrine."[118] What follows are the most common arguments in defense of the much condemned rule.

[2] Deterrence

The most common defense of the felony-murder rule is that it is intended to deter negligent and accidental killings during the commission of felonies.[119] As Holmes explained this theory, the law ought to throw on the felon the peril that if a death results, even an unforeseeable one, she will be punished as a murderer.[120] This enhanced risk, the argument proceeds, will cause a felon to be more careful, i.e., she may commit the felony,[121] but she will do so in a manner less likely to result in death.

---

[113] People v. Harding, 506 N.W.2d 482 (Mich. 1993) (in actual case, original shooting was not accidental).

[114] But see Note 106, *supra*.

[115] Many courts have placed limits on the felony-murder rule. See § 31.06[C], *infra*.

[116] American Law Institute, Comment to § 210.2, at 37.

[117] State v. Maldonado, 645 A.2d 1165, 1171 (N.J. 1994). See Note 108, *supra*, for the most common criticism of the rule.

[118] Roth & Sundby, Note 105, *supra*, at 446.

[119] People v. Washington, 402 P.2d 130, 133 (Cal. 1965).

[120] Oliver Wendell Holmes, The Common Law 59 (1881).

[121] It is important to observe that the felony-murder rule cannot sensibly be defended on the ground that it deters the underlying felony. The rational way to deter *that* offense is to increase the penalty for the felony (or, better still, increase the arrest rate for the felony), and not to increase the penalty for the unintended, and potentially unforeseeable, byproduct of it, the homicide.

Critics of the felony-murder rule reject the deterrence argument. They ask, "[q]uite simply, how does one deter an unintended act?"[122] Of course, the act of committing the felony *is* intended, but the *result* of the death is unintended, and may even be unforeseeable to the most rational and far-sighted felon.

Advocates of the felony-murder rule cannot provide empirical evidence to support the deterrence thesis. Although there is little recent data on point, homicides during the commission of felonies seemingly are rare. According to some admittedly old data, only one-half of one percent of all robberies result in a homicide.[123] Even this figure seemingly overstates the case, because it does not differentiate between homicides intentionally or recklessly caused during the commission of robberies (cases in which murder convictions would be possible without the use of the felony-murder rule) and ones that accidentally or negligently occur. In short, it is hard to make the case for the need for the felony-murder rule on deterrence grounds.

[3] Reaffirming the Sanctity of Human Life

Two commentators[124] defend the felony-murder rule on the ground that it reaffirms the sanctity of human life. The rule reflects society's judgment that the commission of a felony resulting in death is more serious — and, therefore, deserves greater punishment — than the commission of a felony *not* resulting in death. If a criminal is required to "pay her debt" to society, the felony-murderer has a greater debt to pay than the felon who does not take a life.

This argument proves too much. Even if a felony that results in a death should be punished more severely than one that does not result in a homicide, it hardly follows that a felon who accidentally takes a life should be subject to the severe penalties, including death or life imprisonment, reserved for murderers.

In order to calculate a wrongdoer's debt to society, and thus to set an appropriate punishment for an offense, legislators must consider the actor's culpability, and not simply the harm that she has caused.[125] In the context of felony-murder, it must be kept in mind that the offense involves two different social harms: the felony and the homicide. The culpability for each should be analyzed separately. The penalty for the felony serves to punish for the intentional social harm of that crime. The real issue, therefore, is whether it is fair to increase the felon's punishment for the social harm of a death that may have been caused unintentionally, non-recklessly, and non-negligently.

---

[122] Roth & Sundby, Note 105, *supra*, at 451.

[123] Enmund v. Florida, 458 U.S. 782, 799-800 nn. 23-24 (1982) (reporting the data).

[124] Crump & Crump, Note 105, *supra*, at 361-69.

[125] See § 6.03, *supra*.

Consider two pickpockets, *P1* and *P2*. *P1* puts her hand in *V1*'s pocket and finds a wallet containing two hundred dollars. *P2* puts her hand in *V2*'s pocket and discovers a wallet with the same amount of money, but *V2* dies of shock from the experience. The property harm caused is the same — the loss of two hundred dollars. And, the culpability of *P1* and *P2* as to the thefts is identical. Therefore, as to the larcenies, they should be punished alike.

As for the social harm of the death, *P2* is no more culpable than *P1*, as the death was unforeseeable. It is true, of course, that *P2* caused a death, but in terms of *mens rea*, her culpability (as that of *P1*) is that of an intentional thief, and no more. Even if it were concluded that *P2* should pay some debt for the unforeseeable death, it surely violates ordinary concepts of just deserts, and proportional punishment, to treat the unlucky pickpocket as deserving of punishment equal to that of an intentional, premeditated killer.[126]

[4] Transferred Intent

The felony-murder rule is sometimes defended on the basis of the transferred-intent doctrine. The argument is that the felon's intent to commit a felony is transferred to the homicide.[127] Thus, the offense is not one of strict liability but one of intent.

This is a misuse of the transferred intent doctrine. That doctrine provides that an actor's intention to commit a particular social harm (call it Social Harm X) relating to a particular victim (call her Victim *A*) may be transferred to a different, unintended victim (Victim *B*) of the same social harm (Social Harm X).[128] Ordinarily, however, the law does not recognize a transference of intent to cause one social harm (Social Harm X) to a different and greater harm (Social Harm Y), involving the same victim. Thus, when *D* intends to steal rum in a boat (Social Harm X), and in the process accidentally sets fire to the boat (Social Harm Y), she is not guilty of intentionally burning the boat.[129] Yet, this is precisely what occurs with a felony-murder: The felon's intent to commit a felony (Social Harm X) is transferred to the different, and more serious, social harm of a homicide (Social Harm Y).

[5] Easing the Prosecutor's Burden of Proof

Most felony-murder convictions do not involve innocent homicides. For example, a robber may intentionally shoot the victim or a police officer during the

---

[126] See People v. Dillon, 668 P.2d 697, 719 (Cal. 1983) (holding that some felony-murders may not be punished as first-degree murder on the ground that it would constitute cruel and unusual punishment under the state and federal constitutions).

[127] State v. O'Blasney, 297 N.W.2d 797, 798 (S.D. 1980).

[128] See § 10.04[A][3], *supra*.

[129] Regina v. Faulkner, 13 Cox Crim. Cas. 550 (1877).

commission of the crime. In such a case, one may infer that the felon intended to kill or, at least, seriously injure the victim. Thus, malice aforethought can be proven independent of the felony. The felony-murder rule, in short, is unnecessary.

Even when a felon does not intend to kill or seriously injure another person, her felonious conduct will often manifest a depraved heart, i.e., extreme recklessness. For example, an arsonist may burn down a house knowing that the building is probably occupied, or a rapist may wound the victim in order to overcome her resistance.

Yet, even in felony cases involving one of these alternative forms of malice, prosecutors often charge the defendant on the basis of felony-murder. The effect of the doctrine, therefore, if not its explicit rationale, is to ease the prosecutor's burden of proof regarding malice aforethought, by dispensing with the requirement that she show beyond a reasonable doubt that the felon intended to kill or injure the victim grievously or that the felon was aware that her conduct was highly dangerous to human life.[130] All that the prosecutor must do is prove that the defendant committed the felony and that the death occurred during its commission.

[C] Limits on the Rule

Many courts have engrafted limitations on the felony-murder rule, the most significant of which are considered below.

[1] Inherently-Dangerous-Felony Limitation

In order to avoid the potential harshness of the felony-murder rule, many states limit the rule to homicides that occur during the commission of felonies dangerous to human life. This is often described as the "inherently dangerous felony" limitation.

What is an "inherently dangerous" felony? There are two approaches. First, some courts consider felonies in the abstract. That is, to determine whether a felony is inherently dangerous, a court will ignore the facts of the specific case and, instead, consider the elements of the offense in the abstract — that is, look at the offense as it defined by statute. The test is whether the crime, "by its very nature, . . . cannot be committed without creating a substantial risk that some-

---

[130] One other prosecutorial benefit: Most state homicide statutes will permit a prosecutor to charge a defendant with first-degree murder (for example, if the underlying felony is robbery) based on the felony-murder rule in a circumstance in which, absent the rule, the homicide would constitute the lesser offense of second-degree murder (based on depraved-heart).

one will be killed."[131] Or, it has been stated that an offense "carrying 'a high probability' that death will result" is an inherently dangerous felony.[132]

Applying the in-the-abstract rule, one state court has held that theft is not an inherently dangerous felony, even though the felon in the particular case caused the death of a cancer-ridden child by falsely claiming that he had a cure for the disease, which induced the parents to forego traditional medical care.[133] Similarly, the offense of false imprisonment (defined as imprisonment "effected by violence, menace, fraud, *or* deceit") is not dangerous in the abstract, because the offense can be committed in nonviolent fashion (by fraud or deceit).[134] The fact that the felon in the actual case used *force* to imprison the victim was immaterial to the analysis "in the abstract." Likewise, the felony offense of "driving with a willful or wanton disregard for the safety of persons *or property* while fleeing from a pursuing police officer" — an offense that further defined the required wantonness to include any driving-while-fleeing that results in three or more traffic violations of any kind or that causes any damage to property — is excluded from the felony-murder rule because the offense so defined "include[s] conduct that ordinarily would not be considered particularly dangerous."[135] On the other hand, the felony of manufacturing methamphetamine is inherently dangerous to human life because manufacture of the drug "demands the use of hazardous materials."[136]

In contrast to the abstract approach, many states that apply the dangerous-felony limitation determine the dangerousness of a felony by considering "the facts and the circumstances of the particular case to determine if such felony was inherently dangerous in the manner and circumstances in which it was committed."[137] Still other jurisdictions apply both tests: If the felony is dangerous under either approach, it may serve as the predicate for a felony-murder prosecution.[138]

---

[131] People v. Burroughs, 678 P.2d 894, 900 (Cal. 1984), overruled in part on other grounds by People v. Blakeley, 999 P.2d 675 (Cal. 2000); see also Fisher and Utley v. State, 786 A.2d 706, 727 (Md. 2001) (stating that the dangerous-in-the-abstract test "is satisfied only when the elements of the crime, considered in the abstract, do not admit any state of facts under which the crime could be committed without danger to life"). The *Fisher* statement of the test, however, improperly excludes the adjective "substantial" as a modifier of "danger to life."

[132] People v. Patterson, 778 P.2d 549, 558 (Cal. 1989); see also People v. Hansen, 885 P.2d 1022, 1026 (Cal. 1994) (treating this standard and the "substantial risk" standard as interchangeable).

[133] People v. Phillips, 414 P.2d 353 (Cal. 1966), overruled on other grounds by People v. Flood, 957 P.2d 869 (Cal. 1998).

[134] See People v. Henderson, 560 P.2d 1180 (Cal. 1977), overruled on other grounds, People v. Flood, 957 P.2d 869 (Cal. 1998).

[135] People v. Howard, 104 P.3d 107, 113 (Cal. 2005).

[136] People v. James, 62 Cal. App. 4th 244, 264 (Ct. App. 1998).

[137] State v. Stewart, 663 A.2d 912, 919 (R.I. 1995).

[138] State v. Harrison, 564 P.2d 1321, 1324 (N.M. 1977).

Advocates of the in-the-abstract test favor it because, if "a court were to examine the particular facts of the case prior to establishing whether the underlying felony is inherently dangerous, the court might well be led to conclude the rule applicable despite any unfairness which might redound to the defendant by so broad an application."[139] Advocates of the facts-of-the-case test argue that "the abstract approach undermines one of the primary purposes of the modern felony murder rule," namely, "to deter dangerous conduct by punishing as murder a homicide resulting from dangerous conduct in the perpetration of a felony. . . . If the felonious conduct, under all of the circumstances, made death a foreseeable consequence, it is reasonable for the law to infer . . . the malice that qualifies the homicide as murder."[140]

Either version of the inherently-dangerous-felony limitation brings felony-murder very close to the extreme-recklessness concept of malice. A felony the commission of which is likely to result in death is a crime the commission of which is apt to demonstrate the "wickedness of disposition, hardness of heart, cruelty, recklessness of consequences and . . . mind regardless of social duty" that constitutes depraved-heart murder. The reason there is not a perfect overlap is that the depraved-heart form of murder usually requires conscious risk-taking; it is theoretically possible (although rarely the case) that a felon will be unaware of the dangerousness of her actions.

[2] Independent Felony (or Merger) Limitation

Most states[141] recognize an "independent felony"or "collateral felony" limitation on the felony-murder rule. That is, the felony-murder rule only applies if the predicate felony is independent of, or collateral to, the homicide. If the felony is *not* independent, then the felony "merges" with the homicide and cannot serve as the basis for a felony-murder conviction.[142]

One reason for this felony-murder limitation is easy to appreciate upon reflection. Suppose that *D* negligently kills *V*. A criminally negligent homicide constitutes involuntary manslaughter, which is a felony. Because a death occurred during the commission of a felony — involuntary manslaughter — *D* would seemingly be guilty of murder under the felony-murder rule if there were no merger doctrine. That is, without some felony-murder limitation, there could never be an involuntary manslaughter conviction, as the latter offense would *always* convert into felony-murder. To avoid this outcome, a requirement that the felony be independent of the homicide is ordinarily recognized.

---

[139] People v. Burroughs, 678 P.2d 894, 897-98 (Cal. 1984).

[140] Fisher and Utley v. State, 786 A.2d 706, 732 (Md. 2001).

[141] But see State v. Williams, 24 S.W.3d 101 (Mo. Ct. App. 2000) (holding that the "*any* felony" language of the state's felony-murder statute eliminated application of a merger doctrine).

[142] See generally State v. Campos, 921 P.2d 1266, 1269-71 (N.M. 1996) (summarizing various versions of the "independent felony" limitation in different jurisdictions).

Now, consider this situation: *D* arrives home and discovers her husband in bed with *V*. In sudden heat of passion, she shoots and kills *V*. Under normal principles, *D* is guilty of voluntary manslaughter, a felony. Just as with involuntary manslaughter, the felony of voluntary manslaughter should not serve as the basis for a felony-murder prosecution, or else the offense of voluntary manslaughter would disappear. But, may the prosecutor take this case one step further back to avoid this outcome? May she say that the predicate felony is not voluntary manslaughter, but is the felony of "assault with a deadly weapon"? May *that* felony be used to raise *D*'s offense to murder? Unless a jurisdiction applies an "independent felony" limitation, the felonious assault could be used and, again, this voluntary manslaughter would become felony-murder. And, since most criminal homicides involve assaults, a felony-murder rule without some form of independent-felony limitation would effectively destroy the distinctions set up by legislatures between first- and second-degree murder and manslaughter.[143] Most, although not all,[144] jurisdictions hold, therefore, that felonious assault or battery may not serve as the basis for felony-murder.[145]

More difficult questions arise when the predicate felony is not assault or battery, but is a felony that includes assaultive behavior. For example, in *People v. Wilson*,[146] W forcibly entered his estranged wife's home carrying a shotgun, and killed his victim. The entry constituted burglary, as he entered with the purpose of committing a felony (assault with a deadly weapon) inside. The California Supreme Court held that the burglary in this case merged with the homicide. In essence, the fact that the assault took place inside a dwelling — and, thus, converted the offense from assault to burglary — was coincidental and irrelevant to the analysis. Most states, however, have rejected this outcome.[147]

Wilson seemed to suggest that *any* felony that includes-in-fact an assault with a deadly weapon merges with the homicide and, therefore, will not support application of the felony-murder rule. The California Supreme Court, a leader at the time in setting limits on the felony-murder rule, later pulled back from this view, however, and restated the merger rule in a manner followed today by many jurisdictions: A felony does not merge if the assaultive conduct involves

---

[143] People v. Hansen, 885 P.2d 1022, 1028 (Cal. 1994); State v. Ulland, 943 P.2d 947, 950 (Kan. Ct. App. 1997).

[144] E.g., State v. Beeman, 315 N.W.2d 770, 777 (Iowa 1982); Roary v. State, 867 A.2d 1095, 1102-04 (Md. 2005).

[145] E.g., Barnett v. State, 783 So. 2d 929, 929 (Ala. Crim. App. 2000); State v. Essman, 403 P.2d 540, 545 (Ariz. 1965); People v. Morgan, 758 N.E.2d 813, 839 (Ill. 2001); see also People v. Smith, 678 P.2d 886 (Cal. 1984) (applying the merger doctrine to a battery-type felony child abuse statute); State v. Prouse, 767 P.2d 1308 (Kan. 1989) (same).

[146] 462 P.2d 22 (1969).

[147] Commonwealth v. Claudio, 634 N.E.2d 902, 905 (Mass. 1994) (describing *Wilson* as the minority view); State v. Contreras, 46 P.3d 661, 663-64 (Nev. 2002).

"an independent felonious purpose"[148] or as it was later put, "a felony does not merge with a homicide where the act causing death was committed with a collateral and independent felonious design separate from the intent to inflict the injury that caused death."[149] Thus, if a death results during the commission of an armed robbery, the underlying assault does not merge with the homicide since the felonious purpose of the conduct — to take property — is independent of the homicide. Likewise, a kidnapping, even if it involves assaultive conduct, does not merge with the homicide, since the purpose of the conduct is independent of the homicide.[150]

This version of the merger doctrine is sensible. Assuming that the rationale of felony-murder is to reduce the likelihood of accidental deaths occurring during the commission of felonies,[151] the felony-murder rule can only serve *this* deterrent function if the wrongdoer has a felonious purpose independent of the assault. That is, if *D*'s felonious purpose is, simply, to assault *V*, there is no way that the felony-murder rule can serve its function: There is no way to convince *D* to achieve her felonious purpose (attack *V*) safely. On the other hand, if *D*'s purpose is to take *V*'s property — a felonious intent independent of any assaultive conduct — she can seek to obtain the property violently (armed robbery) or nonviolently (theft). Assuming that the felony-murder rule has a deterrent effect, operation of the rule here warns *D* that if she chooses to go ahead with her felonious plan to take another person's property, she should do so in a non-dangerous manner. If she fails to heed the message, and she takes property forcibly and a person accidentally dies during the robbery, the felony-murder doctrine should apply.[152]

[3] The *Res Gestae* Requirement

[a] Overview

The common law felony-murder rule applies when a killing occurs *during the commission or attempted commission* of a felony. Taken literally, this would suggest that the felony-murder rule does not apply if the killing occurs before

---

[148] People v. Burton, 491 P.2d 793, 801 (Cal. 1971) (emphasis omitted).

[149] People v. Hansen, 885 P.2d 1022, 1029 (Cal. 1994).

[150] People v. Escobar, 48 Cal. App. 4th 999, 1012-13 (Ct. App. 1996).

[151] See § 31.06[B][2], *supra*.

[152] Despite the wisdom of the "independent felonious purpose" test for determining whether a felony merges into the homicide, California departed from it in *People v. Hansen*, 885 P.2d 885 P.2d 1022 (Cal. 1994). In *Hansen*, the state supreme court applied a different standard: whether use of the predicate felony in question will "elevate all felonious assaults to murder or otherwise subvert the legislative intent" to carefully graduate homicides. Applying this standard, the court held in *Hansen* that the felony of willful discharge of a firearm at an occupied dwelling — one that did not involve an independent, non-assaultive felonious purpose — which action resulted in death, did *not* merge with the homicide and, therefore, *could* serve as the basis for felony-murder.

the felony is attempted or once the felony has been completed, i.e., when all of the elements of the offense have been committed. In fact, however, courts commonly state that, in order for the felony-murder rule to operate, the homicide must occur "within the res gestae of [things done to commit] the felony."[153] This *"res gestae"* requirement has time, distance, and causal components,[154] discussed below. As will be seen, the *res gestae* rule, if broadly applied, serves as an *extension*, not limitation, of the felony-murder rule.

[b] Time and Distance Requirements

In general, in order for the felony-murder rule to apply, there must be relatively close proximity in terms of time and distance between the felony and the homicide.[155] The *res gestae* period typically begins when the actor has reached the point at which she could be prosecuted for an attempt to commit the felony,[156] and it continues at least until all of the elements of the crime are completed. Thus, the felony-murder rule does *not* apply if the felony was conceived of after the homicide, i.e., as an afterthought of the killing.[157]

On the other hand, for purposes of felony-murder, most courts provide that the *res gestae* of a felony continues, *even after commission of the crime*, while the felon flees the scene until she reaches a place of temporary safety.[158] Thus, an armed robber who flees across urban roofs during the night, may be convicted of felony-murder if a police officer, in hot pursuit, falls into an air shaft on a roof and dies.[159] Likewise, a felon who commits a robbery in a building, leaves, and is confronted outside by a victim of the crime, is guilty of felony-murder if she kills the resisting victim on the street.[160] However, the felony-murder rule is *not* operative if a car thief kills a passenger in another vehicle 280 miles away from the scene of the theft.[161]

---

[153] State v. Leech, 790 P.2d 160, 163 (Wash. 1990).

[154] State v. Griffin, 112 P.3d 862, 870 (Kan. 2005); State v. Hearron, 619 P.2d 1157, 1159-60 (Kan. 1980).

[155] People v. Dudrey, 635 P.2d 750, 752 (Wash. Ct. App. 1982).

[156] Payne v. State, 406 P.2d 922, 924 (Nev. 1965).

[157] People v. Esquivel, 28 Cal. App. 4th 1386, 1396 (Ct. App. 1994); Bouwkamp v. State, 833 P.2d 486, 492 (Wyo. 1992).

[158] People v. Salas, 500 P.2d 7, 15 (Cal. 1972). Some states reach substantially the same conclusion by statute. E.g., Kan. Stat. Ann. § 21-3401(b) (2005) ("Murder in the first degree is the killing of a human being committed . . . in the commission of, attempt to commit, or *flight from* . . . [a] felony. . . .") (emphasis added).

[159] People v. Matos, 634 N.E.2d 157 (N.Y. 1994).

[160] Payne v. State, 406 P.2d 922 (Nev. 1965); see also People v. Bodely, 32 Cal. App. 4th 311 (Ct. App. 1995) (*B* took $75 from supermarket cash register, fled, began to drive away in parking lot, and struck and accidentally killed a supermarket employee who was attempting to stop *B*).

[161] Doane v. Commonwealth, 237 S.E.2d 797 (1977). This case also implicates the causal requirement, discussed in the next subsection.

In terms of the "time" component, however, the critical issue — causation questions aside, which are considered immediately below — is when the *killing* conduct occurred and not when the *death* itself ensued. For example, if a felon snatches a purse from an elderly person, who succumbs days later from a heart attack brought on by the crime, the felony-murder rule is operative.[162]

[c] Causation Requirement

The *res gestae* requirement includes more than a connection in time and place: There must also be a causal relationship between the felony and the homicide.[163]

The but-for causal connection is often easy to satisfy. For example, if V suffers a fatal heart attack brought on by D's felonious conduct, the connection is satisfied, even if the heart failure occurs two hours after the crime.[164] However, for the causation element to be met, the prosecutor must show that it was the felonious nature of the conduct that caused the death. For example, in *King v. Commonwealth*,[165] K, accompanied by accomplice X, piloted an airplane containing marijuana through a thick fog. A crash ensued, in which X died. The court held that the felony-murder rule did not apply. It observed that the crash would have resulted even if they had been transporting legal cargo. That is, K was not flying unduly low to avoid radar sighting, or in any other dangerous manner; the accident was the result of the bad weather.

[4] Killing by a Non-Felon

[a] The Issue

Suppose that *F1* and *F2* enter a liquor store in order to rob it. *F1* points a gun at *X*, a store employee, and threatens to kill her unless she hands over the money in the cash register. To prove her point, *F1* fires warning shots over *X*'s head. In response, *X* justifiably fires a weapon at *F1* to prevent the robbery. Two people — *F1* and V, a customer in the store — are struck and killed by the bullets. May *F2* be convicted of felony-murder of *F1* and V?

---

[162] Matter of Anthony M., 471 N.E.2d 447 (N.Y. 1984); see also State v. Griffin, 112 P.3d 862 (Kan. 2005) (in felony-murder prosecution based on burglary, G and a co-felon unlawfully entered an apartment, pushed over a stove causing a gas pipe to break; after their flight, gas continued to escape, resulting in an explosion and deaths almost three hours later; held: felony-murder rule applies).

[163] State v. Adams, 98 S.W.2d 632, 637 (Mo. 1936).

[164] Stewart v. State, 500 A.2d 676 (Md. Ct. Spec. App. 1985); Matter of Anthony M., 471 N.E.2d 447 (N.Y. 1984) (see the text to Note 162, *supra*).

[165] 368 S.E.2d 704 (Va. Ct. App. 1988).

Notice the problem raised by these facts — the fatal shots were fired by X, rather than by one of the felons. In a literal sense, the killings occurred *"during* the commission or attempted commission of the felony," but they did not occur in *furtherance* of it. The question for consideration, therefore, is whether the felony-murder rule should apply in these circumstances.

[b] The "Agency" Approach

A majority of states that have considered the issue apply the "agency" theory of felony-murder,[166] which provides that the felony-murder rule "does not extend to a killing, although growing out of the commission of the felony, if directly attributable to the act of one other than the defendant or those associated with him in the unlawful enterprise."[167] In short, the felony-murder rule does not apply if an adversary to the crime, rather than a felon, personally commits the homicidal act. Therefore, in the hypothetical described in subsection [a], $F2$ may not be convicted of felony-murder for the deaths of $F1$ and V at the hands of non-felon X. The same result would apply if the shooter were a bystander or police officer, rather than the direct victim of the felony.

Why should a felon escape punishment as a murderer when the shooter is not a felon? Conceptually, the explanation is this: Generally speaking, a person is criminally responsible for her own acts, but not for the actions of others. Therefore, applying this general principle, a felon who does not shoot anyone ($F2$ in the hypothetical) is not responsible for the actions of a non-felon shooter (X).

There is an exception, however, to the latter principle. A person *is* responsible for the acts of another if the actor-shooter is functioning as an agent of the non-shooter. This agency relationship exists when the secondary party is an accomplice of the primary party.[168] Under such circumstances, the primary party's acts are properly imputed to the secondary party. Therefore, in the ordinary felony-murder situation, when a felon kills an innocent person, any co-felons are also responsible for the shooting — the shooting felon acts as an agent of the non-shooting co-felons. (It is as if the non-shooting co-felons said to the shooting felon in advance, "We are in this together, so your acts are our acts.") In the present hypothetical, however, the shooter (X) was *not* an accomplice of the felons: X was acting antagonistically to their interests, *not* as their agent. Therefore, non-agent X's actions (killing $F1$ and V) cannot be imputed to $F2$.

---

[166] State v. Sophophone, 19 P.3d 70, 74-76 (Kan. 2001) (citing this Text, and applying the agency theory); State v. Canola, 374 A.2d 20, 29-30 (N.J. 1977) (applying the agency rule, and citing other cases in support of this approach); State v. Oimen, 516 N.W.2d 399, 407-08 (Wis. 1994) (rejecting the agency approach, but stating that it is the position of the "vast majority of state courts that have addressed this issue").

[167] State v. Canola, 374 A.2d at 23.

[168] See § 30.02[B], *supra*.

The agency approach is supported by two additional arguments. First, the killing cannot truly be said to be within the *res gestae* of the offense, since the killing was not in furtherance of the crime, but in resistance to it. Second, the felony-murder rule can have little or no deterrent effect when the shooter is a non-felon, since the felon has no control over the actions of the innocent person.

[c] The "Proximate Causation" Approach

[i] In General

A minority of courts apply the "proximate causation" theory of felony-murder.[169] Following this approach, a felon is liable for any death that is the proximate result of the felony, whether the shooter is a felon or a third party. This rule is justified on the ground that "when a felon's attempt to commit a forcible felony sets in motion a chain of events which were or should have been within his contemplation when the motion was initiated, he should be held responsible for any death which by direct and almost inevitable sequence results from the initial criminal act."[170]

As with any other proximate-causation issue, the result will depend on the particular facts of the case, and the matter ultimately is one for the jury to decide. For example, in the hypothetical under discussion, *F1* pointed a gun at *X*, threatened her life, and fired warning shots. This conduct could be viewed as the proximate cause of *X*'s reasonable and foreseeable response. If the circumstances were so viewed, *F2* could be convicted of the death of her colleague, *F1*, and of *V*, the innocent bystander. In contrast, the felony-murder rule might not apply if a pickpocket took money and fled, and the crime victim pulled a gun and fired it at the felon, killing a bystander.

[ii] Limited Version

Should a court that permits the operation of the felony-murder rule when the shooter is a non-felon take into consideration *who was shot*? In the hypothetical under discussion, for example, should a proximate-causation jurisdiction distinguish between the deaths of *V* and *F1*, for purposes of *F2*'s felony-murder responsibility? Pennsylvania once drew such a distinction: The rule was that a felon (*F2*) could be convicted of murder in a bystander's (*V*'s) death, but not as

---

[169] E.g., People v. Dekens, 695 N.E.2d 474 (Ill. 1998); Palmer v. State, 704 N.E.2d 124 (Ind. 1999); People v. Hernandez, 624 N.E.2d 661 (N.Y. 1993); State v. Oimen, 516 N.W.2d 399 (Wis. 1994).

[170] People v. Lowery, 687 N.E.2d 973, 976 (Ill. 1997).

to the death of a co-felon *(F1)*.[171] Even today, there is apparent support for this distinction.[172]

This differentiation is presumably based on the principle that when a non-felon kills a felon this homicide is *justifiable*, whereas the death of a bystander accidentally shot by a non-felon is *excusable* homicide. As these italicized words are explained elsewhere in this Text,[173] a justifiable homicide is a proper or permissible killing; an excusable homicide involves a wrongful result for which the actor is not morally accountable. A court that draws this distinction presumably believes that a felon should not be convicted in a justifiable homicide, because it would be as if she were being punished for causing a good result (i.e., the death of a co-felon). This reasoning is hardly self-evident, however, since the felon who would otherwise be convicted wrongfully assisted in creating the condition that made her co-felon's death justifiable.

[d] Distinguishing Felony-Murder from Other Theories (The "Provocative Act" Doctrine)

Even in an agency jurisdiction, a felon may be held responsible for the death of another at the hands of a third party if the basis for the charge is *not* felony-murder, but instead is founded on what is sometimes termed the "provocative act" doctrine, which is simply a form of reckless (depraved-heart) homicide.

For example, in the hypothetical in subsection [a], *F1*'s conduct — pointing a loaded gun at *X*, threatening *X*'s life, and shooting over *X*'s head — arguably manifested an extreme indifference to the value of human life. Consequently, if *F1* had unintentionally killed *X* by her provocative actions, *F1* would have been guilty of murder, not simply on felony-murder grounds, but also on the basis of depraved-heart murder. And, *F2* would have been guilty of the murder as well, under traditional complicity principles, since *F1*'s reckless acts would have been imputed to her.

Suppose, however, that *F1*'s reckless and provocative behavior had caused *X* to fire a gun in self-defense, and further suppose that a bullet from *X*'s weapon

---

[171] See Commonwealth v. Almeida, 68 A.2d 595 (Pa. 1949) (police officer killed another police officer; held: felony-murder rule applies); Commonwealth v. Redline, 137 A.2d 472, 483 (Pa. 1958) (police officer killed co-felon; held: felony-murder does *not* apply); Commonwealth ex rel. Smith v. Myers, 261 A.2d 550 (Pa. 1970) (overruling *Almeida*, and adopting agency theory).

[172] For example, compare two Michigan cases: People v. Podolski, 52 N.W.2d 201, 204 (Mich. 1952) (Felon is guilty of felony-murder in excusable death of Police Officer 1, who was accidentally shot by Police Officer 2); and People v. Austin, 120 N.W.2d 766, 774-75 (Mich. 1963) (Victim justifiably kills Felon 1; co-felons are *not* guilty under felony-murder). New Mexico, as well, seems to draw the distinction. State v. Harrison, 564 P.2d 1321, 1324 n.1 (N.M. 1977) (in dictum, the court stated that the felony-murder rule would apply if a police officer were to kill an innocent bystander while shooting at a felon); Jackson v. State, 589 P.2d 1052, 1053 (N.M. 1979) (Victim killed Felon 1; held: felony-murder charge is properly dismissed against co-felon).

[173] See §§ 16.03-.04, *supra*.

had accidentally struck and killed bystander *V* instead. Now the provocative-act doctrine applies: On these facts, since *F1* recklessly caused *X* to fire the weapon that killed *V*, *F1* would be guilty of reckless murder — her provocative acts proximately caused the result — and *F2* would be held responsible for *V*'s death, since *F1*'s reckless conduct may be imputed to *F2*, her accomplice.[174]

On the other hand, suppose that *X*'s aim had been better, and that she had shot and killed *F1*, as intended, in self-defense. Now, *F2* may *not* be convicted of *F1*'s death at *X*'s hands, because *F1*'s malicious (reckless) conduct did *not* result in the unlawful killing of *another* human being, but rather in her own justifiable homicide. Therefore, in the case of *F1*'s death, there is no criminal homicide to impute to *F2*.[175]

§ 31.07 MANSLAUGHTER: PROVOCATION ("SUDDEN HEAT OF PASSION")[176]

[A] In General

Under common law principles, an intentional homicide committed in "sudden heat of passion" as the result of "adequate provocation" mitigates the offense to voluntary manslaughter.[177] Although the issue rarely arises, the "provocation defense" may also negate other forms of malice aforethought, i.e., cases in which the actor is provoked to inflict grievous bodily injury upon another or to act in an extremely reckless manner, in which death unintentionally results.[178]

The common law defense contains four elements, discussed in the next subsection: (1) the actor must have acted in heat of passion; (2) the passion must have been the result of adequate provocation; (3) the actor must not have had a reasonable opportunity to cool off; and (4) there must be a causal link between the provocation, the passion, and the homicide.[179]

---

[174] People v. Washington, 402 P.2d 130, 133 (Cal. 1965).

[175] People v. Antick, 539 P.2d 43, 50 (Cal. 1975).

[176] See generally Jeremy Horder, Provocation and Responsibility (1992); Pillsbury, Note 47, *supra*, at 125-60; A.J. Ashworth, *The Doctrine of Provocation*, 35 Cambridge L.J. 292 (1976); Joshua Dressler, *Why Keep the Provocation Defense?: Some Reflections on a Difficult Subject*, 86 Minn. L. Rev. 959 (2002); Joshua Dressler, *Provocation: Partial Justification or Partial Excuse?*, 51 Mod. L. Rev. 467 (1988); Joshua Dressler, *Rethinking Heat of Passion: A Defense in Search of a Rationale*, 73 J. Crim. L. & Criminology 421 (1982); Victoria Nourse, *Passion's Progress: Modern Law Reform and the Provocation Defense*, 106 Yale L.J. 1331 (1997).

[177] Comber v. United States, 584 A.2d 26, 42 (D.C. Ct. App. 1990).

[178] People v. Lasko, 999 P.2d 666, 668 (Cal. 2000); State v. Blish, 776 A.2d 380, 386 (Vt. 2001). The defense does not apply in felony-murder cases. The law understandably does not recognize a claim by a felon that she was provoked to kill because the victim of the felony resisted the crime. People v. Balderas, 711 P.2d 480, 510 (Cal. 1985).

[179] Girouard v. State, 583 A.2d 718, 721 (Md. 1991); State v. Mauricio, 568 A.2d 879, 883 (N.J. 1990).

[B] Elements of the Defense

[1] State of Passion

The provocation defense does not apply unless the defendant is in a state of passion at the moment of the homicide.[180] Although anger may be the emotion most often claimed in heat-of-passion cases, the defense is not so limited. "Passion" includes any "[v]iolent, intense, high-wrought, or enthusiastic emotion."[181] This term is "sufficiently broad to encompass a range of emotions[,] including fear,"[182] jealousy,[183] "furious resentment,"[184] and "wild desperation."[185]

[2] Adequate Provocation

[a] Early Common Law Categories

Early English case law defined "adequate provocation" as "an amount of provocation as would be excited by the circumstances in the mind of a reasonable man."[186] Common law courts developed a small and fixed list of categories that met this standard. These "paradigms of misbehavior"[187] were: (1) an aggravated assault or battery;[188] (2) mutual combat;[189] (3) commission of a serious

---

[180] State v. Johnson, 23 N.C. 354, 362 (1840) ("[P]rovocation furnishes no extenuation, unless it produces passion.").

[181] People v. Borchers, 325 P.2d 97, 102 (Cal. 1958) (quoting Webster's New International Dictionary (2d ed. 1950)).

[182] LaPierre v. State, 734 P.2d 997, 1001 (Alaska Ct. App. 1987).

[183] People v. Berry, 556 P.2d 777, 781 (Cal. 1976).

[184] State v. Ritchey, 573 P.2d 973, 975 (Kan. 1977).

[185] People v. Borchers, 325 P.2d at 102.

[186] Regina v. Welsh, 11 Cox Crim. Cas. 336, 338 (1869).

[187] Brown v. United States, 584 A.2d 537, 540 (D.C. Ct. App. 1990).

[188] Stewart v. State, 78 Ala. 436, 440 (1885) (a blow to the face, intentionally inflicted, is adequate provocation to reduce homicide to manslaughter). The line between provocation and self-defense is subtle. If V unjustifiably strikes D with the intent to kill her, D is justified in killing V in self-defense, assuming that she reasonably believes that the attack will continue and that deadly force is necessary. If V commences a *non*deadly attack, D may justifiably use *non*deadly force to protect herself, and if an accidental death ensues she will not be guilty of any homicide offense. If V starts a *non*deadly assault and D, enraged, *intentionally* kills V, her disproportionate response undermines her claim of self-defense, but the provocation defense comes into play.

[189] Mutual combat is "a fight or struggle which both parties enter willingly or in which two persons, upon a sudden quarrel, and in hot blood, mutually fight upon equal terms and death results from the combat." People v. Neal, 446 N.E.2d 270, 274 (Ill. Ct. App. 1983).

crime against a close relative of the defendant;[190] (4) illegal arrest;[191] and (5) observation of spousal adultery.[192]

Among the provocative acts that were *not* considered adequate were: (1) a trivial battery;[193] (2) learning about (but not observing) adultery;[194] (3) observation of the sexual unfaithfulness of a fiancé or other unmarried sexual partner;[195] and (4) words, no matter how insulting or offensive.[196]

[b] Modern Law

[i] In General

The rigid common law categories of "adequate provocation" have given way in most states to the view that the issue of what constitutes adequate provocation should be left to the jury to decide. As one court explained, "[w]hat is sufficient provocation . . . must vary with the myriad shifting circumstances of men's temper and quarrels."[197] No court can "catalogue all the various facts and combinations of facts which shall be held [sufficient]."[198]

Jurors are variously instructed that provocation is sufficient ("adequate") to mitigate an intentional killing to manslaughter if it: "would render any ordinarily prudent person for the time being incapable of that cool reflection that otherwise makes it murder";[199] "might render ordinary men, of fair average disposition, liable to act rashly or without due deliberation or reflection, and from passion, rather than judgment";[200] is "sufficient to cause an ordinary man to lose control of his actions and his reason";[201] or is "'calculated to inflame the passion of a reasonable [person] and tend to cause [that person] to act for the moment from passion rather than reason.'"[202]

---

[190] E.g., State v. Cooper, 36 So. 350 (La. 1904) (rape of a close relative).

[191] John Bad Elk v. United States, 177 U.S. 529, 534 (1900).

[192] Dennis v. State, 661 A.2d 175, 179 (Md. Ct. Spec. App. 1995).

[193] Commonwealth v. Webb, 97 A. 189, 191 (Pa. 1916).

[194] See Holmes v. Director of Public Prosecutions, [1946] 2 All E.R. 124, 127. Observation of "sexual intimacy" or "significant sexual contact" short of intercourse apparently is also insufficient at common law. See Dennis v. State, 661 A.2d at 179-80.

[195] See Rex v. Greening, 3 K.B. 846, 23 Cox Crim. Cas. 601 (1913).

[196] Perkins & Boyce, Note 29, *supra*, at 93.

[197] Commonwealth v. Paese, 69 A. 891, 892 (Pa. 1908).

[198] Maher v. People, 10 Mich. 212, 222-23 (1862).

[199] Addington v. United States, 165 U.S. 184, 186 (1897) (jury instruction apparently approved).

[200] Maher v. People, 10 Mich. at 220 (emphasis omitted).

[201] State v. Guebara, 696 P.2d 381, 385 (Kan. 1985).

[202] Dennis v. State, 661 A.2d 175, 179 (Md. Ct. Spec. App. 1995) (emphasis omitted) (alterations in original) (quoting Girouard v. State, 583 A.2d 718 (Md. 1991)).

Although the clear trend is away from recognizing only a limited number of categories of "adequate provocation,"[203] one common law rule that has persisted in most non-Model Penal Code jurisdictions is that "words alone" do not constitute adequate provocation.[204] This can prove to be a harsh rule. For example, in one incident, *G*, an African-American, killed *V*, his white neighbor, in a rage after *V* informed *G* that he had purposely shot *G*'s dog a few weeks earlier, and that he had done so because "it was bad enough living around niggers, much less dogs."[205] Thus, two types of words were involved in this situation: informational words (words informing the listener of an incident — killing a dog — that might have constituted adequate provocation had it been observed); and highly insulting words. In such circumstances, the words-alone rule would bar an instruction to the jury on manslaughter, even though this "ignores the fact that sometimes words may be even more inflammatory than aggressive actions."[206]

This rule is slowly breaking down. A few courts allow, or suggest that they would permit, the defense to be raised with informational words.[207] Other courts have held open the possibility that insulting words may qualify in extreme circumstances.[208] Also, the "words alone" rule does not apply in jurisdictions following the Model Penal Code.[209]

---

[203] In an example of a counter-trend, one common law category of adequate provocation — observation of spousal adultery — now is deemed *not* to constitute adequate provocation, as a matter of law, in one state. Md. Code Ann., Crim Law § 2-207(b) (2005). This may be part of a more general move to narrow the provocation defense, which is increasingly controversial. See § 31.07[C][3], *infra*.

[204] State v. Horn, 91 P.3d 517, 529 (Kan. 2004); Girouard v. State, 583 A.2d 718, 722 (Md. 1991) (describing this as the "overwhelming" rule).

[205] People v. Green, 519 N.W.2d 853, 856 (Mich. 1994).

[206] State v. Shane, 590 N.E.2d 272, 277 (Ohio 1992).

[207] E.g., Commonwealth v. Berry, 336 A.2d 262, 264 (Pa. 1975) ("[W]ords conveying information of a fact which constitutes adequate provocation when that fact is observed would constitute sufficient provocation."); Commonwealth v. Benjamin, 722 N.E.2d 953, 959 (Mass. 2000) (stating that "in certain circumstances, words may convey information constituting adequate provocation," but warning that "this is very limited exception," one that only applies "where the statements constitute a 'peculiarly immediate and intense offense to [one's] sensitivities'") (alteration in original) (quoting Commonwealth v. Bermudez, 348 N.E.2d 802 (Mass. 1976)).

[208] E.g., People v. Pouncey, 471 N.W.2d 346, 351 (Mich. 1991); see also State v. Shane, 590 N.E.2d at 278 (stating that words will rarely be sufficient, but ruling that, in *any* words-alone case, the "trial judge must determine whether evidence of reasonably sufficient provocation occasioned by the victim has been presented to warrant a voluntary manslaughter instruction").

[209] See § 31.10[C][3][b], *infra*.

[ii] The Nature of the "Reasonable Person"[210]

Who is the "reasonable person" to whom the provoked defendant is compared, in order to determine what constitutes "adequate provocation"? First, it should be observed that the word "reasonable" is an odd term in this context, since the "reasonable man" is sometimes considered to be "the public embodiment of rational behavior,"[211] which is hardly an apt description of a provoked killer. It is more accurate, therefore, to describe the objective character in this context — as some courts do[212] — as an "ordinary" person, one who sometimes, unfortunately, acts out of uncontrolled emotion rather than reason.

Second, to the extent that one seeks to determine the nature of the "reasonable/ordinary person" on the basis of traditional Anglo-American case law, we learn that such a person is: of average disposition,[213] i.e., not exceptionally belligerent;[214] sober at the time of the provocation;[215] and of normal mental capacity.[216]

As in other areas of the criminal law,[217] however, there is a movement to subjectivize the standard, i.e., to include at least some of the defendant's personal characteristics in the "ordinary/reasonable person" standard.[218] Due to the influence of the Model Penal Code,[219] juries are increasingly instructed to test the defendant's reaction to a provocation by the standard of the ordinary person "in the actor's situation." Left ambiguous is what "the actor's situation" might include.

---

[210] See generally B. Sharon Byrd, *On Getting the Reasonable Person Out of the Courtroom*, 2 Ohio St. J. Crim. L. 571 (2005); Joshua Dressler, *When "Heterosexual" Men Kill "Homosexual" Men: Reflections on Provocation Law, Sexual Advances, and the "Reasonable Man" Standard*, 85 J. Crim. L. & Criminology 726 (1995); Kevin Joe Heller, *Beyond the Reasonable Man? A Sympathetic but Critical Assessment of the Use of Subjective Standards of Reasonableness in Self-Defense and Provocation Cases*, 26 Am. J. Crim. L. 1 (1998); Orit Kamir, *Responsibility Determination as a Smokescreen: Provocation and the Reasonable Person in the Israeli Supreme Court*, 2 Ohio St. J. Crim. L. 547 (2005); Robert B. Mison, *Homophobia in Manslaughter: The Homosexual Advance as Insufficient Provocation*, 80 Cal. L. Rev. 133 (1992); William I. Torry, *The Doctrine of Provocation and the Reasonable Person Test: An Essay on Culture Theory and the Criminal Law*, 29 Intl. J. Soc. L. 1 (2001) See also §§ 10.04[D][2][d] and 18.05[A], *supra*, and the cites therein.

[211] Ronald K.L. Collins, *Language, History and the Legal Process: A Profile of the "Reasonable Man"*, 8 Rutgers-Cam. L.J. 311, 315 (1977).

[212] See the text to Note 199-202, *supra*.

[213] Maher v. People, 10 Mich. 212, 220 (1862).

[214] Mancini v. Director of Public Prosecutions, [1941] 3 All E.R. 272, 277.

[215] Regina v. McCarthy, [1954] 2 All E.R. 262, 265.

[216] Rex v. Lesbini, [1914] 11 Crim. App. 7.

[217] See especially §§ 18.05[A]-[B], *supra*.

[218] State v. Thunberg, 492 N.W.2d 534, 536 (Minn. 1992) (noting the trend).

[219] See § 31.10[C][3][a], *infra*.

In this regard it is useful to consider two possible ways a defendant's personal characteristics — "the actor's situation" — might be legally relevant: (1) in measuring the *gravity* of the provocation to the reasonable/ordinary person; and (2) in assessing the *level of self-control* to be expected of a reasonable/ordinary person.

In regard to the gravity of the provocation, how far should such subjectivization be permitted to go? American courts are struggling with this question. In England, however, the door is seemingly wide open: The House of Lords has held that the "reasonable man referred to [in the law] . . . share[s] such of the accused characteristics as [the jury] think[s] would affect the gravity of the provocation to him."[220] Thus, a defendant's height, weight, sex, religion, race, culture, or virtually any other personal factor is incorporated into the "reasonable person," if the jury believes that the factor in question would affect the gravity of the provocation.

Shouldn't there be *some* limits, however? To appreciate the significance of the English approach, consider two American cases. In the first case,[221] the defendant observed two women in lesbian lovemaking. Inflamed, he killed one of the women and wounded the other. He sought to reduce the homicide to manslaughter by introducing psychiatric testimony that, while growing up, he had been rejected by his mother, whom he long suspected had been involved in a lesbian relationship. In effect, the defendant sought to be measured by the standard of a "reasonable/ordinary man who, because of family trauma, has pathological animus towards lesbians." Although the proffered testimony might arguably support a valid diminished capacity claim,[222] it is submitted that subjectivization of the sort sought here is out of place in a provocation case, which focuses on the type of provocation that would cause an ordinary person, with *ordinary* human frailties, to become so inflamed as to lose self-control.[223]

In a second case,[224] the defendant, who had come to the United States from China a year earlier, brutally killed his wife because she refused to have sex with him and admitted that she had been seeing other men. The defense proffered expert testimony of an anthropologist, who asserted that the accused's

---

[220] Director of Public Prosecutions v. Camplin, [1978] 2 All E.R. 168, 175.

[221] Commonwealth v. Carr, 580 A.2d 1362 (Pa. Super. Ct. 1990).

[222] See § 26.03, *supra.*

[223] The trial court did not allow the psychiatric testimony. The appellate court affirmed, observing that "[t]he sight of naked women engaged in lesbian lovemaking is not . . . an event which is sufficient to cause a reasonable person to become so impassioned as to be incapable of cool reflection. A reasonable person would simply have discontinued his observation and left the scene." Commonwealth v. Carr, 580 A.2d at 1364.

[224] People v. Dong Lu Chen, No. 87-7774 (N.Y. Sup. Ct. Dec. 2, 1988) (discussed in Leti Volpp, *(Mis)identifying Culture: Asian Women and the "Cultural Defense"*, 17 Harv. Women's L.J. 57, 64-77 (1994)).

reaction "would not be unusual at all . . . for a normal Chinese in that situation." The defense went on to state that, in part because of the shame or humiliation such a person would feel in the close-knit Chinese community, "one could expect a Chinese to react in a much more volatile, violent way to those circumstances that someone from our own society." Even assuming arguendo the accuracy of this testimony, does this mean that the gravity of the provocation should be measured by the standards of an "ordinary/reasonable man brought up in a Chinese culture"? The trial judge apparently thought so,[225] but decisions of this sort bring the law dangerously close to a slippery slope. In an understandable, even commendable, effort to take cognizance of cultural disparities in our multi-cultural society, and thus to be fair to persons who are not fully integrated into the dominant culture, the law runs the risk of trivializing the normative anti-killing message of the criminal law by permitting juries to evaluate provoked killers on the basis of values generally considered abhorrent in American society.[226]

Courts are far less willing to subjectivize the "reasonable/ordinary person" standard when the factor in question is used to assess the level of self-control to be expected of the defendant, rather than to measure the gravity of the provocation. Are we prepared, for example, to apply a "reasonable drunk person" or "reasonable short-tempered person" standard if the defendant can show she is an alcoholic or otherwise short-tempered? And yet, even here, such a subjectivization movement is underway in the United Kingdom. For example, when a fifteen-year-old male was provoked to kill a man who had sexually assaulted him, the House of Lords ruled that the jury should be instructed to measure the defendant actions by "a person having the power of self-control to be expected of a person of the same age and sex as the accused."[227] More recently, and more remarkably, in a case involving a defendant who suffered from serious clinical depression — a psychiatric condition that reduced his "threshold for erupt-

---

[225] The judge found the defendant guilty of manslaughter, based in considerable part on evidence of the defendant's culture.

[226] One must be careful, however, not to let the risk of over-subjectivization bar claims that would otherwise seem legitimate. Suppose that a male inappropriately touches the testicles of a male stranger, who is provoked to kill as a result. Is this adequate provocation? Some observers would argue such a provoked killer is homophobic and, therefore, it is inappropriate to evaluate the adequacy of the provocation on the basis of how it would affect a "reasonable/ordinary homophobic person." On the other hand, some would argue that an ordinary or reasonable man — even one who is not homophobic — might treat this invasion of bodily privacy as highly provocative, much as a woman might respond to a comparable touching by a man. For debate of this issue, see Mison, Note 210, *supra* (arguing that non-violent homosexual advances should not constitute adequate provocation, as a matter of law), and Dressler, Note 210, *supra* (arguing that advances of the sort described here should go to the jury).

[227] Director of Public Prosecutions v. Camplin, [1978] 2 All ER 168, 175. Is a gender-specific instruction, such as that recommended in *Camplin*, a good idea? If jurors believe that an ordinary woman is less likely than an ordinary man to respond violently to a provocation — a very plausible assumption — a gender-specific instruction might result in requiring female defendants to live up to a higher (less violent) standard than male defendants.

ing with violence" — the House of Lords ruled that the jury should be permitted to take into account the defendant's condition, although it reduced his powers of self-control.[228] It is fair to say, however, that such a ruling renders the objective standard almost entirely and inappropriately subjective.

[3] Cooling Off Time

The defense of provocation involves *sudden* heat of passion. The defense is unavailable if a reasonable person would have cooled off in the time that elapsed between the provocation and the fatal act.[229]

Historically, this element was strictly applied. The homicidal act had to occur "in the first transport of passion."[230] As a result, the defense was unavailable to a person subjected, over an extended period of time, to multiple minor provocative acts that cumulatively caused the individual to boil over; likewise, the provocation defense could not successfully be asserted by one who brooded over the provocation before acting. In one famous case,[231] V sodomized G while the latter was unconscious. For three weeks, V ridiculed G, by informing others of what had taken place. Finally, G could take no more of it, and he killed V in a rage. The appellate court held that G was not entitled to claim provocation, as too much time had elapsed between the original provocative act and the homicide.

As with the issue of adequate provocation, the "cooling off" element of the provocation defense, which used to be resolved by the judge, is typically left to the jury today.

[4] Causal Connection

Even if a person is adequately provoked, the provocation defense is unavailable to a defendant whose motivation for the homicide is causally unrelated to the provocation.[232] For example, suppose that Alice calmly plans to kill Barbara, her business rival. Alice arrives at Barbara's home, gun in hand, with a fully formed intention to kill Barbara. Coincidentally, Alice discovers Barbara committing adultery with Alice's husband. Enraged, Alice kills Barbara. Under these circumstances, Alice is not entitled to claim heat-of-passion. Although observation of adultery is adequate provocation, and Alice was in a state of

---

[228] Regina v. Smith, [2001] AC 146, [2000] 4 All ER 289.

[229] American Law Institute, Comment to § 210.3, at 59.

[230] State v. Yanz, 50 A. 37, 38 (Conn. 1901).

[231] State v. Gounagias, 153 P. 9 (Wash. 1915).

[232] Sometimes the causation element is incorporated into the requirement that the defendant act as the result of "*sudden* heat of passion" (the cooling-off element). E.g., Mo. Rev. Stat. § 565.002(7) (2005) (defining "sudden passion" as "passion *directly caused by and arising out of provocation by the victim* . . . which passion arises at the time of the offense . . .") (emphasis added).

high emotion at the time of the offense, the provocation did not cause Alice to kill Barbara: Alice intended to kill her enemy regardless of the adultery; the preconceived design to kill, and not the provocation, was the impetus for the homicide.

[C] Rationale of the Defense[233]

[1] Partial Justification or Partial Excuse?: Initial Inquiry

The provocation doctrine was developed in order to mitigate the harshness of the death penalty, which originally applied to all unjustifiable homicides.[234] This rationale, however, fails to explain the doctrine's continued vitality in England, which no longer has capital punishment, and in the United States, in which there are no more mandatory death penalty laws.[235]

Why should people who become angry enough to kill when provoked be given a defense (partial as it is) when they intentionally take a human life, and why does the defense apply to some provocations and not to others? The common law sheds little light on the subject. Indeed, as English courts and commentators have observed, the doctrine developed "largely [for] reasons of the heart and of common sense, not [for] reasons of pure juristic logic."[236] Put simply, the doctrine has lacked a clear and consistent rationale.

In an effort to identify a sensible rationale for the doctrine, it is useful to focus initially on the role of the provocative act in stirring the defendant's homicidal conduct. What is the relevance of the provocation? One philosopher has phrased the issue this way:

> Is [the provoker] partially responsible [for the homicide] because he roused a violent impulse or passion in me so that it wasn't truly or merely me "acting of my own accord"? Or is it rather that, he having done me such injury, I was entitled to retaliate?[237]

In essence, the issue comes down to this: Does provocation serve as a partial justification or, instead, a partial excuse for a homicide?[238] In partial-justifica-

---

[233] See generally the citations in Note 176, *supra*.

[234] Royal Commission on Capital Punishment Report, (Cmd. 8932) ¶ 144 (1953).

[235] In states that divide murder into degrees, an impassioned killing should constitute no more than second-degree murder, a non-capital offense, because a person who kills suddenly when provoked does not premeditate or act with the degree of calmness normally associated with first-degree murder. See § 31.03[C], *supra*.

[236] Director of Public Prosecutions v. Camplin, [1978] 2 All. E.R. 168, 180.

[237] J. Austin, *A Plea for Excuses*, "The Presidential Address to the Aristotelian Society, 1956," *reprinted in* Ordinary Language 43 (V. Chappell ed. 1964).

[238] For definitions of "justification defense" and "excuse defense," see §§ 16.03-.04, *supra*; for consideration of the importance of distinguishing between the two types of defenses, see § 17.05, *supra*.

tion terms, do we say that a heat-of-passion killing is a less serious offense than an ordinary homicide, because the decedent (partially) deserved to die? Or, instead, do we partially *excuse* the killer because — although the killing is as unjustified as a murder — we believe that the passion she experienced at the moment of the fatal act makes her less responsible for her conduct?

The answer to the justification/excuse puzzle is that, unfortunately, courts have often failed to state which doctrinal path is involved; or worse, they have explained the doctrine under both theories.

[2] Justification or Excuse: A Deeper Look

[a] The Argument for Provocation as a Partial Justification

Various features of the defense, most notably, the original categories of "adequate provocation,"[239] suggest that a provoked killing is partially justified. For example, upon a husband witnessing his wife in an act of adultery, "if the husband shall stab the adulterer, or knock out his brains, that is bare manslaughter,"[240] but it is murder if a man kills after discovering his fiancé in such a tryst. The common law explanation for the dichotomy was that "adultery is the highest invasion of property,"[241] whereas a man "has no such control" over his faithless lover.[242] In short, a husband is justified in protecting his "property" from a "trespasser."

The other categories of "adequate provocation," as well, involve affronts that, in an earlier era, "men of honour" were expected to respond to by "inflict[ing] proportional . . . retaliation . . . on the perpetrator of the injustice."[243] In other words, provokers deserved to be harmed, but homicide was an over-response; therefore, the provoked actor was only partially justified in taking a life.

Another justificatory feature of the defense is the "misdirected retaliation" rule, which provides that the defense may only be used if the defendant attempts to kill the "right" person, i.e., the person who performed the provocative act. For example, in *Rex v. Scriva*,[244] S observed P, a reckless driver, strike X, S's young child. Provoked, S attempted to attack P with a knife. V, a bystander, intervened. Therefore, S intentionally killed V. The court held that the issue of provocation was properly withdrawn from the jury. Although S

---

[239] See § 31.07[B][2][a], *supra*.

[240] Regina v. Mawdridge, [1707] Kel. J. 119, 137, 84 Eng. Rep. 1107, 1115.

[241] *Id.*

[242] Rex v. Greening, 3 K.B. at 849, 23 Cox. Crim. Cas. at 603.

[243] Horder, Note 176, at 51.

[244] [1951] Vict. L.R. 298.

was adequately provoked, the provoker — the person who (partially) deserved to die — was *P*, and not *V*.[245]

[b] The Argument for Provocation as a Partial Excuse

Various arguments, and language from court opinions, support the proposition that the provocation defense is a partial excuse, and not a partial justification. It is essential at the outset, however, to distinguish between the *anger* (or other passion) that the provoked party experiences and the *homicidal act* arising from it. A person may be justified in becoming enraged when she is provoked[246] — for example, if she is physically or sexually assaulted or is insulted in some deeply provocative way — but this does not mean that the homicidal reaction to the provocation — which, after all, is what serves as the basis for prosecution — is justified, even partially.

Instead, as most modern courts have come to realize, the heat-of-passion defense is "the legal system's recognition of the weaknesses or infirmity of human nature and that those who kill [in sudden heat of passion] . . . are less morally blameworthy than those who kill in the absence of such influence."[247] In short, the anger or other emotion of a provoked defendant is justifiable or, at least, excusable; the homicide is unjustifiable, but partially excusable.

Why are adequately provoked killers less blameworthy? The provocation doctrine is controversial,[248] but two explanations are offered in its defense. First, there is a character-based explanation: A person who kills in such circumstances does not act from a "bad or corrupt heart, but rather from the infirmity of passion to which even good men are subject."[249] The more serious the provocation, the more likely it is that the bad act can be explained by "the extraordinary character of the situation . . . rather than [by] any extraordinary deficiency in . . . [human] character."[250]

A more common and preferable way to explain the defense is in terms of voluntariness. The defense is a "concession to human weakness,"[251] in that the law

---

[245] See also Thibodeaux v. State, 733 S.W.2d 668 (Tex. App. 1987) (*X* told *T*, her common law husband, that he was not the father of *V*, a two-month old baby; devastated by the news, *T* killed *V*; held: *T* was not entitled to an instruction on manslaughter because, by statute, the provocation that incites the homicide must come from "the individual killed or another acting with the person killed").

[246] Dressler, *Why Keep the Provocation Defense*, Note 176, *supra*, at 972.

[247] Simpson v. United States, 632 A.2d 374, 377 n.8 (D.C. Ct. App. 1993).

[248] See § 31.07[C][3], *infra*.

[249] Collins v. State, 102 So. 880, 882 (Fla. 1925).

[250] Wechsler & Michael, Note 1, *supra*, at 1281.

[251] Holmes v. Director of Public Prosecutions, [1946] 2 All E.R. at 128; American Law Institute, Comment to § 210.3, at 55.

recognizes that a person disturbed or obscured by passion is less able to control her actions than one who is in a normal state of mind. Therefore, assuming that the provocation is of a nature that would cause a similar reaction in an ordinary person — a critical element, so that the provoked person cannot be blamed for her emotional state — the provoked actor is not fully to blame for her homicidal act. In essence, she lacks sufficient free choice to be held fully accountable for her actions.

[3] Criticism of the Provocation Doctrine[252]

The provocation defense is controversial. Some criticisms will be summarized here. First, there is utilitarian criticism. The argument is that the defense is counter-utilitarian in that it diminishes the general deterrence incentive of persons to learn self-control in provocative circumstances. Moreover, those who lose self-control as a result of provocation are arguably as dangerous as persons who kill without provocation. A man who kills his wife because she has been sexually unfaithful may be as dangerous as one who kills for money. "One need not believe that all [provoked] killers are likely to repeat their offenses or that all [such] killers find emotional reassurance in the provocation defense, to believe that some do."[253]

Second, some claim that the voluntariness excuse argument is unsatisfactory. If persons truly lose their *capacity* for self-control as the result of adequate provocation — if they are truly acting in a "blind rage" — it would seem that a *full* defense would be necessary. The only way to justify the *partial* defense is to say that provoked persons maintain the capacity for self-control, but that they simply find it harder to control themselves because of the anger. But, if they have the capacity to control themselves, why not fully blame the killer for failing to exercise self-control, at least for failing to direct the anger in a non-homicidal direction?[254]

Abolitionist arguments today come primarily from feminist critics. One opponent of the defense has asserted that "provocation operates as a deeply sexed excuse for murder."[255] The defense, it is said, disadvantages women because

---

[252] See generally, Horder, Note 176, *supra*, at 156-97 (favoring abolition of the doctrine); Dressler, *Why Keep the Provocation Defense*, Note 176, *supra* (favoring retention of the doctrine); Nourse, Note 176, *supra* (favoring narrowing of the doctrine).

[253] Nourse, Note 176, *supra*, at 1374.

[254] This position would be consistent with the common law rule that a person is entitled to no defense — full or partial — if she is coerced to kill an innocent person. See § 23.04, *supra*. Surely, a person's ability to control her conduct is as impaired by the fear of death when is gun is to put to her head as is a person who acts out of provocation-induced anger. Advocates of the provocation defense respond, however, that this argument only demonstrates that the duress rule should be changed to permit a partial excuse in homicidal coercive circumstances.

[255] Adrian Howe, *More Folk Provoke Their Own Demise (Homophobic Violence and Sexed Excuses) — Rejoining the Provocation Law Debate, Courtesy of the Homosexual Advance Defence*, 19 Sydney L. Rev. 336, 337 (1997).

"men are by far the most frequent victimizers [killers], and women the most frequent victims."[256] One need only skim the case law and consider the types of provocation generally considered adequate, to see that the doctrine is mostly a "male defense."

Some feminists would narrow, rather than abolish, the defense. For example, Professor Victoria Nourse argues that a defendant who seeks to have a homicide reduced to manslaughter "asks for our compassion." But, she argues, "[t]o merit the reduction of verdict . . . , the defendant's claim to our compassion must put him in a position of normative equality vis-á-vis his victim. A strong measure of that equality can be found by asking whether the emotion reflects a wrong that the law would independently punish."[257] Thus, for example, as long as the law does not choose to punish adultery, the defense would be unavailable to an enraged person who kills due to infidelity.

§ 31.08 MANSLAUGHTER: CRIMINAL NEGLIGENCE

According to Blackstone, a homicide is manslaughter when "a person does an act, lawful in itself, but in an unlawful manner *and without due caution and circumspection.*"[258] Although common law courts have used many terms to explain the italicized language — including "gross negligence," "culpable negligence," and, confusingly, "recklessness" — the best modern term is "criminal negligence." In states that distinguish between forms of manslaughter, a criminally negligent homicide is "involuntary" manslaughter, a lesser offense than "voluntary" ("sudden heat of passion") manslaughter.

As "criminal negligence" is generally defined,[259] involuntary manslaughter involves a gross deviation from the standard of care that reasonable people would exercise in the same situation.[260] It is "something more than the slight degree of negligence" sufficient to justify tort liability; it must be "so gross as to be deserving of punishment."[261]

On the other end of spectrum, as noted elsewhere,[262] the line most commonly drawn between criminal negligence and the sort of risk-taking that justifies a finding of malice aforethought (and consequent murder) is one founded on the consciousness of the actor's risk-taking. One who is aware that she is taking a substantial and unjustifiable risk to human life, but proceeds anyway,

---

[256] Nourse, Note 176, *supra*, at 1335 (summarizing the author's study of American provocation cases).

[257] *Id.* at 1396.

[258] 4 Blackstone, Note 19, *supra*, at *192 (emphasis added).

[259] See § 10.04[D][2], *supra*.

[260] State v. Hernandez, 815 S.W.2d 67, 70 (Mo. Ct. App. 1991).

[261] Hazelwood v. State, 912 P.2d 1266, 1279 n.16 (Alaska Ct. App. 1996).

[262] See § 31.05[B], *supra*.

manifests an indifference to the value of human life that constitutes malice aforethought; one who should be aware of the risk, but is not, is negligent.

For example, one who playfully fires a gun that she knows has bullets in it, in the direction of another person, may be convicted of murder;[263] if the same person performs the same act believing that the gun is unloaded, she is guilty of manslaughter.[264] Or, if a parent knowingly ignores her child's need for food or medical care to survive, the ensuing death may constitute murder.[265] If the parent is unaware of the peril, but should be, the offense is manslaughter.[266]

§ 31.09 MANSLAUGHTER: UNLAWFUL-ACT (MISDEMEANOR-MANSLAUGHTER) DOCTRINE

An accidental homicide that occurs during the commission of an unlawful act not amounting to a felony (or, at least, not amounting to felony that would trigger the felony-murder rule) constitutes involuntary manslaughter.[267] This is the analogue to the felony-murder rule and, as such, is often termed the "misdemeanor-manslaughter" rule. More accurately, it is characterized as "unlawful-act manslaughter."

The scope of the doctrine varies widely by jurisdiction. Some states permit a prosecution for involuntary manslaughter for all offenses, even when the predicate offense is a minor misdemeanor traffic offense.[268] In such jurisdictions, a driver who fails to stop at a stop sign, in violation of the law, may be convicted of manslaughter if she non-negligently causes the death of a pedestrian.[269] In contrast, some courts limit the unlawful-act misdemeanor doctrine to inherently dangerous misdemeanors.[270] Limited this way, the offense will often overlap involuntary (criminally negligent) manslaughter.[271] Other courts distinguish

---

[263] See § 31.05[A][2], *supra*.

[264] In re Dennis M., 450 P.2d 296, 298 (Cal. 1969).

[265] E.g., People v. Burden, 72 Cal. App. 3d 603 (Ct. App. 1977).

[266] E.g., State v. Williams, 484 P.2d 1167 (Wash. Ct. App. 1971).

[267] See 4 Blackstone, Note 19, *supra*, at *192-93; Comber v. United States, 584 A.2d 26, 49 (D.C. Ct. App. 1990).

[268] E.g., State v. Weitbrecht, 715 N.E.2d 167 (Ohio 1999) (upholding conviction for involuntary manslaughter, and finding no constitutional violation in the maximum penalty of five years' imprisonment, based on deaths resulting from minor misdemeanor traffic offenses).

[269] E.g., State v. Hupf, 101 A.2d 355 (Del. 1953).

[270] E.g., Comber v. United States, 584 A.2d at 51 ("if the manner of its commission entails a reasonably foreseeable risk of appreciable physical injury").

[271] See also State v. Yarborough, 930 P.2d 131, 136, 138 (N.M. 1996) (observing that a majority of jurisdictions now require that the predicate offense in misdemeanor-manslaughter prosecutions involve criminal negligence or recklessness, and holding that criminal negligence is required to convict of involuntary manslaughter in New Mexico).

between misdemeanors *mala in se* and *mala prohibita*, limiting the homicide rule to offenses of the former variety.[272]

The unlawful-act doctrine is not always limited to misdemeanor conduct. In jurisdictions that do not apply the felony-murder rule to some felonies (e.g., non-dangerous felonies), a killing that occurs during the commission of an excluded felony should constitute manslaughter. On the other end of the spectrum, there is limited historical precedent, seemingly not followed today, for the view that morally wrongful, but not criminal, conduct may serve as the predicate for a manslaughter conviction: If a person attempts to commit suicide (an immoral act), she could be convicted of manslaughter if a bystander dies successfully preventing the suicide.[273]

§ 31.10 CRIMINAL HOMICIDE: MODEL PENAL CODE[274]

[A] In General

A person is guilty of criminal homicide under the Model Code if she unjustifiably and inexcusably takes the life of another human being[275] purposely, knowingly, recklessly, or negligently.[276] Unlike the common law, the death need not occur within a year and a day of the homicidal act.[277] The Code recognizes three forms of criminal homicide: murder, manslaughter, and (unlike the common law) negligent homicide.

[B] Murder

A criminal homicide constitutes murder when the actor unjustifiably, inexcusably, and in the absence of a mitigating circumstance, kills another: (1) purposely or knowingly; or (2) recklessly, under circumstances manifesting extreme indifference to the value of human life.[278] Thus, using common law terminology, a homicide is murder (defenses aside) if the actor intentionally takes a life, or if she acts with extreme recklessness (i.e., depraved-heart murder).

---

[272] E.g., Mills v. State, 282 A.2d 147 (Md. Ct. Spec. App. 1971).

[273] Commonwealth v. Mink, 123 Mass. 422 (1877), overruled in part by Commonwealth v. Catalina, 556 N.E.2d 973 (Mass. 1990) (limiting the offense to deaths arising from batteries).

[274] Franklin E. Zimring & Gordon Hawkins, *Murder, the Model Code, and the Multiple Agendas of Reform*, 19 Rutgers L.J. 773 (1988).

[275] The Code applies the common law born-alive definition of "human being." Model Penal Code § 210.0(1). See § 31.01[B][1], *supra*. The Code does not define legal death. See § 31.01[B][2], *supra*.

[276] Model Penal Code § 210.1(1).

[277] Neither the Code provisions on criminal homicide nor causation (§ 2.03) mention the year-and-a-day rule. According to the Commentary, therefore, it does not apply. American Law Institute, Comment to § 210.1, at 9. The common law rule is discussed at § 31.01[C], *supra*.

[278] Model Penal Code § 210.2(1)(a)-(b).

There are no degrees of murder under the Code. However, the offense of murder is graded as a felony of the first degree,[279] which means that the offense carries a minimum sentence of from one to ten years' imprisonment, and a maximum sentence of death[280] or life imprisonment.[281]

The Model Penal Code definition of murder abandons the common law element of malice aforethought. As such, the common law mental state of "intent to commit grievous bodily injury" — one form of malice — has no independent significance under the Code. Any case involving this state of mind would constitute extreme recklessness (i.e., murder) or a lesser form of unintentional homicide (i.e., reckless manslaughter or negligent homicide).[282]

The Code's approach to felony-murder is more complicated. The drafters of the Code were opposed in principle to the rule, but they considered it politically unfeasible to abolish it. Therefore, the Code provides that extreme recklessness (and, thus, murder) is non-conclusively presumed if the homicide occurs while the actor is engaged in, or is an accomplice in, the commission or attempted commission of, or flight from, one of the dangerous felonies specified in the statute.[283] For example, under this provision, if D unintentionally kills V during the commission of a robbery, the jury should be instructed that it may, but need not, infer extreme recklessness from commission of the crime.[284] If the felony was not committed in a manner that manifested an extreme indifference to the value of human life, the felon is not guilty of murder for the resulting homicide.

[C] Manslaughter

[1] In General

A person is guilty of manslaughter if she: (1) recklessly kills another; or (2) kills another person under circumstances that would ordinarily constitute murder, but which homicide is committed as the result of "extreme mental or emotional disturbance" for which there is a "reasonable explanation or excuse."[285] These forms of manslaughter are discussed below. The Code does not recognize

---

[279] Model Penal Code § 210.2(2).

[280] Although the Reporters of the Model Penal Code favored abolition of the death penalty, see American Law Institute, Comment to § 210.6, at 111-17, the American Law Institute took no position on the issue. In order to accommodate pro-death penalty legislatures, procedures for implementing the death penalty for murder were adopted. Model Penal Code § 210.6.

[281] Model Penal Code § 6.06(1).

[282] American Law Institute, Comment to § 210.2, at 28-29.

[283] Model Penal Code § 210.2(1)(b).

[284] See American Law Institute, Comment to § 210.2, at 30.

[285] Model Penal Code § 210.3(1)(a)-(b).

any form of criminal homicide based on the unlawful-act (misdemeanor-manslaughter) rule.

Manslaughter is a felony of the second degree. It carries a minimum punishment of imprisonment from one to three years and a maximum sentence of ten years.[286]

[2] Reckless Homicide

A person who kills another recklessly is guilty of manslaughter. It should be observed, however, that a homicide committed recklessly may also constitute murder under the Model Penal Code. The difference between the two offenses is that, in the case of murder, the recklessness must manifest extreme indifference to the value of human life. This feature is not included in the definition of manslaughter.

Reckless manslaughter is a necessarily-included lesser offense of reckless murder.[287] That is, in any case in which a defendant is prosecuted for reckless murder, she is entitled to a jury instruction regarding reckless manslaughter, and may be convicted of the lesser offense if the jury determines that her conscious risk-taking, although unjustifiable and substantial, was not extreme enough to merit treatment as murder.

In a sharp departure from the common law, liability for manslaughter under the Code cannot be founded on criminal negligence. The drafters of the Code believed that no person should be convicted of an offense as serious as manslaughter in the absence of subjective fault, e.g., *conscious* disregard of a substantial and unjustifiable risk.

[3] Extreme Mental or Emotional Disturbance[288]

[a] In General

A person who would be guilty of murder because she purposely or knowingly took a human life, or because she killed a person recklessly under circumstances manifesting an extreme indifference to the value of human life, is guilty of the lesser offense of manslaughter if she killed the victim while suffering from an "extreme mental or emotional disturbance" (EMED) for which there is "reasonable explanation or excuse." The reasonableness of the explanation or excuse regarding the EMED is "determined from the viewpoint of a

---

[286] Model Penal Code § 6.06(2).

[287] American Law Institute, Comment to § 210.3, at 53.

[288] See generally Nourse, Note 176, *supra*; Richard Singer, *The Resurgence of Mens Rea: I — Provocation, Emotional Disturbance, and the Model Penal Code*, 27 B.C. L. Rev. 243 (1986).

person in the actor's situation under the circumstances as he believes them to be."

The Model Penal Code provides that the defendant has the burden of producing evidence regarding this affirmative defense, after which the prosecution must disprove the defense beyond a reasonable doubt.[289] However, most states that have adopted this provision of the Code require the defendant to prove the affirmative defense by a preponderance of the evidence.[290]

The concept of EMED is intended to incorporate two common law doctrines: (1) sudden heat of passion (but in a much expanded form); and (2) partial responsibility (diminished capacity). The latter form of manslaughter in discussed elsewhere in the Text.[291]

This manslaughter provision has two components, one subjective and the other objective. The subjective component is the EMED. This condition need not involve "a state of mind so far from the norm as to be characteristic of a mental illness."[292] Instead, it is enough that the defendant experienced intense feelings, sufficient to cause loss of self-control, at the time of the homicide.[293]

Second, there must be a "reasonable explanation or excuse" for the EMED, which is the objective portion of the defense. It is critical to observe, however, that this standard relates to the mental or emotional condition, and not to the homicide, i.e., the defense is *not* based on the ground that there is a reasonable explanation or excuse for the homicide, but rather that there is a reasonable explanation or excuse for the EMED that caused the actor to kill.[294] In turn, this objective standard is partially subjective, in that the reasonableness of the explanation is considered from the viewpoint of a person "in the actor's situation under the circumstances as he believes them to be."

The Commentary states that the phrase "the actor's situation" is intended to incorporate the accused's personal handicaps and other relevant external characteristics; however, in order to preserve the normative message of the criminal law, the "idiosyncratic moral values" of the defendant must be excluded. For example, if V touches D on the shoulder and makes a homosexual proposition, D may not claim EMED manslaughter on the ground that his rage was brought on by his "moral" view that gay people deserve to be killed. The drafters took no position regarding less extreme personal characteristics, e.g., abnormal sensi-

---

[289] Model Penal Code § 1.12(2).

[290] 1 Paul H. Robinson, Criminal Law Defenses 483 (1984); American Law Institute, Comment to § 210.3, at 63.

[291] See § 26.03[A][3], *supra*.

[292] State v. Ott, 686 P.2d 1001, 1011 (Or. 1984) (interpreting state statute based on Model Code).

[293] *Id.*; State v. Dumlao, 715 P.2d 822, 828 (Haw. 1986).

[294] People v. Casassa, 404 N.E.2d 1310, 1316 n.2 (N.Y. 1980).

tivity to verbal attacks or "an abnormally fearful temperament." These factors are left to judicial interpretation.[295]

Although the Commentary is not specific in this regard, at least two jurisdiction have held that, upon a finding of EMED, the defendant is always entitled to a jury instruction regarding manslaughter, i.e., the objective element of the defense must be left to the trier of fact to consider.[296]

[b] Comparison of Model Code to Common Law "Heat-of-Passion"

The EMED manslaughter provision is much broader than the common law provocation defense. First, a specific provocative act is not required to trigger the EMED defense.[297] All that must be proven is that the homicide occurred as the result of an EMED for which there is a reasonable explanation of excuse. For example, if a psychiatrist testifies that D killed V, his brother, under the influence of EMED, brought on by a combination of factors, including "child custody problems, the inability to maintain a recently purchased home and an overwhelming fear of his brother,"[298] a jury instruction on manslaughter is warranted, although V did nothing to provoke the incident.[299]

Second, even if there is provocation, it need not involve "an injury, affront, or other provocative act perpetrated upon [the defendant] by the decedent."[300] Therefore, the person may successfully claim the defense if she simply believes, although incorrectly, that the decedent was responsible for the affront, or if there was a provocation and the defendant "strikes out in a blinding rage and kills an innocent bystander."[301]

Third, even if the decedent provoked the incident, it need not fall within any fixed category of provocations; and, contrary to the common law, words alone *can* warrant a manslaughter instruction. For example, if D kills V as a result of EMED, a jury instruction on manslaughter is warranted (although, of course, a *verdict* of manslaughter is not required) if the basis for the EMED was that: (1) V derided D because he was unable to have an erection when he attempted

---

[295] American Law Institute, Comment to § 210.3, at 62-63.

[296] State v. Sawyer, 966 P.2d 637, 645-46 (Haw. 1998); People v. Casassa, 404 N.E.2d at 1317.

[297] State v. Elliott, 411 A.2d 3, 7 (Conn. 1979), but see Foster v. Commonwealth, 827 S.W.2d 670, 678 (Ky. 1992) (a triggering event is required; EMED "based on a gradual victimization from his or her environment" is insufficient "unless the additional proof of a triggering event is . . . shown").

[298] State v. Elliott, 411 A.2d at 5.

[299] See People v. Tabarez, 497 N.Y.S.2d 80 (App. Div. 1985), aff'd, 503 N.E.2d 1369 (1986) (D shot at V while experiencing EMED brought on by depression, prolonged unemployment, a very fragile personality, and an I.Q. of 66).

[300] American Law Institute, Comment to § 210.3, at 61.

[301] Id.

to have intercourse with her;[302] (2) V took D's reserved parking space in an apartment building;[303] or (3) in a restaurant, V demanded money owed to him by D from an earlier drug transaction, a verbal argument ensued, and V placed his hand on D's plate.[304]

Fourth, there is no rigid cooling-off rule. The suddenness requirement of the common law is absent here.[305]

[D] Negligent Homicide

A criminally negligent homicide — involuntary manslaughter at common law — constitutes the lesser offense of negligent homicide under the Code.[306] The offense is graded as a felony of the third degree, which carries a minimum sentence of one to two years' incarceration, and a maximum sentence of five years.[307]

---

[302] People v. Moye, 489 N.E.2d 736 (N.Y. 1985) (based on the facts set out in the text, murder conviction reversed on ground that evidence was sufficient to warrant manslaughter instruction).

[303] State v. Raguseo, 622 A.2d 519 (Conn. 1993) (EMED instruction given; D was convicted of murder; conviction upheld on sufficiency-of-evidence grounds).

[304] People v. Walker, 473 N.Y.S.2d 460 (App. Div. 1984), aff'd in memorandum, 475 N.E.2d 445 (N.Y. 1984) (murder conviction affirmed; no jury instruction on EMED given; this ruling was upheld on ground that there was no evidence that D suffered from EMED; had he experienced EMED, instruction would presumably have been required).

[305] State v. Elliott, 411 A.2d at 7.

[306] Model Penal Code § 210.4.

[307] Model Penal Code § 6.06(3).

Chapter 32

THEFT

§ 32.01 THEFT: HISTORICAL OVERVIEW[1]

This chapter considers three traditional[2] theft[3] offenses: larceny, embezzlement, and false pretenses. As is explained below, larceny is a common law felony; the other offenses find their origins in English misdemeanor statutes.

In very early English history, only *forcible* appropriation of property, i.e., robbery, was punished.[4] By the middle ages, however, jurists expanded the scope of the criminal law to prohibit nonviolent, albeit nonconsensual, dispossessions of personal property, i.e., larceny.

The law of larceny did not develop simply or smoothly. Various economic conditions, originating as early as the fifteenth century, placed pressure on the English courts to expand the scope of theft law in order to deter new forms of dishonest conduct. To a significant extent the courts cooperated with the economic interests of the time. Rather than create new theft offenses, however, the judges manipulated the elements of larceny to encompass the new conduct. The outcome was a law riddled with technicalities and intricacies.

At the same time, judicial displeasure with capital punishment, the penalty for all but the most petty larcenies, deterred English courts from broadening the law to the extent that economic conditions might have justified. Consequently, various lacunae in the law of larceny developed. The "cure" for the gaps was the enactment of statutory "gap-fillers," most importantly the misdemeanor offenses of false pretenses and embezzlement.

In recent years, many legislatures have consolidated the three crimes discussed in this chapter into a single offense, often denominated, simply, as

---

[1] See generally Jerome Hall, Theft, Law and Society (2d ed. 1952); Kathleen F. Brickey, *The Jurisprudence of Larceny: An Historical Inquiry and Interest Analysis*, 33 Vand. L. Rev. 1101 (1980); George P. Fletcher, *The Metamorphosis of Larceny*, 89 Harv. L. Rev. 469 (1976); Lloyd L. Weinreb, *Manifest Criminality, Criminal Intent, and the "Metamorphosis of Larceny"*, 90 Yale L.J. 294 (1980).

[2] Many states have enacted other "theft" crimes to fill in holes in the traditional offenses, particularly with the advent of computer crime. These new statutory crimes, themselves founded on the traditional offenses, are not the subject of this chapter.

[3] The word "theft" is used in this chapter to signify the involuntary and unlawful transfer of property. Unless otherwise noted, the term is not used to describe any particular common law or statutory offense.

[4] Robbery is aggravated larceny, i.e., larceny from the person by use or threatened use of force. People v. Tufunga, 987 P.2d 168, 174 (Cal. 1999).

"theft." These efforts at consolidation are briefly noted later.[5] Notwithstanding the reform movement, lawyers cannot confidently ignore the centuries of theft law that preceded consolidation. "History has its own logic."[6] Many of the substantive doctrines discussed below remain relevant today.

§ 32.02 LARCENY: GENERAL PRINCIPLES

[A] Definition

Common law larceny is the trespassory taking and carrying away of the personal property of another with the intent to permanently deprive the possessor of the property.[7]

It is useful to break this definition down into its components and to become familiar with the different ways that each element is described by judges and commentators. The *actus reus* of larceny is the "trespassory taking and carrying away of the personal property of another." It should be observed that larceny is a "conduct," rather than a "result," crime. That is, it prohibits the conduct of taking and carrying away personal property; the offense is complete when those acts occur. It is not necessary that the property taken be damaged, destroyed, or converted to the personal use of the wrongful taker. Instead, if the offender has the requisite *mens rea*, it is assumed that injury to the property or to the victim's interest in it will occur (if it has not already occurred). In this limited sense, larceny may be viewed as an inchoate offense.

The most complicated legal aspect of the *actus reus* of larceny is the requirement that there be a "trespassory taking." More specifically, the trespassory taking involves the nonconsensual taking *of possession* of the property in question.[8] A person who by trespass obtains title — ownership — to the property of another is guilty, if anything, of obtaining property by false pretenses, a different offense. The element of "taking" is frequently described in the case law as the *caption* of the property.

The element of "carrying away" is often described as the *asportation* of the property. Legal issues regarding this element rarely arise.

Larceny prohibits only the trespassory caption and asportation of another person's *personal* property. Real property is not the subject of larceny law.[9]

---

[5] See § 32.11, *infra.*

[6] American Law Institute, Comment to § 223.1, at 130.

[7] See Lee v. State, 474 A.2d 537, 539 (Md. Ct. Spec. App. 1984); United States v. Waronek, 582 F.2d 1158, 1161 (7th Cir. 1978); 4 William Blackstone, Commentaries on the Laws of England *230 (1769) ("the felonious taking, and carrying away, of the personal goods of another").

[8] See Bell v. United States, 462 U.S. 356, 358 (1983) (noting that the original purpose of larceny law was to prevent breaches of the peace, and the concern of the courts was that violence was more apt to occur when property was taken from the possession of another).

[9] People v. Sanders, 67 Cal. App. 4th 1403, 1415 (Ct. App. 1998).

Moreover, only tangible forms of personal property are encompassed in the common law offense.

Larceny is a specific-intent crime. The actor who takes and carries away the personal property of another must do so with the specific intent to deprive the other of the property on a permanent basis. Sometimes this *mens rea* is described in shorthand, simply, as "the intent to steal," "felonious intent," or by the Latin words, "*animus furandi.*" The wrongdoer must possess this intent at the time of the trespassory caption and asportation.

[B] Grading of the Offense

The common law distinguished between grand and petit (now "petty") larceny. Grand larceny involved the stealing of goods above the value[10] of twelvepence.[11] This amount, now worth well less than ten American cents, equaled the value of a sheep.[12]

Although grand and petty larceny were felonies at common law, the death penalty applied only to grand larceny. In this country, grand larceny is a felony, and petty larceny is a misdemeanor.[13]

§ 32.03 LARCENY: TRESPASS

The act of taking and carrying away the personal property of another is not, in itself, an offense. The beginning point is that "[t]here can be no larceny without a trespass, and there can be no trespass unless the property was in the possession of the one from whom it is charged to have been stolen."[14]

---

[10] The value of property for the purpose of determining whether the offense is "grand" or "petty" is ordinarily based on the stolen item's current market value, or "the price at which the minds of a willing buyer and a willing seller would meet." United States v. DiGilio, 538 F.2d 972, 979 (3d Cir. 1976). Although case law on the point is scant, apparently the thief's belief regarding the value of the property is irrelevant at common law. American Law Institute, Comment to § 223.1, at 145-46. Thus, a thief who steals a Picasso painting, believing it is a nearly valueless copy, is guilty of grand larceny; he is guilty of petty larceny if he takes the nearly worthless copy, believing it is the original.

The Model Penal Code departs from the common law in this regard. Under Section 223.1(2), the value of property is determined on the basis of the "highest value, by any reasonable standard, of the property . . . the actor stole *or attempted to steal.*" Thus, the thief who tries to steal a Picasso, but whose plan is frustrated by the police who substitute a copy, can be convicted of grand larceny. For fuller discussion of this situation, see American Law Institute, Comment to § 223.1, at 144-47.

[11] 4 Blackstone, Note 7, *supra*, at *229.

[12] Rollin M. Perkins & Ronald N. Boyce, Criminal Law 290 (3d ed. 1982).

[13] The Model Penal Code treats theft as a felony if the value of the property exceeds $500 or is a specified type of property (e.g., a firearm or automobile). Below that figure, it is a misdemeanor or (if the amount involved is less than $50) a petty misdemeanor. Model Penal Code §§ 223.1(2)(a)-(b).

[14] People v. Hoban, 88 N.E. 806, 807 (Ill. 1909).

The term "trespass" as used here is not related to the tort or crime of trespass to land. Rather, the origin of the term is the ancient writ of *trespass be bonis asportatis* (trespass for goods carried away), which was the basis for the tort of trespass to chattel. In the larceny context, a "trespass" occurs if one takes possession of the victim's personal property — he dispossesses the other of the property — without consent, or in the absence of a justification for the nonconsensual dispossession.[15]

The concept of trespass originally was limited to acts of stealth. The doctrine of *caveat emptor* ("let the buyer beware") prevailed: One who obtained possession of another person's property by fraud was viewed as a clever person, rather than as a criminal deserving of the death penalty. Gradually this *laissez faire* attitude changed. In 1757, the Parliament enacted the misdemeanor offense of "obtaining property by false pretenses."[16] This offense, however, prohibited the use of deception to obtain *title* to another's property; mere dispossession of personal property by fraud was not covered by the statute.

Fraud became a part of larceny law in 1779 with *Pear's Case*.[17] In *Pear*, *P* rented *V*'s horse for a day with the fraudulent intent to take it and sell it immediately, which he did. Because stealth was not involved, the delivery of the horse to *P* by *V* was outwardly consensual. Nonetheless, a majority of judges in the case concluded that *P* was guilty of larceny or, as it is often identified by statute, "larceny by trick."

The reasoning of *Pear* is disputed.[18] Nonetheless, it is clear that obtaining possession of property by fraud constitutes a trespassory taking that may result in conviction for larceny.

§ 32.04 LARCENY: TAKING (CAPTION)

[A] The Significance of "Possession"

Larceny involves the trespassory taking of personal property from the *possession* of another. Ownership is not the key.[19]

"Possession" is a term of art in larceny law. As a result of competing pressures on the common law courts — the need to broaden the scope of larceny law to meet the economic needs of the time, and yet the desire of judges to avoid

---

[15] E.g., no trespass occurs if a law enforcement officer takes property pursuant to a court order.

[16] See § 32.10, *infra*.

[17] King v. Pear, 1 Leach 212, 168 Eng. Rep. 208 (1779).

[18] See § 32.04[B][5], *infra*.

[19] 2 Frederick Pollock & Frederic William Maitland, History of English Law 498 (2d ed. 1898) ("[T]he crime involves a violation of possession; it is an offence against a possessor and therefore can never be committed by a possessor."); People v. Sanders, 67 Cal. App. 4th 1403, 1415 (Ct. App. 1998); People v. Sheldon, 527 N.W.2d 76, 77-78 (Mich. Ct. App. 1995).

undue use of the death penalty — various legal fictions developed in the law of possession.

In order to understand larceny law, therefore, one must distinguish between the doctrines of "possession" and "custody." It is also important to focus on the relationship of the parties involved in the transfer of property, e.g., whether there is a "master-servant" (employer-employee) or bailor-bailee relationship.

[B] "Custody" versus "Possession"

[1] In General

A person has *possession* of property when he has sufficient control over it to use it in a reasonably unrestricted manner. Possession can be actual or constructive. It is *actual* if the person is in physical control of it; it is *constructive* if he is not in physical control of it but nobody else has actual possession of it, either because the property was lost or mislaid or because another person has mere "custody" of it (as that term is defined immediately below). *All non-abandoned property is in the actual or constructive possession of some party at all times.*

A person has mere "custody" of property if he has physical control over it, but his right to use it is substantially restricted by the person in constructive possession of the property.

Unfortunately, the terms "possession" and "custody" largely represent legal conclusions regarding the comparative rights of the parties; there is no bright-line point at which the degree of control over property shifts from custody to possession.

Whenever a court must ascertain whether larceny has occurred, it must determine who initially had possession of the property that allegedly was stolen, and then it must decide whether, when, and to whom "possession" (as distinguished from "custody") was transferred. If the person charged with larceny *did* obtain possession from another, the issue will be whether such possession occurred trespassorily or lawfully.

As a starting point, a person in physical control of property ordinarily is in *possession* of it. However, a person in physical control of property has mere *custody* of the property if he: (1) has temporary and extremely limited authorization to use the property; (2) received the property from his employer for use in the employment relation; (3) is a bailee of goods enclosed in a container; or (4) obtained the property by fraud. These examples of "custody" are considered immediately below.

[2] Temporary and Limited Use of Property

A person with temporary and extremely limited authority to use a piece of property has mere custody of it.[20] Thus, D, a dinner guest, has only custody of the cutlery used at V's dining room table.[21] Similarly, if V, a jewelry merchant, hands a ring to D, a customer, for inspection, D has custody of the item; V retains constructive possession.[22]

The line between custody and possession can be fuzzy. A critical factor, however, is whether D uses the property in V's presence. Thus, if D test-drives an automobile, D's control over it largely depends on whether V, the car dealer, is in the vehicle during the drive. If he is, D has *custody* of the car. If he is allowed to drive the car alone, *possession* of the car shifts from V to D when D leaves the lot.

Why does it matter whether D has "custody" or "possession"? Reconsider the test-drive hypothetical. Suppose that D test-drives the car in V's presence (i.e., D has custody). When they return to the lot, V gets out of the car, as D speeds away in the vehicle. At the instant of this act, D has dispossessed V of the car; D no longer has mere custody of the automobile, because he is using the property in a manner far in excess of his limited right to test-drive it in V's presence. Consequently, D's act would represent a "taking" of the property, i.e., he has "taken possession" of the vehicle from V. As the taking was nonconsensual, it was "trespassory." Therefore, if D intended to steal the car when he drove away, D would be guilty of larceny.

On the other hand, suppose that D was permitted to test-drive the car alone. As he is driving the car, D decides he likes it so much that he is not going to return it, so he drives it out of town. In this case, there is *no* common law larceny. Here, D took possession of the car from V when he left the lot by himself for the test-drive. This taking was nontrespassory because it was consensual. When he later decided to steal the car and drove it away, no trespassory taking occurred because he already had lawful possession of the property. Although not guilty of larceny, D could be guilty of the statutory offense of embezzlement, which generally prohibits the misappropriation of property by one who obtains possession of it in a nontrespassory manner.[23]

---

[20] United States v. Mafnas, 701 F.2d 83, 84 (9th Cir. 1983).

[21] 1 Matthew Hale, History of the Pleas of the Crown *506 (1736).

[22] Chisser's Case, 83 Eng. Rep. 142 (1678).

[23] See § 32.09, *infra*.

[3] Employers and Employees

[a] Employer to Employee

By necessity employers must frequently furnish their personal property to employees in furtherance of the employment relation. In such circumstances, the employer consensually transfers the property to his employee. This does not fit the paradigm of larceny, i.e., the use of stealth to obtain another's property.

In order to make sure that dishonest employees could be convicted of larceny of property furnished to them by their employers, the common law adopted the fiction that when a master furnishes property to his servant for use by the servant in the master-servant relationship, the master retains *constructive possession* of the property, and the servant has mere *custody* of it.[24]

For example, if *V*, the owner of a pizza-delivery franchise, furnishes *D*, his servant, with a car in order to deliver pizzas, *D* has mere custody of the automobile. If *D* does not return with the car, he violates *V*'s possessory right to the property and, consequently, trespassorily takes possession of it. If the taking was felonious, i.e., with the intent to steal the car, *D* is guilty of larceny.

[b] Third Person to the Employee for the Employer

The rule described in subsection [a] applies when an employer furnishes personal property to his employee. The premise that the employee has limited control over the property because of the employment relation does not apply when an employee receives property from a person who has no special authority over him, but who wants the property delivered to the employee's boss. Ordinarily, therefore, a servant who obtains property from a third person for delivery to the servant's master takes lawful *possession* upon delivery. Therefore, in the absence of some other legal fiction, the servant cannot be convicted of larceny of the property if he carries it away.

Notice how this situation plays out in a banking situation. In the famous *Bazeley* case,[25] *B*, a teller of Bank *X*, apparently took customer *V*'s deposit and, deciding now to keep it, immediately pocketed it. *B* was prosecuted for larceny. Essentially, this is what occurred: *V* had possession of the money when he entered the bank; *B* took actual possession of the property from *V* when it was delivered to him for the purpose of transferring it to *B*'s employer, *X*;[26] as this taking was consensual, it was not trespassory; therefore, no larceny occurred.[27]

---

[24] 2 East, Pleas of the Crown 564-65 (1803); United States v. Mafnas, 701 F.2d at 84.

[25] King v. Bazeley, 2 Leach 835, 168 Eng. Rep. 517 (1799).

[26] See 1 Hale, Note 21, *supra*, at *667.

[27] See Commonwealth v. Ryan, 30 N.E. 364 (Mass. 1892) (Customer gives $4 to *R*, a bartender, for liquor; *R* places the money in a business drawer and shortly thereafter retrieves and pockets it; held: this is embezzlement, not larceny).

Instead, shortly after *Bazeley* was decided, the Parliament enacted an embezzlement statute encompassing *B*'s conduct.[28]

A slight change in the facts in *Bazeley*, however, would have changed the outcome. For example, assume that *B*, having no dishonest intention, places *V*'s deposit in Bank *X*'s bank drawer, as is proper. At the end of the day, however, *B* decides to abscond with the cash, which he does. Now, *B* *is* guilty of larceny.[29] In these circumstances, possession of the money moved nontrespassorily from *V* to *B* to *X* (when it was placed in the drawer for the day). Then, when *B* removed the money from the drawer at the end of the day, possession shifted from *X* to *B*. The latter act, however, constituted a trespassory taking. The victim of the larceny, however, was Bank *X*, rather than *V*.

[4] Bailors and Bailees

The fifteenth century marked a period of economic chaos in England as that country was transformed from a feudal, agricultural society into one in which manufacturing sprung up in every town, and international commercial ties developed.[30] As a result of these changes, members of the European mercantile class were forced to entrust their property to carriers who would transport their goods long distances. Unfortunately for the merchants, with the new industry came a new form of criminal conduct, committed by many carriers. Their *modus operandi* was to take containers, wrongfully open them, remove some or all of the contents so that they could be sold for personal profit, close the containers, and then deliver them.

In terms of larceny law, this presented a problem. The merchant consensually entrusted the goods to the carrier, so there appeared to be a lawful transfer of possession. Beginning with the *Carrier's Case*,[31] therefore, the King's Council of the Star Chamber developed a new legal fiction, the "breaking bulk" doctrine, which expanded larceny law.

The precise reasoning of *Carrier's Case* is a matter of some dispute. The most common interpretation of the case, however, is that when a person is entrusted with a container for delivery in unopened condition, the bailee receives possession of the container but mere custody of its contents. When the bailee wrongfully opens the container and removes the contents, i.e., when he "breaks bulk," a trespassory taking of possession of the contents results.[32]

---

[28] See § 32.09[A], *infra*.

[29] Nolan v. State, 131 A.2d 851 (Md. 1957).

[30] Hall, Note 1, *supra*, at 21.

[31] Anon. v. The Sheriff of London (The Carrier's Case), Year Book 13 Edw. IV pl. 5 (1473), *reprinted in* 64 Selden Soc'y 30 (1945). The case is discussed in great detail in Hall, Note 1, *supra*, at 3-33.

[32] Another interpretation of the case is that the bailee receives possession of *everything*, but that when he opens the container constructive possession springs back to the bailor, so that the subsequent act of taking the contents out of the container is a trespassory taking.

The significance of the breaking-bulk doctrine is that the timing and means used by the carrier to steal goods determines whether larceny has occurred. For example, suppose that C, a carrier, receives property belonging to the bailor, B, for delivery to A, but he improperly sells the unopened container to X (i.e., he does not break bulk). In this case, there is no larceny,[33] because C had lawful possession of the container and he never had legal possession of the contents. On the other hand, if C opens the container prior to delivery and sells the contents to X, C has committed larceny. Similarly, if C delivers the container whole to A, and then takes it from A, larceny has occurred, although the victim is A, who was dispossessed, rather than B.[34]

[5] Fraud

Pear's Case[35] involves another legal fiction regarding the nature of possession of property. In *Pear*, P rented a horse from V with the intent to sell it, which he did immediately. Eleven of twelve judges to whom the case was referred concluded that P's fraudulent conduct constituted a trespass and that, therefore, the taking constituted larceny (or "larceny by trick").

The apparent reasoning of the judges was that, in light of P's fraud, "the parting with the property had not changed the nature of the possession, but that it remained unaltered in the prosecutor [V] at the time of the conversion." In other words, because of P's fraud, constructive possession of the horse remained with V; P received only custody of the steed. When he sold the horse in violation of the arrangement, therefore, P trespassorily took possession of the animal.[36]

Pear creates a substantial hurdle for a prosecutor in a common law jurisdiction, as the prosecutor must charge a defendant with the proper offense. Notice the prosecutor's quandary: If D receives property from V based on a false promise to return it, he receives only custody of the property, and is guilty of larceny

---

[33] Edmond Coke, Third Institute *107 (1644).

[34] 4 Blackstone, Note 7, *supra*, at *230.

[35] King v. Pear, 1 Leach 212, 168 Eng. Rep. 208 (1779).

[36] There is another interpretation of this case. Perkins and Boyce assert that the proper reading of this case should be that P took possession of the horse when he rented it with the fraudulent intent; since this taking was deceitful, it was trespassory. Perkins & Boyce, Note 12, *supra*, at 305. If Professors Perkins and Boyce are right, P was guilty of larceny the moment he rode away, although the authors concede that it would have been difficult to prove P's felonious intent at that time. According to the reading of the case expressed in the text, however, larceny did not occur until P acted in violation of the rental agreement.

If Perkins and Boyce are right, there are other interesting implications. First, if P abandoned his felonious intent after renting the horse (but before he sold it) he would still be guilty of larceny, although it would be much harder to prove the felonious intent. Second, if P loaned the horse for one day to X before selling it, X would be guilty of receiving stolen property, assuming he knew of P's intentions! Under the holding of the case described in the text, neither of these results would follow.

if he appropriates it. On the other hand, if D has an honest intention when he receives the property (and, thus, no fraud is involved), D receives *possession* of the property, and any subsequent misappropriation constitutes embezzlement or no offense.

In these latter two hypotheticals, the objective, external circumstances are the same. The difference — which will determine whether the offense is larceny or embezzlement (if anything) — is a function of when D formed the felonious intent. Even if we put aside the fact that D's moral culpability is the same in either case,[37] the critical fact in the case is one likely to be known only by the defendant. Yet, an error by the prosecutor in charging the defendant with the wrong offense could result in acquittal or reversal of the conviction of an obviously dishonest person.[38]

§ 32.05 LARCENY: CARRYING AWAY (ASPORTATION)

A person is not guilty of larceny unless he carries away the personal property that he took trespassorily from another.[39] However, virtually any movement of the property — even a "hair's breadth"[40] — away from the point of caption is sufficient.[41] Thus, larceny, rather than attempted larceny, occurs if a shoplifter is caught with the merchant's property in his possession while walking to the exit,[42] or if a person pulls an earring from the victim's ear, and moves it only a few inches before it gets snagged in her hair.[43]

The asportation requirement is not satisfied, however, unless the movement of the property constitutes a "carrying away" motion. For example, if D moves a box from the floor to a table in order to open it and steal the contents, this change of position of the property does not meet the asportation requirement; instead, it is an act in furtherance of the process of taking possession of the contents of the container; it was not a "carrying away" motion. Therefore, if D were arrested at this moment, he would be guilty of *attempted* larceny.[44]

In view of the nearly trivial nature of the "carrying away" requirement, one scholar has observed that "it is frequently difficult to see where taking ends and asportation begins."[45] As a consequence, the Model Penal Code does not require

---

[37] Yet, at common law, embezzlement was a misdemeanor; larceny was a capital felony.

[38] This problem is considered in greater detail in § 32.11, *infra*.

[39] People v. Sanders, 67 Cal. App. 4th 1403, 1415 (Ct. App. 1998).

[40] Hall, Note 1, *supra*, at 259.

[41] American Law Institute, Comment to § 223.2, at 164.

[42] People v. Olivo, 420 N.E.2d 40, 44 (N.Y. 1981).

[43] Rex v. Lapier, 1 Leach 320, 168 Eng. Rep. 763 (1784); see Harrison v. People, 50 N.Y. 518 (1872) (pickpocket moved a wallet in victim's pocket a few inches before he was caught).

[44] See Cherry's Case, 168 Eng. Rep. 221 (1781) (defendant picked up a package containing cloth in order to remove the cloth; held: no larceny).

[45] Hall, Note 1, *supra*, at 259.

proof of asportation.[46] This feature of the Code has been followed by most states that have revised their theft laws.[47]

§ 32.06 LARCENY: PERSONAL PROPERTY OF ANOTHER

[A] Personal Property

[1] Land and Attachments Thereto

The common law of larceny does not protect land.[48] By its nature, land is immovable; a wrongdoer cannot carry it away and thereafter damage, destroy or lose it. The underlying purpose of larceny law, therefore, does not apply to real estate. Moreover, land can only be "taken" in the sense that a person may come onto it and evict the rightful possessor, or obtain title to unoccupied land by adverse possession. These injuries can be righted adequately by civil action.

Items attached to the land, such as trees, crops, and inanimate objects affixed in the earth,[49] also fall outside the scope of the offense. Once they are severed from the land, however, they become personal property and subject to larceny law.

Certain fictions were developed by the courts to deal with the taking and carrying away of trees and crops recently severed from the land. For example, suppose *D* wrongfully enters *V*'s land and chops down a tree. Once the tree is severed from the land its legal nature changes from real to personal property. Because *D* is the first person to control the timber after it has become personal property, he is in possession of it. Because *V* never had possession of the severed tree *as personal property*, *D* did not take possession of it trespassorily (or otherwise) from *V*. Even though the severed tree lies on *V*'s land, *D* retains constructive possession of it as long as he remains near it. If he takes the tree from *V*'s land immediately, therefore, he has committed no larceny, although he is liable in tort for trespass to the land.

On the other hand, suppose that *D* leaves the land with the intention of returning the next day to retrieve the timber. As soon as he leaves, *D* loses constructive possession of the timber. Because it sits on *V*'s land in *D*'s absence, possession of the personal property immediately shifts to *V*. When *D* enters the land the next day and carries away the timber with the intent of depriving *V* of it permanently, *D* is guilty of larceny.[50]

---

[46] E.g., Model Penal Code § 223.2(1) (providing that theft occurs if a person "unlawfully takes" another's property).

[47] American Law Institute, Comment to § 223.2, at 165.

[48] 4 Blackstone, Note 7, *supra*, at *232.

[49] E.g., Parker v. State, 352 So. 2d 1386 (Ala. Crim. App. 1977) (wires attached to poles embedded in the earth are real property).

[50] See 2 East, Pleas of the Crown 587 (1803).

The Model Penal Code and many modern statutes dispense with these rules. The Model Penal Code's theft laws cover all property ("anything of value"[51]), including "immovable" property, such as real estate, and "movable" property, "including things growing on, or found in land."[52]

[2] Animals

At common law, animals in the state of nature or *ferae naturae* (e.g., wild deer, wild birds, fish in an open river) were not "property" within the meaning of larceny law. However, once an animal was confined by a person on his land or killed, it became his personal property, subject to the law's protection.[53]

Domesticated animals of a "base nature" also fell outside the scope of the common law definition of larceny. Horses and cattle were subject to larceny laws; dogs were "base."[54] Such distinctions were primarily based on economic factors, but today all domesticated animals and birds are protected by theft statutes.

[3] Stolen Property and Contraband

It is larceny for a person to take and carry away the property of another, even if the "victim" also had no right to possess the property in question. Thus, it is larceny to steal stolen property from a thief, or to steal contraband, e.g., illegal narcotics, that no person has a lawful right to possess.[55]

It is easy to rationalize a contrary result. It might plausibly be argued that thieves, persons who are not bona-fide purchasers of stolen goods, and possessors of contraband, should be deemed to have no possessory interest in wrongfully secured property. Instead, however, theft laws are applicable in order to deter the free-for-all that might ensue if criminals could steal from each other with impunity.[56]

---

[51] Model Penal Code § 223.0(6).

[52] Model Penal Code § 223.0(4). See American Law Institute, Comment to § 223.2, at 166-68.

[53] 4 Blackstone, Note 7, *supra*, at *235.

[54] See 2 East, Note 50, *supra*, at 614.

[55] See People v. Otis, 139 N.E. 562, 562-63 (N.Y. 1923) (involving theft of bootleg liquor during Prohibition); see also Model Penal Code § 223.0(7) (defining property "of another" broadly to include persons who would be precluded from civil recovery of the property because it was used in an unlawful transaction or was contraband).

[56] Commonwealth v. Crow, 154 A. 283, 286 (Pa. 1931) ("To establish the rule that the owner of liquor, illegally held, had no property right therein, would lead to a condition of terror and bloodshed among rival bootleggers far worse than we have known.").

[4] Intangible Personal Property

Because common law larceny involves the wrongful taking and carrying away of personal property, property without a corporeal existence, i.e., intangible property, is excluded from its coverage.[57] For example, labor or services are not the subject of traditional theft laws.[58] Thus, if a college student wrongfully takes a computer print-out that lists the computer-access account numbers of other students, and then uses the numbers to obtain computer services to which he is not entitled, he is not guilty of common law larceny of the computer services, although he is technically guilty of theft of the sheet of paper on which the account numbers were found.[59]

Today the vast majority of larceny statutes follow the Model Penal Code's lead and prohibit the unlawful transfer of intangible personal property rights.[60]

[B] Of Another

It is not common law larceny, of course, to take and carry away one's own personal property. However, because larceny involves the trespassory taking of *possession* of another person's property, a person may be convicted of larceny of property he owns. For example, if *D*, landlord of an apartment building and owner of the furnishings therein, enters an apartment unit leased to *V*, and takes and carries away the furniture in violation of the lease agreement, *D* has taken the personal property "of another" for purposes of larceny law.

The Model Penal Code defines "property of another" broadly to include "property in which any person other than the actor has an interest."[61] This definition includes a possessory or ownership interest. It is also broad enough to make it a crime for a partner to steal partnership funds in which he shares an interest,[62] contrary to the common law rule.[63]

---

[57] 4 Blackstone, Note 7, *supra*, at *234.

[58] United States v. Delano, 55 F.3d 720, 727 (2d Cir. 1995).

[59] See Lund v. Commonwealth, 232 S.E.2d 745 (Va. 1977), superseded by statute, as recognized in Evans v. Commonwealth, 308 S.E.2d 126 (Va. 1983); People v. Tansey, 593 N.Y.S.2d 426 (N.Y. Sup. Ct. 1992) (in prosecution for possession of stolen goods, *T* is not guilty if the "stolen" property is an intangible telephone authorization code).

[60] Model Penal Code § 223.2(2).

[61] Model Penal Code § 223.0(7).

[62] American Law Institute, Comment to § 223.2, at 169.

[63] E.g., People v. Zinke, 555 N.E.2d 263 (N.Y. 1990).

§ 32.07 LARCENY: INTENT TO STEAL (*ANIMUS FURANDI*)

[A] Nature of the Felonious Intent

[1] In General

Courts commonly state that a person is not guilty of larceny unless he takes and carries away the personal property of another with the "specific intent to steal" the property. In this context, "intent to steal" is a shorthand way of describing the felonious intent of larceny, which is the intent to deprive another person permanently of the property.[64] Thus, *D* is guilty of larceny if he trespassorily drives away in *V*'s automobile, with the intent of keeping the car. However, he is not guilty of larceny (although he may be guilty of a statutory offense of "joyriding"), if he intends to keep the vehicle temporarily and then return it.[65]

It should be observed that the felonious intent of larceny is *animus furandi* (intent to deprive), not *lucri causa* (for the sake of gain). That is, it is neither necessary nor sufficient that the thief intended to obtain personal benefit from the taking.[66] For example, if *D* takes and carries away *V*'s valuable vase with the intention of destroying it, he has committed larceny although he may gain nothing (except some nonpecuniary pleasure) from the act. On the other hand, if *D* takes *V*'s framed college diploma off the wall and carries it away with the purpose of using it for a day (and then returning it) to fraudulently obtain money from another, *D* is not guilty of larceny of the diploma although he has taken it for personal gain.

It follows from this, as well, that the *nature* of the property taken can be relevant in determining whether a person has acted with the requisite felonious intent. If property is perishable, for example, cut flowers from a florist shop, an intent to deprive the victim of the property long enough to "appropriate a major portion of its economic value"[67] constitutes the requisite "permanent" deprivation.[68]

---

[64] People v. Brown, 38 P. 518, 519 (Cal. 1894).

[65] Impson v. State, 58 P.2d 523 (Ariz. 1936); see People v. Kunkin, 507 P.2d 1392 (Cal. 1973) (*A*, an employee of the state attorney general, unlawfully took a confidential state document to *B* and *C*, journalists, for their inspection, with the intention of returning the document; held: since *A* lacked the intent to steal the document, he did not commit theft; therefore, *B* and *C* were not guilty of possession of *stolen* property).

[66] See Jupiter v. State, 616 A.2d 412, 416 (Md. 1992); State v. Gordon, 321 A.2d 352, 356 (Me. 1974).

[67] American Law Institute, Comment to § 223.3, at 175 (defining the word "deprive" in the statutory provision).

[68] People v. Avery, 38 P.3d 1, 2 (Cal. 2002) (holding that the intent to take property only temporarily nonetheless constitutes the intent to steal if the actor's intention is to take property "for so extended a period of time as to deprive the owner of a major portion of [the property's] value or enjoyment").

[2] Recklessly Depriving Another of Property Permanently

Courts will frequently uphold a conviction for larceny in circumstances in which the most accurate characterization of the defendant's mental state is that he knew that his conduct would create a substantial risk of permanent loss, i.e., that the actor was guilty of recklessly exposing the property to permanent loss. Although this is a different *mens rea* than "intent to steal," many courts treat these two states of mind alike or, at least, infer the felonious intent from the actor's recklessness.[69]

For example, *D1* is guilty of the larceny of a car if he trespassorily takes *V*'s vehicle in City X, with the intention of driving it to City Y and abandoning it there.[70] Although *D1* may hope that the abandoned car will be returned to *V*, he knows there is a very high likelihood that it will be re-stolen or its component parts taken before it can be recovered. *D1*'s recklessness in this regard is enough to justify a larceny conviction. Similarly, the intent to steal may be inferred if *D2* takes property which does not belong to him, with the intention of "selling" the property back to its owner or returning it only if he is paid a reward.[71]

[B] Concurrence of *Mens Rea* and *Actus Reus*

[1] In General

A larceny does not occur unless the actor possesses the intent to steal the property at the time of commission of the *actus reus* of larceny. For example, if *D* takes and drives away *V*'s car, intending to steal it, *D* has committed larceny. On the other hand, if *D* obtains permission to use *V*'s automobile for the day and, hours later, decides to abscond with it, he is *not* guilty of larceny, because he did not have the felonious intent at the moment he took possession of the car.

[2] Continuing-Trespass Doctrine

Suppose that *D* nonconsensually takes *V*'s car with the intention of keeping it for the day and then returning it. Hours later, *D* decides to keep the auto-

---

[69] See State v. Gordon, 321 A.2d at 357-58; accord Model Penal Code § 223.0(1) (although a person is not guilty of theft unless he acts with the "purpose to deprive" the other of the property, § 223.2(1), the word "deprive" is defined broadly to include disposal of property "so as to make it unlikely that the owner will recover it").

[70] United States v. Sheffield, 161 F. Supp. 387, 390 (D. Md. 1958) (*S* is guilty of larceny, even if he intended to abandon the vehicle six blocks from the site of the original taking).

[71] People v. Davis, 965 P.2d 1165, 1169 (Cal. 1998); State v. Hauptmann 180 A. 809, 819 (N.J. 1935) ("intent to return should be unconditional; and, where there is an element of coercion or of reward, as a condition of return, larceny is inferable"); see American Law Institute, Comment to § 223.2, at 174.

mobile permanently and drives out of town with it. Is D guilty of larceny? On its face, it would seem not. D initially took the car without permission, i.e., a trespassory taking occurred. At the time of the trespassory taking, D had a wrongful intent (intent to keep the car without permission for one day), but he did not have the intent to steal. The felonious intent was an afterthought. Consequently, it would seem that the requisite concurrence of *mens rea* and *actus reus* is missing.

Courts developed the legal fiction of "continuing trespass" to deal with such cases. According to this doctrine, when a person takes possession of another person's property by trespass, every moment that he retains possession of it constitutes a new trespassory taking that continues until he terminates possession of the property.[72] Therefore, in the preceding hypothetical, because D's nonconsensual taking of the vehicle was trespassory, every moment he retained the car he was committing the *actus reus* of larceny anew. Consequently, when he decided hours later to deprive V of the automobile permanently, this intent to steal concurred with the "new" trespassory taking, and D is guilty of larceny.

[C] Claim of Right

[1] In General

A person is not guilty of larceny if he takes property belonging to another person based on a good faith belief that he has a right to possess the property.[73] The actor's belief negates the specific intent to steal.[74] After all, one cannot intend to trespassorily deprive another of property that one believes one has a right to possess.

For example, suppose that D, a landlord, believes that V, a tenant, has failed to pay his rent. In fact, the rent was paid, but D inadvertently failed to credit V's account. As a result, D enters V's premises and mistakenly impounds V's furniture, pursuant to a default clause in the lease that authorizes D to seize a tenant's property and sell it as a way of recovering unpaid rent. Under these circumstances, D is not guilty of larceny. Even if his mistake of fact was unreasonable, the mistake negates the intent to steal.

The same analysis would apply in a landlord-tenant hypothetical if D's mistake related to a matter of law, rather than fact. For example, suppose that V, in fact, had defaulted on the rent. If D enters the premises and seizes V's property and sells it, based on an *incorrect* reading of the lease (D incorrectly thinks the lease permits him to sell V's furniture), D would not be guilty of larceny:

---

[72] State v. Somerville, 21 Me. 14, 19 (1842).

[73] State v. Varszegi, 635 A.2d 816, 818 (Conn. 1993); accord Model Penal Code § 223.1(3)(b). The Code's more expansive "claim of right" defense is discussed at American Law Institute, Comment to § 223.1, at 151-59.

[74] People v. Tufunga, 987 P.2d 168, 174 (Cal. 1999).

Whether his mistake of law was reasonable or not, he believed that he had a right to take the property; therefore, he did not have the intent to permanently deprive *V* of his furniture.[75]

Most claim-of-right cases involve nonviolent action of the sort described above. However, although there is contrary case law on the point, the generally accepted rule is that the specific intent to steal is negated even if a person uses force to retrieve the specific property to which he claims a good-faith right of possession. For example, if *D* believes he is entitled to a car in *V*'s possession, and seeks to obtain it at gunpoint, *D* is not guilty of robbery (i.e., larceny by force),[76] although he may be guilty of aggravated assault inasmuch as the latter offense does not require the intent to steal.[77] Various courts, however, will not permit use of force, even if done in good faith, to satisfy, settle, or collect on a debt, as distinguished from seeking the return of specific property.[78]

[2] Forced Sale

Suppose that *D* takes *V*'s property with the intention of paying fair market value for the item. In this circumstance, *D* intends to deprive *V* permanently of the specific property in question, but he does not intend to deprive *V* of its value. May *D* assert a claim-of-right defense, on the ground that he believed that he had a right to take the property as long as he paid for it?

If the property *D* takes was *not* for sale, *D* should be convicted of larceny, even if he intends to pay fair market value for the item.[79] Nonetheless, the law on the subject is sparse and inconsistent. The case for conviction is strongest, however, if *D* has reason to know that *V* would refuse to accept payment in lieu of the return of the item.

Suppose, however, a good *is* for sale, but the merchant does not want to sell it to *D*. For example, suppose that *D* attempts to purchase a beer from bartender *V*, who refuses to serve *D* because *D* is intoxicated. If *D* takes the beer, and throws down change to pay for the drink, is *D* guilty of larceny? Blackstone sug-

---

[75] See State v. Varszegi, 635 A.2d at 819.

[76] See State v. Bonser, 623 P.2d 1251, 1252 (Ariz. Ct. App. 1981); People v. Tufunga, 987 P.2d at 177. The Model Penal Code is in accord with this rule. Model Penal Code Section 222.1 defines "robbery" as the infliction of serious bodily injury or a threat thereof upon another "in the course of committing a theft." As no theft occurs if there is a claim of right, there can be no robbery in such circumstances. For criticism of the prevailing rule, see State v. Schaefer, 790 P.2d 281 (Ariz. Ct. App. 1990).

[77] Butts v. Commonwealth, 133 S.E. 764, 768 (Va. 1926).

[78] People v. Tufunga, 987 P.2d at 177 (noting that a majority of recent cases refuse to permit use of force in such circumstances).

[79] See Perkins & Boyce, Note 12, *supra*, at 345 (stating that it is robbery to require a person at gunpoint to "sell" property that is not for sale).

gested this would not be an offense;[80] and this is the prevailing, although non-unanimous,[81] American view.[82]

§ 32.08 LARCENY: LOST AND MISLAID PROPERTY

The law is confronted with competing policy concerns when a person loses or misplaces his property. On the one hand, there is the interest of the owner in regaining his property; on the other hand, society has an interest in promoting the relatively unrestricted use or transfer of property. As a result, courts have developed rules that seek to balance these competing interests.

The rights of a finder of lost property depend on two factors: (1) the possessory interest of the owner at the time the property is discovered; and (2) the finder's state of mind when he retrieves the lost property.

Regarding the first factor, an owner of property retains constructive possession of his lost property if there exists a reasonable clue to ownership of it when it is discovered. A reasonable clue to ownership exists if the finder: (1) knows to whom the lost property belongs; or (2) "has reasonable ground to believe, from the nature of the property, or the circumstances under which it is found, that if he . . . deals honestly with it, the owner will appear or be ascertained."[83] Thus, a court is more apt to rule that there exists a reasonable clue to ownership of an expensive piece of jewelry found on the floor of a grocery store than a dollar bill aimlessly blowing down a street.

If there is *no* reasonable clue to ownership of the lost property, the finder may use the property as he wishes; the act of picking up the property and using or disposing of it is not a "taking" (trespassory or otherwise). However, if there is a reasonable clue to ownership of the property, the finder's state of mind upon discovery is critical. When D, the finder, picks up the lost (reasonable-clue-to-ownership) property, he takes possession of it from V, the owner. If D takes possession with the intent to steal the property, he is guilty of larceny.[84] If D picks up the article with the intent to find the owner, the taking is not trespassory; if D subsequently absconds with the property, he is not guilty of larceny since the original taking was lawful. Moreover, because V did not entrust the property to D, D's actions may fall outside the scope of a typical embezzlement statute.[85]

---

[80] 4 Blackstone, Note 7, *supra*, at *242 ("it is doubted, whether the forcing [of a merchant] . . . to sell his wares, and giving him the full value of them, amounts to so heinous a crime as robbery").

[81] See Jupiter v. State, 616 A.2d 412, 414 (Md. 1992) (noting and citing support for the contrary view, and taking no position on the matter).

[82] American Law Institute, Comment to § 223.1, at 158; Perkins & Boyce, Note 12, *supra*, at 345.

[83] Brooks v. State, 35 Ohio St. 46, 50 (1878).

[84] *Id.*

[85] See § 32.09[B], *infra*.

Mislaid property is treated somewhat differently than lost property.[86] An object is "mislaid" if "it is intentionally put in a certain place for a temporary purpose and then inadvertently left there when the owner goes away."[87] Supposedly, there is *always* a clue to ownership of mislaid property: Because it was misplaced, rather than lost, the owner knows where it is, and is likely to return to pick it up once he notices that he has left it behind.[88] Therefore, the lawfulness of the finder's actions depends entirely on his state of mind when he takes possession of the property from the owner. If he takes it with the intent to steal it, he is guilty of larceny;[89] if he picks it up with honest intentions, he is not guilty of any theft offense.

§ 32.09 EMBEZZLEMENT

[A] Historical Background

Embezzlement is not a common law offense. The offense is the result of eighteenth century legislative efforts to compensate for gaps in the law of larceny. As described earlier, common law jurists were willing to punish new forms of dishonest conduct by manipulating the meaning of the term "trespassory taking" to expand the scope of larceny law. But, there were limits to their willingness to stretch the law: In particular, they were not prepared to treat dishonest employees, who appropriated property lawfully entrusted to them by third persons for delivery to employers, as capital felons.

In 1799, shortly after the acquittal of a dishonest bank employee in the *Bazeley* case,[90] Parliament enacted the first general embezzlement statute.[91] The statute provided in pertinent part:

> [I]f any servant or clerk, or any person employed . . . by virtue of such employment receive or take into his possession any money, goods, bond, bill, note, banker's draft, or other valuable security, or effects, for or in the name or on the account of his master or masters, or employer or employers, and shall fraudulently embezzle, secrete, or make away with the same, or any part thereof . . . [he] shall be deemed to have feloniously stolen the same. . . .[92]

---

[86] The Model Penal Code treats lost and mislaid property similarly. See Model Penal Code § 223.5 ("Theft of Property Lost, Mislaid, or Delivered by Mistake").

[87] Perkins & Boyce, Note 12, *supra*, at 310.

[88] *Id.* at 310-11.

[89] If the finder genuinely believes that the item was abandoned by its owner, he lacks the specific intent to steal it. See Model Penal Code § 223.1(3)(a); American Law Institute, Comment to § 223.5, at 227-28.

[90] King v. Bazeley, 2 Leach 835, 168 Eng. Rep. 517 (1799). See § 32.04[B][3][b], *supra*.

[91] Previously, it had enacted statutes prohibiting embezzlement by officers and servants of the Bank of England, South Sea Company, and the post office. Hall, Note 1, *supra*, at 39.

[92] 39 Geo. III, c. 85 (1799).

Subsequent embezzlement statutes were enacted to deal with other persons not encompassed by this law.

Under English law, embezzlement was a misdemeanor. In the United States today, embezzlement is a felony or misdemeanor, depending on the value of the property embezzled.

[B] Elements of the Offense

Because of the statutory nature of the offense, and the piecemeal manner in which embezzlement laws were enacted, no single definition of the crime exists. At a minimum, however, embezzlement involves two basic ingredients: (1) that D came into possession of the personal property of another in a lawful manner; and (2) that D thereafter fraudulently converted the property (i.e., D performed some act that demonstrated his intent to deprive another of the property permanently). Most embezzlement statutes include a third element: that D came into possession of the property as the result of entrustment by or for the owner of the property.

[C] Distinguishing Larceny from Embezzlement

The most significant distinction between larceny and embezzlement is that "[i]n embezzlement, the property comes lawfully into possession of the taker and is fraudulently or unlawfully appropriated by him; in larceny, there is a trespass in the unlawful taking of the property."[93] It is useful to summarize here some of the subtle differences between the two offenses, as developed in earlier sections of this chapter.

First, a person who fraudulently secures property from another obtains mere *custody* of the property. Consequently, the subsequent appropriation of the property, which constitutes a trespassory taking of possession thereof, renders the fraudulent actor guilty of larceny (by trick).[94]

Second, an employee who receives property from his employer for use in the employment relationship ordinarily obtains mere *custody* of the property. Therefore, if the employee takes and carries away the employer's property with the concurrent intent to steal it, he is guilty of larceny, rather than embezzlement.[95]

Third, an employee who receives property *for* his employer from a third person ordinarily receives *possession* of the property. Therefore, if he later decides to convert the property, he is guilty of embezzlement.[96]

---

[93] State v. Smith, 98 P.2d 647, 648 (Wash. 1939) (quoting 18 Am. Jur., Embezzlement § 3 (1938)), overruled in part, State v. Smith, 798 P.2d 1146 (Wash. 1990).

[94] See § 32.04[B][5], *supra*.

[95] See § 32.04[B][3][a], *supra*.

[96] See § 32.04[B][3][b], *supra*.

Fourth, a bailee entrusted with property ordinarily obtains possession of it, except that if the property is enclosed in a container he obtains possession of the container but only custody of its contents.[97] Therefore, if the bailee subsequently decides to sell or otherwise convert the entrusted property in the condition in which it was received (e.g., in its original container if there was one), he is guilty of embezzlement. In contrast, if the bailee wrongfully opens the container and converts the contents, he is guilty of larceny. If he is responsible for delivering the container to a third party, and he does so without opening it, and thereafter decides to steal the property, he is guilty of larceny.

Finally, in jurisdictions in which entrustment is an element of the offense of embezzlement, a person who finds lost or mislaid property, takes it with the intent to find the true owner, and then changes his mind and converts the property to his own use, is guilty of no offense. It is larceny, however, if he had a wrongful intent when he found the property.[98]

§ 32.10 FALSE PRETENSES

[A] In General

The offense of "obtaining property by false pretenses" or, simply, "false pretenses," is statutory in nature. Originally, it was a misdemeanor in England. In the United States, it is now a felony or misdemeanor, depending on the value of the property obtained.

The original false pretenses statute was enacted in England in 1757.[99] According to that statute, any person who "knowingly and designedly" by false pretenses obtains title to "money, goods, wares or merchandizes" from another person "with the intent to cheat or defraud" the other person is guilty of false pretenses. A "false pretense" is a false representation of an existing fact.[100]

[B] Distinguishing False Pretenses From Larceny and Embezzlement

Larceny, embezzlement, and false pretenses may occur as the result of fraud. False pretenses and larceny are alike in one critical way: Fraud is used to *obtain* the property. In contrast, an embezzler obtains property lawfully, but thereafter fraudulently *converts* it to his own use. The primary difference between larceny and false pretenses is that a thief who uses trickery to secure

---

[97] See § 32.04[B][4], *supra.*

[98] See § 32.08, *supra.*

[99] 30 Geo. II, c. 24 § 1 (1757).

[100] See Lund v. Commonwealth, 232 S.E.2d 745, 748 (Va. 1977); American Law Institute, Comment to § 223.3, at 184.

title, and not simply possession, of property, is guilty of false pretenses; one who merely secures possession through fraud is guilty of larceny by trick.[101]

The line between larceny-by-trick and false pretenses is sometimes clear. For example, in *Pear's Case*,[102] *P* fraudulently rented a horse from *V*, intending from the outset to steal the animal. Clearly, this was not false pretenses: The existence of the rental arrangement demonstrates that title to the horse did not pass with possession.

Often the line between the two offenses is very thin. Frequently, a court will rule that, although the thief obtained *possession* of property through fraud, *title* to it did not transfer because some condition had not yet been satisfied. For example, in one case,[103] *H* drove his car to *V*'s gas station and asked the operator to fill his tank. *H* did not intend to pay for the gasoline. After the tank was filled, *H* drove away without paying. The court determined that *H* committed larceny-by-trick rather than false pretenses because *V* did not intend title to the gas to pass until payment was made. In contrast, if *H* had paid for the gasoline with counterfeit money, title would have passed, and the offense would have been false pretenses.

One who provides money to another for a special purpose does not transfer title to it until that purpose is met. For example, in *Graham v. United States*,[104] *G*, a lawyer, obtained money from *V*, his client, for the stated purpose of bribing *X*, a police officer, for *V*'s benefit. Instead, *G* converted the cash to his own use. The court held that *G* was guilty of larceny, not false pretenses: *V* did not intend to part with title to the money until it was delivered to *X* as a bribe.

[C] Elements of the Offense

[1] False Representation

False pretenses requires a false representation. The representation itself may be in writing, orally presented, or in the form of misleading conduct.[105] Usually, *nondisclosure* of a material fact does not constitute false pretenses, even if the omitter of the information knows that the other party is acting under a false impression.[106] However, nondisclosure constitutes misrepresentation if the omitter has a duty of disclosure, such as when he has a fiduciary relationship to the victim.

---

[101] Bell v. United States, 462 U.S. 356, 359 (1983).

[102] King v. Pear, 1 Leach 212, 168 Eng. Rep. 208 (1779).

[103] Hufstetler v. State, 63 So. 2d 730 (Ala. Ct. App. 1953).

[104] 187 F.2d 87 (D.C. Cir. 1950).

[105] In one famous case, *B* obtained property from *V* by giving the false impression that he was an Oxford student by wearing a cap and gown identified with the college. Rex v. Barnard, 173 Eng. Rep. 342 (1837).

[106] People v. Johnson, 150 N.Y.S. 331 (Sup. Ct. 1914).

The representation, of course, must be false. A person is not guilty of false pretenses if he obtains title to property by making a "false" claim that turns out to be true. For example, if *D*, a scam artist, sells a book purporting to be the diary of Hitler, he cannot be convicted of false pretenses if the diary turns out to be genuine, although *D* believed that it was forged. Instead, *D* would be guilty of *attempted* false pretenses.

[2] Existing Fact

[a] Fact versus Opinion

Expression of an opinion, uttered with the intent to defraud another, does not constitute false pretenses.[107] For example, "seller's talk" or "puffing" (e.g., "this is the best product that has ever been manufactured") is not actionable. The justification for this rule is that such statements cannot be taken literally as fact, but must be considered to be the seller's opinion. As such, a listener should not rely on the utterance.

The fact/opinion distinction may also preclude conviction of persons not involved in puffing. For example, a statement by a seller regarding the value of his property is traditionally treated as a non-actionable representation of opinion.[108] This is because the value of property is the price agreed upon by a willing buyer and seller. A representation regarding value, therefore, is no more than an expression of opinion by the speaker of the price he thinks the property would obtain in the market.

As the fact/opinion distinction might suggest, the ethic of *caveat emptor* was strong while the law of false pretenses developed. It is commonly acknowledged today, however, that if this distinction is inflexibly followed it will result in "the clever [person] . . . be[ing] able to steal with impunity."[109] Consequently, many states have expanded the scope of false pretenses. For example, Model Penal Code Section 223.3 provides that a person is guilty of "theft by deception," the Code's equivalent offense, if he creates or reinforces a false impression regarding the value of property. However, puffing is not prohibited unless the statement would deceive an ordinary listener.

[b] Fact versus Promise of Future Conduct

Suppose that *D* purchases an automobile on installment contract[110] and later fails to make payments. Or, suppose that *D* obtains a loan and later fails to meet

---

[107] Regina v. Bryan, 7 Cox Crim. Cas. 312, 317 (1857).

[108] E.g., Commonwealth v. Quinn, 111 N.E. 405, 407 (Mass. 1916).

[109] American Law Institute, Comment to § 223.3, at 192.

[110] Although title technically is retained by the vendor of property until full payment is received on an installment contract, the equitable interest obtained by the purchaser is sufficiently great that the offense of false pretenses applies. Whitmore v. State, 298 N.W. 194, 195 (Wis. 1941).

his obligation of repayment. May *D* be convicted of false pretenses if it can be shown he had no intention of paying his debt when he entered into the agreement?

Conceptually, a promise to make payment in the future is an assertion of the present fact of the speaker's intention to perform a future act. Nonetheless, common law courts were reluctant to treat a debtor's breach of contract as the basis for prosecution for false pretenses. The traditional explanation is that "the act complained of . . . is as consonant with ordinary commercial default as with criminal conduct. . . . Business affairs would be materially encumbered by the ever present threat that a debtor might be subjected to criminal penalties. . . ."[111] The majority rule, therefore, is that the offense of false pretenses does not apply to misrepresentations regarding future conduct.

In recent years, many states have redrafted their theft laws to encompass false promises. The Model Penal Code is typical of this trend. It prohibits deception regarding a person's "intention or other state of mind." The Code expressly provides, however, that deception regarding the intention to fulfill a promise cannot be inferred solely from the fact that the promisor did not perform as guaranteed.[112]

[3] *Mens Rea*

The original false pretenses statute and others modeled on it require proof not only that the actor uttered a false representation of an existing fact, but that it was uttered "knowingly and designedly" and with "the intent to defraud."

The phrase "knowingly and designedly" means only that the actor made the representation knowing that it was false. The phrase "intent to defraud" constitutes the specific intent of false pretenses; it approximates the meaning of "intent to steal" required in larceny prosecutions. Thus, *D* is not guilty of false pretenses if he knowingly utters a false statement in order to obtain property to which he believes he is entitled. In such circumstances, *D* lacks the intent to defraud another.[113]

§ 32.11 CONSOLIDATION OF THEFT OFFENSES

It is virtually impossible to justify theft law as it has developed. Many legal fictions complicate the law of larceny, embezzlement, and false pretenses, and the lines between the offenses are exceedingly thin. And, there is no meaningful difference between the offenses in terms of the culpability of the actors, their dangerousness, or the seriousness of the harm caused.

---

[111] Chaplin v. United States, 157 F.2d 697, 698-99 (D.C. Cir. 1946).

[112] Model Penal Code § 223.3(1).

[113] People v. Thomas, 3 Hill 169 (N.Y. Sup. Ct. 1842).

Making matters worse, the key distinctions between the offenses depend largely on the hidden intentions of the parties. The line between larceny and embezzlement, for example, depends on whether the defendant formed the wrongful mental state prior to, or after, the property was delivered to him. The line between larceny-by-trick and false pretenses, on the other hand, depends on whether title passed in a property transaction; yet this critical fact depends largely on the victim's intent at the time of transfer.

These distinctions have served as mighty encumbrances in the prosecution of wrongdoers. At one time, a prosecutor of a theft offense was required to prove commission of the form of theft alleged in the indictment. Thus, if the indictment charged larceny, the prosecutor could not obtain a conviction for embezzlement or false pretenses. Even if a prosecutor is allowed to allege alternative offenses in an indictment, this is only a slight benefit: He must still convince all of the jurors as to which crime was committed. As a result, thieves sometimes escape punishment because the prosecutor is unable to prove beyond a reasonable whether the wrongdoer had a felonious intent at the time he took possession of property (larceny) or later (embezzlement), or whether the wrongdoer's admitted fraud resulted in transfer of title (false pretenses) or only possession (larceny).

As the result of difficulties of proof, most states have sought to ease the prosecutor's burden by consolidating the three theft crimes (and other property crimes) into a single theft offense. However, lawyers in jurisdictions that have reformed the law in this manner should be wary of what consolidation does and does not do. Specifically, unless a theft statute provides to the contrary, the consolidation may do nothing more than bring the various theft crimes under a single statutory umbrella. The umbrella may actually not eliminate the prosecutor's responsibility to prove the elements of the specific type of theft alleged.[114]

To avoid continued problems of pleading and proof, some states have followed the lead of the Model Penal Code. The Code sets out separate forms of theft — e.g., theft by unlawful taking, theft by deception, theft by extortion — but the offenses are consolidated in that the prosecutor may prove a different form of theft than was specified in the indictment, as long as the defendant's right to a fair trial is ensured.[115] Another approach is to allow the prosecutor to allege simply that the defendant "stole" the property in question, and to support the allegation at trial with evidence of any form of theft.[116]

---

[114] People v. Sanders, 67 Cal. App. 4th 1403, 1416-17 (Ct. App. 1998).

[115] Model Penal Code § 223.1(1).

[116] Mass. Gen. Laws ch. 277, § 41 (2005).

Chapter 33

RAPE

§ 33.01 RAPE: GENERAL PRINCIPLES[1]

[A] Definition: Common Law

Blackstone defined *rape* as "carnal knowledge[2] of a woman forcibly and against her will."[3] At common law, however, a husband who forced his wife to engage in sexual intercourse with him was not guilty of rape.[4] Common law rape is a general-intent offense.

An ancient English felony statute prohibited sexual intercourse by a male with a "woman child" under the age of ten years with or without her consent.[5] This offense has come to be known as "statutory rape," although it is a feature of the common law of the United States.[6]

---

[1] See generally Susan Brownmiller, Against Our Will (1975); Susan Estrich, Real Rape (1987); Stephen J. Schulhofer, Unwanted Sex: The Culture of Intimidation and the Failure of Law (1998); David P. Bryden, *Redefining Rape*, 3 Buff. Crim. L. Rev. 317 (2000); Anne M. Coughlin, *Sex and Guilt*, 84 Va. L. Rev. 1 (1998); Joshua Dressler, *Where We Have Been, and Where We Might Be Going: Some Cautionary Reflections on Rape Law Reform*, 46 Clev. St. L. Rev. 409 (1998); Susan Estrich, *Rape*, 95 Yale L.J. 1087 (1986); Stephen J. Schulhofer, *The Feminist Challenge in Criminal Law*, 143 U. Pa. L. Rev. 2151 (1995). For a searing account of one woman's rape, and an eloquent description of her "road to recovery," see Nancy Venable Raine, After Silence: Rape and My Journey Back (1998).

[2] "Carnal knowledge" is sexual intercourse, i.e., genital copulation. (Anal and oral penetration fall outside the scope of common law rape, but constitute the offense of sodomy.) Sexual penetration by the penis of the vulva is necessary to constitute rape; sexual emission is neither sufficient nor necessary. 1 Matthew Hale, History of the Pleas of the Crown *628 (1736).

Various courts have held that each act of penetration constitutes a separate act of rape if "there are successive impulses, even though all unite in a common course of action." Ricks v. State, 940 S.W.2d 422, 423 (Ark. 1997); People v. Brown, 28 Cal. App. 4th 591, 601 (Ct. App. 1994) (*B*'s penis came out of *V*'s vagina because of *V*'s resistance; *B* repenetrated eight or nine times; held: *B* could be punished separately for each penetration).

[3] 4 William Blackstone, Commentaries on the Laws of England *210 (1769).

[4] 1 Hale, Note 2, *supra*, at *628-29.

[5] 18 Eliz. ch. 7, § 4; see 4 Blackstone, Note 3, *supra*, at *212.

[6] See generally Michelle Oberman, *Regulating Consensual Sex with Minors: Defining a Role for Statutory Rape*, 48 Buff. L. Rev. 703 (2000); Michelle Oberman, *Turning Girls into Women: Re-Evaluating Modern Statutory Rape Law*, 85 J. Crim. L. & Criminology 15 (1994); Frances Olsen, *Statutory Rape: A Feminist Critique of Rights Analysis*, 63 Tex. L. Rev. 387 (1984).

[B] Statutes: Traditional and Reform

American rape statutes vary considerably. In recent years many legislatures have redrafted their rape statutes, often at the urging of feminist critics of the common law and early statutory definitions of rape.[7] The Model Penal Code, which was largely drafted in the 1950s and adopted by the American Law Institute in 1962, long before modern feminist scholarly and public criticism of rape law fully developed, has had little impact on rape law reform.[8] Given modern sensibilities, the Code's sexual offense provisions are seen today by many as relics that "should be pulled and replaced."[9]

Traditional (non-reformed) statutes focus on forcible rape, or sexual intercourse achieved "forcibly," "against the will" of the female, "without her consent." As is considered below,[10] these terms — sometimes all contained in a single statute[11] — are not necessarily synonymous. Traditional rape statutes are also gender-specific: Only males are legally capable of perpetrating the offense,[12] and only females are victims of the crime.

Many states now prohibit other, nonforcible but nonconsensual, forms of sexual intercourse. For example, sexual intercourse by a male with an unconscious or drugged female,[13] and sexual intercourse procured by "fraud-in-the-factum,"[14] will constitute rape. And, increasingly, states have redefined the offense in gender-neutral terms in regard to both the perpetrator and the victim.[15] In the most reformed versions of the law, the offense has been broadened to include all forms of sexual penetration; the name of the crime has been changed (e.g., "criminal sexual conduct" or "sexual assault"[16]); the offense is divided into

---

[7] E.g., State in the Interest of M.T.S., 609 A.2d 1266, 1274-75 (N.J. 1992) (summarizing that state's rape reform, formulated by a coalition of feminist organizations).

[8] For the Code's approach to rape, see § 33.08, *infra*.

[9] Deborah W. Denno, *Why the Model Penal Code's Sexual Offense Provisions Should Be Pulled and Replaced*, 1 Ohio St. J. Crim. L. 207 (2003).

[10] See § 33.04, *infra*.

[11] E.g., Md. Ann. Code of 1957 Art. 27, § 463(a)(1) ("[b]y force or threat of force against the will and without the consent of the other person") (since repealed).

[12] However, a female may be convicted of rape as an accomplice of a male.

[13] E.g., Cal. Penal Code § 261(a)(3)-(4) (Deering 2005).

[14] Cal. Penal Code § 261(a)(4)(C) (Deering 2005) ("fraud in fact"). See § 33.04[C], *infra*.

[15] E.g., Mich. Comp. Laws §§ 750.520a - 750.520*l* (2005); N.J. Stat. Ann. § 2C:14-2 (2005).

[16] Raine, Note 1, *supra*, at 208:

Sexual assault puts the concept of violence into the word *rape*. It reflects a historically recent clinical, political, and social analysis of the phenomenon of rape that attempts to drain off the toxins of blame-the-victim, and to shift the criterion of rape from the behavior of the victim to that of the criminal. It is an attempt to take any ambiguity out of the word *rape*.

degrees; and the marital immunity rule — the common law rule that a husband could not legally rape his wife — has been narrowed or abolished.[17]

Today, "statutory rape" remains an offense, although all states have expanded upon the common law scope of the crime, which only encompassed sexual intercourse with minor girls under the age of ten. Not uncommonly, states apply a two-level approach to this offense: Sexual intercourse with a very young girl (e.g., twelve years of age or younger) remains punishable at the level of forcible rape; intercourse with an older girl (especially if the male is older than the female by a specified number of years) is a felony of a lesser degree.[18]

[C] Grading of the Offense

Under Saxon law, rape was a felony punishable by death. For a short time in the thirteenth century, it was treated as only a trespass punishable by two years' imprisonment and a fine. Subsequently, the offense was treated again as a capital crime.[19]

In the United States, as late as the mid-1920s, eighteen states, the District of Columbia, and the federal government authorized capital punishment for rape. However, "the death penalty [was] reserved overwhelmingly for black defendants, especially those convicted of raping white women."[20] In 1977, the Supreme Court ruled that the penalty of death was unconstitutionally disproportionate to the rape of an adult woman.[21]

Today, rape is treated as a very serious — often the most serious — non-homicide felony. Penalties vary, but most states set the maximum penalty at life imprisonment[22] or a substantial terms of years.[23]

§ 33.02 STATISTICS REGARDING RAPE

Accurate figures on the commission of rape are almost impossible to find.[24] Indeed, the two primary national sources for all United States crime statistics

---

[17] Bryden, Note 1, *supra*, at 321 (and citing statutes). The marital exemption rule is considered in § 33.06, *infra*.

[18] American Law Institute, Comment to § 213.1, at 324-26.

[19] 4 Blackstone, Note 3, *supra*, at *211-12.

[20] James R. Acker, *Social Science in Supreme Court Death Penalty Cases: Citation Practices and Their Implications*, 8 Just. Q. 421, 431 (1991).

[21] Coker v. Georgia, 433 U.S. 584 (1977). See § 6.05[B], *supra*.

[22] E.g., Mich. Comp. Laws § 750.520b (2005).

[23] E.g., N.Y. Penal Law §§ 130.35 (LexisNexis 2005) (defining rape in the first degree as a Class B felony) and § 70.02(3)(a) (LexisNexis 2005) (authorizing imprisonment up to twenty-five years for Class B felonies).

[24] For discussion of some of the problems in this regard, see Helen M. Eigenberg, *The National Crime Survey and Rape: The Case of the Missing Question*, 7 Just. Q. 655 (1990).

— the Uniform Crime Report and National Crime Victimization Survey (NCVS) — have shown "markedly different [rape] trends."[25] What *is* known is that rape is and has been an under-reported crime,[26] although the extent to which it is (and whether it is *more* under-reported than other violent offenses) remains in dispute.[27]

Specifically, the NCVS estimated that 155,000 women, age twelve or older, were victims of consummated or attempted forcible rapes each year between 1973 and 1987.[28] The average annual figure reported in 2002-2003 of the same population was 142,380.[29] Data from a separate study of "sexual victimization of college women" — a random telephone survey of 4,446 college women in 1997 — suggest that 4.9% of female college students are victims of rape or attempted rape in any given calendar year. Extrapolating from this, the report states that "[o]ver the course of a college career — which now lasts an average of 5 years — the percentage of completed or attempted rape victimization among women in higher educational institutions might climb to between one-fifth and one-quarter."[30]

Based on 2003 data, blacks and whites are equally likely per capita to be victims of rape; non-Hispanics are more likely to be victims than Hispanics. Persons between the ages of twenty and thirty-four are victims more than those younger or older; individuals with household annual incomes below $15,000 are more like to be victims than persons better off economically.[31]

---

[25] David P. Bryden & Sonja Lengnick, *Rape in the Criminal Justice System*, 87 J. Crim. L. & Criminology 1194, 1218 (1997).

[26] According to a late twentieth century NCVS estimate, only 32% of all rapes and lesser forms of sexual assault were reported to law enforcement agencies. "The most common reason given by victims of rape/sexual assault for reporting the crime . . . was to prevent further crimes by the offender against them. The most common reason cited by the victim for not reporting the crime . . . was that it was considered a personal matter." U.S. Department of Justice, Bureau of Justice Statistics, Sex Offenses and Offenders (NCJ 163392, Feb. 1997).

[27] A majority of scholars in the field believe that the proportion of rape victims who report their crime has increased in recent years. Bryden & Lengnick, Note 25, *supra*, at 1225. In dispute is whether rape reform legislation, intended in part to have this effect, is responsible. Compare *id.* at 1225-28 ("In sum, the evidence, although mixed, suggests that rape reporting rates are generally unresponsive to changes in a particular jurisdiction's [reform of] rape law. . . .") with Stacy Futter & Walter R. Mebane, Jr., *The Effects of Rape Law Reform on Rape Case Processing*, 16 Berkeley Women's L.J. 72, 73-74 (2001) ("The results of our study strongly suggest that implementation of more liberal and feminist-oriented legal provisions during the years 1970-1991 did, for the most part, increase the number of rape reports that police agencies deemed well-founded.").

[28] U.S. Department of Justice, Bureau of Justice Statistics, Female Victims of Violent Crime (NCJ 126826, Jan. 1991).

[29] U.S. Department of Justice, Bureau of Justice Statistics, Criminal Victimization, 2003 (NCJ 205455, Sept. 2004).

[30] U.S. Department of Justice, Office of Justice Programs, The Sexual Victimization of College Women 10 (NCJ 182369, Dec. 2000) (by Bonnie S. Fisher et al.).

[31] Criminal Victimization, Note 29, *supra*, at 7-8.

§ 33.03 SOCIAL ATTITUDES REGARDING RAPE[32]

[A] Social Harm of Rape

[1] The Original Perspective

The law of rape is rooted in ancient male concepts of property.[33] A virgin daughter was a valuable commodity owned by her father; a wife was a chattel of her husband. As a consequence, rape was a property offense. For example, according to one Biblical passage, the punishment for rape of a virgin daughter was fifty shekels, to be paid to her "owner" (the father), and forced marriage to the victim.[34]

The marital exemption, i.e., the doctrine that a husband is legally incapable of raping his wife, is a manifestation of the view that the husband "owned" sexual rights over his wife. According to this view, the husband had the right to sexual relations with his wife whenever he chose, regardless of her wishes.

[2] Modern Perspective

Lawmakers and feminist scholars have sought to provide a modern explanation of the loss suffered by rape victims. Generally speaking, rape is viewed today as a crime of violence and a privacy/autonomy offense. But, beyond this, controversy abounds.

The conception of rape as a crime of violence is easy to understand. Any rape involves, at a minimum, a battery of the female. When it is committed forcibly, it has all the earmarks of an aggravated battery. According to this view, the social harm of rape is not the sex act itself, but the way in which it is executed: violently. One scholar has gone so far as to claim that rape should be treated "as a variety of ordinary (simple or aggravated) battery because that is what rape is."[35]

However, rape surely involves more than bruises or breaks to the body.[36] Rape is a sexual invasion of the woman's body, in which her "private, personal

---

[32] See generally Michael Davis, *Setting Penalties: What Does Rape Deserve?*, 3 Law & Phil. 61 (1984); John Gardner & Stephen Shute, *The Wrongness of Rape, in* Oxford Essays in Jurisprudence 194 (4th Series 2000); Lynne Henderson, *Rape and Responsibility*, 11 Law & Phil. 127 (1992); Catherine A. MacKinnon, *Feminism, Marxism, Method, and the State: Toward Feminist Jurisprudence*, 8 Signs: J. Women Culture & Soc'y 635 (1983); Stephen J. Schulhofer, *Taking Sexual Autonomy Seriously: Rape Law and Beyond*, 11 Law & Phil. 35 (1992). See also the cites in Note 1, *supra*.

[33] Brownmiller, Note 1, *supra*, at 376; see generally, *id*. at 16-30.

[34] *Deuteronomy* 22:28-29.

[35] Davis, Note 32, *supra*, at 62-63.

[36] A male reader might imagine the experience of being sexually assaulted, for example, in a jail, by another inmate. It is unlikely that the male victim of such a forcible sexual assault would feel that he was *only* battered.

inner space" is violated without her consent.[37] It is an internal assault, an assault on her psyche, and a violation of the privacy of the victim. The act of rape denies the woman autonomy[38] by abridging her right to determine when, with whom, and how she will have sexual intimacy.[39] Perhaps as significantly, rape is a hostile, humiliating, degrading act of sexual domination by the man of the woman.[40]

[B] Perceptions of the Seriousness of the Offense

[1] In General

One's view of the social harm of rape largely determines that individual's perception of the seriousness of the crime. Although rape is considered a serious offense in all states, empirical evidence suggests that not all rapes are considered equally serious. Indeed, even if the force used in a sexual assault remains constant, the perceived character and background of the victim of the rape, and her relationship, if any, to the rapist, impacts attitudes regarding the severity of the crime.

---

[37] Brownmiller, Note 1, *supra*, at 376.

[38] Professor Anne Coughlin believes that none of the conventional explanations of rape law, including the autonomy concept, fully explains the offense as it is traditionally defined. She argues that rape laws were developed at a time when "sexuality was [decreed to be] a force so dangerous that it could not safely be left to self-regulation, but rather should be closely confined, by state law, within marital relationships." Coughlin, Note 1, *supra*, at 6. That is, sexual autonomy — by either sex — was *discouraged*, rather than *valued*. She claims that rape laws arose in a culture that also criminalized adultery and fornication, and she suggests that traditional rape law is explainable if one considers the efforts of that earlier society to regulate all forms of heterosexual intercourse outside the marital union. Because sexual autonomy now *is* valued, Coughlin reasons, rape law can be reshaped.

[39] One victim of rape — a harrowing three-hour sexual assault in her home — powerfully described her loss of autonomy this way:

> The rapist had violated my most basic human need — my bodyright. By destroying my ability to control my own body, he made my body an object. I lost a sense of it as the boundary of self, the fundamental and most scared of all borders. A self without boundaries is like a weak country that has been overrun by a stronger one.

Raine, Note 1, *supra*, at 163. She also wrote, at 206-07, that "[t]he most personal part of being raped had less to do with what happened to my body for three hours . . . , than with what happened to my spirit." She said she lost "faith that there is order and continuity in life. . . . To lose faith in life was, for me, the loss of connection with the intangible world — with soul, spirit, anima, essence, vital force, or what one chooses to call it. . . ."

[40] Brownmiller, Note 1, supra, at 376-78; see State v. Smith, 372 A.2d 386, 389-90 (N.J. Super. Ct. Law Div. 1977), rev'd, 426 A.2d 38 (N.J. 1981) ("Rape is necessarily and essentially an act of male self-aggrandizement. . . . Rape subjugates and humiliates the woman. . . ."). One commentator has described rape as an "act of terrorism" that keeps women dependent on men. Susan Griffin, *Rape: The All-American Crime*, *in* Rape Victimology 36 (L. Schultz ed. 1975).

[2] Blaming the Victim

Both men and women tend to attribute some blame for a rape to the victim, even when the circumstances of the assault do not suggest any causal responsibility on her part. To some extent, victim-blaming occurs with *all* offenses. One explanation for this phenomenon is that people psychically need to believe that the world is just. This belief is cast in doubt when innocent people are victims of crime. Therefore, when a person is victimized, the observer — and even the victim herself — wants to believe that the victim was partially responsible for her own fate.[41]

This phenomenon is exacerbated in rape cases. Various studies suggest that males and females, but especially males, assign significant weight for the occurrence of a rape to the character and behavior of the female victim.[42] For example, in one study,[43] college students were provided descriptions of two rapes. In each, the victim was forcibly attacked by a stranger, late at night, as she walked across campus following an evening college class. In one rape, however, the victim was described as a divorced, topless dancer, out of jail awaiting trial on a drug charge. The other victim was a married social worker.

In terms of gender, the study demonstrated that the respectability of the victim — her supposed character — affected male perceptions of responsibility for the crime. Males placed more blame for the crime on a victim's "low" character (the topless dancer) than did women. In contrast, females were more likely to attribute responsibility for the crime to the victim's behavior, e.g., walking home late at night (the same in both cases), and on matters of chance (simply being in the wrong place at the wrong time).

As might be expected from these findings, when the students were asked to assign a penalty to the rapists, men and women responded differently. The females assigned penalties virtually alike in the two cases, approximately forty-six years' imprisonment (on a 1 to 99 year scale). Male respondents were harsher than females in the case of the rape of the social worker, assigning an average penalty of fifty-four years. They were substantially more lenient, however, in setting the penalty for the rape of the topless dancer (an average eighteen years).

How do we explain the male view that the rape of a topless dancer is three times less serious (based on assigned penalties) than the rape of a social worker?

---

[41] See generally Melvin J. Lerner, *The Desire for Justice and Reactions to Victims, in* Altruism and Helping Behavior (J. Macaulay & L. Berkowitz eds., 1970).

[42] E.g., L.G. Calhoun et al., *The Effect of Victim Physical Attractiveness and Sex of Respondent on Social Reactions to the Victims of Rape*, 17 Brit. J. Soc. & Clinical Psychol. 191 (1978); James Luginbuhl & Courtney Mullin, *Rape and Responsibility: How and How Much Is the Victim Blamed?*, 7 Sex Roles 547 (1981); James W. Selby et al., *Sex Difference in the Social Perception of Rape Victims*, 3 Personality & Soc. Psychol. Bull. 412 (1977).

[43] Luginbuhl & Mullin, Note 42, *supra*.

In part, the answer is that in the minds of the male respondents, she was partially responsible for the rape; therefore, somewhat like a comparative negligence analysis in tort law, the penalty is mitigated.

There may be more. Arguably, some male respondents did not believe that there is as much social harm in raping a person of "low" sexual character than one of "high" character. That is, it is possible that the property aspect of traditional rape law has not entirely given way. To some males, females may still be sexual objects — "prizes" to be won by a male.[44] If so, it would follow that a woman who is believed to be sexually promiscuous is a less valuable prize than a woman of good sexual character.[45] The female respondents, however, focused on the victims' right to physical integrity and sexual autonomy. These interests are not impaired by the woman's sexual history.

[3] Victim's Relationship to Rapist

Other factors affect attitudes regarding rape. For example, in one now-dated study of public attitudes, rape of a stranger was considered a significantly more serious offense than rape of an acquaintance.[46] Respondents treated the forcible rape of a stranger in a park as an extremely serious crime, even more serious than the assassination of a public official. On the other hand, the forcible rape of a neighbor, although still a serious offense, was considered less egregious. Both of these cases, however, were perceived as significantly more serious than the forcible rape of a former wife, the latter offense of which was considered only slightly more serious than "driving while drunk" and "practicing medicine without a license."[47]

---

[44] Comment, *Forcible and Statutory Rape: An Exploration of the Operation and Objectives of the Consent Standard*, 62 Yale L.J. 55, 72 (1952) (suggesting that there exists "a masculine pride in the exclusive possession of a sexual object. The consent [of the female] . . . awards the man a privilege of bodily access, a personal 'prize' whose value is enhanced by sole ownership.") (footnotes deleted).

[45] United States v. Wiley, 492 F.2d 547, 555 (D.C. Cir. 1973) (Bazelon, J., concurring) (criticizing the view that penalties for rape "are high because a 'good' woman is a valued possession of a man").

[46] Peter H. Rossi et al., *The Seriousness of Crimes: Normative Structure and Individual Differences*, 39 Am. Soc. Rev. 224, 228-29 (1974).

[47] An attitudinal study of college students, beginning law students, and students who had taken a course in criminal law, found that the victim's relationship to the rapist was much less important than in the study reported in the text. See Joshua Dressler et al., *Effect of Legal Education Upon Perceptions of Crime Seriousness: A Response to Rummel v. Estelle*, 28 Wayne L. Rev. 1247 (1982). Students who had had a course in criminal law were least likely to consider this factor relevant.

§ 33.04 RAPE: *ACTUS REUS*

[A] In General

Generally speaking, sexual intercourse by a male, with a female not his wife, constitutes rape if it is committed: (1) forcibly; (2) by means of certain forms of deception; (3) while the female is asleep or unconscious;[48] or (4) upon a female incompetent to give consent (e.g., she is drugged, mentally disabled, or too young). The first two criteria are discussed below.

In forcible rape cases, which represent the vast majority of rape prosecutions, the law is undergoing significant change. It is useful, therefore, to distinguish between what might be characterized as traditional rape law and the more expansive definition of forcible rape developing in some jurisdictions.

[B] Forcible Rape

[1] Traditional Law

[a] In General

The traditional rule is that a successful prosecution for forcible rape requires proof that the female did not consent to the intercourse *and* that the sexual intercourse was by force. That is, where there is lack of consent, but no showing of force, a forcible rape conviction is inappropriate.[49]

As explained more fully below, the traditional position is that nonconsensual intercourse is "forcible" if the male uses or threatens to use force likely to cause serious bodily harm to the female (or, possibly, a third person[50]), or if the male uses sufficient force to overcome the female's physical resistance to his actions.

Intercourse secured by a *non*-physical threat does not ordinarily constitute forcible rape. Thus, traditionally it is not "forcible rape" for an adult guardian to threaten to recommit a fourteen-year-old girl to a juvenile detention facility if she does not submit to his advances,[51] or for a high school principal to threaten not to allow a senior to graduate unless she has sex with him.[52]

---

[48] State v. Moorman, 358 S.E.2d 502, 505 (N.C. 1987).

[49] Commonwealth v. Berkowitz, 641 A.2d 1161, 1164 (Pa. 1994); State v. Alston, 312 S.E.2d 470 (N.C. 1984).

[50] Fitzpatrick v. State, 558 P.2d 630, 631 (Nev. 1977).

[51] Commonwealth v. Mlinarich, 542 A.2d 1335 (Pa. 1988) (evenly divided opinion).

[52] State v. Thompson, 792 P.2d 1103 (Mont. 1990).

[b] Lack of Consent

Typically, the elements of nonconsent and force merge in a forcible rape prosecution. The male's use (or threatened use) of grave force proves both elements. Nonetheless, the two concepts are distinct. Two persons might freely consent to participate in sexual intercourse that, by any ordinary sense of the term, includes force (e.g., a mutually feigned rape). On the other hand, a female may not want sex — it is nonconsensual — but passively acquiesce to an act of penetration performed without undue force. Consequently, courts must determine whether consent, separate from force, exists.

Unfortunately, "consent" (or "nonconsent") is a concept of considerable complexity.[53] "Consent" may be understood as an attitudinal, or internal, state of mind. For example, a female may subjectively, in her mind, want intercourse (thus, intercourse was "consensual") or not want it (intercourse was "nonconsensual"), but fail to manifest her wishes objectively. Alternatively, "consent" may be an expressive, or external, concept: It exists when permission is given verbally or by some other external act by the party (a literal or figurative "yes"); it does not exist when permission is refused (a "no" or physical resistance). Unfortunately, courts and legislatures rarely clarify which version of "consent" renders intercourse lawful.[54] And, even if "consent" is regarded as an expressive concept, there remains the issue of how the law should deal with a female's silence. Should the legal onus be placed on the male to obtain affirmative permission, or on the female to deny it? Inevitably, this is a policy question that courts and legislatures have largely failed to address.

Three other "consent" issues may be noted here. First, the attitudinal version of "consent" necessarily can result in miscalculation by the male: He may honestly believe she wants intercourse when she does not, thereby raising *mens rea* issues.[55] The expressive form of consent is less ambiguous, but one cannot entirely avoid the questions of whether "no" always means "no,"[56] and whether "yes" always means "yes."

---

[53] See especially Peter Westen, *Some Common Confusions About Consent in Rape Cases*, 2 Ohio St. J. Crim. L. 333 (2004).

[54] But see State in the Interest of M.T.S., 609 A.2d 1266, 1277 (N..J. 1992) (interpreting "consent" to require proof of "affirmative and freely-given *permission* of the victim to the specific act of penetration") (emphasis added); Vt. Stat. Ann. tit. 13 § 3251(3) (2005) (defining "consent" as "words or actions by a person indicating a voluntary agreement to engage in a sexual act").

[55] See § 33.05, *infra*.

[56] See Charlene L. Muehlenhard & Lisa C. Hollabaugh, *Do Women Sometimes Say No When They Mean Yes? The Prevalence and Correlates of Women's Token Resistance to Sex*, 74 J. Personality & Soc. Psychol. 872 (1988) (finding that 39% of female respondents admitted putting up mild resistance although they intended to engage in intercourse). Particularly if mixed messages are sent with some frequency, males may interpret a "no" as a "yes" or "maybe," raising *mens rea* issues. See George C. Thomas III & David Edelman, *Consent to Have Sex: Empirical Evidence About "No,"* 61 U. Pitt. L. Rev. 579, 616 (2000) (concluding from 1992 and 1997 data that "remnants of the old view that women want sex more than they acknowledge" persists).

Second, "yes" may not always mean "yes" because consent, to be legally valid, must be voluntary; even if externalized, permission must be given freely. Unfortunately, the concept of voluntariness, or its antithesis of duress,[57] is largely a normative concept. In some sense all choices people make are "voluntary" (the woman who accedes to intercourse rather than be injured or killed has in some sense rationally "chosen" intercourse), and likewise are "involuntary" (even in a loving relationship, the women may feel psychological pressure from the circumstances to have intercourse), so the line between consensual and nonconsensual intercourse at the outer edges can be little more than a normative line drawn to distinguish between pressures a person should, and should not, be expected to resist.

Third, even if voluntary consent is granted, it may be withdrawn. If the female withdraws consent before intercourse occurs — *mens rea* issues aside — the male is guilty of rape if he proceeds forcibly to have sexual intercourse. But, what if the female withdraws consent *after* penetration but while the sexual act is proceeding? The traditional rule, apparently still adhered to in most states,[58] is that such late withdrawal of consent does not convert lawful intercourse into rape, even if the female physically resists the male at this point and the male uses force to overcome her resistance.[59] Conceptually, continued intercourse might constitute some lesser offense, such as a battery.

[c] Force and Resistance

Traditionally, courts rarely needed to define the term "force" in forcible rape prosecutions. If the perpetrator used or threatened to use extreme force, i.e., force likely or intended to cause serious injury or death, the element of "force" was (and is) uncontroversially satisfied.

Moreover, in a jurisdiction that applies traditional rape law, a rape conviction will not stand unless it is proven at trial that the female resisted the male's unwanted overtures "and her resistance was overcome by force or . . . she was prevented from resisting by threats to her safety."[60] Thus, even if a sexual encounter does not begin forcibly, or begins with only moderate use of force, the common law resistance requirement imposes on the female the obligation to physically respond in a manner that demonstrates her lack of consent and causes the perpetrator, if he intends to continue notwithstanding her physical

---

[57] See § 23.02[B], *supra*.

[58] See generally Matthew R. Lyon, Comment, *No Means No?: Withdrawal of Consent During Intercourse and the Continuing Evolution of the Definition of Rape*, 95 J. Crim. L. & Criminology 277, 291 (2004).

[59] But see People v. John Z., 60 P.3d 183 (Cal. 2003) (overruling prior case law and holding that late withdrawal of consent nullifies any earlier consent and subjects the male to forcible rape charges if he persists in what has become nonconsensual intercourse), overruling People v. Vela, 172 Cal. App. 3d 237 (Ct. App. 1985).

[60] Hazel v. State, 157 A.2d 922, 925 (Md. 1960).

expression of nonconsent, to use violence (or its threat) in order to overcome her will. It is the latter act by the male that satisfies the force element, if not already proven.

The resistance requirement has traditionally been expressed in different ways by courts. Some courts state that the victim must resist "to the utmost"; some courts only require enough resistance to make the female's lack of consent evident to the male; and still other courts require, simply, "reasonable" resistance under the circumstances.[61] In its most extreme form, the female must "follow the natural instinct of every proud female"[62] to resist the sexual attacker "until exhausted or overpowered,"[63] or resist "the attack in every way possible and continue[] such resistance until she [is] overcome by force, [is] insensible through fright, or cease[s] resistance from exhaustion, fear of death or great bodily harm."[64]

[d] Fear of Force versus Threat of Force

Forcible rape prosecutions may be based on a threat of serious force rather than its infliction. The threat may be verbal or nonverbal (e.g., waving a knife at the victim).[65]

In order for a forcible rape charge to be upheld on the basis of "threat of force," it is not ordinarily enough for the prosecution to show, simply, that the female *feared* serious bodily injury if she resisted. *Fear* is a subjective emotion — a feeling in the mind of the victim — whereas a *threat* is an objective act emanating from another person. In general, both components — the female's subjective apprehension of serious harm, and some conduct by the male that places her in *reasonable* apprehension for her safety — are required.[66] Thus, no forcible rape occurs if a female accedes to intercourse with a male simply "because he is bigger than she is and she is afraid of him."[67] Some courts go further and provide that a forcible rape prosecution is appropriate, even if the female's fears are unreasonable if the male "*knowingly* takes advantage of that fear in order to accomplish sexual intercourse."[68]

---

[61] Bryden, Note 1, *supra*, at 356-57.

[62] State v. Rusk, 424 A.2d 720, 733 (1981) (Cole, J., dissenting).

[63] People v. Dohring, 59 N.Y. 374, 386 (1874).

[64] King v. State, 357 S.W.2d 42, 45 (Tenn. 1962).

[65] People v. Barnes, 721 P.2d 110, 122 (Cal. 1986).

[66] See People v. Iniguez, 872 P.2d 1183, 1188 (Cal. 1994).

[67] People v. Kinney, 691 N.E.2d 867, 870 (Ill. Ct. App. 1998) (dictum); Farrar v. United States, 275 F.2d 868, 876 (D.C. Cir. 1959) ("[F]ear, to be sufficient [to constitute rape], must be based upon something of substance; and furthermore the fear must be of death or severe bodily harm. . . . She must have a reasonable apprehension, as I understand the law, of something real; her fear must be not fanciful but substantial.") (Prettyman, C.J., concurring in denial of rehearing en banc).

[68] People v. Barnes, 721 P.2d at 122 n.20 (emphasis added); see also American Law Institute, Comment to § 213.1, at 310 (recommending that "one who takes advantage of a woman's unreasonable fears of violence should not escape punishment . . .").

[e] Cases Applying the Traditional Doctrine

The strictness of the traditional definition of forcible rape is evident by considering three cases. In *Rusk v. State*,[69] V agreed to give R, a man she met at a bar,[70] a drive home. When they arrived, R invited V upstairs. When she refused, R took the keys from the ignition and asked, "Now will you come up?" V agreed: It was late at night; and, as she was in an unfamiliar neighborhood, she feared for her safety. Inside, R pulled her on the bed and began to remove her blouse. She took off the rest of her clothing when he asked her to do so. Throughout the process, V begged to be allowed to leave, and at one point, as he put his hands lightly on her throat, she asked R, "If I do what you want, will you let me go without killing me?" R said "yes," after which V "proceeded to do what he wanted me to do." R was convicted of forcible rape.

The Court of Special Appeals reversed R's conviction. It applied a traditional analysis to conclude that no forcible rape occurred: V did not physically resist R, nor did the evidence support the claim that she reasonably feared that if she had resisted R would have harmed her. This judgment was reversed, however, by the Court of Appeals, which more sensibly — and somewhat less traditionally — held that the "reasonableness of [V's] apprehension of fear [and, thus, her justification for not physically resisting] was plainly a question of fact for the jury to determine."

State v. Alston[71] provides an even more classic example of pre-reform rape law: A and V had participated in an abusive relationship, in which V sometimes had sexual relations with A "just to accommodate" his violent demands. On those occasions, V "would stand still and remain entirely passive while [A] undressed her and had intercourse with her."

At the time of the incident, V was living with her mother because she wanted out of the relationship. A telephoned her and demanded that V return to him. The next day, A grabbed V in a parking lot, and warned that he would "'fix'" her face "so that her mother could see he was not playing." A escorted V to a friend's house where they had had sexual relations in the past. Inside, A asked her if she was "ready." V said that she did not want to have sex with him, but when A told her to lie down on a bed, she complied, after which A pushed apart her legs and had intercourse. A was convicted of forcible rape.

The appellate court overturned the conviction. It held that there was sufficient evidence that V had not consented to the intercourse, but there was no evidence that A "used force or threats to overcome the will of the victim *to resist the*

---

[69] 406 A.2d 624 (Md. Ct. Spec. App. 1979), reversed, 424 A.2d 720 (Md. 1981).

[70] The Maryland Court of Special Appeals stated V was "bar hopping." *Rusk*, 406 A.2d at 477. As Judge Wilner in dissent suggested, the court may have intended by this language to suggest that V was "on the make." *Id*. at 492.

[71] 312 S.E.2d 470 (N.C. 1984).

sexual intercourse." That is, in a remarkable "example of narrow time-framing and psychological naivete,"[72] the court discounted *V*'s reasonable fear of *A* that was based on his prior use of force, and even ignored his specific threat to "fix" her face because it was not linked directly to a demand for sexual intercourse on the present occasion.

Finally, consider *Commonwealth v. Berkowitz*,[73] a case involving sexual intercourse between two college students in the victim's dormitory room. *B*, who was a friend of *V*'s roommate, came by and, after some conversation, asked *V* to give him a back rub. She refused. While *V* was sitting on the floor, *B* came over and "kind of pushed" *V* down. She described it as a "leaning-type of thing." On the floor, *B* straddled *V*, lifted up her shirt and bra, and began fondling *V*. At various times, *V* objected. *B* unsuccessfully attempted to put his penis in *V*'s mouth. Although *V* did not physically resist, she continued to say "no." *B* got off, locked the door (although it could be opened freely from the inside), and then put *V* on the bed ("kind of like a push"), straddled her, and had intercourse. *V* did not physically resist or cry out. *B* was convicted of forcible rape.

The conviction was overturned. As in *Alston*, there was no consent, but "[i]n regard to the critical issue of forcible compulsion, [*V*'s] testimony [was] devoid of any statement which clearly or adequately describes the use of force or the threat of force against her."[74] As for *V*'s repeated "no's," the state supreme court stated that "while such an allegation of fact would be relevant to the issue of consent, it is not relevant to the issue of force."

Thus, these three cases provide the following clues to the traditional rule in rape cases. First, nonconsent and force are not synonymous. Second, in order to prove force, the female must physically (not merely verbally) resist the male ("no" is not enough), or the male must use or threaten force on the present occasion to an extent that would cause a reasonable female to fear grievous injury if she were to resist sexual intercourse.

---

[72] Dressler, Note 1, *supra*, at 418.

[73] 609 A.2d 1338 (Pa. Super. Ct. 1992), aff'd, 641 A.2d 1161 (Pa. 1994).

[74] *Berkowitz*, 641 A.2d at 1164.

[2] The Law in Transition[75]

[a] Resistance Requirement

As explained above,[76] the common law developed a resistance requirement in forcible rape cases. This resistance requirement has been sharply criticized by some modern courts and many scholars. First, "studies have demonstrated that while some women respond to sexual assault with active resistance, others 'freeze'" and "become helpless from panic and numbing fear."[77] Indeed, some women "do what they were taught to do as girls — to remain passive in the face of a rapist. . . ."[78] Therefore, whether out of fear or training, many females do not resist and, as a consequence, cannot see their attackers successfully prosecuted for forcible rape in jurisdictions strictly enforcing the resistance rule.

Second, resisting a rapist can prove dangerous.[79] Although a female who resists a sexual assault may be less likely to be raped than one who takes no self-protective measures, substantial resistance increases the risk of aggravated injury to the female confronting a determined rapist.

It is difficult to measure the extent to which the resistance rule is eroding. It has been written that "[t]he legal requirement that a woman strongly resist a man's sexual advances to prove that she was raped has largely disappeared from the statute books."[80] And, "[i]n recent decades, statutory reforms nominally have eroded the resistance requirement."[81] But, notice the careful words selected in the preceding quotations: The rule that a female "strongly resist" (what about lesser resistance?) has "largely disappeared" (but not entirely?) from "the statute books" (but what about case law?); and legislative reform has "nominally eroded" the resistance rule.

---

[75] See generally Schulhofer, Unwanted Sex, Note 1, *supra*; Michelle J. Anderson, *Reviving Resistance in Rape Law*, 1998 U. Ill. L. Rev. 953; Vivian Berger, *Rape Law Reform at the Millennium: Remarks on Professor Bryden's Non-Millennial Approach*, 3 Buff. Crim. L. Rev. 513 (2000); Bryden, Note 1, *supra*; Dressler, Note 1, *supra*; Donald A. Dripps, *Beyond Rape: An Essay on the Difference Between the Presence of Force and the Absence of Consent*, 92 Colum. L. Rev. 1780 (1992); Lois Pineau, *Date Rape: A Feminist Analysis*, 8 Law & Phil. 217 (1989); Robin L. West, *Legitimating the Illegitimate: A Comment on Beyond Rape*, 93 Colum. L. Rev. 1442 (1993).

[76] See § 33.04[B][1][c], *supra*.

[77] People v. Barnes, 721 P.2d 110, 119 (Cal. 1986).

[78] Anderson, Note 75, *supra*, at 958.

[79] Schulhofer, Unwanted Sex, Note 1, *supra*, at 19.

[80] Anderson, Note 75, *supra*, at 953 (emphasis deleted) (syllabus to the article).

[81] Bryden, Note 1, *supra*, at 357.

A few jurisdictions by statute[82] or common law interpretation[83] have abolished the resistance requirement. Although many states seemingly retain the resistance requirement — it was a common law embellishment of the statutory force requirement — the trend is to reduce the significance of the rule by lowering the barrier. Today, states rarely require a female to physically resist her attacker "to the utmost" and instead require only "earnest" resistance, or resistance sufficient "to establish that an act of sexual intercourse was without consent and by force,"[84] or resistance that is "reasonable" under the circumstances.[85]

Even as courts and legislatures abolish or soften the resistance rule, a female's resistance — or lack thereof — has not lost its relevance in rape prosecutions. Consider a Pennsylvania statute that provides: "The alleged victim need not resist the actor in prosecutions under this chapter [on sexual offenses]: Provided, however, That nothing in this section shall be construed to prohibit a defendant from introducing evidence that the alleged victim consented to the conduct in question."[86] That is, although substantial resistance may no longer be an essential element in a rape prosecution, it retains evidentiary significance: Proof of the female's resistance may be critical to the prosecutor in proving beyond a reasonable doubt that a rape has occurred, i.e., that the intercourse was forcible and nonconsensual and/or that the defendant was on reasonable notice (possessed the requisite *mens rea*) of the female's lack of consent.

[b] "Force": Changing Its Definition (or Abolishing the Requirement)

Consider the following judicial observation:

> [T]he fundamental wrong at which the law of rape is aimed is not the application of physical force that causes physical harm. Rather, the law of rape primarily guards the integrity of a woman's will and the privacy of her sexuality from an act of intercourse undertaken without her consent. Because the fundamental wrong is the violation of a woman's will and sexuality, the law of rape does not require that "force" cause physical harm. Rather, . . . "force" plays merely a supporting evidentiary

---

[82] E.g., Mich. Comp. Laws. § 750.520i (2005) ("A victim need not resist the actor in prosecution [for rape].").

[83] E.g., People v. Barnes, 721 P.2d at 121 ("This court therefore concludes that the Legislature's purposes in amending [the rape statute] were (1) to relieve the state of the need to establish resistance as a prerequisite to a rape conviction, and (2) to release rape complainants from the potentially dangerous burden of resisting an assailant in order to substantiate allegations of forcible rape.").

[84] Anderson, Note 75, *supra*, at 964.

[85] See generally *id*. at 962-68.

[86] 18 Pa. Cons. Stat. § 3107 (2005).

role, as necessary only to insure an act of intercourse has been undertaken against a victim's will.[87]

This statement expresses the reformist belief that the common law definition of rape, which requires proof of force *and* lack of consent, should be abandoned. Under an autonomy and privacy approach, the only real issue should be whether the female desired intercourse. According to this view, just as resistance should no longer be an element of the offense — it should only be an evidentiary factor that helps determine whether there was lack of consent — so, too, a male's use of force should simply be one way of showing that the female did not consent.

Of course, legislatures can amend their rape statutes, as some have done, to define various forms of nonforcible intercourse as rape.[88] Once they start down this path, the critical issues become: (a) Should all forms of nonconsensual intercourse be criminalized?; (b) How should "non-consent" be proved, without re-instituting *sub silentio* the requirements of force and resistance?; and (c) Should some or all nonforcible forms of prohibited nonconsensual intercourse be graded as a lower degree of rape than the forcible variety?

In states that maintain the statutory requirement of force, problems have newly arisen. At common law, "force" was largely defined in terms of the female's resistance. As courts abolish or soften the "resistance" rule, it becomes necessary to redefine "force." Some courts have redefined the term broadly to include minor physical acts[89] and/or *non*-physical forms of coercion.[90] Still other courts have left the term undefined and invited juries to resolve the issue of force without judicial assistance, or have defined "force" in a manner that essentially reads the element out of the statute, leaving the requirement of nonconsent.

---

[87] People v. Cicero, 157 Cal. App. 3d 465, 475 (Ct. App. 1984); see also Regina v. Park, [1995] 2 S.C.R. 836, 839 ("The primary concern animating and underlying the present offence of sexual assault is the belief that women have an inherent right to exercise full control over their own bodies, and to engage only in sexual activity that they wish to engage in").

[88] One statute make it an offense *either* to "compel the other person to participate in a sexual act without the consent of the other person" or to "compel" the act "by threatening or coercing the other person." Vt. Stat. Ann. tit. 13 § 3252(a)(1)(A)-(B) (2005). It is unclear what the word "compel" adds to the first provision — that it be without consent — but the Vermont sexual assault statute apparently treats nonconsensual sexual intercourse as an offense without proof of force.

[89] E.g., State v. Brown, 420 S.E.2d 147, 152 (N.C. 1992) (in a hospital setting, the court held that *B*'s "actions in pulling back the bedclothing, pulling up the victim's gown, and pulling her panties aside amounted to actual physical 'force' as that term is to be applied in sexual offense cases").

[90] E.g., Commonwealth v. Rhodes, 510 A.2d 1217, 1226 (Pa. 1986) (interpreting the statutory term "forcible compulsion" to include "not only physical force or violence but also moral, psychological or intellectual force used to compel a person to engage in sexual intercourse against that person's will").

For example, in *People v. Griffin*,[91] the California Supreme Court stated that there is nothing "in the common usage definitions of the term 'force,' or in the express statutory language . . . that suggests force . . . actually means force '*substantially* different from or *substantially* greater than' the physical force normally inherent in an act of consensual sexual intercourse." As "force" has "a common usage meaning," *Griffin* holds, "there is no sua sponte duty to specially instruct the jury in a rape case on the definition of that term." Thus, in California, "the prosecution need only show the defendant used physical force of a degree sufficient to support a finding that the act of sexual intercourse was against the will of the [victim]."[92]

California arguably requires somewhat more force — just not *substantially* more force — than is inherent in the sexual act itself. But, a forcible rape prosecution is now possible in at least one jurisdiction *solely* on the basis of the female's lack of permission for the sexual intercourse.[93] The New Jersey Supreme Court ruled in *State in the Interest of M.T.S.*[94] that a person is guilty of forcible sexual assault under the statute if he commits an act of sexual penetration of another person[95] in the absence of affirmative and freely-given permission, either express or implied, for the specific act of penetration. Without such permission, *any* force used, *even the force inherent in the sexual act itself*, justifies a forcible rape prosecution. Thus, under *M.T.S.*, the female is not required to say "no" or physically resist in order to convert lawful sexual intercourse into rape. Nor may the male avoid conviction by proving, simply, that the female concurred in mind and spirit with having intercourse. The key word in *M.T.S.* is "permission."[96] A male commits forcible rape under *M.T.S.* if he has intercourse without securing a "yes" in words or action before proceeding.

M.T.S. is questionable as a matter of statutory construction,[97] but it is consistent with the underlying principle set out at the beginning of this subsection, namely, that the core purpose of modern rape law is to protect the sexual autonomy of the female. The underlying reasoning of *M.T.S.* seems to be this: Just as a person is not required to say "no" when a thief takes her property — a thief cannot successfully claim, "I had the right to take *V*'s unlocked car because she did not object when I entered her car and drove away" — a female should not be

---

[91] 94 P.3d 1089, 1094 (Cal. 2004).

[92] *Id.* (quoting People v. Young, 190 Cal. App. 3d 248, 257-58 (Ct. App. 1987)).

[93] Vermont also seems to criminalize intercourse that is merely nonconsensual, but it does not characterize the offense as *forcible* rape or *forcible* sexual assault. See Note 88, *supra*.

[94] 609 A.2d 1266 (N.J. 1992).

[95] The sexual assault statute is gender-neutral as to the victim. For purposes of clarity, however, the discussion in the text will assume that the victim is female.

[96] Thus, New Jersey requires expressive, not attitudinal, consent. See § 33.04[B][1][b], *supra*.

[97] The statute requires proof of "force or coercion"; "lack of consent" is not an express element. The practical effect of the case, however, is to write "force or coercion" out of the statute, and to replace it with an affirmative permission requirement.

required to object even verbally to the male's sexual advances in order to render a subsequent sexual act of penetration criminally punishable.

As might be expected, *M.T.S.* has adherents and critics.[98] But, if *M.T.S.* is going to be followed, a number of difficult issues remain to be decided. First, what conduct short of an express "yes" is sufficient to prove permission? In *M.T.S.*, two teenagers were involved in consensual "kissing and heavy petting," but the female did not give permission for the *specific* act of sexual penetration, and it was *this* failure that rendered the defendant teenager's actions violative of the forcible rape statute, as interpreted by *M.T.S.* So, again, what *will* suffice short of express permission to have sexual intercourse?

Second, as permission must be given freely, the courts must determine what conduct renders permission tainted. For example, if a female consents to intercourse with her male employer in order to avoid a wrongful reduction in her salary, is this freely-given consent? Does it matter whether the salary reduction is substantial or trivial? Suppose that a female gives permission because he offers her a raise to which she would not otherwise be entitled? Various rules come to mind. First, the rule could be that permission is invalid if it is secured as the result of *any* illegal or tortious act by the male, regardless of whether it has a coercive effect on the female. Second, the standard could be that permission is tainted if it is the result of a threat or offer that would cause a person of reasonable firmness to grant permission. Third, the latter standard could apply but be limited to threats. As Professor Stephen Schulhofer has observed, *M.T.S.* does not ultimately resolve the problem of "identifying the boundary between autonomy and compulsion, between free choice and coerced consent. The innovative New Jersey test, though seemingly straightforward, obscures the problem rather than addressing it."[99]

[C] Fraud[100]

At common law, a seducer is not a rapist.[101] That is, a male may use any nonforcible "sales technique," no matter how deceptive, to obtain the consent of a female to sexual intercourse, and escape criminal punishment as a rapist.[102] It is not common law rape, for example, for *D*, a look-alike of a famous actor, to induce *V* to have intercourse with him by claiming to be the actor. It is not

---

[98] E.g., Schulhofer, Unwanted Sex, Note 1, *supra*, at 94-98 (stating it offers clear benefits, but with reservations); Dressler, Note 1, *supra*, at 422-30 (mostly critical).

[99] Schulhofer, Unwanted Sex, Note 1, *supra*, at 97-98.

[100] See generally Vivian Berger, *Not So Simple Rape*, Crim. Just. Ethics, Winter/Spring 1988, at 69; Bryden, Note 1, *supra*, at 457-75; Dressler, Note 1, *supra*, at 439-42; Patricia J. Falk, *Rape by Fraud and Rape by Coercion*, 64 Brooklyn L. Rev. 39 (1998).

[101] People v. Evans, 379 N.Y.S.2d 912, 919 (N.Y. App. Div. 1975).

[102] Obtaining sexual intercourse by fraudulent inducement may constitute an offense less serious than rape. E.g., Cal. Penal Code § 266 (2005) (procuring female for illicit intercourse by false pretenses; punishable by incarceration not exceeding one year).

common law rape for *D* to pay for intercourse with a prostitute with counterfeit money, or for a doctor to induce a woman to have intercourse with him by falsely claiming that it will cure her of an illness.[103] Each of these examples have one fact in common — the victim knew that she was consenting to sexual intercourse. The fraud was in the *inducement* to have intercourse.

In contrast, a female's consent to engage in sexual intercourse is invalid if, as a result of fraud, she is unaware that she has consented to the act of sexual intercourse — so-called "fraud in the factum," to distinguish it from "fraud in the inducement." For example, *D*, a male physician, is guilty of rape if, by so-called "fraud-in-the-factum," he obtains consent from *V*, a female patient, to "insert an instrument" in her vagina while she is under anaesthesia, if the "instrument" used is his penis.[104]

Courts have struggled with the question of how to deal with a male who engages in sexual intercourse by deceiving a woman into believing that he is her husband or unmarried sexual partner. For example, suppose that *D* enters *V*'s bed at night in the dark, under circumstances in which *D* knows that *V* believes that he is her husband. If she has intercourse with him, is it rape? Some early English cases treated this as fraud-in-the-inducement, since the victim knew that she was consenting to sexual intercourse.[105] Most courts, however, apparently now treat this deception as fraud-in-the-factum (and, therefore, rape), on the ground that the attendant circumstance that the male was not the female's husband is a fundamental aspect of the sexual act.[106] Intercourse with one's spouse is inherently a different "factum" than intercourse with a stranger. Seemingly, it should constitute rape to impersonate anyone with whom the victim has been consensually sexually intimate.[107]

If the law of rape is meant to protect a woman's sexual autonomy, should all forms of fraud-in-the-inducement vitiate consent? The question poses difficult matters of line-drawing and policy. For example, if fraud converts every induced act of sexual intercourse into rape, a person would be subject to prosecution if, allegedly, he falsely claimed love or promised marriage in order to secure the other's consent to intercourse. Prosecutions in such circumstances would result

---

[103] Don Moran v. People, 25 Mich. 356 (1872); see Boro v. Superior Court, 163 Cal. App. 3d 1224 (Ct. App. 1985) (*B* falsely claimed to *V* that he was a doctor, that she had contracted a dangerous, perhaps fatal, disease, and that the only way to treat the disease was through surgery or sexual intercourse with an anonymous donor injected with a serum; *V* agreed to the latter "cure"; *B* had sexual intercourse with *V*; held: charge of rape, based on a rape statute that prohibited intercourse "[w]here a person is at the time unconscious of the nature of the act," dismissed on the ground that *B* committed fraud-in-the-inducement; *V* was conscious of the nature of the act to which she had consented).

[104] See Pomeroy v. State, 94 Ind. 96 (1883).

[105] E.g., Regina v. Barrow, 11 Cox Crim. Cas. 191 (1868).

[106] Regina v. Dee, 15 Cox Crim. Cas. 579 (1884).

[107] Schulhofer, Unwanted Sex, Note 1, *supra*, at 284; R. v. Elbekkay, [1995] Crim. L. R. 163 (impersonation of *V*'s boyfriend to secure intercourse constitutes rape).

in serious problems of proof, and would expend finite judicial resources to deal with failed relationships. As Professor Martha Chamallas has observed, "the most common risk in any sexual relationship is the risk that one party will end the relationship unilaterally. . . ."[108] Quite arguably, the law should not require a person who ends a relationship to bear the risk of a felony rape prosecution in such circumstances.

On the other hand, what if a man fraudulently claims that he is sterile,[109] or what if he fails to disclose that he has a communicable disease,[110] in order to secure consent to intercourse? Some argue that cases of this sort should be resolved, as they are now, in tort actions. And, when the physical harm resulting from fraud is substantial, there may be adequate means to bring the male to justice, e.g., a prosecution for aggravated battery, reckless endangerment, or even attempted murder. The contrary claim is that these prosecutions do not directly redress the victim's interest in sexual autonomy. If fraud in a business context can result in a theft prosecution, the argument proceeds, fraud in this context should result in a sexual assault prosecution, albeit of a lesser degree of the offense than if force were used.

§ 33.05 RAPE: *MENS REA*[111]

Rape is ordinarily denominated as a general-intent offense in non-Model Penal Code jurisdictions.[112] As such, a defendant need not possess an intention that sexual intercourse be nonconsensual.[113] He is guilty of rape if he possessed a morally blameworthy state of mind regarding the female's lack of consent.[114] Therefore, the general rule is that a person is not guilty of rape if he entertained a genuine *and reasonable* belief that the female voluntarily con-

---

[108] Martha Chamallas, *Consent, Equality, and the Legal Control of Sexual Conduct*, 61 S. Cal. L. Rev. 777, 834 (1988).

[109] E.g., Barbara A. v. John G., 145 Cal. App. 3d 369 (Ct. App. 1983) (battery and deceit action, in tort, resulting from pregnancy based on the defendant's claim of sterility).

[110] Kathleen K. v. Robert B., 150 Cal. App. 3d 992 (Ct. App. 1984) (civil suit, based on defendant's false claim that he did not have a venereal disease); R. v. Cuerrier, 162 D.L.R.4th 513 (1998) (Canadian Supreme Court: *C* may be prosecuted for aggravated assault for having unprotected sexual relations, knowing he was HIV-positive, and without disclosing this fact to *V*).

[111] See generally Rosanna Cavallaro, *A Big Mistake: Eroding the Defense of Mistake of Fact About Consent in Rape*, 86 J. Crim. L. & Criminology 815 (1996); Robin Charlow, *Bad Acts in Search of a Mens Rea: Anatomy of a Rape*, 71 Fordham L. Rev. 263 (2002); Victoria J. Dettmar, *Culpable Mistakes in Rape: Eliminating the Defense of Unreasonable Mistake of Fact as to Victim Consent*, 89 Dick. L. Rev. 473 (1984); R.A. Duff, *Recklessness and Rape*, 3 Liverpool L. Rev. 49 (1981); Douglas N. Husak & George C. Thomas III, *Date Rape, Social Convention, and Reasonable Mistakes*, 11 Law & Phil. 95 (1992).

[112] Steve v. State, 875 P.2d 110, 115 (Alaska Ct. App. 1994); State v. Cantrell, 673 P.2d 1147, 1154 (Kan. 1983).

[113] Commonwealth v. Grant, 464 N.E.2d 33, 36 (Mass. 1984).

[114] A less common issue is what *mens rea*, if any, is required as to the element of force. In this regard, see Kit Kinports, *Rape and Force: The Forgotten Mens Rea*, 4 Buff. Crim. L. Rev. 755 (2001).

sented to intercourse with him.[115] This rule conforms with ordinary common law mistake-of-fact principles relating to general-intent offenses.[116]

In recent years, some American jurisdictions have ruled that even a defendant's *reasonable* mistake of fact regarding the female's lack of consent is *not* a "defense."[117] In contrast, in England, the defendant's honest but *unreasonable* mistake of fact *does* exculpate if he was not reckless in his belief.[118]

It is submitted that the American trend is disquieting. In traditional forcible rape cases, the issue of *mens rea* rarely arises. A male of normal intelligence who uses or threatens force likely to cause serious bodily injury will almost always know that the female is not consenting, so his culpability is obvious. Furthermore, if the female resists her assailant, her lack of consent is even more clearly demonstrated. But, with the expansion of rape law to include intercourse secured in the absence of grave force or resistance, particularly in the acquaintance rape context, the issue of *mens rea* becomes more critical. If a male genuinely *and reasonably* believes that the female is consenting, then he is acting without moral culpability. The effect of dispensing with the reasonable-mistake-of-fact doctrine is, effectively, to convert rape, a felony carrying very severe penalties, into a strict liability offense.[119]

Even in states that permit a reasonable-mistake-of-fact defense, it may become more difficult in the future for a defendant to secure a jury instruction in this regard. The California Supreme Court, for example, recently ruled that

---

[115] E.g., People v. Stitely, 108 P.3d 182, 208 (Cal. 2005); State v. Smith, 554 A.2d 713, 717 (Conn. 1989); State in the Interest of M.T.S., 609 A.2d 1266, 1279 (N.J. 1992) ("[T]he State must demonstrate either that defendant did not actually believe that affirmative permission had been freely-given or that such a belief was unreasonable under all of the circumstances."); United States v. Everett, 41 M.J. 847, 852 (A.F.C.M.R. 1994).

[116] See § 12.03[D], *supra*.

[117] Commonwealth v. Ascolillo, 541 N.E.2d 570, 575 (Mass. 1989); Clifton v. Commonwealth, 468 S.E.2d 155, 158 (Va. Ct. App. 1996); see Commonwealth v. Williams, 439 A.2d 765, 769 (Pa. Super. Ct. 1980) ("The charge requested by the defendant [that a reasonable belief that the female consented is a defense] is not now and has never been the law of Pennsylvania. The crux of the offense of rape is force and lack of victim's consent. . . . If the element of the defendant's belief as to the victim's state of mind is to be established as a defense to the crime of rape then it should be done by our legislature which has the power to define crimes and offenses. We refuse to create such a defense."); Charlow, Note 111, *supra*, at 281 n.68 (providing further citations). The word "defense" as used here is a misnomer if rape is a general-intent offense. In such circumstances, "mistake-of-fact" is a failure-of-proof defense. See § 16.02, *supra*.

[118] Regina v. Morgan, [1976] A.C. 182; see Sexual Offenses (Amendment) Act of 1976 (permitting conviction on the basis of knowledge or recklessness as to the victim's lack of consent). See § 12.03[D][4], *supra*.

[119] One court has defended the no-defense rule by arguing that "proof of rape requires proof of intent, . . . [namely,] proof that the accused knowingly and intentionally committed the acts constituting the elements of rape." Clifton v. Commonwealth, 468 S.E.2d at 158. But, of course, the act in question — sexual intercourse — is not a wrongful act in itself, nor is knowingly and intentionally having intercourse in itself the crime of rape. The "act" that is wrongful is a nonconsensual (and, perhaps, forcible) act of intercourse. When the defendant reasonably believes that the other person consented, he is not committing the "act" of rape knowingly and intelligently.

a "reasonable mistake" instruction should not be given in a criminal case unless there is "substantial evidence of equivocal conduct [on the female's part] that would have led a defendant to reasonably and in good faith believe consent existed where it did not."[120] According to this rule, where there is an evidentiary chasm — the defendant says she consented, whereas the female claims a forcible rape occurred, and no evidence is introduced of equivocal conduct by the female that the defendant could mistake for consent — a mistake-of-fact instruction is inappropriate.

§ 33.06 MARITAL IMMUNITY RULE[121]

[A] The Immunity and Its Rationales

[1] Rule

In 1736, Sir Matthew Hale stated that a "husband cannot be guilty of rape committed by himself upon his lawful wife."[122] He cited no authority for this proposition as, indeed, there was none.[123] Nonetheless, the so-called marital immunity rule became a part of the common law, and was adopted by most American legislatures as part of the original definition of rape.

[2] Rationales

[a] Consent/Property Rationale

According to Hale, "by their matrimonial consent and contract the wife hath given up herself in this kind unto her husband, which she cannot retract."[124] However, the concept of irrevocable consent by the wife makes little sense in modern times, if it ever did. The general understanding of marital partners today is that each person consents generally to have sexual intercourse with the other, subject to the right of either to refuse on particular occasions. Moreover,

---

[120] People v. Williams, 841 P.2d 961, 966 (Cal. 1992); see also R. v. Park, [1994] 2 S.C.R. 836 (there must be an "air of reality" to the mistake claim).

[121] See generally Diana H. Russell, Rape in Marriage (Rev. ed. 1990); Melisa J. Anderson, Note, *Lawful Wife, Unlawful Sex — Examining the Effect of the Criminalization of Marital Rape in England and the Republic of Ireland*, 27 Ga. J. Int'l & Comp. L. 139 (1998); Michelle J. Anderson, *Marital Immunity, Intimate Relationships, and Improper Inferences: A New Law on Sexual Offenses by Intimates*, 54 Hastings L.J. 1465 (2003); Lisa R. Eskow, Note, *The Ultimate Weapon?: Demythologizing Spousal Rape and Reconceptualizing Its Prosecution*, 48 Stan. L. Rev. 677 (1996); Jill Elaine Hasday, *Contest and Consent: A Legal History of Marital Rape*, 88 Calif. L. Rev. 1373 (2000).

[122] 1 Hale, Note 2, *supra*, at *629.

[123] Regina v. R., [1991] 4 All E.R. 481, 483 ("There is no similar statement in the works of any earlier English commentator.").

[124] 1 Hale, Note 2, *supra*, at *629.

if a husband uses force to secure intercourse with his wife, he is subject to prosecution for assault or battery; the principle of consent does not carry over to these offenses, so there is no reason why consent should be assumed in the rape context.

The more accurate explanation of the common law marital immunity rule is that the wife was the virtual property of the husband.[125] She was "incorporated and consolidated into that of the husband."[126] Therefore, the husband possessed an unlimited right of sexual access to her.

[b] Protection of the Marriage

Defenders of the marital immunity rule sometimes argue that it is needed to protect "against governmental intrusion into marital privacy," and to promote "reconciliation of the spouses."[127]

This argument vastly overstates the case for the immunity. If a husband's use of force to have intercourse with his wife is an isolated act in an otherwise salvageable marriage, it is unlikely that the wife would seek a rape prosecution of her husband. On the other hand, if the husband is guilty of ongoing physical and sexual abuse, the marriage presumably is not worth saving; at the least, it should be the woman's decision whether to try to preserve it or, instead, seek prosecution. Beyond this, the interest in protecting the safety of the woman certainly outweighs the privacy concern.

[c] Protection of the Husband in Divorce Proceedings

Some advocates of the marital exemption rule assert that if a husband could be prosecuted for rape of his wife, she might use this threat as leverage in property settlement negotiations in divorce proceedings.

This argument is unpersuasive. There is no reason to believe that a woman's ability to take unfair advantage of her husband would be significantly heightened by the repeal of the marital immunity rule. Even in jurisdictions that apply the exemption, a husband may be prosecuted for assault or battery if he uses force to secure intercourse; therefore, a wife could always use the threat of prosecution for these offenses as leverage. Beyond this, it is odd at best for the law to take sides with a wrongdoer against his victim on the unproven assumption that the victims, as a group, will behave improperly in civil proceedings.

---

[125] American Law Institute, Comment to § 213.1, at 343.

[126] 1 Blackstone, Note 3, *supra*, at *430.

[127] People v. Liberta, 474 N.E.2d 567, 574 (N.Y. 1984) (rejecting the argument).

[d] Less Serious Harm

Some advocates of the marital immunity doctrine contend that the existence of the marital relationship "is not irrelevant to the concerns of the law of rape."[128] They reason that an important aspect of the harm of rape is the degradation of the woman that results from forcing her to have sexual intimacy with someone with whom she does not wish such a relationship. Although a female's sexual autonomy, as a male's, should include the right to refuse sexual relations on any given occasion, the marital relationship implies a general willingness — indeed, desire — by the parties to have intercourse with each other. When intercourse is coerced on a given occasion in the marital relationship, the argument proceeds, the wife's autonomy is less seriously violated than if the perpetrator were a stranger or someone with whom the victim had not indicated a general willingness to have sexual relations.

This argument has the aroma of plausibility in the case of nonforcible rape. Nonetheless, there are important reasons for treating nonconsensual sexual intercourse in the marital bedroom as a form of rape. Even in the marriage context, rape causes harm not protected by the laws of assault and battery. Spousal rape impairs the wife's sexual autonomy; and, particularly if the husband's conduct is ongoing, the sex act by the husband becomes a means of subordinating the wife within the marital relationship. Spousal rape is also a violation of the trust and mutual respect implicit in the marital union. These special violations should be denounced by the law, and the offense of rape is better suited to do this than the laws of assault and battery.

[B] Breakdown of the Rule

The marital immunity rule was judicially abolished in England in 1991.[129]

The law in the United States is in transition. According to one fairly recent survey,[130] twenty-four states (and the District of Columbia) have abolished the rule for all sexual offenses. Among the remaining states, some jurisdictions have abolished marital immunity for the specific offense of forcible rape, while retaining immunity for other sexual offenses, such as intercourse with a mentally or physically helpless spouse, as well as with lesser forms of nonconsensual sexual contact. Often, however, when there is a marital immunity rule, it does not apply if the parties are legally separated or living apart at the time of the rape.[131]

---

[128] American Law Institute, Comment to § 213.1, at 344.

[129] Regina v. R., [1991] 4 All E.R. 481.

[130] Anderson, *Marital Immunity, Intimate Relationships*, Note 121, *supra*, at 1468-73, 1486-89 (and citations therein).

[131] *Id*. at 1494-95.

§ 33.07 PROVING RAPE AT TRIAL

[A] Corroboration Rule and Cautionary Jury Instructions[132]

At common law, the testimony of the "prosecutrix" — the alleged rape victim — was sufficient to uphold a conviction for rape; her testimony did not need to be corroborated.[133] However, a minority of states, by statute or case law, have instituted a corroboration requirement. Such a rule provides that a defendant may not be convicted of rape (or, often, of any other sex offense) upon the uncorroborated testimony of the alleged victim.

The corroboration requirement is the result of "legitimate concerns, outdated beliefs, and deep-seated prejudices."[134] Defenders of the rule believe that there is a higher risk of conviction of an innocent person in the prosecution of a sex offense than in the prosecution of other crimes. Lord Hale asserted that rape "is an accusation easily to be made and hard to be proved, and harder to be defended by the party accused, though never so innocent."[135] These words or a paraphrase of them have commonly formed the basis of a cautionary jury instruction given at the conclusion of rape trials in over half of the states.[136] In recent years, however, various courts have jettisoned the cautionary instruction.[137]

Why would some lawmakers believe that conviction of an innocent person is more likely in a rape case than, for example, a robbery? Some of the reasons given are based on entrenched notions of sexuality that suggest that the testimony of a woman in a rape prosecution is particularly suspect.[138] According to this view, some women fantasize being raped and, therefore, genuinely come to believe that they were raped, when in fact the sexual contact was consensual.[139]

---

[132] See generally Denise R. Johnson, *Prior False Allegations of Rape: Falso in Uno, Falsus in Omnibus?*, 7 Yale J.L. & Feminism 243 (1995); Laurie Edelstein, *An Accusation Easily to be Made? Rape and Malicious Prosecution in Eighteenth-Century England*, 42 Am. J. Legal Hist. 351 (1998); Note, *The Rape Corroboration Requirement: Repeal Not Reform*, 81 Yale L.J. 1365 (1972).

[133] American Law Institute, Comment to § 213.6, at 422; State v. Matlock, 660 P.2d 945, 946 (Kan. 1983).

[134] United States v. Wiley, 492 F.2d 547, 552 (D.C. Cir. 1973) (Bazelon, J., concurring).

[135] 1 Hale, Note 2, *supra*, at *635.

[136] A. Thomas Morris, Note, *The Empirical, Historical and Legal Case Against the Cautionary Instruction: A Call for Legislative Reform*, 1988 Duke L.J. 154, 156.

[137] E.g., People v. Rincon-Pineda, 538 P.2d 247, 256 (Cal. 1975); State v. Bashaw, 672 P.2d 48, 50 (Or. 1983).

[138] United States v. Wiley, 492 F.2d at 550.

[139] American Law Institute, Comment to § 213.6, at 426-27; see Brownmiller, Note 1, *supra*, 319-33 (describing this attitude); Comment, *Forcible and Statutory Rape: An Exploration of the Operation and Objectives of the Consent Standard*, 62 Yale L.J. 55, 66 (1952) ("Many women . . . require as a part of preliminary 'love play' aggressive overtures by the man. . . . [T]heir erotic pleasure . . . depend[s] upon an accompanying physical struggle."). A more accurate psychological view is that men fantasize that women fantasize being raped.

Other advocates of the corroboration rule believe that women have a strong motive to "cry rape" falsely. Traditionally, females were expected to avoid sexual relations until marriage; those who violated this moral code were subject to embarrassment, stigmatization, and even ostracism. Therefore, an unmarried female who had sexual intercourse or, more significantly, became pregnant, had an incentive to claim that she was raped, rather than to admit that she had consented to sexual intimacy.

Another aspect of the concern for the accused may be the unfortunate result of racism. Historically, society disapproved of interracial sexual relations. A racist stereotype was that black men were prone to rape white women. A white woman who was known or suspected to have had sexual relations with an African-American male, therefore, was under substantial social pressure to claim that she was raped. The corroboration requirement reduced the risk of racially-motivated convictions.

Opponents of the rule point out that Lord Hale's "comment does not reflect contemporary thought or experience."[140] The premise that women commonly fantasize rape is entirely unfounded, and the other concerns are overstated or outdated. For example, minority group members previously excluded from jury service now serve regularly on juries, which reduces the risk of racially-biased rape convictions. Moreover, today's society is tolerant of premarital sexual activity, so that women have little reason to falsely claim rape. Finally, in light of the stigma still attached to the crime of rape, and embarrassment that rape victims often suffer in the legal system, there is little reason to believe that false claims of rape occur often enough to justify a special corroboration requirement.

Opponents of the corroboration rule appear to be winning the day. A number of states that adopted the rule have since repealed it.[141]

[B] Rape-Shield Statutes[142]

In a criminal trial, two basic principles determine the admissibility of proffered evidence. First, no evidence is admissible unless it is relevant. Second, subject to limited exceptions, relevant evidence is admissible. Evidence is relevant if it has the tendency to prove or disprove any disputed fact at issue, including the credibility of a witness. However, a judge has discretion to exclude relevant

---

[140] State v. Bashaw, 672 P.2d at 49.

[141] American Law Institute, Comment to § 213.6, at 423 (citing nine states in which legislative repeal occurred by 1978).

[142] See generally Ann Althouse, *Thelma and Louise and the Law: Do Rape Shield Rules Matter?*, 25 Loy. L.A. L. Rev. 757 (1992); Elizabeth J. Kramer, *When Men Are Victims: Applying Rape Shield Laws to Male Same-Sex Rape*, 73 N.Y.U. L. Rev. 293 (1998); Cassia Spohn & Julie Horney, *"The Law's the Law, but Fair Is Fair:" Rape Shield Laws and Officials' Assessments of Sexual History Evidence*, 29 Criminology 137 (1991).

evidence if its probative value — its relevance — is outweighed by the risk that it will cause undue prejudice to an opposing party.

In rape trials, defense attorneys have traditionally sought to introduce evidence relating to the alleged rape victim's sexual history and moral character. Specifically, three classes of evidence regarding the complainant might be proffered: (1) her prior consensual sexual acts with the accused; (2) her prior consensual sexual acts with persons other than the accused; and (3) her reputation for lack of chastity.

The first category of evidence has always been admissible if the defendant contends that the female consented to sexual intercourse with him on the present occasion. Thus, if *V* claims that she was raped by *D* on January 15, it is relevant to the issue of guilt that she consented to sexual relations with *D* on January 14. Of course, the fact that she consented on one day does not necessarily mean that she consented on another day; nonetheless, the evidence is of some relevance in determining whether *V* consented on the day in dispute, and it is relevant in determining *D*'s *mens rea* as to *V*'s possible consent. Therefore, the jury is entitled to consider the fact of their prior consensual sexual relations, and to give the evidence as much (or little) weight as it believes is justified. This remains the rule today.

The other two categories of evidence have always been more problematical. In the past, however, many states permitted testimony regarding the complaining witness's prior sexual history with other men and/or her reputation for lack of chastity as substantive evidence relevant to the issue of her consent to intercourse with the accused. The traditional justification for this rule was that "no court can overrule the law of human nature, which declares that one who has already started on the road of [sexual unchastity], would be less reluctant to pursue her way, than another who yet remains at her home of innocence, and looks upon such a [pursuit] . . . with horror."[143] Such evidence was also admissible in the past to impeach the female's credibility, apparently on the peculiar ground that there is a connection between sexual "immorality" and lack of veracity. The practical effect of these rules of evidence was to put the complaining witness on trial along with the defendant.

In the past two decades, however, "rape-shield" laws have been enacted by virtually every state. Although the statutes vary, these laws generally deny a defendant in a rape case the opportunity, absent good cause to the contrary, to cross-examine the complainant, or to offer extrinsic evidence, concerning her prior sexual conduct with others or her reputation for chastity. Rape-shield laws are founded on the view that "[c]onsent to engage in sexual activity with one person does not, without more, give rise to a reasonable claim that consent is more likely with another,"[144] and such sexual activity provides no reason to

---

[143] People v. Abbot, 19 Wend. 192, 196 (N.Y. 1838).

[144] United States v. Lauture, 46 M.J. 794, 800 (A. Ct. Crim. App. 1997).

believe that the woman is less truthful than a "chaste" female. Rape-shield laws also make it more difficult for a defense lawyer to humiliate the accuser in the courtroom, with the resulting hope that such laws will increase the likelihood that rapes will be reported.

Although rape-shield laws reduce the risk of prejudice to rape victims, they also increase the risk that an accused person might be denied the opportunity to introduce evidence that would demonstrate his innocence. In an extreme case, enforcement of a rape-shield law may conflict with the Constitution. Specifically, the Sixth Amendment provides that a defendant is entitled to confront and cross-examine his accuser (in this case, the alleged victim of the rape), as well as to present evidence in his own behalf. However, these constitutional rights are not absolute, and courts have resorted to a balancing test, in which the weighty interests of a rape-shield law are balanced against the defendant's need to introduce the "shielded" evidence in the specific case.

For example, in *State v. Colbath*,[145] *C* and *V* were in a tavern. *V* directed "sexually provocative statements" toward *C* as well as other customers. While in the bar, *V* also allowed *C* to feel her breasts and buttocks, and she rubbed *C*'s penis. Later, the two left the bar together and went to *C*'s trailer, where they had sexual intercourse. When *C*'s live-in companion unexpectedly arrived, she assaulted *V*. *V* sought to explain the situation on the ground that *C* had raped her. In support of *C*'s claim that the sexual acts were consensual, *C* sought unsuccessfully at trial to introduce evidence of *V*'s public sexual behavior with other men in the tavern on the day of the incident, including the fact that she had left the bar with other men in the hours immediately preceding her actions with *C*.

The court held that the rape-shield law had to give way in this case to the defendant's constitutional rights to confront the witnesses against him and to present his own exculpatory evidence. The court emphasized that the evidence involved public acts by *V*: "[E]vidence of public displays of general interest in sexual activity can be taken to indicate a contemporaneous receptiveness to sexual advances that cannot be inferred from evidence of private behavior with chosen sex partners." The court stated that the evidence *C* sought to introduce was more than "merely . . . relevant." Instead, it strongly supported *C*'s claim that *V* had made a false accusation, in light of the "undignified predicament" in which she found herself when she was discovered by *C*'s live-in companion.

Although *Colbath* does not stand alone,[146] rulings of this sort are uncommon absent special facts.[147] In general, courts have ruled that "the probativeness of

---

[145] 540 A.2d 1212 (N.H. 1988) (opinion of Souter, J.).

[146] See also State v. Perez, 995 P.2d 372 (Kan. Ct. App. 1999) (holding that *P* was permitted to introduce evidence that *V* had engaged in sexual intercourse with two other men in full view of *P* and others at a party hours earlier).

[147] In a case somewhat similar to *Colbath*, the rape-shield law prevailed. In *People v. Wilhelm*, 476 N.W.2d 753 (Mich. Ct. App. 1991), *W* and *V* were at a bar, although not together. *W* wished to introduce evidence at the trial that he saw *V* expose her breasts to two men sitting at her table, and

the [defendant's proffered] evidence is so minuscule when weighed against the potential prejudice to the complaining witness that . . . the sixth amendment rights must bend to protect the innocent victims."[148]

§ 33.08 MODEL PENAL CODE[149]

[A] Sex Offenses, In General

Article 213 of the Model Penal Code sets out the sexual offenses recognized under the Code: rape; gross sexual imposition; deviate sexual intercourse; corruption of minors; sexual assault; and indecent exposure. Only rape, deviate sexual intercourse, and some forms of corruption of minors constitute felony offenses. Consensual sexual conduct between adults is not prohibited.

The offenses of rape and gross sexual imposition are summarized here. However, the Code's approach to these offenses has been followed in whole or in part by only a few states.[150]

[B] Rape

[1] In General

A male is guilty of rape if, acting purposely, knowingly, or recklessly regarding each of the material elements of the offense, he has sexual intercourse with a female under any of the following circumstances: (1) the female is less than ten years of age;[151] (2) the female is unconscious; (3) he compels the

---

that she permitted one of them to fondle her breasts. Another witness also observed the activity. However, the court upheld the trial court's exclusion of this evidence. It stated that "we fail to see how a woman's consensual sexual conduct with another in public indicates to third parties that the woman would engage in similar behavior with them." *Id.* at 759. The court distinguished *Colbath* on the ground that the woman in that case had left the bar with various men during the afternoon in question, and that the beating she received from *C*'s girlfriend provided a motive for fabrication.

See also State v. Detonancour, 34 P.3d 487 (Mont. 2001) (evidence proffered by *D* that *V* pulled him onto her lap at a birthday party two days earlier was inadmissible; such "flirtatious" behavior is not evidence of the type of "sexual conduct" between *D* and *V* admissible under the rape-shield law); State v. Thompson, 884 P.2d 574 (Or. Ct. App. 1994) (*T* claimed he had consensual intercourse with *V* in exchange for drugs; held: evidence that *V* had previously offered other men sex in exchange for drugs was inadmissible under the rape-shield statute).

148 State v. Herndon, 426 N.W.2d 347, 361 (Wis. Ct. App. 1988) (stating the general approach of courts, but holding in the instant case that the rape-shield law violated the constitutional rights of the defendant), overruled by State v. Pulizzano, 456 N.W.2d 325 (Wis. 1990) (stating that the rape-shield law is not unconstitutional on its face).

149 See generally Denno, Note 9, *supra.*

150 American Law Institute, Comment to § 213.1, at 299.

151 In an exception to general Code principles, it is no defense that the male did not know the girl was under the age of ten, nor is it a defense that he reasonably believed that she was over the age of ten. Model Penal Code § 213.6(1).

female to submit by force or by threatening her or another person with imminent death, grievous bodily harm, extreme pain or kidnapping; or (4) he administers or employs drugs or intoxicants in a manner that substantially impairs the female's ability to appraise or control her conduct.[152] The Code recognizes a partial marital exemption: The preceding conduct does *not* constitute rape if the female is his spouse, unless the parties are living apart under a formal decree of separation. Moreover, the immunity extends to persons "living as man and wife," although they are not formally married.[153]

Rape is a felony of the first degree (and, thus, graded as seriously as murder) in either of two circumstances: (1) the defendant inflicted serious bodily injury upon the female or another in the course of the rape; or (2) the female was *not* a "voluntary social companion" who had "previously permitted him sexual liberties." In all other circumstances, the offense is a felony of the second degree.

[2] Comparison to Common Law

The Code's treatment of rape is traditional in various regards. First, it is gender-specific, i.e., legally only males can commit the offense, and only females are victims. Second, the Code affirms the general principle that nonconsensual intercourse with a spouse is not rape.

The Code differs from the common law in various respects. First, the term "sexual intercourse" is defined broadly to include genital, oral, and anal sexual penetration by the male of the female.[154]

Second, rape is defined in terms of the male's acts of aggression or overreaching, rather than in the negative terms of the female's lack of consent. The drafters favored this approach because "[t]he deceptively simple notion of consent may obscure a tangled mesh of psychological complexity, ambiguous communication, and unconscious restructuring of the event by the participants."[155] By shifting the focus to the male's conduct, the Code seeks to avoid the common law's emphasis on objective proof of the victim's lack of consent. In particular, the Code does *not* require proof of resistance by the victim, although the Commentary recognizes that evidence of resistance may sometimes be required to convince the jury that the sexual act was compelled.[156]

Third, the definition of rape is broader than the common law in certain respects: The offense is committed if the female submits as the result of violence directed at a third party; and it is rape if the victim submits as a result of a threat to kidnap her or another. On the other hand, sexual intercourse obtained

---

[152] Model Penal Code § 213.1(1).

[153] Model Penal Code § 213.6(2).

[154] Model Penal Code § 213.0(2).

[155] American Law Institute, Comment to § 213.1, at 303.

[156] *Id.* at 305.

by fraud-in-the-*factum* does not constitute the offense of rape, although it does make up the offense of gross sexual imposition, as discussed below.

[C] Gross Sexual Imposition

Subject to the exemptions discussed above relating to spouses and persons living together "as husband and wife," a male is guilty of gross sexual imposition, a felony of the third degree, if he has sexual intercourse with a female in any one of three circumstances. First, he is guilty if the female submits as the result of a "threat that would prevent resistance by a woman of ordinary resolution."[157] Thus, a man who obtains intercourse by threatening a woman with loss of employment, is guilty of gross sexual imposition, assuming the factfinder determines that the threat meets the objective standard defined in the law.

The objective standard — "a woman of ordinary resolution" — is "not a staple of the law,"[158] but the drafters believed it was sufficiently clear to permit the jury to distinguish between serious threats (e.g., loss of a job) and trivial ones (e.g., a threat by a police officer to give the victim a parking ticket). It should also be noted that *offers* do not fall within the scope of the offense; for example, a man is not guilty of gross sexual imposition if he offers a poverty-stricken woman a high-paying job if she submits to intercourse.

Second, gross sexual imposition is committed if a male has sexual relations with a female with knowledge that, as the result of mental illness or defect, she is unable to appraise the nature of her conduct.[159]

Finally, a male is guilty of this offense if "he knows that [the woman] is unaware that a sexual act is being committed upon her or that she submits because she mistakenly supposes that he is her husband."[160] Essentially, this incorporates the common law approach to fraudulent rape.[161]

[D] Proving a Sexual Offense

The Model Penal Code adheres to the highly questionable corroboration requirement, which is followed by a small (and diminishing) number of non-Code jurisdictions.[162] It also requires that juries be instructed to treat a complainant's testimony "with special care in view of the emotional involvement of

---

[157] Model Penal Code § 213.1(2)(a).

[158] American Law Institute, Comment to § 213.1, at 313.

[159] Model Penal Code § 213.1(2)(b).

[160] Model Penal Code § 213.1(2)(c).

[161] See § 33.04[C], *supra*.

[162] Model Penal Code § 213.6(5). The corroboration requirement is discussed at § 33.07[A], *supra*.

the witness and the difficulty of determining the truth with respect to alleged sexual activities carried out in private."[163]

The Code also includes a dubious prompt-complaint rule. A prosecution is barred if an adult complainant fails to bring the offense to the attention of a law enforcement agency within three months of its occurrence.[164]

The Code is silent regarding the admissibility of evidence of the complainant's sexual history or reputation for chastity.[165]

---

[163] Model Penal Code § 213.6(5).

[164] Model Penal Code § 213.6(4).

[165] Rape-shield laws, which generally prohibit the introduction of such evidence, are considered in § 33.07[B], *supra*.

Table of References

Text references are to sections/subsections.

Table of Cases

Text references are to sections/subsections.

U

V

W

Index

References are to pages.

A